AMERICAN CAPITALISM

COLUMBIA STUDIES IN THE HISTORY OF U.S. CAPITALISM

COLUMBIA STUDIES IN THE HISTORY OF U.S. CAPITALISM

Series Editors: Devin Fergus, Louis Hyman, Bethany Moreton, and Julia Ott

---

Capitalism has served as an engine of growth, a source of inequality, and a catalyst for conflict in American history. While remaking our material world, capitalism's myriad forms have altered—and been shaped by—our most fundamental experiences of race, gender, sexuality, nation, and citizenship. This series takes the full measure of the complexity and significance of capitalism, placing it squarely back at the center of the American experience. By drawing insight and inspiration from a range of disciplines and alloying novel methods of social and cultural analysis with the traditions of labor and business history, our authors take history "from the bottom up" all the way to the top.

Capital of Capital: Money, Banking, and Power in New York City, by Steven H. Jaffe and Jessica Lautin

From Head Shops to Whole Foods: The Rise and Fall of Activist Entrepreneurs, by Joshua Clark Davis

Creditworthy: A History of Credit Surveillance and Financial Identity in America, by Josh Lauer

AMERICAN CAPITALISM

New Histories

EDITED BY
SVEN BECKERT AND
CHRISTINE DESAN

Columbia University Press
New York

Columbia University Press
Publishers Since 1893
New York   Chichester, West Sussex
cup.columbia.edu

Library of Congress Cataloging-in-Publication Data
Names: Beckert, Sven, editor. | Desan, Christine, editor.
Title: American capitalism : new histories / edited by Sven Beckert and
    Christine Desan.
Description: New York : Columbia University Press, [2018] | Series: Columbia
    studies in the history of U.S. capitalism | Includes index.
Identifiers: LCCN 2017028907 (print) | LCCN 2017054108 (ebook) |
    ISBN 9780231546065 (ebook) | ISBN 9780231185240 (hardcover : alk. paper)
Subjects: LCSH: Capitalism—United States—History. | United States—
    Economic conditions. | United States—Economic policy. |
    United States—Commerce—History.
Classification: LCC HB501 (ebook) | LCC HB501 .A5698 2018 (print) |
    DDC 330.973—dc23
LC record available at https://lccn.loc.gov/2017028907

∞

Columbia University Press books are printed
on permanent and durable acid-free paper.
Printed in the United States of America

Cover design: Nancy Rouemy

To Morton Horwitz, who brought law and history together to illuminate capitalism ∽

CONTENTS

ACKNOWLEDGMENTS

This book has been made possible by many people and institutions. First, and most important, we want to thank the students, scholars, and other participants who have animated the Workshop on the Political Economy of Modern Capitalism for many years. Their creativity, energy, and insight drove the discussions that made this book possible. A special thanks to Alexander Keyssar, who helped create the Workshop, and to Arthur Patton-Hock, who has provided the managerial prowess that keeps the Workshop going. We are grateful to Larissa Kennedy, Monnikue McCall, and the directors of the Charles Warren Center, Liz Cohen, Joyce Chaplin, Nancy Cott, Walter Johnson, and Vince Brown for their support. We have also benefited from the support of the Harvard Law School, the Harvard University Graduate School of Arts and Sciences, and the David Howe Fund for Business and Economic History for the resources that have enabled us to run the Workshop for so many years. A big thank-you also to the Harvard History Department, including Mary McConnell, for long-running support of the Workshop in general, and of this book in particular.

Many people contributed to the production of this volume, including Shaun Nichols, Rachel Steely, and Martha Shulman. Peter Knight at the University of Manchester, Christopher McKenna at the University of Oxford, and Julia Ott at the New School convened a series of conferences that stimulated the book. We also greatly appreciate the energy and dedication that the speakers and commentators at the 2011 Conference on the New History of American Capitalism brought to Harvard University. Thanks particularly to Seth Rockman,

Amy Dru Stanley, and Suzanne Desan for essential help during formative stages. We are especially grateful to Ashley Fournier Davis and Susan Jane Smith for their adept coordination and support of the entire process.

Bridget Flannery-McCoy was an amazing editor throughout. We appreciate the invaluable support of Christian Winting and Marielle Poss at Columbia University Press; the series editors, Devin Fergus, Louis Hyman, Bethany Moreton, and Julia Ott; and Erin Davis and the team at Westchester Publishing Services for their great work.

Finally, we thank friends and family who coached and cajoled. We imagine that each contributing author would agree. We take the occasion here to thank particularly Robert Husson and Lisa McGirr.

AMERICAN
CAPITALISM

INTRODUCTION

Over the last decade, attention to capitalism as a political economic form has skyrocketed. Newspapers of all political stripes debate the "future of capitalism." Pope Francis has made capitalism a central theme of his papacy. A French economist, Thomas Piketty, has attained rock star status for publishing a book on the manifold inequalities he attributes to "capital." And a cottage industry producing books predicting "the end of capitalism"[1] has emerged. This is a sea change: for decades, respectable commentators avoided the term, and only the most ebullient entrepreneurs embraced it for its positive connotations—thus Malcolm Forbes who emblazoned his private jet, like his journal, with the words: "The Capitalist Tool."[2]

Since the early 2000s, however, debates on capitalism have returned with a vengeance. And historians, ever attentive to the world they live in, have taken note. Driven by student interest, the focus on the history of capitalism emerged first as a teaching field at American universities. Soon the history of capitalism became a framework that organized a burgeoning wave of research perhaps best demonstrated by a surge of conferences on the topic.[3] Just a few years ago, the annual meeting of the Organization of American Historians was dedicated to the exploration of capitalism and democracy. Shortly thereafter, the Social Science History Association focused on histories of capitalism, and in 2014 the premier journal in the field, *The Journal of American History*, ran a roundtable on the topic. These events were followed by an outpouring of monographs, a book series at Columbia University Press, and a number of faculty positions created in the field of the history of American capitalism at Brown University,

Arizona State University, the New School, and elsewhere. So vibrant and large a field had the study of the history of American capitalism become that by 2018 a sizeable body of writing had emerged intended to help readers navigate the burgeoning literature.[4]

The attention to capitalism among historians flows from a convergence of events. Most obviously, since the fall of the Berlin Wall, capitalism has come to predominate throughout much of the world—the end of the Cold War and the collapse of the Soviet Union having undermined competing modes of organizing economic activity. Capitalism of a wide variety of institutional and ideological stripes now characterizes all developed economies. Many in the postcolonial world join in recognizing capitalism's impact, whether they identify it as a model for engendering economic growth or target it as an impediment to sustainable development.[5] The international institutions that most powerfully coordinate financial, trade, and economic relations today overwhelmingly assume capitalist economies as their paradigm. So much has the political economy of capitalism and Western liberalism come to dominate that in 1992 an American political theorist, Francis Fukuyama, argued that we had reached "the end of history." To him, it seemed that the contemporary political economy would structure economic, social, and political relations into the foreseeable future.

Fukuyama's diagnosis was, of course, premature. By the time the new millennium broke, troubling undercurrents in contemporary capitalism had once more risen to the surface, including deep instability, divisive politics, rising inequality, and concerns about the environmental sustainability of present economic practices. The burst of the dotcom bubble at the turn of the millennium, the series of sovereign debt crises that tied poor communities to wealthy American (and other foreign) investors, the devastating crisis of 2008—all of these fed historians' interest in capitalism, motivating them to inquire into how these problems and crises fit into capitalism's longer history. They underscored the urgency of understanding a system that packed such "creative destruction," in Joseph Schumpeter's words. It was in this economic, political, and social context that the historical profession turned to capitalism with renewed intensity.

For much of its history, the United States has been at the epicenter of the political economy of capitalism. "Capitalism came in the first ships," argued historian Carl Degler many decades ago.[6] The "market revolution" of the early nineteenth century transformed America from an agrarian land to an industrializing nation, while America's slave plantations fueled the national economy. By the end of that century, a majority of Americans worked for corporate employers. The rags-to-riches story of entrepreneurial success became an elemental part of American cultural folklore. By 1914, the United States manufactured more goods than the United Kingdom, France, and Germany—

combined. And by 1945 the United States dominated virtually every aspect of the world capitalist economy, first inventing and then defending its elaborate institutional infrastructure. In the disciplinary realm, neoclassical economics gained and maintains its most assertive reach in the American academy. And at the international level, the United States ascended to superpower status on the basis of its economic hegemony, the reach of its corporate enterprises, and the strength of its financial system. Just as understanding capitalism is essential to understanding the history of the United States, understanding the United States is essential to understanding the history of global capitalism.

∗ ∗ ∗

This book is the result of more than a decade of debates at Harvard University on the history of capitalism. In biweekly meetings of the Workshop on the Political Economy of Modern Capitalism, dozens of scholars and hundreds of students discussed the multiple ways that capitalism as a concept can structure investigations of the history of the United States and how the specific history of American capitalism can be interpreted. We reread many of the classics—from Adam Smith to Karl Marx, from Karl Polanyi to Douglass North, from W. E. B. Du Bois to Fernand Braudel. Faculty and students shared their research on a wide range of topics, including the meaning of property and ownership in liberal polities (Greta Krippner), patterns of Gilded Age capitalism (Steven Hahn), the economics of unfree labor in the nineteenth century (Suresh Naidu), the properties of markets (Timothy Mitchell), the long history of inequality (Thomas Piketty), and slavery reparations (Hilary Beckles). We analyzed the origins of modern labor cost accounting on America's slave plantations, the history of economic statistics, transformations of capital, labor and the state at the turn of the twentieth century, the Boston bourgeoisie's investments in the American West, and cycles of industrialization and deindustrialization, among many other topics.[7] Historians, legal scholars, anthropologists, sociologists, political scientists, and economists participated, hailing from universities from across the United States and the world.[8] A rich set of research projects emerged, and as their authors developed and published them and Workshop graduates began teaching, debates that began in the Workshop helped define the field.

The Workshop prospered in an open mode, a model that this book embraces as well. Participants studied many different topics and embraced an equally broad diversity of approaches. While we agreed on the fundamental usefulness of structuring our investigations around capitalism, we never endeavored to create a unified definition or a singular history of that phenomenon. Many participants had theorized their own approaches and advocated the usefulness of particular methodologies—but the Workshop itself opted for methodological and theoretical breadth. We attempted not so much to come to a master narrative of American capitalism as to explore its history in all of its variation. Animated by a desire to understand American history from an array of perspectives, we took an inductive approach that followed the scholarship as it emerged. If there was a point of departure it was the effort to understand capitalism in action, to allow plantation kings and enslaved consumers, empire-building statesmen and beleaguered Native Americans, stock hawkers and unionized New York workers to lead us to new historical insights.

To be sure, capitalism's definition is a central issue for the field. Most of our participants had working definitions to deploy. Sometimes those claims were explicit; other times they were implicit, functional vocabularies that shaped the scope and direction of work. We committed to flagging and debating conflicting definitional claims in an effort to expose their underlying assumptions.

In the debate that ensued, participants embraced understandings of capitalism that conflicted, and debate over those definitions regularly and productively divided the Workshop. For some, capitalism occurred with the spread of wage labor and the ownership of the means of production by capitalists. For others, the categories of wage labor and capital ownership were ambiguous and, at worst, misleading insofar as they obscure developments critical to capitalism in, for example, the slave South. A different group of scholars suggested that capitalism takes shape when "the market" expands to crowd out other means of sustenance, forcing people to produce for the market and extract resources from it. This approach also found its critics, however, who pointed out that it tends to reify categories like "the market" and "money," institutions that have operated very differently over time. Another group of scholars characterized capitalism by emphasized acquisitiveness, the orientation toward profit, or simple greed as distinguishing developments. But there are problems here as well: the drivers of those developments are uncertain, and their institutional perpetuation ambiguous. And the debate continues.

The contest over definitions for capitalism critically informs the project of understanding it. Each alternative puts forward claims about the nature of human agency, the causes of economic change, the interplay of institutions, culture, and ideology, the role of the state, and the power and character of coercion and choice.[9] Each definition carries, as well, implications about capitalism's "edges," the aspects that set it apart from other political economic orders.[10]

That recognition returns us to the operating premise of the Workshop. We believe it has been an advantage, not a defect, to consider capitalism inclusively. If a scholar claimed to focus on capitalism, we were content to read and debate her arguments, including the definition of capitalism she asserted. It may be that the new history of capitalism eventually coalesces around a particular definition. If it does, we believe that convergence will emerge from a contest among many competing proposals rather than an attempt to discipline the field.

Consonant with that approach, the debate over definitions has itself illuminated certain areas of commonality. Dialogue in the Workshop (and, we think, beyond) directs attention to "the market" as an organizing concept often assumed to distinguish private activity from public authority; the sanctification of property and contract as enforceable categories commodifying labor and structuring exchange; the salience of profit and self-interest in the cultural repertoire; the importance of racial and gender hierarchies; the prevalence of imperial power in structuring global markets; and the crucial role of money and credit. Capitalism thus takes shape as a phenomenon of our time that is both distinctive and compelling in significance and that can only be understood historically.

This inductive approach has had rich results. It enabled us to bring varied strands of scholarship together and to facilitate conversations between scholars who all too often operate in different corners of the academy. Substantively, the flow of scholarship that came through the Workshop allowed us to look for patterns beyond the skeletal commonalities identified above. While there are undoubtedly other trends, in this volume we flag a set of intriguing and important themes without attributing to them priority or exclusivity. Put simply, we suggest that new histories of American capitalism tend to approach markets as politically engineered and conceptually informed; they often expose and emphasize efforts by participants to assimilate, contest, or refashion capitalism; a good number of them problematize knowledge of the market and its constitutive aspects, including data, behavioral aggregates, and visualizations; and a significant subset track the transactional momentum and universalizing claims of capitalism across borders.

This volume publishes a sampling of the work that emerged from the Workshop. As a result, the book is neither a manifesto that lays down a single line of argument nor a comprehensive interpretation of the history of American capitalism. Instead it is an introduction to what in recent years has become one of the most vibrant fields in the discipline of history—an introduction to themes and topics as much as approaches and methods.

* * *

Within the discipline of history, attention to American capitalism began to flourish in the 2000s, yet the disciplinary developments that fueled that renewed interest gathered force as early as the 1970s. Perturbed by market dynamics (like stagflation) that Keynesian theory failed to explain, in that decade economists turned sharply toward neoclassical models, hypothesizing that individuals acted as agents with rational expectations and that markets operated efficiently. The approach suggested that economic development occurred predictably, assuming proper support.[11] To be sure, deep disagreements remained on many important issues, including when and how smoothly societies moved toward market-centered organization, whether there had been a transition to capitalism, or if economic life had always been capitalist.[12] Moreover, an important set of authors within economics and political science reconsidered institutions, identifying those practices that seemed most suited to producing stable exchange.[13] But at a deeper level, many scholars viewed exchange organized into markets as a universalizable paradigm, indeed as natural. Such beliefs often went hand in hand with the conviction that, given the right techniques, capitalist economies could be managed by highly skilled technocrats. The confidence seemed warranted by the spread of liberal regimes and rapidly rising world GDP.

In retrospect, the neoclassical approach was almost tailor-made to provoke historians wary of universalizing social realities. The claim that economic change occurred with a kind of constancy itself reignited historians' attention to how capitalism emerged, developed, and differed in many places. The history of capitalism as a field of investigation was, in part, a response to the naturalizing agenda of many economists.

Relatedly, historians have responded to disciplinary developments as varied as the rise of public choice scholarship and the search for "micro" foundations in economics (the commitment to anchor economic dynamics to the behavior of individuals).[14] Those approaches amplified the tendency to read human behavior in the market as all truck and barter, to echo Adam Smith's classic claim. That conception, far from being neutral, brought with it a set of implications about the character of markets and the modes of study that would most fruitfully explain them.

Perhaps most obviously, the tendency to frame markets as the product of innate human activities and interests divided private activity from public structures. Liberal and neoliberal authors prioritized the decentralized activity of buyers and sellers making deals with individuated logics.[15] They approached the state as an institution that, ideally, was organized to support this decentralized activity in the aggregate; in much scholarship, the government's role figured as secondary, epiphenomenal, or obstructionist. Criticism from the left oddly reinforced the trend insofar as it cast the state as an entity largely derivative of economic forces. Emphasizing that the juggernaut of capitalist accumulation required state protection, they could be read to suggest that economic interests consistently produced the requisites instrumental to their success.[16] Given these premises, the idea that governance itself made markets possible or formatted economic activity receded. Rather, exchange seemed something that could be imagined in the abstract or in terms covered by loosely defined social conventions. Reference to the state shrank to a perfunctory note acknowledging that property rights mattered.

The hypothesis that markets could be understood as the aggregation of individual transactions or as a discrete portion of daily life also prioritized certain tools of analysis. Quantification seemed especially useful, since it allowed the abstraction of stipulated traits and behaviors, as did mathematical models.

This new emphasis helped to reorganize the disciplines. Perhaps most conspicuously, economic history began to migrate out of history departments and into departments of economics. Until the 1970s, almost all history departments in the United States included economic historians.[17] Increasingly, however, departments shifted their hiring toward newly vibrant work in social and cultural history. Economics departments meanwhile welcomed scholars who sought to test economic theories against the almost infinite empirical sweep of history. Cliometrics took off as a subdiscipline of economics, using more quantitative and heavily mathematical methods. In 1974, Robert Fogel and Stanley Engerman published *Time on the Cross,* which interpreted slavery through a lens of economic incentive. The book set off a debate that ricocheted between departments and divided scholars. To a significant extent, judgments about Fogel and Engerman's argument correlated with people's disciplinary homes and the methodologies nurtured there.[18]

As one version of economic history flourished in economics departments, history as a discipline moved toward new issues. In the 1970s, social history exploded as scholars reconsidered who and what drives history. Their work generated sophisticated accounts of social structures and conflicts, including attention to formerly marginalized groups—industrial workers, women, immigrants, people of color, among others—a reconceptualization that fundamentally transformed our understanding of the American past. Among other innovations, social historians redefined the corpus of scholarly evidence, recognizing material artifacts, literature, protest practices, and ephemera as essential indicators of human experience. Their work engaged economic pressures and dynamics, but in ways radically different from the scholarship produced by cliometricians.[19]

Social historians sought to ground explorations of social change by emphasizing the complex composition of collectivities, social structures, the force of popular beliefs, and local politics, often through the detailed analysis of particular localities and particular social groups. To be sure, social history and the economic history practiced in economics departments retained some shared interests, including a commitment to material history and, to some extent, the enlightenment project of cumulative knowledge production. But social historians had no use for the rationalizing assumptions that undergirded much of cliometric research, and they fundamentally opposed reducing social life to economic matters.[20]

By the 1980s, with social history flourishing, some historians increasingly drew on and engaged in dialogue with other fields, including anthropology, critical philosophy, and social and literary theory, whose thinkers were reconsidering claims of objectivity. Those scholars doubted naive empiricism, questioned the possibility of a progression toward epistemological consensus, and suggested that a multitude of stories could be told about the past, with no one necessarily superior.[21] As they innovated, at times in explicit critique of social history itself, many scholars began exploring political solidarity and change, and the construction of "the social" as cultural dynamics. Vernacular performance, the gendered nature of power, the layered and disjunctive nature of conventions, the emergence and fragmentation of identities—important new studies by cultural historians captured these and other topics.[22] Over the next few years, economic phenomena themselves came in for reexamination. Joan Scott and others argued that categories like "economics" and "data" were, in fundamental ways, discursive—a methodological momentum that would carry forward to inform some later scholars of capitalism.[23]

At the same time, another group of historians joined sociologists and political scientists in reconsidering the American state. Perhaps the most relevant strand of such research for the history of capitalism was the attempt to rethink the relationship between economic development and the state. While always contested, approaches that cast the United States as exceptional because of its allegedly weak, even insignificant, state had arguably dampened investigation into the plethora of forms that governance took. But in the 1990s, historians and sociologists redressed that neglect—most self-consciously in Charles Tilly's *Coercion, Capital, and European States, AD 990–1990* and Theda Skocpol's call "to bring the state back in."[24] Scholars working in the field of American political development engaged with a similar set of questions, with political scientists such as Richard Bensel making the impact of state structures on economic change a central issue in understanding the nineteenth century.[25]

Legal historians, meanwhile, needed little persuading that the state mattered to economic change; from the 1980s on, they debated with particular intensity the relationship of law to the market. Critical legal scholars interrogated categories like labor along with structures of liberal legal thought and their relationship to economic orthodoxies, often using historical approaches. A seminal work in this field, then and now, was Morton Horwitz's two-volume study, *The Transformation of American Law*, which explored how markets, and even the very conception of property, were legally constructed.[26] At the same time, law and economics developed as a competing methodology, hewing more closely to the tools and goals of mainstream economists.[27]

Another important inspiration for the history of American capitalism came from labor and business historians. Although concerned that their specialties had become more isolated within the discipline of American history, they continued to explore the nation's businesses and workers, forging sophisticated accounts of America's changing businesses, detailing the exploits of individual business leaders, examining union histories, and tracing the history of strikes and other forms of working class collective action. Historians of capitalism would pick up on some of that research, while embedding it into new frameworks—emphasizing the importance of considering labor and capital simultaneously, for example, and of seeing both within the larger framework of the political economy of capitalism.[28]

Finally, writers on American capitalism were deeply influenced by a cohort of historians who had long written on the American political economy. The history of American capitalism was never explicitly at the center of the questions they asked, but the stories they told and the arguments they made invited a rethinking of the history of economic change in North America. From Eric Foner's work tracing struggles over the constitution of new labor regimes after emancipation to Richard White's writings on the history of the American West and the federal government's role in making it accessible and productive to private capital, this work raised new questions about the American political economy. Others grappled with core issues in American capitalism, including Steven Hahn in his work on the economic origins of Southern Populism, Elizabeth Blackmar's writing on the social history of housing in New York, Thomas McCraw's history of twentieth-century business, and Barbara Field's excavations of Reconstruction history in Maryland. In many ways, the questions they identified made possible a return to an engagement with matters of economic change and political economy and provided a fertile ground for the new story of American capitalism.[29]

The new history of American capitalism emerged as scholars in history, law, and political science reconsidered issues that had fragmented the disciplines, as well as the capacities created by the methodologies that had developed. Perhaps most fundamentally, it was the very consolidation of market-based modes of organization, complete with disciplinary subfields dedicated to their explication, that raised a red flag. Scholars preoccupied with the complex nature of power in private and public life, the ineffable impact of experience, identity, and conceptual ordering, and the comparative differences in material and social worlds could only confront universalizing approaches with disbelief. The more powerful capitalism became, the more obviously it demanded renewed exploration by historians.

* * *

The new history of American capitalism builds on these disciplinary trends in history, economics, political science, and law; indeed, it would be unimaginable without them. At the same time, it represents a distinctive departure.

First—and most basically—the history of American capitalism, along with the essays gathered here, reinstalls political economy as a category for analysis. Economic life, all the authors agree, is crucial to understanding the history of the United States. But rather than taking the subject as given, they explore it as politically constituted. If "the market" is neither a discrete phenomenon nor marginal to human experience, then basic structures of governance become important. Rather than assuming that exchange for profit naturally produces a particular infrastructure for transactional activity, new scholarship asks what forces shape modern patterns of economic activity and how those patterns sort people and resources. Instead of reproducing conventional dichotomies, current historians of American capitalism contest the line between public and private that had seemed to neatly divide politics and markets, states and economies.

The connection between markets and political order has been a perennial topic for writers on capitalism, from Progressive historians who argued that elites used the advantages of wealth to skew political structures in their favor to consensus historians who found more widespread support for a market-oriented liberal political order.[30] Echoes of this debate lingered through the late twentieth-century scholarship that sought to locate and date the American "market revolution," contending over the visions of political voice and material development embedded in agrarian, "republican," and "liberal" orientations.[31] Capitalism scholarship revisits many traditional questions with the tools generated by the innovation of past decades, including the relationship between money and power, commerce and politics, exchange and social status. Its effort is to find new ways of exploring how institutions, political movements, and legal formations like debt, contract, and property come into being and inflect material and ideological life.[32]

The study of finance as a concept constructed by law and naturalized by economics is one theme that the new history of American capitalism emphasizes and that exemplifies the great possibilities of understanding capitalism as a political economy. Thomas Piketty locates the roots of growing inequality in the economic returns to capital and stresses the political stakes of distributive justice. "If democracy is someday to regain control of capitalism," he writes, "it must start by recognizing that the concrete institutions in which democracy and capitalism are embodied need to be reinvented again and again." His contribution attends to the role of public debt, other financial investments, and the reach of empire as elements in the maldistribution of modern wealth.[33] Scholars also trace fiscal and regulatory developments, from the rise (and fall?) of progressive taxation to the revisionary engineering of the New Deal. They consider how deeply finance has penetrated into daily life, including the ideological and political forces that made citizens into investors and the confluence of forces that sanctified home owning—and credit—as the path to the American dream.[34]

Other writing identifies as transformative a radical redesign of money and finance that, during the Enlightenment, institutionalized the self-interested activity of investors as the compass for public systems. That experiment generated particular turmoil recently when a series of actions, many profit-driven, others unwitting, accelerated financialization.[35]

Second, the new history of American capitalism targets the lived experience of people and groups as they assimilate—and reshape—the political economy they engage. No generic truck and barter here; scholars find instead distinctive regimes of interaction and peculiar modes of relation. They study capitalism in action.[36] This new focus lies at the intersection of two legacies from the historiography traced above—historians' tendency to expand their subjects of study and their orientation toward methodologies tuned to the experiential dimension. Capitalism scholars today are interested in the narratives created by the interplay of a broad variety of actors, from those who organize businesses to those who consume, trade, plant, and work. They focus on actually existing capitalism, not the ideal types developed by various social scientists during the past two centuries.

One of the prime foci of social history, for example, was the history of labor. The history of capitalism picks up that interest but moves beyond wage labor in an industrial setting. Recent histories look at enslaved workers, sharecroppers, and other nonwaged workers and shift attention from the industrial cities of the Northeast to the nation as a whole.[37] That approach allows scholars to interrogate the connections between slavery and the unfolding of capitalism. The project has undermined one of the deepest dividing lines of American historiography, between Southern and Northern history.[38] The effect is to restore the centrality of violence and coercion to the history of capitalism while problematizing both liberal and Marxist understandings of capitalism as defined by its reliance on wage labor. At the same time, historians have reconceptualized commodification, sale, and ownership, recasting the market as a place of colliding human ambitions, fantasies of wealth, modes of resistance, acts of brutality, tenderness, and heroism.[39]

Slavery's relocation into capitalism is only the beginning point for a group of scholars studying racialization as an enduring American strategy for the coercion and control of labor, particularly African American labor. Race and capitalism is an expanding area, reaching subjects as varied Jim Crow, migration, urban studies, the carceral state, and black property rights movements. Approaches vary greatly, but many scholars attend closely to the subjects who receive, impose, resist, or recast race as a category. Their work erodes the image of exchange between equally situated agents and locates it in a field of power and culturally constructed valuation.[40]

New histories reach other actors in the political economy, including shoppers, businesspeople, financiers, and traders. Thus Liz Cohen, in her *Consumer's*

Republic, looks at the ways consumers helped construct a new kind of political economy—through both individual preferences and politically informed collective action. By following the lines that join purchasers to those who market to them, fund production, and organize economic exchange, scholars have rediscovered financiers, industrialists, and managers, considering them not only as economic actors but also, and especially, as political, ideological, and cultural agents. Slave traders and New York financiers, Boston merchants, and Pittsburgh industrialists feature prominently in many of these accounts.[41]

These accounts not only bring diverse actors into the narrative, they do so to quite different effect than older histories. Alfred Chandler's approach, for example, sometimes presented businesspeople as almost powerless actors who could do little more than watch as modernity restructured American business enterprises. By contrast, new historians of capitalism present businesspeople as influential actors, but situate them within social networks. Scholars draw on Pierre Bourdieu, among others, to investigate how businesspeople accumulated not just wealth but cultural and political capital. The work on the rise of right-wing politics in the United States after the 1970s, for example, makes such political activities and identities of businesspeople visible, and sees them as crucial to the emergence of a new kind of political economy.[42]

A third point of departure in the new literature concerns the production of knowledge. Sometime in the twentieth century most historians lost faith in the notion that they were intermediaries; it no longer seemed possible to conceive of the historian's task as only translating the mysteries of a distant world for those in the present. Now the ways of knowing that held together a particular time, its events and ideas, mattered as well. Equally important was a historian's own interpretative agency, her mode of creating coherence, which inflected the narrative in innumerable ways. History's journey from self-identifying as an objective or naively empirical project wound through the pragmatism of the Progressive era, the critical existentialism of the mid-twentieth century, the efflorescence of social constructivism and the cultural turn in the 1970s and 1980s, through postmodern and postcolonial arguments about the subject.[43]

One of the legacies of that debate is that historians of capitalism routinely subject to scrutiny narrative perspectives and conceptual orthodoxies, both their own and those of others. Modes of organizing and conveying knowledge themselves have become worthy subjects for query. The history of "disciplines, genres, paradigms, and other forms of representation" joins the study of social, cultural, political, and economic phenomena.[44]

Drawing on an influential stream of pioneering works, scholars now problematize in particular the isolation of the economy as a subject matter and economics as a discipline.[45] They have interrogated the relationship of the discipline of economics with the subject it studies and considered how models and images of the market claimed to communicate reality.[46] Timothy Mitchell, for example, explores how the parameters of economic expertise shape the questions the discipline investigates, while others have scrutinized how data and statistics come to represent the authenticity of phenomena.[47] Those studies amplify the argument, notably articulated by feminist scholars who early recognized that household labor had been read out of the record, that determinations about what is identified, measured, and counted create the "real economy." As Susan Buck-Morss observed about the visualization of economic data, "In the crossing of the supply-demand curve, none of the substantive problems of political economy are resolved, while the social whole simply disappears from sight."[48]

In concert with that sensibility, capitalism scholars have interrogated the structures of belief, assumption, and culture that underlie the ascendance of credit, the embrace of speculation, and the legitimation of self-interest as a driver of human behavior.[49] Legal and institutional scholars similarly seek to dereify categories that organize or enable exchange, including property, contract, money, and the classical dichotomy that divides the "real economy" economy itself from its "nominal" counterpart.[50]

Finally, the new history of American capitalism has often taken a more global perspective. That trend draws on the emergence of global history as a thriving research field, one in which economic issues play a central role.[51] Flows of capital, labor, and science linked developments across oceans; trade bound national economies to one another; and financial institutions grounded in particular places colonized the capitalist global economy as a whole, connections that were overlooked by more locally focused histories. Capitalism has not observed boundaries, and now neither do those studying it.[52] Scholars currently working on American capitalism emphasize transnational flows of capital, people, ideas, and institutions, whether they are looking at trade relations in early America or considering the transnational history of neoliberalism. The rich literature on "varieties of capitalism" has fed that comparative perspective. And more recently, histories of various commodities—sugar, rice, tobacco, indigo, and cotton—have embedded the history of American capitalism in a larger global story of the spread and intensification of capitalism.[53]

Within such a global perspective, however, the emphasis on understanding capitalism as a political economy counterbalances some of the more enthusiastic globalization narratives. No matter what the scale of analysis—local, regional, national, or global—the new history of American capitalism's insistence on the importance of the state sees the global market not as an area outside public authority but as one shaped by rules, laws, treaties, and the distribution of power between states. Globalization and state formation constitute one another.

In the process of engaging these issues, historians of American capitalism have reimagined both the spatial divisions common to Americanists and the temporal frame of American history.[54] The focus on capitalism has brought the history of the antebellum North and South into one narrative, for example, while scholars have attempted to integrate the West more broadly into an understanding of American capitalism. Similarly, issues raised by the history of capitalism transcend firm temporal markers such as the Revolution, the Civil War, or the New Deal, even as those events shape political economy in important ways.[55] The project to understand how capitalism both observes and obviates borders at the global level has had, it seems, an impact even in the most local matters.

$$* * *$$

This volume is deeply indebted to long-running conversations between and within the disciplines. It is also indicative of changing understandings of American capitalism and approaches to exploring it. Invited to discuss the phenomenon of American capitalism according to their own lights, our authors spread out across the last three centuries of the American experience. They emphasized developments emblematic of the modern political economy such as bond markets, corporations, the concerns of wage labor, and the Commerce Clause, but they focused as well on subjects outside the traditional repertoire, including slavery, the rights of women, the utopian claims of late-nineteenth-century monopolists, and rationales that recast capitalism as a matter of state. As they worked, they created new approaches to American capitalism.

Part I: Making Markets

Overwhelmingly, scholars in this volume ask how markets are made, rather than taking them as matters that emerge predictably or with a consistent character. Certain essays emphasize that query, including those by Woody Holton, Julie Ott, and Kim Phillips-Fein.

In these essays, two axes of inquiry appear repeatedly. One is the role and democratic legitimacy of public authority in shaping economic exchange: these authors understand material transactions as governed in myriad ways, from what counts as capital to who can own and transfer property. Second, our authors deepen explorations of finance as a critical aspect of capitalism. Credit and debt star in these narratives of American capitalism, identified here as vectors that organize the citizenry along contentious lines of wealth and political influence. The approach contrasts with a major stream of modern scholarship that sees credit less problematically as the sine qua non of developed economies.[56] At the same time, the essays counter another established narrative that considers the rise of credit relations as an important force toward abstraction.

According to this tradition, credit is a form of representation, both monetary and literary, that packages increasingly impersonal market relations.[57] The essays here are less teleological than either of these widespread narratives. Reminiscent of earlier strands of historical political economic scholarship that stressed the contested nature of credit relations, these authors consider how investor interests structure political alignment and action, resistance and re-definition from opponents, and the ideological stakes of the battle.[58]

In the opening essay, "The Capitalist Constitution," Woody Holton launches a broadside against histories that divide market-making from nation-building. As he sees it, market-making *was* nation-building: the Framers designed the U.S. Constitution to make America safe for capital investment. The political architecture they put in place favored creditors over debtors by limiting the propensity of state legislatures to grant their constituents tax relief and debtor-protection, prohibiting states from issuing paper money as lawful tender, giving the national government authority to determine the monetary standard, and making federal law supreme over conflicting state provisions.

Holton's contention compels us to reconsider theories that naively identify democracy with markets, as if highly distributed political power accords natu-rally with decentralized determinations of preference in buying and selling. By moving our focus to investment, Holton reminds us that neither politics nor markets are orders of atomized or one-shot decision-making. Both political and economic decision-making depend on established institutions and draw on expectations of the future. The Framers could only create the market they wanted by structuring political voice and legal rights in particular ways. In-deed, the Constitution remained a work in progress in the following decades, as the courts' efforts to protect creditors provoked an unexpected backlash—the expansion of women's rights as families moved property into their names to protect it from seizure. Across the first American century, then, the market unfolded as an unruly and emphatically political process.

In Julia Ott's narrative ("What *Was* the Great Bull Market?"), the rousing, rising, altogether astonishing capital market of the 1920s gains so much trans-formative significance that it becomes another constitutional moment. In the early twentieth century, less than 1 percent of Americans owned either stocks or bonds, and the capital markets played a limited role in funding most corpo-rate growth. By 1929, fully 25 percent of the population held financial wealth and the participation of American households in the stock market had risen as much as sixteenfold. The efflorescence of securities ownership, the spike in financial values, and the surge in credit extended on collateral set Ott her puzzle: what forces made the capital markets such a vortex for investment during the Jazz Age? The issue is particularly compelling given the crash after the euphoria; the Great Depression decimated the wealth of new investors, arresting economic development, destroying businesses, and turning a quarter of the American workforce out of work. As Ott makes clear, the parallels with the financial crisis of 2008 are striking.

Existing histories of capital market dynamics tend to treat them as phenomena produced by individual investors, whether rational or caught up in a speculative frenzy. But Ott counters that neither the demand for stocks by purchasers nor the supply of corporate value in the form of shares occurs naturally; she exposes the political, institutional, and ideological forces that make the capital markets rather than taking them for granted. Her approach moves public agency to the center of market-making. It was the government's drive to borrow from its citizens during World War I that introduced them to bond holding. As officials promoted Liberty Loans, they equated investment in the government with voting, suggesting that democracy itself depended on market participation. After the Armistice, the politics of the campaign to sell securities morphed and fractured. Some advocated mass-marketed bonds as a way toward nationalized industry and social welfare while others focused on how corporations could sell Americans a stake in industrial capitalism, ensuring respect for private property rights and idealized market forces. In Ott's hands, financialization becomes a drama defined as much by the contingencies of American politics and class as by any recurring pattern of profit-driven decisions.

In "The New York City Fiscal Crisis and the Idea of the State," Kim Phillips-Fein turns the inquiry about market-making inside out, showing that even as politics makes markets, markets (re)make politics. Phillips-Fein excavates New York City's fiscal crisis to reveal how community determinations about how to fund its collective well-being became the vehicle for shifting priorities in governance.

Once again, finance is central. But while public debt offered earlier Americans ways to expand political authority—thus the Federalist initiative in Holton's saga and the wartime surge in patriotic investment in Ott's narrative—in the 1970s it eroded municipal agency. Confronting an array of challenges including declines in manufacturing jobs and steep expenses for social services, New York City turned to borrowing. But as Phillips-Fein shows, that option was anything but natural. The city took loans because the state had pioneered methods of borrowing unmoored from particular revenue streams. Relatedly, the city had to appease commercial elites: members of the New York Stock Exchange threatened to relocate it if they were subjected to a stock transfer tax. From their point of view, the solution was austerity—cutbacks in social services and constraining the power of a strongly unionized public sector. Indeed, the debate over New York City's predicament ultimately escalated, with besieged officials, protesting citizens, and business elites all making their case to state and national governments.

Thus New York City's fiscal crisis returns us to the issue of democracy and its relationship to the market. As Phillips-Fein shows, the crisis was no simple matter of overconsumption or underpayment. At stake were competing visions of communal responsibility for social welfare, the role of public authority in distributing those resources, and the connection between equality and commercial concerns. The balance struck would redefine the political possibilities going forward.

Part II: Claiming and Contesting Capitalism

From the outset, Americans at every level struggled to engage, appropriate, resist, and refashion capitalism. Essays by Richard White, Amy Dru Stanley, Seth Rockman, and Christopher Tomlins revise our assumptions about how Americans understood and affected the modern market order in which they participated, whether intentionally or unwittingly.

Across these essays, a pair of issues is particularly relevant. First, the authors identify market forces that have an almost centripetal pull: a concern with production, exchange, and consumption orients much of modern life. On one level, the concern is familiar. A number of American historians have identified the "market revolution" as the moment when capital owners gained enormous influence over the political process or when the need to produce for exchange compelled farmers and craftspeople to restructure their lives.[59] At the same time, these essays reshape the inquiry. Instead of measuring market presence as a matter of degree, the authors consider how the market comes to be prioritized. Sometimes it appeals as an ideal (White), at other moments, it is a strategic and gendered vocabulary (Stanley), a productive opportunity (Rockman), or a political structure (Tomlins).

Second, many authors in this volume approach capitalism as a struggle over the way that producing, trading, and trafficking configure or should configure human relations. Their orientation pushes back against economic assumptions that individual predisposition to exchange is hardwired, but also against commentators who reduce market relations to the mindless activity of "evaluating, weighing, [and] calculating."[60] By contrast, the authors in this volume open up the daily experience of capitalism, showing people defining the world of exchange—laying claim to it and resisting it, conceptualizing it and deploying it to rich and surprising ends.

In his essay on "Utopian Capitalism," Richard White arrests the attention of readers who assume that business elites have always owned capitalism. He writes a genealogy of American capitalism that shows how small producers and laborers, as well as larger entrepreneurs, embraced the market for its emancipatory potential. The genesis of their faith was the liberal taproot that nourished both Thomas Jefferson and Andrew Jackson. Racialized and gendered, this vision nevertheless permitted white men to dream about a "roughly egalitarian world," at least until the rise of industrial corporations made labor with contract freedom increasingly implausible. In the struggle that followed, antimonopolist reformers split over how to rank ideals like competition, individualism, and equality, while business capitalists advocated a world of orchestrated production. Labor continued throughout to advance its own version of utopian capitalism, with the skilled brotherhoods attempting to assert control over the conditions of work. White's argument explains capitalism's terrific magnetism, portraying the liberal promise that spoke to many Americans who believed in the productive capacity of their own labor.

By the mid-twentieth century, that promise would, to be sure, devolve into the self-justificatory discourse of twentieth-century corporate capitalism. White ends his essay with Joseph Schumpeter's conservative defense of the market's ability to deliver "MORE" in the long run, even if in the short term it degraded laboring people. The conclusion illuminates the normative stakes to the contrasting visions of capitalism that Americans proffered over the course of their history. It becomes tragic, the more so because alternatives existed, that they came to rest with an approach to exchange that sacrificed human relations as the price of future accumulation.

If Richard White convinces us that capitalism had emancipatory potential, Amy Dru Stanley casts that potential as deeply ironic. In "The Sovereign Market and Sex Difference: Human Rights in America," the market's centripetal pull becomes constitutional doctrine of a very odd sort. On one side, lawmakers and jurists used Congress's authority to regulate commerce to legitimate a federal capacity to reach injuries of sex. The national legislature could prohibit violence against women, trafficking, or other wrongs insofar as they affected economic activity that crossed state lines. The White Slave Traffic Act of 1910 and the Hate Crimes Prevention Act of 2009, like the Civil Rights Act of 1964, made human rights protections coextensive with market interaction—thus public power reached as far as private interstate exchange.

On the other hand, the Commerce Clause expanded in emancipatory fashion precisely because the more obvious instrument to police wrongs of sex had been curtailed. Ratified in 1865, the Thirteenth Amendment prohibited slavery and involuntary servitude. As articulated and enforced, however, it was not understood to make more generalized guarantees of equality and liberation. As Stanley argues, this odd constitutional twist reconciled the revolutionary emancipation of African American slaves with women's continued subjugation. Americans fought a bloody war to end the treatment of people as commodities, but in the aftermath of that war, their officials limited the sex injuries they policed to those, like trafficking, that they could analogize to violations of free exchange *in* commodities.

Stanley's argument throws into high relief the question how practices of exchange—producing, trading, and trafficking—define human relations. Here again, paradox abounds. Nineteenth-century jurists refused, for example, to prohibit rape in marriage, construing marriage as a terrain of contract where the legal act of consent vitiated any further right to refuse unwanted sex. By contrast, categorizing women as commodities in transit allowed legislators to avoid questions of agency and prohibit the trafficking of prostitutes early in the next century. By the 1990s, Congress cast the market as boundless, claiming the ability to protect women from domestic terror in the Violence Against Women Act because of federal authority over interstate commerce. When the Supreme Court rejected that argument, it left women's rights advocates in the awkward position of redoubling their efforts to paint the market as pervasive and penetrating. Once human rights were yoked to market exchange, they depended on it for recognition and protection.

Moving from judges to merchants and artisans, Seth Rockman gives new meaning to the phrase "a materialist reading." His portrait of the market's centrality starts with prices and profits and culminates with linens, jerseys, and wools in plaid, plains, and patterns. His essay binds industrialization in the North to the plantation economy of the slaveholding South: New England businessmen cultivated the market for slave goods with painstaking care, catering to the intricate demands of slave-owning clients, molding public policy like the tariff of 1828, and adapting their business strategies in its aftermath. As Rockman shows, the slave economy and the price of cotton drove national developments in insurance, accounting, and manufacturing, not just life on the plantation.

Rockman exposes the web of exchange relations by following merchants and producers into the process of making and marketing "negro" cloth, shoes, and farming equipment. He catches Rhode Island Quakers struggling to identify and accommodate the desires of Southern planters and New England weavers adapting their techniques for plantation products. His method amounts to a meditation on the human experience that was configured by those practices, stunning in its immediacy. Rockman's portrait prompts us to wonder whether those weaving "negro cloth" felt any solidarity with those who would wear it. Conversely, did the deep ties of commerce implicate Northern producers in the brutal bondage of the South? As they collected the knowledge they needed for successful sales, how did they reconcile that daily exposure to slavery's harshness with their own ambitions, values, and needs?

In Christopher Tomlins' portrait of Nat Turner's Virginia, "Revulsions of Capital: Slavery and Political Economy in the Epoch of the Turner Rebellion, Virginia, 1829–1832," capitalism moves south and becomes the center of debates over political representation. By the 1830s, new forms of commodified obligation, including indebtedness and confiscation, had hollowed out old Virginian hierarchies based on land wealth. At the same time, "productive labor" had gained status as a democratic ideal and a path to economic development. As the free white farmers of western Virginia agitated for a greater voice in government, they forced a constitutional debate about the basis of political apportionment and suffrage. The results dethroned land as a special form of wealth and shifted the requirement for political power: "interests" were now valued monetarily. But that reform made two kinds of labor—slave and free—commensurate in that quantitive sense. Plantation owners used the claims of free white men to entrench the value of productive work by slaves: labor of all kinds would be commodified, one sold for wages, the other shipped across state lines to the slave markets inland.

The homogeneity of labor would become an argument used to smooth regional discord in the years that followed. In the immediate aftermath of Nat Turner's Rebellion, escalating anxieties produced a challenge to slaveholding itself: a reformist governor considered proposals for state-supported emancipation. The defense of capital that followed justified slavery as the natural consequence of economic activity, including the acquisition of property and the propensity to trade. Government's task was to tame the "revulsions of capital," not abet them. A political compromise promised internal improvements, the waterways and rails that white farmers sought, along with the argument that the market itself would eventually end slavery as Virginia became more a commercial and less agricultural commonwealth. Here was the tragic version of utopian capitalism, one that rewrote production, trade, and trafficking in slaves as the work that would heal Virginia's white population and that population alone.

Part III: "Knowing" Capital

The narratives in this section exemplify the modern commitment to understanding the production of knowledge. Remarkable for how deeply they penetrate specific fields of knowledge including elite theorizing, popular political propaganda, and the entrepreneurial expertise pioneered by slave owners, these essays also make an intriguing point. In each case, the market knowledge under discussion works to consolidate its orthodoxy by disallowing a variable of disorder, moral unmanageability, or incalculability.

In "Risk, Uncertainty, and Data: Managing Risk in Twentieth-Century America," Mary Poovey recaptures the early-twentieth-century debate about how economists would approach the unknown—particularly notably financial events occurring in the future. That issue was essential to the discipline at a theoretical level because economics posited decision-making by participants with equal access to information. But the issue arose in a highly political context, namely an argument over how corporations should be valued and taxed. In those circumstances, the scholar Frank Knight distinguished "uncertainty" from "risk," arguing that business judgment inhered in the skill that entrepreneurs exercised in making judgments when the results of human activity could not be predicted. That capacity set them apart and justified the corporate profits that critics felt should be returned to society.

Even as it produced this insight, the contest over corporate wealth also promoted new efforts to gather economic information of all types; the resulting empirical richness suggested an increasingly powerful data set. Theorists could model decision-making more and more mechanistically, positing rational agents who acted to further self-interested ends. Those agents would assumedly plug any gaps in their knowledge using probabilistic calculations based on the proliferating data. Thus uncertainty vanished and risk took its place. For Poovey, the shift liberated the discipline of economics to model the world as a math problem instead of confronting its incalculabilities. The results, she suggests, bequeathed us a discipline incapable of understanding the financial crisis of 2008.

With Peter Knight's essay, we move to another knowledge problem faced by corporate capitalism in its infancy. The debate this time was within commercial culture and the issue was how to present modern finance visually, an area inscrutable and elusive to most Americans. In Knight's essay, the communication process *becomes* the epistemological process: Americans were puzzling through the nature of economic life as they pondered how to represent it.

The trend was toward images that rationalized information: charts that made landscapes out of data points, a hydraulic model that found equilibria in flow dynamics, and maps of interlocking corporations. This is the stage on which Poovey's protagonists tried to eradicate uncertainty. As Peter Knight observes, the representations of this period portrayed—and thus created—the market as a totality, an ordered and abstracted whole that was increasingly knowable. By the 1930s, the concept of "economy" had moved from its traditional meaning as a commitment to frugality to its modern meaning as *"the economy"*—a coherent aggregate or sphere of market activity, nationally bounded. But Knight's essay, like Poovey's, also provokes us to think about alternative, less sweetened representations and readings: early caricatures of financiers that turned them into monsters, the inhuman character of mechanistic devices, the "uncannily decentered" network that created corporate power. The question we are left pondering is whether the efforts to tame and replace those alternatives, like the effort to eradicate uncertainty, become essential to capitalism.

Michael Ralph introduces readers to one of the liveliest debates in the new literature on American capitalism—the question of how the development of American capitalism relates to the history of slavery. Ralph adds to this vibrant debate by showing how early American life insurance developed alongside the desire of slave owners to insure slaves they rented out to industrial enterprises and mines. Insurance companies, Ralph shows, embraced the new opportunities provided by the booming slave economy in the South, and slave owners used the insurance to significantly recast the slave economy, moving slave labor into new sectors of the economy and bringing new flexibility to an economy characterized by the commodification not just of labor but of the laborer.

The practice of insuring slaves shaped relations both in the black community and in the free laboring community far into the future. For African Americans, monetary valuations that rendered their lives cheap interfered with their efforts to protect themselves and their families, either through insurance or in mutual aid societies. And all free mining labor would contend, through the twentieth century, with the industry's refusal to make public medical information about the dangers to their workers, a record that would have been richly informative if it had been framed to include those enslaved workers of the previous century.

The essays in this section leave us, then, with a haunting issue. Do the attempts to tame the future, order observations, and sanitize the genealogy of economic techniques and results distinguish capitalism as a knowledge form? If so, how does that affect our efforts to write its history?

Part IV: Refiguring Space from the Local to the Global

For a growing number of scholars, American capitalism has always figured as a global phenomenon. There the agreement ends and the debate begins: should capitalism be cast as trade and competition, contagion, empire, and/or extraction? Our last cluster of essays—by Eliga H. Gould, Peter Coclanis, Michael Zakim, and Kris Manjapra—engages these issues. Like other historians who think globally, these authors demonstrate that we cannot understand capitalism without enlarging the frame of analysis. But against that backdrop, these essays stand out for their willingness to upset the conventional account. In various ways, each narrative inverts the idea of fluidity of capital across space or, in Coclanis's case, time. Along the way, these writers raise a series of questions about what capitalism is—what is this thing that goes global?

Eliga Gould overturns our expectations about the laissez-faire character of early American capitalism with "War by Other Means: Mercantilism and Free Trade in the Age of the American Revolution." His target is the conventional wisdom that the revolutionaries, united behind the liberal economic vision of

Adam Smith, fought to establish "the free flow of commerce." Americans did resist Britain's attempts to police trade with its enemies, but they also acknowledged and ultimately adopted the British conviction that only national naval power and the fiscal muscle to back it up made the seas safe. That was true in wartime, when aggressors targeted home ships, but it was just as true in peacetime, when pirates decimated private wealth and irresponsible merchants freeloaded on the established order without paying their dues. In that sense, free trade itself became an act of war against one's country. Mercantilism, in other words, was a precondition for the market, not an obstacle to it.

In its attention to the value Americans gave to "commercial security," Gould's essay evokes the Holton essay that opens the volume. Like Holton, Gould claims lasting significance for American adherence to mercantilism, expressed through the nineteenth century in the acceptance that British maritime power ultimately set the conditions for free commerce. The implication for capitalism's identity follows: rather than a system of laissez-faire or market autonomy, it becomes a state-sponsored structure of production and commerce. This understanding of capitalism recurs in other essays in the volume, most notably those by Julia Ott, Christopher Tomlins, and Amy Dru Stanley.

If so, Peter Coclanis contests this understanding in "'Innovative Solutions to Modern Agriculture': Capitalist Farming, Global Competition, and the Devolution of the U.S. Rice Industry." For Coclanis, capitalism is something closer to Joseph Schumpeter's "continuously disruptive economic process," a phenomenon driven by entrepreneurs who repeatedly used power advantages to further their own "aggressively commercialized, rent-seeking" ends. Coclanis's claim is that we might understand something about the fundamentals of capitalism by seeing this process play out in the rice industry across time and borders.

That goal leads Coclanis to a methodological experiment, another kind of interruption. Rather than tell the industry's story from inception to modern day, Coclanis starts with present, bioprospecting, as he puts it, from contemporary structures to their precedents. The technique aims to identify the long-term forces and the disruptive events that shaped both rice farming and capitalism itself. Profit-driven entrepreneurs with an appetite for risk, a pattern of economic rationality, and a willingness to act instrumentally start the story, and they reappear throughout, from contemporary farmers open to "science and productivity-enhancing innovations," to the nineteenth-century Midwestern migrants who pioneered capital-intensive techniques in Louisiana, to the early slave-owning planters who engineered tidal irrigation technology along the South Carolina. The potentially redemptive aspect to these morally compromised characters—rice planters held concentrations of slaves that were among the highest in their societies—is that they may, in Coclanis's view, ultimately have produced economic growth and development. Here, the strain of feeding the world's population drives Coclanis's contention that we must take capitalism's self-celebratory claims seriously.

Michael Zakim provides a careful and theoretically sophisticated reading of one event—the New York World's Fair of 1853—as a way to illuminate how Americans navigated the recasting of their economy from one based on artisanal manufacturing and independent farming to one dominated by industrial production controlled by large capitalists. His nuanced reading of the debates that emerged around this ill-fated undertaking, one that showcased both the ingenuity of manufacturers and the increasing dominance of capital over production, focuses our attention on one of the most consequential changes in the American economy and the common narrative that formed around that change. If once artisans proudly displayed their technical ingenuity and innovation, the 1853 World's Fair was a display of things that were made efficiently, inexpensively, and in great quantity. Zakim shows how the tools of cultural history, particularly its attention to narratives and self-perception, can open new understandings of some of the fundamental transitions in American capitalism. Most important, he suggests that the true revolutionaries of the age were not protesting workers or rebelling farmers but the great capitalists who transformed human life, a project that created deep tensions. In the mid-century United States, this celebration of modern material surfeit and its redemptive effects for humanity failed, both to our surprise and that of contemporaries, because the very shape of the commodity form—the "specter of capital"—was still an open question.

It is the last essay that perhaps most profoundly aims to invert our assumptions about how capitalism took its global shape. In "Plantation Dispossessions: The Global Travel of Agricultural Racial Capitalism," Kris Manjapra sets the location for capitalism's expansion in Jamaica Kincaid's "Small Place," the Caribbean, where the plantation complex developed as a system of racialized control, coerced labor, land appropriation, and resource accumulation. Having accumulated wealth there, plantation agents took their money, forms of knowledge, techniques of land acquisition, financial institutions, and political and social networks across the globe. As they moved to South America, Africa, India, and South Asia, they perfected their system of exploitation. The apotheosis of the "West Indian Method" occurred in the late nineteenth century, when multinational corporations consolidated control over vast territories and populations, bureaucratizing coercion to maximize extraction.

Manjapra thus decenters both North America and Europe—in this telling, capitalism flows from relations and methods perfected at the periphery. The plantation complex ultimately colonized the developed world, organizing industrialized populations now dependent on products extracted from the Third World. Moreover, the plantation complex went viral in the aftermath of abolition, just in the wake of emancipation in the Caribbean. That liberatory moment became the event that spewed slave owners worldwide, enriched with the compensation payments they received from the English and French states and in search of new venues for resource accumulation.

Like Coclanis, Manjapra puts the profit-driven actor at the center of his story; unlike Coclanis, the entrepreneur has no redemptive possibility. While other authors investigate capitalism's relationship to state power, the picture here is bleaker, with the state providing essential finance and delegating communal responsibility to the corporation. Capitalism is liberalism subverted, a "force economy," a system of coercion unprecedented in its reach and capacity to extract "life-power from colonized and terrorized flesh, blood, soil and earth." The only question is whether the resistance this capitalism engenders, a Third World universalism, might speak for a humankind so pervasively exploited.

* * *

The essays in this volume, like the interlocking, multidisciplinary and open discussions out of which they grew, represent an invitation or, perhaps, a challenge. They encourage us to engage the endlessly fascinating and enormously complicated history of American capitalism. As American capitalism morphs once more, shedding its industrial past and, perhaps, its central role in the world, we need to continue tracing this great revolution of human affairs. We hope articles in this volume provide some of the tools and the inspiration for doing so.

Notes

1. Lauren Gensler, "Rising Income Inequality Is Throwing the Future of Capitalism into Question, Says World Economic Forum," *Forbes,* January 11, 2017, https://www.forbes.com/sites/laurengensler/2017/01/11/world-economic-forum-income-inequality-capitalism/#63d2a90c5dd3; Jim Yardley and Binyamin Appelbaum, "In Fiery Speeches, Francis Excoriates Global Capitalism," *New York Times,* July 11, 2015, https://www.nytimes.com/2015/07/12/world/americas/in-fiery-speeches-francis-excoriates-global-capitalism.html?_r=0; Thomas Piketty, *Capital in the Twenty-First Century* (Cambridge, Mass.: Belknap Press of Harvard University Press, 2014); for example, Wolfgang Streek, *How Will Capitalism End?: Essays on a Failing System* (London: Verso, 2016).
2. George James, "Malcolm Forbes, Publisher, Dies at 70," February 26, 1990, http://www.nytimes.com/1990/02/26/obituaries/malcolm-forbes-publisher-dies-at-70.html?pagewanted=all.
3. Conferences included a transatlantic series: The Culture of the Market (University of Manchester, Oxford University, New School, Harvard University); Global Capitalism and Global South Graduate Student Conference at the University of Georgia, Athens;

O'Connell Initiative on the Global History of Capitalism at Fordham University; a regular "History of Capitalism" boot camp at Cornell University; a forum on teaching capitalism; and a biannual graduate student conference on the history of American capitalism, both at Harvard University.

4. Seth Rockman, "What Makes the History of Capitalism Newsworthy?," *Journal of the Early Republic* 34, no. 3 (Fall 2014): 439–66; Noam Maggor, "The Great Inequalizer: American Capitalism in the Gilded Age and Progressive Era," *Journal of the Gilded Age and Progressive Era* 15, no. 3 (July 2016): 241–45; Sven Beckert, "History of American Capitalism," in *American History Now*, ed. Lisa McGirr and Eric Foner (Philadelphia: Temple University Press, 2011), 314–35; Jeff Sklansky, "Labor, Money, and the Financial Turn in the History of Capitalism," *Labor* 11, no. 1 (2014): 23–46; Michael Zakim and Gary J. Kornblith, "Introduction: An American Revolutionary Tradition," in *Capitalism Takes Command: The Social Transformation of Nineteenth-Century America*, ed. Zakim and Kornblith (Chicago: University of Chicago Press, 2012), 1–12; William H. Sewell Jr., "A Strange Career: The Historical Study of Economic Life," in "The Next Fifty Years," ed. Brian Fay, special issue, *History and Theory* 49, no. 4 (December 2010): 146–66; Sven Beckert et al., "Interchange: The History of Capitalism," *Journal of American History* 101, no. 2 (September 2014): 503–36.

5. For an analysis assimilating a more capitalist model, see, for example, Hernando de Soto, *The Mystery of Capital: Why Capitalism Triumphs in the West and Fails Everywhere Else* (New York: Triumph Books Group, 2000). For critical approaches, see, for example, Sanjaya Lall, *Learning from the Asian Tigers: Studies in Technology and Industrial Policy* (London: Macmillan, 1996); Kevin P. Gallagher, Stephany Griffith-Jones, and José Antonio Ocampo, eds., *Regulating Global Capital Flows for Long-Run Development* (Boston: Frederick S. Pardee Center for the Study of the Longer-Range Future at Boston University, 2012).

6. Carl Degler, *Out of Our Past: The Forces That Shaped Modern America* (New York: Harper and Row, 1962), 1.

7. Caitlin Rosenthal, "Slavery's Scientific Management: Accounting for Mastery," in *Slavery's Capitalism: A New History of American Economic Development*, ed. Sven Beckert and Seth Rockman (Philadelphia: University of Pennsylvania Press, 2016), 62–86; Eli Cook, *The Pricing of Progress: Economic Indicators and the Capitalization of American Life* (Cambridge, Mass.: Harvard University Press, 2017); Rudi Batzell, "Reconstructing Global Capitalism: Class, Corporations and the Rise of Welfare States, 1870–1930" (PhD diss., Harvard University, 2017); Noam Maggor, *Brahmin Capitalism: Frontiers of Wealth and Populism in America's First Gilded Age* (Cambridge, Mass.: Harvard University Press, 2017); and Shaun S. Nichols, "Crisis Capital; Industrial Massachusetts and the Making of Global Capitalism, 1865–Present" (PhD diss., Harvard University, 2016).

8. For two academic years, we had the additional good fortune of partnering with the Charles Warren Center for Studies in American history, which allowed us to invite groups of postdoctoral fellows to pursue their work on the history of American capitalism.

9. A good introduction to debates on capitalism over the very long run (i.e., the past 150 years) and their intersection with questions of definition can be found in Jürgen Kocka and Marcel van der Linden, eds., *Capitalism: The Reemergence of a Historical Concept* (London: Bloomsbury, 2016), especially the introductory and concluding essays by Kocka and van der Linden. Our own and quite different approaches can be

found in Sven Beckert, *Empire of Cotton: A Global History* (New York: Knopf, 2014) and Christine Desan, *Making Money: Coin, Currency, and the Coming of Capitalism* (Oxford: Oxford University Press, 2014).

10. Tom Cutterham, "Is the History of Capitalism the History of Everything?," *The Junto* (blog), https://earlyamericanists.com/2014/09/02/is-the-history-of-capitalism-the-history-of-everything/.

11. Daniel T. Rodgers, *Age of Fracture* (Cambridge, Mass.: Harvard University Press, 2012), 41–76; Mark Blyth, *Austerity: The History of a Dangerous Idea* (New York: Oxford University Press, 2013), 40–43; see generally Justin Fox, *The Myth of the Rational Market: A History of Risk, Reward, and Delusion on Wall Street* (New York: Harper Collins, 2009); John Cassidy, *How Markets Fail: The Logic of Economic Calamities* (New York: Farrar, Straus and Giroux, 2009).

12. See, for example, Larry Neal and Jeffery G. Williamson, eds., *The Cambridge History of Capitalism*, vol. 1, *The Rise of Capitalism: From Ancient Origins to 1848* (Cambridge: Cambridge University Press, 2014).

13. Douglass C. North, John J. Wallis, and Barry R. Weingast, *Violence and Social Orders: A Conceptual Framework for Interpreting Recorded Human History* (Cambridge: Cambridge University Press, 2013); Daron Acemoglu and James A. Robinson, *Economic Origins of Dictatorship and Democracy* (Cambridge: Cambridge University Press, 2009). For a useful critique see Julian Hoppit, "Compulsion, Compensation and Property Rights in Britain, 1688–1833," *Past and Present* 210, no. 1 (February 2011): 93–128.

14. See, for example, Donald W. Katzner, "Unity of Subject Matter in the Teaching of Intermediate Microeconomic Theory," *Journal of Economic Education* 22, no. 2 (1991): 154–63.

15. See, for example, R. A. Radford, "The Economic Organisation of a P.O.W. Camp," *Economica* 12, no. 48 (November 1945): 189–201; F. A. Hayek, *Individualism and Economic Order* (Chicago: University of Chicago Press, 2012); Milton Friedman, *Capitalism and Freedom* (Chicago: University of Chicago, 2012); N. Gregory Mankiw, *Macroeconomics,* 4th ed. (New York: Worth, 2000).

16. See, for example, Adam Smith, *An Inquiry into the Nature and Causes of the Wealth of Nations* (1776; Chicago: University of Chicago Press, 1976), 521–22; F. A. von Hayek, *The Counter-Revolution of Science: Studies on the Abuse of Reason* (Glencoe, Ill.: Free Press, 1952). For Marxist approaches, see Karl Marx, *Capital: A Critique of Political Economy*, Pelican Marx Library (Harmondsworth, UK: Penguin, 1976); David Harvey, *The Limits to Capital* (London: Verso, 2006).

17. Peter A. Coclanis, "The Audacity of Hope: Economic History Today," *Perspectives on History*, January 2010, 21–22.

18. Herbert Gutman, *Slavery and the Numbers Game: A Critique of Time on the Cross* (Urbana: University of Illinois Press, 1975); Alan L. Olmstead and Paul W. Rhode, "Biological Innovation and Productivity Growth in the Antebellum Cotton Economy," *Journal of Economic History* 68, no. 4 (December 2008): 1123–71.

19. See, for example, Paul E. Johnson, *A Shopkeeper's Millennium: Society and Revivals in Rochester, New York, 1815–1837* (New York: Hill and Wang, 1978); Lawrence Goodwyn, *The Populist Movement: A Short History of the Agrarian Revolt in America* (Oxford: Oxford University Press, 1978); Linda Gordon, *Woman's Body, Woman's Right: A Social History of Birth Control in America* (New York: Penguin, 1977). Innovation flourished in European history as well. See, for example, William H. Sewell Jr., *Work and Revolution in France: The Language of Labor from the Old Regime to 1848* (Cambridge:

Cambridge University Press, 1980); Louise A. Tilly and Joan W. Scott, *Women, Work, and Family* (New York: Routledge, 1987).

20. See, for example, Michael Merrill, "Cash Is Good to Eat: Self-Sufficiency and Exchange in the Rural Economy of the United States," *Radical History Review* 1977, no. 13 (Winter 1977): 42–71.

21. For an overview, see Peter Novick, *That Noble Dream: The "Objectivity Question" and the American Historical Profession* (Cambridge: Cambridge University Press, 1997). For influential sources, see, for example, Michel Foucault, *Discipline and Punish: The Birth of a Prison* (New York: Vintage, 1995); Clifford Geertz, *The Interpretation of Cultures: Selected Essays* (New York: Basic Books, 1973); Peter Winch, *The Idea of a Social Science and its Relation to Philosophy* (London: Routledge and Kegan Paul, 1960).

22. See, for example, Jeanne Boydston, *Home and Work: Housework, Wages, and the Ideology of Labor in the Early Republic* (Oxford: Oxford University Press, 1994); John F. Kasson, *Rudeness and Civility: Manners in Nineteenth Century Urban America* (New York: Hill and Wang, 1990); Lizbeth Cohen, *Making a New Deal: Industrial Workers in Chicago, 1919–1939* (New York: Cambridge University Press, 1990); Karen Halttunen, *Confidence Men and Painted Women: A Study of Middle-Class Culture in America, 1830–1870* (New Haven, Conn.: Yale University Press, 1982).

23. Joan W. Scott, "A Statistical Representation of Work: La Statistique de l'Industrie a Paris, 1847–1848," in *Gender and the Politics of History* (New York, Columbia University Press, 1988), 133–38; see also Mary Poovey, *A History of the Modern Fact: Problems of Knowledge in the Sciences of Wealth and Society* (Chicago: University of Chicago Press, 1998). For a critical take on economic categories as legally constituted, see Duncan Kennedy, "The Role of Law in Economic Thought: Essays on the Fetishism of Commodities," *American University Law Review* 34, no. 4 (1985): 939–1001.

24. Charles Tilly, *Coercion, Capital and European States, AD 990–1990* (Oxford: Blackwell, 1990); Theda Skocpol, "Bringing the State Back In: Strategies of Analysis in Current Research," in *Bringing the State Back In*, ed. Peter B. Evans, Dietrich Rüschemeyer, and Theda Skocpol (Cambridge: Cambridge University Press, 1985); see also Stephen Skowronek, *Building a New American State: The Expansion of National Administrative Capacities, 1877–1920* (Cambridge: Cambridge University Press, 2003).

25. See Karen Orren and Stephen Skowronek, *The Search for American Political Development* (Cambridge: Cambridge University Press, 2004; Richard Franklin Bensel, *Yankee Leviathan: The Origins of Central State Authority in America, 1859–1877* (Cambridge: Cambridge University Press, 2003); see also Julian Zelizer, *The American Congress: The Building of Democracy* (Boston: Houghton Mifflin, 2004); Daniel Carpenter, *Reputation and Power: Organizational Image and Pharmaceutical Regulation at the FDA* (Princeton, N.J.: Princeton University Press, 2014); Elizabeth Sanders, *Roots of Reform: Farmers, Workers and the American State, 1877–1917* (Chicago: University of Chicago Press, 1999); Meg Jacobs, *Pocketbook Politics: Economic Citizenship in Twentieth-Century America* (Princeton, N.J.: Princeton University Press, 2005); Brian Balogh, *The Associational State: American Governance in the Twentieth Century* (Philadelphia: University of Pennsylvania Press, 2015); and William J. Novak, *The People's Welfare: Law and Regulation in Nineteenth-Century America* (Chapel Hill: University of North Carolina Press, 1996).

26. See, for example, Morton J. Horwitz, *The Transformation of American Law, 1780–1860* (Cambridge, Mass.: Harvard University Press, 1977); Morton J. Horwitz, *The Transformation of American Law, 1870–1960: The Crisis of Legal Orthodoxy* (New York: Oxford University Press, 1992); Robert Steinfeld, *The Invention of Free Labor: The Employ-

ment Relation in English and American Law and Culture, 1350–1870 (Chapel Hill: University of North Carolina Press, 1991); Kennedy, "The Role of Law In Economic Thought"; Robert W. Gordon, "Critical Legal Histories," *Stanford Law Review* 36 (1984): 57–125; Barbara H. Fried, *The Progressive Assault on Laissez Faire: Robert Hale and the First Law and Economics Movement* (Cambridge, Mass.: Harvard University Press, 1998).

27. See, for example, George L. Priest, "The Common Law Process and the Selection of Efficient Rules," *Journal of Legal Studies* 6, no. 1 (1977): 65–82.

28. See, for example, Marcus Rediker, *Between the Devil and the Deep Blue Sea: Merchant Seamen, Pirates, and the Anglo-American Maritime World, 1700–1750* (Cambridge: Cambridge University Press, 1987); Boydston, *Home and Work*; see also Simon Middleton and Billy G. Smith, *Class Matters: Early North America and the Atlantic World* (Philadelphia: University of Pennsylvania, 2008).

29. Eric Foner, *Reconstruction: America's Unfinished Revolution, 1863–1877* (New York: Harper and Row, 1988); Richard White, *Railroaded: The Transcontinentals and the Making of Modern America* (New York: W. W. Norton, 2010); Steven Hahn, *The Roots of Southern Populism: Yeoman Farmers and the Transformation of the Georgia Upcountry, 1850–1890* (Oxford: Oxford University Press, 1983); Elizabeth Blackmar, *Manhattan for Rent: 1785–1850* (Ithaca, N.Y.: Cornell University Press, 1989); Thomas K. McCraw, *Prophets of Regulation: Charles Francis Adams, Louis D. Brandeis, James M. Landis, Alfred E. Kahn* (Cambridge, Mass.: Belknap Press of Harvard University Press, 1984); Barbara J. Fields, *Slavery and Freedom on the Middle Ground: Maryland During the Nineteenth Century* (New Haven, Conn.: Yale University Press, 1985).

30. Charles A. Beard, *An Economic Interpretation of the Constitution of the United States* (New York: Macmillan, 1913); Oscar Handlin and Mary Handlin, *Commonwealth: A Study of the Role of Government in the American Economy: Massachusetts, 1774–1861* (New York: New York University Press, 1947); Louis Hartz, *The Liberal Tradition in America: An Interpretation of American Political Thought since the Revolution* (New York: Harcourt, Brace, 1955); Harry N. Scheiber, *The State and Freedom of Contract* (Stanford, Calif.: Stanford University Press, 1998); Irwin Unger, *The Greenback Era* (Princeton, N.J.: Princeton University Press, 1964).

31. See, for example, Joyce Oldham Appleby, *Capitalism and a New Social Order: The Republican Vision of the 1790s* (New York: New York University Press, 1984); Gordon S. Wood, "Was America Born Capitalist?," *Wilson Quarterly* 23, no. 2 (1999): 36–46; Allan Kulikoff, *The Agrarian Origins of American Capitalism* (Charlottesville: University Press of Virginia, 1992).

32. Richard R. John, "Ruling Passions: Political Economy in Nineteenth-Century America," *Journal of Policy History* 18, no. 1 (2006): 1–20; Richard R. John, *Network Nation: Inventing American Telecommunications* (Cambridge, Mass: Belknap Press of Harvard University Press, 2015); David A. Moss, *Socializing Security: Progressive-Era Economists and the Origins of American Social Policy* (Cambridge, Mass.: Harvard University Press, 1996); Robin L. Einhorn, *American Taxation, American Slavery* (Chicago: University of Chicago Press, 2006); L. Ray Gunn, *The Decline of Authority: Public Economic Policy and Political Development in New York, 1800–1860* (Ithaca, N.Y.: Cornell University Press, 1988); Steven W. Usselman, *Regulating Railroad Innovation: Business, Technology and Politics in America, 1840–1920* (New York: Cambridge University Press, 2002); Colleen Dunlavy, *Politics and Industrialization: Early Railroads in the United States and Prussia* (Princeton, N.J.: Princeton University Press, 1994).

33. Thomas Piketty, *Capital in the Twenty-First Century*, trans. Arthur Goldhammer (Cambridge, Mass.: Belknap Press of Harvard University Press, 2014): 570.

34. See, for example, Ajay K. Mehrotra, *Making the Modern American Fiscal State: Law, Politics, and the Rise of Progressive Taxation* (Cambridge: Cambridge University Press, 2013); Timothy Mitchell, *Rule of Experts: Egypt, Techno-Politics, Modernity* (Berkeley: University of California Press, 2002); Julia Ott, *When Wall Street Met Main Street: The Quest for an Investors' Democracy* (Cambridge, Mass.: Harvard University Press, 2011); Louis Hyman, *Debtor Nation: The History of American in Red Ink* (Princeton, N.J.: Princeton University Press, 2012).

35. Christine Desan, *Making Money*; Greta Krippner, *Capitalizing on Crisis: The Political Origins of the Rise of Finance* (Cambridge, Mass.: Harvard University Press, 2011).

36. For "capitalism in action," see Beckert, *Empire of Cotton*, xv.

37. See, for example, Seth Rockman, *Scraping By: Wage Labor, Slavery and Survival in Early Baltimore* (Baltimore, Md.: Johns Hopkins University Press, 2009); Seth Rockman, "Class and the History of Working People in the Early Republic," *Journal of the Early Republic* 25, no. 4 (Winter 2005): 527–35.

38. The dichotomy was most famously put forward by Eugene Genovese. By contrast, see Beckert, *Empire of Cotton*; Edward E. Baptist, *The Half Has Never Been Told* (New York: Basic Books, 2014); Walter Johnson, *River of Dark Dreams: Slavery and Empire in the Cotton Kingdom* (Cambridge, Mass.: Harvard University Press, 2013).

39. See Walter Johnson, *Soul by Soul: Life in the Antebellum Slave Market* (Cambridge, Mass.: Harvard University Press, 1999).

40. See, for example, Paula Chakravartty and Denise Ferreira da Silva, "Accumulation, Dispossession, and Debt: The Racial Logic of Global Capitalism—An Introduction," *American Quarterly* 64, no. 3 (2012): 361–85; Nathan Connolly, *A World More Concrete: Real Estate and the Remaking of Jim Crow South Florida* (Chicago: University of Chicago Press, 2014). Earlier influential work abounds. See, for example, Cedric J. Robinson, "Introduction," and "Racial Capitalism," in *Black Marxism: The Making of the Black Radical Tradition* (Chapel Hill: University of North Carolina Press, 2000), 1–7, 9–24.

41. Lizabeth Cohen, *A Consumer's Republic: The Politics of Mass Consumption in Postwar America* (New York: Knopf, 2003); Calvin Schermerhorn, *The Business of Slavery and the Rise of American Capitalism, 1815–1860* (New Haven, Conn.: Yale University, 2015); Sven Beckert, *The Monied Metropolis: New York City and the Consolidation of the American Bourgeoisie, 1850–1896* (Cambridge: Cambridge University Press, 2003); Noam Maggor, *Brahmin Capitalism: Frontiers of Wealth and Populism in America's First Gilded Age* (Cambridge, Mass.: Harvard University Press, 2017).

42. Bethany Moreton, *To Serve God and Wal-Mart: The Making of Christian Free Enterprise* (Cambridge, Mass.: Harvard University Press, 2010); Nelson Lichtenstein and Elizabeth Tandy Shermer, eds., *The Right and Labor in America: Politics, Ideology and Imagination* (Philadelphia: University of Pennsylvania, 2012); Ott, *When Wall Street Met Main Street*; Hyman, *Debtor Nation*; Ben Waterhouse, *Lobbying America: The Politics of Business from Nixon to NAFTA* (Princeton, N.J.: Princeton University Press, 2013); Kim Philips-Fein, *Invisible Hands: The Businessmen's Crusade Against the New Deal* (New York: W. W. Norton, 2010).

43. See, for example, Novick, *That Noble Dream*; Dorothy Ross, *The Origins of American Social Science* (Cambridge: Cambridge University Press, 1992); Dipesh Chakrabarty, *Provincializing Europe: Postcolonial Thought and Historical Difference* (Princeton, N.J.: Princeton University Press, 2000).

44. Sklansky, "The Elusive Sovereign," 241.

45. For important influences on capitalism scholars in the history of science and technology, sociology, institutional history, and social theory see, for example, Donald A. MacKenzie, Fabian Muniesa, and Lucia Siu, eds., *Do Economists Make Markets? On the Performativity of Economics* (Princeton, N.J.: Princeton University Press, 2007); Michael A. Bernstein, *A Perilous Progress: Economists and Public Purpose in Twentieth-Century America* (Princeton, N.J.: Princeton University Press, 2001); Geoffrey Ingham, "On the Underdevelopment of the 'Sociology of Money,'" *Acta Sociologica* 41, no. 1 (1998): 3–18; and of course, Karl Marx, *Capital: A Critique of Political Economy*, Pelican Marx Library (Harmondsworth, U.K.: Penguin Books, 1976).

46. See, for example, Michel Callon, ed. *The Laws of the Markets* (Oxford: Blackwell, 1998); Philip Mirowski, *More Heat than Light: Economics as Social Physics, Physics as Nature's Economics* (Cambridge: Cambridge University Press, 1989).

47. Timothy Mitchell, "Economentality: How the Future Entered Government," *Critical Inquiry* 40, no. 4 (2014): 479–507; Mitchell, *Rule of Experts*; Walter Friedman, *Fortune Tellers: The Story of America's First Economic Forecasters* (Princeton, N.J.: Princeton University Press, 2014); Eli Cook, *The Pricing of Progress: Economic Indicators and the Capitalization of American Life* (Cambridge, Mass.: Harvard University Press, 2017).

48. Susan Buck-Morss, "Envisioning Capital: Political Economy on Display," *Critical Inquiry* 21, no. 2 (1995): 463.

49. See, for example, Jessica M. Lepler, *The Many Panics of 1837: People, Politics, and the Creation of a Transatlantic Financial Crisis* (Cambridge: Cambridge University Press, 2013); Jonathan Levy, *Freaks of Fortune: The Emerging World of Capitalism and Risk in America* (Cambridge, Mass.: Harvard University Press, 2012); Marieke de Goede, *Virtue, Fortune, and Faith: A Genealogy of Finance* (Minneapolis: University of Minnesota Press, 2005).

50. See, for example, Jeffrey Sklansky, *Sovereign of the Market: The Money Question in Early America* (Chicago: University of Chicago Press, 2017); Laura F. Edwards, "Textiles: Popular Culture and the Law," *Buffalo Law Review* 64 (January 2016): 193–214; Roy Kreitner, *Calculating Promises: The Emergence of Modern American Contract Doctrine* (Stanford, Calif.: Stanford University Press, 2007); Desan, *Making Money*, 23–69; Peter Knight, *Reading the Market: Genres of Financial Capitalism in Gilded Age America* (Baltimore, Md.: Johns Hopkins University Press, 2016).

51. Ken Pomeranz's *The Great Divergence* effected a sea change here, modeling for American historians a way to engage both comparative and connected perspectives to understand several centuries of world economic change.

52. An excellent discussion of the connections between the history of capitalism and more global understandings of American history can be found in Paul A. Kramer, "Embedding Capital: Political-Economic History, the United States, and the World," *Journal of the Gilded Age and Progressive Era* 15 (July 2016): 331–62.

53. Peter Hall and David Soskice, eds., *Varieties of Capitalism: The Institutional Foundations of Comparative Advantage* (Oxford: Oxford University Press, 2001); Sidney W. Mintz, *Sweetness and Power: The Place of Sugar in Modern History* (New York: Penguin Books, 1985); Peter Coclanis, *The Shadow of a Dream: Economic Life and Death in the South Carolina Low Country, 1670–1920* (New York: Oxford University Press, 1989); Beckert, *Empire of Cotton*; Sven Beckert and Dominic Sachsenmaier, *Global History, Globally: Research and Practice Around the World* (London: Bloomsbury, 2018); Richard Follett, *The Sugar Masters: Planters and Slaves in Louisiana's Cane World, 1820–1860* (Baton Rouge: Louisiana State University Press, 2005); Barbara Hahn, *Making Tobacco Bright: Creating an American Commodity, 1617–1937* (Baltimore, Md.: Johns

Hopkins University Press, 2011); James Fichter, *So Great a Proffit: How the East Indies Trade Transformed Anglo-American Capitalism* (Cambridge, Mass.: Harvard University Press, 2010); Philip Mirowski and Dieter Plehwe, *The Road from Mont Pèlerin: The Making of the Neoliberal Thought Collective* (Cambridge, Mass.: Harvard University Press, 2015).

54. Rockman, "What Makes the History of Capitalism Newsworthy?," 443.

55. For a reflection on the dangers of dismissing such boundaries, see James Livingston, "What Is Called History at the End of Modernity?," pt. 3, http://s-usih.org/2015/03/what-is-called-history-at-the-end-of-modernity-part-iii.html.

56. In the view of Douglass North and other institutional economists and economic historians, the "credible commitment" of a sovereign government to repay its debts is critical because it signals the agreement of those authorities more generally to acknowledge and protect the property rights of individuals. See Douglass C. North and Barry R. Weingast, "Constitutions and Commitment: The Evolution of Institutions Governing Public Choice in Seventeenth-Century England," *Journal of Economic History* 49, no. 4 (1989): 803–32. This view generated a flood of literature seeking to prove, disprove, or amend its contentions. See, for example, David Stasavage, "Credible Commitment in Early Modern Europe: North and Weingast Revisited," *Journal of Law, Economics, and Organization* 18, no. 1 (2002): 155–86; D'Maris Coffman, Adrian Leonard, and Larry Neal, eds., *Questioning Credible Commitment: Perspectives on the Rise of Financial Capitalism* (Cambridge: Cambridge University Press, 2013).

57. See, for example, Mary Poovey, *Genres of the Credit Economy: Mediating Value in Eighteenth- and Nineteenth-Century Britain* (Chicago: University of Chicago Press, 2008); Bruce H. Mann, *Neighbors and Strangers: Law and Community in Early Connecticut*, Studies in Legal History (Chapel Hill: University of North Carolina Press, 1987).

58. See, for example, Beard, *An Economic Interpretation of the Constitution*; Jackson Turner Main, *The Antifederalists: Critics of the Constitution, 1781–1788* (Chapel Hill: University of North Carolina Press, 1961).

59. See, for example, Michael Merrill, "Putting 'Capitalism' in Its Place: A Review of Recent Literature," *William and Mary Quarterly* 52, no. 2 (1995): 315–16, 322; Christopher Clark, *The Roots of Rural Capitalism: Western Massachusetts, 1780–1860* (Ithaca, N.Y.: Cornell University Press, 1992); see also John J. Clegg, "Capitalism and Slavery," *Critical Historical Studies* 2, no. 2 (Fall 2015): 281–304. See generally Karl Polanyi, *The Great Transformation: The Political and Economic Origins of Our Time* (Boston: Beacon, 2001).

60. Georg Simmel, *The Philosophy of Money*, 3rd rev. ed. (London: Routledge, 2004), 444. On the liberal approach, see Adam Smith, *The Essential Adam Smith*, ed. Robert L. Heilbroner (Oxford: Oxford University Press, 1986), 109–21, 167–90; see also, for example, Winifred Barr Rothenberg, *From Market-Places to a Market Economy: The Transformation of Rural Massachusetts, 1750–1850* (Chicago: University of Chicago Press, 1992).

PART I

MAKING MARKETS

CHAPTER 1

THE CAPITALIST CONSTITUTION

WOODY HOLTON

I n 1776, when thirteen North American colonies broke out of the British Empire, each became a sovereign state. Barely a decade later, these thirteen newly independent countries joined together under the U.S. Constitution, establishing an empire of their own. Why? Modern Americans' estimations of the motives behind the adoption of the Constitution tend to reflect their own priorities, be they the First Amendment freedoms, "the equal protection of the laws," or gun rights. Actually, none of these civil liberties received any protection in the document that the Constitutional Convention presented to the nation on September 17, 1787. The Framers decided not to open the Constitution with a bill of rights, and their later acquiescence in the first ten amendments is best described as a strategic concession.

What, then, were the actual motivations that brought the authors of the Constitution to Philadelphia in May 1787? One way to approach that question is to examine the constitutional clauses that elicited the most extravagant praise from its authors and from the Federalists (the Americans who championed the Constitution in the ratification debate). The clear winner of the most-popular-clause contest is something of a dark horse, virtually unknown among twenty-first-century Americans. It is Article I, Section 10, which prohibits the state assemblies from (among other things) printing paper money, making "any Thing but gold and silver Coin a Tender in Payment of Debts," or adopting any "Law impairing the Obligation of Contracts." In the close-fought ratification struggle, Federalists routinely referred to the ban on paper money and the Contracts Clause as "the best in the Constitution," "the soul of the Constitution," and "Sufficient to outweigh all Objections to the System."[1] "Nothing, in the whole Federal Constitution, is more necessary than this very section," a New Jersey Federalist claimed. Two Pennsylvania signers of the Declaration of Independence, attorney James Wilson and physician Benjamin Rush, independently concluded that even if the Constitution had done nothing more than ban paper money, that alone would still have been, in Rush's words, "eno' to recommend it to honest men."[2]

In the early twentieth century, Charles A. Beard and other so-called Progressive historians argued that the reason the authors of the Constitution were so eager to get rid of paper currency and other legislative impediments to debt collection was that they themselves were creditors. Many were, but there is abundant evidence that the Framers had a larger motive for writing a procreditor Constitution: making America safe for capitalist investment. The Framers believed that the economic troubles that beset the United States during the 1780s were the result of ill-advised legislation adopted by the thirteen state assemblies. Nearly 90 percent of eighteenth-century Americans tilled the soil for a living. During the recession that followed the Revolutionary War, farmers frequently asked their representatives for relief from their obligations to the tax man and their debts to local stores. According to the men who wrote the U.S. Constitution, its thirteen state-level counterparts were so democratic—all of the state constitutions except South Carolina's required legislators to face the voters at least once a year—that state assemblymen had no choice but to accede to their constituents' demands for tax and debt relief.

The obvious victims of relief legislation were the owners of government bonds (whose notes could not be serviced when the states eased up on taxpayers) and private creditors—mostly storekeepers who had sold merchandise on credit. But tax and debt relief also had a disastrous secondary effect, scaring off the investment dollars that were needed to pull the American economy out of recession. By the mid-1780s, many prominent citizens believed the only way to reopen the credit valve, attracting investors both to government bonds and to private enterprise, was to adopt a new national charter that prohibited state assemblymen from coming to the aid of debtors and taxpayers. The Constitution did just that, effectively transferring several key governmental responsibilities—from regulating the relationship between debtors and creditors to levying sufficient taxes to pay off the Revolutionary War debt—from the states to the federal government. To make sure that this new national government would not adopt its own tax and debt relief measures, or at least would not look the other way when individual states did so, the authors of the Constitution made it much less amenable to pressure from ordinary farmers.

Most Americans agreed with the Framers that the economy was in deep trouble in the years after the Peace of Paris in 1783 and that the thirteen state legislatures were largely to blame. But the Framers' explanation of the government's role in the recession—that state representatives had enacted irresponsible legislation because they were too responsive to their constituents—by no means commanded universal assent. In fact many Americans took the opposite view: that assemblymen had exacerbated the postwar downturn by coming down too hard on farmers. In particular, they had tried to pay off the war debt by imposing taxes that were, on average, three times higher than Americans had ever paid as British colonists.

The debate over the origins of the 1780s recession raised crucial questions about American governance. When prominent citizens, including future delegates to the Constitutional Convention, asserted that the state governments had adopted disastrous policies because they were too democratic, farmers and their defenders took the contrary position: that elected representatives could have pulled the United States out of the postwar recession much sooner if they had only listened to their constituents.

The Contracts Clause and the constitutional ban on fiat currency contributed mightily to the nineteenth century's storied economic growth. Yet when state as well as federal judges gradually cracked down on debtors—who were the intended beneficiaries of the only two nonprocedural state laws struck down by state courts during the 1790s, of the first two state laws overturned by federal circuit courts, and of the first state statute voided by the Supreme Court—many Americans began to see the procreditor Constitution as at best a mixed blessing. The creation of the new national government also had unintended consequences—and not just in the political and economic realms. Indeed the Contracts Clause and the ban on state currency adopted at the Constitutional Convention in Philadelphia during the summer of 1787 set the stage for the married women's property acts that the state legislatures began enacting a half century later.

Making America Safe for Investment

Given the widespread modern conception of the Constitution as a democratic document, it is jarring to read the Federalists' descriptions of the affliction it was designed to cure. During the 1780s, Federalists characterized the United States as "a headstrong democracy," awash in a "prevailing rage of excessive democracy," a "republican frenzy," "democratical tyranny," and "Democratic licentiousness."[3] In a letter to George Washington, former Revolutionary War general Charles Lee prayed for "a quiet and peaceable transition from the present American government, into another more powerful and independent of the people."[4] Often the American Revolution and the people who had made it were compared to bucking broncos. To Silas Deane, an American expatriate in London, it seemed "the reins of Government" were held with too "feeble a hand" in the United States.[5] Washington agreed. "Let the reins of government . . . be braced in time," he wrote, "& held with a steady hand." Numerous other supporters of the Constitution (and even some opponents) agreed that the fundamental problem of the 1780s was (to quote a phrase uttered at the Constitutional Convention by both Elbridge Gerry, a future Anti-Federalist, and by hyper-Federalist Alexander Hamilton) an "excess of democracy."[6]

Whether the Federalists were correct that American officeholders of 1780s were too susceptible to pressure from their constituents is a matter of perspective, but it is objectively true that the state constitutions adopted during the founding era were much more democratic than the federal charter ratified in 1788. In every state except South Carolina, every member of the lower house of assembly had to face the voters at least once a year, which made it difficult for representatives to stray far from the views of their constituents.[7] Within the state governments, assemblymen reigned virtually supreme. The senates were weak, and almost none of the governors (several of whom were chosen by legislators) had the power to veto laws. The concept of judicial review was undeveloped, and any bill that made it through the annually elected lower house of assembly was almost certain to become law.[8] Independent America was not ancient Athens, but whether the thirteen state governments that emerged from the American Revolution are compared to their colonial predecessors or to the United States Constitution, they look highly democratic.

The Framers of the Constitution are often portrayed as devising it only after poring over tomes of ancient and modern history and then engaging in learned discussions of the ideas found therein. This portrait is not inaccurate, but the Constitution was also a practical solution to real-world problems. When the Framers pronounced the thirteen state governments too democratic, they were not just speaking theoretically but judging the tree by its fruit. In their view, the democratization of the thirteen state assemblies had led to the adoption of policies that gave American farmers temporary respite but damaged the American economy. Modern historians have likened the recession that followed the War of Independence to the Great Depression of the 1930s, and the most prominent men in America believed the downturn was primarily a result of the relief legislation coming out of the thirteen state legislatures.[9]

The aid that farmers extracted from their state assemblymen took two principal forms: tax relief and protection against creditors' lawsuits. Paper money provided relief both to taxpayers and to private debtors.

Seldom did legislators respond to taxpayers' complaints by simply reducing the amount they had to pay. Instead they allowed residents to pay their taxes using farm produce and (even more commonly) various forms of government paper, much of which had depreciated to a fraction of its face value. The benefits to the taxpayer were obvious, but in the Framers' eyes, tax relief came at an intolerable cost. State governments that eased taxpayers' burdens disabled themselves not only from covering their current expenses but, even worse, from paying off the enormous debts they had incurred fighting the Revolutionary War. In many cases, so little tax revenue came in that the states were not even able to pay the owners of state government securities their interest, much less redeem the principal. Under the Articles of Confederation (1781–1789), Congress could not service the federal war debt, either, because its only real source of revenue was the insolvent state governments. In the immediate aftermath of the War of Independence, most of the states made valiant efforts to hand over the money that Congress requisitioned from them, but as farmers deploying everything from petitions to violence convinced assemblymen to grant them tax relief, the states not only stopped servicing their own debts but also defaulted on their payments to Congress.[10]

The authors of the Constitution believed investors in federal bonds would never receive the money they deserved until the responsibility for raising and disbursing those funds was shifted from the excessively democratic state legislatures to a reformed central government that had both the statutory power to levy taxes and the political will to actually do so. During the ratification debate, some of the Constitution's supporters pointed out that it would also give Congress the option of assuming the state debts, which in fact it did on August 4, 1790. The state and federal bonds were replaced with new securities, and the U.S. government faithfully paid interest on these until it was able to redeem them.[11]

Early in the twentieth century, when the historian and political scientist Charles Beard noticed the windfall that the Constitution showered on investors in state and federal government bonds, he was moved to pose a seemingly obvious question: did the Framers themselves own government securities? At the offices of the U.S. Treasury, Beard found ample evidence that many of the authors of the Constitution were indeed government creditors who benefited directly from its adoption. Beard reported his findings in *An Economic Interpretation of the Constitution of the United States*, which appeared in 1913 and became the most talked-about American history book of the twentieth century—and one of the most controversial. Critics pointed out that the correlation between bondholding and support for the Constitution, both at the federal convention during the summer of 1787 and in the subsequent ratifying conventions out in the states, was far from perfect. Some of the largest holders of government bonds, such as Elbridge Gerry of Massachusetts, opposed the Constitution, while many of its champions—including Alexander Hamilton, James Madison, and John Jay, the authors of the *Federalist Papers*—owned few or none.[12] The Constitution drew more support from investors in government securities than any other group, yet it also appears that the primary reason the framers of the document were so determined to protect the bondholding class was not that they belonged to it but in order to persuade moneyed men and women to make additional loans to the state and federal governments in the future.

The American economy as a whole was also having trouble attracting investors in the years before the Constitution was adopted, and the Framers were sure they knew why. The excessively democratic state assemblies had caved in to far too many of their agrarian constituents' demands for debt relief legislation, especially stay laws (which prevented deputy sheriffs from repossessing debtors' property on behalf of their creditors), property tender legislation (allowing debtors to satisfy their creditors with property instead of scarce gold and silver coin), and, most egregious of all, paper money. James Madison's conviction that state assemblymen would never be able to resist the temptation to provide relief to distressed farmers was the basis for one of his most controversial proposals to the Constitutional Convention: that the U.S. Senate be empowered to veto any legislation coming out of the thirteen state assemblies. The federal convention rejected Madison's federal veto of state laws; some delegates worried that it would jeopardize ratification, while others feared it would put too much power in the hands of the new national government. But the convention accomplished Madison's purpose by voting, on the same day that it rejected his federal veto, to make the Constitution the supreme law of the land, obligating state judges to overturn all laws contravening it. When the convention later adopted Article I, Section 10, it committed the federal and state judiciaries to preventing state assemblymen from printing paper money or granting distressed debtors most other forms of relief.[13]

Today most Americans believe that the primary reason the Constitution was adopted in 1787 and ratified the following year was that the previous federal government, under the Articles of Confederation, had proved too weak. But to examine the writings and speeches of the men who wrote the Constitution and then campaigned for its ratification is to discover another more pressing motive. Early in the Constitutional Convention, James Madison urged his colleagues to tackle "the evils . . . which prevail within the States individually as well as those which affect them collectively."[14] The "injustice" and "the mutability of the laws of the States" had, Madison declared shortly after leaving Philadelphia, "contributed more to that uneasiness which produced the Convention, and prepared the public mind for a general reform, than those which accrued to our national character and interest from the inadequacy of the Confederation."[15]

Madison's preoccupation with what he later called the "the internal administration of the States" was by no means unique.[16] On the eve of the federal convention, expressions of concern about the weakness of Congress, numerous as they were, appear to have been outnumbered by complaints against the state governments. "What led to the appointment of this Convention?" Maryland delegate John Francis Mercer asked his colleagues. Was it not "the corruption & mutability of the Legislative Councils of the States"?[17]

Charles Beard uncovered records showing that many of the authors of the Constitution were creditors for large sums. Like his evidence that numerous

Framers owned government bonds, this discovery encouraged his belief that they wrote the Constitution at least in part to benefit themselves. It is certainly true that private creditors joined the possessors of government securities in enthusiastic support for the Constitution. Yet it appears that the primary reason the Framers protected creditors was not to facilitate their own debt collection but to attract investment capital to the American economy. In this sense, the Constitution was more the work of debtors—prospective debtors, that is—than creditors.[18]

The dire shortage of investment capital in post-Revolutionary America received emphasis from all three authors of the *Federalist Papers*. Without the guarantees that the Constitution would supply, John Jay stated, "scarcely any man can borrow of his neighbor." In the last *Federalist*, Alexander Hamilton praised Article I, Section 10 for its "precautions against the repetition of those practices on the part of the state governments, which have undermined the foundations of property and credit."[19] Cracking down on debtors and taxpayers, James Madison claimed, would not only end the terrible recession that had followed the Revolutionary War but fuel rapid economic growth—a matter that for him was intensely personal.

In the spring of 1787, the thirty-six-year-old Madison still lived at Montpelier, his father's estate in Orange County, Virginia. Eager to acquire the wealth that would allow him to live both comfortably and not with his parents, he had recently embarked on a classically American get-rich-quick scheme: land speculation. The venture fell far short of Madison's expectations, however—for reasons that had nothing to do with the quality of the soil. In the fall of 1784, Madison accompanied the Marquis de Lafayette up the Hudson and Mohawk Rivers to Fort Stanwix, in present-day Rome, New York, to witness a conference where U.S. Indian agents extracted land from the Six Nations of the Iroquois.[20] As he sailed the Mohawk River, Madison could not help noticing the richness of the soil in what had once been the Iroquois heartland. A year after Stanwix, on a visit to Mount Vernon, he asked George Washington about the advisability of buying land in the region. Madison could not have come to a better place. "The greatest Estates we have in this Colony," Washington had discovered back when he was Madison's age, were made "by taking up and purchasing at very low rates the rich back Lands."[21] "If he had money to spare and was disposed to deal in land," he now told Madison, the Mohawk Valley was "the very spot which his fancy had selected out of all the U.S." Indeed, Washington and a partner had just purchased their own Mohawk River tract.[22]

Madison formed a partnership with Virginia congressman James Monroe in the spring of 1786, and the two "made a small purchase"—nine hundred acres—on the Mohawk River nine miles from the site of the Stanwix treaty. Madison and Monroe knew their plan contained a fatal flaw. Shortly after they made their initial purchase, in August 1786, Madison wrote his friend Thomas Jefferson saying "nothing but the difficulty of raising a sufficient sum restrained us from making a larger one." The young entrepreneurs had run up against well-to-do Americans' growing reluctance to lend money to their fellow citizens. Madison himself came from the wealthiest family in Orange County, Virginia, but it was becoming harder and harder for men like him to convert their land and slaves into cash. In fact Madison had had to rely on Monroe for the entire down payment, and repaying him took Madison much longer than anticipated.[23]

It occurred to Madison that Jefferson, who was then the American envoy to France, might have better luck "raising a sufficient sum" in Europe. Assuring Jefferson there was "prospect of advantage to your self as well as to us," Madison invited him to become a partner. This involved Jefferson "borrowing say, four or five thousand louis" d'or (French coins named for the king)—oh, and putting up a portion of his own considerable estate as collateral. Madison reminded Jefferson that "scarce an instance has happened in which purchases of new lands of good quality and in good situations have not well rewarded the adventurers."[24]

Jefferson had once exhibited a voracious appetite for Indian land, but he passed on Madison's proposal, for he knew the "Monied men" of Europe would be no likelier than their American counterparts to invest in it. Jefferson had recently tried to interest wealthy Parisians in a similar loan request from George Washington's Potomac River canal company. Yet he soon found that no one would lend to the canal builders when they could earn the same interest rate on French government bonds, on which interest was paid "with a religious punctuality." Louis XVI's financial prospects would soon darken, but Jefferson could understand why French bankers and aristocrats would rather invest at home than in Virginia. If a Parisian lent a large sum to a man like Madison and the two of them ever landed in a Virginia court, the judges' "habitual protection of the debtor would be against" the investor, Jefferson said.[25]

James Madison had a personal stake in governmental reform, but he was not among the creditors to whom Professor Beard famously ascribed the movement for the Constitution. Indeed, Madison and many of the most passionate advocates for the Constitution were more or less the opposite of what Beard depicted them as being: not creditors but debtors—*wannabe* debtors, to be precise.[26] Madison's central insight was that, no matter how impeccable his personal credit rating, he would never be able to borrow substantial sums of money until American legislators and judges enforced the collection of earlier loans. On May 3, 1787, when Madison, who was then a member of Congress, left Federal Hall in New York City, headed to Philadelphia and the federal convention, his most fundamental demand was for the right to lose a lawsuit.

It seems likely that Madison's frustration was not only economic but psychological. Prevented by America's poor investment climate from borrowing the money he needed to escape his father's patriarchal care, the man who was about to become "the father of the Constitution" was, economically speaking, still a child.[27] It must have been humiliating. Madison would not really reach manhood until he became the head of his own household, and to do that he would first need to establish a gilt-edged credit rating, not only for himself but for the nation as a whole.

Madison recognized that thousands of Americans shared his frustration. Under the Articles of Confederation, he declared in *Federalist Paper* No. 62, "no great improvement or laudable enterprise, can go forward," because the lack of "confidence in the public councils damps every useful undertaking."[28] If that confidence could be restored, if ambitious men like Madison could obtain the loans they needed to buy land, expand their trade networks, and develop manufacturing enterprises, they would set in motion a commercial revival that would shower its bounty on even the poorest tenant.

The Constitution does not prevent the federal government itself from caving in to grassroots demands for tax cuts, debtor relief, or other legislation that the Framers deemed irresponsible. But the Framers inhibited the adoption of national relief legislation by insulating the federal government against grassroots pressure with a series of firewalls. Members of Congress represented between ten and twenty times as many voters as their counterparts in the much more accessible state legislatures.[29] And even if a debtor relief law made it out of the House of Representatives, it could still be defeated by the Senate, president, or Supreme Court—none of whom ever had to face the voters directly (senators were appointed by the state legislatures until 1913) and all of whom served and continue to serve long terms. In trying to prevent Congress from enacting prodebtor legislation except in the direst of emergencies, the Framers were notably successful. For example, the federal government printed no paper money until 1862.

Bricks Without Straw

It will never be possible to say for sure whether the authors of the U.S. Constitution were correct that the primary factor hobbling the American economy in the immediate aftermath of the Revolutionary War was the failure to attract private capital. What *is* certain is that many of the Framers' contemporaries— most likely a majority—disagreed with their analysis. By 1786 nearly everyone concurred that the economy was in terrible shape and that the primary culprits were the thirteen state governments. But many newspaper writers, state assemblymen, and ordinary farmers offered diagnoses of their state governments' failings that were very nearly the opposite of those presented by men like James Madison. Even as the Framers and Federalists wagged their fingers at the debt and tax relief measures that the state assemblies adopted in the mid-1780s, other Americans pointed to the very different fiscal and monetary programs that many of those same legislatures had embraced just a few years earlier.

Within months of breaking off from Great Britain under the banner of "no taxation without representation," elected representatives in the former colonies levied taxes that were, on average, three times higher than Americans had ever been asked to pay as British colonists. By the mid-1780s, some Americans were saying they had actually been better off under colonial rule. Since the primary purpose of the taxes levied by the state assemblies was to service the war debt, most of which had been bought up by speculators at pennies on the dollar, every new levy transferred wealth from the countryside (home to most taxpayers) to the great port cities (where most speculators in government securities lived) and from the poor and middling to the wealthy. State legislators initially imposed tight monetary policies as well, and taxpayers likened the punishing combination of high taxes and tight money to having to make bricks without straw.[30]

This lesser-known explanation for the economic downturn that led to the adoption of the Constitution—that the state legislatures had taxed the economy into recession—merits serious consideration. Surely a modern U.S. Congress that tripled taxes while reducing the money supply would harm not only individual taxpayers but the entire economy. In particular, the heavy taxation and monetary famine of the mid-1780s deprived farmers of their means of production (deputy sheriffs tasked with collecting debts and taxes preferred to seize farm animals, since they transported themselves) and even their own labor (delinquent debtors were jailed), which not only harmed individual families but held down what would later be known as the gross domestic product. Moreover, news stories about farmers' distress discouraged Europeans from immigrating to America—and everyone understood that economic growth depended on a constant infusion of labor.[31]

Many opponents of the harsh measures adopted by the assemblies in the early 1780s argued that they reduced the labor supply in another way as well: farmers whose livestock or other property was seized by the sheriff to satisfy the tax collector or a private creditor had trouble mustering sufficient enthusiasm for the day's challenges and chores. A group of Delaware petitioners described themselves as "disabled, dispiritted and cast down, bereft of our Peace and Tranquility . . . incapable of doing any farther good, for Ourselves, Families, or Country." Even the Massachusetts legislature, which in March 1786 approved its largest tax increase ever, soon provoking the taxpayer revolt popularly known as Shays' Rebellion, rejected proposals to demand even more money from farmers out of fear that "increasing the demands might rather tend to dishearten them, and to lessen [their] exertions."[32]

Today the recession of the 1780s is often viewed as an all but inevitable sequel to the American War of Independence; most other eighteenth-century wars ended the same way.[33] But Americans who complained about the heavy taxes and tight monetary policies levied by the state assemblies in the early 1780s were only too happy to join the men who wrote the Constitution in attributing the nation's troubles not to inevitable economic rhythms but to state action. They would not have agreed with Charles Beard and other Progressive and neo-Progressive historians who insisted more than a century later that the state assemblymen who served during the 1780s were actually responsible stewards of the economy.[34] From their perspective, state representatives really had hobbled the economy, not by adopting tax and debt relief (as the Framers contended) but with earlier legislation—especially unprecedented taxes and tight monetary policies—that created a crying need for relief. In their view, the only way to save the economy was to ease up on taxpayers and debtors.

The dispute over whether tax and debt relief were the causes or cures of the nation's economic ills was especially stark when it came to paper currency. Even as the men who wrote the Constitution repeatedly warned that the threat of runaway inflation was scaring off investors, other Americans argued that an economy that was chronically deficient in circulating gold and silver coin desperately needed paper currency as a medium of exchange, especially for inland farmers who might go weeks without seeing an actual coin and who had no other means with which to pay the extraordinarily high taxes imposed on them during the 1780s. The currency advocates acknowledged that paper money issued as promissory notes to fund wars usually depreciated, sometimes spectacularly. But during the colonial era, several of the British provinces had found that paper money lent out during peacetime, and only to inhabitants who could guarantee their loans by mortgaging real estate, fostered rather than stunted economic growth.[35]

Seven of the thirteen states printed paper money during the half decade between the Peace of Paris in 1783 and the ratification of the Constitution in 1788, and the fate of this currency provided fodder for both sides of the monetary debate. The enemies of paper money and friends of the Constitution often rehearsed the sad fate of Rhode Island, where a May 1786 emission was almost universally rejected by the state's merchants and had already lost much of its value by the time the federal convention assembled a year later. Georgia's and North Carolina's paper money also depreciated, but the currency issued by South Carolina, New Jersey, Pennsylvania, and New York either held its value or inflated at a slow and fairly predictable rate.[36] No member of the New York assembly pleaded more passionately against the adoption of paper money than Alexander Hamilton, soon to be the lead author of the *Federalist Papers*. But in April 1786, New York legislators went ahead and voted to issue currency. In February 1787, Hamilton, recalling his previous certainty that the money would depreciate, candidly acknowledged that "the event has, however, turned out otherwise."[37]

Hamilton's forthright admission that he had been wrong about New York's paper currency did not deter him from the ongoing crusade against tax and debt relief, including paper money. But when he and other advocates for the U.S. Constitution attributed the recession of the 1780s to excessively democratic state legislators acquiescing in farmers' demands for relief legislation that scared away investment, they were not stating a consensus view. The implications of this simple fact are large. The philosophical basis for the creation of the Constitution—the Founding Fathers' conviction that ordinary Americans had demanded and received a shot at self-government, only to bungle their way into a vivid demonstration of the perils of popular rule—was, to say the least, debatable.

Intended and Unintended Consequences

Nearly everyone who examined the American economy in the 1780s agreed that the state legislatures had exacerbated the recession that followed the Revolutionary War. The question was whether they had done so by enacting excessively harsh fiscal and monetary policies early in the decade or by later granting relief to debtors and taxpayers. It appears that the Rhode Island economy was damaged both by the assembly's initial austerity measures and by its later decision to emit paper money; a similar pattern may have held in other states. In any event, the foregoing description of the relief debate of the 1780s raises an obvious question. More than anything else, the U.S. Constitution was a grand effort, launched more than a century before the creation of the welfare state, to mobilize the power of government to fundamentally transform the American economy, primarily by prohibiting state-level tax and debt relief.[38] Was the experiment a success?

It may never be possible to determine whether the Constitution produced a net economic benefit for ordinary Americans. But we can at least list its largest benefits and costs. For farmers, the most positive impact of ratification was fiscal. One of the Framers' goals had been to empower the federal government to levy sufficient taxes to pay off the war debt, their thinking being that national legislators would be more willing than their state-level counterparts to extract the needed sums from America's agrarian majority. But as a small number of Federalists had predicted, customs revenue proved so abundant that the federal government was able to fund its debt without levying the internal taxes that farmers found so painful. The one great exception was the excise on whiskey and other domestically distilled spirits that Congress adopted in March 1791 to finance its assumption of the state war bonds.

For many farmers, the excise was a replay of the early 1780s, when state assemblymen levied taxes that had to be paid in scarce gold and silver. A farmer running a small distilling operation and bartering bottles of whiskey for labor and merchandise would have experienced no undue hardship if he could have paid the new tax with whiskey. But excise officers only accepted hard money, which hardly circulated in the countryside and became even scarcer as the excise transferred gold and silver to bondholders in the port cities.[39] Farmers in several states refused to pay the new levy, and in 1794, President Washington decided to make an example of tax protestors in western Pennsylvania. Appropriately enough, the army that marched west to suppress the insurrection was accompanied by Alexander Hamilton. As the lead author of the *Federalist Papers*, he had done as much as anyone to procure for the federal government the independent taxing authority it needed to "ensure domestic tranquility" by military means. As secretary of the treasury, Hamilton had devised the debt-assumption plan. And he was now responsible for collecting the excise. It was also Hamilton who gave the farmers' uprising its disparaging name: the Whiskey Rebellion.

The drama of the newly unified nation's first agrarian uprising should not obscure the fact that congressional assumption of the state debts in August 1790 allowed the thirteen states to cut taxes by as much as 90 percent, since most of their revenue had been used to service government securities that were now the responsibility of the federal government. During the ratification fight, the Anti-Federalists had warned their fellow citizens not to allow Congress and the state governments concurrent access to taxpayers' pocketbooks, but as it turned out, the adoption of the Constitution led to a dramatic reduction in most farm families' overall tax burden.[40]

When the focus shifts from taxation to the impact of the Constitution on the broader economy, the evidence is more ambiguous. During the period between the ratification of the new national charter and the outbreak of the Civil War, American productivity as well as output increased at rates that have never been surpassed.[41] The Constitution deserves much of the credit for this expansion. It fostered the growth of a national market and enabled the federal government to negotiate favorable trade deals with other nations, drive Indians from their land, enact protective tariffs, subsidize manufacturing, and support roads, canals, railroads, and other infrastructure. More important than all of these, the Constitution made America safe for capitalist investment.

But as indicated by the rapid economic growth of the British North American colonies (not to mention Britain itself) in the seventeenth and eighteenth centuries, the Constitution was by no means a necessary condition for the nineteenth-century boom.[42] It is best seen as restoring the external supervision of debtor-creditor relations that the colonies had thrown off when they declared independence in 1776. Moreover, the contention that adoption of the Constitution was essential to American economic growth must contend with the fact that ratification coincided with Old World crop failures that massively increased demand for American grain.[43] Then in 1789, with the outbreak of the French Revolution, Europe entered an era of nearly constant warfare that persisted for more than two decades. Vessels flying the flags of the two principal combatants, France and Britain, became easy targets for enemy raiders, vastly increasing their owners' insurance costs and thus opening up new opportunities for American ships to carry Caribbean as well as North American produce. The United States would have received most of these benefits from Europe's troubles even if it had not adopted the Constitution. The American commercial surge resulting from Europe's wars also deserves much of the credit for the new government's remarkable success at bringing in customs revenue. Moreover, by 1794, the year of revolutionary France's Reign of Terror, the United States would have become a refuge for European investment—not to mention investors— even if the Constitution had not been ratified.[44]

It must also be acknowledged that even as the Constitution helped spur unprecedented growth, it also exacerbated an already robust boom-bust cycle. Although peacetime financial panics were by no means rare in the colonial era—the South Sea Bubble (1720) and a 1772 credit crisis ramified throughout the British Empire—it was only after the new federal government was organized that peacetime recessions outnumbered those brought on by wars. One reason for the intensification of the boom-bust cycle was that the guarantees that the Constitution afforded investors emboldened them to speculate on an unprecedented scale.[45] Moreover, by yoking the states more firmly together, the Constitution increased the likelihood that each would share the others' fate.

Another provision of the Constitution that intensified the boom-bust cycle was the ban on state-issued "bills of credit." As intended, this prohibition prevented the emission of fiat currency, but it also had the perverse effect of vastly increasing the money supply, often to unhealthy levels. Since the Constitution permitted private banks to continue issuing their own currency, its adoption amounted to privatization of the money supply.[46] In the early nineteenth century, the continuing need for investment capital as well as circulating currency led to the proliferation of banks and bank notes. In January 1818, the Kentucky legislature chartered forty new banks—quickly dubbed the "Forty Thieves"—and the next month, it created six more.[47] By the 1850s, more than 10,000 different kinds of commercial paper circulated in the United States. Unlike the state-backed bills of credit of the 1780s, private currency was not blamed for chasing away investment capital, since creditors had the right to refuse it. But the privatization of the money supply entailed its own evils, including an explosion in counterfeiting. Even worse, by flooding the market with currency that sometimes lost its value overnight, the new banks exacerbated the boom-bust cycle.[48]

The adoption of the Constitution aggravated the volatility of the American economy in other ways as well. In 1791, Treasury Secretary Hamilton persuaded

President Washington and Congress to create a national bank. A small down payment procured the investor a certificate entitling him or her to claim bank stock upon paying the remaining installments. These down-payment certificates, popularly known as "scrip," were transferrable, and they immediately became the objects of intense speculation. The real value of scrip quickly receded into insignificance as investors focused on the dramatic spike in its market price, which promised rich returns to all those who could sell their scrip before the wave crested.[49] The inevitable collapse that came in 1792 was the newly unified nation's first financial panic. Like the peacetime panics of 1797, 1819, 1837, and 1857, "scripomania" wreaked havoc on a scale that Americans had rarely experienced as British colonists.

In the wake of each of nineteenth-century America's iconic financial panics, state representatives attempted to do what they had done before the Constitution was adopted: provide relief to their indebted constituents. They scored some important initial victories, but legislative efforts to protect debtors from creditors were ultimately doomed, both because paper money was off the table and because as the nineteenth century wore on, state as well as federal judges—and even some state assemblymen—grew increasingly determined to enforce the Contracts Clause at all costs.

Historians have made much of the fact that the U.S. Supreme Court did not strike down a single act of Congress during the half century between *Marbury v. Madison* (1803) and *Dred Scott v. Sandford* (1857).[50] But the court proved considerably more willing to overturn state laws, especially legislation protecting debtors. In 1796, the justices unanimously voided a 1777 Virginia statute allowing any citizen to liquidate a debt to a British merchant by giving the state government a nominally equivalent sum in depreciated paper money. The court ruled that Virginia's "sequestration" act violated the 1783 peace treaty with Britain and thus the Supremacy Clause. As William Treanor notes, *Ware v. Hylton* was "the first case in which the Supreme Court invalidated a state statute."[51]

No clause of the Constitution justified more judicial intervention in state legislation than Article I, Section 10. Some of the best-known contracts cases, including *Fletcher v. Peck* (1810) and *Trustees of Dartmouth College v. Woodward* (1819), did not involve debtor relief.[52] But others did. In the 1819 case of *Sturges v. Crowninshield*, the U.S. Supreme Court struck down New York's bankruptcy law.[53] Eleven years later, the justices clarified that state legislatures could not get away with printing paper money simply by giving it a different name.[54] Debtors did score some successes. In the 1827 case of *Ogden v. Saunders*, the court upheld a New York bankruptcy law on the basis of its only applying to debts contracted after its adoption. In *Mason v. Haile*, the justices allowed states to eliminate debtor's prison. But *Ogden*—the only Supreme Court decision on a matter of constitutional interpretation from which Chief Justice

John Marshall ever dissented—and *Mason* were the debtors' last major victories at the Supreme Court until after the Civil War. The Contracts Clause was coming into its own.[55]

Granted, the Supreme Court rarely stepped in to overturn state debtor relief legislation, but it did not need to do so, because lower courts, state as well as federal, were equal to the task.[56] In both of the first two instances of federal circuit courts striking down state laws, the legislators had been trying to protect debtors. North Carolina assemblymen voted during the Revolutionary War to enable citizens to discharge any debt owed to a Loyalist by paying the state government a nominally equivalent sum. In February 1791, the Rhode Island assembly adopted legislation granting a man named Silas Casey a three-year respite from his debts, including one owed to British merchants Champion & Dickason, and the firm sued. Federal courts voided both laws in 1792.[57] The Vermont assembly responded to the Panic of 1819 by adopting a stay law, but a U.S. court overturned it as an impairment of contract.[58]

Nor did federal judges stand alone in this fight. Article VI makes the Constitution and all federal treaties and statutes the supreme law of the land and mandates that "the Judges in every State shall be bound thereby," and over time state-level justices became increasingly bold about ruling debtor relief unconstitutional. Only twice in the 1790s did state courts find constitutional grounds for overturning state laws other than those interfering in judicial procedure; in both cases, Rhode Island justices nullified paper money statutes that violated the Contracts Clause. Article I, Section 10 was also the basis for the North Carolina Supreme Court's decision to overturn an 1812 statute halting executions against debtors.[59] Often state judges who struck down debtor relief legislation came in for private abuse or even public censure. In 1815, when a panel of superior court judges ruled that Georgia's eight-year-old stay violated "The 10th section of the 1st article" of the Constitution, its members received a formal reprimand from the state assembly.[60] In July 1822, Missouri circuit court justices found the state's stay laws unconstitutional, leading many Missourians to call for their dismissal.[61]

By all accounts, the state where the judiciary generated the most turmoil by rigorously enforcing the Contracts Clause was Kentucky. In 1820, the assembly adopted a replevin law (allowing debtors whose property had been confiscated to recover it upon discharging the debt), only to see it ruled unconstitutional by two circuit judges, one of whom, James Clark, insisted that previous to the adoption of the Constitution, "the frequent interference of the state legislatures with the private rights of individuals, the property laws of some, and the suspension laws of all, had, in a great degree, impaired public faith, and destroyed the regular course of business," a malady that Article I, Section 10 had remedied by placing "the private contracts of men out of the reach of legislative control."[62]

Relief advocates in the legislature initiated a move to fire Clark and the other judge who had overturned the replevin law, but they fell just short of the required two-thirds majority. When the court of appeals, the highest tribunal in the state, affirmed the two lower court decisions, its members were also saved from removal only by the requirement of a supermajority. But regular legislation only needed a simple majority, so in December 1824, the Kentucky legislature abolished the appeals court altogether, replacing it with a new panel whose members would be appointed by prorelief governor Joseph Desha. The existing appeals court judges ruled that this legislation was itself a violation of the state constitution; they refused to disband, and for the next two years Kentucky had two competing appeals courts.

Shortly after the autumn 1825 election, the controversy took a violent turn. Early on the morning of November 7, hours before the assembly was due to convene, Solomon Sharp, the legislative leader of the "New Court" faction, was murdered at the door of his Frankfort home. Sharp's widow and brother accused the "Old Court" faction of having instigated the murderer, Jereboam Beauchamp, by telling him that Sharp was spreading a rumor that Beauchamp's wife had given birth to a mixed-race child. The 1826 election yielded a clear victory for the Old Court faction, which proceeded to repeal the legislation creating a debtor-friendly appeals court.[63]

The federal and state judges' growing adherence to the Contracts Clause provoked many Americans to advance the "agency" theory of representation, which requires public officials to view themselves not as trustees who best know the true interests of their constituents but as agents whose highest calling is to do the voters' bidding. Some debtor-relief advocates even denied the legitimacy of judicial review. The Kentucky House of Representatives drew a sharp contrast between the state's judges, who served life terms, and its own members, who had to face the electorate every single year. Annual elections allowed the representatives' constituents to "test the fidelity of their agency" every year, the assemblymen affirmed. By contrast, the inevitable effect of judicial review by lifetime judges was to "make regents of the agents, and vassals of the people."[64]

Opponents of the various relief schemes contended that the best way to avoid judicial review was to not create a need for it by enacting unconstitutional statutes, and these fast friends of the Contracts Clause were increasingly to be found even in the state legislatures. After more than 450 New Castle County, Delaware, citizens responded to the Panic of 1819 by petitioning the assembly for relief, a legislative committee investigated various schemes and concluded that none would pass constitutional muster. None was adopted.[65] A proposal to prohibit the sale of debtors' property below three quarters of its assessed value came before the Virginia House of Delegates early in 1820. Opponents branded the legislation a clear violation of the Contracts Clause, one delegate reminding his colleagues that "laws similar in their character to the present bill had been pronounced to be unconstitutional." The battle over the property valuation bill coincided with the Missouri crisis, and supporters of the legislation mustered states-rights rhetoric in its defense. A delegate from Kanawha County challenged his fellow Virginians not to allow the federal government to "deny to the states the power to regulate the process of their own courts." In the end, though, constitutional and other qualms led the House of Delegates to defeat the bill, 113 to 74.[66]

By serving in effect as debt collector of last resort, the U.S. government made its presence felt in every home and business in America. Indeed, given that few nineteenth-century Americans paid federal taxes or received federal help, it may well be that the areas where ordinary citizens most felt the force of their national government were the constitutional ban on fiat currency and the federal courts' intensifying enforcement of the Contracts Clause, which in turn had an immeasurable but important chilling effect on state judges and even legislators.

The gradually escalating judicial assault on debtor relief legislation also produced unintended consequences—and not just in the realms of economics and traditional politics. Perhaps most spectacularly, the adoption and, over time, the enforcement of Article I, Section 10 contributed in unexpected ways to the erosion of patriarchy and the establishment of a more equitable relationship between American women and men. As federal and state judges closed off more and more of the state assemblies' options for alleviating their indebted constituents' distress, legislators had to become increasingly creative. One solution that gradually dawned on them was to allow families to put some of their property in the wife's name, shielding it not only from the husband but from his creditors.

Although English common law, which prevailed in most American states even after 1776, did not allow married women to own personal property, it permitted wives who could obtain their husbands' consent to establish "separate estates"; typically the woman's father would deposit property in a trust for the wife's sole benefit. By the time Thomas Jefferson and Benjamin Franklin wrote their wills, both men's sons-in-law were insolvent, which meant that anything bequeathed to Martha Jefferson Randolph or Sarah Franklin Bache would be fair game for their husbands' creditors. So Jefferson and Franklin both established separate estates, and both of Abigail Adams's sisters had them, too.[67] More and more women acquired separate estates in the early nineteenth century, but setting them up was expensive, so, starting in 1839, the state legislatures began adopting legislation allowing married women to own and control property without having to go to the trouble and expense of establishing trusts.[68]

That conservative Mississippi was the first state to adopt a married women's property act may seem surprising, but the state's leading role made sense for several reasons. State senator Thomas Hadley, the sponsor of the Mississippi law, had previously lived in Louisiana, where the prevailing civil law allowed women to retain property even after marrying. Apparently he and his wife Piety were impressed with the civil system and wished to move Mississippi in the same direction.[69] In addition, Mississippi's highest court had recently allowed one segment of the state's female population, those who had married under Chickasaw law, to continue owning property even after marrying.[70]

By far the most important reason Mississippi became the first state to adopt a married women's property act was its heavy dependence on the cultivation of cotton, which was America's most valuable crop but also one of the most volatile. Rising prices drove Mississippi's cotton production from 85 million pounds in 1834 to nearly 200 million pounds in 1839, by which time Mississippi produced more cotton fiber than any other state.[71] But then the Panic of 1837 brought the cotton boom to a screeching halt, and in Hinds County, Mississippi, alone, more than 1,000 debt suits were filed.[72] Hinds County farmers insisted that their sheriff, whose duties included seizing debtors' property on behalf of their creditors, resign his position, and they "threaten[ed] vengeance against any one who will accept the office." Similar demands were made in other Mississippi counties, and there was even an unconfirmed report that Yazoo County citizens "had torn down their Court-house." Rumors about these debtor revolts made it all the way to John Prentiss, the editor of the *New-Hampshire Sentinel*, putting him in mind of the agrarian rebellion in neighboring Massachusetts fifty years earlier. If the rumors were true, Prentiss mused, then Mississippians were in "'the midst of a revolution'—Daniel Shays' time come again."[73]

The married women's property act that Mississippi adopted in February 1839 fell far short of giving wives the same rights as husbands. Only one type of personal property that the bride brought to the marriage—slaves—would remain her own, and any wages she earned went to her husband. But the Mississippi statute was an important first step.[74]

Over the next four years, only two more states (Rhode Island and Texas) and one territory (Arkansas) granted married women permission to own property. Then on February 23, 1843, the Supreme Court handed American debtors their most devastating defeat yet. After the death of Chief Justice John Marshall in 1835, President Andrew Jackson had named Roger B. Taney to succeed him. Although best known as the author of the infamous *Dred Scott vs. Sandford* (1857) decision, Taney is generally seen as more sympathetic than his predecessor to states' rights and to the plight of ordinary white farmers. But in *Bronson v. Kinzie*, the Taney court did something Marshall and his colleagues had never done: it ruled that state valuation laws, which halted sheriffs' sales when no one bid above a certain amount, violated the Framers' intent to "maintain the integrity of contracts and to secure their faithful execution throughout this Union by placing them under the protection of the Constitution of the United States."[75]

Bronson v. Kinzie was evidence of intensifying judicial determination to enforce the Contracts Clause; it also became an important if overlooked mile-
stone in the history of family law. Over the next five years, fifteen more state
assemblies enacted married women's property legislation. Although most of
these statutes did more for wives than Mississippi had, none gave them the
same property rights as men. Still, the early married women's property acts
were a necessary step toward more comprehensive reform. And they might
never have been adopted in the absence of constitutional provisions prohibiting the state assemblies from shielding male debtors in more conventional ways
that preserved their gender privileges.[76]

After the Civil War that the Constitution was designed in part to prevent,
the ratification of the Thirteenth, Fourteenth, and Fifteenth Amendments set
in motion the painfully slow process by which the document that had been
written largely with the intention of attracting wealthy investors became something like its opposite: a guardian of the poor and powerless. The journey to
the underdog's Constitution was most remarkable for its countless detours. For
example, in the late nineteenth and early twentieth centuries, Supreme Court
justices found that they could use even the Fourteenth Amendment, which was
written to safeguard the civil rights of former slaves, for purposes that called
to mind the Founding Fathers' commercial motives for writing the Constitution in the first place.[77]

∗ ∗ ∗

Shortly after the Revolutionary War, the United States sank into a deep recession, and most well-to-do Americans could see only one way to extricate the
nation from its financial rut. They must transfer several of the state governments' key functions—from determining the money supply to levying taxes to
pay off the war debt—to a new national government that would be much less
susceptible to the influence of ordinary citizens. Only with this radical reform
could Americans attract sufficient investment capital to end the recession and
spur growth. But not everyone agreed, either with the Framers' elitist diagnosis of the nation's economic woes or with the remedy they prescribed. Many
Americans challenged the Framers' assumption that during the 1780s, farmers
and their state representatives had proven themselves incapable of self-
government. And they questioned whether the benefits of living under a capitalist Constitution justified the considerable costs.

As it turned out, both sides' predictions proved correct: the Constitution
spurred rapid economic growth, and disabling the state assemblies from coming
to the aid of indebted farmers entailed considerable pain. As the nineteenth-
century economy lurched between soaring summits and deep troughs, Americans could see that the Federalists had accurately forecast the booms—and that

with equal clarity, the relief advocates had foreseen the busts. But the ratification of the Constitution also led to unforeseen and even unimaginable consequences. Perhaps most astonishingly, the elimination of state-based paper money and the adoption of the Contracts Clause set the stage for the epochal enactment of the first round of married women's property acts. In one of its most liberating, albeit unintended, consequences, the Constitution had advanced the emancipation of America's nominally free women by increasing the likelihood that their husbands would lose everything they had.

Notes

1. U.S. Const., art. I, § 10; William Davie, speech in the North Carolina ratifying convention, July 29, 1788, in *The Records of the Federal Convention of 1787*, ed. Max Farrand, (New Haven, Conn.: Yale University Press, 1911), 3:350; Charles Pinckney, speech in South Carolina ratifying convention, May 20, 1788, in *The Debates in the Several State Conventions on the Adoption of the Federal Constitution*, 2nd ed., ed. Jonathan Elliot (Washington, D.C., 1836), 4:333; Edmund Pendleton to James Madison, October 8, 1787, in *The Documentary History of the Ratification of the Constitution* (hereinafter *DHRC*), ed. John P. Kaminski and Gaspare J. Saladino (Madison: State Historical Society of Wisconsin, 1993), 10:1773.

2. Extract of a letter from Salem County, West Jersey, October 22, 1787, *Pennsylvania Herald*, October 27, 1787, *DHRC*, 3: 140–41; Benjamin Rush to Jeremy Belknap, February 28, 1788, in *The Debate on the Constitution: Federalist and Antifederalist Speeches, Articles, and Letters during the Struggle over Ratification*, vol. 2, *January to August, 1788*, ed. Bernard Bailyn (New York: Library of America, 1993), 256; James Wilson, speech in Pennsylvania ratifying convention, December 4, 1787, *DHRC*, 2:500; John Fiske, *The Critical Period of American History, 1783–1789* (Boston, 1888), 272–75. To state that Article I, Section 10 was a major reason why Federalists supported the Constitution is not to say that this clause figured prominently in the opposition to the document. It did in some regions, but Anti-Federalists had a host of other, more pressing, reasons to oppose the Constitution. Indeed many of them, including Elbridge Gerry of Massachusetts and George Mason of Virginia, were themselves fervent opponents of paper money and other debtor relief legislation. George William Van Cleve, "The Anti-Federalists' Toughest Challenge: Paper Money, Debt Relief, and the Ratification of the Constitution," *Journal of the Early Republic* 34, no. 4 (Winter 2014): 529–60.

3. Henry Knox to Rufus King, June 8, 1787, in *The Life and Correspondence of Rufus King*, vol. 1, *Comprising His Letters, Private and Official, His Public Documents and His Speeches, 1755–1794*, ed. Charles R. King (New York: G. P. Putnam's Sons, 1894), 222; "Extract of a Letter from a Gentleman in Washington County," *Albany Gazette*, June 21, 1787, *DHRC*, 13:141; Theodore Sedgwick to Nathan Dane, July 5, 1787, Sedgwick Family Papers, Massachusetts Historical Society, Boston; *United States Chronicle* (Hartford), June 1, 1786; Edmund Randolph, speech, June 12, 1787, in Farrand, *Records of the Federal Convention of 1787*, 1:218.

4. Charles Lee to George Washington, April 11, 1788, *Founders Online*, National Archives, last modified June 29, 2017, http://founders.archives.gov/documents/Washington/04-06-02-0181; Roger H. Brown, *Redeeming the Republic: Federalists, Taxation, and the*

Origins of the Constitution (Baltimore, Md.: Johns Hopkins University Press, 1993), 259.

5. Silas Deane to Samuel B. Webb, July 16, 1785, in *Correspondence and Journals of Samuel Blachley Webb*, vol. 3, *1783–1806*, ed. Worthington Chauncey Ford, (New York, 1893), 49; Samuel Wales, "A Sermon Preached Before the General Assembly of the State of Connecticut, at Hartford," May 12, 1785, in *Political Sermons of the American Founding Era, 1730–1805*, ed. Ellis Sandoz (Indianapolis: Liberty Fund, 1998), 1:852.

6. George Washington to Henry Lee Jr., October 31, 1786, *Founders Online*, National Archives, last modified June 29, 2017, http://founders.archives.gov/documents/Washington/04-04-02-0286; Elbridge Gerry, speech, May 31, 1787, and Hamilton, speech, June 18, 1787, in Farrand, *Records of the Federal Convention of 1787*, 1:48, 301.

7. Assemblymen served for two years in South Carolina, six months in Connecticut, and one year in the other eleven states. The first state constitutions are usefully summarized in Bailyn, *Debate on the Constitution*, 2:1087–92 and are printed in full in Francis Newton Thorpe, ed., *The Federal and State Constitutions, Colonial Charters, and Other Organic Laws of the States, Territories, and Colonies Now or Heretofore Forming the United States of America*, 7 vols. (Washington, D.C.: Government Printing Office, 1909). They are available online at http://avalon.law.yale.edu.

8. In some states, the upper house of the legislature was known as the council. Two states—Pennsylvania and Georgia—had no upper house. The Pennsylvania constitution of 1776 placed executive authority in the hands of a twelve-member supreme executive council; there was no governor. Pennsylvania constitution, September 28, 1776, Georgia constitution, February 5, 1777, available at http://avalon.yale.edu.

9. John J. McCusker and Russell R. Menard, *The Economy of British America, 1607–1789* (Chapel Hill: University of North Carolina Press, 1985), 373–74.

10. Brown, *Redeeming the Republic*.

11. Anonymous essay, *Massachusetts Centinel*, October 13, 1787, *DHRC*, 4:70; William Cranch to John Quincy Adams, November 26, 1787, *DHRC*, 4:319.

12. Robert E. Brown, *Charles Beard and the Constitution: A Critical Analysis of "An Economic Interpretation of the Constitution"* (Princeton, N.J.: Princeton University Press, 1956); Forrest McDonald, *We the People: The Economic Origins of the Constitution* (Chicago: University of Chicago Press, 1958); E. James Ferguson, *The Power of the Purse: A History of American Public Finance, 1776–1790* (Chapel Hill: University of North Carolina Press, 1961), 340–41; George Athan Billias, *Elbridge Gerry: Founding Father and Republican Statesman* (New York: McGraw-Hill, 1976), 131–32; Forrest McDonald, *Alexander Hamilton: A Biography* (New York: W. W. Norton, 1979), 137. For an effort to revive Beard's interpretation, see Robert A. McGuire and Robert L. Ohsfeldt, "Economic Interests and the American Constitution: A Quantitative Rehabilitation of Charles A. Beard," *Journal of Economic History* 44, no. 2 (1984): 509–19; Robert A. McGuire, *To Form a More Perfect Union: A New Economic Interpretation of the United States Constitution* (Oxford: Oxford University Press, 2003).

13. Charles F. Hobson, "The Negative on State Laws: James Madison, the Constitution, and the Crisis of Republican Government," *William and Mary Quarterly* (hereinafter *WMQ*) 36, no. 2 (April 1979): 215–35.

14. James Madison, June 19, 1787, in Farrand, *Records of the Federal Convention of 1787*, 1:318.

15. James Madison to Thomas Jefferson, October 24, 1787, *Founders Online*, National Archives, last modified June 29, 2017, http://founders.archives.gov/documents/Madison/01-10-02-0151; Gordon S. Wood, *The Creation of the American Republic, 1776–1787* (Chapel Hill: University of North Carolina Press, 1969), 467.

16. James Madison, "Preface to Debates in the Convention of 1787," in Farrand, *Records of the Federal Convention of 1787*, 3:548.

17. John Francis Mercer, speech, August 14, 1787, in Farrand, *Records of the Federal Convention of 1787*, 2:288–89; Donald S. Lutz, *Popular Consent and Popular Control: Whig Political Theory in the Early State Constitutions* (Baton Rouge: Louisiana State University, 1980), 119; Lance Banning, *The Sacred Fire of Liberty: James Madison and the Founding of the Federal Republic* (Ithaca, N.Y.: Cornell University Press, 1995), 114.

18. In assessing the economic origins of the Constitution, many scholars focus on a series of needs that went unmet under the Articles of Confederation: protecting American shipping against the Barbary pirates; retaliating against British trade barriers in hopes of bringing them down; creating a national market by eliminating the tariffs that the thirteen states had (allegedly) begun to levy on each others' goods—and let us not forget that old chestnut, standardizing a currency system that was supposedly too diverse and too complex. The historians who offer these explanations generally downplay or altogether ignore the imperative that was most frequently articulated by the Framers themselves: the need to make the United States a more attractive place in which to invest. Douglass C. North, *The Economic Growth of the United States, 1790–1860* (Englewood Cliffs, N.J.: Prentice-Hall, 1961), 20; Curtis P. Nettels, *The Emergence of a National Economy, 1775–1815* (New York: Harper and Row, 1962), 65–66, 72–75, 91–92; Stuart Bruchey, *The Roots of American Economic Growth, 1607–1861: An Essay in Social Causation* (New York: Harper and Row, 1965), 94–108; Frederick W. Marks, III, *Independence on Trial: Foreign Affairs and the Making of the Constitution* (Baton Rouge: Louisiana State University Press, 1973), 52–95; Drew R. McCoy, *The Elusive Republic: Political Economy in Jeffersonian America* (Chapel Hill: University of North Carolina Press, 1980), 124–26; Brown, *Redeeming the Republic*, 144; Jack N. Rakove, *Original Meanings: Politics and Ideas in the Making of the Constitution* (New York: Knopf, 1996), 26–27. My thanks to Stephen Gillette for the notion of the Constitution as a debtors' document.

19. John Jay, *An Address to the People of the State of New York on the Subject of the Constitution Agreed Upon at Philadelphia*, 1788, in *Pamphlets on the Constitution of the United States, Published During its Discussion by the People, 1787–1788*, ed. Paul Leicester Ford (Brooklyn, N.Y., 1888), 73; Alexander Hamilton, speech in New York legislature, April 12, 1787, in *The Papers of Alexander Hamilton*, vol. 4, *January 1787–1788*, ed. Harold C. Syrett (New York: Columbia University Press, 1962), 145; Alexander Hamilton, *Federalist* No. 85, *The Federalist Papers*, ed. Jacob E. Cooke (Middletown, Conn.: Wesleyan University Press, 1961), par. 3 (henceforth cited by author, *Federalist*, essay:paragraph).

20. Jack N. Rakove, *James Madison and the Creation of the American Republic* (New York: Harper Collins, 1990), 32.

21. George Washington, quoted in Woody Holton, *Forced Founders: Indians, Debtors, Slaves, and the Making of the American Revolution in Virginia* (Chapel Hill: University of North Carolina Press, 1999), 3. On Washington's land speculation, see Charles A. Beard, *An Economic Interpretation of the Constitution of the United States* (New York: Macmillan, 1913), 144; Holton, *Forced Founders*, 3–11, 37, 210, 215; Charles Royster, *The Fabulous History of the Dismal Swamp Company: A Story of George Washington's Times* (New York: Knopf, 1999).

22. George Washington, quoted in James Madison to Thomas Jefferson, August 12, 1786, *Founders Online*, National Archives, last modified June 29, 2017, http://founders.archives.gov/documents/Madison/01-09-02-0026.

23. Madison to Jefferson, August 12, 1786; James Madison to James Monroe, February 24, 1786, *Founders Online*, National Archives, last modified June 29, 2017, http://founders. archives.gov/documents/Madison/01-08-02-0262; Irving Brant, *James Madison: The Nationalist, 1780–1787* (Indianapolis: Bobbs-Merrill, 1948), 339–40.
24. Madison to Jefferson, August 12, 1786.
25. Thomas Jefferson to James Madison, December 16, 1786, *Founders Online*, National Archives, last modified June 29, 2017, http://founders.archives.gov/documents /Jefferson/01-10-02-0461. On Jefferson's land speculation, see Holton, *Forced Founders*, 3–13, 32–37.
26. Beard, *Economic Interpretation of the Constitution*. My thanks to Stephen Gillette for this insight.
27. Charles Jared Ingersoll (1825), quoted in Drew R. McCoy, *The Last of the Fathers: James Madison and the Republican Legacy* (Cambridge: Cambridge University Press, 1989), 73.
28. James Madison, *Federalist* 62:17.
29. James Madison, *Federalist* 10; Woody Holton, "Divide et Impera: The Tenth *Federalist* in a Wider Sphere," *WMQ* 62 (April 2005): 175–212.
30. "Answer of the Town of Greenwich to the Circular Letter from Boston," *Worcester Magazine* 2, no. 35 (last week of November 1786): 422; David Daggett, *An Oration, Pronounced in the Brick Meeting-House, in the City of New-Haven, on the Fourth of July, A.D. 1787* (New Haven, Conn., 1787), 4–5, 14; Robert A. Becker, "Currency, Taxation, and Finance, 1775–1787," in *The Blackwell Encyclopedia of the American Revolution*, ed. Jack P. Greene and J. R. Pole (Cambridge, Mass.: Blackwell, 1991), 367; Brown, *Redeeming the Republic*, 33–36; Max M. Edling, *A Revolution in Favor of Government: Origins of the U.S. Constitution and the Making of the American State* (Oxford: Oxford University Press, 2003), 155–58; Woody Holton, "'From the Labours of Others': The War Bonds Controversy and the Origins of the Constitution in New England," *WMQ* 61, no. 2 (April 2004): 271–316.
31. Woody Holton, *Unruly Americans and the Origins of the Constitution* (New York: Hill and Wang, 2007), 103, 122–23.
32. Sussex County citizens, petition, January–February 1787 legislative petitions, record group 1111, reel 8, frames 341–43 (first quotation); Delaware citizens, petition, May–June 1786 legislative petitions, Delaware Public Archives, reel 7, frame 448; "Proceedings of the General Court," *Boston Magazine* 3 (March 1786): 139 (second quotation); Daggett, *Fourth of July Oration*, 12; Lancaster town meeting, representative instructions, January 22, 1787, *Worcester Magazine* 2, no. 44 (first week of February 1787): 532.
33. Terry Bouton, "The Trials of the Confederation," in *The Oxford Handbook of the American Revolution*, ed. Edward G. Gray and Jane Kamensky (Oxford: Oxford University Press, 2013), 372–74.
34. Beard, *Economic Interpretation of the Constitution*, 47–48; Merrill Jensen, *The New Nation: A History of the United States during the Confederation, 1781–1789* (New York: Knopf, 1950), 423–24; Wood, *Creation of the American Republic*, 394–95.
35. William F. Hixson, *Triumph of the Bankers: Money and Banking in the Eighteenth and Nineteenth Centuries* (Westport, Conn.: Praeger, 1993), 46–58; Terry Bouton, *Taming Democracy: "The People," the Founders, and the Troubled Ending of the American Revolution* (Oxford: Oxford University Press, 2007), 17–21.
36. Ferguson, *Power of the Purse*, 244; Holton, *Unruly Americans*, 113.
37. Alexander Hamilton, speech in New York assembly, February 18, 1787, *American Museum* 1 (June 1787): 524.

38. Morton J. Horwitz argues that the Constitution fostered capitalist development not only in the ways its authors intended but also in an unexpected manner. Ratification set the stage for congressional enactment of the Funding and Assumption Acts of 1790–1791, which gave an immense boost to the value of government securities, leading in turn to an important change in the way American courts viewed contracts. Securities speculation produced windfall profits for some, devastating losses for others—and a barrage of lawsuits that provoked judges to abandon their long-standing practice of considering whether a particular contract was fair, an approach that had often led them to allow the parties to recover only what they had brought to the deal. Henceforth judges would define their duty differently, as ensuring that both parties received everything the contract had promised them, and this new approach fostered capitalist development. Morton J. Horwitz, *The Transformation of American Law, 1780–1860* (Cambridge, Mass.: Harvard University Press, 1977), 160–77.

39. Thomas P. Slaughter, *The Whiskey Rebellion: Frontier Epilogue to the American Revolution* (New York: Oxford University Press, 1988); William Hogeland, *The Whiskey Rebellion: George Washington, Alexander Hamilton, and the Frontier Rebels Who Challenged America's Newfound Sovereignty* (New York: Scribner, 2006); Bouton, *Taming Democracy*, 219–26.

40. Brown, *Redeeming the Republic*, 236; Edling, *Revolution in Favor of Government*, 211–14.

41. North, *Economic Growth of the United States*, 36–54; Stephen Mihm, *A Nation of Counterfeiters: Capitalists, Con Men, and the Making of the United States* (Cambridge, Mass.: Harvard University Press, 2007), 15.

42. Hixson, *Triumph of the Bankers*, 91–92.

43. Richard S. Chew, "Certain Victims of an International Contagion: The Panic of 1797 and the Hard Times of the Late 1790s in Baltimore," *Journal of the Early Republic* 25, no. 4 (Winter 2005): 574.

44. Scott Reynolds Nelson, *A Nation of Deadbeats: An Uncommon History of America's Financial Disasters* (New York: Knopf, 2012), 35; Michael A. Blaakman, "The Marketplace of American Federalism: Land Speculators, Governments, and the Post-Revolutionary Mania in Lands" (paper presented at "'So Sudden an Alteration': The Causes, Course, and Consequences of the American Revolution," Massachusetts Historical Society conference, Boston, April 9–11, 2015, 28.

45. Richard B. Sheridan, "The British Credit Crisis of 1772 and the American Colonies," *Journal of Economic History* 20, no. 2 (June 1960): 161–86. On the nineteenth-century boom-bust cycle, see Nelson, *Nation of Deadbeats*.

46. Hixson, *Triumph of the Bankers*, 91–92; Christine Desan, "From Blood to Profit: Making Money in the Practice and Imagery of Early America," *Journal of Policy History* 20, no. 1 (January 2008): 34–36.

47. Arndt M. Stickles, *The Critical Court Struggle in Kentucky, 1819–1829* (Bloomington: Indiana University Press, 1929), 10.

48. Mihm, *Nation of Counterfeiters*, 3.

49. Joseph Stancliffe Davis, "William Duer, Entrepreneur, 1747–99," in *Essays in the Earlier History of American Corporations* (Cambridge, Mass.: Harvard University Press 1917), 1:202–3; Nelson, *Nation of Deadbeats*, 3–5, 26–32.

50. R. Kent Newmyer, *The Supreme Court Under Marshall and Taney* (New York: Crowell, 1968), 31; Theodore W. Ruger, "'A Question Which Convulses a Nation': The Early Republic's Greatest Debate about the Judicial Review Power," *Harvard Law Review* 117, no. 3 (January 2004): 826–97, esp. 831n21.

51. *Ware v. Hylton*, like most of those in which federal courts overturned state debtor re-lief legislation, began with a prodebtor decision by a state court that the creditor then appealed in federal court. Ware v. Hylton, 3 U.S. 243 (1796); Charles F. Hobson, "Ware v. Hylton," in *The Oxford Guide to United States Supreme Court Decisions*, 2nd ed., ed. Kermit L. Hall and James W. Ely Jr. (Oxford: Oxford University Press, 2009); quo-tation from William Michael Treanor, "Judicial Review Before *Marbury*," *Stanford Law Review* 58, no. 2 (November 2005): 554, http://www.stanfordlawreview.org/print /article/judicial-review-before-marbury.

52. Many of the early contract cases, including *Fletcher* and *Dartmouth*, involved con-tracts to which the state government was itself a party. "T. M.," "Art. 1–Law of Contracts—Obligation of Contracts," *American Jurist and Law Magazine* 24 (Janu-ary 1841): 257–80, esp. 264–69; Christopher Tomlins, "Republican Law," in *Oxford Handbook of the American Revolution*, 555. Mark Douglas McGarvie demonstrates that American courts, including the Supreme Court, frequently justified the separation of church and state by invoking the Contracts Clause—more often, in fact, than they justified it using the First Amendment. Mark Douglas McGarvie, *One Nation Under Law: America's Early National Struggles to Separate Church and State* (DeKalb: North-ern Illinois University Press, 2004).

53. Sturges v. Crowninshield, 17 U.S. 122 (1819); Richard H. Chused, "Married Women's Property Law: 1800–1850," *Georgetown Law Journal* 71 (June 1983): 1402. All U.S. Supreme Court decisions are available at https://supreme.justia.com.

54. Craig v. Missouri, 29 U.S. 410 (1830).

55. Wayman v. Southard, 23 U.S. 1 (1825); Bank of the United States v. Halstead, 23 U.S. 51 (1825); Ogden v. Saunders, 25 U.S. (1827); Mason v. Haile, 25 U.S. 370 (1827); Stickles, *Critical Court Struggle in Kentucky*, 33; Larry D. Kramer, *The People Themselves: Popular Constitutionalism and Judicial Review* (New York: Oxford University Press, 2004), 150–51. Dwight Wiley Jessup observes that around 1825, the Marshall Court, in ap-parent response to public pressure, dropped its campaign to extend the reach of the Contracts Clause. But among Jessup's numerous examples of judicial "accommoda-tion," only *Ogden v. Saunders* involved debtor-creditor relations. Jessup, "Reaction and Accommodation: The United States Supreme Court and Political Conflict, 1809–1835" (PhD diss., University of Minnesota, 1978), 324–26.

56. Debt relief legislation is the one glaring exception to legal historians' generalization that U.S. courts were slow to assert the power of judicial review. But as with other kinds of cases, the process by which federal judges assumed the authority to overturn state debtor relief legislation was gradual, and it only reached fruition with *Bronson v. Kinzie* in 1843. William E. Nelson, "Changing Conceptions of Judicial Review: The Evolution of Constitutional Theory in the States, 1790–1860," *University of Pennsylva-nia Law Review* 120 (June 1972): 1166–85; Kramer, *The People Themselves*.

57. *Providence Gazette*, June 16, 23, 1792; Treanor, "Judicial Review before *Marbury*," 518–21; Steven R. Boyd, "The Contract Clause and the Evolution of American Federalism, 1789–1815," *WMQ* 44, no. 3 (July 1987): 529–48, esp. 539–40; Gordon S. Wood, *Empire of Liberty: A History of the Early American Republic, 1789–1815* (Oxford: Oxford Uni-versity Press, 2009), 409n.

58. Walter Hill Crockett, *Vermont: The Green Mountain State* (New York: Century His-tory, 1921), 3:181.

59. As Stephen Boyd points out, the Constitution did not immediately eliminate all debt relief legislation, but there were many "fewer interferences in contracts" after 1788 than before, and state paper money—seen by many as the plague of the pre-Constitution

era—was eliminated; Boyd, "Contract Clause and the Evolution of American Federalism," 542, 548. See also *Providence Gazette*, June 25, July 9, 1791; Treanor, "Judicial Review before *Marbury*," 502–3; A. H. Feller, "Moratory Legislation: A Comparative Study," *Harvard Law Review*, 46, no. 7 (May 1933): 1061–85, esp. 1072, 1081–85.

60. "Opinion of the Judges of the Superior Court of the State of Georgia, Pronounced in the Superior Court of Richmond County, January Term, 1815," *Augusta Herald*, January 19, 1815, 1 (both quotations); Milton Sydney Heath, *Constructive Liberalism: The Role of the State in Economic Development in Georgia to 1860* (Cambridge, Mass.: Harvard University Press, 1954), 168–69.

61. Murray N. Rothbard, *The Panic of 1819: Reactions and Policies* (New York: Columbia University Press, 1962), 46.

62. Clark noted that the replevin law also violated the 1799 Kentucky state constitution, which contained a provision adopted in conformity to the federal contracts clause. Decision in *Blair v. Williams* (1822), quoted in "The Case of Judge Clark," *Niles Weekly Register*, 23, supplement (1823): 153–54 (reprinted from the *National Intelligencer*) (both quotations); Stickles, *Critical Court Struggle in Kentucky*, 25–26, 30–31.

63. Blair v. Williams, 14 Ky. 34 (1823) and Lapsley v. Brashears, 14 Ky. 47; "The Case of Judge Clark," 153–60; Stickles, *Critical Court Struggle in Kentucky*, 32–33, 40, 47–48, 57–61, 79, 88–103; Matthew G. Schoenbachler, *Murder and Madness: The Myth of the Kentucky Tragedy* (Lexington: University Press of Kentucky, 2009), 151.

64. Kentucky General Assembly, "Preamble and Resolution Vindicating the Constitutionality of Replevin Laws, and the Right of the Legislature to Remove Judges for Error of Opinion, in Reply to the Response of the Judges of the Court of Appeals," *Acts Passed at the First Session of the Thirty-Third General Assembly for the Commonwealth of Kentucky* (Frankfort, Ky., 1825), 250 (first quotation), 273 (second quotation); Ruger, "Question Which Convulses a Nation," 859–60.

65. Rothbard, *Panic of 1819*, 32; Boyd, "Contract Clause and the Evolution of American Federalism," 542, 546.

66. Debate in the Virginia House of Delegates, January 29, 1820, *Richmond Enquirer*, February 1, 1820, 3 (first and second quotations), February 3, 1820, 2 (third and fourth quotations); Rothbard, *Panic of 1819*, 35–38, 212n49. Such attempts to link the relief battle to national politics were rare. In the South, at least, debtor-protection measures, including the married women's property acts, won support from Democrats as well as Whigs. Elizabeth Bowles Warbasse, *The Changing Legal Rights of Married Women, 1800–1861* (New York: Garland, 1987), 149–50.

67. Jefferson's financial affairs were not in much better shape than Randolph's, so most of his property, including proceeds from the sale of Monticello and of most of his slaves, ultimately went to his creditors rather than his daughter. Thomas Jefferson, last will and testament, with codicil, March 16, 17, 1826, accessed August 7, 2017, http://www.monticello.org/site/research-and-collections/last-will-and-testament Steven Harold Hochman, "Thomas Jefferson: A Personal Financial Biography" (PhD diss., University of Virginia, 1987), 283–88; Cynthia A. Kierner, *Martha Jefferson Randolph, Daughter of Monticello: Her Life and Times* (Chapel Hill: University of North Carolina Press, 2012), 200–201; Benjamin Franklin, last will and testament, July 17, 1788 and codicil, June 23, 1789, accessed August 7, 2017, http://franklinpapers.org; Woody Holton, *Abigail Adams* (New York: Free Press, 2009), 296–97, 339.

68. In some areas, including South Carolina, the number of marriage settlements remained unchanged in the early nineteenth century. Marylynn Salmon, "Women and Property in South Carolina: The Evidence from Marriage Settlements," *WMQ* 39, no. 4

(October 1982): 660, 666; Chused, "Married Women's Property Law," 1361; Suzanne Lebsock, *The Free Women of Petersburg: Status and Culture in a Southern Town, 1784–1860*
(New York: W. W. Norton, 1984), 57, 60.

69. J. F. H. Claiborne, *Mississippi, as a Province, Territory, and State: With Biographical
Notices of Eminent Citizens* (Jackson, Miss.: Power and Barksdale, 1880), 1:475–76; Sara
Brooks Sundberg, "Women and Property in Early Louisiana: Legal Systems at Odds,"
Journal of the Early Republic 32, no. 4 (Winter 2012): 633–65.

70. Megan Benson, "*Fisher v. Allen*: The Southern Origins of the Married Women's Property Acts," *Journal of Southern Legal History* 6 (1998): 97–122 (quotation from *Fisher
v. Allen* at 102); Sandra Moncrief, "The Mississippi Married Women's Property Act of
1839," *Journal of Mississippi History* 47 (May 1985): 110–25; Robert Gilmer, "Chickasaws,
Tribal Laws, and the Mississippi Married Women's Property Act of 1839" (senior thesis, University of North Carolina at Asheville, 2003). Native practices contributed to
the fight for married women's property rights in other states as well. Sally Roesch
Wagner, "The Iroquois Influence on Women's Rights," in *Gone to Croatan: Origins
of North American Dropout Culture*, ed. Ron B. Sakolsky and James Koehnline (New
York, 1993), 225–50.

71. Adam Rothman, *Slave Country: American Expansion and the Origins of the Deep
South* (Cambridge, Mass.: Harvard University Press, 2005), 45–51; Joshua D. Roth-
man, *Flush Times and Fever Dreams: A Story of Capitalism and Slavery in the Age of
Jackson* (Athens: University of Georgia Press, 2012), 3–4.

72. The Mississippi legislature did, however, halt the importation of slaves into the state,
a measure that emphasized the slave traders' essential role in the cotton boom that
led to the Panic of 1837. Lacy K. Ford, *Deliver Us from Evil: The Slavery Question in the
Old South* (New York: Oxford University Press, 2009), 453–58.

73. *New Orleans American*, April 5, 1837, quoted in *The Causes of the Present Crisis, Shown
by an Examiner* (Philadelphia, 1837), 15 (first quotation); *Richmond Enquirer*, May 5,
1837 (second quotation); *New-Hampshire Sentinel*, May 11, 1837 (third quotation).

74. The Mississippi act was also limited in the protection it afforded financially strapped
farm families. Most crucially, it only applied to any property that the wife might acquire in the future. "An Act for the Protection and Preservation of the Rights and
Property of Married Women," February 15, 1839, in *A Digest of the Laws of Mississippi,
Comprising All the Laws of a General Nature, Including the Acts of the Session of 1839*,
ed. T. J. Fox Alden and J. A. Van Hoesen (New York, 1839), 920–21. Without this
concession, creditors might well have gotten the law overturned as a violation of Article
I, Section 10. Still, the Mississippi statute allowed married women to do something
they could not previously have done without going to the trouble and expense of creating a separate estate: place property beyond the reach of their husbands' creditors.

75. Bronson v. Kinzie, 42 U.S. 311, quotation at 318 (1843); Charles W. McCurdy, *The Anti-
Rent Era in New York Law and Politics, 1839–1865* (Chapel Hill: University of North
Carolina Press, 2001), 107–9; "Justice," "Relief—The Currency—Better Times, &c.,"
no. 13, *Indiana State Sentinel*, April 18, 1843, 3.

76. For an extended version of this argument, with greater emphasis on such other factors
as agitation by women's rights advocates, see Woody Holton, "Equality as Unintended
Consequence: The Contracts Clause and the Married Women's Property Acts," *Journal of Southern History* 81, no. 2 (May 2015): 313–40.

77. Santa Clara County v. Southern Pacific Railroad, 118 U.S. 394 (1886); Pembina Consolidated Silver Mining Co. v. Pennsylvania, 125 U.S. 181 (1888).

CHAPTER 2

WHAT *WAS* THE GREAT BULL MARKET?

Value, Valuation, and Financial History

JULIA OTT

The rise and fall of financial markets punctuate our histories of capitalism. Time and again, it seems, a rapacious few lure the unwary masses into acquiring overpriced assets that they can neither afford nor understand. A credit-fueled frenzy of speculation lifts asset prices far above what the "fundamentals" of the "real" economy can support. When prices plummet, a financial crisis may ensue. It wrecks lives, tests governments, and upheaves far-flung economic arrangements. From episode to episode, only the type of asset, the magnitude of price fluctuation, and the final date of reckoning vary.

One episode stands out. For nearly a century, the Great Bull Market of the 1920s and the Crash of 1929 have stood as standards by which we measure all other financial manias and crises.[1] The financial turmoil spilling from the U.S. mortgage market in 2007 triggered a torrent of references to the stock market crash of 1929, for example. Both episodes were preceded by a period of rising asset prices fueled by unsustainable debt. In each incidence, beliefs about the efficiency of financial markets blinded policymakers, financial institutions, and investors to those dangers. In both cases, the collapse of asset markets brought hundreds of financial institutions across the country and around the world to ruin or its brink.

And yet, the Jazz Age stock market was unique. Both the rate of increase in stock prices and the extent of public participation in the stock market were exceptional by historical standards. Between 1921 and 1928, the average rate of annual return in the stock market hit 23.7 percent. The number of U.S.

households owning equity may have increased as much as *sixteen*fold during the 1920s.[2]

Ever since, commentators have reflected upon on the 1920s stock market as they have contemplated questions of price, value, and valuation. Why do the prices of assets fluctuate? Where does financial value come from?

Nothing could be more central to the history of capitalism than capital itself. Property—whether tangible or intangible—becomes capital when it is recognized as an asset, as something that possesses the ability to generate value in the future. Capitalism requires processes and practices of valuation. These create value even as they measure it. Even so, valuation orders *and* disorders markets. Propitious predictions about the generation of value in the future *produce* value in the present, while foreboding predictions destroy it.[3] Valuation is never spontaneous, nor uniform, nor timeless. Valuation—the imaginative, complex, conflictual, and profoundly *social* process by which something attains value—warrants historical scrutiny.[4]

This re-examination of the Great Bull Market of the 1920s reveals how financial values emerge from—and remake—their political, institutional, and ideological context. Changes in popular saving practices and beliefs about financial securities and markets spurred the stock market in the 1920s. The federal government's campaigns to sell war bonds to fund the First World War set these transformations in motion. Distributors of corporate stock echoed those war loan drives after Armistice as they issued newly credible promises about the bright future that mass investment would secure: renewed citizenship, social mobility and stability, and the reconciliation of democracy and industrial corporate capitalism. As the decade wore on, stocks grew more desirable—and valuable—as utopian narratives about mass stock ownership circulated and credit flowed. Corporations, banks, brokerages, and investment trusts marketed stock and extended credit to millions of Americans for the first time not simply because they spied opportunities for profit. Rather, they aimed to resolve key political controversies in their favor. They imagined a future in which broad-based stock ownership would reverse and discredit Progressive Era and wartime constraints on the power of corporations and financial institutions.

* * *

Standard accounts of the Jazz Age stock market—indeed, most financial history—explain changes in asset values and asset prices by extrapolating from presumptions about the psychological state of investors. Some view the high stock prices of the late 1920s as a product of increased demand in response to strong economic "fundamentals" including U.S. corporations' robust earnings, strong dividends, and profitable commercialization of new technologies like radio, aviation, talking pictures, automobiles, and consumer durables.[5]

Most standard accounts, however, see little rational analysis in the singular surge in stock ownership and share prices during the 1920s—or in any financial asset bubble.[6] Economist John Kenneth Galbraith famously characterizes the Great Bull Market as a "mass escape into make-believe" when Americans tossed fundamentals aside in a fit of "seminal lunacy."[7] In a more thoughtful and broader theorization, the financial instability hypothesis of economist Hyman Minsky holds that during any economic expansion, investors come to expect ever-increasing returns on assets and adopt a willingness to borrow more to acquire those assets.[8] Lenders "live in the same expectational climate" and extend credit readily. "Euphoria" ensues as creditors and investors "accept liability [debt] structures" and asset valuations that they would have rejected previously.[9] Debt-fueled demand then ignites a rapid rise in asset prices. Similarly, Charles Kindleberger posits that "the expansion phase of a business cycle" triggers "euphoria" or "mania" in asset markets, especially when investors can easily and cheaply obtain credit from lenders afflicted with the same naive sanguinity.[10] More recently, economists Carmen Reinhart and Kenneth Rogoff finger a "this time is different mentality" for what happened to U.S. stocks in the late 1920s and for dozens of other episodes across countries and centuries.[11]

In standard accounts, historical context helps explain the emergence of belief in everlasting economic growth, asset price appreciation, and credit availability. Hyman Minsky theorizes that a "displacement" or a "shock" that "changes horizons, expectations, anticipated profit opportunities, and behavior" can trigger fanciful valuations that yield inflated asset prices.[12] Historians Maury Klein and Steve Fraser argue that in the 1920s, shocks included not only the new commercial technologies but also a general sense that World War I had abolished the "old rules" of society.[13] (In fact, however, the corporations and financial firms that marketed corporate shares most aggressively in the 1920s presented stock ownership as the expression of traditional, even conservative, American values like industriousness, thrift, egalitarianism, and freedom.)

However logical, these standard accounts share two flawed assumptions. The first—grounded in efficient markets theory—holds that large and rapid changes in asset prices occur because investors ignore fundamental data when rapid social or technological change (and/or humans' natural tendency toward herding behavior) suddenly blocks rational judgments about value. This, in turn, short-circuits the market's natural tendency to price assets properly. The second assumption—grounded in neoclassical economics—holds that the movements of a market can be explained by generalizing from the behavior of individual economic agents.[14]

Efficient markets hypothesis would lead us to expect that for any asset there exists a fundamental value—grounded in fundamental data—toward which market prices gravitate (unless investors depart from rational analysis of those fundamentals).[15] This view assumes that investors *concur* about what information qualifies as fundamental and that all investors enjoy equal access to that data. Efficient market hypothesis also assumes that investors share a valuation framework for processing fundamental information to determine the value of an asset. This framework is most often understood to involve the use of discounting calculations. In these calculations, investors determine the value of an asset by using fundamental data to estimate the returns that an asset will likely generate in the future.[16] Investors then "discount" those future returns by a rate they select—based on projections of risk and future interest rates—over an appropriate period of time. In the case of the stock market, the resulting value might be divided by the number of shares available in a company to calculate the value-per-share. If value-per-share exceeds the current stock price, a rational investor would buy the stock. Asset values vary because investors alter their projections of future returns in response to new fundamental data. (Efficient markets hypothesis offers little explanation for financial manias and panics.)

But as Hyman Minsky recognizes, economic agents act according to "models of the economy" that they construct "out of their experience and their observations of the 'world.'"[17] Multiple, various, and conflicting models—beliefs about what qualifies as fundamental and valuation frameworks or formulas for determining value—coexist.[18] An individual may select and apply models inconsistently. Empirical and interdisciplinary research by behavioral economists and psychologists has shown that irrational thinking and noneconomic motivations like social norms, identity, and bias all condition economic decisionmaking, including the valuation of assets.[19] These are not momentary departures from rational calculations of the probabilities of possible future payouts. Irrational cognition, heuristics, and noneconomic impulses *always* influence investors' behavior.

Ultimately, neither the presumption of individual rationality or irrationality can provide satisfying answers about why asset values vary, why asset prices periodically spike or plummet, or how valuation works. Inferences about the psychological state or cognitive shortcomings of individuals—even if these can be verified with historical evidence—can only explain so much about the behavior of *markets*. Markets do not simply express as prices the aggregation of individual decisions about value. Markets are complex social phenomena, shaped in historically and culturally specific ways by politics and policy, institutions, norms and ideology, and relationships of class, race, and gender.

The Marxian approach to questions of value and valuation differs in significant ways from the standard accounts examined above. Still, it too presumes that a solid basis for value lies beneath the turbulent waters of financial markets. In the Marxian tradition, all value under capitalism originates in surplus-value, the "socially necessary labor-time" that workers impart to commodities they create. Capitalists seize this surplus-value in the form of money when commodities sell.[20] Capitalists may divert some of this money-capital into the credit system. It then becomes interest-bearing capital that may be borrowed by other capitalists (or households, as neo-Marxists observe of contemporary financialization).[21] Acting as the "common capital of the class," interest-bearing capital is accessible to any capitalist in return for interest payments to the finance capitalists (especially banks) who control it. For Marx, the amount of surplus-value each category of capitalist (industrial, commercial, financial) commands—and the prevailing interest-rate on interest-bearing capital—are outcomes that vary historically, based on the distribution of political and social power among these three types of capitalists.[22]

Although Marx locates the origins of interest-bearing capital in the production of surplus-value, he allows that interest-bearing capital may behave independently.[23] For example, a corporation may sell its stock (a form of "fictitious capital") to obtain interest-bearing capital to put to use in production. In doing so, the corporation commits to distributing surplus-value periodically to shareholders in the form of returns.[24]

For Marx and his followers, the periodic and uncertain nature of these distributions explains why the market price of stocks and other financial assets vary. Gesturing to discounting techniques of valuation, Marx wrote that the market price of an asset represents the present value of "the anticipated revenue as reckoned in the advance," then discounted by the "going rate of interest."[25] Because investors' calculations of the present value involve *anticipation* about the production and capture of surplus-value in the future, asset values (and ultimately, prices) vary as investors' expectations change.[26]

Both standard and Marxian accounts hold that asset prices possess an essential foundation in values that themselves are grounded in either fundamental data or surplus-value. Both traditions understand valuation as a process that involves discounting calculations by individuals, with competitive markets reconciling the disparate values that result, then registering this reconciliation as asset price.[27]

In contrast, valuation studies centers its analysis on the *social construction* of value.[28] This emerging interdisciplinary field maintains that competing perspectives on what has value (and why) coexist at a given moment, as do contradictory techniques of valuing. Prices *do not* arise spontaneously because competitive markets reconcile the values generated by disparate valuation frameworks.[29] Rather, valuation frameworks *interrelate* in complex and contingent ways that both are shaped by *and* shape social phenomena: technical devices and arrangements, organizations, networks and institutions, heuristics alongside formal rules and routines, intellectual and ideological justifications, moral and ethical norms, and, especially, prevailing distributions of power.[30]

Value begins when property is recognized as valuable—as a valid means for fulfilling a legitimate end—not only by its current or its prospective owner but also by others. No estimate of value stands alone. This is especially true in financial markets, where rising values and prices often *attract* demand (the so-called Veblen effect) rather than suppressing it, as standard microeconomic theory maintains.[31] As economist John Maynard Keynes famously observed, valuation incorporates belief about *others'* beliefs about value, not unlike a newspaper contest in which the entrants receive a prize if they pick the faces that the readership selects as the most attractive.[32] Just as the outcome of Keynes's contest depends more on assessments of judges' judgment than it does on appraisals of beauty, the "the process of exchange itself" generates and validates the value of an asset.[33]

Valuation references the valuations of others; value draws from other, non-economic values. Sociologist Jens Beckert theorizes that an asset attains "symbolic value" on account of connections imagined between the asset and socially recognized moral norms, aesthetic values, and/or political ideals. An asset gains "relational value" when it is socially recognized as enhancing the social standing of its owner. And valuation at once reflects and contributes to an asset's "imaginative value," that is, an asset's socially recognized potential to alter the future for the better.[34] Certainly agents imagine future profits, forthcoming payments, prospective gains, and enhanced exploitation of labor.[35] Even so, their predictions range beyond monetary returns and often assume narrative form.[36]

Assets—units of capital, tangible or intangible—gain value when agents create, adopt, or adapt narratives about the ability of the asset to shape the future. Particular narratives attain legitimacy and make sense at their specific historical moment and within their particular social context.[37] Capitalism depends, then, upon imagination, the imaginary, and narrative as much as it does on rational, probabilistic calculation—maybe even more.[38] Imagination disturbs capitalism, too. Narratives that sustained values fall apart when forecasts fail. Prices tumble. Creditors refuse further loans. Value disappears but debt remains. Obligations based on discredited narratives about the future weigh down the present.

What "imagined futures" circulated during the Great Bull Market? Who made promises about corporate stock ownership, and why?[39] How did these narratives achieve validity and creditability? In the 1920s, *first* nonfinancial corporations and *then* financial institutions suddenly encouraged mass stock ownership because they anticipated that universal investment would preserve the private administration of industrial corporate capitalism against threats posed by organized labor, radicalism, and the expansion of the regulatory and administrative state. The three key dimensions of the Great Bull Market—the explosion in the number of investors, the soaring prices of shares, and the surge in credit extended on stock collateral—must be understood in the context of prevailing societal concerns, shifting norms and ideology, relations between government and private-sector institutions, and struggles over economic policy.

Before World War I, neither the stock nor the bond markets played much of a direct role in how the vast majority of U.S. households saved money. Less than 1 percent of the population owned either form of financial security, whether issued by a government or by a corporation.[40] Financial securities markets remained peripheral to how most firms raised capital.[41] Americans judged both the bond and stock markets as marginal, even parasitical to the "real" economy of production and commerce.

Concerted efforts by mobilized groups of citizens, prodded by their wartime state, shifted prevailing sentiments and changed savings practices. During the Great War, nearly 20 million Americans pledged to buy a liberty or victory bond (priced for as little as fifty dollars).[42] War Savings, the second program conducted by the Treasury Department's War Loan Organization, sold savings stamps and certificates (priced for as little as five cents) to over 30 million men, women, and children.[43]

Treasury Department officials seized on mass investment in federal debt as a means of encouraging and making evident a widespread sense of identification with the war effort, and indeed, with the nation itself. "The backbone of the whole matter will be the small investor," the war loan engineers explained.[44] Through mass distribution of liberty bonds and war savings stamps and certificates, the War Loan Organization aimed to mobilize all the inhabitants of the United States behind the Great War, even those lacking full political rights. Women, African Americans, Native Americans, recent immigrants, and children could all signify their consent and loyalty by acquiring war debt, War Loan Organization officials imagined.

The war loan drives framed investment as an act that both made and manifested citizenship. At a historical moment marked by passionate debate over the meaning of citizenship, pervasive paranoia about radicalism, and racial conflict, war loan leaders dreamed that the dispossessed, the disenfranchised, and the disaffected would enter into the social contract when they invested in war debt. Universal ownership of federal securities would inculcate in every citizen investor a sense that he or she held a direct stake in the war, in the nation, and in the institution of private property, war loan architects anticipated. As individuals acquired and promoted war bonds, stamps, and certificates, they would gain the sense that they belonged in a national political culture grounded in the shared practice of investment. Universal investment in federal debt would distinguish the American people, superseding all cultural, ethnic, racial, or religious particularities.[45]

In countless speeches, on posters, and through other forms of publicity and pageantry, the war loan campaigns associated investment with suffrage. When Americans subscribed to Liberty loans, one pamphlet pronounced, they endorsed the war "more effectually as if they put a piece of paper in the ballot box.[46] Orators likened the liberty bond to a share in "the greatest, the most glorious, the most honorable and most successful corporation in the world." This "share in America" trope cast the nation as a corporation in which every citizen investor held a share, even if he or she could not cast a vote.[47]

Many opposed American entanglement in Europe. Others deemed Wilson's strategy for financing the war improper.[48] Criticism compelled the War Loan Organization to defend the merit of financial investment as a set of attitudes and practices that would yield a better future for individuals and for the nation as a whole. War loan rhetoric and imagery articulated and dramatized a theory of political economy in which investors' resolve to forego expenditure and their decisions about how to invest set the nation's economic course.[49] Not just federal bonds, stamps, and certificates but financial securities in general were promoted as tools of individual economic freedom, instruments of macroeconomic prosperity and stability, and bulwarks against bolshevism. Indeed, concerns about immigrants and workers sympathizing with the Russian Revolution led directly to the Treasury's establishment of the small-denomination War Savings program in December 1917.

The challenge of mass distribution "would have been hopeless," Treasury Secretary William G. McAdoo later recollected, "if we had not had the willing cooperation" of "an army of volunteer salesmen."[50] An enormous array of private associations mobilized citizen investors en masse. Most important were those organizations representing groups whose fealty the state sought to secure.

Women's, labor, African American, and ethnic associations laid claim to new rights as they roused their members to raise money for the war. The visions of the future that they articulated cast financial instruments and markets as means of achieving and securing those rights. Women's suffragists jockeyed for women's dollars in order to gauge—and to encourage—women's receptivity to the vote. Ethnic societies countered "100 percent American" jingoism by celebrating their ancestral heritages in war loan pageants and parades. Labor unions developed a "back of it all" trope that identified workers' contributions to the war effort as essential. Union leaders anticipated that robust subscription totals would secure the right to organize on a permanent basis after the war. African Americans voiced demands for civic inclusion, political rights, and the destruction of Jim Crow. The editor of the *Savannah Tribune* envisioned a future in which ownership of federal bonds certificates would convey "vast wealth and improved economic and industrial status" to blacks, leveling "the hierarchy of groups" in society and abolishing racial "troubles and friction and oppression."[51]

War loan publicity, imagery, and spectacle fixed associations between investment and citizenship and between securities markets and political democracy. But it was not foreordained that citizen investors would flock to the stock market after the Armistice.

In fact, a number of schemes to transform society through mass investment circulated in the immediate postwar period. Progressives and rail unionists devised the "Plumb plan." It proposed that the federal government buy out the railroads with the proceeds of a mass-marketed bond issue.[52] Federal and state governments sold bonds to fund workers' compensation, maternal and infant health care, pensions for soldiers, mothers, and the elderly, and subsidized farm mortgages.[53] Union locals launched experiments in worker finance and worker ownership. Marcus Garvey and his United Negro Improvement Association sold shares in enterprises like the Black Star Line with the ultimate goal of establishing self-sufficiency among African diaspora communities. The Treasury Department's U.S. Government Savings division continued to market small-denomination federal stamps and certificates as tools of social mobility and security until 1924.[54]

Economic recession and political suppression squashed promises that mass investment would steer society in a progressive direction. The deep economic downturn of 1920–21 hit hard both organized labor and union-led "labor capitalism." FBI harassment led to Marcus Garvey's arrest for mail fraud in 1924, crushing his attempt to create an autonomous "black capitalism." In that same year, banking industry lobbyists convinced the Republican Congress to terminate the successful U.S. Government Savings program.[55]

A new narrative about the promise of mass investment emerged in response to the recession, anticommunist hysteria, labor strife, race riots, and xenophobia that plagued the nation after Armistice.[56] Harvard economist and leading war loan theorist Thomas Nixon Carver first suggested that shares of corporate stock could convey a political-economic stake to disaffected Americans more effectively than public debt. Carver envisioned a "new proprietorship," a future in which universal investment would collectivize the ownership of U.S. corporations and democratize their management. This "silent revolution," Carver promised, would respect private property rights and natural market forces, quite unlike developments in the former Russian Empire.[57]

For Carver and his many disciples, corporate stock seemed to offer the last, best hope for securing propertied status for all Americans and for inducing corporations to align their actions with the public interest.[58] His more progressive adherents believed that federal regulation of the securities markets and a strong labor movement would be required for mass investment to renew economic citizenship in industrial America. Corporate and financial leaders disagreed.

New proprietorship narratives guided a remarkable transformation in financial culture. They inspired a variety of stock distributors to turn their attention—and to extend credit—to novice investors of modest means for the first time in the 1920s. But as corporations and financial firms put Carver's theory into practice, they bent it toward conservative political goals. The "silent revolution" muzzled criticism of industrial corporate capitalism, for a time.

After World War I, as French economist Thomas Piketty demonstrates, both income and wealth inequality fell in the industrialized nations of the West. The obliteration of tangible assets during the war and postwar policies like nationalization and heavy taxation of capital gains suppressed the returns and the value of all forms of capital. But this did not happen in the United States, where sustained political and ideological effort blocked policies that might devalue investments and advanced others that aimed to enhance investments.[59]

In the years following World War I, stock distributors believed that capitalism as they knew it faced a crisis. In 1919, 4 million men and women—nearly one-fifth of the labor force—participated in approximately 3,500 strikes. Rail unionists endorsed the "Plumb plan" to nationalize the railroads while the United Mine Workers called for a federal takeover of the mines. Whether the nation's telecommunications infrastructure would revert to private control remained in question.[60]

Promising that widespread stock ownership would harmonize class interests, U.S. corporations and financial institutions sold corporate stock further down the socioeconomic ladder. But as they did so, they aimed to preserve prevailing structures of economic wealth and power. Although roughly one-quarter of U.S. households owned corporate stock by 1929, the share of all income (capital gains included) received by the top 1 percent rose to 23.9 percent—a level never seen before nor seen again until 2007.[61]

AT&T led the charge to distribute corporate stock. In 1919, it had faced down demands to make wartime nationalization of the telephone system permanent and a massive operator strike. But the political climate remained uncertain. AT&T responded with Bell Telephone Securities Company, led by David F. Houston, the former secretary of the treasury. The subsidiary introduced employee and customer stock ownership programs to increase the number of AT&T shareholders. Simultaneously, AT&T showcased shareholders in its institutional advertising.[62]

Just as he had done as secretary of the treasury, Houston continued to promote the urgent necessity of government austerity and individual thrift. Even after the economy picked up in 1922, Houston continued to counsel fiscal conservatism and frugal investment as surefire methods for preventing inflation and perpetuating prosperity. As the chairman of Bell Telephone Securities,

Houston took up Thomas Nixon Carver's notion that the mass distribution of corporate shares offered the best mechanism for transforming every worker into a capitalist, for sustaining thrift as a national virtue, and for democratizing American capitalism. Universal stock ownership would fortify "the foundation of democracy itself" by providing every American "salvation against dependence" and "a stake in society," Houston avowed. He envisioned that dispersed shareholding would reestablish the link between property ownership and citizenship.[63]

AT&T reworked the war loans "share in America" trope in its advertisements, casting itself as a political democracy populated by citizen shareholders. Associating the "future independence of many citizens of small means" with AT&T dividend payments, the company implied that the investors were management's top priority.[64] Bell Telephone Securities financed employees and customers who wished to pay for AT&T shares over time, just as they had acquired Liberty and Victory bonds. This transformed AT&T into "a new democracy of public service ownership," David F. Houston declared, "a partnership of the rank and file who use the telephone service and the rank and file employed that service."[65]

In 1929, AT&T boasted that a half million persons owned its stock (with 400,000 added since World War I). *Printer's Ink* reported that the company's strategy effectively silenced "government ownership talk." Among major industrial nations, only the United States retained private ownership of its telecommunications infrastructure.[66]

David F. Houston presented AT&T's initiatives as just a single example of a general corporate commitment to instantiate the economic democracy that war loan boosters and new proprietorship theorists had promised. As share ownership spread, Houston predicted, the economic interests of the public would meld with those of corporate stockowners. The perennial "problem of the relation of labor and capital" would resolve itself. Individual investment in corporate stock enabled men of small means "to acquire a financial stake in society" and "ownership of one's self," an economic independence that assured both "the financial salvation" of the individual and "the permanence of democracy."[67]

Bell Telephone Securities sparked a surge of customer and employee ownership plans among U.S. corporations in the 1920s. Corporations seized on the proposition that they too could conjure a more hospitable political climate if they distributed their stock directly to the public. These companies did not face any shortage of capital. In fact, large industrial corporations of the period funded outlays with retained earnings.[68] When corporations introduced employee stock ownership plans, they sought to repel unionization. Those adopting customer stock ownership plans sought to avoid antitrust suits, to quash unfavorable regulatory action, and to counteract proposals for federal, state, or municipal ownership (all of which executives likened to bolshevism).

By 1928, nearly 800,000 employee owners at 315 firms held $1 billion worth of employers' stock.[69] Corporate managers looked back to the war loan drives as they devised ways to administer employee share ownership plans—with the notable exception that they did not make use of labor unions.[70] According to ESOP enthusiasts, stock ownership would nurture loyal feelings and the "profit motive" in the hearts of workers. Employee stock ownership plans might also dissolve any sense of collective solidarity as each employee investor received a fair share of corporate profits in proportion to that individual's resolve to resist consumption and invest.[71] Companies that instituted ESOPs presented themselves as sponsors of a private enterprise solution to the problem of social welfare.

Because "open" shops and company unions often accompanied ESOPs, organized labor viewed employee ownership with extreme suspicion. Employee ownership programs promised to deepen workers' financial dependence on the employer. But the corporation did not incur extended, expensive commitments as it might with pension benefits or group insurance. Once laborers subscribed to employers' stock, they had something more to lose if they left or were fired.[72]

Worker-owners invested according to their own motivations. Some chased short-term profits by trading their employers' stock. Those who acquired shares through an installment plan sometimes sold partially paid-for shares short, anticipating a drop in share price.[73] When employees sold, shorted, or speculated in their employers' stock, they discarded the suggestion that they should save soberly. A distinct economic self that fell outside the wage relationship emerged. This was not the financial freedom that ESOP engineers intended. Still, it associated financial markets with individual economic self-realization.

As in the case of AT&T, customer stock ownership plans (COPs) often accompanied employee stock ownership plans. Customer plans also adopted mass-marketing techniques inspired by the war loan drives such as direct mail, partial payment, sales contests, sensational giveaways, and thrift education campaigns. COPs experimented with new media like radio.[74] By 1929, one and a half million customers owned shares in 230 utility companies, according to the National Electric Light Association (NELA), a utility industry association[75]

Inspired by the new proprietorship, utility and transportation executives boasted of their customer owners as they opposed municipal-, state-, or federally owned power and transportation facilities, resisted regulatory incursions, and sought favorable action in regard to rates. Railroad lines introduced employee and customer ownership plans in response to the 1919 Plumb plan for railroad nationalization. In the power and light industries, NELA promoted customer ownership throughout the 1920s as it lobbied for the privatization of the Muscle Shoals hydroelectric dam and nitrate plants and against proposals for federal development of another dam on the Colorado River.

At stake were fundamental questions about the legitimacy of privately administered capitalism and the viability of state ownership and operation. According to utility corporations and industry associations, government-owned and -operated utilities suffered from inherent inertia, inefficiency, and ineptitude. National, state, or municipal ownership and operation could never provide the "vast supply of low-priced power" that Americans deserved, NELA warned. "'Public ownership' in its true sense" could only be achieved when "individuals who desired to become partners" chose to invest in utility stocks, rather than imposing ownership on taxpayers.[76] In regard to rates, the public interest could best be served if government agencies set utility rates to secure a "fair wage," or return, for the capital contributed by millions of customer owners, NELA argued. NELA viewed the customer owner as a "political asset" on all these questions. Accordingly, member utilities often included information "combating attacks on the company whether political, business, or personal in character" in their dividend mailings.[77]

Although executives and publicists cast employee ownership and customer ownership as a means of democratizing particular corporations, no plan ever embraced more democratic forms of corporate governance. In fact, these plans often involved non-voting stock. The possibility that new shareholders might exercise influence—much less control—never troubled the corporate executives who launched COPs and ESOPs.[78]

For the most part, financial firms watched from the sidelines as U.S. corporations enlarged their shareholder ranks in the early 1920s. Investors of modest means required financing in order to trade shares and it was risky to extend credit (or "margin") to them. And because financial firms regularly lent to each other, systemic risk increased if more firms borrowed in order to lend to novice investors of modest means.[79]

Once financial firms witnessed the success of nonfinancial corporations in distributing their stock, and as the economy recovered at mid-decade, financial firms changed course. The Great Bull Market took off when millions more Americans decided to acquire more shares in more corporations—and to borrow in order to do so. By the end of the decade, perhaps 2 million Americans had acquired shares in an investment trust, while 3.5 million had opened a brokerage account with a brokerage firm, a bank, a bank's security affiliate, or some other investment firm.[80]

Much like the nonfinancial corporations that preceded them, financial firms pursued new investors in an effort to influence political culture. Progressivism did not perish in World War I. In the 1920s, the federal government continued to rely on direct, progressive taxation of personal and corporate income for revenue. The passage of the federal Soldiers' Bonus Act in 1924 signaled an important federal foray into social policy. Combined government spending on nonveteran pensions—disabled, government employee, maternal, and old age—increased by 65 percent between 1922 and 1927. By 1929, per capita federal expenditures net of military and interest expenses stood at four times pre–World War I levels. In 1924, Robert M. La Follette Sr. even managed to capture 16 percent of the popular vote as the presidential candidate of the Progressive Party, which advocated government ownership of the rails, mines, and utilities.[81]

The state's expanded role in the postwar economy alarmed members of the financial securities industry. Economist Frank H. Sisson of Guaranty warned that the tax increases or bond issues needed to pay out new benefits or to buy out sectors threatened to suck up all available funding, stifling "large industrial institutions" and railroads "in their legitimate expansion" and introducing "the menace of government ownership" with all "its assured inefficiencies and political tragedies."[82] Herbert H. Houston, president of the Associated Advertising Clubs of America, advised bankers like Sisson that if American held "a stake in the country" in the form of corporate stock, then "bolshevism" would never make "the slightest inroads," not even in the cloaked forms of welfare, entitlements, government ownership, or regulation.[83]

The institutional innovation of the investment trust fired up the Great Bull Market. In exchange for shares in the investment trust, investors contributed their savings to a common portfolio that professional managers invested in a range of corporate stocks. Securities salesmen found investment trusts exceedingly attractive because trust sponsors—including banks, brokerages, and other independent investment houses—provided salesmen with generous sales incentives and national advertising campaigns. One promoter later identified "the slogan of 'participating in the future growth of American prosperity'" as "the fetish around which the somewhat hectic scramble" to sell trust shares—the "same old stocks, but in a different package"—unfolded.[84] After 1924, the number of these new investment vehicles grew exponentially. U.S. investment trusts raised approximately $3 billion in 1929 alone. At the time of the Great Crash, two million American households owned shares in 770 investment trusts.[85]

Because investment trusts used investors' funds to acquire shares in a range of corporations, they appeared particularly capable of delivering a "share in America" to every American. Adapting that war loan trope for their advertising and marketing, investment trusts promised to tap the ever-certain, ever-expanding wealth of the U.S. corporate economy. Investment trusts claimed to forge a connection between the individual citizen shareholder and the corporate economy at large. When a citizen shareholder considered an investment in American Basic-Business shares, for example, it was as if "the President, or a director, of United States Steel," of "AT&T" and of "the great Du Pont Company" all asked "to go into partnership with him." The stocks contained in the trust portfolio allegedly embodied an active claim of ownership and a manly assumption of risk.[86] Investment trusts promised to erect an "industrial democracy . . . a Sovietism far more enlightened and direct than the experiment so freshly originated in Russia," according to one promoter.[87] Any discord between capital, labor, and consumer would dissolve as investment trusts universalized corporate share ownership (albeit in an indirect form). Acquisition of trust shares would sustain—perhaps even enhance—the investor's standard of living and class status in an era of rapidly escalating inequality.[88] Thrift and consumption had stood at odds in the war loan drives. No longer, explained Incorporated Investors' "The American Birthright" advertisement:

> Never were man's horizons wider, his opportunity for the finer things of life greater—because never was wealth, upon which these enjoyments depend, so open to attainment. . . . The creation of new wealth in fabulous quantities is America's special faculty . . . *and anyone may participate.* Incorporated Investors provides an ideal method.[89]

And as seasoned trust managers sagely allocated the savings of small investors, promoters contended, a far less volatile stock market and much more stable economy would result.[90]

As the investment trust movement gained momentum in the second half of the 1920s, banks and brokerages launched initiatives that encouraged citizen shareholders to open brokerage accounts so they might trade corporate stocks as individuals. By 1929 an estimated 3.5 million Americans held an account with a brokerage, a bank, a bank's security affiliate, or some other investment firm that offered brokerage service.

Firms newly offering service to the public looked upon the brokerage account as "the greatest assurance of law and order yet developed in the nation" because their clients held "something to lose by social upheavals." Securities investment fortified "the position of the individual, obviating the possibility of his becoming a public charge in his old age, stabilizing his thinking, stimulating his enterprise, and improving his sense of civic responsibility," one Kidder, Peabody executive opined. He predicted that citizen shareholders would reject dangerous political experiments like government takeovers or state-based social insurance.[91] Financial firms seized hold of the "back of it all" trope developed by organized labor during World War I. Advertisements depicted the vast, complex wonders of modern corporate industry. But figures representing workers or the state—which had been showcased in the war loans—were replaced with that of the securities salesman.[92]

Brokerage advertisements also reworked norms around masculine economic responsibility.[93] The investor often appeared as an ambitious corporate-ladder climber whose portfolio returns positioned him to "capitalize" his "earnings as a preparation for a larger opportunity" ahead.[94] Only through stock investments could men secure the means—and the right—to retirement, presented as cessation of labor and devotion to self-betterment and cultured leisure. "In later years," income from investments bestowed "the privilege of leisure and culture," the "time to think and read and ponder and dream," Caldwell and Company explained. If a man steadfastly earned, denied, and invested, he eventually secured both the justification and the "income sufficient" to indulge both "needs" and "whims." This portrait of retirement reconfigured the economic independence of American men as a stream of future income from investment. As returns compounded in the investment portfolio "to the end of time," Ames, Emerich and Company imagined, "income coming from sources outside" one's "own efforts" might "last forever," securing perpetual stewardship of descendants. Neither state-based old-age insurance nor even corporate pensions could compete with such lavish fantasies of financial immortality.[95]

In the 1920s, first corporations and then financial firms spun stories that pitted mass investment against regulation, government-owned enterprise, the welfare state, labor unions, and even, at times, welfare capitalism. Universal acquisition of corporate stock via privately administered securities markets could accomplish key social goals—individual security and opportunity, macroeconomic prosperity, and social stability—in the most efficient and democratic manner, stock distributors pledged. They upheld the maximization of shareholder value as a proper—even primary—goal of corporate policy. Recasting war loan rhetoric and imagery, repurposing new proprietorship theory, and retold countless times, these narratives about the stock market achieved creditability because they were familiar.[96]

The ideal of shareholder democracy provided the ideological context within which millions of Americans altered their savings practices in the 1920s. Corporate stock distributors, and possibly investors, came to share a vision of the future grounded in broad-based ownership of corporate stocks. They did not, however, share any framework for valuing these assets. Some business schools had introduced discounting techniques for determining the present value of assets like stocks, but before the 1950s, corporate financial officers and investors applied these infrequently.[97]

Still, the shareholder democracy ideal might have amounted to nothing but a Jazz Age sales pitch if the New York Stock Exchange had not overhauled its institutional identity, mission, and message to promote mass investment after 1921. A public relations crisis drove this departure. In the spring of 1920, NYSE member Allan A. Ryan cornered the stock of Stutz Motor Car Company, of which he was the chairman. When penalized by the governors of the New York Stock Exchange, the charismatic Ryan charged them with acting arbitrarily to recoup their own losses. Much to the consternation of the NYSE commission houses—those firms that executed the trades of clients for a commission—the press threw its support behind Ryan. In Washington, D.C. and in Albany, law-makers introduced bills for the regulation of stock exchanges.[98]

" 'What we must give is service to the public,' " insisted the commission houses who strained against Exchange regulations prohibiting marketing and extending credit to retail investors. More was at stake than potential profits or even the prospect of regulation, they claimed. "Extreme radicalism" in the form of "government ownership" and "government operation" of enterprise and infrastructure threatened the "age-old right of private property," one ad-vertising agent observed. But if that right were "universally exercised," it would "be universally defended." When the public owned corporations on a private ownership basis then "a true democratic state when industry and finance are democratic as well as government" would emerge. Mass investment in corpo-rate stocks would dissipate demands for financial regulation and turn the tide against radical statism in favor of capitalism and democracy, the commission houses believed.[99]

Beginning in 1922, the NYSE governors relaxed their censorship. They launched a public relations campaign to support commission houses in pur-suit of retail investors. Growing national networks of branch offices provided the Exchange with a conduit for its finance-centered variant of laissez-faire. In its public relations, the stock exchange presented itself not only as the "free and open market"—as it had since 1913—but as "the people's market." As the Ex-change professed universal stock ownership as its core mission, its members extended brokerage service—and billions of dollars in credit—to retail inves-tors in the hopes of cultivating political allies.

Like customer and employee share ownership plan boosters, investment trust sponsors, and nonmember banks and brokerages, the New York Stock Exchange repurposed war loan tropes and new proprietorship theory. It recast citizenship as share ownership and the stock market as both the hallmark and the handmaiden of a democratic polity and an equitable economy. Exchange leader and publicists concurred that every man could best preserve his politi-cal stature and economic security as a shareholder. NYSE publicists also up-held the maximization of shareholder returns as the proper goal of economic policy and corporate management. This particular vision of shareholder de-mocracy stressed the absolute necessity of preserving Exchange self-governance against any form of financial regulation. Indeed, the NYSE categorically denied that *any* form of state oversight or intervention in the economy might ever be beneficial.

NYSE representatives crisscrossed the nation to promote members' broker-ages, to preempt regulation, and to secure a steady flow of brokers' loans to NYSE members. They visited professional associations, business organizations, high schools, colleges, and other civic organizations and gatherings. The Ex-change communicated also through the branch offices of NYSE commission houses, the Better Business Bureau system, and mass media outlets. In the late 1920s, roughly one million Americans viewed a film about the New York Stock Exchange.[100]

The citizen investor assumed center stage in NYSE public relations. Through the "people's market," Exchange orators explained, the "collective judgment" of the "vast investing public" determined the value of each NYSE-listed corporation and delivered a "daily health report" on the "state of modern American capitalism." Although stock market trades in fact involve transactions between investors, the stock exchange insisted that its market delivered the "savings of the people" directly to corporations. Because shareholders could sell their shares if they grew dissatisfied, publicists claimed, a "representative form of government" existed within listed corporations.[101] And because member brokerages stood ready to lend to so that any man might assume whatever risks he chose, only the privately administered New York Stock Exchange could instantiate a true shareholder democracy.[102]

Any argument for state oversight of financial securities markets was an elitist attack on shareholder democracy, according to NYSE spokesmen. "The public has infinitely more to fear from the arbitrary actions of a few men in artificially 'regulating'" the stock market than from "the average judgment and courage of the whole people of the country," Exchange officials insisted. Any "artificial attempt" by the state "to control and regulate" the prices of securities—or the amount of credit available to stockbrokers or their customers—would "pervert and interfere with" the financial self-determination of citizen shareholders. The state could only constrain the market, the true sphere of freedom.[103]

The New York Stock Exchange engaged issues far beyond its own self-governance. Its envoys condemned Henry Ford's $5-a-day policies for placing the wage cart before the profit horse.[104] NYSE representatives damned the incipient welfare state as a "drift toward paternalism," a "delusion that government is the source of all blessings" or "a fairy godmother whose magic wand" could "banish" the necessity of industry and thrift.[105] Acquisition of stock through private markets could meet every social need on an appropriately individual basis.[106] The stock exchange even harbored deep suspicions about Commerce Secretary Herbert Hoover's "associative" model of the state. Hoover believed that economic stability and growth could be ensured if firms, business associations, and government agencies voluntarily shared data and coordinated strategy.[107] This vision of state-facilitated (but privately conducted) macroeconomic planning alarmingly implied inefficiency in privately administered markets like the New York Stock Exchange.[108]

The Great Bull Market did not run on rhetoric alone. It consumed vast quantities of credit. As the market soared in the late 1920s, stockbrokers borrowed heavily to finance their own speculations and to extend credit to customers who wished to trade on margin. By the end of 1928, NYSE members together owed $6.4 billion.[109]

Brokers' loans paid double-digit rates of interest and generally could be called in for payment by the lender at any time. Critics damned these loans for depriving industry and trade of affordable credit. From the floor of the Senate, Robert M. Lafollette Jr. (Republican-Wisc.), Hendrick Shipstead (Farmer-Laborite, Minn.), and J. Thomas Helfin (Democrat-Ala.) all condemned loans to brokers.[110] Proposals to restrict brokers' loans appeared in Democratic and progressive Republican platforms in 1928. Throughout 1929, the Federal Reserve raised interest rates, attempting to deter brokers' borrowing by increasing the cost of doing so.[111]

By raising interest rates, the Fed hoped to signal to lenders that brokers' loans carried dangerous risks and thereby precipitate a reduction in loan volume. The Fed's member banks pulled back. But nonmember banks and corporations flooded the market.[112] For most of 1929, more than half of the brokers' loans reported to the Federal Reserve originated from nonbank sources.[113] Standard Oil lent an average of $69 million per day in 1929.[114] The total known volume of brokers' loans rose to $11.5 billion (11.0% of GDP) in September 1929. As a group, NYSE brokers owed $8.5 billion (8.1% of GDP).[115]

NYSE representatives worked tirelessly to influence lenders' perceptions and expectations regarding brokers' loans. "Stock market call loans are without question the safest form of investment known in this country," NYSE president E. H. H. Simmons swore. Any obstruction of the flow of credit to stockbrokers would compromise the liquidity and perhaps even the solvency of the banks and companies that parked their "surplus capital and credit" in brokers' loans. Drain this "flexible reservoir" Simmons cautioned, and that surplus would flood commodity or real estate markets, causing inflation.[116] Brokers' loans served "a safety valve for our entire economic system," Simmons contended. Critics in Congress and on the Federal Reserve Board risked "blowing out the whole boiler," he warned.[117]

Simmons allowed that as banks increased loans to brokers, the amount of commercial paper they granted to businesses declined. But, he instructed, this reorientation of the banking system toward the stock market simply meant that the U.S. financial system had evolved. Modern bankers must adapt to new modes of financing business.[118] Greatly exaggerating the role of the stock market in providing corporations with funds, Simmons asserted that "stock market loans" enabled NYSE members to acquire shares of newly listed corporations so these could receive "working capital" immediately.[119] Fortified with credit, NYSE brokers then gradually distributed these new stock issues "to the American investing class."[120] But Simmons could offer no proof that increases in brokers' loans caused an "expansion in new security offerings" rather than driving up the prices of established corporations' stock.[121] What of it, Simmons demanded, if brokers' loans enabled the masses to borrow and to assume greater risks?

> Some of us have talked a great deal . . . about creating a nation of investors. . . . These new investors have intelligence and ideas of their own. . . . They do not need to be lectured to or patronized by anyone. . . . Many . . . will speculate. . . . I do not see any reason to raise our hands in horror over this suggestion. It may be that we all have much to learn in regard to what that hackneyed phrase "a nation of investors" really means anyway.[122]

As the stock market teetered near its peak, rising share prices—and growing numbers of shareholders—appeared to endorse valuations and to confirm predictions that a shareholder democracy was imminent.

✳ ✳ ✳

During the Great Bull Market, lofty claims about the stock market, grand promises about stock ownership, and hopeful narratives about the better future guaranteed by universal investment all contributed value to shares in U.S. corporations. Lenders credited these narratives, too, and they lent to novice investors so these investors could acquire shares at market prices everyone judged consistent with value.

The bond drives that funded the First World War validated the value of financial securities as possible means for realizing important goals and ideals like victory, citizenship, nationhood, and social cohesion. During the Great Bull Market, corporate stock distributors launched marketing, advertising, and public relations initiatives that drew upon war loan precedents to associate share ownership with political and economic liberty. They presented corporate stock ownership as a tool of social mobility that conveyed economic security and liberated the innate entrepreneurialism of American men. Banks, brokerages, investment trusts, and corporations all promised that universal investment would bring about a better future: more equitable, less volatile, and free of social conflict.

In the tales that they told, Jazz Age distributors of corporate stock admitted that concentrations of wealth and power threatened democratic political traditions. They acknowledged that tensions existed between producer and consumer, labor and capital, small proprietor and big business. Their ideology of shareholder democracy superficially conceded populist and progressive critiques of finance. It distorted promises about mass investment that Americans had made to one another in the bond drives that funded the First World War. And it presented mass investment in the stock market as the only solution consistent with American commitments to private property, private initiative, and progress.

In the 1920s, stock distributors aimed to influence the nation's political culture as much as they sought after profits.[123] Before the New Deal—not in reaction to it—distributors of corporate stock and their ideological allies urged Americans to renounce the regulatory or welfare state as an agent for managing economic risk across society. After the Crash of 1929, the analogies that linked market and nation, corporation and polity, trade and vote, investor and citizen were reinterpreted once more. New Dealers used them to justify their demands for the federal government to assume responsibility for safeguarding citizen investors. It did so with the establishment of the Securities and Exchange Commission in 1934.

The Great Bull Market marked a moment of financialization that anticipated the structural transformation of the U.S. economy at the end of the twentieth century.[124] In the later part of the 1920s, banks reoriented toward the stock market as they opened securities affiliates and extended loans on stock collateral. Nonfinancial corporations channeled resources into financial activities, including loans to consumers, shareholders, and stockbrokers. Theories about the efficiency of financial markets and the prioritization of shareholder value appeared. Inequality peaked as the stock market ensnared an estimated quarter of U.S. households.[125]

In light of the Great Bull Market, financialization appears as something other than a post-1970s phenomenon that marks a final (or uniquely fragile) and all-encompassing stage of capitalism.[126] Financialization recurs periodically under capitalism, but not mechanistically according to some internal, inalterable, and ahistorical logic.[127] Neither a decline in rates of profit nor an increase in international competition accounts for the turn toward the financial markets taken by both U.S. banks and nonfinancial corporations in the 1920s.[128] The Jazz Age expansion of stock ownership did not respond to the dismantling of the welfare state; it resulted from efforts to keep social democracy at bay. Financialization represents a recurring tendency within capitalism, true, yet it can coexist alongside another regime of accumulation without displacing it.

Notes

1. Carmen Reinhart and Kenneth Rogoff, *This Time Is Different: Eight Centuries of Financial Folly* (Princeton, N.J.: Princeton University Press, 2009); Carmen M. Reinhart and Vincent R. Reinhart, "When the North Last Headed South: Revisiting the 1930s," *Brookings Papers on Economic Activity* 2 (Fall 2009): 251; Reinhart and Rogoff, "The Aftermath of Financial Crises," *American Economic Review* 99, no. 2 (May 2009): 466–72; Carmen M. Reinhart and Vincent R. Reinhart, "After the Fall," (NBER working paper no. 16334, National Bureau of Economic Research [NBER]: International Finance and Macroeconomics [IFM], Monetary Economics [ME], September 2010), 6; John Kenneth Galbraith, *The Great Crash of 1929* (Boston: Houghton Mifflin, 1961), 61;

Maury Klein, *Rainbow's End: The Crash of 1929* (Oxford: Oxford University Press, 2003), 154–56; Justin Fox, *The Myth of the Rational Market: A History of Risk, Reward, and Delusion on Wall Street* (New York: Harper Business, 2009).

2. Julia Cathleen Ott, *When Wall Street Met Main Street: The Quest for an Investors' Democracy* (Cambridge, Mass.: Harvard University Press, 2011), 2.

3. Francois Vatin, "Valuation as Evaluating and Valorizing," *Valuation Studies* 1 no. 1 (2013): 31–50; "Hans Kjellberg and Alexandre Mallard, "Valuation Studies? Our Collective Two Cents," *Valuation Studies* 1, no. 1 (2013): 11–30; Patrik Aspers and Jens Beckert, "Value in Markets," in *The Worth of Goods: Valuation and Pricing in the Economy*, ed. Aspers and Beckert (New York: Oxford University Press, 2011), 3–40.

4. Value at once assesses and establishes worth, while prices register, in quantitative form, one assessment of value at which parties transact (vs. a bid or an offer to transact). See David Stark, "What's Valuable?," in Beckert and Aspers, eds., *The Worth of Goods*, 319–38; Claes-Fredrik Helgesson and Fabian Muniesa, "For What It's Worth: An Introduction to Valuation Studies," *Valuation Studies* 1 no. 1 (2013): 1–10; Michele Lamont, "Toward a Comparative Sociology of Valuation and Evaluation," *Annual Review of Sociology* 38, no. 1 (2012): 201–21; Vatin, "Valuation as Evaluating and Valorizing," 31–50; John Dewey, *The Later Works of John Dewey* (Carbondale: Southern Illinois University Press, 2008), 189–252. For a similar call to bring valuation to the fore in the history of capitalism, see Jonathan Levy, "Capital as Process and the History of Capitalism," *Business History Review* 91, no. 3 (2017): 1–28.

5. Harold Bierman Jr., *The Causes of the 1929 Stock Market Crash: A Speculative Orgy or a New Era* (Westport, Conn.: Greenwood, 1998).

6. J. Bradford De Long and Andrei Shleifer, "The Stock Market Bubble of 1929: Evidence from Closed-End Mutual Funds," *Journal of Economic History* 51, no. 3 (September 1991): 675–700.

7. Galbraith, *The Great Crash of 1929*, 4, 8, 16.

8. Hyman P. Minsky, "Finance and Profits: The Changing Nature of American Business Cycles" (Paper 63, Hyman P. Minsky Archive, Levy Institute, Bard College, Annandale-on-Hudson, N.Y., 1980), 212. http://digitalcommons.bard.edu/cgi/viewcontent.cgi?article=1062&context=hm_archive.

9. Hyman P. Minsky, "Fundamental Reappraisal of the Discount Mechanism: Financial Instability Revisited; The Economics of Disaster" (paper prepared for the Steering Committee for the Fundamental Reappraisal of the Discount Mechanism Appointed by the Board of Governors of the Federal Reserve System, 1970), 8, 10, accessed July 3, 2016, https://fraser.stlouisfed.org/files/docs/historical/federal%20reserve%20history/discountmech/fininst_minsky.pdf.

10. Charles P. Kindleberger and Robert Aliber, *Manias, Panics and Crashes: A History of Financial Crises,* 5th ed. (Hoboken, N.J.: Wiley, 2005), 12, 14, 42.

11. Reinhart and Rogoff, *This Time is Different*, xxxiv, xil.

12. Kindleberger and Aliber, *Manias*, 43, 53.

13. Maury Klein, *Rainbow's End*, xviii, 1–16, 26; Steve Fraser, *Every Man a Speculator: A History of Wall Street in American Life* (New York: Harper Collins, 2005), 366.

14. Eli Cook identifies American economist Irving Fisher as a key figure in erasing "both society and history from the study of economics." Eli Cooke, "The Neoclassical Club: Irving Fisher and the Progressive Origins of Neoliberalism," *Journal of the Gilded Age and Progressive Era* 15 (2016): 252.

15. Eugene Fama is credited with developing the efficient market hypothesis, but it was introduced in vernacular form by members of the financial community as early as the

1910s and developed further by Friedrich Hayek in the 1940s. Eugene Fama, "The Behavior of Stock Market Prices," *Journal of Business* 38, no. 1 (January 1965): 34–105; Ott, *When Wall Street Met Main Street*, chap. 2; Friedrich Hayek, "The Use of Knowledge in Society," *The American Economic Review* 35, no. 4 (September 1945): 519–30.

16. Returns may take the form of dividends, interest, or an increase in the price of the asset.

17. Hyman P. Minsky, "Uncertainty and the Institutional Structure of Capitalist Economies" (working paper no. 155, Levy Institute, Bard College, Annondale-on-Hudson, N.Y., 1996), accessed July 3, 2016, http://www.levyinstitute.org/pubs/wp155.pdf.

18. Daniel Beunza and Raghu Garud, "Security Analysts as Frame-makers" (Economic Working Papers, Department of Economics and Business, Universitat Pompeu Fabra, Barcelona, Spain), accessed August 16, 2017, http://econpapers.repec.org/paper/upfupfgen/733.htm.

19. George A. Akerlof and Robert J. Shiller, *Animal Spirits: How Human Psychology Drives the Economy and Why It Matters for Global Capitalism* (Princeton, N.J.: Princeton University Press, 2010), 4, 5, 12; George A. Akerlof and Rachel Kranton, *Identity Economics: How Our Identities Shape Our Work, Wages, and Well-Being* (Princeton, N.J.: Princeton University Press, 2010).

20. David Harvey, *A Companion to Marx's Capital* (New York: Verso, 2013), 20.

21. Paulo L. dos Santos, "On the Content of Banking in Contemporary Capitalism," *Historical Materialism* 17, no. 2 (2009): 180–213.

22. Costas Lapavitsas, *Profiting Without Producing: How Finance Exploits Us All* (New York: Verso, 2014); dos Santos, "On the Content of Banking," 189.

23. David Harvey, *A Companion to Marx's Capital, Volume 2* (New York: Verso, 2013).

24. dos Santos, 208.

25. Karl Marx, *Capital*, vol. 3 (London: Electric Book, 2001), 621–38, accessed May 22, 2017. ProQuest ebrary.

26. Stock prices appear illusionary to Marx and many of his adherents because this "fictitious capital" bears no direct relationship to the production of surplus-value. Ibid., 532–54, 594–620.

27. dos Santos, "On the Content of Banking," 209.

28. Lamont, "Toward a Comparative Sociology of Valuation and Evaluation," 202–3; Vatin, "Valuation as Evaluating and Valorizing," 32; Gordon Haywood et. al, "Valuation Studies: A Collaborative Valuation in Practice" *Valuation Studies* 2 no. 1 (2014): 73, 78, 80. Valuation studies draws upon the analytic concepts of embeddedness and performativity, as well as the social studies of finance literature. Mark Granovetter, "Economic Action and Social Structures: The Problem of Embeddedness," *American Journal of Sociology* 91 (November 1985): 481–520; Michel Callon, *The Laws of Markets* (London: Blackwell Publishers, 1998); Alex Preda, *Framing Finance: The Boundaries of Markets and Modern Capitalism* (Chicago: University of Chicago Press, 2009); Donald Mackenzie, *An Engine Not a Camera: How Financial Models Shape Markets* (Cambridge: MIT Press, 2006); Donald MacKenzie, Fabian Muniesa, and Lucia Siu, eds., *Do Economists Make Markets: On the Performativity of Economics* (Princeton, N.J.: Princeton University Press, 2008); Donald MacKenzie, *Material Markets: How Economic Agents Are Constructed* (New York: Oxford University Press, 2009); Judith Butler, *Excitable Speech: A Politics of the Performative* (New York: Routledge, 1997); J. L. Austin, *How to do Things with Words* (Oxford: Clarendon, 1962).

29. Aspers and Beckert, "Value in Markets," 3–40.

30. Kjellberg and Mallard, "Valuation Studies? Our Collective Two Cents," 11–30; Alexander Styhre, "The Economic Valuation and Commensuration of Cultural Resources:

Financing and Monitoring the Swedish Culture Sector," *Valuation Studies* 1, no. 1 (2013): 51–81; Fabian Muniesa, "Setting the Habit of Capitalization: The Pedagogy of Earning Power at the Harvard Business School, 1920–1940," *Historical Social Research* 41, no. 2 (2016): 196–217.

31. Aspers and Beckert, "Value in Markets," 10.

32. John Maynard Keynes, *The Essential Keynes* (New York: Penguin Classics, 2015), 155.

33. Aspers and Beckert, "Value in Markets," 15. This assertion comports with behavioral economists' finding that economic agents construct their preferences *during* the decision-making process, not prior.

34. Ibid., 15, 5–16. See also Jens Beckert, *Imagined Futures: Fictional Expectations and Capitalist Dynamics* (Cambridge, Mass.: Harvard University Press, 2016); Jens Beckert, "The Transcending Power of Goods: Imaginative Value in the Economy," in Aspers and Beckert, eds., *The Worth of Goods*, 106–25.

35. Walter Johnson, *Soul by Soul: Life Inside the Antebellum Slave Market* (Cambridge, Mass.: Harvard University Press, 2001); Ed Baptist, *The Half Has Never Been Told: Slavery and the Making of American Capitalism* (New York: Basic Books, 2014).

36. Caitlin Zaloom, *Out of the Pits: Traders and Technology from Chicago to London* (Chicago: University of Chicago Press, 2006).

37. Beckert, "The Transcending Power of Goods," 106–25; Aspers and Beckert, "Value in Markets."

38. For the concept of the social imaginary, a broadly shared understanding of collective social life, see Charles Taylor, *Modern Social Imaginaries* (Durham, N.C.: Duke University Press, 2003).

39. Aspers and Beckert, "Value in Markets," 10–16.

40. Ott, *When Wall Street Met Main Street*, 2; H. T. Warshow, "Distribution of Corporate Ownership in the United States," *Quarterly Journal of Economics* 39, no. 1 (November 1924): 15–38; Gardiner C. Means, "Diffusion of Stock Ownership in the United States," *Quarterly Journal of Economics* 44, no. 4 (1930): 561–600; David F. Hawkins, "The Development of Modern Financial Reporting Practices among American Manufacturing Corporations," *Business History Review* 37, no. 3 (Autumn 1963): 145. National Industrial Conference Board (NICB), *Employee Stock Purchase Plans in the United States* (New York: NICB, 1928), 2, 35–36; Charles Amos Dice, *New Levels in the Stock Market* (New York: McGraw Hill, 1929), 198; National Electric Light Association, *Political Ownership and the Electric Light and Power Industry* (NELA), (New York: NELA, 1925), 20; U.S. Securities and Exchange Commission, *Investment Trusts and Investment Companies* (Washington, D.C.: Government Printing Office [GPO], 1939), 362, 370; Senate Committee on Banking and Currency, *Stock Exchange Practices*, S. Doc. No. 1445, 9–10 (1934); Thomas F. Huertas and Harold van B. Cleveland, *Citibank: 1812–1970* (Cambridge, Mass.: Harvard University Press, 1985), 120; Twentieth Century Fund, *The Securities Markets* (New York: The Fund, 1935), 50, 56–57; Edwin Burk Cox, *Trends in the Distribution of Stock Ownership* (Philadelphia: University of Pennsylvania Press, 1963), 33.

41. Mary O'Sullivan, *Contests for Corporate Control: Corporate Governance and Economic Performance in the United States and Germany* (New York: Oxford University Press, 2000), 75; Leslie Hannah, "The 'Divorce' of Ownership from Control from 1900 Onwards: Re-Calibrating Imagined Global Trends," *Business History* 49, no. 4 (2007): 406.

42. Charles Gilbert, *American Financing of World War I* (Westport, Conn.: Greenwood, 1970), 140; Minutes of War Loan Organization Conference, June 13, 1919, folder "General Files Related to Liberty Loans and War Savings Bonds, 1917-25–1917-1920

Conferences," box 26, General Files Relating to Liberty Loans and War Savings Bonds, 1917–1925 (Entry NC-120, 622), Records of the Bureau of Public Debt (Record Group 53) (henceforth GFRG53), National Archives (NA), College Park, Md., 345; U.S. Department of the Treasury Bureau of Publicity, *Weekly Press Matter,* no. 55 (August 7, 1918).

43. U.S. Department of the Treasury, *Annual Report* (Washington, D.C.: GPO, 1919), 71; U.S. Department of the Treasury, *Report of the National Woman's Liberty Loan Committee for the Victory Loan Campaign* (Washington, D.C.: GPO, 1919), 9; Hugh Rockoff, "Until It's Over, Over There: The US Economy in World War I," in *The Economics of World War I,* ed. Stephen Broadberry and Mark Harrison (New York: Cambridge University Press, 2005), 316.

44. John E. Gardin, *Liberty Bonds and Civilization* (Buffalo, N.Y.: National City Bank, October 1, 1917), 6.

45. Christopher Capozzola, *Uncle Sam Wants You: World War I and the Making of the Modern American Citizen* (New York: Oxford University Press, 2008); Christopher Capozzola, "The Only Badge Needed Is Your Patriotic Fervor: Vigilance, Coercion, and the Law in World War I America," *Journal of American History* 88, no. 4 (March 2002): 1354–82. War Savings Committee of Massachusetts, *Bay State Bulletin,* November 7, 1918, folder "Bulletins," box 13, GFRG53; Macy Campbell, "Thrift Talk No. 5," folder "War Savings leaflets 7th District," box 16, GFRG53; "War Savings Societies—A Home Defense," *War Savings Society Bulletin,* no. 4 (1918); "Outline for an Address on the Liberty Bond Situation," (memorandum) folder 1, box 124, GFRG53; Robert F. Herrick to B. Nason Hamlin, March 30, 1918, folder "War Savings Leaflets 7th District," box 13, GFRG53; "The Country and the Loan," *New York Times,* October 15, 1917; untitled clipping, *New York Tribune,* April 4, 1918 in Guy Emerson scrapbook, vol. 1, Library of Congress. War Savings was specifically designed for the propertyless immigrant. See transcript, Conference on War Savings Certificates, October 12, 1917, box 25, GFRG53.

46. "War Savings Societies—A Home Defense," *War Savings Society Bulletin,* no. 4 (1918).

47. U.S. Department of the Treasury, *The Second Liberty Loan of 1917,* 25, 1917; John Muir, *How to Raise the Money: The Third Liberty Loan Drive* (New York, 1918), 7; "Message of the Secretary of the Treasury to all Liberty Loan workers," June 6, 1918, folder "Directors' Correspondence—4," box 34, GFRG53.

48. Ajay K. Mehrotra, "Lawyers, Guns, and Public Moneys: The U. S. Treasury, World War I, and the Administration of the Modern Fiscal State," *Law and History Review* 28, no. 1 (2010): 173–225; Ajay K. Mehrotra, *Making the Modern American Fiscal State: Law, Politics, and the Rise of Progressive Taxation, 1877–1929* (New York: Cambridge University Press, 2013).

49. Ott, *When Wall Street Met Main Street,* 68–73.

50. William Gibbs McAdoo, *Crowded Years: The Reminiscences of William G. McAdoo* (New York: Houghton Mifflin, 1931), 378, 385.

51. Ibid., 75–100; William G. McAdoo, *Crowded Years: The Reminiscences of William G. McAdoo* (New York: Houghton Mifflin, 1931), 375, 385. "What Savings May Mean," *Savannah Tribune,* May 4, 1918, 4.

52. William G. McAdoo, *Extension of Tenure of Government Control of the Railroads: Statements of Honorable W. G. McAdoo before the Interstate Commerce Commission of the United States Senate, January 3 and 4, 1919* (Washington, D.C.: Government Printing Office, 1919), 5, 11–17, 28, 30, 31; Glenn E. Plumb, *Labor's Plan for Government Ownership and Democracy in the Operation of the Railroads* (Washington, D.C.:

Plumb Plan League, 1919); Richard Waterman, "Proposed Plans for Railroad Legislation," *Annals of the American Academy of Political and Social Science* (henceforth AAAPSS) 86 (November 1919): 92.

53. James B. Morman, "Coöperative Credit Institutions in the United States," *AAAPSS* 87 (January 1920): 182; Vincent P. Carosso, *Investment Banking in America: A History* (Cambridge, Mass.: Harvard University Press, 1970), 229; Edward H. Thomson, "American Farmers' Need for Capital," *AAAPSS* 87 (January 1920): 89–94; Theda Skocpol, *Protecting Soldiers and Mothers: The Political Origins of Social Policy in the United States* (Cambridge, Mass.: Belknap Press of Harvard University Press, 1992); Edward Berkowitz and Kim McQuaid, *Creating the Welfare State: The Political Economy of Twentieth-Century Reform*, 2nd ed. (New York: Praeger, 1988), 115–26; William J. Barber, *From New Era to New Deal: Herbert Hoover, the Economists and National Economic Policy, 1921–1933* (New York: Cambridge University Press, 1985); Colin Gordon, *New Deals: Business, Labor and Politics in America, 1920–1935* (New York: Cambridge University Press, 1994); and Mark Allen Eisner, *From Warfare State to Welfare State: World War I, Compensatory State Building and the Limits of the Modern Order* (University Park: Pennsylvania State University Press, 2000); Lynn Dumenil, *The Modern Temper: American Culture and Society in the 1920s* (New York: Hill and Wang, 1995); Jennifer Klein, *For All These Rights: Business, Labor, and the Shaping of America's Public-Private Welfare State* (Princeton, N.J.: Princeton University Press, 2006), 17, 20, 66, 80; Theda Skocpol, *Protecting Soldiers and Mothers*, 194–202, 234–37, 424–80; Barbara J. Nelson, "The Origins of the Two-Channel Welfare State: Workmen's Compensation and Mothers' Aid," in *Women, The State, and Welfare,* ed. Linda Gordon (Madison: University of Wisconsin Press, 1990), 123–51; Lorraine Gates Schuyler, *The Weight of Their Votes: Southern Women and Political Leverage in the 1920s* (Chapel Hill, N.C.: University of North Carolina Press, 2006), 208–210; Alice Kessler-Harris, *In Pursuit of Equity: Women, Men, and the Quest for Economic Citizenship in Twentieth-Century America* (New York: Oxford University Press, 2001).

54. Frank, *Purchasing Power*, 66–75; Judith Stein, *The World of Marcus Garvey: Race and Class in Modern Society* (Baton Rouge: Louisiana State University Press, 1986); Otis B. Grant, "Social Justice Versus Social Equality: The Capitalistic Jurisprudence of Marcus Garvey," *Journal of Black Studies* 33 (March 2003): 490–98; Jeffrey D. Howison, " 'Let Us Guide Our Own Destiny': Rethinking the History of the Black Star Line," *Journal of the Ferdinand Braudel Center* 28 (2005): 29–49; Ramla Bandele, *Black Star: African American Activism in the International Political Economy* (Urbana, Ill.: University of Illinois Pres, 2008).

55. U.S. Department of the Treasury, *Annual Report* (Washington, D.C.: GPO, 1924), 83–84.

56. Ott, *When Wall Street Met Main Street,* chap. 5.

57. Thomas Nixon Carver quoted in Harold Callender, "America May Soon Become an Economic Utopia," *New York Times*, September 13, 1925, BR5.

58. Thomas Nixon Carver, *Elementary Economics* (Boston: Ginn, 1920); Thomas Nixon Carver, *The Present Economic Revolution in the United States* (Boston: Little, Brown, 1925), 11; William Z. Ripley, *Main Street and Wall Street* (Boston: Little, Brown, 1927). See also *Proceedings of the Academy of Political Science* 11 (April 1925).

59. Thomas Piketty, *Capital in the Twenty-First Century* (Cambridge, Mass.: Belknap Press of Harvard University Press, 2014), 8–15, 20, 24, 116–17, 128, 141–49, 151–55, 291–92, 299–300, 348–49, 368, 373, 499.

60. David Montgomery, *The Fall of the House of Labor: The Workplace, the State, and American Labor Activism, 1865–1925* (Cambridge: Cambridge University Press, 1989);

Leo Wolman, *Growth of the American Trades Unions, 1880–1923* (New York: National Bureau of Economic Research, 1924); Beverly Gage, *The Day Wall Street Exploded: A Story of America in Its First Age of Terror* (New York: Oxford University Press, 2009); Ann Hagedorn, *Savage Peace: Hope and Fear in America, 1919* (New York: Simon and Schuster, 2007); Dana Frank, *Purchasing Power: Consumer Organizing, Gender, and the Seattle Labor Movement, 1919–1929* (New York: Cambridge University Press, 1994); Anthony Read, *The World on Fire: 1919 and the Battle with Bolshevism* (New York: W. W. Norton, 2008); Robert Whitaker, *On the Laps of Gods: The Red Summer of 1919 and the Struggle for Justice That Remade a Nation* (New York: Crown, 2008); Francis Russell, *A City in Terror: Calvin Coolidge and the 1919 Boston Police Strike* (New York: Viking, 1975); Stuart D. Brandes, *American Welfare Capitalism, 1880–1940* (Chicago: University of Chicago Press, 1976), 29; Lizbeth Cohen, *Making a New Deal: Industrial Workers in Chicago, 1919–1939* (New York: Cambridge University Press, 1990), 161–65; Sanford M. Jacoby, *Modern Manors: Welfare Capitalism Since the New Deal* (Princeton, N.J.: Princeton University Press, 1997); Nikki Mandell, *The Corporation as Family: The Gendering of Corporate Welfare, 1890–1930* (Chapel Hill: University of North Carolina Press, 2002); Andrea Tone, *Business of Benevolence: Industrial Paternalism in Progressive America* (Ithaca, N.Y.: Cornell University Press, 1997), 243; Gerald Zahavi, *Workers, Managers, and Welfare Capitalism: The Shoeworkers and Tanners of Endicott Johnson, 1890–1950* (Urbana: University of Illinois Press, 1988); Robert MacDougall, *The People's Network: The Political Economy of the Telephone in the Gilded Age* (Philadelphia: University of Pennsylvania Press, 2014).

61. http://piketty.pse.ens.fr/files/capital21c/en/pdf/supp/TS8.2.pdf.

62. Ott, *When Wall Street Met Main Street*, chap. 7; Roland Marchand, *Creating the Corporate Soul: The Rise of Public Relations and Corporate Imagery in American Big Business* (Berkeley: University of California Press, 1998), 43–85; Stephen H. Norwood, *Labor's Flaming Youth: Telephone Operators and Worker Militancy, 1878–1923* (Urbana: University of Illinois Press, 1990); MacDougall, *The People's Network*. While AT&T institutional advertising dated from 1908, shareholders were not featured until 1919. See folders 1–3, box 21, N. W. Ayer Advertising Agency Records, Archives Center, National Museum of American History, Smithsonian Institution, Washington, D.C.

63. Lawrence L. Murray, "Bureaucracy and Bipartisanship in Taxation: The Mellon Plan Revisited," *Business History Review* 52, no. 2 (Summer 1978): 200–225; "Estimated Expenditures," June 11, 1920, folder "Estimated Expenditures," (GFRG53); David F. Houston, "Every Worker a Capitalist," *World's Work,* January 1925; David F. Houston, "The City of AT&T," *The Outlook,* January 20, 1926; David F. Houston, untitled address before the Investment Bankers' Association Conference (unpublished manuscript, New York, 1923), box 3, David F. Houston papers, MS Am1510, Houghton Library, Harvard University, Cambridge, Mass.; David F. Houston, "Speech on the Bell System" (unpublished manuscript, Bond Club of New York, New York, October 22, 1925), box 3, David F. Houston papers MS Am1510, Houghton Library, Harvard University, Cambridge, Mass; David F. Houston, "Mr. Houston's Talk: Bell System Education Conference" (unpublished manuscript, July 24, 1926), box 3, David F. Houston papers, MS Am1510, Houghton Library, Harvard University, Cambridge, Mass.; David F. Houston, "The Telephone as a Factor in Modern Business" (unpublished manuscript, 1926), box 3, David F. Houston papers MS Am1510, Houghton Library, Harvard University, Cambridge, Mass; David F. Houston, "The Meaning and Strength of America" (unpublished manuscript Commercial Club, Chicago, Ill., January 1, 1927), box 3, David F. Houston papers, MS Am1510, Houghton Library, Harvard University, Cambridge, Mass.; David F. Houston (unpublished manuscript, Convention of

National Edison Light Association, Atlantic City, N.J., June 8, 1927), box 3, David F. Houston papers, MS Am1510, Houghton Library, Harvard University, Cambridge, Mass.; David F. Houston, "Financing the War" (Washington, D.C., 1921), box 2, David F. Houston papers, MS Am 1510), Houghton Library, Harvard University, Cambridge, Mass.; David F. Houston, "What You Need to Know About Federal Taxation," *World's Work*, October 1922; U.S. Department of the Treasury, *Annual Report* (Washington, D.C.: GPO, 1920).

64. American Telephone and Telegraph [AT&T], "Our Triple Responsibility" (1920); AT&T, "Our Stockholders" (1919); AT&T, "A Community of Owners Nationwide;" AT&T, "Democracy," all in folder 2, box 21, N.W. Ayer Advertising Agency records, Archives Center, National Museum of American History, Smithsonian Institution, Washington, D.C.

65. Houston, "Mr. Houston's Talk," 345; Houston, "Every Worker a Capitalist," 24–26. For corporations' service ideal in the 1920s, see Marchand, *Creating the Corporate Soul*, 45, 164–66, 201.

66. AT&T, "In the Service of All the People" (1929); folders 3, box 21, N.W. Ayer Advertising Agency records, Archives Center, National Museum of American History, Smithsonian Institution, Washington, D.C.

67. David F. Houston, "Creating Good Will Between Capital and Labor," *Magazine of Wall Street,* December 30, 1924; Houston, "Mr. Houston's Talk," 345; Houston, "Every Worker a Capitalist," 24–26; Houston, "The City of AT&T," 5–9.

68. O'Sullivan, *Contests for Corporate Control*, 79; De Long and Shleifer, "The Stock Market Bubble of 1929," 695.

69. Robert F. Foerster and Else H. Dietel, *Employee Stock Ownership in the United States* (Princeton, N.J.: Princeton University Industrial Relations Section, 1926), 6–8; National Industrial Conference Board, *Employee Stock Purchase Plans in the United States* (New York: National Industrial Conference Board, 1928); Sanford Jacoby, *Modern Manors*, 3; Brandes, *American Welfare Capitalism*, 83.

70. Gorton James, Henry S. Dennison, Edwin F. Gay, Henry P. Kendall, and Arthur W. Burritt, *Profit Sharing and Stock Ownership for Employees* (New York: Harper, 1926), 1; Metropolitan Life Policyholders' Service Bureau, "A Report on Employee Stock-Ownership Plans" (New York: Metropolitan Life, 1923), 8.

71. Jacoby, *Modern Manors*, 13, 24; James et al., *Profit Sharing and Stock Ownership,* vii, 23; Brandes, *American Welfare Capitalism,* 85.

72. Robert W. Dunn, *The Americanization of Labor: The Employers' Offensive Against Trade Unions* (New York: International, 1927); NICB, *Employee Stock Purchase Plans in the United States,* 169; James et al., *Profit Sharing and Stock Ownership,* 26.

73. NICB, *Employee Stock Purchase Plans and the Stock Market Crisis of 1929* (New York: NICB, 1930), 29, 33, 56. NICB, *Employee Stock Purchase Plans in the United States,* 59, 142; Foerster and Dietel, *Employee Stock Ownership in the United States,* 14, 54, 56, 66; Arthur Williams, "Labor's Share in Ownership," *Proceedings of the Academy of Political Science [PAPS]* 11 (April 1925): 364.

74. John D. Long and John Eden Farwell, *Fundamentals of Financial Advertising* (New York: Harper, 1927), 256, 262; Frank LeRoy Blanchard, "Radio for Financial Advertising," *Proceedings of the Financial Advertisers Association [FAA] Annual Convention* (Chicago: FAA, 1928), 263–64.

75. NELA, *Political Ownership and the Electric Light*, 20; John T. Broderick, *A Small Stockholder* (Schenectady, N.Y.: Robson and Adee, 1926), 26; Howard T. Sands, "Consumer Ownership and Corporate Management," *PAPS* 11 (April 1925): 499; NICB, *Employee Stock Purchase Plans in the United States,* 44, 135–38.

76. A. Emory Wishon, "Now and Tomorrow with Customer Ownership," *PAPS* 11 (April 1925): 409, 411, 416.

77. AT&T, "Owned by Those It Serves"; Sands, "Consumer Ownership and Corporate Management," 496; David F. Houston, "Some Aspects of the Telephone Business and Its Financing" (address before the Massachusetts Bankers' Association, Boston, January 7, 1925), 8–9, box 2, David F. Houston papers, MS Am 1510, Houghton Library, Harvard University, Cambridge, Mass.; Wishon, "Now and Tomorrow," 410; Frederick H. Wood, "The Small Investor and Railroad Ownership and Management," *PAPS* 11 (April 1925), 440.

78. NELA, *Political Ownership and the Electric Light*, 20; Broderick, *A Small Stockholder*, 26; Sands, "Consumer Ownership and Corporate Management," 499; NICB, *Employee Stock Purchase Plans in the United States*, 44, 135–38; Charles Amos Dice, *New Levels in the Stock Market* (New York: McGraw-Hill, 1929), 198.

79. For these reasons, the governors of the New York Stock Exchange actively discouraged their members from offering retail brokerage services by censoring NYSE members' advertising and marketing. Sure enough, liberal lending during the war loan drives drove several NYSE brokerages to the brink of bankruptcy. See Transcript, November 6, 1921, folder 4, Committee on Business Conduct [CBC] Hearings, NYSE Archives, New York.

80. Ott, *When Wall Street Met Main Street,* chap. 8; Steven L. Osterweis, "Securities Affiliates and Security Operations of Commercial Banks," *Harvard Business Review* 11 (October 1932): 124–32; Carosso, *Investment Banking in America*, 271–281.

81. Randall G. Holcombe, "The Growth of the Federal Government in the 1920s," *Cato Journal* 16 (Fall 1996): 6, 10; Ajay K. Mehrotra, "Lawyers, Guns, and Public Moneys: The U.S. Treasury, World War I, and the Administration of the Modern Fiscal State," *Law and History Review* 28, no. 1 (February 2010), 173, 177, 180, 186, 223; Anne L. Alstott and Ben Novick, "War, Taxes, and Income Redistribution in the Twenties: The 1924 Veterans' Bonus and the Defeat of the Mellon Plan," *Tax Law Review* 59 (Summer 2006), 373, 376, 380, 431, 433; Dora L. Costa, *The Evolution of Retirement: An American Economic History, 1880–1990* (Chicago: University of Chicago Press, 1998), 17, 166–67; Price Fishback, Samuel Allen, Jonathan Fox, and Brendan Livingston, "A Patchwork Social Safety Net" (NBER working paper no. 15696, 2010), 37–39; Theda Skocpol, *Protecting Soldiers and Mothers*, 446, 457; William H. Chafe, "Women's History and Political History: Some Thoughts on Progressivism and the New Deal," in *Visible Women: New Essays on American Activism,* ed. Nancy A. Hewitt and Suzanne Lebsock (Urbana: University of Illinois Press, 1993), 101–18; Seth Koven and Sonya Michel, "Womanly Duties: Maternalist Politics and the Origins of Welfare States in France, Germany, Great Britain, and the United States, 1880–1920," *American History Review* 95, no. 4 (1990): 1080–81; Patrick Wilkinson, "The Selfless and the Helpless: Maternalist Origins of the U.S. Welfare State," *Feminist Studies* 25, no. 3 (Autumn 1999): 571–97; U.S. Bureau of the Census, *Historical Statistics of the United States,* 4th ed. (New York: Cambridge University Press, 2000), accessed July 3, 2016, http://hsus. cambridge.org.proxy.wexler.hunter.cuny.edu/HSUSWeb/toc/tableToc.do?id =Ea61–124.

82. *Proceedings of the FAA Annual Convention* (Chicago: FAA, 1922), 10; Francis H. Sisson, "Financial Advertising and the Public," *Proceedings of the FAA Annual Convention* (Chicago: FAA, 1917), 3, 8.

83. Herbert H. Houston, "The Man in the Street and Financial Advertising," *Proceedings of the FAA Annual Convention* (Chicago: FAA, 1920), 18–20; *Proceedings of the FAA Annual Convention* (Chicago: FAA, 1922), 41.

84. Earl Newsom, "Market Study and Merchandise Developments," *Proceedings of the FAA Annual Convention* (Chicago: FAA, 1930); W. W. Townshend, "Advertising and Merchandising Activities of the Fixed Investment Trusts," *Proceedings of the FAA Annual Convention* (Chicago: FAA, 1930), 271–73, 276–78.

85. Paul Cabot, interview by Andrew Tosiello, October 22, 1971, transcript, 1–2, 4, 13, 14, Baker Library, Harvard Business School, Boston, Mass.; William Howard Steiner, *Investment Trusts and the American Experience* (New York: Adelphi, 1929), 59, 61; H. Burton and D. C. Corner, *Investment and Unit Trusts in Britain and America* (London: Elek, 1968); Carosso, *Investment Banking in America*, 281–95; Leland Rex Robinson, *Investment Trust Organization and Management* (New York: Ronald, 1926), 548; Harold E. Wood, "Investment Banking in the Next Ten Years," *Proceedings of the FAA Annual Convention* (Chicago: FAA, 1930), 268.

86. Lemon L. Smith, "Present and Future of Investment Trusts," *Investment Trusts: Issued Monthly by Bankers' Investment Trust of America,* March 1928, folder "B—Bankers R," box 1, Edgar Higgins Investment Trust Collection [HIT] (Mss 783), Baker Library Historical Collections, Harvard Business School, Boston, Mass.

87. Newsom, "Market Study and Merchandise Developments," 255.

88. Piketty, *Capital in the Twenty-First Century*, 291, 292, 299, 300.

89. Incorporated Investors, "The American Birthright," August 14, 1929, folder "Incorporated Investors," box 2, HIT.

90. Steiner, *Investment Trusts,* 10–11; "Address of the President [American Founders Corp.] to the Annual Meeting of Stockholders," April 8, 1929, folder "America A to America F," box 1, HIT.

91. Investment Research Committee of the FAA, *Advertising Investment Securities* (New York: Prentice-Hall, 1928), 52.

92. National City Bank, "I Shouldn't Decide It Alone" and "What Is a Logical Investment for Me?," in *Kundenwerbung Amerikanischer Banken,* ed. Carl Hundhausen (Berlin: L.Weiss, 1929), appendix.

93. Kidder, Peabody, and Co. circular, December 29, 1926, Kidder Peabody Circulars, vol. 24, 71, Kidder Peabody collection, Baker Library, Harvard Business School, Boston, Mass.

94. National City Bank, "Taking the Broader View," in Hundhausen, *Kunderwerbung*, appendix; Halsey Stuart, "The Capable Young Investor," *Harper's Magazine* (March 1921): 26.

95. Ethel R. Scully, "Appealing to the Accumulators Rather than the Conservators," *Proceedings of the FAA Annual Convention* (Chicago: FAA, 1924), 120; Edmond Boushelle, "The Place of Direct Mail in the Distribution of Investment Securities," *Proceedings of the FAA Annual Convention* (Chicago: FAA, 1924), 112; Milton Harrison, "Development of Thrift Facilities," *AAAPSS* 87 (January 1920): 169–70; H. B. Matthews, "Investment Advertising," *Proceedings of the FAA Annual Convention* (Chicago: FAA, 1922), 61; "A Thoughtful Christmas Present," *Coast Investor and Industrial Review*, November 1929, 59.

96. For the importance of stories about the economy in shaping investors' preferences and bolstering or destroying confidence, see Akerlof and Shiller, *Animal Spirits*, 3–4, 12, 51–55, 66, 119–22; Robert Shiller, *Irrational Exuberance* (Princeton, N.J.: Princeton University Press, 2000), 21–27, 96–98, 138–40, 148–51, 162. For the susceptibility of savings decisions to narrative framing, see Richard H. Thaler and Shlomo Benartzi, "Save More Tomorrow," *Journal of Political Economy* 112, no. S1 (February 2004): S164–87; Brigitte C. Madrian and Dennis F. Shea, "The Power of Suggestion: Inertia in 401(k)

Participation and Savings Behavior" (NBER working paper no. 7682, 2000); Sendhil Mullainathan and Andrei Schleifer, "Persuasion in Finance" (NBER working paper no. W11838, 2005); Richard Thaler and Nicholas Barberis, *Survey of Behavioral Finance* (Cambridge, Mass.: NBER, 2002), 1073–81. For the significance of norms in economic decisionmaking, see George A. Akerlof, "The Missing Motivation in Macroeconomics," *American Economic Review* 97, no. 1 (March 2007): 5–36.

97. Discounting techniques for valuing assets first emerged within a small circle of engineering economists working for railroad lines in the late nineteenth century. S. P. Dulman, "Development of Discounted Cash Flow Techniques in American Industry," *Business History Review* 63, no. 3 (Autumn, 1989) 555–87; Jonathan Levy, "Accounting for Profit and the History of Capital," *Critical Historical Studies* 1, no. 2 (Fall 2014): 174–214.

98. "Allan Ryan on Wall Street," *New York World,* April 18, 1920; "Allan Ryan's Statement," *Evening Mail,* April 24, 1920; "Ryan Quits Seat on Stock Exchange," *New York Times,* April 24, 1920, 1; "Stutz Corner" scrapbook, NYSE Archives, New York.

99. Transcript, Special Committee on Ways and Means: Subcommittee on Odd Lots, folder 7, box 3, NYSE Archives; CBC minute books, vol. 1–7, NYSE Archives; "Report of the Special Committee on Odd Lots," 1921, folder 9, box 3, NYSE Archives, 413; Herbert S. Houston, "How to Maintain the Confidence of the Public" (address before the members of the New York Stock Exchange and their partners, New York, April 7, 1922), 4, 5, 11–13.

100. Committee on Publicity minute book, vol. 2–4; "Some Comments on the Addresses of Jason Westerfield," 4, New York Stock Exchange archives, New York.

101. E. H. H. Simmons, "Modern Capitalism" (speech) (New York: NYSE, 1926), 11–12, 14–15; Simmons, "Listing Securities on the New York Stock Exchange" (New York: NYSE, 1927), 6, 14–15, 20, 21; "Simmons Advanced Views Like Ripley's," *New York Times,* August 26, 1926; "Bids Corporations Tell Income Often," *New York Times,* June 5, 1926.

102. Jason Westerfield, "The Stock Exchange in Its Relation to the Public" (speech) (New York: NYSE, 1924), 6; Jason Westerfield, "Dangerous Delusions" (speech) (New York: NYSE, 1924), 10, 15; J. Edward Meeker, *The Work of the Stock Exchange* (New York: Ronald, 1922), 494–97; Westerfield, "The Good Old Days," in *Four Talks on Wall Street* (New York: NYSE, n.d.), 21–22; Simmons, "The Stock Exchange and American Agriculture" (speech) (New York: NYSE, 1928), 6–8; Westerfield, "Wall Street Is Main Street," in *Four Talks on Wall Street,* 9.

103. Simmons, "Modern Capitalism," 15; E. H. H. Simmons, "The Stock Exchange and the People" (speech) (New York, NYSE: 1924), 15; E. H. H. Simmons, "Stock Market Loans" (speech) (New York: NYSE, 1929), 10, 11, 16; E. H. H. Simmons, "Financing Industrial Development" (speech) (New York: NYSE, 1929), 162–65; E. H. H. Simmons, "New Aspects of American Corporate Finance" (speech) (New York: NYSE, 1929).

104. Scholars generally understand shareholder maximization ideology as a very recent phenomenon. William Lazonick and Mary O'Sullivan, "Maximizing Shareholder Value: A New Ideology for Corporate Governance," *Economy and Society* 29, no. 1 (2000): 13–35; Gerald F. Davis and Christopher Marquis, "The Globalization of Stock Markets and the Convergence in Corporate Governance," in *The Economic Sociology of Capitalism,* ed. Victor Nee and Richard Swedberg (Princeton, N.J.: Princeton University Press, 2005); Gerald F. Davis, *Managed by the Markets: How Finance Reshaped America* (New York: Oxford University Press, 2009).

105. Westerfield, "Dangerous Delusions," 3–4; Westerfield, "Wall Street of Fact and Fiction" (speech) (New York: NYSE, n.d.), 4; Westerfield, "Synthetic Ghosts" (speech)

(New York: NYSE, n.d.,), 8. For the American welfare state, see Klein, *For All These Rights*; Theda Skocpol, *Protecting Soldiers and Mothers*; Nelson, "The Origins of the Two-Channel Welfare State."

106. Westerfield, "Dangerous Delusions," 3–4; Westerfield, "Wall Street of Fact and Fiction," 4; Westerfield, "Synthetic Ghosts," 8.
107. William J. Shultz, *Financial Development of the United States* (New York: Prentice Hall, 1937), 535, 593; Victoria Saker Woeste, *The Farmer's Benevolent Trust: Law and Agricultural Cooperation in Industrial America, 1865–1945* (Chapel Hill: University of North Carolina Press, 1998); "Incorporated Farm Studied," *Los Angeles Times,* March 14, 1929, 3.
108. Ellis Wayne Hawley, *The Great War and the Search for a Modern Order: A History of the American People and Their Institutions, 1917–1933* (Prospect Heights, Ill.: Waveland Press, 1997), 78–96; Ellis W. Hawley, "Herbert Hoover, the Commerce Secretariat, and the Vision of an 'Associative State,' 1921–1928," *Journal of American History* 61, no. 1 (June 1974): 116–40; Guy Alchon, *The Invisible Hand of Planning: Capitalism, Social Science, and the State in the 1920s* (Princeton, N.J.: Princeton University Press, 1985); William Leach, *Land of Desire: Merchants, Power, and the Rise of a New American Culture* (New York: Vintage, 1993).
109. Louis H. Haney, Lyman S. Logan, and Henry S. Gavens, *Brokers' Loans: A Study in the Relation Between Speculative Credits and the Stock Market, Business, and Banking* (New York: Harper, 1932), tables 1 and 2.
110. U.S. Congress, Senate Committee on Banking and Currency, *Brokers' Loans,* 70th Cong., 1st sess., 1928.
111. Atack and Passell, *A New Economic View*, 587.
112. Ibid., 606; Cedric B. Cowing, *Populists, Plungers, and Progressives: A Social History of Stock and Commodity Speculation* (Princeton, N.J.: Princeton University Press, 1965), 133–34, 143–49, 188; Eugene White, "Banking and Finance in the Twentieth Century," in *The Cambridge Economic History of the United States*, vol. 3, *The Twentieth Century,* ed. Stanley L. Engerman and Robert E. Gallman (New York: Cambridge University Press, 2008), 757–58; Haney, Logan, and Gavens, *Brokers' Loans*, 220–21 (table 1).
113. Haney, Logan, and Gavens, *Brokers' Loans*, 220–221 (table 1).
114. Galbraith, *The Great Crash of 1929*, 27–37, 72.
115. Haney, Logan, and Gavens, *Brokers' Loans*, 234 (table 5) and 225 (table 2). This number captures only a portion of the money lent on stock market collateral. Funds lent to investment trusts and holding companies rather than brokers, for example, are not included. Bierman, *The Causes of the 1929 Stock Market Crash*, 71–101. In 2014, eight largest banks' assets totaled 65 percent of GDP. See Pam Martens, "Hoenig: Wall Street Banks 'Excessively Leveraged' at 22 to 1 Ratios," Wall Street on Parade, May 9, 2014, http://wallstreetonparade.com/2014/05/hoenig-wall-street-banks-%E2%80%9Cexcessively-leveraged%E2%80%9D-at-22-to-1-ratios/.
116. Simmons, "Stock Market Loans," 13, 15, 26.
117. Simmons, "Speculation in Securities," 8–9.
118. Simmons, "New Aspects of American Corporate Finance," 11.
119. Simmons, "Stock Market Loans," 8; Guy Morrison Walker, *Brokers' Loans and the Federal Reserve* (New York: A. L. Fowle, 1929), 3.
120. Simmons, "Stock Market Loans," 12.
121. E. H. H. Simmons, "New Aspects of American Corporate Finance," 13; Haney, Logan, and Gavens, *Brokers' Loans*, 8–9.
122. Simmons, "Speculation in Securities," 21.

123. For the significance of culture in shaping frameworks of political belief, see Joseph E. Lowndes, *From the New Deal to the New Right: Race and the Southern Origins of Modern Conservatism* (New Haven, Conn.: Yale University Press, 2008), 140.

124. In her invaluable review of the relevant literature, Natascha van der Zwan delineates three meanings of the term "financialization": a new regime of accumulation, the ascendency of shareholder value orientation, and the financialization of everyday life. Natascha van der Zwan, "Making Sense of Financialization," *Socio-Economic Review* 12, no. 1 (2014): 99–129.

125. Ott, *When Wall Street Met Main Street*; Louis Hyman, *Debtor Nation: The History of America in Red Ink* (Princeton, N.J.: Princeton University Press, 2011); Louis Hyman, *Borrow: The American Way of Debt* (New York: Vintage, 2012); Martijn Konings, *The Development of American Finance* (New York: Cambridge University Press, 2011), 62–63; Piketty, *Capital in the Twenty-First Century*, 299–301.

126. Brett Christophers, "Limits to Financialization," *Dialogues in Human Geography* 5, no. 2 (2015): 183–200.

127. Greta Krippner, *Capitalizing on Crisis: The Political Origins of the Rise of Finance* (Cambridge, Mass.: Harvard University Press, 2011); Giovanni Arrighi, *The Long Twentieth Century: Money, Power and the Origins of Our Times* (New York: Verso, 2010); Robert Brenner, *The Boom and the Bubble: The U.S. in the World Economy* (New York: Verso, 2003); David Harvey, *Seventeen Contradictions and the End of Capitalism* (New York: Oxford University Press, 2014); David Harvey, *The Limits to Capital* (New York: Verso, 2007); Ian Baucom, *Specters of the Atlantic: Finance Capital, Slavery, and the Philosophy of History* (Durham, N.C.: Duke University Press, 2005).

128. "Net Profits of All Corporations for United States," *FRED, Economic Research*, accessed July 3, 2016, https://research.stlouisfed.org/fred2/series/Q09048USQ144NNBR. Over the years 1923–1929, corporate profits as a whole rose by over 62 percent, while corporate dividends increased by 65 percent. See George Soule, *Prosperity Decade: From War to Depression, 1917–1929* (New York: Rinehart, 1947), 326–27; Lewis Corey, *The Decline of American Capitalism* (New York: Covici Friede, 1934), 184.

CHAPTER 3

THE NEW YORK CITY FISCAL CRISIS AND THE IDEA OF THE STATE

KIM PHILLIPS-FEIN

I n April 1975, only a few weeks before the world would learn that New York City was almost bankrupt, a woman named Lyn Smith wrote a letter to New York senator Jacob Javits describing the housing conditions in a South Bronx neighborhood near her home. "When a house burns down they don't destroy the frame, they leave it standing—you never know when it's going to fall. A little boy we know or knew named Ralphy lives in the South Bronx he was playing in one of the broken down houses and he fell through the floor he's dead now but if that building had been torn down he wouldn't be dead." Yet despite the terrible events that she described, the tone of Lyn Smith's letter was not angry, but resigned. "I don't know why I wrote this letter you'll probably never read."[1] Javits forwarded the letter to Abraham Beame, the mayor of New York City. His response would likely not have been too comforting to Lyn Smith or other residents of the South Bronx, which was becoming known nationwide as a center of urban misery: "You are, of course, aware of the recent rash of fires in the South Bronx which have resulted in a large number of burned out buildings. The Department of Buildings has personnel in the area to inspect for unsafe buildings but the procedure is a time-consuming one." He assured the senator that the city would continue to search for dilapidated buildings and to tear them down, when need be.[2]

But in fact, even as Smith wrote her letter, New York City was on the edge of losing the very funds that it needed to be able to engage in such basic maintenance. Every month, New York went to the banks that marketed its debt—

which included First National City Bank, Chase Manhattan Bank, Morgan Stanley, Bankers Trust, and Chemical Bank—to try to negotiate new offerings of short-term notes. The banks were charging the city ever-higher interest rates, which the mayor and comptroller denounced as exorbitant. In the late winter of 1975, a note offering was canceled when the underwriting banks requested information on property tax collections that the city said it could not easily provide. In March 1975, bankers from First National City Bank met with officials from the Treasury Department and with congressional representatives to warn that the city would soon be shut out of the credit markets. In May, Mayor Beame and Governor Hugh Carey traveled to Washington, D.C. to try to persuade the Ford administration to extend aid to New York. Persuaded by his advisors, Ford refused, and by the summer of 1975, New York had been plunged into a fiscal crisis. Throughout most of the rest of 1975, there seemed a real possibility that the city would go bankrupt. Only in the late fall, after New York appeared clearly committed to a new program of austerity, after the city had worked out agreements whereby its unions and the major banks would purchase large quantities of bonds, and after the state government had imposed a moratorium on the repayment of principal of the city's debt, did the federal government agreed to a program of "seasonal" loans.

The fiscal crisis had a profound impact on the scale and ambition of New York City's government, which had previously been the most extensive municipal government in the nation. As a result of the crisis, the city reduced its payroll by more than 69,000 people (out of 294,595) between 1975 and 1978, imposed tuition at the City University of New York, made cutbacks in police and fire protection, slowed capital spending and abandoned ongoing construction projects, closed several of the city's public hospitals, reduced sanitation services, defunded day care centers, and hiked transit fares.[3] But the impact of the crisis was felt far beyond New York. During the 1970s, the fundamental presumptions that had shaped the life of the country during the postwar years—of steady economic growth, mass consumption, military dominance in the Cold War, the easy availability of energy, and the social norm of the two-parent nuclear family—were suddenly called into question. New York City's fiscal crisis seemed a sign of the larger crisis of the postwar order. That New York—the capital of American finance—could experience such financial difficulties was widely seen as evidence of the weakness of the American economy and political system. As Christopher Lasch wrote in his 1979 *The Culture of Narcissism*, "Those who recently dreamed of world power now despair of governing the city of New York."[4] More than this, the crisis of New York City was widely understood and described as a turning point—evidence that the old way of organizing social life could not endure, that the expectations of the past simply could not govern the future.[5]

The fiscal crisis certainly changed much in the assumptions governing political life in New York, and it reflected a broader shift in thinking about politics throughout the nation. It was perceived at the time and afterward as a crisis—a term which denotes, as political scientist Janet Roitman puts it, a fundamental point of rupture between past experience and future possibility. Yet another way to see it is as the latest in a long series of struggles within the city over the scope of the local welfare state, and the question of who would pay for it.[6] The program of austerity that advanced during the fiscal crisis had been unfolding in the early 1970s, even before the crisis began to dominate headlines. The crisis itself was precipitated by the turn to finance as opposed to taxation in the late 1960s and early 1970s, undertaken by the city's elected leaders as they became increasingly reluctant to tax the city's business class. In these ways, rather than mark a turning point, the crisis represented the culmination and emergence into public view of a set of conflicts that previously had been kept out of sight.

Nor did the crisis simply compel a new antistate consensus, or bring about the easy ascendance of a neoliberal perspective. Ideas about government during the 1970s remained fiercely contested. The view of the dominant voices within the Ford administration that New York City should be permitted to go bankrupt met with substantial skepticism from national and international elites, as well as those within the city itself. But the vision of the legitimate scope of government was contested on the ground as well. Working-class New Yorkers greeted the cuts in social programs with resistance framed in terms of their rights as taxpayers and their sense that their very presence as a working-class population within the city was endangered by austerity. Thus the crisis at once demonstrated the weakness of the local government and its growing dependence on the bond markets, while at the same time reflecting the profound discomfort—both within the city and nationally—with the full implications of this position.

Three aspects of the fiscal crisis show how it was embedded in a much longer struggle over the scope of the welfare state and the appropriate role of government both in the city and nationally. First is the reliance of New York City's government on debt financing even as the market for municipal bonds was starting to contract, which the fiscal crisis exposed in spectacular manner, and the contest over the local welfare state that was being staged in the city during the late 1960s and early 1970s. Second is the ambivalence of national elites about the prospect of New York City's bankruptcy. Finally is the anger that the cutbacks provoked within the city itself. Yet while the fiscal crisis revealed a set of changes that had been going on beneath the surface but that had not previously permitted to govern the life of the city, it did lead to the elevation of fiscal responsibility over ideas about social obligation as the final arbiter for thinking about social policy. The crisis was but one step in the transformation of the city's politics; that it could happen at all demonstrated how much had truly changed.

* * *

The American state has long relied on the bond market to achieve its aims, using private financing to bolster its own power and security. For much of American political history, public debt has been a sign of strength rather than of weakness, symbolizing the support of private business rather than something that might shake its confidence. This has been true for both federal and local government. The massive public borrowing campaigns of World War I and World War II, for example, were necessary from a fiscal standpoint, but they also helped to develop popular support for the wars and to deepen the investment of citizens in the state itself. To take a very different example, cities in the early twentieth century expanded their capacity to borrow in order to invest in the infrastructure their business communities deemed essential. Yet while the expansion of the public sector through private credit markets demonstrates the ways that governments sought to use the private sector to bolster their own capacity, the fiscal crisis in New York City shows that the opposite relationship was equally possible—that investors, banks, and the bond market could come to be more powerful than the governments they supported and could use that financial power to bring about changes in government policy.[7]

The basic causes of New York City's fiscal crisis lay in the changing economic base of the city, which became evident by the early 1970s. In the years immediately after the war, the city's economy had been powered by a diverse industrial base quite different from those of cities such as Detroit. New York was populated by small factories in a wide range of industries—garment production, food production, printing and publishing, and electronics. But throughout the 1960s and early 1970s, these companies were shutting down or leaving the city. While during the 1960s the city gained new service sector jobs, these generally were not as well paid as the manufacturing jobs it was losing. The city's job loss became more severe in the early 1970s as it was caught in the national recession. Between 1969 and 1977, the city lost more than 600,000 jobs.[8] The flight of middle-class—and mostly white—New Yorkers to surrounding suburbs drained the city of resources and tax dollars.

This economic crisis had especially serious fiscal consequences in New York because of the city's unusually broad social welfare programs and network of public institutions—its municipal hospitals, free city university system, and extensive mass transit and public housing as well as day care and other city services. Throughout the late 1960s and early 1970s, local social movements pressed the city government for expanded social services. Even as the city's revenues became strained, it undertook a major expansion of its public university system with the adoption of an open admissions policy in 1970. Public employ-ment also helped to offset the employment decline; throughout the 1960s, em-ployment grew more rapidly in local government than in any other sector. The Great Society also created new imperatives for city government. Because New York State law mandated that local governments pay about 25 percent of their Medicaid costs, the city was responsible for an unusually high proportion (rel-ative to other states) of health care expenses for poor people.[9] This is not to say that all local government expenses were rooted in social welfare—there were also high subsidies to certain kinds of businesses, such as the renovation of Yankee Stadium (which cost $100 million and was one of the only capital proj-ects that was continued during the years that followed the fiscal crisis).[10] But the extent and ambition of the city's public sector was unique in the country in the postwar years, and there were recurrent questions throughout the decade about who would pay to support this public sector. New York's political leaders did expand taxes in the city over the 1960s, gaining the reluctant permission of the state government to impose a city income tax, stock transfer taxes, and vari-ous new sales taxes on services. The city also received increased funds from the federal government during the Great Society years. But these taxes and revenues were not sufficient to counter the loss of jobs and population over the 1960s, especially after the onset of recession in 1969.

Although the gap between revenues and expenditures was well known prior to 1975, the long-standing fiscal difficulties of the city were finally transformed into the dramatic crisis of 1975 and 1976 by New York's increasing reliance on short-term debt to finance its affairs.[11] The expansion of short-term borrowing in New York is often dated to the final term of Mayor Robert F. Wagner, who turned to the credit markets in 1965 when facing a budget shortfall, promising that he would not permit the city's fiscal situation to "set the limits of its commit-ment to meet the essential needs of the people of the city."[12] There were relatively few regulations of municipal debt at this time, and the range of instruments available for borrowing expanded considerably over the 1960s. Instead of stan-dard general obligation bond issues—which citizens had to approve with a vote—the city began to market a variety of kinds of short-term debt, in partic-ular tax-anticipation notes, bond-anticipation notes, and revenue-anticipation notes, which were respectively backed by revenues anticipated but not yet col-lected from taxes, bonds, and transfer payments from the state and federal governments. As the city's volume of short-term debt grew, so did the fiscal pressure, as the notes often carried high interest rates.

In turning to debt financing, New York City was following the lead of Albany in the 1960s. Bonds and short-term debt had played a critical role in financing the expansion of the state university system; the building of new state government buildings in Albany; the construction of highways, Battery Park City, and the United Nations; and the building of hospitals, nursing homes, and mental health facilities throughout New York state. The municipal bond market in the 1960s was booming, as banks and insurance companies sought these investments for their supposed safety and stability as well as their tax benefits. But New York State voters early in the decade failed to vote in favor of bonds to fund housing projects. On the advice of bond lawyer (later attorney general under Richard Nixon) John Mitchell, Nelson Rockefeller decided to create a new kind of bond.[13] Known as "moral obligation" bonds, these were not guaranteed by the full faith and credit of the state, and were not backed by any particular revenue stream, so they did not need to be approved by voters. Instead, they could be issued by public corporations in the name of the state, even though there was no collateral for them but the promise that the state would redeem them when the time came. By 1973, the state had $5.6 billion in outstanding debt issued in these ways—compared to $3.4 billion that had been issued with the approval of voters.[14] New York City's move to start relying on short-term debt in a new way took place in the broader context of the expansion of debt throughout New York State.

The banks that underwrote and marketed this debt to the public were generally quite happy to do so throughout the late 1960s and early 1970s. But the era was also one when a range of new financial opportunities for banks were starting to open up. Since World War II, the financial sector had operated according to fairly routine rules and regulations—interest rates on deposits were capped, banks focused most of their business on the domestic United States, regulations governing who could access credit were tight. In the 1970s, however, these constraints were starting to give way, as policymakers relaxed the regulations in response to the spreading economic slowdown.[15] At the same time, banks were beginning to experiment with ways around the regulations dating from the New Deal that limited the interest commercial financial institutions could pay on deposits. Ceasing simply to hold deposits and make loans, banks were becoming the purveyors of all kinds of new financial products.[16] Although the stock market remained mired in a decade-long slump, the banks were attracted by new financial instruments such as real estate investment trusts that promised higher returns than the older and more predictable investments. At the same time, the recession of the 1970s was starting to make many financiers anxious about their investments. Especially after the collapse of the Franklin National Bank in 1974, the bankruptcy of the Penn Central Railroad in 1970, and the meltdown of another New York State agency (the Urban Development Corporation) in February 1975, the city's bankers became much more wary about the municipal loans they were underwriting.

Alongside these larger transformations of the financial industry, the specific market for municipal and state bonds was changing as well. Throughout the 1960s, commercial banks had been the largest market for new bond issues.

Municipal bonds were appealing to banks because the banks did not need to pay federal income tax (and in many cases, state and local income tax) on the interest income from the bonds. In a time of high corporate tax rates, the value of this tax-free income was significant. Drawn by the tax shelter promised by municipal and state bonds, banks had switched much of their holdings of U.S. government bonds for those of the cities and states in the postwar era. But by the 1970s, the increased range of possibilities open to banks—and in particular, the expansion of income from international banking, which often fell outside the U.S. tax structure, with companies counting their foreign tax payments as credits against their income taxes—meant that commercial banks no longer wanted or needed to hold as many municipal bonds.[17] The appeal of municipal bonds was declining. Cities and states would need to look elsewhere for customers for their bonds: to pension funds, life insurance companies, and high-income individuals, for example. By becoming so dependent on the bond markets for the operation of its government, at the very moment when the banks and municipal markets were undergoing a profound set of changes, New York City effectively opened itself up to the possibility of a financial crisis, as finally happened in 1975.[18]

The turn to finance itself reflected the increasing conflict over the scope of the city's public sector. Even before the crisis erupted in 1975, the nature of New York's welfare state had been the subject of great controversy and discontent—a political anxiety about who benefited from the city's government was ultimately expressed in terms of the problem of who would pay for its programs. Business leaders feared that the costs of the city's services would fall increasingly on them, while politicians in the city and state alike grew anxious about the discontent of business.

For many in the city's business circles, the causes of the city's problems were only too obvious: the expansion of the services provided by the city and the rising cost of a recently unionized public sector workforce. For more than a decade, business groups in the city had cautioned that a crisis was imminent. In 1960, the New York Chamber of Commerce warned that the city's expense budget was growing too rapidly, and that "to continue the present trend for any length of time is to court financial disaster."[19] The Citizens Budget Commission predicted a coming fiscal crisis as early as 1964.[20] When Mayor John Lindsay imposed a stock-transfer tax on the financial markets, the leaders of the New York Stock Exchange seriously considered relocating and leaving the city. The president of the Stock Exchange, George Keith Funston, was highly concerned about the city's future. "What troubles me as a New York-based businessman is the fact that New York's potential as a business center isn't being fully realized," he wrote to the president of the Economic Development Council, a business organization devoted to giving New York's businessmen more voice in the city. "We have the people, the capital resources, the tradition of business service, the know-how and the proper geography. But one overriding problem—the deterioration of the climate for business, especially in the realm of taxes—undermines the effectiveness of these many favorable elements."[21] In another letter, Funston observed that, in his opinion, the central problem the city faced was not one of inflexible revenues but of rising expenses. "Our economic development efforts will bear a short crop indeed, if we have nothing to show to any potential or existing employer, but a record of rising expenses that require more elastic taxes."[22] Trying to dissuade the Stock Exchange from departing, Mayor Lindsay established a committee dubbed the Keep the New York Stock Exchange in New York City Committee. However, the participants from the New York Stock Exchange were disheartened by their experience. In a final report, they wrote that there was no hope for repeal of the stock transfer tax. The "pressures from other quarters to keep taxes down on real estate, sales and incomes, to maintain the 20 cents subway fare and to provide welfare and other City services are so great" that the city had to "pursue a most expedient course and forsake no alternative revenue sources." Given this, the best course of action for the board of governors of the NYSE would be to proceed "with all deliberate speed" to explore relocating the NYSE outside of New York State.[23]

The acute awareness of the need to maintain a competitive environment for investment that the NYSE was trying to create was felt at the level of the state government by the early 1970s. Governor Nelson Rockefeller was growing deeply concerned about the flight of industry from New York State, and he decided to make a stand against major tax increases at the state level—to protect the "business climate" of New York. In his budget messages and addresses to the legislature, he warned against a potential exodus of jobs and business from New York, one that would "destroy the very basis of our revenue structure and our ability to meet human needs."[24] He tracked the ways that neighboring industrial states were solving their budget dilemmas, to make sure that the city would not adopt anything out of line with what they wanted to do.[25] His commerce commissioner argued that New York State should maintain a corporate franchise tax below 9 percent, so that the state could be "loudly" competitive with Massachusetts, Connecticut, and Pennsylvania. Along with substantial tax breaks for industries that were expanding their facilities in New York State, this tax (lower than in surrounding states) gave the commissioner a "very effective 'sales pitch'" to use to attract new business.[26] For Rockefeller, New York City was a prime target. When Mayor Lindsay approached him in 1971 asking for the right to impose new taxes, the governor responded by reminding the legislature: "The citizens of our state already pay the highest taxes—state and local combined—in the Nation." No one should forget that "people overburdened with taxes can easily move out of a state." The only appropriate solution was federal aid, which would not be forthcoming: "Tragically, the Congress has demonstrated no sense of urgency or even awareness of the profound human implications of this fiscal crisis." The result was that there was no choice but to cut services. All involved had to keep in mind the ultimate consequence of such fiscal irresponsibility: He warned that everyone should remember that it was quite possible for local governments—and even for states—to go bankrupt.[27]

By the early 1970s, then, the struggle over New York City's finances was already under way. Local business elites were resentful and hostile toward the city's programs, even as poor and working-class people in the city mobilized for expanded and improved services. The state government viewed the city's propensity to tax as a threat to its "business climate." As a result, the city government sought to evade open conflict by turning to the credit markets—even though the market for municipal bonds was contracting. These tensions came into open view during the fiscal crisis, but they had been building for years before: they suggested the weakness of the state in comparison to business and the private markets.

* * *

Yet the expectations that had been generated during the postwar boom and the Great Society years did not immediately dissipate with the onset of fiscal crisis. The crisis provided a dramatic illustration of the weakness of the city's government. Local and national elites alike made the case for government action to save New York from bankruptcy. At the same time, within the city, New Yorkers responded to the crisis by trying to articulate the legitimacy of their claims on city services, despite all they were being told about the new fiscal limits. The fiscal crisis did not mean a collapse of government authority; on the contrary, it was met by a new insistence on the importance of finding ways to make demands on the local and national state governments.

The Gerald Ford administration monitored the situation in New York City closely throughout the year, gathering information about the city's adoption of budget cuts, local political developments, and the likely impact of default on banks across the nation.[28] Although there were some people within the administration who believed that it might ultimately be necessary to find a way to provide loans to the city to keep it from default, the strongest voice became that of Treasury Secretary William Simon, a former municipal bond dealer himself (he had worked at Salomon Brothers). Simon's stance was supported by Donald Rumsfeld (Ford's chief of staff until November 1975, when he became secretary of defense) and Alan Greenspan (the chairman of the Council of Economic Advisers). Simon was deeply committed to free-market economic ideas, and he viewed the financial problems of the city as a harbinger of a coming national fiscal crisis. In a speech to the Economic Club of New York in September 1975, he said little about New York's own crisis, instead describing the dangers he felt the country faced as a result of the "visceral negative reaction" that could be provoked in some quarters by "mention of corporate profits, capitalism and even free enterprise." The federal government, he warned, "has been living beyond its means for far too long," and the result was runaway inflation.[29] Simon was very reluctant to extend federal aid to New York. He believed that default would not have a serious impact on the rest of the country, and that extending aid would ultimately be a political and economic mistake because it would legitimate the kinds of public spending that New York had previously undertaken. His position was bolstered by the mail he received from people around the country urging him to stick to a hard line in response to the city's difficulties. For example, one municipal underwriting firm in Pittsburgh suggested that a default on the part of New York City would have a "sobering effect on municipal financing," whereas a bailout for such a "spend-thrift local government" would establish a dangerous precedent.[30] This was the attitude reflected by President Gerald Ford's press secretary, who compared the city to "a wayward daughter hooked on heroin. You don't give her $100 a day to support her habit. You make her go cold turkey."[31] After Simon left national office, he wrote a book (*A Time for Truth*) directed at rallying American business-people to become politically active, which included a chapter on the fiscal crisis entitled "New York: Disaster in Microcosm."[32] For Simon, the problems of New York City were simply those the United States as a whole would face should it continue to expand the welfare state.

But there was no national or elite consensus around a denial of federal aid. Mayor Abraham Beame and New York State Governor Hugh Carey approached Washington in May 1975 for aid, making the case that the city's fate was a matter of national concern and that private entities had previously received bailouts. As Beame put it, "The federal government has not hesitated to rush in and assist banks with cash flow problems, or to provide emergency funds to Lockheed or the Penn Central."[33] Early in the summer of 1975, New York State created the Municipal Assistance Corporation, which was empowered to market bonds (backed by sales taxes) to refinance the city's debt. The MAC was led by business leaders and financiers who promoted themselves as bringing technocratic expertise and rationality to city affairs, a neutral and depoliticizing force to counter the power of labor unions and the old working-class machine. They suggested they had the independence and the force to simply do what was needed to regain the trust of investors and the marketplace. As William Ellinghaus, the chief executive of AT&T who served on MAC, argued, "To balance the budget, to restore the confidence of the financial community whose resources we need in order to survive, to guarantee the survival of New York City there is an urgent need to alter the traditional view of what city government can and should do. What is required is a fundamental rethinking of the level and quality of services this city provides its citizens."[34] In one 1976 speech, investment banker Felix Rohatyn outlined what such a plan might be, describing the need to make New York "a tourist Mecca" for the rest of the country, and also to appeal to the "tens of thousands" of European tourists "who view with alarm the leftward drift of their respective governments. This time around, New York City should look to Europe and say, 'Give me your rich!'"[35] More immediate to the crisis, at a meeting with Beame in July 1975 Rohatyn argued that the more dramatic the city's cuts the better—"overkill" might be necessary to have the proper "shock impact," convincing banks and investors that New York City had changed its ways. He recommended raising the subway fare and ending free tuition at CUNY, noting that it was apparent from what the banking community had said that "the City's way of life is disliked nationwide."[36]

Yet at the same time, this increased involvement of business in the city's government and the press for retrenchment at the local level did not dissuade business leaders from making the case for greater federal involvement. MAC had a great deal of difficulty selling its bonds in the summer of 1975, and it became clear that federal aid would still be needed to avoid default. Rohatyn and others involved with MAC were in close touch with federal officials, and by midsummer 1975 Simon and others in the Treasury Department were concerned that MAC had become too much a lobbying force requesting aid for the city. As one Treasury advisor put it, MAC had become "an impotent and divided group, the most vocal faction of which seems to be lobbying for a 'federal involvement.'"[37] Rohatyn even made the case that the federal government should assume all of New York City's welfare costs, as this would significantly reduce the fiscal burden on the city.[38]

Many other business leaders in and out of New York City argued that federal action was unavoidable. The city simply could not be permitted to declare bankruptcy—this would have an irrevocably terrible effect on bondholders, the municipal bond markets around the entire country, and the broader image of New York and of the United States in the rest of the world. Some framed their worries in terms of the potential for social crisis and racial violence: "If the city stops services and welfare payments, we will have riots in the streets," one executive wrote to Simon. "Certainly the fact that high welfare payments have attracted so many people from Puerto Rico and the South should not be a cause for punishing New York City and its bondholders."[39] Tom Clausen, the president of the Bank of America, told the Senate Committee on Banking, Housing and Urban Affairs, "The effects of a New York City default may well be grave and enduring, not only in terms of our economy and financial markets, but also of public confidence in government and loss of international prestige." Default, he said, "most certainly must be averted in the national interest."[40] A default by New York City would be a financial event of the first magnitude, surpassing anything of like character since the banking holiday of 1933," wrote the

Public Finance Committee of the Securities Industry Association.[41] In the fall of 1975, Charles Luce, the chairman of Con Edison, wrote to Ford to plead with him not to allow New York to go bankrupt, arguing that it would have wide-ranging and unpredictable financial effects and that "Governor Carey and Mayor Beame already have placed management of the City's finances in the hands of some of the ablest business executives in the country."[42] The chancellor of West Germany, Helmut Schmidt, criticized the Ford administration publicly for failing to do more to aid New York, saying that the city's default would have national and even international economic ramifications.[43]

The problems of New York and the question of appropriate government response were also being fiercely debated in the national press.[44] Over the course of the summer, New York's crisis became an opportunity for a referendum on the problems of American cities and the nature of the welfare state. The city was compared to a bankrupt corporation. As the *St. Louis Post-Dispatch* put it, "New York City, the financial capital of the nation if not the world, is on the verge of bankruptcy. Unlike a company that goes broke and whose assets are sold off to pay creditors, New York presumably will not be put on the auction block. After all, who would buy it?"[45] The *Washington Post* sneered at the "myth so deeply embedded in New York's politics that things are 'free' if government provides them."[46] The *Miami Herald* suggested that New York City resembled "a drunk in the family who loses most of his paycheck on the way home every Friday," citing the "million people" on welfare in the city and the city's insistence on clinging to free tuition at CUNY.[47] The *Chicago Tribune* attacked the city's public sector unions: "New York City is writhing in financial agony—some say it is dying—but the municipal unions that have been carving their pounds of flesh out of the city's emaciated body for years are unwilling to make the slightest sacrifice to help the city now." The paper went on to accuse public employee unions across the country of the same sins, citing strikes in San Francisco and elsewhere.[48] In another editorial, the *Tribune* argued that the problems of New York were those facing cities across the country: "Any city can get into New York City's plight by acting as that city did—expanding 'free' services and entering into union contracts beyond its ability to pay. The lesson is clear. In public finance there is no Santa Claus. There really is an end somewhere to a city's capacity to write checks."[49] The *Baltimore Sun* made the comparison to the federal government explicit: "The day may come when the federal government will face a crisis similar to the one New York faces now. And no government will be able to bail Uncle Sam out."[50]

At the same time, newspapers reflected the idea that the city should not simply be allowed to go bankrupt and that this could have dire consequences for the country as a whole. The *Boston Globe* stated that there was nothing so distinctive about New York's situation: "New York's problems are not so very different from those of other big cities—it is just suffering them earlier and harder."[51] The *Washington Post* ultimately came to recommend some kind of bailout for the city, warning that unless the federal government was willing to act as a "lender of last resort" the entire municipal and state bond market might collapse.[52] Even the *Sun* pointed out that "the consequences of a New York bankruptcy could be so harmful for other state and local governments which borrow to live, the federal government has some responsibility here."[53] The pressures of the Cold War, too, came to bear on New York. The *New York Times* reported that *Pravda* was informing people in the Soviet Union of the city's plight with glee, and the *New York Law Journal* (a publication for city lawyers and judges) advertised a special issue devoted to the crisis in the *Times*: "How Would Russia Look If Moscow Failed?"[54]

In the end, these forces prevailed with Ford. The city and state took various actions over the fall of 1975—creating a state-appointed Emergency Financial Control Board to guarantee that the city would progress toward a balanced budget, making arrangements with pension funds and banks to purchase city bonds, passing a moratorium (later found unconstitutional) on the repayment of principal—which persuaded Ford to approve seasonal loans to the city.[55] The pressures of the Cold War and the sense of anxiety about the economic and political image of the United States proved stronger than the purist antigovernment position in the 1970s. Indeed, when Ford met with other international leaders for an economic summit in November 1975 in Rambouillet, France, he reassured them that he had adopted a tough line with New York City only in order to make sure that it would take the necessary steps. "The only way we have achieved results is to be difficult," he said. "This has been a sort of brinksmanship by the Administration forcing New York City and New York State to take responsible action."[56]

Just as there was no easy consensus in national politics about denying aid to New York, within the city, the crisis of the city government did not simply lead to a rise in antigovernment politics. Instead, it resulted in a range of competing groups intensifying their demands on the local state. Many cutbacks in services, closings of fire and police stations, and reductions in city personnel were greeted with outrage and calls to reinstate the benefits that were threatened or had been taken away. Here, too, the fiscal crisis intensified trends that had been taking place within the city previously. The city government had, for example, closed or threatened to close fire stations in 1972 and again in 1974, before the crisis became public. These closings also met with intense neighborhood protest. There had been cuts planned for the city university system as well in 1974, which also met with protest and resistance from students and faculty alike. By the time the fiscal crisis began there was already an ongoing struggle about resources in the city.

The desire to defend and protect public resources became much more immediate with the onset of the crisis. When Beame announced the first serious cuts in the city workforce early in July, wildcat strikes raged throughout the city. Out-of-work police officers rampaged across the Brooklyn Bridge, blocking traffic, throwing beer bottles at their brethren in uniform, and using flagpoles to puncture the tires of motorists stalled in traffic. Garbage began to pile up in the South Bronx and on the Upper East Side alike. The police printed a "survival guide" for tourists calling New York "Fear City" and threatened to hand it out at the airports, detailing the mayhem that would break out if the layoffs of police officers were allowed to stand.[57] When day care centers were closed in the spring of 1976, Robert Abrams, the borough president of the Bronx, wrote an angry letter to Beame: "We have just heard that mail-o-grams have been received by a number of day care centers with the opening words 'we regret to inform you' and telling them that they will be closed. Perhaps it is appropriate to echo the chilling telegrams sent to families of servicemen."[58] Plans to shutter Fordham Hospital in the Bronx elicited a similarly strong response from local politicians: "We are calling on you to give us hope. Where private industry will not tread government cannot be equally insensitive by turning its back on her poor and low income people."[59] Some New Yorkers made donations to the city government in the hope of rescuing it.[60] They affirmed their need for public services: "Please do not close any libraries. I cannot afford to go out and buy any book I wish to read."[61] They wrote in defense of night English programs that were threatened with closure. There were several different neighborhood occupations of firehouses that the city planned to close, by far the longest one being the sixteen-month sit-in and neighborhood mobilization at Engine Company 212 in Williamsburg, which ultimately rescued the fire station. At Hostos Community College in the Bronx, students organized an occupation of the campus buildings to protest plans to merge the newly created bilingual college with the Bronx Community College. In some cases, the people who wrote to the mayor presented themselves as a beleaguered middle class, whose police, fire, and sanitation services were being cut while people on welfare were still collecting benefits. As one woman wrote to Beame, "Our new slogan can be read as follows: Come to Bankrupt City, Crime and Filth are On the Rise."[62] Middle-class people feared that the withdrawal of public services would mean the "decline" of their neighborhoods. "We are petrified," wrote one Queens resident. "WE NEED THE 107th PRECINCT. The feeling in the area . . . is that the Middle Class is being driven out of New York."[63]

At the same time, the vivid illustration of the city government's weakness led to a reinvigorated interest in finding alternatives to government to cope with various different social problems. The "Citizens Committee for New York City," founded in November 1975 by New York senators James Buckley and Jacob Javits in a direct response to the fiscal crisis, sought to organize volunteer efforts and "community self-help" projects on behalf of the city.[64] Army recruiters contacted the city, indicating that laid-off public workers should consider joining up with "the nation's largest employer."[65] The Manhattan Institute—the think tank founded in 1977 with support from British activist Antony Fisher that sought to advance free-market solutions to urban problems—became a key voice in city politics throughout these years.[66] Time and again, Beame answered the many letters that came to him by saying simply that the city had no money to restore programs and that the fiscal crisis necessitated cutbacks at all levels, across the board. Justice or social obligation was no longer the standard. Regardless of the claims that were made on it, the city government would no longer be able to act as it had in the past.

✳ ✳ ✳

The political importance of the New York City fiscal crisis of 1975 has to do with the dynamics of fiscal crisis and the contradictory attitudes they reveal about the state. On the one hand, moments of fiscal crisis such as that in New York City in 1975 call into question the very capacity of citizens to make demands on the state. They dramatically reveal the weakness of the state and its dependence on financial markets, and suggest the impossibility of using government to redress social grievances. These public demonstrations of the incapacity of the state are thus moments of austerity, both in terms of literal devolution and the cutback of the public sector and in terms of the mood and imagination that they engender. The city's crisis suggested the ultimate reliance of New York City on debt rather than on its own taxing authority and the political commitments of its citizens.

Yet at the same time, the consensus around reducing the scope of government was neither straightforward nor universal. Rather than accept a shrunken version of their city, many New Yorkers engaged in a range of economic protests to resist the contraction of the public sphere. Even the political and economic elite within the city ultimately focused on getting aid from the federal government, albeit in ways that would enforce the contraction of local services. National and international elites also were shocked by the idea that the federal government would do so little to aid the city and by the willingness to embrace this image of public weakness—especially in the context of the Cold War. The city's elite sought to find a way to assert the authority of the state at a time when it seemed to be challenged at the deepest level, even as their goal was to transform and reorient the priorities of the city. The attempt of the city to withdraw services where they were expected led people to assert their claim to resources all the more vigorously. The fiscal crisis, in all these ways, was less a singular turning point and more a moment when a set of contests and struggles over the state that had been taking shape all throughout the early 1970s came into public view. Such conflicts continued throughout the 1980s and beyond. As New York's economy recovered, the city's budget began to grow again during the 1980s until by the end of the decade its spending levels were close to what they had been (adjusting for inflation), leading to new warnings of fiscal disaster and cuts in the early 1990s. But even though spending might recover, the sense of the expansive potential of city government did not. The history of the fiscal crisis meant that the divide between the new reality of the city—both in terms of its economy and who held power—and the old expectations and assumptions about city life could no longer be sustained. The life of the city could not go back to what it had been. The expectations, the assumptions, and the practices of the city had been shifted by the experience and the politics of the fiscal crisis.

Notes

1. Lyn Smith to Jacob Javits, April 16, 1975, roll 5, Abraham Beame Papers (hereafter ABP), New York City Municipal Archives and LaGuardia and Wagner Archive, LaGuardia Community College, Queens, New York. Throughout this chapter, I draw on research that also appears in Kim Phillips-Fein, *Fear City: New York's Fiscal Crisis and the Rise of Austerity Politics* (New York: Metropolitan Books, 2017).

2. Abraham Beame to Jacob Javits, July 31, 1975, roll 5, ABP, Municipal Archives and LaGuardia and Wagner Archive.

3. See Joshua B. Freeman, *Working-Class New York: Life and Labor since World War II* (New York: New Press, 2001), 256–87 for the best short treatment of New York and the fiscal crisis. Also see Roger E. Alcaly and David Mermelstein, eds., *The Fiscal Crisis of American Cities: Essays on the Political Economy of Urban America with Special Reference to New York* (New York: Vintage, 1977); William K. Tabb, *The Long Default: New York City and the Urban Fiscal Crisis* (New York: Monthly Review, 1982); Eric Lichten, *Class, Power & Austerity: The New York City Fiscal Crisis* (South Hadley, Mass.: Bergin & Garvey, 1986); Kim Moody, *From Welfare State to Real Estate: Regime Change in New York City, 1974 to the Present* (New York: New Press, 2007); Miriam Greenberg, *Branding New York: How a City in Crisis Was Sold to the World* (New York: Routledge, 2008); Julian Brash, "Invoking Fiscal Crisis: Moral Discourse and Politics in New York City," *Social Text* 21, no. 3 (Fall 2003): 76; Alice O'Connor, "The Privatized City: The Manhattan Institute, the Urban Crisis, and the Conservative Counterrevolution in New York," *Journal of Urban History* 34, no. 2 (January 2008): 333–53; Jamie Peck, "Pushing Austerity: State Failure, Municipal Bankruptcy and the Crises of Fiscal Federalism in the USA," *Cambridge Journal of Regions, Economy and Society* 7, no. 1 (2014): 17–44; and John Krinsky, "Neoliberal Times: Intersecting Temporalities and the Neoliberalization of New York City's Public-Sector Labor Relations," *Social Science History Review* 35, no. 3 (Fall 2011): 381–422. Suleiman Osman, *The Invention of Brownstone Brooklyn: Gentrification and the Search for Authenticity in Postwar New York* (New York: Oxford University Press, 2011) does not discuss the fiscal crisis, but provides an excellent interpretation of the transformation of New York's liberalism during the postwar years. Other important accounts of the fiscal crisis in New York City politics include Ester R. Fuchs, *Mayors and Money: Fiscal Policy in New York and Chicago* (Chicago: University of Chicago Press, 1992); Martin Shefter, *Political Crisis/Fiscal Crisis: The Collapse and Revival of New York City* (New

York: Columbia University Press, 1992); Peter D. McClellan and Alan L. Magdovitz, *Crisis in the Making: The Political Economy of New York State Since 1945* (New York: Cambridge University Press, 1981); Seymour P. Lachman and Robert Polner, *The Man Who Saved New York: Hugh Carey and the Fiscal Crisis of 1975* (Albany: State University of New York Press, 2010). There are also a set of major journalistic accounts of the crisis mostly written in its immediate aftermath: Jack Newfield and Paul Du Brul, *The Abuse of Power: The Permanent Government and the Fall of New York* (New York: Penguin Books, 1978); Ken Auletta, *The Streets Were Paved With Gold* (New York: Vintage Books, 1980); Fred Ferretti, *The Year the Big Apple Went Bust* (New York: Putnam, 1976); Charles Morris, *The Cost of Good Intentions: New York City and the Liberal Experiment, 1960–1975* (New York: W. W. Norton, 1980). Three important recent PhD dissertations address the crisis as well: Benjamin Holtzman, "Crisis and Confidence: Reimagining New York City in the Late Twentieth Century" (Brown University, 2016); Lana Povitz, "Movement Stirrings: Food Activism in New York City, 1969–2003" (New York University, 2016); and Michael Reagan, "Capital City: New York City in Fiscal Crisis, 1966–1978" (University of Washington, 2017).

4. Christopher Lasch, *The Culture of Narcissism: American Life in an Age of Diminishing Expectations* (New York: W. W. Norton, 1979), xiii. For more recent scholarship on the 1970s, see Jefferson Cowie, *Stayin' Alive: The 1970s and the Last Days of the Working Class* (New York: New Press, 2010); Judith Stein: *Pivotal Decade: How the United States Traded Factories for Finance in the Seventies* (New Haven, Conn.: Yale University Press, 2010); Bethany Moreton, *To Serve God and Wal-Mart: The Making of Christian Free Enterprise* (Cambridge, Mass.: Harvard University Press, 2009); Natasha Zaretsky, *No Direction Home: The American Family and the Fear of National Decline, 1968–1980* (Chapel Hill: University of North Carolina Press, 2007); Greta R. Krippner, *Capitalizing on Crisis: The Political Origins of the Rise of Finance* (Cambridge, Mass.: Harvard University Press, 2011).

5. The 1970s was widely felt as a time of crisis, but initially the idea was often employed by the Left, and in some ways the term "fiscal crisis" represented the claiming of the language of systemic failure by the Right. For writing about crisis in the 1970s, see especially James O'Connor, *The Fiscal Crisis of the State* (New York: St. Martin's, 1973); Fred Block, "The Fiscal Crisis of the Capitalist State," *Annual Review of Sociology* 7, no. 1 (1981): 1–27; Jürgen Habermas, *Legitimation Crisis*, trans. Thomas McCarthy (Boston: Beacon, 1973); Sheldon Wolin, "Political Theory as a Vocation," *American Political Science Review* 63, no. 4 (December 1969): 1062–82. For the implications of the crisis in New York, see David Harvey, *A Brief History of Neoliberalism* (New York: Oxford University Press, 2005), 44–45; Doug Henwood, *Wall Street: How It Works and For Whom* (New York: Verso, 1998), 295–97.

6. Janet Roitman, "Crisis," *Political Concepts: A Critical Lexicon* no. 1, accessed August 6, 2017, http://www.politicalconcepts.org/issue1/crisis/.

7. William Novak, "The Myth of the 'Weak' American State," *American Historical Review* 113, no. 3 (June 2008): 752–72; Julia Ott, *When Main Street Met Wall Street: The Quest for an Investors' Democracy* (Cambridge, Mass.: Harvard University Press, 2011); James T. Sparrow, *Warfare State: World War II Americans and the Age of Big Government* (New York: Oxford University Press, 2011); Gail Radford, "From Municipal Socialism to Public Authorities: Institutional Factors in the Shaping of American Public Enterprise," *Journal of American History* 90, no. 3 (December 2003): 863–90.

8. Roger Sanjek, *The Future of Us All: Race and Neighborhood Politics in New York City* (Ithaca, N.Y.: Cornell University Press, 2000), 86.

9. Jonathan Soffer, *Ed Koch and the Rebuilding of New York City* (New York: Columbia University Press, 2010), 150–51.

10. Ibid., 152.

11. Robert Bailey, *The Crisis Regime: The MAC, the EFCB, and the Political Impact of the New York City Financial Crisis* (Albany: State University of New York Press, 1984), 4.

12. Robert F. Wagner, quoted in Nicholas P. Giuliano, Timothy J. Heine, and Tammy Elaine Tuller, "The Constitutional Debt Limit and New York City," *Fordham Urban Law Journal* 8, no. 1 (1979): 185.

13. Mitchell is perhaps best known for his role in the Watergate break-in and cover-up, for which he ultimately served nineteen months in prison.

14. State of New York Department of Audit and Control, *Debt-Like Commitments of the State of New York*, issue 2, New York State Comptroller's Studies on Issues in Public Finance (New York: Office of the State Comptroller, 1973).

15. Charles N. Stabler, "Developing Debt," *Wall Street Journal*, September 28, 1976.

16. Krippner, *Capitalizing on Crisis*, esp. 75 for discussion of Citibank.

17. Mary Saunders Turner to Mr. Thomas Huertas (memorandum), 1978, in "Reduction in Citibank Income Tax Burden, 1956–1970," RG 12, Citibank Book, Mary S. Turner, Memoranda and Drafts, Citibank Archives.

18. Freeman, *Working-Class New York*, 257.

19. Ferretti, *The Year the Big Apple Went Bust*, 30.

20. Shefter, *Political Crisis, Fiscal Crisis*, 241.

21. G. Keith Funston to Clarence Francis, May 23, 1966, box 3, folder 3, G. Keith Funston Papers, New York Stock Exchange [NYSE] Archives.

22. G. Keith Funston to Clarence Francis, December 5, 1966, box 3, folder 3, G. Keith Funston Papers, NYSE Archives.

23. Henry Harris, George Leness, and Henry Watts to Board of Governors, "Final Report on the Mayor's Committee to Keep the New York Stock Exchange in New York City," March 8, 1967, box 6, folder 6, G. Keith Funston Papers, NYSE Archives.

24. Statement by Nelson A. Rockefeller, March 15, 1971, RG 15, series 10.3, box 13, folder 146, Nelson Aldrich Rockefeller Papers, Gubernatorial Series (hereafter NAR), Rockefeller Archive Center, Sleepy Hollow, New York.

25. Robert Douglass to Governor Rockefeller, March 11, 1971, "Tax Problems and Actions in Neighboring States," RG 15, series 10.3, box 13, folder 196, NAR.

26. Neal Moylan to Robert Douglass, March 24, 1971, RG 15, series 10.3, box 13, folder 146, NAR.

27. Special Message to the Legislature, April 20, 1971, RG 15, series 10.3, box 18, folder 172, NAR.

28. For divisions within the Ford administration, see Charles J. Orlebeke, "Saving New York: The Ford Administration and the New York City Fiscal Crisis," in *Gerald R. Ford and the Politics of Post-Watergate America, Vol. 2*, ed. Bernard J. Firestone and Alexej Ugrinsky (Westport, Conn.: Greenwood, 1993), 359–85.

29. William Simon to the Economic Club of New York, address, September 23, 1975, drawer 24, folder 32, William Simon Papers, Lafayette College.

30. Edwin F. Scheetz Jr., of Moore, Leonard & Lynch, to William Simon, October 2, 1975, drawer 24, folder 33, William Simon Papers, Lafayette College.

31. Martin Tolchin, "Ford Again Denies Fiscal Aid to City," *New York Times*, October 18, 1975, 61.

32. William E. Simon, *A Time for Truth* (New York: McGraw-Hill, 1978).

33. Ronald Smothers, "Simon's Rejection of City's Aid Plea Scored by Beame," *New York Times*, May 12, 1975, 1.

34. William Ellinghaus, statement on MAC Program, July 31, 1975, "MAC Material" binder, Jack Bigel Papers, Baruch College Archives, CUNY.

35. Felix Rohatyn, address to National Policy for Urban America conference, May 21, 1976, "Felix Rohatyn" binder, Jack Bigel Papers, Baruch College, CUNY.

36. "Meeting with MAC," minutes, July 17, 1975, box 070013, folder 11, ABP, Municipal Archives and LaGuardia and Wagner Archive.

37. "Report on New York City: Memorandum for the President," Edwin H. Yeo III, Presidential Handwriting Files, box 28, folder "Local Government, NYC," Gerald Ford Presidential Library, Ann Arbor, Michigan.

38. Steven Weisman, "MAC Calls on US to Pay for Relief," *New York Times*, August 10, 1985.

39. Jesse Werner, GAF Corporation, to William Simon, October 13, 1975, drawer 24, folder 33, NYC 1975 (October), William Simon Papers, Lafayette College. The letter cites another friend who denounced Simon to Werner: "Just where did he make his fortune? And how did he do it? Selling bonds!"

40. Statement of A. W. Clausen, president, BankAmerica Corporation, San Francisco, California, before the Senate Committee on Banking, Housing, and Urban Affairs, October 18, 1975. Hearings Before the Committee on Banking, Housing, and Urban Affairs, U.S. Senate, 94th Cong., 1st sess. on S. 1833, S. 1862, S. 2372, @. 2514, and S. 2523 (Washington, D.C.: Government Printing Office, 1975) at 666.

41. Press release, October 9, 1975. MAC binder, Jack Bigel Papers, Baruch College, CUNY.

42. Charles Luce to Gerald Ford, telegram, November 4, 1975, "Default & Bankruptcy (articles, notes and correspondence) binder, May 1975–Dec 1976," Jack Bigel Papers, Baruch College, CUNY.

43. Memorandum of conversation, October 3, 1975, National Security Adviser's Memoranda of Conversation Collection, box 15, folder "October 3, 1975—Ford, Kissinger, FRG Chancellor Helmut Schmidt," Gerald Ford Presidential Library, Ann Arbor, Michigan. Also see David Binder, "Schmidt Fears Effects of City Crisis," *New York Times*, October 5, 1975.

44. The material in the following paragraphs also appears in Phillips-Fein, *Fear City*, 145–46.

45. Editorial, *St. Louis Post-Dispatch*, May 29, 1975.

46. Editorial, *Washington Post*, June 2, 1975.

47. "NY's Big Mac Is 'Cold Turkey,'" *Miami Herald*, June 11, 1975.

48. "Contagious New Yorkitis," *Chicago Tribune*, August 21, 1975.

49. "Lessons from New York, Cont.," *Chicago Tribune*, September 8, 1975.

50. Editorial, *Baltimore Sun*, July 24, 1975.

51. "Mr. Ford on New York," *Boston Globe*, August 6, 1975.

52. "A Safety Net for New York," *Washington Post*, September 15, 1975.

53. Editorial, *Baltimore Sun*, July 24, 1975.

54. Malcolm W. Browne, "Soviet Sees Gains in Woes of West," *New York Times*, July 13, 1975; also see advertisement in *New York Times*, October 15, 1975.

55. Charles J. Orlebeke, "Saving New York," 359–86.

56. All references from memorandum of conversation, November 14 to 17, 1975, Rambouillet, France, "Economic Summit," box 16, folder: "November 15–17, 1975, Rambouillet Economic Summit," National Security Adviser Memoranda of Conversation Collection, Gerald Ford Presidential Library.

57. Fred Ferretti, "City's 10,000 Sanitationmen Strike; Police and Firemen Also Discuss Job Actions to Protest Layoffs," *New York Times*, July 2, 1975; Selwyn Raab, "Ex-Policemen Block Brooklyn Bridge," *New York Times*, July 2, 1975; "Welcome to Fear City," folder: "Layoffs 1975," in District Council 37 Archives, privately held at District Council 37, American Federation of State, County and Municipal Employees.

58. Robert Abrams to Abraham Beame, May 27, 1976, roll 10, ABP, Municipal Archives and LaGuardia and Wagner Archive.

59. Stephen B. Kaufman to Abraham Beame, May 6, 1976, roll 10, ABP, Municipal Archives and LaGuardia and Wagner Archive.

60. W. Bernard Richland to Abraham Beame, "Mrs. Sarah A. Wilson of 410 Westminster Road, Brooklyn, has offered the City a gift of $78, her entire Medicare refund, to help it in its fiscal difficulties," October 27, 1976, roll 2, ABP.

61. Chana Klajman to Abraham Beame, May 9, 1976, roll 12, ABP, Municipal Archives and LaGuardia and Wagner Archive.

62. Maureen Cullen to Abraham Beame, June 9, 1975, roll 12, ABP, Municipal Archives and LaGuardia and Wagner Archive.

63. Edith Kalur to Abraham Beame, November 5, 1975, roll 12, ABP, Municipal Archives and LaGuardia and Wagner Archive.

64. Statement by Osborn Elliott, Editor-in-Chief, Newsweek, and Chairman, Citizens Committee for New York City, undated. Citizens Committee for New York City Archives. Privately held at Citizens Committee for New York City offices, New York City.

65. Lt. Colonel Williard M. Bulerson, N.Y. District Recruiting Command; Lt. Colonel Calvin Hosner III, Newburgh District Recruiting Command; and Lt. Colonel William King, Newark District Recruiting Command, to Abraham Beame, March 28, 1976, roll 7, ABP, Municipal Archives and LaGuardia and Wagner Archive.

66. Alice O'Connor, "The Privatized City: The Manhattan Institute, the Urban Crisis, and the Conservative Counterrevolution in New York," *Journal of Urban History* 34, no. 2 (2008): 333.

PART II

CLAIMING AND
CONTESTING CAPITALISM

CHAPTER 4

UTOPIAN CAPITALISM

RICHARD WHITE

W hat is the purpose of an economy? In the twenty-first century United States, outside of environmental circles with only marginal political influence, so thorough has been the triumph of corporate capitalism that the question seems nearly nonsensical. Economists, pundits, and politicians have so naturalized the economy that it has become a kind of social pair of lungs, producing the goods and services necessary to sustain human society. Asking the purpose of the economy has become like asking the purpose of breathing. We breathe to live. The economy produces our social oxygen. The bigger and more efficient our economy, the better off we will be.[1]

But over large periods of American history the question was quite immediate and very pertinent. Americans assumed that a democratic republic demanded a republican economy of independent producers, but the contest between the free-labor North and the slave South made the meaning of independence increasingly contested. The Civil War resolved this issue in favor of free labor and contract freedom, but, with the growth of industry, contract freedom became a chimera for wage laborers and the meaning of free labor itself became contested. The result was the rise of antimonopolism, whose attempt to maintain free labor ultimately transformed it. Antimonopolists insisted that in a republic the economy had to produce free men and not just abundant goods. Finally, in the late nineteenth and early twentieth centuries, largely under pressure from Samuel Gompers and the American Federation of Labor, workers shifted the antimonopolist concentration on production to a new emphasis on consumption, in which the measure of the success of the economy was the living wage and an acceptable level of mass consumption. And, in an ironic development, Gompers' doctrine of more would be assimilated into a conservative defense of capitalism in which the deprivation of workers became necessary for the capitalist utopia of their grandchildren.

As a dynamic and revolutionary system, capitalism has always been a threat to existing orders. From the late seventeenth through the early nineteenth centuries it had been the ally of republicans and democrats seeking to overthrow monarchies, aristocracies, and hierarchical orders. By the late nineteenth and early twentieth century, corporate capitalism in the United States seemed a threat to a democratic republic for more and more Americans. One result was a split among liberals, who had earlier regarded capitalism as merely democracy in an economic sphere. Some, despite their worries, regarded corporate capitalism as a change in degree but not in kind from an older system of competition between small producers. Others, among them the first antimonopolists, regarded the corporation as an aberration spawned by corruption in the political system itself. A return to honest competition would eliminate corporations and the danger they represented. Eventually a third group emerged who thought corporations had fundamentally changed the economy. Neither corporations nor wage labor would disappear anytime soon, but, unless restrained and disciplined, they would destroy the Republic.

These reactions to corporate capitalism all sprang from liberal roots. The more radical critics would alter elements of capitalism—limiting the play of the market, nationalizing some elements of private property, even abolishing wage labor—but relatively few would step over the line into socialism or communism. They simply imagined other capitalisms. In particular they imagined utopian capitalisms. Antebellum liberals had imagined an American utopia of roughly equal, independent small producers; after the Civil War, some still sought this world, but the more radical antimonopolists embraced another utopian capitalism that imagined a democratic corporation in which workers retained control of their working lives. In a republican country, utopian capitalism remained the once and future king.

Until the last ten or fifteen years, most scholars have condescended to the late nineteenth-century capitalist critics of corporations as romantics, reactionaries, or people too muddled to realize that they should be socialists. This has changed. What makes a book like Charles Postel's *Populist Vision* so refreshing is that it neither tries to make the Populists into socialists nor dismisses them as doomed, romantic reformers. He both locates the Populists within a capitalist business tradition and makes them trenchant critics of the corporate order. Populists were just one among many at the time who asked what an economy was for and judged the existing economy wanting.[2] Those living through the rise of the corporation did not agree on the form capitalism would take.

What has largely faded from historical consciousness, except perhaps among labor historians, was a fundamental challenge by working people to the corporate order itself. Workers imagined changes at the bottom rather than the top, on the factory floor—or on the railroad train—rather than in the boardroom or executive offices. Such workers demanded control over not only the conditions of their work, but their work itself. They did so within the corporation, and although some of them belonged to unions such as the Knights of Labor, which imagined an end to the wage system, most belonged to the so-called brotherhoods of skilled and semiskilled workers now so often dismissed as conservative or accommodationist. Managers and owners of nineteenth-century corporations had an accurate view of what was at stake. Charles Francis Adams of the Union Pacific was not being hysterical when he said that the issue in the railroad's dealing with labor unions was whether management or labor organizations would be "controlling the operations of the road." Other executives in other railroads shared his opinion.[3]

Adams as well as the workers could envision very different orders within the corporate form, but unlike Henry George, the era's leading antimonopolist intellectual who saw no necessity of conflict between capital and labor, Adams recognized that despite the goals he might share with his workers, the ultimate issue was one of control. At stake were the rights of capital to determine not only the division of profits within the corporation but how work was to be organized. The struggle over rights and control were really struggles over the organization of capitalism itself and the economy's purpose. It was a struggle that corporations ultimately won, but their victory was neither uncontested nor inevitable.

Recovering and understanding these historical possibilities means revisiting familiar historical terrain but looking at a different set of signposts. Instead of searching for markers for the impending twentieth-century struggle between socialism or communism and capitalism, we need to look for the markers of the struggle between different forms, imagined or real, of capitalism. We need particularly to understand the appeal of utopian capitalisms—forms of capitalism embraced because they seemed to sustain rather than threaten democratic societies.

What Is the Purpose of an Economy? Utopian Capitalism 101

In the antebellum United States liberals agreed that a republican political order demanded a republican economy. And since they believed that a whole set of values they clustered under the rubric of white manhood—independence, virtue, and more—provided the cultural foundation of the Republic, then any economy that threatened white manhood was also a danger to the Republic.

Both Thomas Jefferson and Andrew Jackson regarded competitive markets and white manhood as essential elements of the Republic. Their liberalism did not target wealth—both were by the standards of the time wealthy if often indebted men—as much as older hereditary orders and emerging privilege. Jefferson's chosen opponents were the rich, wise, and wellborn. Jackson's battle with the Bank of the United States previewed the fear of monopoly that would loom so large in the Gilded Age. Jefferson, Jackson, and their followers embraced the earliest American version of utopian capitalism.

In its Jeffersonian and Jacksonian formulations utopian capitalism was racialized and gendered. It could tolerate gross inequality as long as that inequality did not threaten white men. Jeffersonians and Jacksonians imagined a world of small producers in which the paradoxical combination of a free market and local control over the economy produced a roughly egalitarian world of white men. This was the economic ideal for the *herrenvolk* democracy that the American historian George Fredrickson described. The marriage between the economy and the political order seemed strong and mutually sustaining.[4]

In fact, the combination of laissez-faire capitalism, white manhood, general white male equality, and republican government was dangerously brittle. The combination of a slave economy in the South with the free-labor economy of the North proved impossible to sustain. The house divided could not stand. Most northern liberals came to regard a slave economy as incompatible with white male equality and a republican government.[5]

That the house divided could not stand and did not stand was the great insight and achievement of Abraham Lincoln. Our modern focus on racial equality has to some extent blinded us to Lincoln's focus on slavery rather than black freedom. As Eric Foner's *Fiery Trial* demonstrates, Lincoln's attack on slavery as incompatible with republican government was unrelenting; his devotion to racial equality was hesitant and tentative.[6]

When antimonopolists, particularly antimonopolist workers, thought about the purpose of the economy after the Civil War, they predictably embraced the version of utopian capitalism that was intrinsic to the free-labor ideology of the Republican Party that Lincoln articulated and symbolized. Lincoln expressed the utopian ideal in New Haven in 1860: "I am not ashamed to confess that twenty-five years ago I was a hired laborer, mauling rails, at work on a flatboat—just what might happen to any poor man's son. . . . [But in the free states a man knows that] he can better his condition. . . . There is no such thing as a freeman being fatally fixed for life, in the condition of a hired laborer. . . . The man who labored for another last year, this year labors for himself, and next year he will hire others to labor for him." If a man "continues through life in the condition of the hired laborer, it is not the fault of the system, but because of either a dependent nature which prefers it, or improvidence, folly, or singular misfortune." The "free labor system opens the way for all—gives hope to all, and energy, and progress, and improvement of condition to all."[7]

Free labor, as the very term indicates, rooted itself in work. The right of a worker to the fruits of his labor formed perhaps its central value. The traditional liberal formulation of this came from Locke: "Each individual is naturally entitled to do as he pleases with himself and the fruits of his labor." As Lincoln put it more pithily to Cassius Clay, "I always thought that the man who made the corn should eat the corn." Slavery was antithetical to a republic.[8]

The devotees of utopian capitalism embraced the market—at least in theory— as fully as any laissez-faire liberal in large part because they were laissez-faire liberals. Locally, Americans were willing to regulate the market and control the uses of property, and nationally Whigs and ex-Whigs like Lincoln were more than willing to intervene in markets to foster growth, but none of this really challenged their overall view of competitive markets as benign.[9] Lincoln's market, as long as uncorrupted by privilege or special advantage, would yield progress, well-being, and general equality. The United States would be a society of small producers in which both great wealth and extreme poverty would be anomalous.[10]

The rise of large industrial corporations, largely in the form of railroads, challenged the utopian capitalism of free labor. It was initially hard for many believers in the power of free markets to understand how such large corporations arose. Competition supposedly should have suppressed them. It was harder still to recognize that they had done so not only under the party of Lincoln but also under the Lincoln administration. The first task of the critics of corporations was, in effect, to produce a history of corporate origins. The second was to produce a catalog of corporate sins.

Andrew Jackson had prepared the prelude for this history during his battle with the Bank of the United States. Large and powerful corporations emerged only by the granting of public goods as private favors to an elite. This was the essence of corruption, and corruption was thus essential to this explanation of the growth of large corporations. By chartering a private corporation, the Bank of the United States, and entrusting it with the surplus revenues of the United States, Congress had done what the founders had feared: created and sustained a privileged class, and the rich had corrupted government. In denouncing the Bank, Jackson had defended a republican economic order. "It is to be regretted that the rich and powerful too often bend the acts of government to their selfish purposes. Distinctions of society will always exist under every just government. Equality of talents, of education, or of wealth can not be produced by human institutions. In the full enjoyment of the gifts of heaven and the fruits of superior industry, economy, and virtue, every man is equally entitled to protection by law; but when the laws undertake to add to these natural and just advantages, artificial distinctions, to grant titles, gratuities, and exclusive privileges to make the rich richer and the potent more powerful, the humble members of society—the farmers, mechanics, and laborers—who have neither the time nor the means of securing like favors to themselves, have a right to complain of the injustice of their government."[11]

Jackson foreshadowed what became the classic antimonopolist critique of corporations. The Bank of the United States was corrupt and dangerous because it allowed "a few Monied Capitalists" to trade on the public revenue "and enjoy the benefit of it, to the exclusion of the many." By giving these capitalists the ability to influence elections and make loans to Congressmen, the bank gave them the "power to control the Government and change its character." It needed to be defeated to vindicate "the great principles of democracy."[12]

Even as Jackson battled the Bank of the United States, however, a more complicated history was evolving. Corporations were moving from being entities chartered and given special privileges to achieve public purposes—cities, universities, and certain businesses, for example—to becoming largely private organizations. The struggle over the Bank of the United States and the spectacular collapse of state-aided corporations in the late 1830s had sparked a reaction against the prodigality of state legislatures in granting aid and special charters to banks, canals, and early railroads. The prescribed cure was to prohibit state aid to corporations in many states and to democratize corporate charters by making them a form of business organization open to anyone who met the law's qualifications. Corporations thus would supposedly no longer be able to tap state treasuries or secure special privileges. They would not grow large and dangerous.

The reaction against the excesses and failures of the 1830s, however, proved only partial. The federal government retained the power to charter and aid corporations. And most of the new states that entered the Union after the 1840s did not have constitutional prohibitions against aid to private corporations. Subsidies, both state and federal, to corporations returned in the 1850s and increased during the Civil War as the Republicans chartered and subsidized railroads. During the war, the government chartered the Union Pacific, complete with bond guarantees to it and the Central Pacific. Congress bestowed immense land grants on these and other railroads chartered by the states. Railroad corporations in general, and these heavily subsidized western railroads in particular, became the focus of antimonopolists.[13]

The initial antimonopolist critique of the railroads remained thoroughly liberal. The antimonopolist refrain was competition without special privilege or discrimination. In 1886, a journalist, James Hudson, published *Railways and the Republic,* which summarized much of the conventional antimonopoly thinking of the 1870s and early 1880s. As fully as any laissez-faire economist, Hudson believed in competition. For him, it was a moral value, rooted in a sense of equity, individualism, freedom, and a hatred of special privileges bestowed by government.[14]

The regulation that antimonopolists proposed were not so much attacks on laissez-faire and individualism as attempts to restore and protect them. The reformers attacked special privilege in the form of railroad land grants. They targeted unfair railroad rates as distortions of competition. Reformers justified railroad commissions as legitimate tools for restraining the anticompetitive practices of railroads, which were "a restraint on individual freedom." When the Supreme Court upheld these commissions in the so-called Granger cases of 1877, it marked the railroads as a specific class of property "clothed with a public interest" and holding monopoly power, in the sense that the public had no choice but to make use of their services.[15]

The economic sins of corporations were also political: they struck at the rights of American citizens. At the heart of the antimonopoly argument for competition was a single word: discrimination. The idea of discrimination entered most powerfully into American political discourse in the late nineteenth century not in regard to race or gender, but rather in regard to the prices railroads charged their customers. That there was an economic gain as overall railroad rates fell was not the issue. The issue was equity. When the Senate Select Committee on Interstate Commerce reported its investigations in 1886, it concluded that the "essence of the complaints" against railroads was "the practice of discrimination in one form or another." The "great desideratum is to secure equality."[16]

Charges of discrimination had resonance because they touched both the material interests of millions and basic notions of republican equity. Because railroads were chartered by the state, because the government used its powers of eminent domain to aid the railroads, because governments granted land to railroads and extended some railroads credit, and because the railroads were public highways under common law, they had obligations to the public much greater than those of normal businesses. Critics claimed it was unjust for railroad corporations to set rates that discriminated against the citizens of the governments that gave them life.[17] "When railroads charged more to some shippers than to others and more per mile from one place to another," then, as Hudson argued, "the equality of all persons is denied by the discriminations of the corporations which the government has created." Wealth was "not distributed among all classes, according to their industry or prudence, but is concentrated among those who enjoy the favor of the railway power; and general independence and self respect are made impossible." When such influences undercut "the establishment of a nation, of intelligent, self-respecting and self-governing freemen" the result was "little better than national suicide."[18] Hudson denounced discrimination among things as "prescriptive and unreasonable," discrimination among places as "burdensome and dangerous," and discrimination among persons as "corrupt and criminal."[19] The railroads' ability to discriminate against citizens violated both political equity and basic rules of the market.

Critics of corporations saw the power to discriminate as inextricably bound up with the monopolies that they regarded as the products of special privilege. A monopoly was thus almost by definition corrupt since antimonopolists believed that special privilege "in the last analysis rested upon legislative, executive and judicial favoritism." Such privilege could take the form of tariffs, land grants, loans or other subsidies that favored a few and hurt many, or corporate charters that gave the railroads public aid without concomitant public control. By the 1870s special privilege and monopoly had become synonymous with corporations.[20]

A monopoly possessed the ability to destroy, limit, or distort competition. The competition in question was not simply that between the railroads themselves or between railroads and other forms of transportation; it was competition between all those businesses that used the railroads. By manipulating rates, the railroads could decide who succeeded in business and who failed. Monopoly has to be understood within its nineteenth-century context. In the nineteenth century the word "monopoly" had a wider meaning than it had in the twentieth century. Monopolies did not just, or even primarily, dominate some field of productive activity, it was rather that they laid claim to technologies or institutions necessary for the functioning of the economy itself. At best they exacted rents, but at worst they determined the outcome of economic competition itself, selecting winners and losers.

The final liberal critique of corporate capitalism concerned labor and was most closely associated with Henry George. George arose from an antimonopoly tradition concerned with land monopoly, but his core question in his bestselling *Progress and Poverty* (1879) was how in the midst of technological progress the United States was producing growing numbers of poor. This was a labor question, and it would become part of a larger argument that large corporations degraded labor itself, depriving republican citizens of control not only over the fruits of their labor but of the very conditions of their labor itself. The result was an argument that contract freedom meant little within these new conditions and a resurgence of the old language of wage slavery.

The critiques of both Hudson and George were liberal and laissez-faire. In the late nineteenth century laissez-faire was still making its strange transition from a doctrine of radicals and democrats to a doctrine of conservatives fearful of popular politics. Thomas Jefferson or Adam Smith had feared government intervention in the economy as always and necessarily favoring the rich. Jefferson had valued property because its possession bestowed more than access to things. Liberalism extolled independence, which represented, in R. Jeffrey

Lustig's words, "a stake in productive wealth, a chance to exercise initiative, do valuable work and earn standing in a community." These values seemed precisely what corporations and corporate property threatened. They made people dependent.[21]

Antimonopoly and the Evolution of Utopian Capitalism

The rise of corporations and the popular unrest apparent in the great strikes of the late nineteenth century fractured liberalism and changed the valence of laissez-faire. In the original liberal version of the economy, there was no contradiction between republican government and an economy formulated on the basis of free labor, contract freedom, and laissez-faire, but with the evolution of antimonopolism, the contradictions became glaring. Lyman Abbott outlined the problem in 1879: "Politically America is a democracy; industrially America is an aristocracy." The worker might make political laws but "he is under industrial laws. At the ballot box he is a king; in the factory he is a servant, sometimes a slave." This was the core of what was known as the labor question: how to reconcile the democratic promise of the nation with the profoundly undemocratic organization of industry. In involved the old issue of creating a republican economy.[22]

In reaction to such arguments and attempts to implement them, small "l" liberalism became conservatism. The liberals who worried about democracy and threats to property were not reactionaries. Nor were they enamored with corporations and men who grew wealthy from them. But where Jeffersonians and Jacksonians had made property the means to freedom, the liberals who were making their transition to Gilded Age conservatives regarded property as the reward of freedom. It became a proof of virtue and part of a lineage that Max Weber connected with the Protestant Reformation and which stretched from Edmund Burke to William Graham Sumner and Herbert Spencer. Conservatives, reluctantly at first, but then with increasing enthusiasm given the alternatives, embraced the rich.

It was conservatives who first accepted the demise of the older American version of utopian capitalism and the birth of a new corporate order, but they were not united on the cause of death. Nor were they in agreement on which liberal premises still held and which were outmoded in the new age. The two major conservative accounts of the new economy did not provide a version of the meaning and purpose of the economy that would be popular in a democracy.

The first account of the new economy was a neo-Darwinian narrative popularized by Herbert Spencer and William Graham Sumner. It did not so much abandon utopian capitalism as relocate it onto international markets, where the gold standard would keep national economies honest, ensure the enforcement of economic laws, and punish those who violated them. It remained liberal insofar as it embraced individualism, competition, and progress. It thus maintained links to earlier liberal Jeffersonian and Lincolnian narratives of progress, but it turned the older narratives in much darker directions.[23]

Sumner, in particular, retained liberal premises. He believed in contract freedom; he believed in competition; he believed in the market; he believed in individualism. He believed in these things as eternal verities. He, like Jefferson, equated them with laws of nature. But these were no longer the laws of Jefferson's Enlightenment nature; rather, they were what Sumner took to be the evolutionary laws revealed by Darwin. That Sumner utterly misunderstood Darwinian biology is beside the point. What is more pertinent is that he could make this nature seem consistent with the American liberal tradition. He sounded much like Jefferson and Jackson in that he wanted a laissez-faire economy with minimal federal government interference in the competition between individuals in the market. And he sounded like Lincoln in his praise of contract freedom and self-ownership.

What was profoundly different in Sumner was that he was not trying to justify an egalitarian society, at least among whites, but instead a society of increasing inequality as industrialization and corporate capitalism took hold. In retrospect, Sumner recognized the social realities of his age. He did not deny that industrial capitalism was making life worse, not better, for large numbers of American workers. He did not deny inequality. He regarded this as inevitable. It was the price of progress. He, in effect, noticed the same things that Henry George noticed and proclaimed them right and necessary.

Sumner's essays were in many ways quintessential nineteenth-century liberal tracts. When he asked what social classes owe each other, the answer to his question was nothing. It was not an answer that a classical conservative would give, but it was the logical answer from a new conservative whose intellectual heritage was liberal. Jackson had used laissez-faire and individualism to argue for a society of largely equal white men, and Lincoln had mobilized contract freedom to attack slavery, but Sumner used these ideas to justify inequality. "Let it be understood," Sumner wrote elsewhere, "that we cannot go outside of this alternative; liberty, inequality, survival of the fittest, not liberty, equality, survival of the unfittest. The former carries society forward and favors all of its best members; the latter carries society downwards and favors all of its worst members."[24]

In severing liberty and equality, Sumner made inequality the price of liberty and progress. Sumner's poor had nobody to blame but themselves. They would remain poor and perish.

Many are frightened at liberty, especially under the form of competition, which they elevate into a bugbear. They think it bears harshly on the weak.

They do not perceive that "the strong" and the "weak" are terms which admit of no definition unless they are made equivalent to the industrious and the idle, the frugal and the extravagant . . . If we do not like the survival of the fittest, we have only one possible alternative and that is the survival of the unfittest.[25]

Sumner's version of liberalism had rather spectacular limits in a democratic polity where the poor, despite the efforts of other liberals, could still vote, but political dangers also lurked in a very different defense of the new corporate capitalism that dispensed with the liberal pieties that Sumner cherished. John D. Rockefeller was not an intellectual, but he certainly was a capitalist, and he had no time for liberalism or utopian capitalism. He did not believe in individualism. He believed in organization.

John D. Rockefeller and his partners were capitalists of legend. Rockefeller was a Baptist, but most of his executives were stern Presbyterians. They worked six days a week and, initially, shunned any sort of ostentation. Their ethics embraced what might be called Business Christianity. Henry Flagler, Rockefeller's partner, kept a quote from a popular novel, *David Harum*, on his desk: "Do unto others as they would do unto you—and do it first."[26]

Rockefeller had no patience with what he called "academic enthusiasts"— by which he meant economists—and sentimentalists, including Sumner and the ideologues of contract theory and open competition. They knew nothing about how businesses operated. Rockefeller had even less patience with their competitive models. He saw himself as acting to stop a competition that would prove ruinous. In the case of Standard Oil, consolidation was, he said, "forced upon us. We had to do it in self-defense. The oil business was in confusion and daily growing worse. Someone had to make a stand."[27]

Standard Oil was, he proclaimed, the future. "This movement was the origin of the whole system of economic administration. It has revolutionized the way of doing business all over the world. The time was ripe for it. It had to come, though all we saw at the moment was the need to save ourselves from wasteful conditions. The day of the combination is here to stay. Individualism has gone never to return."[28]

Charles Francis Adams managed to give the corporation a utopian twist. Working from premises similar to Rockefeller's, Adams, the president of the Union Pacific and a conventional liberal in many respects, concocted an evolutionary scheme very different from Sumner's. Adams combined Auguste Comte and John Stuart Mill in a way that allowed him to combine liberalism with his sense that organizations were replacing individuals as basic social units. Progress would come from recognizing the laws of human society. Adams adjusted easily enough to the idea that cultivated minds would lead human society in recognizing these laws, never doubting that his mind was among the most cultivated. But where Comte dismissed laissez faire and the "so-called rights of the individual"—the hallmarks of Gilded Age liberalism—as purely "metaphysical," Adams, reading Comte through Mill, could hold on to them as corollaries to social laws, an "inference from the laws of human nature and human affairs." He could have both his liberalism and his positivism.[29]

Social laws yielded for Adams a constrained individualism; instead of blindly pursuing self-interest, humans in society would seek the "cooperation of mankind one with another, by the division of employments and interchange of commodities and services." Human society, in short, sounded a lot like a railroad corporation. Cooperation was the source of progress; and it reached its fulfillment when "the true methods of positive science were applied to society."[30] Adams adopted Mill's view that the market might be a temporary practical necessity for settling workers' share of production, but it was certainly not a moral ideal, and society was striving for a moral ideal whose model was the military, since until "laborers and employers perform the work of industry in the spirit in which soldiers perform that of any army, industry will never be moralized and military life will remain . . . the chief school of moral cooperation."[31]

Adams, too, regarded the dominance of the market as but a phase of human existence and looked elsewhere for principles of social organization. In the late nineteenth century liberals like Mill as well as radical writers like Edward Bellamy, who borrowed heavily from the Knights of Labor, praised the army as a social model. This stress on cooperation and the unwillingness to see the market as a template for society distanced Charles Francis Adams from laissez-faire businessmen like Charles Perkins, president of the Chicago, Burlington, and Quincy Railroad. Ideals of a cooperative society based on military analogies and embraced by former military officers like Adams conveyed, however, a rather constricted view of cooperation.

Lecturing at Harvard College, Adams portrayed the late nineteenth century as a time in which the old freebooters of American capitalism were yielding to a new generation of managers and college-educated professionals. Organization was now everything, and he told Harvard undergraduates that the genius of the modern corporation was that "the individual withers, and the whole is more and more." As president of the corporation, his job was to keep the whole operating in harmony.[32] This was as utopian as anything on the left.

Sumner, Rockefeller, and Adams were all willing to admit that the world had changed. Where Rockefeller and Adams differed from Sumner was in their claim that many of the old verities no longer applied. Competition and individualism—the basis of the older liberal utopian version of capitalism—simply could not account for the new organization of production.

Rockefeller and Adams assumed that the reorganization of work under corporate capitalism would proceed from above. The new cooperative order would be hierarchical and bureaucratic. Adams, however, worked in an industry with organized workers, and he recognized that a challenge to his order would come from below. Historians have paid a great deal of attention to those groups that challenged capitalism and the private ownership of the means of production. They have given considerable attention to the Knights of Labor, with their advocacy of the end of the wage system and the advent of a cooperative order far different from what Rockefeller and Adams had in mind, and to socialists. They have given less attention to the brotherhoods of skilled workers. The brotherhoods did not challenge the capitalist order and often went out of their way to present themselves as conservative. Regarded as the first steps toward an acquiescent bread-and-butter unionism, the railroad brotherhoods tend to be dismissed as lapdogs compared to the Knights of Labor, the American Railway Union, and the unions connected to the Socialist Party.

But it is precisely the brotherhoods' reluctance to challenge either capitalism or the corporation that make them interesting. They were convinced that they could control work within the corporation, and their attempts to do so alarmed corporate managers. They had their own version of the Knights of Labor ideal of citizens as producers and producers as citizens. In practical terms, they imagined a workers' version of utopian capitalism in which workers, as befitted the citizens of a democratic republic, would control their working lives as they controlled their political lives and where accepting wages did not mean the loss of independence.

Workers challenged the military analogies that corporate officials in the nineteenth century favored in their correspondence and which Charles Francis Adams, Comte, and John Stuart Mill elevated to social theory. Military analogies turned workers into soldiers. Their job was to take orders. They had no control over their work, how it was done, or when it was to be performed. In selling their labor they had passed through a filter that negated the social rules that governed the rights and duties of republican citizenship. They became a different kind of being; they were no longer, in the workers' terms, men. Their opinions did not matter. Conditions they would never accept in their civic or public life were to be the conditions of their working lives. Employers might be benevolent, but that was the employers' decision.

Both workers and managers understood the great stakes involved in this struggle over work. Adams always recognized that what was at stake in his dealings with the unions was whether management or "labor organizations" would be "controlling the operations of the road."[33]

The struggle over the control of work became a struggle over the nature of corporate capitalism. In effect, workers sought to recreate a utopian capitalism within the corporation. In thinking of themselves as republican citizens who did not surrender their rights or autonomy when they went to work, the members of the brotherhoods did not differ substantially from the Knights of Labor, whose goal, as expressed by George McNeill, was "to engraft republican principles into our industrial system."[34] As a miner in a Union Pacific coal mine in Rock Springs Wyoming put it, forcing employees to sign papers allowing the company to control where they worked and how they worked and to assess penalties when they complained or refused was an attack on the independence that was at the root of workers' identity. It was asking a man to sign away "his free speech, his liberty and his manhood."[35]

Work was the stuff of both principle and of quotidian struggle. Workers grasped both the conditions of the new economy and the implications of the new doctrines of marginalism taking root among economists, even if they would not have recognized the term.[36] A columnist for the *Union Pacific Employes* [sic] *Magazine* wrote, as a hypothetical worker out of employment seeking a job, that an employer would grant a job "if I can produce for you a tithe more than you will pay me in wages; no, if I produce a tithe less." Employers would hire additional workers only if it was to their gain. With the deflationary tendency of the late nineteenth-century economy and a surplus of workers, the price of labor and the wages of workers would continually fall. The wage paid the last worker hired would become the governing wage. In bold language that workers could easily understand, the writer spelled out the consequences for workers:

> So long as [the workers] recognize the right of a man to hire them, they must recognize his right to refuse. He will rarely refuse when it is to his gain. The amount he will pay is regulated in a measure by that and the number seeking his service. Consequently by recognizing this right to hire they indirectly recognize his right to fix the pay, for it can never be above what he demands as gain, no matter how wasteful his management may be, on which the hired service might improve; the servant is helpless before the recognized right of the employer.[37]

Workers were groping toward a situation that, in a sense, restored collectively the conditions that had supposedly pertained individually in the older vision of utopian capitalism. Workers needed to be independent and men. They would have a say in the conditions, timing, and conduct of work. Workers would have a say in who obtained work and who did not. The unilateral right to hire and fire could not be conceded nor could the right to unilaterally set wages or to control the terms of work. The groups who were in the strongest position to make a stand were the brotherhoods of skilled workers.

This challenge to the operation of the corporate order was more than theoretical; in the nineteenth century it was an issue of praxis. The workers battled daily for control of the operation of the railroad and the compensation given workers. Because work rules and compensation could not be easily separated, the more complex work rules became, the more the brotherhoods stood to gain in negotiations. On the western railroads by the early 1880s both trainmen and managers had agreed that the basic unit of compensation would be some measure of mileage, but how this was to be measured became a matter of dispute. As Henry B. Stone, the general manager of the Chicago, Burlington, and Quincy Railroad argued, "Nothing . . . could be more fallacious than the claim that a mile run on one railroad should be paid at the same rate as a mile run on another, and that a mile run on one part of a large system should be paid at the same rate as a mile run on another part, regardless of all other circumstances."[38] Variations in equipment, schedules, types of trains, whether the trains were through or local, and whether they ran on main or branch lines all resulted in differing amounts of labor. Freight trains, except for livestock trains, always ran more slowly than passenger trains, and thus their crews worked longer hours on runs of similar distance. Scheduled freight crews, however, had it better than unscheduled, or "wild," freights whose runs took longer yet because they had to yield the right of way to virtually all other traffic and thus spent hours on sidings.[39]

Nature, too, influenced practice and thus how men organized work. The frequency of snowstorms, hills, and mountains, traveling at night rather than during the day, and the strain and danger of moving freight and switching cars on slopes all added up to distinctions in labor. Workers on the Northern Pacific in 1893 gave a detailed geography of difference that they, rather than managers, knew intimately. Edgeley, North Dakota, for example, was "a very hard place to do switching. . . . The 'Y' there is about ¾ of a mile away from the station and it is a very steep grade." On runs west of Mandan "the topography of the country, and the difficulties under which the work is performed, justify the higher rate [of pay]." Near Fertile there were "two very bad hills" that were hard on short crews. The run in Canada from Winnipeg to Portage "is in continual snow. They have to run a snowplow nearly everyday ahead of it." Each division was different; each run was different, sometimes very different. In Washington Territory the Palouse branch was "a branch peculiar to itself." And natural differences mattered not just because of work but also because of where workers had to live. Wallula "being a very undesirable place to live in" meant its workers deserved more hours paid at overtime rates. Specific differences in compensation had to be added to balance the scales. Equity demanded the recognition of difference.[40]

Recognizing difference was not the same thing as agreeing on how to compensate for it, and the result was the endless negotiations over work rules that served the brotherhoods so well. The rules could become quite arcane. Many western railroads paid trainmen by the run and then equalized the difference between the runs with so-called arbitraries. Arbitraries were fictitious miles added to long runs or runs made under difficult conditions. It appears that engineers negotiated the first systematic schedule of arbitraries on the St. Paul, Minneapolis, and Manitoba Railway in 1885. Until 1894 both the Northern Pacific and Union Pacific trainmen could appeal directly to the general manager with regard to disputes over work rules, and on the Northern Pacific, so the general manager claimed, such appeals took up "more than half his time." By coupling grievances with demands for extra compensation, workers and their representatives made small but cumulatively substantial gains, since "the determination of these matters at these meetings necessarily takes the form of a compromise . . . with the net result that the men have continually gained ground."[41] After ten years of negotiating with the brotherhoods on the Northern Pacific, the managers of that railroad found that the incremental changes in the work schedules had helped to increase the wages of trainmen over 20 percent by 1893. Other classes of employees, without elaborate work rules, had gained far less, and section workers nothing at all. The situation was similar on the Atchison, Topeka & Santa Fe Railroad.[42]

The workers valued the increases in compensation that came from their ability to exert control over work rules, but they valued their autonomy even more. In the crisis brought by the economic collapse of 1893, the Northern Pacific fought to end of the brotherhood's power to control the terms and conditions of their work. The company wanted a simplification of the rules, a reduction of wages, and a standardization of wage schedules. The workers recognized what was at stake. The engineers stated that they did not "care so much about their reduction in wages, as they . . . about the loss of their rights." Similarly, the "trainmen east of Mandan object to the schedule principally because they were not consulted." The switchmen were "very much discontented. They allege as a reason for this that if they concede the Company's right to make any decrease whatsoever in their pay, they must expect that future reductions will be made, and it is reported to me that the statement is commonly made that if they submit to this, their condition will soon be no better than serfs."[43]

This attempt by workers to establish control over their working lives and an equality with management within the corporation represented an attempt to instill the values of the earlier free-labor version of utopian capitalism into corporate capitalism. It would fail with the suppression of militant workers and the rise of bread-and-butter unionism, Fordism, and Taylorism. Attempts to control the corporation in the United States fell to government and its regulatory apparatus.

"We Want More"

Even bread-and-butter unionism had its utopian aspects. Despite his own proclaimed pragmatism, Samuel Gompers imagined a reformed and regulated capitalism that would, through a living wage, guarantee a baseline of prosperity for all workers. It became the American Federation of Labor's doctrine of "more," which was nearly as utopian in its aims as it was prosaic in its presentation. Gompers believed that "liberty can be neither exercised nor enjoyed by those who are in poverty." "More" expanded for Gompers so that by the end of the 1890s it meant "better homes, better surroundings, higher education, higher aspirations, nobler thoughts, more human feelings, all the human instincts that to make up a manhood that shall be free and independent and loving and noble and true and sympathetic. We want more."[44]

In its final apparition utopian capitalism would, unlike its Jeffersonian and worker antimonopoly versions, be conservative, justifying inequality far more successfully than Sumner or Rockefeller had done and commandeering Gompers's doctrine of "more." Lincoln had celebrated the rise into republican independence and manhood; the new version would create Ayn Rand characters that strode the earth like Titans. It celebrated exactly the kind of figures Jefferson had feared and organized workers had fought.

Joseph Schumpeter created the most sophisticated version of this twentieth-century variant. It is easy to forget that Joseph Schumpeter's *Capitalism, Socialism, and Democracy* was a defensive book written in 1942, when he considered capitalism a system under siege from socialism, communism, and the New Deal regulatory state. Schumpeter's defense of capitalism was as brilliant as it was simple. He both granted the basis of much of the antimonopolist critique of monopolies and derided the critique as "extra-rational."[45] The justification for capitalism, he argued, can never be comprehended by have-nots who were not fully rational because they necessarily think in the short run, and "any pro-capitalist argument must rest on long-run considerations." In the short run "profits and inefficiencies . . . dominate the picture." But in the long run society as a whole benefits. What "the masses" cannot grasp, quite understandably according to Schumpeter, is that "the long-run interests of society are . . . entirely lodged with the upper strata of bourgeois society."[46] The interests of the elite—and by the twentieth-century particularly the corporate elite—were and are the interests of the society as a whole.

Schumpeter returned by a kind of backdoor to the basic question of the purpose of an economy. His answer, like Gompers's, was *more*: more goods, higher GNP, greater productivity. He argued that the interests of the mass of people and the interests of the upper strata of the bourgeois converged over the long term.[47] Where he differed from Gompers was that Gompers saw the provision of more in the present as the salvation and justification for capitalism, while Schumpeter saw the immediate denial of material benefits to workers and the immediate bestowal of rewards on the bourgeoisie as the engine that drove progress. The bourgeoisie, from the nature of the system, needed benefits now; the mass of people would have to sacrifice their present for the future.

Schumpeter rested his case on material prosperity. He pointed to the rising standards of living of members of industrial societies over the long term to justify the inequities and inefficiencies of the short term. He connected them through the figure of the entrepreneur, who had to have vast and seemingly obscene gains in the present to ensure the well-being of society in the future. Those who suffered from present injustice would be compensated by the greater material well-being of their grandchildren.

Written in the 1930s and early 1940s, *Capitalism, Socialism, and Democracy* was necessarily defensive, but read and popularized during the prosperity of the 1940s and 1950s, it made sense. The 1950s were, after all, more prosperous than the 1890s. If the criteria of an economy was "more," then American capitalism had succeeded spectacularly in the long run. A book written to justify capitalism in an age of declining incomes and scarcity—the Depression—found an audience in a period of prosperity. Its defensiveness was largely unnecessary.

Schumpeter provided a utopian capitalism for conservatives. Like Spencer and Sumner, he thought workers would need to wait, but he did not think them unfit or unworthy, just short-sighted. It was nothing personal. Like Sumner and Rockefeller, he accepted the inevitable destructiveness and disorder of capitalism, but he reunited capitalism with progress, individualism, and mass prosperity. Rockefeller might see himself as the antithesis of individualism, but Schumpeter made him an entrepreneur and yanked him back up on the pedestal he had abdicated. He was as enamored of the corporation as Rockefeller, and he lauded Rockefellerian efficiency as the necessary condition for mass prosperity. He wanted nothing to do with Sumner's dark social Darwinism.

"More," not in Gompers's expansive sense but in Schumpeter's more narrow sense, became the modern answer to the purpose of an economy. Equality and the laborer's control of work had nothing to do with it. Schumpeter's conservative version of utopian capitalism largely erased antimonopoly and co-opted Gompers. If workers disliked their work and hated their bosses; if they felt disenfranchised and if, increasingly by the late twentieth century, they felt that corporations rather than citizens controlled the polity, they still had the compensation of "more." As "more" becomes "less," the conservative version of utopian capitalism may find itself challenged.

Notes

1. This chapter draws on material previously included in my book *Railroaded: The Transcontinentals and the Making of Modern America* (New York: W. W. Norton, 2011).
2. Charles Postel, *The Populist Vision* (Oxford: Oxford University Press, 2007). The change can be gauged by comparing Postel to a range of earlier treatments: Richard Hofstadter, *The Age of Reform: From Bryan to F.D.R.* (New York: Knopf, 1955); Lawrence Goodwyn, *Democratic Promise: The Populist Moment in America* (New York:

Oxford University Press, 1976); Norman Pollack, *The Populist Response to Industrial America: Midwestern Populist Thought* (New York: Norton, 1962).

3. Charles Francis Adams to S. R. Callaway, September 8, 1885, Union Pacific Railroad, Office of the President, Outgoing Correspondence, v. 32, ser. 2, r. 27, Nebraska State Historical Society, Lincoln, Nebraska.

4. George M. Fredrickson, *White Supremacy: A Comparative Study in American and South African History* (New York: Oxford University Press, 1981). *Herrenvolk* refers to a system democratic in form where only the majority racial or ethnic group, in this case white men, gets to participate.

5. Eric Foner, *Free Soil, Free Labor, Free Men: The Ideology of the Republican Party Before the Civil War* (New York: Oxford University Press, 1970).

6. Eric Foner, *The Fiery Trial: Abraham Lincoln and American Slavery* (New York: W. W. Norton, 2010).

7. James M. McPherson, *Battle Cry of Freedom: The Civil War Era* (New York: Oxford University Press, 1988), 28.

8. Mark Fiege, *The Republic of Nature: An Environmental History of the United States* (Seattle: University of Washington Press, 2012), 179–81.

9. William J. Novak, *The People's Welfare: Law and Regulation in Nineteenth-Century America* (Chapel Hill: University of North Carolina Press, 1996), 34–39; Foner, *The Fiery Trial*.

10. Foner, *The Fiery Trial*, 36–40.

11. Sean Wilentz, *The Rise of American Democracy: Jefferson to Lincoln* (New York: W. W. Norton, 2005), 370.

12. Ibid., 361.

13. Richard White, *Railroaded: The Transcontinentals and the Making of Modern America* (New York: W. W. Norton, 2011).

14. James F. Hudson, *The Railways and the Republic* (New York, 1886), 107–24; Herbert Hovenkamp, *Enterprise and American Law, 1836–1937* (Cambridge, Mass.: Harvard University Press, 1991), 139–48.

15. George H. Miller, *Railroads and the Granger Laws* (Madison: University of Wisconsin Press, 1971), 172–93.

16. *Report of the Senate Select Committee on Interstate Commerce . . . (with Appendix) . . . [and Testimony]* 49th Cong., 1st Sess., ed. Shelby M. Cullom (Washington, D.C.: Government Printing Office, 1886), 182, 215–16; John Lauritz Larson, *Bonds of Enterprise: John Murray Forbes and Western Development in America's Railway Age*, exp. ed. (Iowa City: University of Iowa Press, 2001), 135–43.

17. Hudson, *The Railways and the Republic*, 107–24, 35–38; Hovenkamp, *Enterprise and American Law*, 139–48; *Report of the Senate Select Committee on Interstate Commerce*, 175–80.

18. Hudson, *The Railways and the Republic*, 9.

19. Ibid., 55.

20. Chester McArthur Destler, "Western Radicalism, 1865–1901: Concepts and Origins," *Mississippi Valley Historical Review* 31, no. 3 (December 1944): 335–68, esp. 340–41, quote, 356. R. Jeffrey Lustig, *Corporate Liberalism: The Origins of Modern American Political Theory, 1890–1920* (Berkeley: University of California Press, 1982), 42–46; William Larrabee, *The Railroad Question: A Historical and Practical Treatise on Railroads, and Remedies for Their Abuses*, 10th ed. (Chicago: Schulte, 1898), 317; Hudson, *The Railways and the Republic*, 287.

21. Lustig, *Corporate Liberalism*, 18, 43.

22. Karen Orren, *Belated Feudalism: Labor, the Law, and Liberal Development in the United States* (Cambridge: Cambridge University Press, 1991), 110–17; Rosanne Currarino, *The Labor Question in America: Economic Democracy in the Gilded Age* (Urbana: University of Illinois Press, 2011), 2–4, 80–81; Mark Hendrickson, *American Labor and Economic Citizenship: New Capitalism from World War I to the Great* Depression (New York: Cambridge University Press, 2013), 16–17.

23. Christine Desan, *Making Money: Coin, Currency, and the Coming of Capitalism* (New York: Oxford University Press, 2014), 411, 430.

24. William Graham Sumner, *The Challenge of Facts and Other Essays*, ed. Albert Galloway Keller (New Haven, Conn.: Yale University Press, 1914), 25.

25. William Graham Sumner, "The Influence of Commercial Crises on Opinions about Economic Doctrines," in *The Forgotten Man: And Other Essays*, ed. Albert Galloway Keller (New Haven, Conn.: Yale University Press, 1919), 225.

26. Ron Chernow, *Titan: The Life of John D. Rockefeller, Sr.* (New York: Random House, 1998), 109–17. The novel is by Edward Noyes Westcott, *David Harum: A Story of American Life* (New York: D. Appleton, 1899).

27. Ibid.

28. Ibid.

29. John Stuart Mill, *The Positive Philosophy of Auguste Comte* (Boston: Spencer, 1866), 72; Charles Francis Adams, *Charles Francis Adams, 1835–1915: An Autobiography* (Boston: Houghton Mifflin, 1916), 179.

30. Mill, *The Positive Philosophy of Auguste Comte*, 87–89.

31. Ibid., 135.

32. Anita Haya Patterson, *Race, American Literature and Transnational Modernisms* (Cambridge: Cambridge University Press, 2011).

33. Charles Francis Adams to Callaway, September 8, 1885, in Union Pacific, President's Office, Outgoing Correspondence, v. 32, ser. 2, r. 27, Nebraska State Historical Society.

34. Kim Voss, *The Making of American Exceptionalism: The Knights of Labor and Class Formation in the Nineteenth Century* (Ithaca: Cornell University Press, 1993), 82–83; Robert E. Weir, *Knights Unhorsed: Internal Conflict in a Gilded Age Social Movement* (Detroit: Wayne State University Press, 2000), 161; John P. Enyeart, *The Quest for "Just and Pure Law": Rocky Mountain Workers and American Social Democracy, 1870–1924* (Stanford, Calif.: Stanford University Press, 2009), 41, 42, 46, 47, 50–54; Craig Phelan, *Grand Master Workman: Terence Powderly and the Knights of Labor* (Westport, Conn.: Greenwood, 2000), 118–19.

35. Craig Storti, *Incident at Bitter Creek: The Story of the Rock Springs Chinese Massacre* (Ames: Iowa State University Press, 1991), 84–85. For Knights and manhood, see Weir, *Knights Unhorsed*, 36 ff; Robert Weir, *Beyond Labor's Veil: The Culture of the Knight of Labor* (University Park: Pennsylvania State University Press, 1996), chap. 1.

36. John Bates Clark, "Possibility of a Scientific Law of Wages," *Publications of the American Economic Association* 4, no. 1 (March 1889): 39–69.

37. "The Helplessness of Labor," *Union Pacific Employes' Magazine* 8 (September 1893): 229.

38. H. B. Stone to C. Perkins, February 18, 1888, in *Chicago, Burlington, and Quincy Railroad Company, Burlington Archives*, Chicago: Newberry Library, box 33, 1880, 9.11.

39. John H. White, *The American Railroad Freight Car: From the Wood-Car Era to the Coming of Steel* (Baltimore, Md.: Johns Hopkins University Press, 1993), 6–77.

40. "Conference Between the Management of the Northern Pacific Railroad and the Employees in Its Train Service . . . January 11, 1894," 11.A.5.6 F, 138.H.8.8 (F), Northern Pacific Railway Corporate Records, 1861–1970, Minnesota Historical Society, St. Paul, Minnesota, 2, 10, 14, 24, 28 40–41, 50.

41. T. F. Oakes to Receiver, August 18, 1893, 11 A.5.6 E, 138 H.8.8. (F) Northern Pacific Railway Corporate Records, 1861–1970, Minnesota Historical Society, St. Paul, Minnesota.

42. M. C. Kimberly to W. G. Pearce, October 21, 1893, 11.A.5.6 F, 138.H.8.8 (F) Northern Pacific Railway Corporate Records, 1861–1970, Minnesota Historical Society, St. Paul, Minnesota; James H. Ducker, *Men of the Steel Rails: Workers on the Atchison, Topeka & Santa Fe Railroad, 1869–1900* (Lincoln: University of Nebraska Press, 1983), 112.

43. J. W. Kendrick to T. F. Oakes, August 28, 1893, Kendrick to T. F. Oakes, H. Payne, H. House, December 12, 1893, with attachments, see pp. 18–20 for workers' reactions. Kendrick to W. G. Pearce, October 21, 1893, all in *General Manager's Records: Labor, Pullman, Northern Pacific Railway Corporate Records*, St. Paul, Minnesota: Minnesota Historical Society.

44. Kathleen G. Donohue, *Freedom from Want: American Liberalism and the Idea of the Consumer* (Baltimore, Md.: Johns Hopkins University Press, 2003), 27–29; Currarino, *The Labor Question in America*, 87–94.

45. Joseph A. Schumpeter, *Capitalism, Socialism, and Democracy*, 3rd ed. (1950; repr., New York: Harper, 1976), 140–41.

46. Ibid., 144–45.

47. Ibid., 143–45.

CHAPTER 5

THE SOVEREIGN MARKET AND SEX DIFFERENCE

Human Rights in America

AMY DRU STANLEY

Since the abolition of chattel slavery, the progress of human rights in America has been peculiarly attached to the traffic in commodities. Guarantees of rights considered universal in nature, as belonging to all humanity, bear a trademark of commerce. As a consequence, the rules of the market economy have come to penetrate ever more deeply into social existence, and the distinction between persons and things has eroded—a distinction at the heart of the difference between slavery and freedom.[1]

At issue in this essay are not institutions of capital: corporations, contracts, money, or wage labor. Instead it explores the legal and moral perplexities posed by acts of Congress that connect vindications of the rights of persons to the free flow of commerce. It illuminates the counterpoint between two constitutional grants of power—the Commerce Clause, which gives Congress plenary power to regulate interstate and foreign commerce, and the Thirteenth Amendment, which gives Congress power to enforce the prohibition of slavery and involuntary servitude.[2] The essay traces how the American nation-state has made human wellbeing commensurate with the exchange of goods across state borders and with untrammeled wealth accumulation.

Put bluntly, I argue that the Commerce Clause has become a charter of human rights where the reach of the Thirteenth Amendment ends.[3] Particularly, it is wrongs of sex that have connected human rights to commodity conceptions of personhood rather than calling forth antislavery prohibitions. For a century, Congress has invoked the commerce power in legislating against women's subjection—from the ban on white slave trafficking to the ban on violence against women—making the flow of trade a source of protection against violations of free will and invasions of the body.[4] As justified by the rules of commerce, human rights doctrine has carried the ethos of the market into the most private recesses of social exchange.

The development of this commerce-laden rights tradition involves deep contradictions: On the one hand, treating human beings as commodities—at its most extreme—counts as slavery. On the other hand, yoking fundamental rights to the commerce power adds new moral legitimacy to economic values, though on behalf of human dignity. Paradoxically, guarantees of human rights have come to underwrite the sway of the market.

This is a puzzle unstudied in jeremiads on the market's dominion. Today philosophers argue that market values have overreached their moral limits, observing that the "logic of buying and selling no longer applies to material goods alone but increasingly governs the whole of life."[5] The warning echoes classic historical critiques of market society. Quoting Aristotle's *Politics*, the political economist Karl Polanyi lamented a world that had been lost—where markets had been "mere accessories" to household economy—and condemned the destruction of "organic forms of existence."[6] Such claims take no account of human rights that owe their guarantee to market relations. Yet a century and a half ago, at the end of the Civil War, appeals for universal freedom as an outcome of slave emancipation anticipated the predicaments of sex. There were "no new arguments to be made on human rights," explained Elizabeth Cady Stanton to the American Equal Rights Association, except to "teach man that woman is not an anomalous being."[7]

By outlawing wrongs of sex as burdens on commerce, Congress has at once guaranteed rights and extended the logic of buying and selling.[8] In other words, the creation of this rights tradition enshrines a limitless market but also establishes the emancipatory sovereignty of the nation-state founded on the flow of commerce. Precisely because the situation of women remains anomalous, Congress has acted under the commerce power rather than the antislavery amendment. My account of the making of this human rights tradition begins with the contemporary problem of hate violence, which sets in relief the counterpoint between the Thirteenth Amendment and the Commerce Clause. Next it turns back to the era of slave emancipation, and then proceeds by following the paths of congressional lawmaking and constitutional jurisprudence, while also looking outward to international treaties that have shaped American guarantees of rights.

Although this is a distinctly American story, it may well prompt broader reflection on cosmopolitan political authority, global capitalism, and protection against both states and private actors in safeguarding human rights. At the least, it casts new light on the equation of social exchange and economic intercourse. And it reveals how sex confounds the opposition of freedom and bondage.[9]

* * *

Consider the Hate Crimes Prevention Act of 2009, a law enacted by Congress to safeguard the right of all persons within the jurisdiction of the United States to freedom from violence based on bias. It bars violent acts motivated by animus on account of gender, sexual orientation, or gender identity, as well as on account of race, color, religion, national identity, or disability. The traits fueling hate may be either actual or perceived. The prohibited violence involves willfully inflicting bodily injury on any person, or trying to do so, through the use of dangerous weapons, fire or firearms, or other explosive or incendiary devices. Punishment ranges from a fine to life in prison. The statute is also known as the Matthew Shepard and James Byrd, Jr. Act, in memory of the murders in 1998 of a gay man, Shepard, who was beaten with a pistol, tied to a fence like a scarecrow, and left to die by the side of a road in Laramie, Wyoming, and of a black man, Byrd, who was beaten, chained to a pickup truck, and dragged behind it, on a road in Jasper, Texas, until his body ripped apart.[10]

In Congress, arguments on behalf of the legislation drew on both international and American ideals of human rights. It would uphold the charter of the United Nations in protecting "the dignity of the human person." It would guarantee the "inalienable rights framed in the Declaration of Independence." It was universalist in principle, though realized within the domain of a nation, as a project of "garnering the civil and human rights of all Americans." The reasoning linked together inherent rights with rights depending on membership in the nation. It also relied on empirical data revealing that across the country a hate crime occurred roughly every hour of every day. The legislation was a decade in the making, opposed as a violation of principles of free speech, impartial justice, and federalism, but supported by a broad coalition of civil rights, religious, and law enforcement groups. "We have for centuries strived to live up to our founding ideal, of a nation where all are free and equal and able to pursue their own version of happiness," said President Obama in signing the measure into law. "A nation in which we're all free to live and love as we see fit."[11] Under the legislation, the right to happiness would entail not only liberty and bodily security but free love, unqualified by race or sex difference.

The Hate Crimes Act reaches into a private sphere once fenced off from national authority. The Reconstruction Amendments were designed to empower Congress to enforce the abolition of slavery and its vestiges, and to guarantee rights of national citizenship, suffrage, due process, and equal protection of the law. Yet sex-based crimes—if not carried out across state lines or involving state action—remained within the traditional police power of the states. To the states was reserved authority for protecting the right to bodily security long defined as essential to liberty. A hate crimes law of 1968, enacted by Congress after the murder of Martin Luther King, Jr., addressed race, color, religion, and national origin alone, and covered only federally protected activities: suffrage, jury service, employment, interstate travel, pursuit of public education, enrollment in government programs, and use of public accommodations. The new measure, sponsored by John Conyers and Edward Kennedy, proceeds further. It grants all persons, in all places, a right to freedom from hate violence.[12]

The expansive hate crimes enactment rests on two constitutional pillars, each supporting the power of Congress to overcome states' rights doctrine. The prohibition of violence animated by hate due to race, color, religion, or national origin rests on the Thirteenth Amendment. But the prohibition of violence animated by hate due to gender, sexuality, or disability rests on the Commerce Clause. Bias alone is a sufficient warrant for congressional action against hate crime under the antislavery amendment.[13] But bias must affect buying and selling—the flow of commodities across state borders—for Congress to ban hate violence motivated by sex under the commerce power.[14]

The language of the statute is nothing if not explicit. Where the Thirteenth Amendment does not apply—to violence based on sex—the commerce power operates.

The legislative findings that introduce the act highlight the intersection of violence, slavery, and race that empowers Congress under the Thirteenth Amendment to trespass on state authority in legislating against hate crime in order to purge the nation of the vestiges of chattel bondage:

> For generations, the institutions of slavery and involuntary servitude were defined by the race, color, and ancestry of those held in bondage. Slavery and involuntary servitude were enforced, both prior to and after the adoption of the 13th amendment to the Constitution of the United States, through widespread public and private violence directed at persons because of their race, color, or ancestry. . . . Accordingly, eliminating racially motivated violence is an important means of eliminating, to the extent possible, the badges, incidents, and relics of slavery and involuntary servitude.[15]

Notably absent from the findings is the designation of wrongs of sex as a badge of slavery and involuntary servitude that falls within the sphere of congressional authority under the Thirteenth Amendment. Notably absent, too, is any claim about a racial hate crime affecting the stream of interstate commerce.

By contrast, the statute highlights the intersection of the market, sex, and violence that empowers Congress to reach hate crimes under the Commerce Clause. Describing the nature of offenses bearing on sex, the language of the act grows specific and detailed, not simply about bodily injury and the use of dangerous weapons, firearms, and incendiary devices but also about the channels, facilities, and instrumentalities of commerce, and about crimes that interfere with "economic activity" and "purchasing goods and services" and "sustaining employment" and "commercial activity"—about violence that "affects interstate or foreign commerce." Such violence must involve some kind of "Circumstances" demonstrating a market nexus and/or the circulation of people or things among states or nations:

> (i)   the travel of the defendant or the victim
> > (I)   across a State line or national border; or
> > (II) using a channel, facility, or instrumentality of interstate or foreign commerce;
>
> (ii) the defendant uses a channel, facility, or instrumentality of interstate or foreign commerce . . .
>
> (iii) . . . the defendant employs a firearm, dangerous weapon, explosive or incendiary device, or other weapon that has traveled in interstate or foreign commerce; or
>
> (iv) the conduct . . .
> > (I)   interferes with commercial or other economic activity in which the victim is engaged at the time of the conduct; or
> > (II) otherwise affects interstate or foreign commerce.[16]

Notably absent from the explanation of circumstantial evidence of economic activity is violence involving slavery's badges. Notably absent, too, is any assumption that market exchange stands apart from the private sphere.

Under the Hate Crimes Act, therefore, where the relics of bondage prohibited by the Thirteenth Amendment are not at issue—in violence due to sex—the commerce nexus entitles Congress to safeguard freedom from bodily injury. By definition, the market's ways must pervade social life traditionally belonging to the sphere of domestic relations governed by the states to create the authority of the nation to prohibit hate violence.

So the attorney general of the United States testified in congressional hearings, endorsing the measure's constitutionality on the eve of its passage. Violent acts motivated by bias, Eric Holder told the Senate Judiciary Committee, "deny the humanity that we all share." On the dual sources of congressional power, he explained:

1. Thirteenth Amendment
Congress has authority under Section 2 of the Thirteenth Amendment to punish racially motivated violence as part of a reasonable legislative effort to extinguish the relics, badges, and incidents of slavery. . . .

2. Commerce Clause Jurisdiction

The interstate commerce element . . . would ensure that Federal prosecutions for hate crimes based on sexual orientation, gender, gender identity . . . would be brought only in those particular cases in which a Federal interest is clear.

The extension of national authority would hinge on "proof of a nexus to interstate commerce."[17]

For a decade, Congress had heard testimony on the legislation. Witnesses told of violence with a connection to interstate commerce. A husband beat his wife while driving back and forth across state lines; a rapist held a gun that had traveled in interstate commerce. The central question was the source of congressional authority over acts of private violence, with no relation to state action. "The 13th amendment can be legitimately invoked insofar . . . as the bill involves racial hate crimes," the law professor Cass Sunstein said in House judiciary hearings in 1998. Explaining the split in the statute, in reply to a query from a black congresswoman, Sheila Jackson Lee, he spoke of both antislavery doctrine and the commerce power:

> *Ms. Jackson Lee.* . . . You mentioned the commerce clause not being in 1 and being in 2. Give me some comfort, and maybe I can't get any comfort, I would like it not to be in 2 . . . and making 1 and 2 the same.
> *Mr. Sunstein.* . . . The question would be whether clause 2, which does not involve race or color, could be supported by the 13th amendment. . . . The 13th amendment isn't about those areas of discrimination. . . . The commerce clause . . . would be a legitimate basis for asserting authority given certain findings on the connection between these kinds of hate crimes and interstate commerce.
> *Ms. Jackson Lee.* . . . You can cite the commerce clause . . . and we would be on safer grounds?
> *Mr. Sunstein.* That is right.

The lesson was plain; wrongs of sex had no constitutional link to slavery—"the 13th amendment isn't about those areas of discrimination." Instead a connection to commerce—"private violence may well interfere with the interstate movement of both people and goods"—validated national authority by linking the right to bodily security with the traffic in goods.[18]

Consider the outcome of the odd cleft in the structure of the Hate Crimes Act. Surely it would count as a hate crime if a black person were murdered at home by a white killer using bare hands and uttering racial epithets. But suppose a wife were slain by a husband of the same race during a rape. That would count as a hate crime only if her death occurred from an object that had traveled in interstate commerce. Or if the private violence interfered with economic activity.

That asymmetry is the price of the counterpoint between the Thirteenth Amendment and the Commerce Clause as sources for securing human rights. Under the Hate Crimes Act, only a market nexus overcomes the limits of antislavery constitutionalism, making protections of freedom from sex-based violence an accessory of interstate commodity exchange.

* * *

The sweep of the Thirteenth Amendment has been circumscribed since its inception. That Congress would come to circumvent those limits by associating the freedom of persons with the traffic in merchandise appears all the more perverse because abolitionism had long taught that the essence of slavery was reducing human beings to commodities.

As the American Anti-Slavery Society declared at its founding in 1833, "No man has a right to enslave or imbrute his brother—to hold or acknowledge him, for one moment, as a piece of merchandise." Under the slave system, human beings existed "as marketable commodities."[19]

This principle echoed in Congress as sectional crisis deepened before the Civil War. Above all, it was the figure of the ravaged bondswoman—and the creation of wealth through slave breeding—that symbolized the evil of treating people as merchandise. Slavery ruined "the image of God in the human soul," as Congressman Horace Mann argued, describing the debasement of slave women who lacked the liberty to obey the Apostle's rule: "Wives shall submit themselves to their husbands." Such claims echoed accounts by former slaves, who disclosed how their masters compelled, as Frederick Douglass recalled, "unmitigated fornication" to produce human chattel as "a marketable commodity."[20]

But sex disappeared as Congress framed the Thirteenth Amendment, making explicit the reconciliation of emancipation with woman's subjection. The debate over the amendment's phrasing anticipated its limits, as antislavery statesmen refused language that would have provided, "All persons are equal before the law, so that no person can hold another as a slave"—an affirmation of freedom modeled on the French *Declaration of Rights* of 1789. For that expansive guarantee implied that any woman, even a wife, would be "as free as a man."[21]

After the war, Congress reinforced the Thirteenth Amendment's limits, defining slave emancipation to forbid wrongs of labor, contract, property, and race—but not of sex. According to the inventory of unfreedom named in the Senate, denying rights to "the colored man . . . to buy or to sell, or to make contracts . . . to own property . . . were all badges of servitude made in the interest of slavery."[22] Drawing on the Thirteenth Amendment, the architects of

Reconstruction enacted laws meant to complete the work of abolition: the Civil Rights Act of 1866, the Anti-Peonage Act of 1867, the Enforcement Act of 1870, the Ku Klux Klan Act of 1871, the Padrone Act of 1874, the Civil Rights Acts of 1875. But none struck at torments based on sex. Neither wifely submission nor unmitigated fornication figured as badges of slavery. [23]

At the moment of abolition, then, Congress began narrowing the meaning of slavery. And the limits of the Thirteenth Amendment soon became etched in constitutional doctrine, as the Supreme Court delineated freedom's guarantees and slavery's badges. In the *Slaughterhouse Cases* of 1873, the Court declared the antislavery amendments "additional guarantees of human rights," while tethering their emancipatory force to the extinction of racial forms of bondage and the legacies of chattel slavery. The intent of the Thirteenth Amendment—"this grand yet simple declaration of the personal freedom of all the human race"—was to bar "all shades and conditions of African slavery," the Court found, adding that its sanctions would also forbid bondage that might emerge from "Mexican peonage" and "Chinese coolie labor," although "negro slavery alone was in the mind of the Congress which proposed the thirteenth article." But slaughterhouse laws that affected white butchers fell outside the amendment's prohibitions. *Slaughterhouse* did not speak of subjection on account of sex. Instead it established that the "pervading spirit" of the Thirteenth Amendment aimed at "freedom of the slave race." Yet that spirit too had boundaries. In the *Civil Rights Cases* of 1883, the Court rejected the Thirteenth Amendment as a source of congressional power to outlaw Jim Crow, ruling that to forbid race discrimination in "matters of intercourse or business" as a relic of bondage would be "running the slavery argument into the ground."[24]

But it was the companion case to the *Slaughterhouse Cases* that made evident the anomalies of being a woman and the exclusion of women from antislavery guarantees. In *Bradwell v. the State*—where the deprivation of the right to pursue employment and to contract freely involved a white wife rather than white butchers—the badges of slavery never arose at all. Rather, the Court infamously affirmed that slave emancipation left intact the different spheres and destinies of the sexes. It found that barring women from practicing law in state courts no more violated fundamental rights of United States citizenship than regulating the butchering of pigs in city slaughterhouses. The difference between men and women emanated from "nature itself," Justice Bradley reasoned in concurrence, noting the annihilation of a wife's independent legal existence under the principle of coverture and the persistence of "special rules of law flowing from and dependent upon this cardinal principle."[25] *Bradwell* marks the conspicuous absence in Thirteenth Amendment doctrine of matters of sex difference.

Far less famous is a rape case that came before the Supreme Judicial Court of Massachusetts in 1870.[26] Yet it stands as an exemplar of the special rules that shielded the household—and private violence animated by sex—from the guarantees of the Thirteenth Amendment. It spoke of a bond of master and subject unaltered by abolition.

The Massachusetts court bluntly set forth the definition of rape prevailing across the country in the era of slave emancipation. "The simple question . . . is, Was the woman willing or unwilling?" The crime consisted in the violation of her body and denial of her will: "enforcement of a woman without her consent."[27]

And deciding if the sex was at will depended first on whether the violated woman was a wife. The rule, with the exception for marriage, declared, "A man who has carnal intercourse with a woman (not his wife) without her consent . . . is guilty of rape." This common law rule was centuries old, appearing in *Historia Placitorum Coronæ*, a treatise on capital crimes written by the lord chief justice of the Court of the King's Bench in the seventeenth century, and published posthumously in 1736: "But the husband cannot be guilty of a rape committed by himself upon his lawful wife, for by their mutual matrimonial consent and contract the wife hath given up herself in this kind unto her husband, which she cannot retract." The criminal law of the king's court incorporated the Apostle's gospel on wifely submission, and the tenet endured in American law. "In no State of the Union has the wife the right to her own person," protested a Declaration of Rights for Women presented on the centennial of Independence Day.[28]

In the eyes of the law, unfree sex could not exist within marriage as a bond founded on contract and consent. The intercourse between husband and wife represented the antithesis of slave breeding, for the illusion of perpetual consent turned violence into a legitimate taking. A woman could not be ravished by her own husband, just as a slave master could never be guilty of raping his chattel property: the essential difference was wives were assumed always to be willing, but slaves to have no will of their own.[29]

In the era of slave emancipation, therefore, wrongs of sex fell beyond the limits of the Thirteenth Amendment, and Congress claimed no power to govern home life, but for enforcing the dissolution of the bonds of slavery. Meanwhile, in the *Civil Rights Cases* of 1883, the Supreme Court broached—yet left unanswered—the question of whether the commerce power might ground congressional rights decrees where the antislavery amendments could not: "Whether Congress, in the exercise of its power to regulate commerce amongst the several States, might or might not pass a law regulating rights . . . is not now before us." Presciently, Justice Harlan noted in dissent, "It may become a pertinent inquiry."[30]

From that pertinent inquiry would develop the emancipatory use of the commerce power, a path of governance that led away from the antislavery amendments. In regulating commerce among the states, Congress came to enact laws that created a human rights tradition connecting the intercourse of persons with the circulation of pieces of merchandise.

＊＊＊

Irony lies in the title of the White Slave Traffic Act of 1910, for the legislation was not premised on the Thirteenth Amendment. Instead, Congress drew on the Commerce Clause to ban the transport of women across national and state borders for the purposes of prostitution. The act expanded the commerce power, beyond regulating objects such as steamboats, railroads, and livestock, to reach illegitimate human intercourse. Its full title clarified the intent: "An Act to Further Regulate Interstate and Foreign Commerce by Prohibiting the Transportation Therein for Immoral Purposes of Women and Girls, and for Other Purposes." It made a felony of enticing, coercing, and conveying, as well as buying a ticket for the transport of white slaves.[31]

Congress adopted the act to uphold a treaty, a 1904 agreement signed in Paris by the nations of Europe and providing for global repression of the commerce in white women, *Traite des Blanches*. International conferences on the trade—Paris in 1902, 1904, and 1906, Brussels in 1907, Vienna in 1909, and Madrid in 1910—condemned the unregulated movement of people across state borders, warning of both sexual bondage and racial disorder. In 1908, the United States formally adhered to the Paris treaty.[32] Today it belongs to the covenants of the United Nations against trafficking in persons.

Calls for suppression did not come from the trafficked women. But the treaty drew support from the International Council of Women, which advocated the abolition of white slavery throughout the world. At a meeting in Berlin in 1904, the council pledged to "keep the question of the White Slave Traffic on the International programme." A resolution adopted by council delegates representing nations on every continent assailed the trade as "a disgrace to humanity and a slur on all women."[33]

A vast market existed in involuntary prostitutes, according to American documents of state proposing legislation that would honor the Paris treaty and supplement laws restricting immigration. *Suppression of the White-Slave Traffic*—a message from the president of the United States presented to Congress in 1910—denounced the "condition of virtual slavery," estimating that more than a hundred thousand immoral women were imports from foreign nations. A Senate report summed up the findings of Congress by declaring that the treaty bound the United States to liberate "women who are owned and held as property and chattel" and to suppress the "business . . . of selling them outright." Accounts in newspapers and reform tracts described how prostitutes were shipped interstate and held captive in brothels, how a white slave would be flayed "until the skin across her back and shoulders cracked." The business was abhorred as "bestial degradation."[34]

Yet the Thirteenth Amendment never figured in the making of the white slave traffic legislation. The congressional debate on its constitutional validity examined the moral contradictions of the chattel principle—the dualisms of free will and coercion, of persons and property, of humanitarianism and market exchange. And the debate blurred divisions of creed and region that dated from the era of the Civil War. But the project of abolishing sex trafficking produced no resolve to summon the antislavery amendment rather than the commerce power as a source of congressional authority.[35]

In re White-Slave Trade, a legislative memorandum prepared by the commerce committee of the House of Representatives in 1909, set forth the approach of Congress. In explaining the measure's constitutionality under the Commerce Clause, the memorandum advanced three main claims. First, a prostitute transported "unwillingly" was the legal equivalent of an inanimate commodity, with both representing "the subject of commerce." Second, the traffic in women "directly connected" to the flow of interstate commerce. Third, because the trade was at once "national in its character" and a peril to "civilized nations," the assertion of federal authority would not infringe on state police power. Therefore, the commerce power afforded Congress ample authority to prohibit sex trafficking.[36]

Particularly, *In re White-Slave Trade* dwelled on the parity between persons and property, and on the opposition between consent and coercion. It began with the principle that commerce encompasses the conveyance of passengers, further positing that the power of Congress over "the transportation of property of course applies to the transportation of persons." It stressed that white slaves suffered "sale and exploitation" and "force and restraint," that they were objects of sexual commerce "against their will," that they were made to be "literally slaves . . . women owned and held as property." They were utterly unlike willing wives. Accordingly, the commerce power extended to their circulation, like merchandise—articles with exchange value but without volition.[37]

Oratory in Congress decried illegitimate wealth creation, filthy lucre begotten by unfree sex. That it was an evil practice to "make merchandise of a human soul" had become an article of faith, as statesmen with antislavery and proslavery pedigrees joined in mounting a new abolitionism, speaking of "a horror which the devil would be ashamed of." The crimes of the "black-slave trade," claimed the author of the anti-trafficking act, Congressman James Mann of Illinois, chairman of the House Commerce Committee, "pale into insignificance as compared to the horrors of the so-called 'white-slave traffic.'" So, too, a Virginia congressman, Edward Saunders, who was born on a tobacco plantation worked by some fifty slaves, called on Congress to ban "this traffic in human flesh, a traffic which oppresses the conscience of humanity."

Citing the opinion of Justice Marshall a century earlier in *Gibbons v. Ogden*, the Virginian argued, "Intercourse is commerce."[38]

But on the use of the commerce power there was dissent—legal and moral and philosophical. It was unconstitutional, found a minority report of the Commerce Committee, for Congress to interfere with the domestic affairs of the states to legislate against vice under the "guise of regulating commerce"; nor was the intrusion on state authority justified by the Paris agreement and the treaty-making power.[39]

In particular, the argument against the White Slave Traffic Act denied the analogy between persons and property, and discredited the equivalence between immoral intercourse and interstate commerce. The heart of the argument was that human beings—endowed with free will—differed from commodities. That difference meant Congress could not usurp states' rights by invoking the commerce power to reach relations among persons or wrongs of sex as "commercial intercourse." Allegedly, the legislation rested on a false premise, "that prostitution is commerce." Congress must not "assume jurisdiction," an Ohioan said. But it was Southerners, who had lived among chattel slaves, who most fully explained the difference between trafficking in women and "chattels, something that has no volition in the transaction at all." The interstate transit of an "immoral person," a Georgian said, bore no resemblance to the unlawful trade in harmful articles such as "diseased cattle" that were "commercial in their nature." An Alabaman elaborated on the dissimilarity between cotton and a prostitute:

> When you ship . . . a bale of cotton . . . that is commerce between citizens of different States. What is the commerce here? . . . Simply the vague, indefinite statement that she is going to start from a place in one State and is going to another for immoral purposes.

By such reasoning, not even an impure woman amounted to a piece of merchandise, "a commodity subject to interstate commerce."[40]

Put simply, the point was that some intercourse did not constitute commerce. Furthermore, it was asked why women should not be held culpable for their own transit, along with the traffickers who purchased their tickets, since even a white slave was not a thing—like cotton or cattle—with "no volition." If Congress aimed to "purify commerce," impartial justice required punishing an interstate prostitute as a person possessing a will of her own and containing no "inherent quality" rendering her equivalent to diseased, guiltless livestock.[41]

The counterargument hardly resolved the perplexities of the legislation—of delivering freedom by equating women with articles of commerce. Perversely, the justification for the act deplored the merchandising of souls but ratified the dominion of commerce, relying on the likeness of persons and things. It condemned the sinfulness of trafficking as sexual enslavement while defending the constitutionality of classifying women with impure commodities—contaminated cattle, spoiled food, lottery tickets—all objects of interstate commerce banned by Congress as it exercised greater regulatory authority in the Progressive Era. Fervent rhetoric paired the spiritual with the material. A white slave was an "imprisoned soul that is being carried from one State to another" through the enterprise of a "demon, in human form, who is . . . to sell her body and soul into hell." Yet she would be liberated within the broad expanse of the commerce power, due to the principle that "the power to regulate *the transportation of persons* is the same as the power to regulate *the transportation of things*." Again southern statesmen, versed in the ways of the old slave system, spoke of property and person but affirmed the analogy in defending the abolition of "diabolical traffic." In the words of Congressman Saunders of Virginia:

> What is this interstate traffic? . . . Transportation of insensate objects for a consideration, from one State to another, is clearly commerce; and yet when it is proposed to carry from State to State, sentient beings for the purposes of degradation, and dishonor, and in order that the image in which they have been created, shall be defaced . . . gentlemen seek to make a distinction, and assert that this transport across state lines of living beings for immoral purposes, is not commerce, and cannot be reached under authority of the interstate commerce clause of the Constitution.

Telling of a vast syndicate that carried women to market across the country, and that profaned the stream of trade, the Virginian abjured "subtle distinctions" between inanimate and sentient objects of commerce.[42]

Still, nothing was said of the Thirteenth Amendment. For all the protest against the chattel condition of involuntary prostitutes—and all the argument about property and personhood—Congress did not contemplate prohibiting the traffic in women as a badge of slavery or form of involuntary servitude. Rather, antislavery internationalism found a new weapon against sexual bondage in the American commerce power.

The Supreme Court upheld the White Slave Traffic Act in 1913, construing interstate commerce to consist of traffic and intercourse and to include the transportation of both persons and property. Explicitly, the Court approved the analogy between "enslavement in prostitution" and "contagion of diseased cattle" as matters of congressional legislation, dismissing the difference between people and things: "Of course it will be said that women are not articles of merchandise, but this does not affect the analogy; the substance of the congressional power is the same." That year, in a sensationalized trial in Chicago, a white slave was protected from an alleged black trafficker, Jack Johnson, the boxer. Two years later, the Court ruled that a woman could be punished for trafficking herself interstate—as a voluntary conspirator. The decision was written by Justice Oliver Wendell Holmes, in *United States v. Holte*, an obscure case involving a woman's transit from Illinois to Wisconsin. Yet it illustrated the ambiguities of grouping persons with merchandise. The trial court held a woman could not be "both slave and slaver." But the Supreme Court found to the contrary. As Justice Holmes wrote, "We abandon the illusion that the woman always is the victim."[43] In the law's eyes, a white slave could be both the unfree object and willing agent of unlawful sexual commerce.

Emancipated not by the Thirteenth Amendment but by the Commerce Clause, the white slave became an anomalous being indeed. In fulfilling the Paris treaty, Congress made apparent the limits of the amendment and extended the province of the commerce power, striking at unfree interstate intercourse. The anti-trafficking act marked the burgeoning of an American humanitarianism that connected the protection of persons to the flow of commerce. It abolished a wrong of sex unrecognized as a vestige of slavery under the Thirteenth Amendment. By extending market values to human intercourse, it gave new moral stature to commodity conceptions of personhood.

✳ ✳ ✳

Not until the end of the twentieth century did freedom from bodily subjection based on sex become a right guaranteed by the American nation-state. Appeals for that right were as old as calls for slave emancipation, and as new as international declarations of human rights. Emerging from the outcry of women against violence, the rights guarantee reached beyond wrongs of interstate transit to the sphere of home and marriage, and into the most private forms of intercourse.[44]

But again commerce held sway as Congress transposed an international affirmation of human dignity into American law: the Violence Against Women Act of 1994. The language of the United Nations hardly resonated in the congressional legislation, though both condemned the violation of fundamental rights to bodily security and autonomy.

The General Assembly of the United Nations adopted the Declaration on the Elimination of Violence against Women in 1993. A year later, complying with the international mandate, Congress enacted the prohibition on violence against women. An American delegation testified to the United Nations Human Rights Committee that the legislation fulfilled global agreements binding nations to protect "inalienable rights," promoting universal respect for the inherent dignity of the human person.[45]

The United Nations declaration against violence speaks of "human rights" and the "fundamental freedoms of women" and "historically unequal power relations between men and women" and the "dignity of all human beings." It enjoins all nations to condemn and eliminate and punish gender-based violence, which it defines in terms of deprivation of liberty and physical, sexual, and psychological harm, "occurring in public or in private life." It states that violence encompasses not only sexual trafficking, coercion, and brutality within the "general community," but also intimacies at home and within the precincts of marriage, in particular the wrong of marital rape. According to the United Nations, all violence against women violates human rights.[46]

In contrast, the American act speaks of "crossing a state line," not of human rights. Like the United Nations declaration, it extends beyond the public sphere into private life. Originally, it was titled A Bill to Combat Violence and Crimes Against Women on the Streets and in Homes, and rhetorically it recognizes a fundamental right to freedom from crimes of violence motivated by gender, including domestic violence. But the rights guarantee reaches only to sex-based violence "affecting interstate commerce."[47]

The prosaic language reflects how Congress asserted national authority in domestic life, trenching on state police power by drawing on the Commerce Clause in tandem with the Fourteenth Amendment's equal protection and enforcement clauses. In addressing private wrongs of sex, the anti-violence act recalls the white slaving act. But the subjection outlawed stems from physical terror, rather than immoral transport, and the intent was to affirm rights, not simply punish wrongs, through an unprecedented reach of congressional power into the household. The legislation was conceived by lawyers at the Legal Defense Fund of the National Organization of Women, and introduced by then-Senator Joseph Biden. Support came from women's rights and civil rights groups, and from a multitude of religious, labor, family advocacy, health, and community organizations. The commerce power, as an author of the act later said, was the "constitutional hook."[48]

At congressional hearings, women spoke of their own experiences and aspirations. "Black eyes, bruises, a broken ear drum, and, yes, also being beaten while I was pregnant," a witness told the Senate Judiciary Committee. She testified that "the problem hits too close to home and many men still feel that his home is his castle, where he is the ruler and all who live under him should obey, or else." Reading aloud from a document she titled Rights of a Battered Woman, she said, "I have the right not to be abused. . . . I have the right to freedom from fear of abuse. I have the right to request and expect assistance from police. . . . I have the right to privacy. . . . I have the right to develop my individual talents and abilities. I have the right to legally prosecute the abusing person. I have the right to be." Such statements reiterated claims made for more than a century. "Can there be anything sacred at that family altar," as Elizabeth Cady Stanton had objected, "where the chief-priest who ministers makes sacrifices of human beings." Testimony on behalf of the legislation often began with statistics: a rape every six minutes; a woman beaten by a husband or partner every 15 seconds.[49]

Newly, the Violence Against Women Act made "interstate domestic violence" a federal crime, defined as causing bodily injury to a spouse or intimate partner and involving some kind of travel across state lines.[50] Simultaneously, Congress created a new private right of action—a civil rights remedy—for victims of violence fueled by gender animus. That newfound private right entitled a woman to sue her assailant, rather than relying on the process of criminal justice, and to pursue her claims in the federal courts. The legislation annulled age-old exceptions for sexual violence within marriage, allowing no immunity to a husband who ravished his wife, overturning a proprietary claim.[51]

Under the Violence Against Women Act, therefore, the sweeping commerce power became an instrument of liberation, which reached into the home. It pierced into a private sphere of social exchange left untouched by the Thirteenth Amendment. "The Commerce Clause is a broad grant of power allowing Congress to reach conduct that has even the slightest effect on interstate commerce," stated the Senate Judiciary Committee.[52] But that expansive national power had never before been invoked to intrude on household bonds by connecting wellbeing with interstate commerce.

Congress designed the act expressly to safeguard freedom from sexual brutality as a fundamental right of personhood, and the guarantee drew no distinction between violence done by a stranger and a one-time lover. According to the rights clause, "All persons within the United States shall have the right to be free from crimes of violence motivated by gender." For the first time, every woman would be entitled to enforce that right, rather than depending on police and prosecutors. An unwilling wife would acquire a right to sue her husband for rape, even in states that still adhered to the rule that rape was ravishing a woman without the consent assumed in marriage—a majority when the act was passed. Her status would be nothing like that of a white slave punishable for trafficking herself. Domestic wrongs, as Congresswoman Patricia Schroeder said, were "human rights abuses."[53]

The Violence Against Women Act collapsed the distinction between the market and the household while eroding classical dualisms of the law: the division between public and private, and between national and local. The act gave a wealth of new meaning to the old dictum of Justice Marshall in *Gibbons v. Ogden*—the case concerning steamboats plying the waters between New York and New Jersey—that the commerce power of Congress embraced more than "buying and selling . . . the interchange of commodities." In the words of Justice Marshall, "Commerce, undoubtedly, is traffic, but it is something more: it is intercourse."[54]

Such was the constitutional logic of the anti-violence act—that traffic meant intercourse—in vindicating the rights of women. Congress based the act on the theory that all violence due to sex, even rape committed in marriage, inside a bedroom's privacy, affects interstate commerce. The legislation extended the market's reach, grounding the right to freedom from violence in the power of Congress to assure the free flow of commerce. The declared intent was "to protect the civil rights of victims of gender motivated violence and to promote public safety, health, and activities affecting interstate commerce."[55]

At congressional hearings the market logic was summed up in a single phrase: "Sexual violence takes a toll on interstate commerce." The act's criminal sanctions hinged on the circumstance of interstate travel. But the rights clause did not carry that condition, resting instead on the premise that even violence committed at home burdens the interstate exchange of commodities; so long as the offense constituted a felony and was motivated by animus "because of gender," it was immaterial where the injury occurred and whether it involved the passage of persons or objects across state borders. "Gender-based violent crimes meet the modest threshold required by the Commerce Clause," the Senate Judiciary Committee found, "effect on interstate commerce."[56]

Only for a moment was there testimony proposing the Thirteenth Amendment as a constitutional basis for the prohibition. The theory was that the amendment embodied a "moral imperative" and that sexual violence was "analogous" to the incidents of chattel bondage as a "crude form of physical subordination." But the antislavery approach had no purchase in Congress. It was too subversive in impinging on private relations of domination and dependence, too disruptive of settled doctrine in "generalizing slavery" to the situation of women, recalled its proponent, the constitutional law professor Burt Neuborne, who was then Special Counsel to the Legal Defense Fund of the National Organization of Women. With provisions of the Fourteenth Amendment serving as "simply backstops," the rights clause took shape as a protection of interstate commerce rather than as a ban on slavery's badges.[57]

Not the least of the reasons why the commerce power appeared so compelling as a basis for barring violence against women was that it had authorized prior protections of rights. It underlay the constitutional transformation of the New Deal era, when Congress legislated against capitalist crisis by guarantying labor rights and regulating the market in labor as necessary to promoting interstate commerce. "Affecting commerce," the Supreme Court affirmed in upholding the legislation, "means in commerce, or burdening or obstructing commerce or the free flow of commerce." The commerce power also grounded the Civil Rights Act of 1964, enabling Congress to reach beyond state action and to resurrect protections that the Supreme Court had struck down in the *Civil Rights Cases* of 1883 as unconstitutional under the Thirteenth and

Fourteenth Amendments. And the market logic of the 1964 act—that discrimination adversely affected interstate commerce—withstood scrutiny by the Court, which in turn cited the ban on white slave trafficking as a precedent for moral governance by Congress under the Commerce Clause.[58]

The Violence Against Women Act remade this body of doctrine, swelling the commerce power, creating rights involving neither the production and exchange of goods nor the circulation of persons across state borders, bringing the force of economic values into home life and across the threshold of marriage, to intercourse distant from the marketplace. The Senate Judiciary Committee offered a remarkably expansive justification for the rights clause: "The Commerce Clause gives Congress authority to act even if the proposed law, on its face, has nothing do with 'commerce.'" Surely, on its face, the wrong of rape appeared remote from steamboats and railroads, or bales of cotton and diseased livestock—objects of the commerce power long recognized by the Supreme Court. But as the judiciary committee explained, "Even the fear of gender-based violence affects the economy."[59]

In other words, the power of Congress to outlaw unfreedom due to sex presupposed a boundless market. The ban on violence against women at once amplified the cash nexus and augmented the authority of the national government to remedy private wrongs—private in a double sense, of involving no state action and of occurring in private places. The rights clause presumed that the stream of interstate commerce connected violence against women "purely local in nature" with the national economy, and that market values mediated between private life and the public sphere. This was its "rational basis," as formulated in congressional hearings. The notion was not that a rape, in itself, affects economic intercourse, but that unfree sex, in the aggregate, obstructs the free flow of commerce, inhibiting women from acting in the marketplace, interfering with buying and selling, diminishing the exchange of goods. The problem was the cumulative effect of women's subjection on "our economic lives."[60]

No debate arose on the ethics of attaching the rights of persons to the traffic in commodities. Disagreement concerned the power of the national government and the presence of domestic disputes in the federal courts. Suppose that "every rape" were litigated as a rights claim?[61] But there were no arguments against the moral legitimacy of associating sentient women with articles of merchandise.

On the contrary, the anti-violence act affirmed the connection between human intercourse and interstate commerce. Again and again, it was said in Congress that the suffering of women burdened the economy. That rape and domestic violence imposed "enormous economic costs." And that the freedom of economic man should not be forfeited by women *"because of their sex."* The rights guarantee would protect both the exchange of goods and the autonomy of women, reducing the "high price for being female."[62]

∗ ∗ ∗

Today, the rights clause is no longer part of the Violence Against Women Act. The Supreme Court struck it down as unconstitutional in a rape case, *United States v. Morrison*, in 2000.[63] The Court reined in the commerce power and also denied that the Fourteenth Amendment applied to private wrongs, revoking the right of women to seek justice, at their own will. With *Morrison*, the anti-violence act became a negative landmark in the path of the law connecting human rights to market exchange.

The Court spoke categorically: violent crime against women was not "economic in nature"—"not, in any sense of the phrase, economic activity"—and fell outside the authority afforded by the commerce power.[64] The causal connection between violence due to sex and the flow of commerce was too indirect.

What troubled the Court was the specter of a congressional leviathan fed by a commodity fiction. Writing for the majority, Justice Rehnquist envisioned the expansion of congressional power into spheres far beyond its constitutional bounds—from murder to marriage—by virtue of "every attenuated effect upon interstate commerce." The commerce power would invade private life, obliterating the boundary between "what is truly national and what is truly local." Conversely, the dissent measured the cost of domestic violence, money lost to the economy from the suffering of women, then about $5 billion a year, and viewed the national and local as joined. Writing for the dissent, Justice Souter disputed the restraint on the commerce power—the "economic/noneconomic distinction"—and the separation of market and household. "Deaths of 2,000 to 4,000 women annually at the hands of domestic abusers," he observed, adversely affected "supply and demand for goods in interstate commerce." His point was that sexual violence was always "economic."[65]

Turning the specter of a limitless market into an affirmation of the plenary power of Congress to safeguard the right of all persons to freedom from violence, the dissent linked the guarantee of women's human dignity to expansive market values. Justice Souter wrote of "an integrated economic world" as the basis of a sweeping commerce power. A mistake of "categorical formalism" accounted for the "limits to 'commerce.'"[66]

But in striking down the rights guarantee of the Violence Against Women Act, the majority adhered to a categorical distinction between the spheres of commerce and domestic life. It was the nightmare of a limitless commerce power encroaching on state control of marriage—and rooted in a boundless conception of the economic—that the Court evoked in *Morrison*. The rights clause lacked even a "jurisdictional element," a requirement of circumstantial proof demonstrating a connection to "things or persons" involved in interstate commerce. Wholesale, the Court rejected the notion "that Congress may regulate noneconomic, violent criminal conduct," discounting the aggregate effect of domestic violence on interstate commerce.[67] In sum, unfree intercourse had no bearing on the free flow of commodities.

Arguments on behalf of human rights were just as unconvincing to the Court. Uselessly, amicus briefs spoke of "binding commitments under international law" and "violations of international human rights." Admonitions that it was improper to "read the Commerce Clause to invalidate an Act of Congress that advances our treaty and customary international commitments" came to nothing.[68] Dissociating the exchange of goods and the rights of persons by defining subjection due to sex as "noneconomic," *Morrison* not only limited congressional authority to remedy private wrongs but refused the fulfillment of global human rights agreements. The dissent lamented the "ebb of the commerce power."[69]

The constitutional question, then, appeared settled. Enabling a woman to enforce her right to freedom from sex-based violence fell beyond the sphere of national sovereignty that is grounded in commodity exchange. As once Congress had insisted on the difference between a wife and a freed slave, so the Court now insisted on the boundary between domestic bonds and the flow of commerce.

✳ ✳ ✳

Again consider the Hate Crimes Prevention Act, based on the two pillars of the Thirteenth Amendment and the Commerce Clause. As Congress debated the legislation, the ruling came down from the Court in *Morrison*, making it appear that a ban on hate violence extending to sex and home life would be a dead letter.[70]

With the delimiting of the commerce power, the theory was no longer that Congress was entitled to regulate private life simply because the wrongs at stake affected the flow of interstate commerce, however remote the intercourse from the market itself. New objections emerged after *Morrison*: that committing hate crimes "is in no sense economic or commercial but instead is noneconomic and criminal in nature" and that a congressional prohibition would be "struck down by the Supreme Court as violative of the Constitution." There were more warnings about a flood of rape cases entering the federal courts, although the hate crimes measure contained no self-enforcing rights guarantee, only criminal sanctions.[71]

Therefore the act was rewritten, and the commerce nexus spelled out more distinctly in the section on hate crimes based on sex. Congress shored up its authority by requiring direct circumstantial proof that the forbidden activity was both economic in nature and crossed state lines, rather than relying on the concept of aggregate effect. It added a jurisdictional element absent from the defunct rights clause of the Violence Against Women Act.

The dualism of the hate crimes act thus grew more explicit—the juxtaposition of the commerce-saturated section on sex with the antislavery-infused section on race. "In light of *United States v. Morrison*," a Justice Department memorandum stated, the prohibition of sex-based hate crime "would *not* be based 'solely on that conduct's aggregate effect on interstate commerce,' but would instead be based on a specific and discrete connection between each instance of prohibited conduct and interstate or foreign commerce." Along with a motive of animus, not desire, the economic nature of the violence would have to be manifest. Explaining how the legislation had been altered to assure its constitutionality, its authors spoke of "sadistic murders" that possessed a "commerce nexus."[72]

As enacted in 2009, the Hate Crimes Act enumerates multiple ways that violence animated by sex might involve or affect commerce across the borders of states and nations. Shaped by the Court's rebuke in *Morrison*, it deals in detail with both things and persons: channels, facilities, and instrumentalities of commerce; purchase of goods and services; interference with commercial or other economic activity; conduct affecting interstate or foreign commerce; use of a weapon or incendiary device that has traveled in interstate or foreign commerce; and travel of persons among states and nations.[73]

It is an inventory of the market's expanse that does not accompany the description of hate crimes based on race. For there, owing to the act's cleft structure, the badges of slavery do the work of commodity relations, and the Thirteenth Amendment stands in place of the Commerce Clause. But hate crimes based on sex must connect directly to the flow of interstate commerce to constitute intercourse subject to the power of the nation-state. An article of merchandise—use of a weapon that had crossed state borders—would transform even a rape at home into violence sufficiently economic in nature for Congress to forbid it. In the market's reach into private life lay the necessary justification for both the authority of the national government and the protection of persons.

The Hate Crimes Act has been upheld under both the Thirteenth Amendment and the Commerce Clause, as courts have approved the congressional interpretation of the badges of slavery and weighed the circumstantial evidence of an interstate commerce nexus. It was a reasonable conclusion "that physically attacking a person of a particular race . . . is a badge or incident of slavery," held the United States Court of Appeals for the Tenth Circuit, while stressing that the ban on "non-racial" hate violence emanated from the commerce power, for otherwise "nearly every hurtful thing . . . might be analogized to slavery." And it was the channel of a highway and instrumentality of a car—as proof of a commerce nexus—that led a United States District Court in Kentucky to uphold the act in a case involving hate violence directed at a gay man. Although denying that the flow of commerce should be treated as "talismanic," the ruling spoke of the "interstate transportation routes through which persons and goods move" and the "quintessential instrumentalities of modern interstate commerce" in finding private "non-economic activity" punishable by the national government. As the court observed, "the Interstate Commerce Clause continues to cast a very large shadow, indeed."[74]

No hate crimes case has reached the Supreme Court, however; nor has a ruling on hate violence at home come from any court.[75] As a constitutional question, the breadth of the commerce power has scarcely been settled.

∗ ∗ ∗

What remains as well is a historical question—why the law of commodities has served as a charter of human rights. Why Congress has forbidden violations of personhood in the name of market values. Why wrongs redolent of slavery—trafficking in and raping women—count as burdens on commerce.

Those are the puzzles that I have sought to elucidate in exploring the counterpoint between the Thirteenth Amendment and the Commerce Clause. My argument is that the flow of commerce has become a source of human rights where the antislavery amendment has never reached—to the wrongs of sex and inside the home and across the threshold of marriage. The situation of women is still anomalous.

A legacy of slave emancipation, then, is a human rights order that rests on the spread of commerce into all spheres of social life. The economy has become sovereign, and principles of buying and selling prevail, where the liberating law of antislavery ends. Since the era of the Civil War, the freedom of persons has depended increasingly on the expansive commerce power of Congress.

The paradox revealed by my argument is that a boundless market is morally unimaginable, but the limits of antislavery constitutionalism have produced an American human rights tradition that values an unbounded market as a wellspring of individual rights. And the paradox is most acute where the wrongs of women are at stake. Sex has been potent in rendering human rights a commodity fiction.

Notes

1. For their insights and criticisms, I thank Craig Becker, Richard R. W. Brooks, Daina Coffey, Chris Desan, Dirk Hartog, Tim Murphy, Emily Remus, Dan Rodgers, Bill Sewell, Kristin Warbasse, and Barbara Welke; and I am grateful for discussions with

members of the Princeton University Center for Human Values, the Columbia University Legal History Workshop, the Gilder Lehrman Center for the Study of Slavery, Resistance, and Abolition at Yale University, and the University of Minnesota Legal History Workshop.

2. The Thirteenth Amendment states: "Section 1. Neither slavery nor involuntary servitude, except as a punishment for crime whereof the party shall have been duly convicted, shall exist within the United States, or any place subject to their jurisdiction. Section 2. Congress shall have power to enforce this article by appropriate legislation." The Commerce Clause, Article I, Section 8, states: "The Congress shall have Power . . . to regulate Commerce with foreign Nations, and among the several States, and with the Indian Tribes."

3. On the Commerce Clause, see Jack M. Balkin, "Commerce," *Michigan Law Review* 109, no. 1 (October 2010): 1–51; James Gray Pope, "The Thirteenth Amendment versus the Commerce Clause: Labor and the Shaping of American Constitutional Law, 1921–1957," *Columbia Law Review* 102, no. 1 (January 2002): 1–122. On the limited reach of the Thirteenth Amendment, see Akhil Reed Amar, "Women and the Constitution," *Harvard Journal of Law and Public Policy* 18, no. 2 (1995): 465–74; George Rutherglen, "State Action, Private Action, and the Thirteenth Amendment," *Virginia Law Review* 94, no. 6 (October 2008): 1367–1406.

4. White Slave Traffic Act, Pub. L. No. 61-277, 36 Stat. 825 (1910); Violence Against Women Act, Pub. L. No. 103-322, 108 Stat. 1796 (1994) (hereafter: VAWA); Matthew Shepard and James Byrd, Jr. Hate Crimes Prevention Act, Pub. L. No. 111-84, 123 Stat. 2190 (2009) (hereafter: Hate Crimes Act). Other landmark statutes based on the Commerce Clause include the National Labor Relations Act of 1935, Pub. L. No. 74-198, 49 Stat. 449, and the Civil Rights Act of 1964, Pub. L. No. 88-352, 78 Stat. 241.

5. See Michael J. Sandel, *What Money Can't Buy: The Moral Limits of Markets* (New York: Farrar, Straus and Giroux, 2012), 5, 6; Debra Satz, *Why Some Things Should Not Be for Sale: The Moral Limits of Markets* (New York: Oxford University Press, 2010).

6. Karl Polanyi, *The Great Transformation: The Political and Economic Origins of Our Time* (Boston: Beacon Press, 1944), 163, 54.

7. Elizabeth Cady Stanton, Susan B. Anthony, and Joslyn Matilda Gage, eds., *History of Woman Suffrage, 1861–1876* (New York: Fowler and Wells, 1887), 2: 349.

8. While the Trafficking Victims Protection Act of 2000 condemns trafficking in persons as "a contemporary manifestation of slavery" and broadens the antipeonage statute, and while Congress cited both the effect of human trafficking on interstate and foreign commerce and the abolition of slavery by the Thirteenth Amendment in the findings section of the act, the operative provisions of the act criminalizing sex trafficking apply only to trafficking that is "in or affecting interstate commerce." See Pub. L. 106-386, Div. A, § 102(a), 112 (amending 18 U.S.C. § 1589), 114 Stat. 1466, 1486, § 102(b)(12), (22), 114 Stat. 1467, 1468, and § 112, 114 Stat. 1487 (amending 18 U.S.C. § 1591). The Trafficking Victims Protection Reauthorization Act of 2003, House Report 108-264, Pt. 1 & 2 (2003); Henry Andrés Yoder, "Civil Rights for Victims of Human Trafficking," *University of Pennsylvania Journal of Law and Social Change* 12, no. 2 (2008–2009): 146–47, 160.

9. See Andrew Clapham, ed., *Human Rights and Non-State Actors* (Cheltenham, UK: Edward Elgar, 2013); Seyla Benhabib, *Dignity in Adversity: Human Rights in Troubled Times* (Cambridge: Polity, 2011).

10. Hate Crimes Act, § 4707 (a).

11. *Cong. Rec.*, 106th Cong., 2nd Sess. (2000) at 11412; *Cong. Rec.*, 111th Cong., 1st Sess. (2009) at 11076; *Hate Crimes Prevention Act of 1997: Hearing on H.R. 3081, Before the Committee on the Judiciary 105-131*, 105th Cong., 2nd Sess. (1998) at 80–81; "Remarks by the President at Reception Commemorating the Enactment of the Matthew Shepard and James Byrd, Jr. Hate Crimes Prevention Act," October 28, 2009, http://www .whitehouse.gov/the-press-office/remarks-president-reception-commemorating -enactment-matthew-shepard-and-james-byrd. For empirical data, see *Cong. Rec.*, 111th Cong., 1st Sess. (2009) at 11210, 11220; *Matthew Shepard Hate Crimes Prevention Act of 2009: Hearing on 111-464 Before the Senate Judiciary Committee.*, 111th Cong., 1st Sess. (2009) at 5; Leadership Conference: http://archives.civilrights.org/hatecrimes /llehcpa/legislation/. There were some three hundred civic, religious, and law enforcement organizations that supported the Hate Crimes Act; see *Cong. Rec.*, 111th Cong., 1st Sess (2009) at 10865. Opposition is summed up in Local Law Enforcement Hate Crimes Prevention Act of 2009, House Report 111-86, 111th Cong., 1st Sess. (2009) at 38–47. See International Covenant on Civil and Political Rights: http://www.ohchr .org/EN/ProfessionalInterest/Pages/CCPR.aspx. See also Valerie Jenness and Kendal Broad, *Hate Crimes: New Social Movements and the Politics of Violence* (New York: Aldine de Gruyter, 1997).

12. Christopher G. Tiedeman, *A Treatise on State and Federal Control of Persons and Property in the United States: Considered from Both a Civil and Criminal Standpoint* (St. Louis: The F.H. Thomas Law Book Co., 1900), 2:1019; *Cong. Rec.*, 111th Cong., 1st Sess. (2009) at 11089, 10863. The Civil Rights Act of 1968 contained a hate crimes provision at 18 U.S.C. § 245 (1968).

13. Hate Crimes Act, § 4702 (7) (8), § 4707 (a).

14. Ibid., § 4702 (6), § 4707 (a).

15. Ibid., § 4702 (7).

16. Ibid., § 4702 (6), § 4707 (a) (2).

17. *Matthew Shepard Hate Crimes Prevention Act of 2009*, Senate Judiciary Hearing 111-464, 5, 175–76.

18. *Hate Crimes Prevention Act of 1997: Hearing on H.R. 3081*, at 51, 116, 50, 116–117, 51.

19. *Declaration of Sentiments of the American Anti-Slavery Society, adopted at the Philadelphia Convention, December 4, 1833* (New York: American Anti-Slavery Society, 1833), 1–2.

20. *Speech of Mr. Horace Mann, of Mass., on the Subject of Slavery in the Territories, and the Consequences of the Threatened Dissolution of the Union. Delivered in the House of Representatives, February 15, 1850* (Washington, D.C.: Gideon & Co., 1850), 12, 4, 3; Frederick Douglass, "Reception Speech at Finsbury Chapel, Moorsfield, England, May 12, 1846," in *My Bondage and My Freedom* (New York, 1855), 217–19, 408.

21. *Cong. Globe*, 38th Cong., 1st Sess. (1864) at 1488. See Amy Dru Stanley, "Instead of Waiting for the Thirteenth Amendment: The War Power, Slave Marriage, and Inviolate Human Rights," *American Historical Review* 115, no. 3 (June 2010): 742–44; Nancy F. Cott, *Public Vows: A History of Marriage* (Cambridge, Mass.: Harvard University Press, 2001), 80; Michael Vorenberg, *Final Freedom: The Civil War, the Abolition of Slavery, and the Thirteenth Amendment* (New York: Cambridge University Press, 2001), 57; Joyce E. McConnell, "Beyond Metaphor: Battered Women, Involuntary Servitude, and the Thirteenth Amendment," *Yale Journal of Law & Feminism* 4, no. 2 (Spring 1992): 207–8; Norma Basch, "Marriage and Domestic Relations," in *The Cambridge History of Law in America*, vol. 2, *The Long Nineteenth Century (1789-1920)*, ed. Michael Grossberg and Christopher Tomlins (New York: Cambridge

University Press, 2008), 269; Tera Hunter, *Bound in Wedlock: Slave and Free Black Marriage in the Nineteenth Century* (Cambridge, Mass.: The Belknap Press of Harvard University Press, 2017).

22. *Cong. Globe*, 39th Cong., 1st Sess. (1866) at 322. See George A. Rutherglen, "The Badges and Incidents of Slavery and the Power of Congress to Enforce the Thirteenth Amendment," in *The Promises of Liberty: The History and Contemporary Relevance of the Thirteenth Amendment*, ed. Alexander Tsesis (New York: Columbia University Press, 2010), 163–81.

23. Civil Rights Act of 1866, 14 Stat. 27 (1866); Peonage Abolition Act, 14 Stat. 546 (1867); Enforcement Act of 1870, 16 Stat. 140 (1870); Ku Klux Klan Act of 1871, 17 Stat. 13 (1871); Civil Rights Act of 1875, 18 Stat. 335 (1875).

24. *Slaughterhouse Cases*, 83 U.S. 36 (1873) at 67, 69, 72, 71; *Civil Rights Cases*, 109 U.S. 3 (1883) at 24–25.

25. *Bradwell v. State of Illinois*, 83 U.S. 130 (1873) at 141.

26. *Commonwealth v. Burke*, 105 Mass. 376 (1870).

27. Ibid., 376.

28. Ibid., 376; Matthew Hale, *Historia Placitorum Coronæ: The History of the Pleas of the Crown* (London: 1736) 1:629; "Declaration of Rights for Women by the National Woman Suffrage Association, read aloud by Susan B. Anthony," in *The History of Woman Suffrage*, 3:33. See Jill Hasday, "Contest and Consent: A Legal History of Marital Rape," *California Law Review* 88 (October 2000): 1373–1505; Estelle B. Freedman, *Redefining Rape: Sexual Violence in the Era of Suffrage and Segregation* (Cambridge, Mass.: Harvard University Press, 2013), 7, 54, 63–66.

29. On the legal presumption of slaves' lack of will, see *State v. Mann*, 13 N.C. 263 (1830) at 266.

30. *Civil Rights Cases*, 19, 61.

31. White Slave Traffic Act. On earlier federal restrictions on the immigration of prostitutes under the Page Act of 1875, see Kerry Abrams, "Polygamy, Prostitution, and the Federalization of Immigration Law," *Columbia Law Review* 105, no. 3 (April 2005): 641–716.

32. "Proclamation of President Theodore Roosevelt," in House Report No. 61-47, 61st Cong., 2nd Sess. (1909) at 15–16. See "The Protection of Girls: Action of European Powers," *The Manchester Guardian*, September 15, 1905; "Poster Warning Girls of White Slave Traffic to be Posted in All Countries," *Chicago Daily Tribune*, November 22, 1903; *Suppression of the White-Slave Traffic*, Senate Document No. 61-214, pt. 2, 61st Cong., 2nd Sess. (1910) at 14; "'White Slave' Congress," *New York Times*, October 24, 1906; "The White Slave Traffic: The Brussels Conference," *Manchester Guardian*, October 30, 1907; "To Stop White Slave Trade. Government Is Planning Co-operative Measures with European Nations," *New York Times*, June 7, 1908; "To Discuss White Slave Traffic," *Washington Post*, October 6, 1909. Also see Gunther W. Peck, "Feminizing White Slavery in the United States: Marcus Braun and the Transnational Traffic in White Bodies, 1890–1910," in *Workers Across the Americas: The Transnational Turn in Labor History*, ed. Leon Fink (New York: Oxford University Press, 2011), 221–44; Valeska Huber, *Channeling Mobilities: Migration and Globalisation in the Suez Canal Region and Beyond, 1869–1914* (New York: Cambridge University Press, 2013), 302; Brian Donovan, *White Slave Crusades: Race, Gender, and Anti-vice Activism, 1887–1917* (Urbana: University of Illinois Press, 2006); Eileen Boris and Heather Berg, "Protecting Virtue, Erasing Labor: Historical Responses to Trafficking," in *Human Trafficking Reconsidered: Rethinking the Problem, Envisioning New Solutions,*

ed. Kimberly Kay Hoang and Rhacel Salazer Parreñas (New York: International Debate Education Association, 2014), 19–29; Tara Zahra, *The Great Departure: Mass Migration from Eastern Europe and the Making of the Free World* (New York: W. W. Norton, 2016); Frederick K. Grittner, *White Slavery: Myth, Ideology, and American Law*
(New York: Garland, 1990); David J. Langum, *Crossing over the Line: Legislating Morality and the Mann Act* (Chicago: University of Chicago Press, 2006); Daina K. Coffey,
"With or Without Her Consent: Women and the Mann Act in Chicago, 1910–1917"
(manuscript in the author's possession, University of Chicago, 2013).

33. International Council of Women, *Report of Transactions during the Third Quinquennial Term Terminating with the Third Quinquennial Meeting Held in Berlin, June, 1904,
with an Introduction by May Wright Sewall, Retiring President* (Boston, 1909), 1:173–75.

34. *Suppression of the White-Slave Traffic,* Senate Document No. 61-214, pt. 2, 61st Cong.,
2nd Sess. (1910) at 14; *White Slave Traffic*, Senate Report No. 61-886, 61st Cong., 2nd
Sess. (1910) at 11; "Women Terribly Beaten: Make Charges Against a White Slave
Trader in Paterson, N.J.," *New York Times*, June 25, 1906; "Pleads for Laws to Stamp
out 'White Slave' Traffic," *Chicago Daily Tribune*, March 13, 1908; "No More White
Slaves. Crusade Begun in Chicago Will Wipe Out Immoral Traffic," *Chicago Daily
Tribune*, July 5, 1908; "To Curb White Slavery. Taft Consulted on Plan to Reach Traf-
fic through Inter-State Commerce Law," *New York Times*, November 25, 1909; Edito-
rial, *Watson's Magazine,* April, 1906, 171; Frederick Martin Lehman, *The White Slave
Hell; or, With Christ at Midnight in the Slums of Chicago* (Chicago: The Christian
Witness Co., 1910); E. Norine Law, *The Shame of a Great Nation: The Story of the
"White Slave Trade"* (Harrisburg, Pa.: United Evangelical, 1909). On allegations of
white slavery in Chicago and the investigations of the Commerce and Labor Depart-
ment, see also *Report of the National Woman's Christian Temperance Union, Thirty-
Fifth Annual Convention, October 23–28, 1908*, 126–27, 140. See Ruth Rosen, *The Lost
Sisterhood: Prostitution in America, 1900–1918* (Baltimore, Md.: Johns Hopkins University Press, 1983).

35. Congress did not act to ban child labor under the Thirteenth Amendment either; see
Dina Mishra, "Child Labor as Involuntary Servitude: The Failure of Congress to Leg-
islate Against Child Labor Pursuant to the Thirteenth Amendment in the Early
Twentieth Century," *Rutgers Law Review* 63, no. 1 (Fall 2010): 59–128.

36. United States, *Memorandum in re White-Slave Trade. Printed by Order of Committee
on Interstate and Foreign Commerce* (Washington, D.C.: Government Printing Office, 1909), 3, 4, 7, 9, 10. Reprinted in House Report No. 61-47 and Senate Report
No. 61-886.

37. Ibid., 9, 11.

38. *Cong. Rec.*, 61st Cong., 2nd Sess. (1910) at 812, 821, 1040, 1038; *Gibbons v. Ogden*, 22
U.S. 1 (1824) at 21. See also *Smith v. Turner*; *Norris v. Boston* (collectively, *Passenger
Cases*), 48 U.S. 283 (1849). On Saunders and Bleak Hill plantation, see Virginia State
Bar Association, *Proceedings of the Annual Meeting of the Virginia State Bar Association* (Richmond, Va.: Richmond Press, 1922), 34:82; United States National Park Service, "National Register of Historic Places Registration Form for Bleak Hill," esp.
9–10, http://www.dhr.virginia.gov/registers/Counties/Franklin/033-0002_Bleak_Hill
_2002_Final_Nomination.pdf.

39. "Views of the Minority," in House Report No. 61-47, 1, 4.

40. *Cong. Rec.*, 61st Cong., 2nd Sess. (1910) at 519, 820, 521, 522, 527, 818. See Tom Blake
(transcriber), "Largest Slaveholders from 1860 Slave Census Schedules and Surname
Matches for African Americans on 1870 Census," Jasper County, Georgia, http://

freepages.genealogy.rootsweb.ancestry.com/~ajac/gajasper.htm; William J. Northen, ed., *Men of Mark in Georgia: A Complete and Elaborate History* (Atlanta: A. B. Caldwell, 1908), 4:371–76; Greg Schmidt, "William Richardson," *Encyclopedia of Alabama*, last updated December 16, 2014, http://www.encyclopediaofalabama.org /article/h-3445.

41. *Cong. Rec.*, 61st Cong., 2nd Sess. (1910) at 820, 818.

42. Ibid., 812, 820, 1037, 1038, 1037, 1040. See Thomas I. Parkinson, "Congressional Prohibitions of Interstate Commerce," *Columbia Law Review* 16, no. 5 (May, 1916): 367–385; *Hipolite Egg Co. v. United States*, 220 U.S. 45 (1911); *Lottery Case*, 188 U.S. 321 (1903).

43. *Hoke v. United States*, 227 U.S. 308 (1913) at 320, 322–33; *United States v. Holte*, 236 U.S. 140 (1915) at 145; the lower court holding is included in *Transcript of Record, Supreme Court of the United States, October Term, 1914, No. 628. The United States, Plaintiff in Error, v. Clara Holte, In Error to the District Court of the United States for the Eastern District of Wisconsin, filed September 19, 1914*, at 6. See "Year in Cell for Johnson," *New York Times*, June 5, 1913; Kevin J. Mumford, *Interzones: Black/White Sex Districts in Chicago and New York in the Early Twentieth Century* (New York: Columbia University Press, 1997), 3–18.

44. See "Event Transcript: A Symposium Celebrating the Fifteenth Anniversary of the Violence Against Women Act," *Georgetown Journal of Gender and Law* 11, no. 2 (2010): 511–31; Reva B. Siegel, "The Rule of Love: Wife Beating as Prerogative and Privacy," *Yale Law Journal* 105, no. 8 (June 1996): 2117–207; Judith Resnik, "Sisterhood, Slavery, and Sovereignty: Transnational Antislavery Work and Women's Rights Movements in the United States During the Twentieth Century," in *Women's Rights and Transatlantic Anti-Slavery in the Era of Emancipation*, ed. Kathryn Kish Sklar and James Brewer Stewart (New Haven, Conn.: Yale University Press, 2007), 19–54; Jeannie Suk, *At Home in the Law: How the Domestic Violence Revolution is Transforming Privacy* (New Haven, Conn.: Yale University Press, 2009).

45. VAWA, Subtitle A, § 40101; VAWA, Subtitle B, §40201; United Nations Human Rights Committee, 53rd Sess., *Summary Record of the 1401st Meeting*, April 17, 1995, CCPR/C/SR. 1401 at ¶¶ 4, 29; International Covenant of Civil and Political Rights, 999 U.N.T.S. 171(1966) at preamble and articles, 6, 7, 8, 9. The United Nations Declaration against violence is not a binding treaty. Notably, the American delegation also testified that the Convention on the Elimination of All Forms of Discrimination against Women (CEDAW) was then being considered by the Senate. CEDAW did not expressly address the problem of violence. A binding convention, CEDAW still remains unratified by the United States. Reverence for state domestic jurisdiction, along with contradictions between international law and national sovereignty, underlies American assertion of reservations on global human rights conventions; see Judith Resnik, "Categorical Federalism: Jurisdiction, Gender, and the Globe," *Yale Law Journal* 111 (December, 2001): 619–80.

46. UN General Assembly, Resolution 48/104, "Declaration on the Elimination of Violence against Women," adopted by the General Assembly., 48th Sess., December 20, 1993, preamble and articles 1–4. According to the declaration, violence against women violates the principles enshrined in the Universal Declaration of Human Rights, the International Covenant of Civil and Political Rights, and the Convention on the Elimination of all Forms of Discrimination Against Women, which has been signed but not ratified by the United States.

47. VAWA, § 2261 (a) (1) (2); VAWA, § 40302, codified at 42 U.S.C. § 13981.

48. *Crimes of Violence Motivated by Gender: Hearing Before the Subcommittee on Civil and Constitutional Rights of the Committee on the Judiciary, House of Representatives,* 103d Cong., 1st Sess. (1993) at 4, 8; *The Violence Against Women Act of 1993,* Senate Report 103–138, 103rd Cong., 1st Sess. (1993), at 44; Senator Joseph Biden, *Turning the Act into Action: The Violence Against Women Law* (Washington, D.C.: Senate Judiciary Committee, 1994), 3; telephone interview, January 16, 2015, with Sally Goldfarb, then senior staff attorney at NOW Legal Defense and Education Fund, now professor of law at Rutgers Camden Law School; *Women and Violence, Hearings on Legislation to Reduce the Growing Problem of Violent Crime Against Women, Before the Senate Judiciary Committee,* 101-939, pt. 2, 101st Cong., 2nd Sess. (1990) at 57. For organizations supporting the measure, see House Hearing 102-42, 19–23. And see Reva B. Siegel, "She the People: The Nineteenth Amendment, Sex Equality, Federalism, and the Family," *Harvard Law Review* 115, no.4 (February 2002): 957, 961, 1025–27; Sally Goldfarb, "The Civil Rights Remedy of the Violence against Women Act: Legislative History, Policy Implications, and Litigation Strategy," *Journal of Law and Social Policy* 4, no.1 (1996): 395. On the legislative history of VAWA, see "Event Transcript: A Symposium," 511–31; Fred Strebeigh, *Equal: Women Reshape American Law* (New York: W. W. Norton, 2009), 339–51.

49. *Senate Judiciary Committee Hearing* 101-939 at 91, 96, 89, 90, 141; *The History of Woman Suffrage,* 1:719. For a citation of statistics on incidence of rape and other sexual assaults, see *Senate Hearing* 101-939. See also *Violence Against Women: Hearing Before the Subcommittee on Crime and Criminal Justice of the House Committee on the Judiciary, House of Representatives,* 102nd Cong., 2nd Sess. (1992); *Violence Against Women: Victims of the System, Senate Judiciary Committee Hearing* 102-369, 102nd Cong., 1st Sess. (1991). On privacy, see Suk, *At Home in the Law.*

50. VAWA, Subtitle B, chap. 2, § 2261 (a)(1)(2); Senate Report 103-138 at 43, 61.

51. VAWA, Subtitle C, § 40302 (a) (b) (c); *Violence Against Women Act of 1991,* Senate Report 102-197, 102nd Cong., 1st Sess. (1991) at 53–54; Senate Report 103-138 at 43, 61.

52. Senate Report 102-197 at 52, 53; Senate Report 103-138 at 54, 55.

53. VAWA, Subtitle C, § 40302 (b); House Hearing 103-51 at 94. On the civil rights clause as the centerpiece of the statute, see statement of Judge Mary Schroeder of the United States Court of Appeals for the Ninth Circuit, "Event Transcript: A Symposium," 546. See also *Crimes of Violence Motivated by Gender Hearing,* House Hearing, at 3, 6, 8; Linda Jackson, "Marital Rape: A Higher Standard is in Order," *William and Mary Journal of Women and the Law* 1 (Fall 1994), 194–97; Goldfarb, "The Civil Rights Remedy," 397. By 1993, marital rape had become a criminal offense in all states, through statutory reform and court rulings, but a majority of states retained some form of exception, requiring particular circumstances—living apart, the use of force, an ongoing divorce proceeding—or classified marital rape as a lesser crime than rape outside of marriage. More than a decade later, a majority of states still retained some form of immunity for husbands who rape wives. See National Clearinghouse on Marital and Date Rape, "State Law Chart, May 2005," at http://www.ncmdr.org/state_law_chart.html; Lalenya Weintraub Siegel, "The Marital Rape Exemption: Evolution to Extinction," *Cleveland State Law Review* 43, no. 2 (1995): 367–69; Jennifer J. McMahon, "Marital Rape Laws, 1976–2002: From Exemptions to Prohibitions" (master's thesis, University of Georgia, 2005), appendix, 67–69. See also Robin West, "Legitimating the Illegitimate: A Comment on 'Beyond Rape,'" *Columbia Law Review* 93, no. 6 (October 1993): 1442–59; Susan Brownmiller, *Against Our Will: Men, Women, and Rape* (New York: Simon and Schuster, 1975); Hasday, "Contest and Consent"; Freedman, *Redefining Rape,* 281–82.

54. *Gibbons v. Ogden*, 22 U.S. 1 at 134, 226. See Frances Olsen, "Constitutional Law: Feminist Critiques of the Public/Private Distinction," *Constitutional Commentary* 10, no. 2 (1993): 319–27; Janet Halley, "What Is Family Law?: A Genealogy Part I," *Yale Journal of Law & the Humanities* 23, no. 1 (Winter 2011): 1–109; Janet Halley, "What Is Family Law?: A Genealogy Part II," *Yale Journal of Law & the Humanities* 23, no. 2 (Summer 2011): 189–293.

55. VAWA, Subtitle C, § 40302 (a), (d) (1) (2).

56. Senate Judiciary Hearing 102-369 at 104; VAWA, Subtitle C, § 40302 (a), (d) (1) (2); Senate Report 103-138 at 54.

57. Senate Judiciary Hearing 102-369 at 90, 102, 101, 102, 97, 88. VAWA, Subtitle C, § 40302 (a), (d) (1) (2); Senate Report 103-138, 54; telephone interview with Burt Neuborne, January 20, 2015. See Jack M. Balkin and Sanford Levinson, "The Dangerous Thirteenth Amendment," *Columbia Law Review* 112, no. 7 (November 2012): 1459–99. Some legal scholars adopted the Thirteenth Amendment theory; see Marcellene Elizabeth Hearn, "A Thirteenth Amendment Defense of the Violence Against Women Act," *University of Pennsylvania Law Review* 146, no. 4 (April 1998): 1097–167.

58. *NLRB v. Jones & Laughlin Steel Corp.*, 301 U.S. 1 (1937) at 31; *Heart of Atlanta Motel v. United States*, 379 U.S. 241 (1964) at 256–257. See also *Wickard v. Filburn*, 317 U.S. 111 (1942). On constitutional transformation in the New Deal era, see Bruce Ackerman, *We the People,* vol. 2, *Transformations* (Cambridge, Mass.: Belknap Press of Harvard University Press, 1998), 297–382; on the 1964 Civil Rights Act, see George Rutherglen, "The Thirteenth Amendment, the Power of Congress, and the Shifting Sources of Civil Rights Law," *Columbia Law Review* 112, no. 7 (November 2012): 1559–68.

59. Senate Report 102-197, 52; Senate Report 103-138, 54.

60. Senate Report 102-197, 53–54; Senate Report 103-138, 54; Senate Judiciary Hearing 102-369 at 103, 115, 119, 125, 86, 96–97.

61. *Crimes of Violence Motivated by Gender Hearing*, House Hearing, at 107. See Judith Resnik, "Drafting, Lobbying, and Litigating VAWA: National, Local, and Transnational Interventions on Behalf of Women's Equality," *Georgetown Journal of Gender and the Law* 11, no. 2 (2010): 557–69.

62. Senate Hearing 101-939, pt. 1 at 68, 62.

63. *United States v. Morrison,* 529 U.S. 598 (2000).

64. Ibid., 613. The Court drew directly on its prior ruling invalidating the Gun-Free School Zones Act of 1990 *in United States v. Lopez*, 514 U.S. 549 (1995). On *Morrison*, see Sally Goldfarb, "'No Civilized System of Justice': The Fate of the Violence Against Women Act," *West Virginia Law Review* 102, no. 3 (Spring 2000): 499–546; Julie Goldscheid, "*United States v. Morrison* and the Civil Rights Remedy of the Violence Against Women Act: A Civil Rights Law Struck Down in the Name of Federalism," *Cornell Law Review* 86, no. 1 (November 2000): 109–39; Catherine Mackinnon, "Disputing Male Sovereignty: On *United States v. Morrison*," *Harvard Law Review* 114, no. 1 (November 2000): 135–77; Robert C. Post and Reva B. Siegel, "Equal Protection by Law: Federal Antidiscrimination Legislation after *Morrison* and *Kimel*," *Yale Law Journal* 110, no. 3 (December 2000): 441–526.

65. *Morrison*, 529 U.S. at 615–16, 617–18, 632, 644, 636, 644. Also see the dissent of Justice Breyer, *Morrison*, 529 U.S. at 656.

66. Ibid. at 644, 639.

67. Ibid. at 613, 618, 609, 617.

68. Brief *Amici Curiae* on Behalf of International Law Scholars and Human Rights Experts in Support of Petitioners, *United States v. Morrison*, Nos. 99-5, 99-29 (November 16, 1999), 1, 29. See also Brief *Amici Curiae* of Law Professors in Support of Peti-

tioners, *United States v. Morrison*, Nos. 99-5, 99-29 (November 12, 1999). See also Harold H. Koh, "1998 Frankel Lecture: Bringing International Law Home," *Faculty Scholarship Series* (1998); Resnik, "Sisterhood, Slavery, and Sovereignty."

69. *Morrison*, 529 U.S. at 613, 654.

70. *Cong. Rec.*, 106th Cong., 2nd Sess. (2000) at 11214–15.

71. Ibid. at 11226, 11218. On the concern about every rape as a federal hate crime, see also *Hate Crimes Prevention Act of 1998, Senate Judiciary Hearing* 105-904, 105th Cong., 2nd Sess. (1998) at 10, 44, 53, 59, 60; *Matthew Shepard Hate Crimes Prevention Act of 2009, Senate Judiciary Hearing* 111-464, 111th Cong., 1st Sess. (2009) at 8, 33, 159, 429, 446.

72. *Cong. Rec.*, 106th Cong., 2nd Sess. (2000) at 11230, 11229, 11230, 11219, 11223, 11212. See Amendment SA 3473, Senate, 106th Cong., 2nd Sess. (June 19, 2000); U.S. Department of Justice Office Legal Counsel, "Constitutionality of the Matthew Shepard Hate Crimes Prevention Act: Memorandum Opinion for the Assistant Attorney General Office of Legislative Affairs," June 16, 2009.

73. Amendment SA 3473, Senate, 106th Cong., 2nd Sess. (June 19, 2000); Hate Crimes Act, § 4702 (6), § 4707 (a) (2).

74. *United States v. Hatch*, 722 F.3d 1193 (10th Cir. 2013), 1206, 1205, 1204; *United States v. Mason*, 993 F.Supp.2d 1308 (D.Or. 2014); *United States v. Jenkins*, 909 F. Supp. 2d 758 (E.D. Ky. 2012), 767, 771, 773. On the courts' validation of the Thirteenth Amendment basis, see also *United States v. Cannon*, 750 F.3d 492 (5th Cir. 2014); *United States v. Maybee*, 687 F.3d 1026 (5th Cir. 2012); *United States v. Henery*, 60 F.Supp.3d 1126 (D. Idaho 2014); *United States v. Beebe*, 807 F. Supp. 2d 1045 (D.N.M. 2010), 1048–57. On the courts' validation of the Commerce Clause basis, see also *United States v. Metcalf*, 2016 U.S.Dist.LEXIS 25950 (N.D. Ia. 2016); *United States v. Mullet*, 868 F. Supp. 2d 618 (N.D. Ohio 2012).

75. The Supreme Court denied review in *United States v. Hatch*, 722 F.3d 1193 (10th Cir. 2013), *cert. denied*, 134 S. Ct. 1538 (2014).

CHAPTER 6

NEGRO CLOTH

Mastering the Market for Slave Clothing
in Antebellum America

SETH ROCKMAN

"It is our intention to make cheap goods for Southern planters,"
announced Isaac P. Hazard, the Rhode Island textile manufacturer who helped to establish plantation provisioning as big business in industrializing New England. Entering what contemporaries called the
"Southern market" in the early 1820s, Isaac Hazard and his brother Rowland
cultivated customers among the largest slaveholders in South Carolina,
Georgia, Alabama, Mississippi, and Louisiana.[1] An 1845 report on American
woolen manufacturing attested to the Hazards' success in catapulting Rhode
Island to preeminence in cloth for the coerced: nearly half of that small state's
woolen enterprises specialized in "negro kerseys." When Frederick Law Olmsted toured the plantation South in the 1850s, he observed slave clothing was
"mostly made, especially for this purpose, in Providence, R.I." Olmsted's im-
precise geography—manufactories were concentrated in the southernmost
parts of the state (shipping from Stonington, Connecticut) and north of Providence along the Blackstone River's path into Massachusetts—scarcely changes
the fundamental fact: the lives and livelihoods of Rhode Island's entrepreneurs, hand-weavers, and seamstresses were inextricably linked to those of the
planters and slaves who constituted the dual consumers of their "negro cloth."[2]

In nineteenth-century parlance, "negro cloth" was an ill-defined category
of textiles varying by composition, texture, color, and pattern, but united by
its explicit purpose of outfitting enslaved people. Some fabrics like *osnaburg* (a
linen fabric produced in Osnabrück and knocked off by Scottish manufacturers in the mid-eighteenth century) had been standard-issue plantation provi-

sions since the colonial era, but by the 1820s the term "negro cloth" said more about the presumptive market than about the textile itself. In fact, as the Hazards were experimenting with linen, cotton, and woolen fabrics early in their manufacturing careers, they acknowledged as much: "We intend applying our Factory altogether to the manufacture of Negro Clothing when we can find the kind that best answers." Ultimately, a dozen fabrics—some made from slave-grown cotton, others from wool imported from Smyrna, Adrianople, and Buenos Aires—would constitute the Hazards' product line, with an array of color and pattern choices further multiplying the possibilities. While the coarse and monochromatic nature of slave clothing figured prominently in both abolitionist exposés and recollections of former slaves, extant fabric samples and purchasing orders suggest that negro cloth ran the gamut from smooth cotton plaids of bright orange and blue hues to drab woolens so abrasive they could draw blood from the skin of their wearers. Nineteenth-century American genre paintings convey the spectrum of fabric provisions. For example, Richard Caton Woodville's *War News from Mexico* (1848) features an enslaved man in a substantial red shirt and blue trousers sitting next to a little girl in a white tattered shirttail.[3]

Woodville's red, white, and blue composition might well have attested to the fact that textile manufacturers flying the Union Jack and the Star-Spangled Banner were in bitter competition to provision plantation markets. The commercial interruptions of the Embargo Act of 1807 and the War of 1812 helped develop the American woolens industry, as did the modest protection offered in the tariff legislation of 1816 and 1824. Still, British imports—Welsh plains and Kendal cottons (woolens that had been "cottoned" by having their nap teased upward)—maintained market dominance, especially through long-standing mercantile networks connecting London to Charleston. Imported fabrics helped cotton and rice exporters attain a balance of trade, but they also possessed a dedicated following among planters who considered them field-tested and appropriately inexpensive.[4] As a result, American manufacturers had to break into an existing market, one whose politicization over tariffs and the morality of slavery itself added layers of complexity to the general obstacles of product design, marketing, and distribution. Even after improving their fabrics, lowering their prices, and establishing a network of loyal merchants and planters, the Hazards would hear time and again about the "prejudices" preventing adoption of their fabrics in Southern markets. The story of negro cloth, then, attests to the range of work—that of entrepreneurs and engineers, of planters and politicians, of mill hands and field hands, among others—involved in making markets in the formative era of American capitalism.[5]

By encompassing the overlapping political economies of the Northern mill village, the Southern plantation, and the nation-state itself, negro cloth generates three important interventions into the broader history of American capitalism. The first is a renewed, if reconceived, attention to New England industrialization. The surge of new scholarship on capitalism has foregrounded consumption and financialization, leaving behind the once-indispensable Industrial Revolution and its reorganization of labor, technology, and environment in one small corner of the United States. Perhaps it is correct to discount mechanized factory production as the emblematic feature of early American capitalism, but the emergence of manufacturing in small Massachusetts, Rhode Island, and Connecticut communities reveals an important history of strategic business innovation involving market research, supply chain management, and flexible production.[6] Turning attention from the adoption of advanced machinery to halting processes of experimentation and tinkering, scholars like David Jaffee and Nina E. Lerman have embedded the history of industrialization in the design and production of commonplace goods that summoned diffused forms of expertise and social power into material form. The commodity history of something like negro cloth illuminates the paths of information connecting an enslaved plantation seamstress to a free Rhode Island weaver, making New England industrialization a collaborative venture of national dimensions—albeit one promising radically divergent outcome to participants located differently in space and the social matrix.[7]

Second, by reflecting the intimate relationship of industrialization and plantation agriculture, negro cloth testifies to slavery's central role in American economic development. The history of nineteenth-century capitalism is being rewritten at the intersection of nominally discrete sectional economies whose fortunes were inextricably linked through the interregional flows of capital and commodities. Such links are vivid in the circulation of cotton from plantation to factory to plantation once again in the form of Lowells, the generic label for plain cotton fabric (often in imitation of that milled along the Merrimack) and appearing regularly in plantation account books and runaway advertisements. Northern manufacturers would come to have a stake in the price of cotton comparable to that of their slaveholding customers, and just as next year's cotton crop financed speculation in lands and slaves along the plantation frontier, so too did it shape the prospects of Connecticut tool manufacturers, Massachusetts shoemakers, and the families braiding palm-leaf hats in New Hampshire. Numerous New England communities thrived in the production of hoes, brogans, and negro cloth, and while slavery's importance to U.S. economic development owed to more than the plantation market for manufactured goods, the provisioning trade nonetheless moved the relationship of slavery and capitalism out of the realm of abstract political economy and into specific locations like South Kingstown, Rhode Island, where few families stood outside the carding, spinning, and weaving requiring for making negro cloth.[8]

The third implication for the history of capitalism is the central role of state policy (and perhaps more important, its attendant politics) in shaping the terrain of business and enterprise. Negro cloth played a disproportionately large role in national political economy, especially when viewed from the halls of a Congress devoting its power of taxation to the question of who would dress the nation's slaves. Of all the infant industries whose protection generated rancor in the tariff debates of the 1820s and 1830s, none seemed as "inflammatory"— to quote Virginia's William Archer—as the proposed tax on imported "coarse woolens" for slave clothing. "Must the distress and ruin of the wool growing industry and cloth making interest of the nation go unrelieved," asked Rhode Island representative Tristam Burges, "lest the workers at growing rice, cotton, [and] tobacco might be obliged to wear cloth made by Pennsylvanians, New Yorkers, and Yankees?" Yes, answered the Charleston (S.C.) Chamber of Commerce, for "the duty on the coarser description of woolens is an additional burden on [the Southern planter] in the ratio of the number of slaves he employs in cultivation." The implementation of substantial duties on low-grade raw wool and woolen fabrics in 1828 yielded minimal benefit to Northern manufacturers like the Hazards, but situated their attempt to enter the Southern textile market in a charged political context, one of vital importance to scholars seeking to foreground the nation-state in the history of early American capitalism.[9]

Beginning in the late 1810s and accelerating in the 1820s, manufacturers in Pennsylvania, New York, Massachusetts, and Rhode Island fought for openings in the negro cloth market. Firms aggressively solicited information on the qualities of successful slave textiles, sent experimental fabrics to plantation markets to be tested, and cultivated reliable merchants and slaveholders who would recommend American-made goods to their clients and neighbors. In terms of composition, color, and weave, very little distinguished the textiles produced for markets in Ohio or Veracruz from those they sent to Charleston and Natchez. However, firms scrambled to develop and market a product "made expressly for the Southern market" and then to differentiate their textiles further in hopes of meeting the presumptively different needs of slaveholders and slaves in places like Richmond, Mobile, or Nashville. How did it come to pass, for example, that a Pennsylvania manufacturer might provide a Louisiana planter with goods "particularly adapted to your State"? Or that a Rhode Island firm would conclude that it had finally cracked the code to produce a fabric good enough to sell in Georgia's Sea Islands?[10] The research and development process for negro cloth reveals a network of informants who connected the plantation and factory in ways that are rarely understood in the history of American capitalism. For the Hazards, whose foray into the manufacture of negro cloth organizes this essay, the opportunities and uncertainties of plantation provisioning were both alluring and frustrating. By the mid-1830s, they stumbled on an unprecedented opportunity to produce ready-made clothing for slaves in the new cotton districts of the southwest. The reorientation of the Hazards' business toward ready-made attests to the dexterity of New England manufacturers in developing new products for new markets, but further embeds the history of Northern industrial production in that of the Southern slave plantation. If, as even the most enthusiastic supporters of American manufacturing freely admitted, the United States would need many years to develop the expertise to compete with higher quality British textiles, then low-grade coarse woolens—negro cloth—would serve as the proving ground for the nation's textile industry.

Product Development

How did aspiring negro cloth manufacturers like the Hazards gain entry into the plantation market? Like manufacturers of other provisions such as hoes and shovels, they drew on a network of remote informants to develop a competitive, differentiated product that merited patent protection, that could be marketed in places like Charleston by brand name, and that could credibly be claimed to be "particularly calculated to resist the effects of the cotton plant picking time or the sugar cane crop time."[11] The design history of the Hazards' negro cloth points to a collaborative process involving slaveholders and slaves, wholesalers and other merchandisers, and Northern manufacturers and laborers. It is difficult to attribute a particular innovation—for example, the double twisted cotton warp and single woolen weft of the Hazards' patented double kersey—to a single enterprising Peace Dale weaver, insightful New York dry goods dealer, "scientific" planter, or enslaved seamstress whose voice might only faintly be heard in a letter sent from Georgia to Rhode Island. The Hazards' signature fabric might be rethought as the agglomeration of numerous kinds of social knowledge "made durable," as a function of "distributed problem solving and group learning," or even as the outcome of countless "transactions" between human, plants, and animals, to borrow from scholarship at the intersection of science studies and material culture. While a flock of sheep, the rough stem of a cotton plant, and the heat-retaining potential of wool fibers might ultimately belong in the history of negro cloth, of foremost concern to the Hazards was the "useful knowledge" (a common nineteenth-century category) generated by a far-flung network of informants engaged with one another as coreligionists, relatives, potential business partners, employers and employees, patrons and dependants, owners and slaves. Yet the seemingly transparent flow of information between a Georgia planter and a Rhode Island manufacturer (and recoverable in the massive archive of written correspondence) belies the much wider range of participation in the Hazards' process of product development.[12]

The Hazards first sought guidance from dry goods wholesalers and retailers. In 1818, a Boston acquaintance had advised the Hazards to focus on New York and Philadelphia because mid-Atlantic merchants were more likely to have direct connections to Southern storekeepers, factors, and planters. Introducing Peace Dale fabrics to Southern purchasers in 1821, the Philadelphia firm Wilkins & Black apologized for having to accept lower prices and longer credit terms than the Hazards would have preferred, but offered a consoling observation that "it will certainly be a great advantage to introduce them among the slaveholding states." An urgent letter later that summer insisted that the Hazards send "what Blk & orange & blue you have on hand immediately on receipt of this, as the Southern people begin to make their appearance in our market." Firms like Wilkins & Black could gather information through Southern correspondents, as well as from the planters and factors who made buying trips to Northern cities. These conduits of information brought word that the Hazards' fabric "will make as cheap clothing for negroes as can be obtain'd." Intensifying their efforts to gather mercantile intelligence in New York and Philadelphia, the Hazards plied Anson Blake, a Brooklyn merchant and fellow Quaker, "to obtain what information thee can for us from thy Southern Friends respecting the kind of Goods suitable for their market."[13]

Yet by 1823, the Hazards had begun to eliminate the middleman by opening their own direct lines of communication to merchants in Charleston, Savannah, Richmond, Alexandria, and Baltimore, not to mention in such smaller markets as Huntsville, Alabama and Beaufort, South Carolina. "Should it be in your line of business to assist us in disposing of some negro Cloths at Augusta," the Hazards wrote to a recommended but unacquainted firm, "[we] would thank you to give us such information as you may possess on the subject. What is the colour+width of the article most approved of by the Planters in the neighbourhood? What price should it sell at to meet the views of the purchasers (presuming the quality suits them)?" Such queries were regularly accompanied by money-back guarantees, declarations of improved quality, boasts of accelerating adoptions, and denunciations of rival manufactures whose poor techniques "tend to injure the credit of American Negro Cloth."[14]

From the outset, the Hazards were savvy, if not shrewd, marketers. They embraced a loss-leader strategy, especially if it meant putting their product into the hands of influential planters. In some cases, they manufactured cloth specifically out of raw material purchased from a potential customer. The Hazards incorporated the cotton of one attractive South Carolina planter into their warps precisely as "the means of introducing the goods into his neighbourhood." Likewise, they purchased overpriced wool from another merchant because "it will be of advantage to us in the end." A more general strategy for the Hazards was to reverse-engineer fabrics already on the market using samples provided by Southern merchants. Gabriel Winter sent specimens of a woolen cloth popular in Natchez to the Hazards, who promised to "imitate" it, as well as to produce a cotton cloth "to answer the sample" recently arrived in Rhode Island. Whether meeting with planters passing through Newport or traveling to Charleston to view the British products on the shelves of that city's leading firms, the Hazards anticipated an expanded market for their goods. When cotton prices dipped in 1826 and Charleston merchants reported that some planters had "set their wheels & looms agoing to make their own cloth," the Hazards sought to have fabrics forwarded to rice planters "as the low price of cotton does not effect [sic] them." Success in one region of the South served marketing campaigns in others. Buyers in Savannah were informed that the Hazards had many satisfied customers in New Orleans, while those in New Orleans learned that Sea Island planters had recently abandoned English imports for Rhode Island double kerseys.[15]

As early as 1825, Rowland Hazard recognized the enormous possibilities along the cotton frontier and strove to develop new contacts in New Orleans and Natchez, where planters were "men of business who calculate so as to make money every year which they generally expend again in the purchase of land and negroes."[16] Indeed, as the entrepreneurial planters of the southwest dedicated their slaves to cotton cultivation at an unprecedented pace, New England seamstresses would soon assume clothes-making responsibilities that elsewhere fell to enslaved women themselves. But in their good fortune, the Hazards would also learn that the market for negro cloth was geographically varied: fabrics that flew off the shelves in Charleston collected dust in Mobile; products that satisfied planters along the Mississippi were roundly scorned in the Carolina Lowcountry. Mastering those differences required cultivating more informants, this time on the plantation itself.

Plantation correspondents were among the Hazards' earliest tutors, and they spoke in different idioms than did the urban merchants who also offered detailed assessments of Rhode Island fabrics. Whereas merchants talked about planters, planters talked about slaves, and they did so in ways that confirm a scholarly assessment of slave consumption as the political space "in which slave and master negotiated the limits of each other's power."[17] For example, when Phineas M. Nightingale, a Sea Island rice planter of distinguished Rhode Island lineage, wrote in 1823 to complain of the inadequacies of the Hazards' fabric, he acknowledged, "I should render our negroes discontented and unhappy by giving it to them." Another Sea Island planter, James Hamilton Couper, suggested "the present feeling respecting the treatment of Negroes, does not admit of any retrograde movement in respect to the supply of their wants." Couper spoke in the language of paternalism, the preferred trope for planters to describe how they thought slavery worked, even in the face of abundant evidence it did not. Couper's language was a performance (for himself, his neighbors, his New England business associates, and his slaves), albeit one that belied the process of struggle and negotiation that placed "the comfort of our people" on the agenda of their legal owners. Couper was insistent that New England firms would have to make a better product if they expected success. "From the specimens which I have seen offered for Negro Clothing, our Manufacturers appear impressed with the idea that any thing will do, if it be but sufficiently *coarse* and *very cheap*. This is a mistaken idea," he explained.[18] Implicit was the fact that Northern provisioning firms like the Hazards operated in a classic (and fortuitously named) "moral hazard" situation: hundreds of miles removed from the plantation, they did not assume the risks of "discontented" slaves. One wonders whether the Hazards were able to discern the plantation politics that made slaves into the virtual coauthors of Couper's notion of the "qualities to be sought for in Negro Clothing." Even when slaveholders did not ventriloquize their slaves (e.g., "my people say . . ."), they were nonetheless conceding the reality of slaves as "involuntary consumers" capable of effecting market outcomes.[19]

The Hazards had a nose for scientific planters, men with developed systems of plantation management, reputations for being improvers, and proclivities to experiment. Within their first decade of business, they could count men like Thomas Spalding of Sapelo Island or Dr. Stephen Duncan in Natchez as design collaborators in negro cloth. It did not hurt that these men were also enormously wealthy and capable of purchasing thousands of yards of fabric annually to provision their multiple plantations. To evaluate three new samples from Peace Dale, Spalding distributed them "to three several Boys accustomed to wear out their clothing very frequently." J. Hamilton Couper eagerly tested new versions of the Hazards' product among his slaves. "The result of our trial of the articles will be communicated to you, and it will afford us pleasure should it prove to be favourable," wrote Couper, reiterating his interest in "obtaining some articles of American manufacture, as a substitute for the English plains, and oznaburgs, which we have heretofore employed as winter and summer clothing for our people." The only way to displace the English imports was to combine "strength, weight, and cheapness," never forgetting though that a "certain degree of softness is required." Couper provided specific critiques of the Hazards' products (they "wanted firmness in the twist of the thread and compactness in the weaving; they were sufficiently heavy, but soon chafed out") and helped them settle on a cotton-wool blend for their signature kersey.[20]

Ultimately, in the quest to design a suitable negro cloth, the Hazards went south for themselves. Renting a storefront in Charleston in 1824, Isaac Hazard received a remarkable, if potentially misleading education. Speaking of local planters, Isaac Hazard observed, "We have little Idea how particular such persons are in purchasing for their Negroes. It appears they would sooner purchase an article for their own use that did not exactly suit than for their Negroes." Day after day, Isaac Hazard heard that the slaves were the arbiters of textiles. One planter reported that he "never saw any American cloth that his negroes would wear," advising Hazard that his product "must be very thick and stout or the negroes will complain." Fabric color was another point of contention. Another South Carolina planter came to Hazard looking for an American-made linsey in blue: "It must be blue or their negro woman would not have it," he reported. Perhaps most surprising to Hazard was the planter who "concluded to bring his negroes [to the store] and let them take their choice" of fabrics. And when he did, the group of South Carolina field hands gave Hazard an earful on the liabilities of the cotton-wool fabric being made in Rhode Island.[21] Enslaved people were discerning customers, astutely aware of how different textiles performed under arduous conditions of labor and themselves suffering the direct, physical costs of fabric failures. For scholars following Walter Johnson's call to "understand enslaved people's actions and ideas" within "the material conditions of their enslavement," such exchanges are tantalizing, for they center what another scholar has called "the stuff of slaves' 'politics'" on actual stuff.[22]

Wintering in Charleston and traveling both inland and along the coastline, Isaac Hazard toured plantations to see the handiwork of Rhode Island weavers firsthand. "I went through the cotton fields when they were gathering cotton and to the gin and sorting house and saw the whole operation," he reported to his brother back home after visiting an Ashley River plantation in 1824. Conducting business near Savannah a few years later, Hazard heard complaints that dirty wool marred Rhode Island-made fabrics. "We shall have but few of the *Burr* & *Stick* wool quality for you next season," promised Hazard in response to the "hint" offered by an enslaved child. Hazard's visit to the Sea Islands at the end of 1828 was both gratifying and revelatory. In the vicinity of Darien, "every body appeared to know me and when I handed my letters [of introduction] I was always told they were entirely unnecessary as my name was quite sufficient." Everywhere he looked, there were slaves wearing the Hazards' double kersey fabric. "More of our goods are used in this than in any other neighborhood I have ever been in," he reported home. This trip allowed Hazard to visit the nation's foremost "showcase" plantations such as the enormous Pierce Butler estate (soon to receive the famed Fanny Kemble as reluctant mistress). With guide Roswell King Jr. declaring that his foremost goal was to "make the negroes comfortable and happy," Hazard appeared to confirm a sense of his own undertaking as a form of amelioration, not as the skimming of profit from atop a corrupt system of labor exploitation. The more that slaveholders stressed the urgency of negro cloth in terms of "warmth" and "comfort," the more the Hazards imbued their manufacturing with a philanthropic urgency on behalf of the slave.[23]

What remains unclear is how deeply, if at all, such views were shared by the Rhode Island men and women making their living at the Hazards' looms. Oddly the most opaque contributions to negro cloth came from those working and living in the closest vicinity to the Hazards themselves. Over the first six months of 1821, for example, the brothers contracted Sarah Sweet, Henry Gardner, Frances Albro, and John Castle's wife, among others, to weave in exchange for store credit; later that year, Joseph Potter, an African-American man, arrived on the payroll as a wool carder. Scholarship on textile production has recovered the craft expertise involved in winding yarn on to a warping board or threading a heddle, yet the transfer of tacit knowledge between workers and employers remains elusive. One wonders about the collaboration between, say, Sarah Sweet and Isaac Hazard in attaining the closeness of weave that planters (and implicitly, slaves) demanded from Northern-made woolens. Could Hazard dictate the number of warp ends necessary to satisfy the complaints of a New York merchant? Or did Sweet convey to Hazard what was in the realm of the possible based on her different relationship to the productive process? Greater research is necessary into the Hazards' labor management practices, as well as their own practical knowledge of weaving (rather than merchandising) cloth; but it is nonetheless clear that for the Hazards to enter the negro cloth market, a spectrum of expertise—Sarah Sweet's, an enslaved child's, James Hamilton Couper's, a Philadelphia merchant's, for starters—would accumulate in the fabric itself.[24]

The Tariff Debate

Other kinds of knowledge were being gathered and deployed in the nation's capital just as the Hazards were gaining a footing in the Southern trade at the end of the 1820s. The antebellum tariff debate marked what one historian famously called the "prelude to Civil War," as politicians rehearsed arguments about state power that would lay the groundwork for secession and the federal government's military response.[25] Few policy issues generated as much verbiage in Congress as tariff schedules, for despite the pretense of making national economic policy, almost everyone presumed that import duties were zero-sum such that one state or region's gain would be another's loss. No commodity illustrated this more clearly than negro cloth, a fact obscured by the euphemism used by politicians and customhouse officials: coarse woolens. However, when the term "negro cloth" is substituted, it becomes clear that slave clothing garnered significant attention at the highest levels of government.

On January 17, 1827 Congressional debate began on a hugely protective Woolens Bill that would potentially double duties on coarse imported "plains," which, as described on an official schedule, were "worn generally by sailors, watermen, and by the negroes in the Southern States." It is noteworthy that woolens were singled out for a radically higher tariff only three years after modest protection was offered to a range of American manufactures. Introduced by Rollin Mallary, Vermont's representative and chair of the Committee of Manufactures, the Woolens Bill passed the House (106 to 95) after three weeks of heated debate and proceeded to the Senate for consideration. There the bill stalled and was ultimately tabled in the spring of 1827 with the tie-breaking vote of Senate President John C. Calhoun.[26] In its short life, the bill generated remarkable rhetoric. "After the passage of the tariff of 1824, the People, at least from that section of the country from which I come," explained South Carolina's James Hamilton Jr., "supposed that they were to have a respite, and repose for several years, from the agitations of this vexatious and disgusting topic." While some tariff advocates contended that they were seeking an enforcement remedy for the failure of customhouses to collect the 1824 duties, others cast wool cloth manufacturing as a national interest and lambasted the "hue and cry" coming from "the planting interest." In a tense moment, South Carolina's Thomas Mitchell called out Mallary for having "alluded to the article of negro-cloth." Affronted, Mitchell "[took] this opportunity of informing that gentleman, that the People of the South, in their opposition to a public measure, were never actuated by mercenary motives." The bill's opponents also included some Northern Jacksonians, including New York's Churchill Cambreleng, who called the proposed tariff "a bill for the relief of the incorporated companies of New England." No disagreement came from Virginia's Burwell Bassett: "The great capitalists of the east got up this bill, which will accrue chiefly to their emolument," he told his constituents. An alternative explanation was that the bill originated with Boston merchants who already had "an immense stock of imported cloth on hand." In the Senate, Robert Hayne found an ingenious way of canceling the bill's effects: if the rates on imported coarse cloth would be nearly prohibitive, so too should the rates on the low-grade imported wool that manufacturers like the Hazards purchased for making negro cloth.[27]

The Woolens Bill's failure generated something remarkable in the summer of 1827: a national convention of tariff advocates in Harrisburg, Pennsylvania. This gathering, by one scholar's account, attested to "the organization of the woolen textile industry into a modern lobbying group based on an interstate, interindustry [sic] coalition that included key legislators and the press."[28] The meeting brought together leading economic nationalists, men committed to an American system whose tariffs, banks, internal improvements—and also legalized slavery—would foster national economic development. Hezekiah Niles, publisher of the national paper of record, *Niles' Register*, penned the convention's address. "On the White mountains of New Hampshire we find the sugar of Louisiana, and in the plains beyond the Mississippi the cotton cloths of Rhode

Island are domesticated," he rhapsodized. Negro cloth received specific mention in the proceedings, namely the fact that under tariff protection since 1816, the price to planters of both domestic and foreign coarse fabrics had fallen by as much as a third. Meanwhile, attesting to the magnitude of the market, the report touted the one million pounds of low-grade wool that Boston's Canton Manufacturing Company (an early negro cloth rival of the Hazards') had already imported from Smyrna in only the first five months of 1827.[29]

With the imminent return of a woolens bill to the Congressional floor, the legislation's opponents also sought to marshal public sentiment. During summer and fall 1827, public meetings generated memorials to be sent to Washington. Citizens in South Carolina's Newberry District threatened a boycott on Northern goods. The Alabama General Assembly sent a remonstrance decrying "the proposed woolens bill as a species of oppression little less than legalized pillage on the property of her citizens." The Chamber of Commerce of Charleston, South Carolina offered perhaps the most remarkable petition, equating a tariff on coarse woolens with a tax on slaveholding itself, "an impost on capital under the guise of a tax on consumption"[30]:

> The slave of the Southern planter must be clothed according to that standard of comfort which both interest and feeling prescribe. This is an inevitable tax on his owner, under all circumstances imaginable—in periods of adversity as well as seasons of prosperity—in all conditions of the market for the produce of the labor of the slave. There is this peculiarity, then, which attaches a tax on the consumption of the slave: it is one that cannot be got rid of, even under the most adverse state of things; nor does the burden admit of diminution, as in other taxes on consumption, by a reduction of expenditure; the expense of clothing the slave is brought within the narrowest limits of an economy that is consistent with humanity. All duties, therefore, which enhance the cost of clothing the slave fall with unmitigated pressure on his owner.[31]

The Charleston merchants behind this petition clearly had little anxiety about being seen as mercenary. They departed from the euphemistic "tax on agriculture" argument deployed by antitariff memorialists elsewhere, and acknowledged a woolens tariff as a tax on slavery itself. Tariff revenue, added a group of memorialists from the Fairfield District, was "wrested from the planting class, who are the chief consumers, and who are subjected to the humiliation of seeing the gains which they have honestly acquired transferred, by the magic of enactments, into the pockets of those who grasp at it contrary to every dictate of honesty."[32]

Politicians had already turned their attention to the upcoming presidential contest when the Twentieth Congress convened in late 1827, assuring that the ensuing tariff bill would be a product of election-year scheming, its origins less in sound policymaking and more in legislative gamesmanship intended to saddle opponents with political liabilities. This was especially true in regard to proposed duties on the raw wool used to make slave clothing. Early in the legislative process, the House Committee on Manufactures took testimony from Delaware's E. I. du Pont, Massachusetts's Aaron Tufts, and several other textile producers. Asked specifically about "negro cloths," these manufacturers explained its composition of "the coarsest kind" of wool imported from Smyrna, Adrianople, and Buenos Aires. They contended that American flocks generated a fiber better than what was necessary to make "negro clothing," and to that end, no advantage would come to any American grower by limiting the importation of low-grade raw wool.[33] Nonetheless, exclusionary rates were reported out of committee, which some saw as a poison pill introduced by antitariff forces to split New England's mercantile and manufacturing interests. Others believed that the bill was designed to bolster Andrew Jackson's credibility where he needed it (the mid-Atlantic) and to undermine John Quincy Adams's where he could not afford to lose it (New England). Yet others contended that the bill was never intended to pass, especially as Southern legislators wrote enormous duties into the bill as to make it so burdensome that the very premise of protective tariffs would forever be discredited.[34]

The proposed legislation effectively doubled the cost of a pound of low-grade wool, and made it cheaper to import English cloth, even when it too was subject to a hefty tariff. Several petitioners foresaw the end of American negro cloth production: "We doubt the policy of excluding the Smyrna wool and that of a similar description, inasmuch as we understand it to be used (and capable of *little* if of any other use) in the coarser kinds of negro clothing," argued an assembly of Pennsylvania sheep ranchers. At the same time, Pennsylvania representative James Stevenson contended that rates on imported negro cloth needed to be held low on behalf of the slave: "[W]ill those who feel, or affect to feel, superior sympathy, forget that it may be an act of wide-spreading practical humanity to keep down the value of the clothing usually bestowed?" Should the price of negro cloth be held too high, it would "tempt the master to stint the man," Stevenson added. However, in a testament to the sectional recriminations that would help shape Jackson's election later in the year, Rhode Island's Tristam Burges berated the representatives from Pennsylvania and New York for saddling New England with too high a tariff on raw wool and too low a tariff on imported textiles "as to enable Southern slavery to be clothed in the woollens of foreign looms." Complaints like those of Burges altered the bill's movement through the Senate, resulting in Daniel Webster's timely amendment to increase the duties on imported negro cloth. The bill secured the minimum support it needed from New Englanders to pass, while retaining its substantial backing from mid-Atlantic and western legislators.[35]

Thus the "Tariff of Abominations" became law, setting off a political crisis as South Carolinians eventually claimed the right to "nullify" federal law. Not surprisingly, the slaveholding advocates of "States' Rights" waged their campaign on the plane of abstract political theory, not in the mundane realm of plantations' rising provisioning costs. However, protectionists regularly invoked negro cloth in their dismissal of antitariff arguments, and editor Hezekiah Niles scarcely missed an opportunity to contest the claim that the tariff had driven up the price of slave clothing. The rhetorical invocations of negro cloth in the Nullification debate and the ensuing renegotiation of tariff rates deserve substantially more attention, but suffice it to say, numerous Congressional floor speeches used slave clothing to denounce greedy Northern manufacturers or idle Southern slaveholders. John Quincy Adams penned a particularly doleful, if sarcastic, report for the House Committee on Manufactures in 1832, incredulous that South Carolinians would see themselves more allied with British manufacturers than their own countrymen. In Adams's parody, the antitariff slaveholder says, to the Northerner, "I will not bear a tax upon the negro cloths of Manchester to enable you to supply me the same article equally cheap because your gain must be my loss." This zero-sum logic appeared to Adams as a Hobbesian "satire on human nature." Floor debates over the Tariff of 1832 and the Compromise Tariff of 1833 witnessed several proposals to maintain tariffs on everything *but* negro clothing and cotton bagging. "Find what are the articles exclusively of Southern consumption and important to the Southern economy," urged Massachusetts's Rufus Choate, and exempt them. Two items immediately came to mind: "negro clothing" and "cotton bagging" for wrapping bales of slave-picked cotton for export. "For so much let there be no tariff and let them be fabricated in England, that the American Union may be preserved." However, by this point, Southern congressmen could hardly accept such a deal without undermining their principled opposition to protective tariffs in the abstract.[36]

Throughout the tariff debate, Southerners claimed they would be forced to manufacture provisions for themselves, especially once they implemented local nonconsumption pacts to boycott Northern goods. "We import a very large amount of manufactures from the Northern States, which every principle of sound policy, and every dictate of patriotism, will urge us to make within ourselves, if this bill shall become a law," South Carolina's George McDuffie had warned in 1828, drawing attention to some $500,000 of "negro shoes" imported annually into his state and neighboring Georgia. Public meetings throughout South Carolina in the wake of the 1828 tariff resolved "to purchase no woollen goods manufactured North of the Potomac" or to "rely, as much as possible, on the productions of our own labor and industry for the articles of our consumption."[37]

Such threats buoyed the prospects of the South's cadre of aspiring manu-facturers, struggling to overcome a substantial regional bias against industrial pursuit. Manufacturing "require[s] a peculiar way of thinking on subjects of economy,—and a yet more peculiar art in practicing it, which can seldom be imbibed in these Southern States," warned the *Southern Agriculturalist and Register of Rural Affairs* in an 1828 editorial denouncing the tariff but warning fellow resisters "not to meddle with manufacturing for profit, or to be con-cerned in manufactories, even for the supply of their own plantations." While a famed generation of Southern entrepreneurs would emerge in the late 1830s and 1840s, a cadre of earlier manufacturing advocates had used the tariff de-bates to foster regional self-sufficiency.[38] North Carolina's Charles Fisher im-plored legislators in his state to grant acts of incorporation for manufacturing companies. "Look to Waltham, to Taunton, to Patterson, Manyunk, and a hundred other places in New England and Northern States, where this system is diffusing wealth and prosperity, and improving the moral condition of soci-ety," Fisher urged in hopes of reversing North Carolina's economic stagnation. Already Henry A. Donaldson's Fayetteville Manufacturing Company was producing cotton yarn, but opportunities abounded for the production of fab-ric, especially utilizing the state's black population. The presumptive incapac-ity of slaves to perform factory labor was nothing more than the propaganda of Northern firms seeking to discourage Southern investment in manufactur-ing, explained Fisher. "With the blacks, there is no turning out for wages, and no time lost in visiting musters, and other public exhibitions," all of which recommended their use over white operatives.[39]

The South Carolina manufactory of David Rogerson Williams had been using slave labor since the 1810s and gained national attention from Hezekiah Niles, who instructed disgruntled planters to purchase negro cloth from Williams "at prices most essentially anti-tariff." A congressman, general, and governor, Williams opposed the tariff, but held even less sympathy for his disunionist neighbors. "Let us then manufacture our own clothes, and be wise enough to wear them," he implored in public. But in private, Williams had little faith that local planters would buy Southern: "99 out of 100 go for cheapness wholly." As a result, he lamented, "we may preach, till the cows come home about staple and tariff imposers, &c. &c.; if we do not sell cheaper we shall have no preference; if only as cheap we stand on the same foot, with 'our brethren of the north.'" Despite Williams's success, the inability—or inadvisability—of the South manufacturing for itself remained a key argument of those opposing the tariff on negro cloth. "They have not, they cannot, in self-defence [*sic*] erect manu-facturing establishments. The nature of their population forbids it," asserted the report of an 1832 "free trade" convention.[40]

Those like Williams who thought otherwise were notable for their connection to the center of the American negro cloth industry: Rhode Island. Williams had been educated at Brown University, married the daughter of one of Providence's leading mercantile families, gathered intelligence on manufacturing during an 1805 visit to Rhode Island, and perhaps most important, recruited local operatives and mechanics to bring their expertise south. A group of Rhode Island migrants arrived in Spartanburg District in the 1810s to begin making cotton yarn, while the orphaned William Bates came from Pawtucket in 1819, spent a decade working in piedmont-area mills, and then began work on Batesville in the early 1830s. And as the tariff controversy spawned new interest in Southern industry, the Hazards emerged as useful informants to aspiring manufacturers. They offered substantial technical advice to E. S. Hoppin of Wilkes County, Georgia, and also put him in touch with Peyton H. Skipwith, a Tennessee manufacturer who was related by marriage to the family of General Nathanael Greene of Rhode Island. To John E. Colhoun of Pendleton, South Carolina, the Hazards provided one of their employees, Daniel Rodman, on contract to assist in a woolen blanket-making operation. "I shall take pleasure in giving you all the Facilities in my Power to accomplish your objects," wrote Isaac warmly, inviting Colhoun to spend the following summer in Newport, where he could vacation and "look among the manufacturers and machinists."[41]

Technology transfer appears to be a strange strategy for a fledgling New England textile enterprise. Like many other woolen manufacturers, the Hazards suffered with the high tariff on raw wool, and the ensuing political controversy lost them a number of existing customers in South Carolina. Yet they eagerly shared their expertise with potential rivals, mapping a new circuit of information between North and South in the manufacture of negro cloth. Their motives remained unstated. Textile production was widely understood to progress through evolutionary stages, with manufacturers advancing from coarser to finer fabric as they perfected their machinery, trained their workers, and coordinated their supply chain. However, the Hazards were nowhere close to leaving low-grade woolens behind in favor of better products such as the broadcloth to which so many other manufacturers aspired. Indeed, their commitment to the Southern market would only intensify over the next decade, especially once the tariff issue appeared to settle.

Mastering the Market

For the Hazards, the challenge of the late 1820s and early 1830s was navigating a business climate made uncertain by the tariff controversy. Well before the proposed Woolens Bill, the so-called Tariff of Abominations, or the Nullification crisis, the Hazards were being called to account for the tariff. One Ashley River planter told Isaac Hazard in 1824 that "a number of his Friends had concluded to buy American goods this year but the Tariff bill having passed they had re-solved not to use them at any rate." "I believe many persons here are in favor of a separation of the Union and if such an event should take place, we shall loose [*sic*] our markets," Isaac wrote with alarm to his brother. As policy debates intensified, the Hazards sought to assure South Carolina customers of their own antitariff credentials. "We are opposed to the Tariff, but do not think it will have the effect upon Domestics, generally supposed," they explained to a Charleston correspondent, noting that "additional duties would increase com-petition to our injury." Sounding all the right notes, they worried aloud about the costs of an enlarged state. "Excessive duties will so change things as to re-quire numerous officers, Navy &c. & heavy Taxes," which meant that "the Tar-iff will increase the price of woollens but not to the exclusive Benefit of us to the North as you think at the South." One Charleston merchant kept a letter from the Hazards on file to share with skeptical customers. "Col. Cross was in my store yesterday and I shewed him what you had written on the subjects; he was much pleased to find your sentiments corresponding with his own," re-ported James McCarter, adding that the letter "has been of some service to me in combatting the silly arguments of some of our Carolinian gentry who are constantly harping about the 'South paying tribute to the North' and similar expressions." For the Hazards, instability in Washington, D.C. undermined their decision-making, as the constant potential for rate revisions interrupted the certainty of their supply chain. And of course, political strife harmed sales in their largest markets. "As manufacturers we would prefer being left alone by Government," they protested.[42]

After writing soothing letters to planters and encouraging letters to mer-chants, the Hazards sent illicit ones to eastern Mediterranean and European merchants as they tried to circumvent the duty on low-grade wool. Isaac had located a loophole: "I can find but one list of duties that mentions matresses," he informed Rowland at the start of 1828, ". . . but the Tariff furnished by the Treasury Department to the Custom House at Savannah does not mention them." Accordingly, they sought to contract for 100,000 lbs. of wool in the form of "negro mattresses." They instructed their Smyrna supplier to make 500 mattresses—each filled with upward of 150 lbs. of raw wool—"in the cheapest possible manner[,] the cloth just sewed together stitched through with strong twine in few places." Another order for slightly disguised bags of wool went to Gothenburg in Sweden. This was part of a specific strategy to enact, in the Haz-ards' own words, "various perplexing evasions of the Tariff Law."[43]

As the 1828 tariff went into operation, the Hazards suffered from the high cost of raw wool, going so far as to import British wool yarn made cheaper by a lower duty. They caught a break when their major rival, the Canton Manufac-turing Company outside of Boston, reoriented its production of coarse wool-ens for the Northern market. They were also lucky to have preexisting markets in Louisiana where the tariff was not nearly so unpopular as to elicit boycotts of Northern goods. The more dicey markets appeared in South Carolina, the more they sought to cultivate new customers on the cotton frontier. Nonetheless, the impossibly high price of raw wool was cause for despair. "[W]e do not expect to buy another pound this year and shall cease to make Negro Cloths very soon," they told a South Carolina friend on an unhappy Independence Day in 1828. The complexity of the tariff schedule closed other opportunities as well. For example, the Hazards had begun to make blankets for the Southern market, but as the cost of wool skyrocketed, they were quickly undersold by English blanket manufacturers whose product was relatively undertaxed. "The new Tariff will have we fear a very unfavorable effect upon the manufacturers of course woolens," they told anyone who would listen, warning "that the manufacturers+Northern+Eastern people generally will suffer by the measure." Within a year, the Hazards had been forced into bankruptcy, prompting a reorganization of their enterprise, bringing in new partners among a wider network of family in Rhode Island.[44]

Despite suspending payments and having their firm put into assignment, the Hazards remained convinced of the lucrative opportunities in plantation provisioning. Once "we can get our old most disastrous affairs arranged," they told one customer, "we expect to continue the manufacture of negro cloths." Rising wool prices on the global market were affecting British manufacturers as well, and as the cost of imported fabrics rose (all the more so with the help of the tariff), American manufacturers proved competitive—especially as competitors disappeared. "[O]ur Family are making half or more of all that are made in the Northern states," they told a Savannah merchant. "This year it has paid a fair profit[;] last year it was ruinous." The Hazards had largely recovered from the tariff by 1830, "as tho' it never had been passed." But the Nullification crisis undermined their gains. "What effect political excitements, which is increasing, will have on sales of negro cloths of Northern fabrics it is yet impossible to surmise," advised William Ravenel, a Charleston merchant, in June 1832, warning "there is no telling how soon the Union may be dissolved." By December, Ravenel was even more direct: "I must however advise you not to ship at this time but to wait until we can discover the course that nullification will probably take."[45]

Nullification may have nudged the Hazards toward their most ambitious strategy yet: ready-made clothing for the plantation frontier. Ready-made shirts, pants, frocks, and jackets were a bold gamble against the traditional allocation of women's plantation labor toward clothing manufacturing, but a move nonetheless suited to the culture of the cotton frontier. Ready-made slave clothing sat on merchants' shelves in Charleston, but proved irresistible in Mississippi and Louisiana, especially as influential planters became early adopters. Taking advantage of the ever-intensifying allocation of slave labor to cotton production in the southwest, the Hazards contracted with the largest planters in the Mississippi River Valley, and cemented their customer base with annual sales visits. Once again, a range of knowledge and expertise came together in the jackets and frocks fabricated in Rhode Island for plantation wear. And more than ever before, the lives and livelihoods of free and slave would be intertwined within American capitalism.

Notes

1. The author is grateful for discussions about this paper with audiences at Georgetown University, Harvard University, the Massachusetts Historical Society, the University of Michigan, the New School for Social Research, the University of Tennessee, Wesleyan University, and the Zuckerman Salon, as well as for specific feedback from Chandra Manning, David Quigley, Leonard Rosenband, Calvin Schermerhorn, Ashli White, and Jeremy Zallen.

2. Isaac Peace Hazard [hereafter IPH] to Anson Blake, September 10, 1822, Peace Dale Manufacturing Company Records, Mss 483, sg 36, Box 1, folder 1, Rhode Island Historical Society, Providence, R.I. [hereafter PDMC-RIHS]; *Statistics of the Woollen Manufactories in the United States* (New York: W. H. Graham, 1845), 33–39; Frederick Law Olmsted, *The Cotton Kingdom: A Traveller's Observations on Cotton and Slavery in the American Slave States*, 2nd ed. (New York: Mason Brothers, 1862), 1:105. For an introduction to the Hazards' business, see Susan Oba, "'Mostly Made, Especially for this Purpose, in Providence, R.I.': The Rhode Island Negro Cloth Industry" (honors thesis, Brown University, 2006); Christy Clark-Pujara, "The Business of Slavery and Antislavery Sentiment: The Case of Rowland Gibson Hazard—An Antislavery 'Negro Cloth' Dealer," *Rhode Island History* 71, no. 2 (Summer/Fall 2013): 35–55. For the geography of Rhode Island's provisioning trade, see Seth Rockman, "Slavery and Abolition along the Blackstone," in *A Landscape of Industry: An Industrial History of the Blackstone Valley*, ed. Worcester Historical Museum (Lebanon, N.H.: University Press of New England, 2009), 110–31.

3. IPH to James Hamilton, April 8, 1823, Isaac P. Hazard Papers, Mss 483, sg 12, Box 1, folder 9, RIHS [hereafter IPH-RIHS]. For the history of slave textiles, see Chris Evans, "Negro Cloth," in *World of a Slave: Encyclopedia of the Material Life of Slaves in the United States*, ed. Martha B. Katz-Hyman and Kym S. Rice (Santa Barbara, Calif.: Greenwood, 2011), 351–53; Robert S. DuPlessis, *The Material Atlantic: Clothing, Commerce, and Colonization in the Atlantic World, 1650–1800* (New York: Cambridge University Press, 2016), chap. 4; Karol K. Weaver, "Fashioning Freedom: Slave Seamstresses in the Atlantic World," *Journal of Women's History* 24, no. 1 (Spring 2012): 44–59; Linda Baumgarten, "Plains, Plaid and Cotton: Woolens for Slave Clothing," *Ars Textrina* 15 (July 1991): 203–22; Madelyn Shaw, "Slave Cloth and Clothing Slaves: Craftsmanship, Commerce, and Industry," *Journal of Early Southern Decorative Arts* 33 (2012), http://www.mesdajournal.org/2012/slave-cloth-clothing-slaves-craftsmanship-commerce-industry/; Gerilyn G. Tandberg, "Field Hand Clothing in Louisiana and Mississippi During the Ante-Bellum Period," *Dress* 6, no. 1 (1980): 89–103; Helen Bradley Foster, *"New Raiments of Self"*: *African American Clothing in the Antebellum South* (Oxford: Berg, 1997); Katie Knowles, "Fashioning Slavery: Slaves and Clothing in the U.S. South, 1830–1865" (PhD diss., Rice University, Houston, Texas, 2014). On visual representation,

see Maurie D. McInnis, *Slaves Waiting for Sale: Abolitionist Art and the American Slave Trade* (Chicago: University of Chicago Press, 2011); Justin P. Wolff, *Richard Caton Woodville: American Painter, Artful Dodger* (Princeton, N.J.: Princeton University Press, 2002), 107–9.

4. George H. Gibson, "The Mississippi Market for Woolen Goods: An 1822 Analysis," *Journal of Southern History* 31, no. 1 (February 1965): 80–90; Chris Evans, *Slave Wales: The Welsh and Atlantic Slavery, 1660–1850* (Cardiff: University of Wales Press, 2010), 46–54.

5. This article draws on analytical approaches put forward in Paul Duguid, "Networks and Knowledge: The Beginning and End of the Port Commodity Chain, 1703–1860," *Business History Review* 79, no. 3 (Autumn 2005): 493–526; Charles F. Sabel and Jonathan Zeitlin, "Stories, Strategies, Structures: Rethinking Historical Alternatives to Mass Production," in *World of Possibilities: Flexibility and Mass Production in Western Industrialization*, ed. Charles Sabel and Jonathan Zeitlin (New York: Cambridge University Press, 1997), 1–33; Chris Evans, "The Plantation Hoe: The Rise and Fall of an Atlantic Commodity, 1650–1850," *William and Mary Quarterly* 69, no. 1 (January 2012): 71–100.

6. A scholarly generation ago, the new labor history had made New England industrialization central to the "transition to capitalism" in such works as Paul G. Faler, *Mechanics and Manufacturers in the Early Industrial Revolution: Lynn, Massachusetts, 1780–1860* (Albany: State University of New York Press, 1981); Mary H. Blewett, *Men, Women, and Work: Class, Gender, and Protest in the New England Shoe Industry, 1780–1910* (Urbana: University of Illinois Press, 1988); and Thomas Dublin, *Transforming Women's Work: New England Lives in the Industrial Revolution* (Ithaca, N.Y.: Cornell University Press, 1994). Historians of technology had also given a place of primary importance to New England: David A. Hounshell, *From the American System to Mass Production, 1800–1932: The Development of Manufacturing Technology in the United States* (Baltimore: Johns Hopkins University Press, 1984); Donald R. Hoke, *Ingenious Yankees: The Rise of the American System of Manufactures in the Private Sector* (New York: Columbia University Press, 1990); Carolyn C. Cooper, *Shaping Invention: Thomas Blanchard's Machinery and Patent Management in Nineteenth-Century America* (New York: Columbia University Press, 1991). To be sure, New England inventors, entrepreneurs, and the Industrial Revolution never disappeared from the historiography: Janet Siskind, *Rum and Axes: The Rise of a Connecticut Merchant Family, 1795–1850* (Ithaca, N.Y.: Cornell University Press, 2002); David R. Meyer, *The Roots of American Industrialization* (Baltimore, Md.: Johns Hopkins University Press, 2003); Barbara M. Tucker, *Industrializing Antebellum America: The Rise of Manufacturing Entrepreneurs in the Early Republic* (New York: Palgrave Macmillan, 2008); Anthony J. Connors, *Ingenious Machinists: Two Inventive Lives from the American Industrial Revolution* (Albany: State University of New York Press, 2014); Lindsay Schakenbach Regele, "Manufacturing Advantage: War, the State, and the Origins of American Industry," *Enterprise & Society* 17, no. 4 (2016): 721–33. For histories of industrialization more generally that bridge production and a wider range of business practices, see Carlo Poni, "Fashion as Flexible Production: The Strategies of the Lyons Silk Merchants in the Eighteenth Century," in Sabel and Zeitlin, *World of Possibilities*, 37–74; Jeff Horn, Leonard N. Rosenband, and Merritt Roe Smith, eds., *Reconceptualizing the Industrial Revolution* (Cambridge, Mass.: MIT Press, 2010).

7. David Jaffee, *A New Nation of Goods: The Material Culture of Early America* (Philadelphia: University of Pennsylvania Press, 2010); Nina E. Lerman, "Categories of Difference, Categories of Power: Bringing Gender and Race to the History of Technology,"

Technology and Culture 51, no. 4 (October 2010): 893–918. More generally, see Kenneth Lipartito, "Reassembling the Economic: New Departures in Historical Materialism," *American Historical Review* 121, no. 1 (February 2016): 101–39, as well as note 12, below.

8. Sven Beckert and Seth Rockman, eds., *Slavery's Capitalism: A New History of American Economic Development* (Philadelphia: University of Pennsylvania Press, 2016); Ronald Bailey, "The Slave(ry) Trade and the Development of Capitalism in the United States: The Textile Industry in New England," *Social Science History* 14, no. 3 (Autumn 1990): 373–414; Martin H. Blatt and David Roediger, eds., *The Meaning of Slavery in the North* (New York: Garland, 1998); Anne Farrow, Joel Lang, and Jennifer Frank, *Complicity: How the North Promoted, Prolonged, and Profited from Slavery* (New York: Ballantine Books, 2005); Calvin Schermerhorn, *The Business of Slavery and the Rise of American Capitalism, 1815–1860* (New Haven, Conn.: Yale University Press, 2015); Christy Clark-Pujara, *Dark Work: The Business of Slavery in Rhode Island* (New York: New York University Press, 2016). Economic historians have had difficulty agreeing on the extent to which southern demand propelled northern industrial development. For a reasonable summation of the early debate, see Paul J. Uselding, "A Note on the Inter-Regional Trade in Manufactures in 1840," *Journal of Economic History* 36, no. 2 (1976): 428–35. My approach is consistent with Uselding's recognition that for certain industries it makes less sense to look at aggregate demand than at the ways southern markets stimulated northern industry "via technology transfers, scale, learning, and other dynamic effects" (435). On provisioning in a broader context, see Bertie Mandelblatt, "A Transatlantic Commodity: Irish Salt Beef in the French Atlantic World," *History Workshop Journal* 63, no. 1 (2007): 18–47; Bertie Mandelblatt, "'Beans from *Rochel* and Manioc from *Prince's Island*': West Africa, French Atlantic Commodity Circuits, and the Provisioning of the French Middle Passage," *History of European Ideas* 34, no. 4 (2008): 411–23; Evans, *Slave Wales*; Eric B. Kimball, "'An essential Link, in a vast Chain': New England and the West Indies, 1700–1775" (PhD diss., University of Pittsburgh, 2009).

9. 3 *Cong. Deb.* 750 (1829), "No. 808. Against Increase of Duties on Imports," *American State Papers: Finance*, 5:708; Tristam Burges, *Speech of Mr. Burges, of Rhode Island, in Committee of the Whole on the State of the Union, March 29, 1828, on Mr. Mallary's Motion to Amend the Bill on Wool and Woolens* (Washington, D.C.: Peter Force, 1828), 19. For efforts to take the tariff debate seriously, see Brian Schoen, *The Fragile Fabric of Union: Cotton, Federal Politics, and the Global Origins of the Civil War* (Baltimore, Md.: Johns Hopkins University Press, 2009), 100–147; Nicholas Greenwood Onuf and Peter Onuf, *Nations, Markets, and War: Modern History and the American Civil War* (Charlottesville: University of Virginia Press, 2006); Daniel Peart, "Looking Beyond Parties and Elections: The Making of United States Tariff Policy during the Early 1820s," *Journal of the Early Republic* 33, no. 1 (Spring 2013): 87–108. On why legislative debate and public discourse matter in evaluating the role of the state in capitalism, see Vivien A. Schmidt, "Putting the Political Back into Political Economy by Bringing the State Back in Yet Again," *World Politics* 61, no. 3 (July 2009): 516–46. For the state in early American capitalism, see Richard R. John, ed., *Ruling Passions: Political Economy in Nineteenth-Century America* (University Park: Pennsylvania State University Press, 2006); Brian Balogh, *A Government out of Sight: The Mystery of National Authority in Nineteenth-Century America* (New York: Cambridge University Press, 2009); Gautham Rao, *National Duties: Customhouses and the Making of the American State* (Chicago: University of Chicago Press, 2016).

10. William R. Rodman to William Kerner & Co., April 14, 1824; to Jonathan Hagan & Co., March 8, 1827, William R. Rodman Letterbook, 1806–1835, ms. N-805, Massachusetts Historical Society, Boston, Mass.; IPH to James A. Maxwell, May 28, 1827, Box 1, folder 3, PDMC-RIHS.

11. For the Hazards' double kersey and its patent, see Rowland Gibson Hazard [hereafter RGH] to IPH, October 30, November 16, December 9, 1828, Box 1, folder 25, IPH-RIHS. Unfortunately, the patent application itself (granted December 6, 1828) does not survive. For branded marketing, see the "Wm. Y. Ripley Dry Goods Store, No. 324 King-Street, Charleston, SC" card, undated, Box 1, folder 26, PDMC-RIHS. IPH to William Jemieson Jr., September 27, 1832, *Letterbook, Vol. 147*, Peace Dale Manufacturing Company, Historical Collections, Baker Library, Harvard Business School, Boston, Mass. [hereafter PDMC-BL] ("calculated").

12. Timothy Webmoor and Christopher L. Witmore, "Things Are Us! A Commentary on Human/Things Relations under the Banner of a 'Social' Archaeology," *Norwegian Archaeological Review* 41, no. 1 (2008): 64 ("durable," "transactions"); Chandra Mukerji, "Cartography, Entrepreneurialism, and Power in the Reign of Louis XIV," in *Merchants and Marvels: Commerce, Science, and Art in Early Modern Europe*, ed. Pamela H. Smith and Paula Findlen (New York: Routledge, 2002), 260 ("distributed problem solving and group learning"). On creole technologies and slave expertise, see Angela Lakwete, *Inventing the Cotton Gin: Machine and Myth in Antebellum America* (Baltimore, Md.: Johns Hopkins University Press, 2003); Daniel B. Rood, *The Reinvention of Atlantic Slavery: Technology, Labor, Race, and Capitalism in the Greater Caribbean* (New York: Oxford University Press, 2017); Gloria Seaman Allen, "Slaves as Textile Artisans: Documentary Evidence for the Chesapeake Region," *Uncoverings: Research Papers of the American Quilt Study Group* 22 (2001): 1–36.

13. Nathan Willcox to IPH, January 1, 1818, Box 1, folder 1, IPH-RIHS; Wilkins & Black to IPH, July 2, September 4, 1821, Box 1, folder 4, IPH-RIHS; IPH to Anson Blake, September 10, 1822, Letterbook, Box 1, folder 1, PDMC-RIHS.

14. IPH to Megrath and Fitzsimmons, February 4, 1827, Box 8, folder 15, IPH-RIHS; IPH to Andrew McDowall August 3, 1826, Letterbook, Box 1, folder 3, PDMC-RIHS.

15. IPH to William Y. Ripley, June 17, 1826, Letterbook, Box 1, folder 3, PDMC-RIHS (cotton deal); IPH to RGH, December 23, 1825, Isaac Peace Hazard Papers, folder 1, South Caroliniana Library, University of South Carolina, Columbia, S.C. [hereafter IPH-SCL] (wool deal); IPH to Gabriel Winter, March 23, 1823, Box 1, folder 1, PDMC-RIHS (specimens); William Y. Ripley to IPH and RGH, May 31, 1826, Box 1, folder 16, IPH-RIHS (looms); IPH to William Y. Ripley, August 8, 1826, Letterbook, Box 1, folder 3, PDMC-RIHS (rice); IPH to J. B. Herbert & Co., October 10, 1827, Letterbook, Box 1, folder 3, PDMC-RIHS (Savannah); IPH to D. W. Urquhart, June 6, 1826, Box 1, folder 3, PDMC-RIHS (New Orleans).

16. RGH to IPH, January 23, 1825, Box 1, folder 13, IPH-RIHS.

17. Kathleen M. Hilliard, *Masters, Slaves, and Exchange: Power's Purchase in the Old South* (New York: Cambridge University Press, 2014), 2.

18. P. M. Nightingale to IPH, December 6, 1823, Box 1, folder 10, IPH-RIHS; J. Hamilton Couper to IPH, November 12, 1823, Box 1, folder 10, IPH-RIHS. For Couper, see John Solomon Otto, *Cannon's Point Plantation, 1794–1860: Living Conditions and Status Patterns in the Old South* (Orlando, Fl.: Academic, 1984); and for a credulous interpretation of his "paternalism," James E. Bagwell, *Rice Gold: James Hamilton Couper and Plantation Life on the Georgia Coast* (Macon, Ga.: Mercer University Press, 2000).

19. For "involuntary consumers," see John Styles, "Lodging at the Old Bailey: Lodgings and Their Furnishing in Eighteenth-Century London," in *Gender, Taste, and Material Culture in Britain and North America, 1700–1830*, ed. John Styles and Amanda Vickery (New Haven, Conn.: Yale University Press, 2006), 62; see also Sophie White, "Geographies of Slave Consumption: French Colonial Louisiana and a World of Goods," *Winterthur Portfolio* 45, no. 2/3 (Summer/Autumn 2011): 229–48.

20. On scientific planters, see Martha Jane Brazy, *An American Planter: Stephen Duncan of Antebellum Natchez and New York* (Baton Rouge: Louisiana State University Press, 2006); E. Merton Coulter, *Thomas Spalding of Sapelo* (Baton Rouge: Louisiana State University Press, 1940); Spalding to IPH, October 8, 1833, Box 1, folder 33, IPH-RIHS; Couper to IPH, November 12, 1823, Box 1, folder 10, IPH-RIHS.

21. IPH to RGH, February 27, 1824 ("no idea" and "blue"); February 21, 1824 ("never saw"), December 5, 1824 ("take their choice"), Rowland G. and Caroline (Newbold) Hazard Papers, Mss 483, sg 5, Box 1, folder 2, RIHS [hereafter RGH-RIHS].

22. Walter Johnson, "Agency," in *Slavery's Ghost: The Problem of Freedom in the Age of Emancipation*, ed. Richard J. Follett, Eric Foner, and Walter Johnson (Baltimore, Md.: Johns Hopkins University Press, 2011, 28; Steven Hahn, *A Nation Under Our Feet: Black Politics Struggles in the Rural South from Slavery to the Great Migration* (Cambridge, Mass.: Belknap Press of Harvard University Press, 2003), 15.

23. IPH to RGH, December 5, 1824, Box 1, folder 2, RGH-RIHS; IPH to James A. Maxwell, May 28, 1827, Box 1, folder 3, PDMC-RIHS; IPH to RGH, December 29, 1828, Box 1, folder 10, RGH-RIHS; IPH to RGH, January 8, 1829, Box 1, folder 12, RGH-RIHS.

24. On the expertise involved in textile production (presented with a generosity to the uninitiated), see Adrienne D. Hood, *The Weaver's Craft: Cloth, Commerce, and Industry in Early Pennsylvania* (Philadelphia: University of Pennsylvania Press, 2003), 85–111; Gail Fowler Mohanty, *Labor and Laborers of the Loom: Mechanization and Handloom Weavers, 1780–1840* (New York: Routledge, 2006) 27–44, 176–186. Ultimately this seems to beg the classic question in capitalist labor relations (and ensuing labor history) regarding how to excise the manager's brains from under the workman's cap (with apologies to both Big Bill Haywood and David Montgomery). IPH to James A. Maxwell, May 28, 1827, Box 1, folder 3, PDMC-RIHS; IPH to Maxwell, October 11, 1823, Box 1, folder 1, PDMC-RIHS; Weaving and Carding Accounts, 1821, Box 5, folder 9, IPH-RIHS.

25. William W. Freehling, *Prelude to Civil War: The Nullification Controversy in South Carolina, 1816–1836* (New York: Harper and Row, 1966).

26. 3 *Cong. Deb.* 731, 1099 (1829); "Importations of Sheep's Wool on the Skin," Committed to the House of Representatives, January 17, 1827, No. 768, *American State Papers: Finance*, 5:594.

27. 3 *Cong. Deb.*, quotes on 779, 866, 871, 1021, 1054; Bassett, as quoted in Noble E. Cunningham, Jr., ed., *Circular Letters of Congressmen to their Constituents, 1789–1829*, vol. 3, *Fifteenth Congress–Twentieth Congress, 1817–1829* (Chapel Hill: University of North Carolina Press for the Institute of Early American History and Culture, 1978), 1369.

28. Grant D. Forsyth, "Special Interest Protectionism and the Antebellum Woolen Textile Industry: A Contemporary Issue in a Historical Context," *American Journal of Economics and Sociology* 65, no. 5 (November 2006): 1035.

29. *General Convention, of Agriculturalists and Manufacturers, and Others Friendly to the Encouragement and Support of the Domestic Industry of the United States* (Baltimore, 1827), 15, 47, 57. The Harrisburg Convention (as it was known) attracted a remarkable assemblage of delegates, including Mathew Carey, Abbott Lawrence, and Alvan Stew-

art (whose pre-abolitionist career deserves more study). On slavery in the Whig (or proto-Whig) political economy, see Andrew Shankman, "Capitalism, Slavery, and the New Epoch: Mathew Carey's 1819" in Beckert and Rockman, *Slavery's Capitalism*, 243–61. There was some New England opposition to the Harrisburg Convention tariff proposals, notably in *Report of a Committee of the Citizens of Boston and Vicinity, Opposed to a Further Increase of Duties on Importations* (Boston: Nathan Hale, 1827).

30. No. 862, *American State Papers: Finance*, 5:876; No. 847, 5:849; No. 808, 5:708.

31. No. 808, *American State Papers: Finance*, 5:707–708.

32. No. 788, *American State Papers: Finance*, 5: 658.

33. No. 843, *American State Papers: Finance*, 5:795–796, 805–806, 828. Rhode Island representative Tristam Burges argued that American farmers would produce no such wool unless Congress "reduce[d] them to the condition of Russian Boors or Turkish slaves." See Burges, *Speech* , 28.

34. Robert V. Remini, "Martin Van Buren and the Tariff of Abominations," *American Historical Review* 63, no. 4 (July 1958): 903–17. The standard accounts of political history devote a few pages to these machinations, but invariably place Martin Van Buren's aspirations for an Andrew Jackson presidency at the center of the action. See Sean Wilentz, *The Rise of American Democracy: Jefferson to Lincoln* (New York: W. W. Norton, 2005), 298–300; Daniel Walker Howe, *What Hath God Wrought: The Transformation of America, 1815–1848* (New York: Oxford University Press, 2007), 274–75; Charles Sellers, *The Market Revolution: Jacksonian America, 1815–1846* (New York: Oxford University Press, 1991), 295–96.

35. For rates, see F. W. Taussig, *The Tariff History of the United States* (New York: G. P. Putnam's Sons, 1931), 89–95. No. 878, *American State Papers: Finance*, 5:902. No. 883, *American State Papers: Finance*, 5:942; 4 *Cong. Deb.* 1768 (1828); Burges, *Speech*, 27.

36. *Niles' Register*, February 7, 1829, November 20, 1830, December 31, 1831; *Journal of the Proceeding of the Friends of Domestic Industry, in General Convention Met at the City of New York, October 26, 1831* (Baltimore, Md.: H. Niles, 1831), 70; 8 *Cong. Deb.* (1833), 3525 (Choate), 3272 (Stewart of Penn.), 3707 (Bates of Mass.).

37. 8 *Cong. Deb.* (1833), 2900 (McDuffie); *Southern Excitement, or a View of the Opinions and Designs of the Friends of General Andrew Jackson* (n.p., 1828) contains resolutions passed in several South Carolina districts.

38. Editorial, *Southern Agriculturalist and Register of Rural Affairs* 1 (August 1828): 357. For Southern manufacturing over the next several decades, see Herbert Collins, "The Southern Industrial Gospel before 1860," *Journal of Southern History* 12, no. 3 (August 1946): 386–402; Michele Gillespie, "Building Networks of Knowledge: Henry Merrell and Textile Manufacturing in the Antebellum South," in *Technology, Innovation, and Southern Industrialization: From the Antebellum Era to the Computer Age*, ed. Susanna Delfino and Michele Gillespie (Columbia: University of Missouri Press, 2008), 97–124; Tom Downey, *Planting a Capitalist South: Masters, Merchants, and Manufacturers in the Southern Interior, 1790–1860* (Baton Rouge: Louisiana State University Press, 2006); Curtis J. Evans, *The Conquest of Labor: Daniel Pratt and Southern Industrialization* (Baton Rouge: Louisiana State University Press, 2001).

39. *Report on the Subject of Cotton and Woollen Manufactories, and the Growing of Wool in North Carolina* (Raleigh: Lawrence and Lamay, 1828), 7–16. Philadelphians in the orbit of Mathew Carey believed slave labor to be the key to southern manufacturing. See *Slave labour employed in manufactures . . . [Signed] Hamilton, Philadelphia, Oct. 2, 1827* (Philadelphia, 1827); Thomas P. Jones, *An Address on the Progress of Manufactures and Internal Improvement, in the United States; and particularly, On the Advantages*

to be Derived from the Employment of Slaves in the Manufacturing of Cotton and Other Goods. Delivered in the Hall of the Franklin Institute, November 6, 1827 (Philadelphia: Judah Dobson, 1827), 11.

40. *Niles Register*, February 7, 1829; Harvey Toliver Cook, *The Life and Legacy of David Rogerson Williams* (New York: Country Life, 1916), 251; David Williams to Col. James Chesnut, February 10, 1830, D. R. Williams Mill, 1828–1835, File Material F-4-6, Mss. 442, Historical Collections, Baker Library, Harvard Business School; *Memorial of a Committee Appointed by the Free Trade Convention, Held in Philadelphia in September and October, 1831, upon the subject of the present tariff of duties*, H.R. Doc. No. 82, 22nd Cong., 1st Sess. (1832), 51.

41. J. B. O. Landrum, *History of Spartanburg County: Embracing an Account of Many Important Events, and . . . Biographical Sketches of Statesmen, Divines at ot.* (Atlanta, Ga.: Franklin, 1900), 158; Cook, *David Rogerson Williams*, 141; IPH to Peyton H. Skipwith, 5 December 15, 1830; IPH to E. S. Hoppin, October 8, 1832; IPH to John E. Colhoun, August 23 and November 8, 1830, Letterbook, vol. 147, PDMC-BL.

42. IPH to RGH, December 5, 1824, Box 1, folder 2, RGH-RIHS; IPH to John Frazer & Co., September 3, 1827; IPH to T. & C. Winthrop, July 10, 1828, Box 1, folder 3, PDMC-RIHS; James J. McCarter to IPH, August 4, 1827, Box 1, folder 24, IPH-RIHS.

43. IPH to RGH, January 24, 1828, Box 2, folder 5, RGH-RIHS ("I can but find . . ."); IPH to Joseph Landon, June 17, 1828, Box 1, folder 3, PDMC-RIHS ("negro mattresses"); IPH to Isaac Winslow, June 18, 1828, Box 1, folder 3, PDMC-RIHS (Gothenburg); "By Tariff of 1828," Box 56, folder 10, PDMC-BL ("perplexing evasions"). If U.S. consul in Smyrna, David Offley, knew anything about wool smuggling, he made no mention in his annual reports to the State Department. The number of bags of wool exported from Smyrna grew from 523 in 1824 to 4,154 in 1831. U.S. State Department, *Despatches from US Consuls in Smyrna, 1802–1906*, reel 1, National Archives and Records Service, General Services Administration.

44. IPH to James Hamilton, July 4, 1828; IPH to John Potter, May 27, 1828; IPH to T. & C. Winthrop, July 10, 1828, Box 1, folder 3, PDMC-RIHS.

45. IPH to Jacob Wood, November 9, 1829 ("disastrous affairs"); IPH to Robert Habersham, November 8, 1830 ("half or more"); IPH to James McCarter December 15, 1830 ("never had been passed"), Letterbook vol. 147, PDMC-BL. See also *Niles Register*, October 2, 1830 on rising cloth prices. William Ravenel to IPH, June 14, 1832, Box 1, folder 29, IPH-RIHS. Ravenel to IPH, December 3, 1832, folder 1-legal, IPH-SCL.

CHAPTER 7

REVULSIONS OF CAPITAL

Slavery and Political Economy in the Epoch of the
Turner Rebellion, Virginia, 1829–1832

CHRISTOPHER TOMLINS

*Who could have anticipated, that the bloody horrors of the Southampton
massacre, instead of suggesting plans for stricter discipline, would give
birth to schemes of emancipation?*

—[Benjamin Watkins Leigh], *The Letter of Appomatox*

*These doctrines, whenever announced in debate, have a tendency to
disorganize and unhinge the condition of society, and to produce uncertainty and alarm; to create revulsions of capital;[1] to cause the land of Old
Virginia, and real source of wealth, to be abandoned; and her white
wealthy population to flee the state, and seek an asylum in a land where
they will be protected in the fruits of their industry.*

—Thomas Roderick Dew, *Review of the Debate in the Virginia Legislature
of 1831 and 1832*

Local opinion held that the landscape upon which Nat Turner's slave
rebellion erupted in August, 1831 was "calm and peaceful."[2] It was
not. Forty years of migration into Virginia's mountainous western
regions had given state politics an increasingly sectional cast that pitted the west's
"peasantry"—recently settled and predominantly nonslaveholding—against the

long-settled east and its planter "aristocracy," heavily invested in slave labor since the late seventeenth century.[3] Local antipathies complemented the sectional, particularly in the eastern region of the state where mercantile and artisanal interests rubbed up against planter preeminence.

Virginia's strains can all be traced to the gradual decomposition of the eighteenth century's hierarchical and premodern political economy, built on uneven accumulations of land and slaves, under the persistent battering of commercial capitalism.[4] Decomposition was particularly evident in the erosion of freehold in land as the principal manifestation of the ideal of propertied independence central to republican Virginia's political and legal structures, and the growth in prominence of a rival "democratic" idealization of productive labor. In the case of the merchant, the artisan, and the western yeoman farmer, the labor that validated their claim to political recognition was their own—the self-possessed, self-disposing labor of the free contracting individual; in the case of slaveholders, in contrast, claims to continued political ascendancy rested not on their labor at all but on their wealth in land and, particularly, in the embodied labor of their slaves.

Turner's rebellion occurred in the midst of seething white discord over the appropriate relationship between free white labor and slaveholding wealth in the distribution of political power. White manhood democracy first confronted slavery, indirectly, in the Virginia Constitutional Convention of 1829–1830. In the rebellion's aftermath, confrontation became open conflict over the political economy of slavery itself as, for the first (and last) time the state legislature openly debated the possibility of emancipation.

The emancipation debate did not bring an end to slavery in Virginia, not even gradually; rather the reverse. As free labor, in the form of white male self-possession, moved to the center of political debates over representation and enfranchisement, slaves were involuntarily annexed to the politics of civic status to qualify *their* possessors too. The outcome was a new political and economic equilibrium, centered not on propertied hierarchy but on property's commodification, notably commodified labor, both free and slave.

In the case of self-possessed white labor, commodification meant increased circulation, whether in the region's limited free-labor market, or in competition with enslaved labor, or in migration elsewhere. In the case of enslaved labor, commodification also meant increased circulation, though with the important proviso that the enslaved laborer lacked self-possession and therefore choice in the matter. But this did not mean there was no change in the terms of possession. No longer harnessed exclusively to custom (in the shape of common law property claims), or positive municipal law, or paternal stewardship, slavery became transactional—modern—albeit the transaction could never be closed, because it turned on a debt that could never be paid off. Slavery was "the price of subsistence," as Nathaniel Beverley Tucker succinctly put it, a quid pro quo, as it were, between creditor master and perpetually indebted slave.[5] Creditors of course will tend to seek the best return on their advances. So when Virginia slaveholders, always uneasy at their labor's insurrectionary inclinations, found their investment could earn better returns elsewhere than were available in their own agricultural economy, they began to send their labor, via enforced migration or the domestic slave trade, deeper into the maw of the cotton kingdom—Alabama, Mississippi, Louisiana, Texas. Slaveholders' revulsion at their own human capital for its rebelliousness became a more discriminating revulsion in political economy's classic sense—a redistribution of capital in the direction of greater opportunity.[6]

No longer mediated by freehold in land, planters' civic membership in an increasingly democratic Virginia polity was founded on the ownership of slaves—property in services perpetually owing. Simultaneously, slaves' labor power joined white labor as a circulating commodity: in their case, a capitalized investment—literally human capital—seeking a return. This double character had been imperfectly revealed at Virginia's Constitutional Convention. There the discourse of political economy had conflated the slave's two abstracted bodies—the political and the economic—as one, denominated "wealth." The emancipation debate, in contrast, produced a decisive differentiation of the economic from the political, the commodified laborer from the civic identity slave labor bestowed on its beneficiary. The reason differentiation could become overt—made so in the analysis of the emancipation debate written in its aftermath by Thomas Roderick Dew[7]—was the appearance of the slave's third body, the real, material, threatening body of the rebel.

The Lie of the Land

Virginia's eastern and western sections meet more or less at the Blue Ridge Mountains. Cash crop monoculture and the slave labor that sustained it lay overwhelmingly to the mountains' east. The west's economy, in contrast, was predominantly one of pastoral family farming. With the exception of Norfolk, at the mouth of the Chesapeake, Virginia's major towns (such as they were)—Richmond, Petersburg, Fredericksburg—all sat on the fall line that divided eastern Virginia's upcountry Piedmont from the flat Tidewater. By 1830, slaves outnumbered whites in both Piedmont and Tidewater regions. Eastern Virginia's towns supported merchants, minor manufactories, and a white artisan class much less invested in slavery than the cash-cropping planters of the surrounding countryside.[8] What eastern planters sought from the state government, simply put, was security: security as slaveholders from the antipathies of nonslaveholders and the discontents of their slaves; security as men of wealth from the demands of others on that wealth. The more planters felt outnumbered in the state, the more stubbornly they relied on institutionalized maldistributions of political power to preserve their ascendancy.

The western section of the state had its own variety. Between the Blue Ridge and the Allegheny Mountains lay the fertile Shenandoah Valley region, on its way to becoming a third concentration of slave-based agriculture, but much smaller and much less dense than either Tidewater or Piedmont. To the west of the Valley lay the vast Trans-Allegheny region of mountains and upland plateau, now the state of West Virginia. What the west sought from Virginia's government was capital investment in transportation and communications improvements that would facilitate the commercial development of its farming sector. Repeated frustration in this quest for improvements was the principal thorn that spurred western politicians to seek a distribution of representation and a definition of suffrage "fairer" to their section.[9]

Amid this fractious collection of white societies, Virginia's 1776 Constitution seemed antiquated: a system of county-based representation with no regard for geographical extent or population, and a suffrage qualified by freehold in land that perpetuated the ascendancy of Tidewater slaveholders and their Piedmont counterparts over everyone else. As the other sections of the state gained population and developed their own distinct interests this constitutional containment vessel was called increasingly into question.

Freehold suffrage long predated the Revolution, but the resonance of "freeholder" changed markedly in the Revolutionary epoch. In place of the common-law definition of freeholder as a tenant in possession of a life estate, revolutionary Virginia substituted an "allodial" theory of absolute private ownership. Allodial possession was embodied in two bills enacted in 1779 governing the disposition of vacant lands and settling title to western lands; in the abolition in 1785 of primogeniture and entail; and in the Manumission Act of 1782, which authorized private manumission of slaves, thus confirming the absolute property rights of their owners. The allodial revolution meant that the freeholders whose economic independence was supposed to underpin republican governance would enjoy unencumbered authority over the disposition of the assets underlying their independence. Unfortunately, the consequences were fatal to the ideal. As Christopher Curtis has written, "freeholders once possessed of absolute control over their land proved unable to retain it." Whether due to the capital demands of commercial agriculture or to speculation, "personal debt proliferated. . . . Mortgages and liens on estates grew more abundant." Land lost its peculiar political distinctiveness as property and became simply "a form of capital." Freeholder republicanism was hollowed out by commerce.[10]

In light of land's precariousness, what was to be the fate of the freehold qualification as the key to Virginia's republican polity? What form of suffrage might replace the freeholder? Given the variety of economic interests competing for political leverage, what might follow from so fundamental an alteration to the state's political institutions? These were the questions white Virginians debated with increasing vigor during the early decades of the nineteenth century. Nat Turner's rude intervention lent their conversation a new coloration and a new direction. Virginia abandoned the attempt to shoehorn multiple economies into a single polity and instead began to debate the merits of one economy in particular, the political economy of slavery.

A Constitutional Convention, 1829–1830

The Turner Rebellion occurred nineteen months after the Virginia Constitutional Convention of 1829 amended the state's suffrage qualifications and the basis for apportionment of representation, and sixteen months after the new state constitution was ratified. The rebellion was not, of course, caused in any direct sense by the Constitutional Convention or its reforms. But it *was* the cause of the emancipation debate that dominated the first weeks of the 1831 session of the newly apportioned House of Delegates. To that extent the rebellion and the two phases of antebellum Virginia's public appraisal of the consequences of slavery are intimately entangled.[11]

The 1829 constitutional convention was the culmination of years of agitation for reform of the freeholder suffrage and county-based representation provisions of the 1776 constitution. For forty years, Virginia's Tidewater "gentry" had resisted all but the most marginal alterations to the distribution of political power. Throughout, the Tidewater's plurality of counties had ensured it would remain by far the best-represented region, normally able to control the House of Delegates through alliances with like-minded representatives from the southern Piedmont.

That control slipped in 1828. Having ignored—or fought off—calls for a state convention in 1816 and again in 1825, the General Assembly finally agreed to allow a referendum on the issue. Participation was defined by existing freehold suffrage laws, but the convention still gained the approval of 57 percent of those voting. Having at last obtained their convention, however, reformers saw it organized on a basis that favored their opponents: freeholders elected four convention delegates from each of the state's twenty-four senate districts, which were apportioned according to the distribution of the white population in 1810, and hence left uncounted twenty years of population growth in the west.

The objective of the convention's democracy advocates was white basis apportionment, which meant replacement of the existing county-based system of legislative representation with representation in accordance with the actual distribution and concentration of population, and white manhood suffrage, which meant enfranchisement of all white adult males. They were met with a variety of counterproposals: no change; moderate reapportionment in accordance with moderate revision of property qualifications on suffrage; "federal basis" apportionment, which meant white population plus three-fifths of slaves counted as "other persons" (disparaged by its opponents as the "black basis"); and "mixed basis" apportionment, which was white population plus an additional allowance for slaves counted as taxable property (again disparaged as the "black basis," also as "the money basis").[12] White basis apportionment and white manhood suffrage prevailed in committee, but once on the convention floor both were fiercely resisted by mixed basis advocates, led by Benjamin Watkins Leigh and Abel Upshur, who advocated explicit representation for white wealth. Wealth meant slaves, which Upshur called "a great, and important, and leading interest" (74) in Virginia east of the Blue Ridge: "almost the whole productive labor" (75) of the section. Including wealth in legislative reapportionment and in suffrage definitions would prevent "numbers alone" (75) from dominating the legislature and levying taxes on the wealth of the east to finance the west's demands for road and canal construction (53).

From the moment of the introduction of the reform recommendations, the convention was deadlocked. Proponents of white manhood democracy repeatedly proclaimed it a natural right, the realization of an original principle of government. Opponents retorted that it was mere "theory" (94), that government was entirely conventional, that its only proper test was practical utility, that it had no original principles. "The principles of Government are those principles only, which the people who form the Government choose to *adopt and apply to themselves*" (69, emphasis in original). The principle that eastern slaveholders chose to adopt and apply was the representation of all essential interests, including their slaves. They let it be known that the alternative was division of the state (566).

Once mixed-basis apportionment had been embraced as the preferred response to white basis, population—not land—was confirmed as the criterion for legislative reapportionment on both sides of the argument. On the mixed-basis side, of course, this was population, in large part, held as property. White basis proponents stressed this would mean a "negro Senate," a "negro House of Delegates" (637, 685). Mixed-basis proponents professed to see little difference, from the perspective of "*political economy*" or capacity for self-government, between the enslaved agricultural laborers of the east and the propertyless white "peasantry" and "day-labourers" of the west (158, emphasis in original). Each was bereft of self-direction, dependent. If the peasants were to be included in calculations of apportionment, so must the slaves.

Neither side had a decisive majority. After weeks of fruitless debate the deadlocked convention settled for reapportionment of the existing county-based House of Delegates according to the white population as counted in the 1820 federal census. It made no provision for future reapportionment. This meant the legislature would remain, as before, in the hands of Tidewater and

Piedmont slaveholders, for as long as further reapportionment could be resisted, and assuming no significant intrasectional rifts upset the status quo.

Whether significant rifts might indeed occur would depend on who were to
be recognized as voters, and the extent to which local solidarity rather than
distinctions of class or interest governed their behavior. In this matter a memorial from nonfreeholder citizens of the city of Richmond, introduced in the
second week of the convention, effectively summarized what was at stake. Non-
freeholders, said the memorial, were "probably the majority, of male citizens
of mature age." Yet they had been "passed by, like aliens or slaves, as if destitute of interest" because they did not own the requisite "certain portion of
land" that carried with it enjoyment of the suffrage.[13]

Western white basis proponents embraced the arguments of the Richmond
petitioners against freehold suffrage in their own arguments for white manhood
suffrage. Just as population had eclipsed land in the apportionment debate, when
the convention turned to suffrage population eclipsed land here too. Yet it did so
without handing the advantage to reformers, for they too bowed before certain
sacred restrictions. "For obvious reasons, by almost universal consent, women
and children, aliens and slaves, are excluded" the Richmond petitioners had observed. "What is concurred in by those who constitute the society, the body politic, must be taken to be right." Just not, they lamely concluded, when it came to
themselves. And what of paupers, goaded Upshur and others. What of convicts?
What of free blacks? Should they also be enfranchised?[14]

Deadlocked again, between advocates and opponents of white manhood
suffrage, the convention inched toward a compromise: the addition of a taxpayer basis to the freehold suffrage. Possession of taxable property, rather than
landed property per se, became the criterion for suffrage expansion. Alongside
those already enfranchised, who were qualified by acreage, the suffrage was
extended to include every adult white male citizen "possessed of an estate of
freehold in land *of the value of twenty-five dollars*"; and also any who the preceding year had been "a house-keeper and head of a family . . . *and shall have
been assessed with a part of the revenue of the Commonwealth*." The significance
of the reformulation lies first in the substitution of dollar value for acreage in
the freehold qualification, and second in its recognition of self-possessed productive labor—assessed house-keepers and heads of family—as another property
interest worthy of enfranchisement. The two innovations went together, in
that each depended on the restatement of its subject as capital: by expressing
landed property qualifications in dollar values rather than physical acreage,
the convention accepted land's productive capacity as capital in the hands of a
proprietor; and by embracing self-possessed productive (taxable) labor as
property, it too became a form of capital in the hands of a proprietor.[15]

And in that same equivalence one can detect a further form of ownership of productive capacity claiming recognition within the body politic: slave ownership as

such. Abel Upshur had told the convention that eastern slaveholdings represented "an interest of imposing magnitude" in a statement that equated property in slaves with wealth and resisted white basis apportionment on grounds that it rendered slaveholders' wealth vulnerable to "oppressive and unequal taxation." Here was the usual argument "that property should possess an influence in Government." But Upshur's case for that influence was in equal part not usual at all. Slaves were "an interest of imposing magnitude" not simply to the eastern districts of the state, but to the state as a whole. As nearly the whole productive labor of the east, slaves represented "the whole productive labour of one half of the *Commonwealth*." It made no difference, said Upshur, "whether a certain amount of labour is brought into the common stock, by four hundred thousand slaves, or four hundred thousand freemen" because the increase "is the same to the aggregate wealth." For Upshur, slave labor was of as much importance to the general welfare as that of free white labor. Each expressed the same quantum of value added. Each was a form of productive capacity—capital—enfranchising its possessor: "our property, so far as slaves are concerned . . . affords almost a full half of the productive labour of the State." It was "the interest of the whole Commonwealth, that its power should not be taken away."[16]

Arguments at Virginia's constitutional convention suggest, then, a refounding of state government on the basis of the contributions made by different "interests"—different forms of productive capacity—to the general welfare. The state's predominantly agricultural economy furnished the measure of productive land, expressed in capital values rather than freehold acreages; the state's mercantile and manufacturing economy furnished the measure of productive labor, expressed in the capacity of the self-possessed producer to pay taxes as a house-keeper, or as a head of a family. The state's owners of slave labor, too, claimed the measure of productive labor—in the form of the labor of their slaves. Theirs, indeed, was the largest bid of all, for as Upshur stressed, they held in their hands "the whole productive labour of one half of the Commonwealth." The question in the wake of the acrimonious convention was whether slave owners had indeed gained the decisive endorsement of their interest's "imposing magnitude" that they had demanded; whether it had indeed been recognized as an "interest of the whole Commonwealth." This was the question that would be raised—and settled—in the debate on emancipation that followed the Turner Rebellion.

The Virginia Slavery Debate, 1831–1832

The Virginia General Assembly convened in Richmond on December 5, 1831, a bleak Monday. On the second day of the session the legislature received Governor John Floyd's annual message, devoted to "the crisis in which your country is placed." Floyd's "crisis" referenced the Turner Rebellion, of course, but much more besides. His crisis was actually a compound of the rebellion and of "great subjects" left unresolved from the previous legislative session, with "the unpleasant aspect of our Federal Relations." His message describing his hopes for the session to come encompassed both.[17]

Floyd's first annual message to the General Assembly as governor had been delivered the previous December in a flush of anticipation attending passage of the new state constitution. Himself a westerner,[18] Floyd then had left no doubt where energies unleashed by reform should be directed: to transportation improvements that would unify the state, extending to all inhabitants "those facilities which open every market to . . . industry and enterprise." Floyd was aware, of course, that internal improvements were not in fact productive of unity among the legislators to whom his message was addressed at all: eastern opposition to taxation to pay for western transportation projects had been the essential sticking point throughout the constitutional convention. But Floyd swept sectional disagreement aside: "Arguments resting upon the inequality of contribution . . . from different portions of the State, fail utterly. . . . Let markets be opened for the agricultural products of any country, and *instantly* the subjects of taxation will become common to it."[19]

The governor, preoccupied in December 1830 by the task of uniting the state around a grand scheme of government investment in economic growth, was, a year later, a governor reelected to an unprecedented three-year term, hence an executive actually able to plan with some sense of continuity, yet required to contemplate the impact on his plans of events completely beyond his control: "the relentless fury of assassins and murderers . . . a banditti of slaves."[20]

Floyd had been mulling the impact of the rebellion on Virginia more or less since the moment of its occurrence, and not just as a question of public order but as a matter of the first importance to the state's economic future. In a letter dated September 2 devoted largely to a discussion of military strategy, for example, Floyd allowed a distinct thought to interject itself: "What the effect of this insurrection is to be upon the commercial credit of the state, upon individual credit, is a point of view not at all pleasant, to say nothing upon interest upon loans for the state itself, should she ever wish to borrow."[21] If long-term state investment in capital projects was to become a reality, Floyd knew that the state would wish to borrow—he already wished to borrow—and for some considerable time into the future. His next clear thought on the consequences of the rebellion, more deliberately composed, appears in a letter dated November 19 (a week after Turner's execution) to James Hamilton, the governor of South Carolina. Reviewing his plans for his December message to the legislature, Floyd told Hamilton he would recommend that the legislature "substitute the surplus revenue in our Treasury for slaves, to work for a time upon our Rail Roads etc etc and these sent out of the country . . . as the first step to emancipation."[22] Well aware that for several weeks memorials had been appearing in Virginia newspapers urging the emancipation and colonization of Virginia's slaves, Floyd seemed about to propose a scheme for gradual emancipation and deportation that in the interim would procure a state-funded slave labor force for his program of internal improvements. In Floyd's mind, quite clearly, advocacy of gradual emancipation and advocacy of internal improvements were linked.

When it came to his annual message, Floyd held back from public avowal of emancipation. The proposal, he had told Hamilton, would require caution. So far as commentary on slavery was concerned, Floyd's annual message emphasized only security. He would indeed try to use the rebellion to achieve his objectives, but indirectly, working through legislative allies—"talented young men"—largely drawn from the state's western districts.[23]

Floyd's efforts bore fruit. On December 16 his diary notes, "Some of the members begin to talk of a loan for improving the State in Railroads"; and, on December 26, "The question of the gradual abolition of slavery begins to be mooted."[24] The first of these entries spoke to the central plank of Floyd's December 6 message, which, after traversing the rebellion, had reemphasized, with great vigor, his theme from the previous year that the state's future depended on transportation improvements. Unmistakably, Floyd took the "melancholy subject" of the rebellion, which had "filled the country with affliction, and . . . mourning," and deployed it in support of his campaign for economic development, as an energizing call to action.[25]

As to the second diary entry, Floyd knew perfectly well that vested slaveholding interests did not share his view that the state's economic future was tied to state-funded pan-sectional pursuit of commerce. To avoid jeopardizing his economic program by antagonizing slaveholders sensitive to attacks on their property rights, Floyd had abstained from public advocacy of gradual abolition. Privately, however, he saw gradual abolition as a necessary complement to commercial prosperity. "It must come if I can influence my friends in the Assembly to bring it on."[26]

Postrebellion public support for the expulsion of Virginia's African population offered an opportunity to weaken the sectional interests that stood athwart Floyd's grand plan for the commonwealth's economic advancement. By mid-December petitions calling for legislative action were turning up in Richmond from all parts of the state. Citizens demanded the removal from the state of free people of color (all petitions), state purchase of "a few hundred" slaves annually and their removal (approximately 40 percent of the petitions), and an end to slavery (approximately 15 percent). Of those demanding state purchase and removal of slaves, signatories identified themselves as slaveholders seeking a remedy against the "appalling and increasing evil" of black population growth. Those concentrating their opposition on free people of color condemned them as a grotesque oddity, "neither free men nor Slaves," who were "incompatible with the tranquility of society."[27]

As the petitions arrived in Richmond they were referred to a select committee created by the House of Delegates to consider and report on "so much of
the governor's message as relates to the insurrectionary movements of the
slaves." The earliest petitions all concentrated on the removal of free persons
of color and occasioned no controversy. But on December 14, William H.
Roane, of Hanover, introduced a petition from the Society of Friends of Charles
City County seeking gradual emancipation of all slaves. After extended debate
of the question whether emancipation in any form was within the select committee's terms of reference, the House voted to refer the petition to the select
committee, thus widening the committee's terms of inquiry to the future of
slavery in the state.[28]

The issue was joined in early January. William Goode, of Mecklenburg, declared his opposition to the "dangerous" course on which the select committee
was embarked, and moved that it be discharged from any further consideration
of the matter of gradual emancipation. Thomas Jefferson Randolph, of Albe-
marle, then moved that instead the committee be instructed to report on the
expediency of polling all qualified voters on "the propriety of providing by law"

> that the children of all female slaves who may be born in this state on or after
> the fourth day of July, 1840 and detained within the limits of Virginia, shall
> become the property of the commonwealth, males at the age of twenty-one
> years, and females at the age of eighteen . . . to be hired out until the net sum
> arising therefrom shall be sufficient to defray the expense of their removal be-
> yond the limits of the United States.[29]

Randolph's proposal was silent on the question whether or not commonwealth
assumption of ownership of the mature *postnati* would be accompanied by
compensation for their owners.

Floyd noted that his "young friends" in the legislature were confident that
the House might be brought to debate emancipation. And indeed, in discussing
whether to take up Goode's motion of discharge—and hence, also, Randolph's
amendment—the House found itself in the midst of a substantive exchange on
the merits of emancipation. The subject already broached, the House bowed to
the inevitable and voted to take up the motion of discharge and the accompanying substitute. Floyd was delighted. "The slave party have produced the very
debate they wished to avoid."[30]

Floyd's sense of triumph over the eastern interests that had obstructed his
internal improvements program proved both short-sighted and exceedingly
short-lived. Within two weeks alarm had replaced celebration. Within three,
the grand agenda to solve Virginia's crisis proclaimed in his December 6 message lay in ruins.

The hinge on which debate turned was, of course, the proposition that the
children of female slaves born in the state should eventually become the property

of the commonwealth. The slave party treated the idea as uncompensated confiscation of capital assets. According to James Gholson of Brunswick, "The owner of land has a reasonable right to its annual profits; the owner of orchards, to their annual fruits; the owner of brood mares, to their product; and the owner of female slaves, to their *increase.*" Children were a return on a slaveholder's investment in their parents. Slaves were the east's marketable "capital stock," realizable for "the discharge of our just obligations." Adoption of legislation unfriendly to slavery would result in the expulsion of Virginia from the interstate slave trade, which would destroy the east's economy.[31]

The governor's allies defended Randolph's proposal as both moderate and essential to the revival of the commonwealth's fortunes. They argued that improvements would be the savior of the eastern economy by "drawing the produce of Middle and Western Virginia to the market towns of the East."[32] Their unity, however, was tested by William Brodnax, chair of the select committee, who criticized both sides of the debate for impetuous extremism and offered a distinct scheme, not of gradual emancipation but of population control. Brodnax would deport annually 6,000 Africans from Virginia at state expense—"commencing, of course, with our free persons of color"—which he calculated to be equivalent to the annual increase of the entire African population, free and enslaved. Three days later Brodnax reported to the House that the select committee had come to the conclusion "that it is inexpedient for the present to make any legislative enactments for the abolition of slavery."[33]

Brodnax's attempt to steer the debate toward expulsion of an undesired population and away from expropriation of slaveholders' property was resisted by emancipationist delegates. Attempting to turn the slave party's deprecation of natural rights in the state convention against it, Charles Faulkner of Berkeley proposed a test of "practical utility." Property was "the creature of civil society." Slaves were held not as of any natural right "but solely by virtue of the acquiescence and consent of the society in which [slaveholders] live." The rebellion had proven slave property a threat to public safety. Property that endangered social order could not be "tolerated." Nor did slaveholders enjoy any irrevocable right to compensation: the community was not required to pay for property "removed or destroyed because it is a nuisance and found injurious to that society." Floyd greatly appreciated Faulkner's speech. "This is a fine talented young gentleman."[34]

In response, slave party rhetoric heated up. Alexander Knox of Mecklenburg condemned "the wild and revolutionary measures sought to be imposed on the people of this Commonwealth." Slavery was no "evil . . . preying upon the vitals of the body politic," he said. Slavery, rather, was the foundation of the Commonwealth's "high and elevated character . . . indispensably requisite in order to preserve the forms of a Republican government," emblematic of the inevitable human distinction "between him who drives, and him who rides within the coach."[35]

"Nothing now is talked of or creates any interest but the debate on the abolition of slavery," Governor Floyd noted in his diary, adding, hopefully, "All is well." But all was not well. The exchanges continued with increasing bitterness and threats of state division. Floyd's diary suddenly became a succession of increasingly anxious entries: the debate was "engendering bad and party feelings" and displaying "erratic tendencies"; "the slave part of the state . . . must not be hurt," simply "held in check"; the debate had become angry—"It is not good that it should be so."[36]

The debate ended abruptly on January 25 after a series of votes showed the emancipationist position lacked a majority. The sequel was disaster for Floyd's hopes for vigorous prosecution of internal improvements—the cause that had led the governor to put his weight behind the gradual abolition initiative in the first place. The next week the House considered and approved a resolution "that the best interests of the Commonwealth demand the immediate commencement and rigorous prosecution of a line of commercial intercourse . . . uniting the navigable waters of the Ohio with the tide-water of the James River." The House then rejected the accompanying resolution "that this measure . . . be executed under the direction of the Government, [employing] funds to be provided upon the faith and credit of the Commonwealth." Floyd's diary noted despondently that the bill had been defeated by the House's eastern members "in revenge for the debate on the negro subject of abolition."[37]

A further expression of eastern disaffection appeared the following day, February 4, in the shape of a long letter "To the People of Virginia" written by Benjamin Watkins Leigh under the pseudonym "Appomattox" and published in the *Richmond Enquirer*. Leigh's letter signaled new trouble for Governor Floyd, for it was written not simply as a general defense of the position of the eastern slaveholders, but specifically to rally "the people of eastern and southern Virginia" in the forthcoming April elections against "all projects for abolition, present or prospective," so putting the cork in the bottle indefinitely.[38] Floyd responded rather as he had when the emancipation issue had first arisen the previous November: He took no public position himself, but instead put the matter in other hands. By mid-February Floyd seems in any case to have been either exhausted, or discouraged (or both) by Virginia's internal affairs. For much of the next five weeks Floyd was ill; for the rest of 1832 his diary contains little other than observations on federal politics. Nothing further of the General Assembly session warrants mention.

The hands into which Floyd shoveled the whole mess—the aftermath of Turner's rebellion, the debate over slavery and gradual abolition, Virginia's suffering economy and sectional discord over internal improvements—were those of Thomas Roderick Dew. Plainly Floyd was not seeking an immediate political solution, for Dew was no General Assembly crony but a professor (of history, metaphysics, and political law) at the College of William and Mary in Williamsburg. Apparently in search of advice on how to proceed, Floyd had latched on to another "talented young man" who might help him recover from the disaster the debate had dealt his attempts to tackle the state's long-term economic development.[39]

Dew responded, as any academic would, by writing an essay. Entitled "Abolition of Negro Slavery," it appeared in the *American Quarterly Review* for September 1832, where it occupied a significant seventy-six pages. But the *Quarterly* had edited Dew's manuscript substantially, while Dew himself continued adding to it. By December it had grown into a 130-page pamphlet. It was published in Richmond under a new title, *Review of the Debate in the Virginia Legislature of 1831 and 1832.*[40]

Dew's pamphlet was an extended critique of the House of Delegates' debate, grounded on a stadialist history of human development in general and of servile labor forms in particular. From these materials, Dew developed two major arguments. The first was a comparative efficiency argument *for* slavery. Slavery was a creature of climate and economic culture. Its future could not be determined by a legislature. The emancipation debate, hence, had been a colossal waste of time, emancipation itself a catastrophic loss of invested capital, fortunately averted. Dew's second argument addressed the amelioration of sectional discord within the state and its long-term economic future. Here his conclusion—the strategic importance of internal improvements to the pursuit of common economic advantage—repaid Floyd's faith in him.

Cannily, Dew comforted each of the protagonists in the emancipation debate. Eastern slaveholders saw slavery put beyond political intervention; its comparative efficiency proved slavery was indeed an interest of the whole commonwealth. Western suffragists had their sectional emphasis on internal improvements affirmed as a matter of common economic advantage; improvements were another interest of the whole commonwealth. Nor did Dew have to compromise his mode of analysis in order to reach this clever solution. Dew's comparative efficiency argument restated labor as a homogenous commodity. As a matter of political economy its form—free or slave—would always be determined by its economic circumstances, not by law or politics.

The Confessions of Thomas Roderick Dew

The principal weight in Dew's argument was contemporary, founded on the demography and political economy of slavery as it existed in Virginia. This was preceded in the pamphlet, however, by a lengthy discourse on the "Origin of Slavery and its Effects on the Progress of Civilization." Here Dew disposed of the contention that slavery was "unnatural and horrible." Slavery was divinely authorized; it was usual and ordinary; it had been and remained the condition of "by far the largest portion of the human race." His method was classically stadialist, in the Scottish eighteenth-century conjectural tradition. Describing successive historical stages of human development—hunter/gatherer, pastoral, agricultural, and urban/commercial—Dew focused on the effects across time of four legal/institutional conditions productive of servile labor (Dew did not distinguish slavery from serfdom or other forms of involuntary labor rent): the laws of war, habits of property, propensity to trade, and criminal punishment. His objective was to demonstrate "that slavery is inevitable in the progress of society, from its first and most savage state to the last and most refined."[41]

The purpose of Dew's historical argument was to normalize slavery as a form of human labor. In normalizing slavery, Dew's stadial account of its "origin and progress" necessarily situated the conditions for its eventual disappearance outside the realm of politics and law: "Something else is requisite to convert slavery into freedom, than the mere enunciation of abstract truths" (46). His objective in the next part of the pamphlet was to demonstrate conclusively the impotence of wishful thinking in the face of political economy's clear-eyed empirical truths. Plans for abolition were "puerile conceits" (64) destined for defeat by "the elastic and powerful spring of population" (5).

The 1830 census counted Virginia's slave population at 470,000. At an average capital value of $200, and allowing for recent population growth, this meant a total capitalization of slave labor in 1832 of $100,000,000. The assessed value of all lands and improvements in the state was $206,000,000. Slaves hence constituted one-third of the state's accumulated wealth. They also constituted the laboring population that earned all invested capital its return, hence maintaining its value. Remove the slaves "and you pull down the atlas that upholds the whole system" (48). Advocates of emancipation and deportation proposed to avoid such a sudden shock by commencing emancipation at levels that would simply remove the increase of the black population. At 6,000 per annum and $200 per capita, allowing a transportation cost of $30 per capita, and $200 in colonization costs, the cost of removing 6,000 slaves became $2,500,000, an annual expenditure "sufficient to destroy the entire value of the whole property of Virginia" (81). In any case, Virginia was already exporting some 6,000 slaves per annum to the southwestern slave states. By entering the market to purchase 6,000 slaves for emancipation and deportation the state government would simply redirect the flow of slaves already available for purchase, abating this outflow "so salutary to the state, and such an abundant source of wealth" (49), and instead incurring a deadweight capital loss. Moreover, by competing for the available 6,000, government would elevate the price of slaves, "and consequently the [rearing] of them would become an object of primary importance throughout the whole state" (54). The spring of population would simply produce more slaves.

Emancipationists proposed to avoid the crushing cost of gradual emancipation and expulsion by imposing it on the slaves themselves, requiring them to cover the cost of their own expulsion by taking them into state ownership on maturity and requiring that they work for hire, administered by the state, until the cost of expulsion had been met. Dew denounced the idea as a confiscation of slave property; a destruction of the slave's realizable capital value (for no one would buy a slave destined to be assumed by the state); an uncompensated imposition of the costs of rearing on the slaveholder; and an ill-advised reliance for the recovery of the cost of expulsion on the superintendence of government, "the most miserable of all managers" (63). Worst of all was the variation on gradual emancipation that deemed property subject to society's right to abate as a nuisance any property that endangered the greater good. The object of government, said Dew, was the protection of property not its abatement. Here was a threat that imperiled the entire economy, calculated to "disorganize and unhinge the condition of society . . . to produce uncertainty and alarm . . . to create revulsions of capital" (68).

If deportation was wholly impracticable, what of emancipation without deportation? Virginia's slaves, said Dew, were utterly unfit for freedom among the white population. Referencing James Mill, Dew pronounced the measure of fitness to be a person's capacity to engage voluntarily in labor sufficient to "supply . . . necessaries and conveniences" (87). The example of Virginia's free people of color—"worthless and indolent . . . *drones* and *pests*"—established that freed slaves could not meet the necessary standard (88, emphasis in original). The same had been proven by the experience of Haiti, which in the forty years since the Haitian Revolution had recorded a continuous and precipitous decline in the production of sugar, coffee, and cotton. Freed slaves simply had no propensity to accumulate. Nor was the unfitness of bound labor for freedom a question merely of racial incapacity: Polish peasants freed by the 1791 constitution had also become "degraded and wretched" (97–98). The "prematurely liberated" bound laborer was, for Dew, a Frankenstein's monster, "a human form" endowed by naïve legislators "with all the physical capabilities of man," but completely lacking in moral sense and capacity (105).

So what was to be done? Even if slavery were a proven injustice and economic calamity, precipitate emancipation would produce more of both. But Dew denied that slavery was in fact either unjust or calamity. It was sanctioned by the Bible; it was assuredly a republican institution for "the perfect spirit of equality" it created among whites (112); and, properly directed, it was in no way inferior to free labor. The efficiency of free labor depended on its propensity to accumulate. The English had learned to accumulate, the Irish far less so, the Spanish and Italian not at all. In southern staple-producing countries slave labor was more efficient—it meant more accumulation—than free labor (125–6).

Slavery's comparative advantage in southern climes meant that despite ruinous federal tariff policies, it had a long-term future in the United States. Dew thought Virginia "too far north" for slavery to exist there indefinitely (126).

And indeed, though the black population was growing, the majority white population had begun to grow faster. But at least in the short term, Virginia's comparative demography was more ambiguous because although the state's white population had been growing faster, it had also been emigrating west-ward in large numbers. Dew recognized this as an important economic prob-lem. Black migration occurred principally through the agency of the internal slave trade, an emigration that "furnishes every inducement to the master to . . . cause the greatest possible number to be raised" (120). Through sale on the market the slaveholder received back the capital invested in the slave, while the spring of black population growth created an equivalent to take the place of the departed. In the case of white emigration, in contrast, the state lost both a laborer, usually in the prime of life, and the capital invested in the laborer by his family in the form of rearing and education, and was thus doubly impover-ished by the migrant's departure (120–21).

Eventually, however, white emigration would be checked, and the demise of slavery in the state encouraged, by two factors: first, the filling up of vacant western territory; and second, internal improvement. Of these, it was internal improvement that in Dew's mind was decisive, for it would bring about the fi-nal crucial shift in Virginia's political economy, from agriculture to commerce, that stadial political economy predicted. For the east it would mean the rise of cities and manufactures, the immigration of free labor, increased density of population and division of labor, growing urban demand for local foodstuffs, and a breakdown of plantation agriculture in favor of truck farming, all of which would decrease demand for enslaved agricultural labor. For the west it would mean the opening of markets and the substitution of commercial agriculture for subsistence pastoralism. Virginians should reject the foolish prattling of politi-cians and wait patiently while the historical logic of political economy unfolded. "Time and internal improvement will cure all our ills" (24).

Dew's *Review of the Debate* has been described as a decisive reorientation of Southern proslavery argument "from the defense of a necessary evil to the as-sertion of a positive good."[42] This seems to me not so much incorrect as beside the point. Dew was applying a mode of analysis in which he was well-versed to a problem in contemporary political economy. Using that mode of analysis his objective was to demonstrate the profound and damaging error of imagining that legislative politics was the realm within which the matter in debate (slav-ery) should be addressed or could be resolved. Government should abstain from interventions in economic activity because its actions would always result in consequences—in this case disastrous revulsions of capital—unanticipated by their advocates. In the short term outcomes were driven by the operation of self-interest and the spring of population, in the long term by the gradual ac-cumulation of social and institutional change that conformed to the classic human progression that began in the "savage" society of hunting and ended in commerce. Slavery in Virginia would eventually wither away because Virginia would eventually make the transition from an agricultural to a commercial stage of development. When that occurred, free labor would take slave labor's place. For as long as Virginia's cash cropping plantation sector remained its principal source of wealth, however, the comparative advantage of slave over free labor in plantation agriculture would ensure that the state *as a whole* would find its economic interests best served by maintaining its commitment to slavery.

Circulations of Labor

Dew's *Review* drew a line under the argument over gradual abolition by answering conclusively the question left hanging by the state convention two years earlier. The convention's slanted reapportionment and suffrage compromises had guaranteed slaveholders sufficient political resources to protect their interest, and the slave party had used them to wrestle the postrebellion bid for gradual emancipation to a standstill. But the damage had been severe—east and west equally embittered, the state brought to the edge of division, Floyd's improvements scheme destroyed. Here was no foundation on which those who held in their hands a full half of Virginia's "productive labour" might hope to see their particular interest acknowledged as an "interest of the whole Commonwealth." Dew had provided the way back: his *Review* unreservedly endorsed internal improvements as the means to knit the sections together again, and set the commonwealth on a new path to wealth and prosperity; slavery, meanwhile, stood endorsed just as unreservedly as an interest of the whole; not a liability but the source of Virginia's comparative advantage for as long as it remained a predominantly agricultural state. Emancipation was suicide. Instead let east and west "steadily unite in pushing forward a vigorous system of internal improvement."[43]

Unite, at least in enthusiasm, they would. After the halting commitments and elaborate displays of legislative indifference of the 1820s and early 1830s, Virginia finally embarked on substantial infrastructure investment—canals, railroads, and banks. But the pattern of development did not bridge the state's sectionalism. Improvement projects were privately managed and funded locally. Localities with capital to draw on prospered, but major interregional projects withered on the vine. In the mid-1830s, when the state government finally began to overcome the legislature's reluctance to invest directly in internal improvements, it did so by pandering to those same local interests. By 1860, largely by deficit finance, the state had invested $40 million in internal improvements. Yet it had no central trunk railroad or water transportation network connecting east and west, Ohio and James Rivers, to show for it. Nearly 70 percent of the state's funds had been expended on projects east of the Blue Ridge, and more than half of the remainder (18 percent) in the Valley. State funding of improvements in the Trans-Allegheny west lagged badly behind the rest of the state.[44]

The absence of real pan-sectional accommodation in improvement outcomes meant that antagonism toward the slave party continued to fester. But it had no further legislative expression. To that considerable extent, Dew's other main purpose, the declaration that slavery was an interest of the whole, was substantially achieved. As important, however, was the direction to Virginia slavery imparted by his comparative efficiency analysis of the slave as human capital—commodified labor, shorn of customary or paternal obligation, expressible as a return on investment that might be realized either through work or, just as rationally, sale. Six thousand per annum was Dew's estimate, earning more than $2.5 million—not an insignificant figure, given that the state's total (nonhuman) exports in 1829 had amounted to less than $3.8 million, equal to its balance of payments deficit for that year.[45] Others had different figures. During the legislative debate, some had said more than 8,000, others more than 9,000, still others more than 10,000.[46]

What *were* the numbers? Using the federal census it is possible roughly to estimate the increase in population one might anticipate from census to census and compare this figure with the actual increase in population.[47] This method suggests that in the 1820s approximately 7,500 slaves per year were sold or sent out of the state. In the 1830s this figure jumped to nearly 12,000, before falling back to around 9,000 in the 1840s and 8,000 in the 1850s. There is no reason to suppose annual figures were uniform across each decade. Nevertheless Dew's figure of 6,000 in 1832 is conservative given the average for the previous decade and the slope of a rising demand curve, corresponding to the rapid extension of cotton cultivation in the states of the southwest that peaked between 1835 and 1836 as cotton prices doubled between 1830 and 1835. Forced slave migration might well have reached 25,000 per year at the 1830s peak, when Virginia slave prices exceeded $1,000, before falling off rapidly with the collapse of cotton prices in the late 1830s. A slow recovery in cotton prices began in the mid-1840s and continued for fifteen years, during which it is likely that the bulk of the 1840–1860 interstate slave sales occurred, at prices rising from $500 to $1,200.[48]

The movements of slaves, when correlated with staple prices, slave prices, and land values in states of origin and reception, suggests that in 1832 Dew knew well of what he wrote. Enslaved bodies were entirely commodified. Slaveholders chose to realize the full value of their embodied capital when the return on it as capital exceeded its anticipated rate of return as labor. What white labor could do on its own behalf—circulate in search of advantage—was done to black labor by its owners, and on theirs. It was not done en masse because, as

Philip Doddridge had bitterly remarked during the constitutional convention, slaves made their owners sovereigns,[49] and because Virginia slaveholders could still make a living, and in the 1840s and 1850s rather more than a living, from their own land. But it was done easily enough to prove Dew's point, and the doing of it earned slaveholders considerable returns.

Dew and his slave party fellow travelers went to some considerable trouble to pronounce Turner's rebellion an aberration, the event itself "trifling and farcical," the fears attending it but a passing phase "of short, *very short* duration."[50] The market behavior of Virginia slaveholders in the 1830s seemed to prove them right. The number of slaves they forced into circulation did increase quite substantially, from 17 percent of total population in the 1820s to 25 percent in the 1830s, before falling back toward 17 percent over the next two decades, suggesting a heightened propensity to sell in the wake of the rebellion. But this was no panic selling—it actually represented a net decrease in Virginia's contribution to the total number of slaves in interregional motion, one that arrested the secular growth of the slave population but did not put it into decline. Virginia's slaveholders were selling into a rising market, engaged in a rational realization of returns on their invested capital.

Still, before accepting the slave party's elaborate contempt for the Turner Rebellion as gospel, we should also consider the words of John Thompson Brown of the town of Petersburg on the seventh day of the emancipation debate. Brown reminded the House of Delegates that Virginia's slaves were "the net proceeds of the labor of our ancestors and ourselves, [from] the foundation of the colony at James Town, to the present moment." They had taken the soil, he said, and cultivated it, and invested the proceeds—$100,000,000—in slaves.

> We derive our subsistence from the labour of our slaves, precisely in the same manner that we would live on the interest of our money if the one hundred millions had been invested in bank stock.

One can hear Brown's voice quaver as he considered the possibility that a rebellious slave might actually induce a majority of his fellow delegates to reconsider their toleration of his investment. "Take from us these slaves without compensation" he pleaded, "and what have we left?"[51] At that moment, perhaps, the fear—the revulsion—was all too frighteningly real.

Notes

1. "Revulsion (n): The action or process of drawing back or away (*from*) . . . a sudden violent change of feeling." *Oxford English Dictionary*, accessed December 29, 2014, http://www.oed.com/view/Entry/164997?redirectedFrom=revulsion#eid (entry #2a).

Thomas Roderick Dew's usage of the term is taken from Adam Smith's *Wealth of Nations* (London, 1776), where it signifies a convulsive redistribution of capital in the direction of a more efficient employment. See Adam Smith, *An Inquiry into the Nature and Causes of the Wealth of Nations*, ed. R. H. Campbell and A. S. Skinner (Indianapolis: Liberty Classics, 1981), 2:596, 609. The implicit violence of "revulsion" underscores Dew's dismay, like that of Benjamin Watkins Leigh, that "the bloody horrors" of the Turner Rebellion could give rise not to "plans for stricter discipline" but instead "schemes of emancipation."

2. Thomas Ruffin Gray, *The Confessions of Nat Turner* (Baltimore, Md., 1831), 4.

3. "Freeholder aristocracy" was common political rhetoric during the 1829–1830 Virginia Constitutional Convention debates, just as "peasantry" was an equally tendentious description of the population of the Trans-Allegheny west. See, for examples, *Proceedings and Debates of the Virginia State Convention, of 1829–30* (Richmond, 1830), 54–62 ("aristocracy"); 158 ("peasantry") [Hereafter *PDVSC*].

4. Christopher Michael Curtis, *Jefferson's Freeholders and the Politics of Ownership in the Old Dominion* (Cambridge: Cambridge University Press, 2012), 13–15.

5. Nathaniel Beverly Tucker, "Note to Blackstone's Commentaries," *Southern Literary Messenger* 1, no. 5 (January 1835): 228.

6. See note 1.

7. Thomas R. Dew, *Review of the Debate in the Virginia Legislature of 1831 and 1832* (Richmond, 1832). See below notes 39–42 and accompanying text.

8. Alison Goodyear Freehling, *Drift Toward Dissolution: The Virginia Slavery Debate of 1831–1832* (Baton Rouge: Louisiana State University Press, 1982), 24.

9. Ibid., 16–17; Curtis, *Jefferson's Freeholders*, 100–101; Carter Goodrich, "The Virginia System of Mixed Enterprise," *Political Science Quarterly* 64, no. 3 (September 1949): 376.

10. Curtis, *Jefferson's Freeholders*, 86, and see generally 53–87.

11. The constitutional convention opened on October 5, 1829 and concluded January 15, 1830. The new state constitution was ratified in April 1830. The first legislative election held under the new constitution occurred in October 1830 for the legislative session beginning December 6, 1830. The legislature for the session beginning December 5, 1831, was elected August 1, 1831. The Turner Rebellion took place August 21–23, 1831.

12. *PDVSC*, 82–3, 123.

13. "The Memorial of the Non-Freeholders of the City of Richmond, respectfully addressed to the Convention, now assembled to deliberate on amendments to the State Constitution," in *PDVSC*, 25–31.

14. *PDVSC*, 30, 68, 92.

15. See "An Amended Constitution, or Form of Government for Virginia (adopted by the Convention January 14th, 1830)," Article 3.14, in *PDVSC*, 900 (emphasis added); Curtis, *Jefferson's Freeholders*, 116.

16. *PDVSC*, 75.

17. *Journal of the House of Delegates of the Commonwealth of Virginia, Begun and Held at the Capitol, in the City of Richmond, on Monday, the Fifth Day of December, One Thousand Eight Hundred and Thirty-One* (Richmond, 1831), 9.

18. Floyd resided in Montgomery County, where he pursued commercial grazing. Though a slaveholder, he observed that "in this mode of drawing a revenue from the soil . . . few slaves are necessary, and more than can be employed in the daily routine [of stock rearing] is a bad investment of capital in such a country. Hence a slave is seldom purchased unless his labor is wanted from some specific purpose." Charles H. Ambler,

The Life and Diary of John Floyd, Governor of Virginia, an Apostle of Secession, and the Father of the Oregon Country (Richmond, Va.: Richmond Press, 1918), 85.

19. Journal of the House of Delegates of the Commonwealth of Virginia, Begun and Held at the Capitol, in the City of Richmond, on Monday, the Sixth Day of December, One Thousand Eight Hundred and Thirty (Richmond, 1830), 8, 9 (emphasis added).

20. Journal of the House of Delegates of the Commonwealth of Virginia, Begun and Held at the Capitol, in the City of Richmond, on Monday, the Fifth Day of December, One Thousand Eight Hundred and Thirty-One (Richmond, 1831), 9.

21. John Floyd to Colonel W. J. Worth. Commanding 1st Battalion U.S. 2nd Artillery, Norfolk, Virginia, in Henry Irving Tragle, ed., The Southampton Slave Revolt of 1831: A Compilation of Source Material (Amherst: University of Massachusetts Press, 1971), 271–72.

22. John Floyd to James Hamilton Jr., November 19, 1831, in Tragle, The Southampton Slave Revolt, 276.

23. Ambler, Life and Diary of John Floyd, 173.

24. Ibid., 172.

25. Journal of the House of Delegates (1831–32), 10.

26. Ambler, Life and Diary of John Floyd, 172.

27. A full list of petitions received (beginning December 6, 1831 and ending February 20, 1832, all but one received before the end of January 1832) appears in Appendix B of Eva Sheppard Wolf, Race and Liberty in the New Nation: Emancipation in Virginia from the Revolution to Nat Turner's Rebellion (Baton Rouge: Louisiana State University Press, 2006), 242–47.

28. Journal of the House of Delegates (1831–32), 15, 29; Wolf, Race and Liberty, 207–09.

29. Erik S. Root, ed., Sons of the Fathers: The Virginia Slavery Debates of 1831–32 (Lanham, Md: Lexington Books, 2010), 25 [Hereafter VSD]; Richmond Enquirer, 12 January 1832.

30. Ambler, Life and Diary of John Floyd, 174.

31. VSD, 45, 55 (emphasis in original).

32. Ibid., 58.

33. Ibid., 79; Journal of the House of Delegates (1831–32), 99.

34. VSD, 106, 107; Ambler, Life and Diary of John Floyd, 174.

35. VSD, 141, 147, 148.

36. Ambler, Life and Diary of John Floyd, 174–75.

37. Journal of the House of Delegates (1831–32), 131 (February 3, 1832); Richmond Enquirer, February 4, 1832; Ambler, Life and Diary of John Floyd, 177.

38. Richmond Enquirer, February 4, 1832, subsequently published as The Letter of Appomatox to the People of Virginia (Richmond, 1832).

39. Floyd and Dew were acquainted. See Ambler, Life and Diary of John Floyd, 167. In his commentary on Floyd's life, Ambler notes (92) that Floyd wrote to Dew in April 1832, "inviting his attention to the subjects of slavery and abolition as set forth in the debates of the Assembly of 1831–1832."

40. Thomas Roderick Dew, "Abolition of Negro Slavery," The American Quarterly Review 12, no. 23 (September 1832): 189–265; Thomas Roderick Dew, Review of the Debate in the Virginia Legislature of 1831 and 1832 (Richmond, 1832).

41. Dew, Review of the Debate, 28.

42. Eugene D. Genovese, Western Civilization Through Slaveholding Eyes: The Social and Historical Thought of Thomas Roderick Dew (New Orleans: Graduate School of Tulane University, 1986), 1.

43. Dew, *Review of the Debate*, 124.

44. John David Majewski, *A House Dividing: Economic Development in Pennsylvania and Virginia before the Civil War* (Cambridge: Cambridge University Press, 2000), 3, 8–11, 12–36, 59–70, 124–40; Goodrich, "The Virginia System of Mixed Enterprise," 367, 371–74.

45. Dew, *Review of the Debate*, 61; Ulrich B. Phillips, *Life and Labor in the Old South* (Boston: Little, Brown, 1963), 177. Virginia slave prices bottomed out at $400, 1825–1829, before beginning their climb toward $1,000 in 1837.

46. *VSD*, 116, 139, 221, 230, 259.

47. Estimates are from Michael Tadman, *Speculators and Slaves: Masters, Traders, and Slaves in the Old South* (Madison: University of Wisconsin Press, 1989), 12 (table 2.1).

48. On slave and cotton price movements, see Phillips, *Life and Labor*, 177.

49. "What would the citizen of another state think, or how would he feel, at the sight of an hundred wretches exposed to sale . . . if in addition to the usual commendations of the auctioneer to encourage bidders, he should hear him tell them, that if they should purchase his goods, they would instantly become Sovereigns in this free land." *PDVSC*, 88.

50. *VSD*, 259; Dew, *Review of the Debate*, 125 (emphasis in original).

51. *VSD*, 170.

PART III

"KNOWING" CAPITAL

CHAPTER 8

RISK, UNCERTAINTY, AND DATA

Managing Risk in Twentieth-Century America

MARY POOVEY

In 1921, Frank H. Knight, an economist at the University of Chicago, introduced a distinction that could have dramatically affected the discipline of economics as we know it today. Knight's distinction—between "uncertainty" and "risk"—sought to discriminate between kinds of events that lie beyond the scope of human knowledge and a category of events that, while not directly knowable, can be calculated with the help of statistics and probability. Had Knight's distinction taken hold, economists might have qualified the confidence they now place in mathematical modeling with a more cautious attitude toward the applicability of probability theory, especially in the arena of financial markets, where the unknowable future looms so large. Knight's attempt to separate uncertainty from risk did not fare well, however, both because dramatic advances in data collection in the 1920s seemed to shrink the domain of uncertainty and expand the domain of calculable risk and because other economists, eager to make their discipline more scientific, devised ways to apply mathematical and statistical tools to nearly everything—even the decision-making process that Knight considered the most important effect of uncertainty. At one level, Knight seems to have anticipated the failure of his theoretical intervention, but no one, including himself, could have known in advance the staggering consequences of this failure or the ironies that swirl around it. To see why the distinction between uncertainty and risk was potentially so consequential for the discipline of economics and the rise of capitalism in the United States, and why the evisceration of this distinction has proved decisive for economists' failure to predict financial events like the crash of 2008, we need to place Knight's work in its historical context: the rise of the giant corporations in early twentieth-century America.

Risk, Uncertainty, and Profit: Knight's Theoretical Breakthrough

The theoretical challenge Frank Knight first tackled in his doctoral thesis was to explain why capitalism, which was supposed to flourish when competition was unfettered, generated profit.[1] According to neoclassical economic theory, profit would not exist in an ideal situation—that is, in conditions of perfect competition where market participants have equal access to information—because, in such conditions, the law of supply and demand would lead consumers and producers to agree on prices, and the economy would reach its natural state of equilibrium. "It is self-evident that in ideal exchange the quantities exchanged are equal in value terms, and there is no chance for anything like a 'profit' to arise," Knight explained.[2] In the actual conditions in which real businesses operated, of course, market participants did—and do—not have perfect information about all the conditions that do or will obtain, and, as a consequence, they always have to deal with unknowns. Some of these unknowns can be calculated, while others cannot. In the kind of unknowns that constitute "risk," "the distribution of the outcome of a group of instances is known (either through calculations *a priori* or from statistics of past experience)." The kind of unknowns that belong to "uncertainty," by contrast, defy this principle—"the reason being in general that it is impossible to form a group of instances, because the situation dealt with is in a high degree unique" (232).

According to Knight, this ineluctable uncertainty explains both why companies turn profits and why those responsible for tackling uncertainty should be well compensated for doing so. "Profit arises out of the inherent, absolute unpredictability of things, out of the sheer brute fact that the results of human activity cannot be anticipated and then only in so far as even a probability calculation in regard to them is impossible and meaningless" (311). In the face of such incalculable conditions, some member of every company has to make estimates, pass judgment, and take control. Knight called this individual the entrepreneur—a figure he declared to be new in the history of commerce. "The function of making these estimates and of 'guaranteeing' their value to the other members of the group falls to the responsible entrepreneur in each establishment, producing a new type of activity and a new type of income entirely unknown in a society where uncertainty is absent" (276). While uncertainty undeniably presents challenges, in Knight's account, this is a cause for celebration, not regret, for uncertainty turns out to be the engine of social improvement, the goad that disrupts the stupid torpor of mindless repetition. "With the introduction of uncertainty—the fact of ignorance and necessity of acting upon opinion rather than knowledge—into this Eden-like situation, its character is completely changed. With uncertainty absent, man's energies are devoted altogether to doing things; it is doubtful whether intelligence itself would exist in such a situation. . . . With uncertainty present, doing things, the actual execution of activity, becomes in a real sense a secondary part of life; the primary problem or function is deciding what to do and how to do it" (268). In Knight's account, making decisions and passing judgment, the entrepreneur's primary activities, are elevated to a new status, and every order by which judgment can be raised augments the importance of the ultimate decider. "The problem of judging men's powers of judgment overshadows the problem of judging the facts of the situation to be dealt with. . . . The receipt of profit in a particular case may be argued to be the result of superior judgment. But it is judgment of judgment, especially one's own judgment" (292, 311).

The Entrepreneur and the New Corporations

The philosophical, even biblical language in which Knight expressed many of his ideas makes the distinction between risk and uncertainty seem like a universal principle, conjured by the deductive method then favored by economists. If we place Knight's argument in its historical context, however, we can see that he was actually engaged not in philosophical deduction but with two secular debates that continued for most of the first two decades of the twentieth century. Both were generated by the rise of the new corporations, which had dramatically altered the U.S. economy by the time Knight began graduate study in 1913, and both raised questions about fairness and social justice. The first debate, which began in the late nineteenth century, turned on how to value the new corporations and how to distribute the wealth they generated: should a corporation be valued by its tangible assets, like buildings and machinery, or by its intangible assets, like earning potential and the goodwill the new corporation carried over from the companies it absorbed? The second debate, which intensified in successive waves—first, in anticipation of the 1909 Corporate Income Tax Act and then again during the lead-up to World War I—focused on how corporations should be taxed: Should a corporation be taxed on its annual "net profits" or on its "excess profits" (however these terms were defined)? Or should it be taxed on its "capitalization," which according to many economists included not only present income but the corporation's anticipated future income as well?[3] While Knight's distinction between risk and uncertainty does not seem, on the face of things, to address questions of fairness, corporate valuation, or taxation, it implicitly does because arguing that the entrepreneur's compensation derived from the magnitude of uncertainty he faced justified both the outsized profits the new corporations generated and their almost unanimous decision to direct large returns to the company's guiding entrepreneurs rather than return some to society at large.

Knight's defense of corporate profit may seem commonsensical today, but in the first decades of the twentieth century this was by no means the majority view. Many contemporaries, legislators among them, argued that some of the income the new companies earned should be redistributed so as to serve the greater social good, and many insisted that the federal government should use taxation to encourage social justice. The debates about corporate valuation and taxation were thus debates about the relationship between private property and fairness, which had enormous impact on the way capitalism developed in the United States. Knight's attribution of profit to a combination of incalculable uncertainty and the labor of an expert decision maker implicitly justified not only paying the expert for his judgment but also allowing the market to operate without legislative interference or undue taxation. The free-market positions Knight anticipated in his 1921 book were eventually articulated in the so-called Chicago School of economics and the Mont Pelerin Society, both of which Knight helped found.

In the debate about corporate valuation, the figure Knight called the entrepreneur was most often referred to as the company promoter. Knight acknowledged that these terms were interchangeable when he applauded the "insurer's" judgment: "The 'insurer' (entrepreneur, speculator, or promoter) now substitutes his own judgment for the judgment of the man who is getting rid of the uncertainty through transferring it to the specialist. In so far as his knowledge and judgment are better, which they almost certainly will be from the mere fact that he is a specialist, the individual risk is less likely to become a loss" (258–59). At the beginning of the century, to those more critical of corporations than Knight, the promoter's activities seemed far more dubious. One of the primary duties of a company promoter was to value the shares of a new company, and, far too often, the value he assigned seemed primarily to advance his own interest. Contemporaries referred to the inflation of a company's shares as "stock watering," and they suspected company promoters of watering shares because the entire process of company valuation was so new and mysterious. A company could water its shares by declaring a dividend without putting additional capital into the company; by issuing bonds purportedly to finance an expansion, then distributing to shareholders the income it raised by selling the bonds without retiring the underlying debt; or simply by generously estimating the value of the intangible assets, like goodwill, the company acquired as it grew. In practice, the company promoter had a stake in setting the value of the shares as high as possible both because he had to attract investors and because the promoter was typically paid at least partly in the new company's shares. Since he could realize his compensation only when he sold the shares, the promoter wanted to push the initial valuation as high as possible—often, contemporaries suspected, by inflating the company's overall worth.

Between 1899 and 1900 alone, a contemporary reported, twenty-eight books, pamphlets, and reports were published about corporate valuation, "together with a flood of periodical articles that will reach probably one hundred and fifty titles."[4] To understand the intensity of this debate, it is helpful to remember just how novel the corporate form was at the beginning of the century. In the 1890s, the majority of companies were private; they were owned by a single individual or a group of individuals often related by blood. Between 1895 and 1904, as many as 1,800 of these companies disappeared through consolidation.[5] The capital the new corporations collectively added to the U.S. economy was thought to be in excess of $3.5 trillion, and many corporations were believed to approach monopoly control in their respective industries. The new companies were able to become so powerful so quickly in part because of a series of legal decisions: beginning with the Santa Clara decision in 1886, the Supreme Court indemnified corporations as legal "persons" with all the rights an individual enjoyed. In addition to this new legal status, the corporations were also characterized by a series of features that distinguished them from the businesses they absorbed. Unlike partnerships, in which a few individuals oversaw the management of a company and fully participated in its profits and losses, the new corporations were funded by a novel combination of promoters, underwriters, and shareholders, whose interest in the company was limited to the liability their original investment entailed. Unlike a partnership, which existed only as long as the partners lived, the corporation was considered an ongoing entity, or going concern, which would endure and be productive beyond the interests of its original investors. Finally, the new corporations were managed by increasingly specialized experts who valued efficiency, cost control, and accountability over the protection of the company's workers or founders. To place a dollar amount on the value of a company, and to oversee its ongoing operations, these experts invested in new technologies, including new accounting procedures, that could keep track of the costs of complex production processes, distinguish the capital that kept the corporation afloat from the income eligible for disbursement as dividends, and gauge the relative effectiveness of the company's financial decisions in addition to its production processes. To these experts—Knight's "entrepreneurs"—the profits the corporation earned in the context of uncertainty self-evidently belonged in their entirety to those who wrested something out of nothing, who made decisions and created something new.

Taxing the Corporations

The very nature of the corporations made them objects of wonder and anxiety to contemporaries in every walk of life, but the debt they might be said to owe to society soon became a matter of legislative concern as well. In a series of cases decided between 1886 and 1900, the U.S. Supreme Court had gradually expanded the definition of "property" to include the right to a reasonable return on investment in intangible assets like goodwill and earning potential. Like the court's decisions to grant corporations the status of a legal person and to limit shareholders' liability, this redefinition of property helped make corporations prominent targets for reform-minded and revenue-hungry officials.[6] At the beginning of the century, the federal government was still relatively weak and perennially cash-starved because, in 1895, the Supreme Court had abolished the personal income tax, which had only been in effect for one year. The court decided that the tax violated Article I, Section 9 of the Constitution, which linked any direct taxation of property to "apportionment"—that is, taxes had to be proportionately divided among the states according to population. In response, President Theodore Roosevelt, who wanted to both limit the corporations' power and increase the power of the federal government, began to promote passage of a corporate income tax, which, as an indirect tax, could presumably sidestep the Constitutional impediment. While Roosevelt was not able to get the corporate tax passed, his successor, William A. Taft, embraced the cause as soon as he took office in 1909. Many members of Congress already supported this tax—not primarily because it could increase federal revenue or power, but because it would redistribute wealth.[7] Led by the Democratic first-term member from Tennessee, Cordell Hull, congressional supporters argued that it was unfair to exempt intangibles, one of the primary forms of corporate wealth, from the "property" subject to taxation.

Taft explicitly viewed the Corporate Income Tax Act as a vehicle for regulating corporations.[8] He did so because, like many of his contemporaries, Taft considered publicity, and the collection of information more generally, an effective curb on all kinds of abuses, corporate excesses among them. In this view, information seemed like an instrument of power both because the government could use data to devise and enforce more efficient rules in areas it was already overseeing, like interstate commerce and tariffs, and because, in the case of corporations in particular, information about capital on hand, bonded debt, and net income would enable investors to decide whether or not to purchase shares in a company. Such information, in short, would help quiet the public's fears about stock-watering at the same time that it would help the government develop more "rational" and "scientific" oversight. Far from seeming like the federal government's attempt to overstep its bounds, the 1909 Corporate Income Tax Act seemed to many contemporaries to encourage a kind of competition that would ultimately promote social justice and the kind of equilibrium economists associated with a self-regulating market.

The act that passed in 1909 did draw corporate assets into the big tent of the nation's resources, but the bite it took out of corporate wealth was relatively small: the act established a flat rate of 1 percent on every corporation's "entire net income over and above five thousand dollars." In so doing, the legislation both rendered corporate income a taxable asset under federal law and set off a fierce debate about how to calculate the value of this new resource. But while the revenue initially generated by the tax was comparatively small, it had a far-reaching impact on the collection of data in a volume and at a level of detail unprecedented in American history.

In order to determine what constituted the taxable 1 percent of a corporation's wealth, someone had to define the concept of "entire net income." Company promoters might have successfully established their prerogative to value the initial capitalization of a corporation, but the decision about how to value its net income soon fell to a combination of legislators and academic economists. Over a number of years, various courts, including but not limited to the Supreme Court, passed judgment on the definition of "business income," but they failed to reach a definitive conclusion. The Supreme Court, in the 1920 *Eisner v. Macomber* case, did establish what is now considered the classic legal definition of corporate income, but federal and state courts continued to issue new rulings through the 1960s.[9] Another effort to reach a decisive conclusion about how to define corporate income also failed in the 1910s, this one using theoretical arguments instead of legal precedent or intent. This other effort failed both because its participants—academic economists—could not agree on the principles involved in corporate income and because the discipline of economics had yet to achieve sufficient social prestige to make its voice heard. The debate among economists provided yet another context for Knight's work, and, ironically, the lessons its failure conveyed helped establish the path by which the discipline was soon to augment its authority.

Academic economists were invited to weigh in on defining corporate income after passage of the 1917 Revenue Act, which signaled the U.S. government's decision not to follow Britain's example of levying a wartime tax to finance the military campaign. Instead of imposing a wartime tax, which was tied to the duration of active hostilities, Congress decided to levy an "excess profits" tax on corporations, because this promised more flexibility. Of course, it was impossible to determine what level of profits was "excessive" unless someone could define what ordinary or "normal" profits were. In the face of this theoretical dilemma, William G. McAdoo, the secretary of the treasury, turned to Professor T. S. Adams of Yale, who consulted with other prominent members of his discipline. Given the fractured nature of economic opinion at the time, it is probably not surprising that American economists could not agree. By the end of 1919, Adams came to the conclusion that it was impossible for economists to define the normal rate of corporate profit so that the excess could be taxed.[10] Despite this failure, the debate did inspire several important contributions to economic theory. Columbia University's J. B. Clark, America's leading representative of the marginalist theories developed in Europe, used marginalist principles to defend a progressive income tax; Irving Fisher, an economist at Yale, supplied the foundational definition that reoriented the concept of "wealth" to include anticipated future income;[11] and Frank Knight defined "uncertainty" in such a way as to justify virtually any amount of profit the new corporations could generate and, implicitly at least, to keep these profits out of the government's hands.

The Fate of Uncertainty in Economic Theory and Ironies That Will Not Die

Knight's distinction between uncertainty and risk has not had a profound impact on the discipline of economics. John Maynard Keynes, one of the most prominent economists of the 1920s and 1930s, did ponder the role uncertainty must play in any economist's deliberations, but, by and large, the concept has been relegated to an increasingly marginal position in economic theory—and this in almost direct proportion to the growth of the attention paid to calculable risk. Part of the reason uncertainty has fared so poorly has to do with a development whose potential Knight acknowledged but which he deemed impossible: the growth of the kind of data mandated by the 1909 Corporate Income Tax Act. Instead of imagining that data would play a central role in the brave, new, unfettered corporate world, Knight considered what we call big data an impossible dream.

> One of the principal gains through organized speculation is the provision of information on business conditions, making possible more intelligent forecasting of market changes. Not merely do the market associations or exchanges and their members engage in this work on their own account. Its importance to society at large is so well recognized that vast sums of public money are annually expended in securing and disseminating information as to the output of various industries, crop conditions, and the like. Great investments of capital and elaborate organizations are also devoted to the work as a private enterprise, on a profit-seeking basis, and the importance of trade journals and statistical bureaus and services tends to increase, as does that of the activities of the Government in this field. The collection, digestion, and dissemination in usable form of economic information is one of the staggering problems

connected with our modern large-scale social organization. It goes without saying that no very satisfactory solution of this problem has been achieved, and it is safe to predict that none will be found in the near future. (260–61)

Knight might have been pessimistic about the feasibility of collecting data, but some of his contemporaries had already launched projects that would augment the government's collection of tax information. Ironically, these projects helped make Knight's speculations about uncertainty seem irrelevant at the same time they allowed corporations—and economists—to acquire even greater social power than they enjoyed when Knight's book appeared. Most prominent among the new mavens of data was the Columbia University economist Wesley Clair Mitchell. By 1920, Mitchell had made a name for himself with two long, data-filled volumes: one examined the U.S. government's nineteenth-century experiment with the fiat currency known as greenbacks, and the other focused on business cycles. Mitchell's campaign to collect and make data available gathered momentum in 1917, when he was appointed chief of the Price Statistics Section of the War Industries Board. In this capacity, Mitchell conducted extensive price and cost studies of the actual profits corporations were making during the war. Along with Edwin F. Gay, an economist trained in Germany who was the first dean of the Harvard Business School, Mitchell helped establish the Central Bureau of Planning and Statistics, a clearinghouse for the information collected by various agencies during the war. At war's end, this bureau was abolished, much to Mitchell's disappointment, but in 1921 he and Gay responded by founding a new organization: the nongovernmental, not-for-profit National Bureau of Economic Research (NBER).

The first NBER project to yield results was a study that directly engaged the old subject of income distribution and, by extension but only indirectly, the topic of corporate wealth. Published in 1921, the same year Knight's book appeared, this two-volume work on income clearly expressed the values Mitchell had come to embrace: a commitment to gathering and making available data that was as objective and comprehensive as possible; and the conviction that social justice, in the form of an equitable distribution of wealth, should balance the profit-seeking activities of corporations.[12] To ensure the impartiality of his data, Mitchell put two teams of researchers to work on two different sets of sources. Only when the two research groups arrived at the same results independently did Mitchell accept them, and he refused to make any policy recommendations in the report itself.[13] Despite his repudiation of policymaking, Mitchell's conviction that the distribution of the nation's income mattered as much as its total amount is visible in the goal explicitly set out in the introduction to *Income in the United States*: the report was designed, its authors explained, to discover "whether the National Income is adequate to provide a decent living for all persons, whether this income is increasing as rapidly as the population, and whether its distribution among individuals is growing more or less unequal" (ix).

Despite the challenges the researchers faced and the limitations of the study they ultimately produced, the brisk sales of the completed volume indicated that such data was in great demand. Whether those who bought the report were government officials, members of the business community, or simply interested citizens, they clearly embraced this kind of information because it promised to help them know more about an economy increasingly dominated by the great corporations. This and subsequent studies published by the NBER also supported government efforts to plan the activities of an economy explicitly viewed as national, not as composed of regional economies or divided by special interests.

While Mitchell never embraced the statist-planning agenda that came to dominate U.S. government policy during the New Deal, he did serve on the President's Research Committee on Social Trends, which President Hoover established in 1929 and which recommended the creation of a national planning board. Franklin Roosevelt also turned to Mitchell to help lead the experiment in New Deal planning conducted from 1933 to 1943.[14] Throughout these attempts to treat the national economy as a single unit, which could be managed and measured in ways similar to those Mitchell associated with the giant corporations, Mitchell remained committed both to collecting data that was impartial—and thus useful to a variety of groups with varying motivations—and to his understanding that some form of equitable income distribution was essential to national well-being. That these two commitments might pull in different directions—one toward a free-market economy in which large corporations' ability to use the increasingly extensive databases of available information would enable them to calibrate their products to an ever-more calculable (and more easily manipulated) public demand and the other toward some kind of government oversight of income redistribution—may well have been beyond even Mitchell's ability to grasp.

Today's readers will recognize that we now reap the dubious legacy of the way the early twentieth-century debates about corporate wealth, valuation, and data were resolved. Although U.S. corporations are heavily taxed, relative to companies in some other nations, their abilities to both act as empowered agents and benefit from ever-growing collections of digital data surely exceed what their early defenders could have imagined. Today, the idea that taxation should be used to redistribute corporate wealth represents a minority, if sporadically vocal, position, and any vestigial outrage over corporations' claim to legal personhood has been marginalized by the Supreme Court's 2010 decision in the *Citizens United* case. A second legacy of these early debates may be less obvious today, but it also casts a shadow long and dark enough to merit attention. This legacy may seem to affect primarily the discipline of economics, but, given the influence economists have gained in the last half-century, through them, it affects us all.

We have seen that the concept of uncertainty was critical to Knight's original argument: for him, uncertainty explained both how a competitive economy could generate profits and why corporations—and the aspiring entrepreneurs who launched them—should be allowed to keep the revenue they earned. According to Knight, uncertainty creates a demand for judgment, and judgment, always in short supply, deserves rewards commensurate with the benefits it confers. In Knight's account, the very nature of uncertainty means that the entrepreneur's judgments defy calculation: by definition, entrepreneurial decisions exceed the statistically calculable world of risk, for they address and constitute that which lies beyond statistics—situations that are "in a high degree unique" (232).

In the 1930s and 1940s, a few influential theorists began to expand the domain of the calculable not simply by gathering data but in theoretical terms. As they did so, the category of risk came to encompass even the process of decision making, which, for Knight, was the distinctive activity of the entrepreneur. Rehearsing the details of this theoretical revolution would take us too far afield, but it may suffice to say that during the early decades of the century, the Hungarian mathematician John von Neumann worked out a way to use axiomization, set theory, and topology to describe the decision-making process as a series of logically coherent, mathematically calculable steps. Given certain foundational assumptions—that all participants are alike in seeking to maximize self-interest and that equal knowledge is available to everyone—the resulting account of decision making allowed von Neumann to calculate the likelihood of various results. With Oskar Morgenstern, von Neumann published his account of game theory in 1944, in a volume entitled *Theory of Games and Economic Behavior.* As the title suggests, this book was eventually (although not immediately) to influence the discipline devoted to economic behavior and, as economists used game theory to model economic behaviors and predict outcomes, to enhance the prestige of the discipline as a whole.

Jacob Marschak, another European theorist and émigré to the United States, was one of the first economists to recognize that game theory could transform economics from a largely deductive enterprise, with some inductive data-collecting on the side, into a mathematical science. That Marschak developed this insight through applications to financial decision making is even more remarkable, for the future-oriented nature of finance adds an extra element of uncertainty to every financial decision: at the moment of choosing, no one can know what the payoff of a financial investment will be because this will occur in the future, the nature of which is unknown. In the most general terms, Marschak brought even financial decisions into the domain of the calculable simply by treating uncertainty as risk. He did so by elaborating the definition of rationality central to the work of von Neumann and Morgenstern: in Marschak's account of financial decisions, the rational self-maximizer is also versed in probability theory. He may not know for certain the outcome of his choices, but he knows that some outcomes are more likely to occur than others. "Instead of assuming an individual who thinks he knows the future events, we assume an individual who thinks he knows the probabilities of future events."[15]

Once uncertainty was translated into risk, the latter could be measured as the volatility of a financial time series and later, with more sophisticated mathematics, treated as the random expression of a stationary stochastic process. Both the process of making decisions, financial decisions included, and the movements of prices on exchanges could then be modeled. In the process, any anxieties raised by our inability to know the future could be managed by economists' assurance that, with the proper tools, they would be able to negate the deleterious effects of risk through calculation and planning. As Peter Miller has remarked, in today's "risk society" to manage risk "means no longer to resign oneself to blows of fate or providence, but to take responsibility for one's affairs by developing the means to avoid and repair its effects. To manage risk means, above all, to have available a set of tools or technologies that allow one to intervene in the name of risk."[16]

This expansion of the domain of the calculable, of course, so that it includes even finance, effectively obliterates Knight's category of uncertainty. In pushing uncertainty away, economists and financial theorists have created the image of a world that, if not quite rational, can at least be modeled mathematically (within a probability range). As the master theorists of this world and architects of ever more complex models, today's economists exercise extraordinary social authority—an authority barely shaken when events in the actual world spectacularly fail to conform to their models.[17] Because they play an outsized role in the way we live now—greater even than what Knight imagined for company entrepreneurs—economists have a special responsibility to learn from the history of their discipline, acknowledge the limitations of their tools, and face up to the reality of things none of us can know.

Notes

1. Knight wrote the dissertation from which he drew *Risk, Uncertainty, and Profit* while he was a graduate student at Cornell, between 1913 and 1916. While Knight was no doubt primarily responsible for the argument of his thesis, it is worth noting the two different kinds of input his two primary advisors might be assumed to have provided. Knight began the thesis under the direction of Alvin S. Johnson, who was politically progressive, if not radical. Johnson helped found the New School in New York after he left Cornell; Johnson also actively encouraged European economists fleeing Nazi Germany to settle in America. When Johnson left Cornell, the economist Allyn J.

Young took over supervision of Knight's thesis. Young had studied economics under the politically progressive Richard A. Ely at Wisconsin, and he went on to direct the Bureau of Statistical Research for the War Trade Board from 1917 to 1918. In contrast to both his advisors, Knight was resolutely antiprogressive.

2. Frank Knight, *Risk, Uncertainty, and Profit* (1921; rpt. Chicago: University of Chicago Press, 1971), 86. References cited by page number.

3. The expansion of the terms "capital" and "wealth" to include anticipated future income originated with Irving Fisher's 1906 *The Nature of Capital and Income* (New York: Macmillan). In the debates about corporate taxation, one of the leading proponents of using Fisher's definition as the basis for taxation was E. R. Seligman. See T. S. Adams, "Federal Taxes upon Income and Excess Profit," *American Economic Review* 8, no. 1, supplement (March 1918): 18–35.

4. Charles J. Bullock, "Trust Literature: A Survey and a Criticism," *Quarterly Journal of Economics* 15, no. 2 (1901): 168.

5. Naomi R. Lamoreaux, *The Great Merger Movement in American Business, 1895–1904* (Cambridge: Cambridge University Press, 1985), 2. Historians refer to this period as "the first merger movement," although they also note that the railroads, which began to expand in the 1840s, were the nation's first corporations. See Alfred D. Chandler, *The Visible Hand: The Managerial Revolution in American Business* (Cambridge, Mass.: Belknap Press of Harvard University Press, 1977), pt. 2; and Martin J. Sklar, *The Corporate Reconstruction of American Capitalism, 1890–1916: The Market, the Law, and Politics* (Cambridge: Cambridge University Press, 1988), chap. 1. On the scholarly controversy about how to date the merger movement, see Sklar, *Corporate Reconstruction*, 46; and Lawrence E. Mitchell, *The Speculation Economy: How Finance Triumphed over Industry* (San Francisco: Berrett-Koehler, 2007), 283–84n12. Mitchell also discusses the controversy about the number of corporations and the amount of capitalization added to the U.S. economy during this brief period (*Speculation Economy*, 12 and 284n12). Also essential to this subject is Jonathan Barron Baskin and Paul J. Miranti Jr., *A History of Corporate Finance* (Cambridge: Cambridge University Press, 1997), especially chapters 4 and 5. For contemporaries' estimates about numbers of corporations and the amount of wealth they added to the economy, see John Moody, *The Truth about the Trusts: A Description and Analysis of the American Trust Movement* (New York: Moody, 1904), 485–89.

6. Sklar, *Corporate Reconstruction*, 49–50. As Sklar explains, the Santa Clara decision was crucial to the emergence of the corporations. "The corporate reorganization required proprietors to surrender ownership of their physical units or assets in exchange for securities that, as equities, were claims upon a share of earnings. Upon that claim, in turn, rested the exchange value of the securities. That value found itself enhanced in the market in proportion as the consolidated prestige, goodwill, and reinforced market power, of previously separated enterprises, raised the putative earning power of the new corporation. The legal protection of the value of intangibles as essential to property rights, along with the court's strengthening of limited stockholder liability in its 'natural entity' doctrine, reduced the risk and enhanced the value of corporate stock, and thereby facilitated the exchange of tangibles for securities and hence the separation of operational control from legal ownership characteristic of the corporate form of property" (50). Despite this procorporate decision, as Sklar explains, between 1897 and 1911 the Supreme Court also inhibited corporate-administered markets through its construction of the Sherman Anti-Trust Act (see Sklar, *Corporate Reconstruction*, chap. 3). In the meantime, states could and did pass legislation

that either promoted corporate formation, as was the case with New Jersey, Delaware, and New York, or inhibited it, as was the case with Massachusetts in particular.

7. See W. Elliot Brownlee, "Economists and the Formation of the Modern Tax System in the United States: The World War I Crisis," in *The State and Economic Knowledge: The American and British Experiences*, ed. Mary O. Furner and Barry Supple (Cambridge: Cambridge University Press, 1990), 401–35.

8. This view of the 1909 act is persuasively set out in Marjorie E. Kornhauser, "Corporate Regulation and the Origins of the Corporate Income Tax," *Indiana Law Journal* 66, no. 1 (1990): 52–136. Kornhauser's discussion of the role of publicity appears on 69–80, 97–99, and 113–18.

9. Willard J. Graham, "Some Observations on the Nature of Income, Generally Accepted Accounting Principles, and Financial Reporting," *Law and Contemporary Problems* 30, no. 4 (Autumn 1965): 652–73. In the *Eisner v. Macomber* decision, Justice Pitney wrote: "'Income may be defined as the gain derived from capital, from labor, or from both combined,' provided it be understood to include profit gained through a sale or conversion of capital assets. . . . Here we have the essential matter: *not* a gain *accruing* to capital, not a *growth* or *increment* of value *in* the investment; but a gain, a profit, something of exchangeable value *proceeding from* the property, *severed* from the capital however invested or employed, and *coming in*, being '*derived*'; that is, *received* or *drawn by* the recipient . . . for his *separate* use, benefit and disposal:—*that* is income derived from property." Graham notes that the essential elements of this definition turn on realization ("to be income it must be severed from the capital"), gain (it must be above costs), production (the gain must be realized from labor or capital or both), appreciation of the capital assets that is realized (taken by the owner), and a monetary concept (654–55). In subsequent decisions, Graham states, courts have insisted that net incomes are not all the same and should not be treated as such. "There is no one legal concept of business income. The courts are concerned with the intent of the various statutes and not with what the measurement of income ought to be." Eisner v. Macomber, 252 U.S. 189 (1920) at 655.

10. Brownlee chronicles the impact that these events had on the profession of economics. See "Economists and the Formation of the Modern Tax System," 406–26.

11. On Clark and progressive taxation, see Mary Murname, "The Mellon Tax Plan: The Income Tax and the Penetration of Marginalist Economic Thought into American Life and Law in the 1920s" (PhD diss., Case Western Reserve University, 2006; UMI ProQuest 2007), 52, 80–88. Fisher's redefinitions of "capital" and "property" appear in Fisher, *The Nature of Capital and Income*.

12. The work was coauthored by Wesley Mitchell, Willford I. King, Frederick R. Macaulay, Oswald W. and Knauth, but the project was directed by Mitchell. See *Income in the United States, Its Amount and Distribution, 1909–1919*, vol. 1 (New York: Harcourt, Brace, 1921).

13. See Mark C. Smith, *Social Science in the Crucible: The American Debate over Objectivity and Purpose, 1918–1941* (Durham, N.C.: Duke University Press, 1994), 65. The NBER did accept financial support from foundations like the Rockefeller Foundation, but Mitchell refused to allow his sponsors to influence the bureau's research. See also *Income in the United States*, 1:9–10, in which the authors explain their method and state that the maximum discrepancy allowed between the two parts of the parallel investigations was 7.0 percent.

14. See Patrick D. Reagan, *Designing a New America: The Origins of New Deal Planning, 1890–1943* (Amherst: University of Massachusetts Press, 1999), 83.

15. J. Marschak, "Neumann's and Morgenstern's New Approach to Static Economics," *Journal of Political Economy* 54, no. 2 (April 1946): 109.

16. The phrase "risk society" comes from Ulrich Beck, *Risk Society: Towards a New Modernity*, trans. Mark Ritter (Thousand Oaks, Calif.: Sage, 1992), 23. Peter Miller, Liisa Kurunmäki, and Ted O'Leary, "Accounting, Hybrids, and the Management of Risk," *Accounting, Organizations, and Society* 33, no. 7–8 (2008): 943.

17. A group of social scientists has offered a telling analysis of the "superiority" economists now enjoy. See Marion Fourcade, Etienne Ollion, and Yann Algan, "The Superiority of Economists," MAXPO Discussion Paper 14/3 (2014), http://www.maxpo.eu/pub/maxpo_dp/maxpodp14-3.pdf. On the limitations of this approach to uncertainty, especially with regard to financial markets, see Nassim Nicholas Taleb, *The Black Swan: The Impact of the Highly Improbable* (New York: Random House, 2007) and Elie Ayache, *The Blank Swan: The End of Probability* (Chichester, UK: Wiley, 2010).

CHAPTER 9

REPRESENTATIONS OF CAPITALISM IN THE GILDED AGE AND PROGRESSIVE ERA

PETER KNIGHT

In his overview of the new history of American capitalism, Jeffrey Sklansky identifies four broad aspects that need to be considered.[1] First, there are ways of being (the forms of selfhood that create and are shaped by capitalism); second, ways of believing (the role of emotions such as trust, confidence, and duplicity in forging a market society); third, ways of ruling (the role of the state and other institutions in framing the political and legal structures of capitalism); and finally, ways of seeing (the disciplines, discourses, and representations that frame knowledge of capitalism).[2] Although the four strands are necessarily interrelated, this essay focuses on capitalism's ways of seeing in the Gilded Age and Progressive Era in the United States. The reason for this spotlight is that, despite its increasing ubiquity and encroachment into many aspects of daily life, American capitalism became increasingly difficult to "see" in this period. As Marieke de Goede has argued, the task of a historical genealogy of capitalism should be to denaturalize the "truths" of economic knowledge that have come to be taken for granted and thus become in many ways invisible.[3] The advantage of examining the vernacular culture of capitalism in the decades around the turn of the twentieth century is that some of the features our contemporary moment of capitalism that have long since become part of the economic landscape were in their infancy then, still in the process of being constructed by proponents and contested by critics.

The increasing omnipresence but also odd invisibility of capitalism in the Gilded Age was in large part the result of the emergence of a recognizably modern form of financial capitalism.[4] Wall Street became the symbolic capital of capital, with the stock market standing in synecdochically for the whole of the economy. The stock market has often been perceived as elusive, mysterious, and spectral because it seems to conjure value out of paper promises, dealing primarily in abstractions that resist realist representation. From the 1880s onward, traders were not necessarily buying wheat or steel as such, but futures and options, paper instruments whose value often exceeded by many multiples the actual production of the nation's farms and factories. Farmers complained bitterly about the vast fortunes being made by speculation in what they termed "wind wheat" on the Chicago Board of Trade, a form of financial commodity that seemed to bear no relation to the actual crops they grew.[5] It is arguable that financial capitalism more generally creates recurrent crises of representation, when the faith that is necessary to maintain belief in the value of the numerous fictive substitutes and abstractions of "real" value (paper money, credit instruments, futures contracts, and so on) periodically begins to crumble.[6] This process quickened pace in the late nineteenth century in the United States when the stock market became abstracted from the particular locations and people of actual open-cry exchanges as, quite simply, there was less to see. Finding representational analogues for the increasingly abstract forms of speculative capitalism thus became more difficult around the turn of the twentieth century with the emergence of vast new industrial trusts and the rise of a popular fascination with Wall Street, even before mass participation in the markets.[7]

Although some interesting work has been done on market society's "ways of seeing," an actual visual culture of capitalism sprang up in the Gilded Age and Progressive Era. The four case studies discussed here include both representations of financial capitalism created by critics and outsiders, and some of the new representational technologies developed by financial insiders in this period. The first is a satirical cartoon of Jay Gould published in *Judge* magazine in 1886; the second is a Babsonchart, an early attempt from the first decades of the twentieth century to provide a visualization of the patterns supposedly inherent in the fluctuations of prices of securities; the third is the economist Irving Fisher's hydraulic machine, which was designed to show the operations of the economy as a whole; and the final example is a diagram produced by the Pujo Committee investigations into the so-called Money Trust in 1912. These representations did not merely create new ways of visualizing the stock market; they helped reconfigure and rationalize the very idea of the market and later the economy as coherent, predictable, and self-sustaining entities. Many of these representations worked by simultaneously abstracting and humanizing the problem of finance.

Bulls, Bears, and Giants

Although the full history of how the stock market has been represented in visual culture has yet to be written, it is possible to sketch out some of the main modes, themes, and images.[8] The allegorical approach to depicting finance in satirical cartoons that accompanied the Financial Revolution in eighteenth-century Britain was adopted in a transformed mode in the United States in the nineteenth century, not least in response to the recurrent financial panics that rocked the nation. Visual depictions of the operations of finance frequently use a register that is either natural (storms, floods, animals) or providential (gambling wheels, lady luck, and other feminizations of finance). One of the most common modes of allegorizing the market in the Gilded Age and Progressive Era was anthropomorphization, with the individuals, generic types, or even abstract traits of speculative capitalism appearing in the guise of animals. Many nineteenth-century depictions of financial panics focus on the herd-like behavior of market crowds, in which the violence of the struggle for financial survival on the floor of the exchange resembles the Darwinian jungle. The most notable portrayal of bestial finance is undoubtedly William Holbrook Beard's painting *The Bulls and Bears in the Market* (1879), which weds the visual allegory of political cartoons to the dramatic narrative and realism of late nineteenth-century high art.[9]

Although bull and bear imagery was the most common in popular depictions of the stock market, other animal metaphors were deployed, the most prominent of which was the octopus. The octopus combined a notion of evil individual intentionality with a suggestion that corporate malfeasance was part of a complex, many-armed system. These cartoon images of the corporation as a monstrous cephalopod also captured antimonopolist fears that the new industrial combinations and the financial apparatus that created them threatened republican virtues of individual enterprise and self-sufficiency because of their unprecedented size and reach. The octopus is scary, the images suggest, because it can insert its tentacles into the entire business and politics of the nation, and even the globe.[10] While some of the octopus cartoons present a particular corporation as a beast with a will and a mind of its own, others identify the octopus with particular robber barons, giving a name and a face in an uncanny fashion to the anthropomorphic embodiment of corporate will.

These renditions of recognizable "captains of industry" were in keeping with other popular depictions of the period that also identified the stock market in general with particular people. Despite efforts by Wall Street apologists to redefine the popular image of finance as professional and impersonal, the American public continued to focus on prominent individuals as the embodiment of the stock market. Portraits of robber barons such as Daniel Drew, Jim Fisk, Cornelius Vanderbilt, and Jay Gould in the 1870s and 1880s, and of John D. Rockefeller and J. P. Morgan in the 1890s and 1900s dominated the public imagination of the stock market, presenting them as giants who loomed over Wall Street, in the view of a satirical cartoon of 1903, for example. The cartoons repeatedly concentrated on the personal power of particular Wall Street titans, showing them sometimes in a celebratory fashion as an all-powerful colossus, but at others in a more critical vein as sinister monsters or puppet masters controlling the fate of mere mortals. If the vast new corporations that were created around the turn of the twentieth century endeavored to hide behind the legal protection of limited liability and collective identity, muckrakers insisted—in the legal terminology of the age—on "piercing the corporate veil," to expose to the harsh light of criticism the individuals they felt were to blame for corporate wrongdoing, and who, they suspected, were hiding behind the legal fiction of corporate personality. At the same time, however, an obsessive focus on the might of particular individual corporate figureheads ended up fetishizing their power, turning them into bogeymen who haunted the popular imagination and made it hard to think of the complexities of financial capitalism in any other way.

When they were not evoking the inscrutable mysteries of Providence, popular explanations for sudden market movements that created or wiped out fortunes tended from the eighteenth century onward to rely on the idea of plotting and scheming behind the scenes by powerful "insiders," seeing the conspiring agency of a hidden hand in place of the abstract convergence of aggregate supply and demand that constituted the "invisible hand" of more orthodox economic theory. It comes as little surprise, therefore, that images of finance focus on the controlling hand of the market manipulator. When they were not, like J. P. Morgan, trying to hide from public display or sink into anonymity behind the façade of their corporate identity, the nation's industrial and financial leaders sought to portray themselves as dignified and professional. Jay Gould, for instance, had himself painted as a respectable and kindly bourgeois businessmen by the Royal Academician Sir Hubert von Herkomer (ironically now best known as the painter of *Hard Times*, a searing portrayal of rural poverty). The public, however, thought of the notorious stock market operator as the "Mephistopheles of Wall Street," a cold and calculating devil manipulating the market with sublime ease. A satirical illustration from *Judge* magazine in 1886 calls to account the outrageous claim made by Gould that he never speculated.[11] The cartoon shows a caricatured version of Gould seated in the bell jar of a gigantic stock ticker machine where, unseen by the frenzied stock market players beneath, he dictates market prices directly onto the ticker tape itself. Gould is thus rendered in caricature as both himself and the very personification of market manipulation. The cartoon

9.1 Grant E. Hamilton, "'I Never Speculate'—Jay Gould," *Judge* 9, January 9, 1886, back cover. Harvard College Library

suggests that stock prices are moved not by the invisible hand of supply and demand but by the visible hand of the Mephistopheles of Wall Street himself. The cartoon thus ironically confirms Gould's scandalous denial: he would have no need to engage in risky speculations if he were able to accurately predict price movements because he was creating them himself.

Plotting the Market

The cartoon of a larger-than-life Gould literally writing the prices on the ticker tape provides an imaginary view of what Populist critics feared was really taking place in the stock market. It resembled the view from the visitors' gallery of the stock exchange, but it promised to reveal what could not be seen with the naked eye from that privileged vantage point. Earlier in the nineteenth century, the visitors' gallery had offered the best view of the stock market, although the amateur observer was only able to gain a general impression of market movements rather than any detailed knowledge of individual transactions, and at worst was overwhelmed by the incomprehensible spectacle. With the introduction of the stock ticker in the late 1860s, however, the general public were barred from the floor of the New York Stock Exchange (so that the NYSE could maintain its precious monopoly on the price information its members produced).[12] This made it impossible for nonmembers to observe market transactions in any detail while they were taking place. However, the development of the stock ticker permitted a new vantage point on the activity of Wall Street, allowing tape readers to observe from afar individual transactions taking place on the floor of the exchange in near real time through the medium of printed symbols on the tape. The stock ticker thus enabled readers to follow all the action in the market from a privileged bird's-eye viewpoint, and thus to begin to see "the market" in a different way, not as the record of personal struggles between identifiable traders but as an abstract and endless procession of fluctuating numbers coming over the tape. It was not simply a more efficient way of transmitting and representing price information but was part of an emerging cluster of representational technologies, discourses, and practices that reconfigured the very market that the ticker was purported to represent more accurately. The stock ticker encouraged an abstract understanding of the market, coupled with a disciplining of the economic subject into habits of rational calculation and unceasing concentration to the endless flow of prices.[13]

The endless flow of price fluctuations on the tape thus prompted a form of reading the market up close. Other commentators, however, warned that the optic provided by the stock ticker was in danger of giving a distorted picture of the market, in the way that it created a view from a microscope rather than a telescope.[14] *The Ticker* magazine (aimed at teaching ordinary Americans how to decipher the ticker tape) warned that "the greatest difficulty of the tape-reader is that he becomes so sensitive from working close to the tape, that his judgment is rendered narrow. He endeavors to catch every small fluctuation in the market."[15] From the 1890s onward the fledgling industry of technical analysis began instead to recommend the stock chart as providing the best perspective on the market. "Charts are simply a bird's-eye view of market movements," H. M. Williams declared in *The Key to Wall Street Mysteries*, while the bucket shop operator Lewis Van Riper averred that "in this way one is able to comprehend at a glance every stock movement of importance in the same way that a picture describes to the mind the events which could only be told imperfectly, though requiring hours to relate."[16] The story that the charts promised to reveal, however, was not simply the record of the trading in a particular day, month, or year, nor even the truth about hidden manipulation by market insiders. Read in the right way their patterns instead promised to reveal trends and forces that operated according to their own logic, far removed from individual intentions.

The charting of financial data in the form of line graphs was pioneered in the early twentieth century by the American businessman and statistician Roger Ward Babson, whose first Babsonchart was issued in 1907. Babson's charts turned the flow of price data into the now familiar patterns of mountains and valleys, a sublime landscape of economic highs and lows that simultaneously invites and rejects human identification. The early chartists (as they became known) were keen to promote their special expertise, emphasizing what they believed was their objectivity and statistical rigor. Babson adopted the language of Newtonian physics in his production of charts that plotted the cyclical motion of the action and reaction in stock prices, along with indices of various "business conditions." Dealing with abstract patterns, Babson's charts were promoted as capturing with scientific accuracy the underlying statistical regularities that were not otherwise visible to even the most experienced of tape readers. Babson argued that the aim of drawing the "Normal Line" (now more commonly known as a trend line) was to make immediately manifest the equal and opposite shaded areas above and below the line; according to his theory, the area of a boom matched the area of the subsequent bust. Yet deciding where to draw the line was presented not as a matter of mechanically applying statistical laws but an act of interpretation based on experience, an art rather than a science. Moreover, if the line could only be inked in once a cycle had completed, it meant that using such charts to predict future stock price movements was impossible, as indeed academic studies of the predictive accuracy of chartism have since demonstrated.[17]

Although the work of the early chartists might have been based on mistaken statistical reasoning, it nevertheless contributed to an important reconfiguration of the vernacular epistemology of the stock market. In addition to their simultaneous appeal to both projection and identification, the charts helped rationalize "the market," making speculation seem sensible because price movements were at least intelligible, if not always entirely predictable. In the eyes of their proponents, the charts seemed to provide instant visual evidence of a profound order to the financial universe, a regularity that could not be seen by those immersed in either the tumult of the trading floor or the ebb and flow of prices on the ticker tape. In effect chart reading developed a theory about the representational

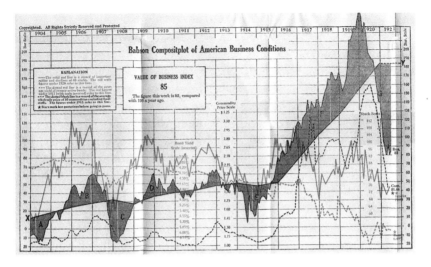

9.2 Babson Compositplot of American Business Conditions (1921), Roger W. Babson, Business Barometers Used in the Accumulation of Money (Wellesley Hills, Mass.: Babson Institute, 1921), inset after page 106. Harvard College Library

capacity of securities prices themselves. The price fluctuations shown on the charts were not the reflection and the result of important political events taking place outside the realm of the market nor even representations of the fundamental underlying value of particular corporations or the economy as a whole. Instead they registered movements that were intrinsic to the market itself. In short, these abstract diagrams of market events worked not through the genre of realism but were in an important sense self-referential artifacts, akin to forms of modernist art that were beginning to emerge at the same time.

If the charts did represent something beyond their immediate selves, however, it was "the market" in its totality, even as an omniscient being with a life and a mind of its own. In the same way that securities prices and the stock ticker itself were repeatedly personified in popular financial advice literature, so too were technical charts often described in decidedly human terms, such as the "head and shoulders" formation. Even when the patterns of abstract data were not read in directly anthropomorphic ways, the shorthand names and instantly recognizable shapes lent a homely familiarity to a statistical knowledge that had promised to reveal the uncanny, inhuman patterns inherent in the aggregated data. In their most abstract, depersonalizing form, the graphs of stock market prices nevertheless tempted readers into an affective identification with impersonal data, which was often figured in distinctly personal terms.

The stock market charts did not so much reflect a preexisting financial universe as help call the very idea of the market as a coherent entity into being, even a person, a living creature that could be grasped at a glance. As the historical sociologist Alex Preda notes in a discussion of why chartism has persisted into the twenty-first century despite the fact that its theories have been disproven by academic economists, the appeal of technical analysis lies not in its ability to accurately represent financial reality but as a coping mechanism for would-be investors in the face of market uncertainties. The result of the increasing popularity—but not necessarily the accuracy—of chart theory, Preda argues, is that "the market" is created in its image: "In the process of using the theory as an uncertainty-processing instrument, new entities are created, corresponding to the theory's representations."[18]

The chartists drew their inspiration from the work of Charles Dow, whose creation of the Dow Jones Industrial Average (DJIA) likewise contributed to the performative construction of the market in this period. In his editorial in the first edition of the *Wall Street Journal*, Jones declared that it would "present in its market article, its tables, and its advertisements a faithful picture of the rapidly shifting panorama of the Street."[19] Although his paper did contain hands-on reporting of the personalities and events of the New York Stock Exchange, its inclusion from the first edition of the Dow average meant that it also attempted to present through the language of statistical averages a panoramic overview of "the Street." Wall Street was now conceived less as a geographically specific place prone to fraud and manipulation of insiders, than as a shorthand for the entirety of the market, which, crucially, operated through its own impersonal laws that could be discovered by plotting them in tables and charts. The shares picked by Dow (twelve originally, increased to thirty in 1928) were deemed by him to be leaders in their respective fields and representative of the market as a whole, although the relationship between the average and what it represented remained opaque as Dow did not reveal which stocks the average contained and expressed the average in terms of index points rather than actual prices. Leaving aside the issue of the accuracy of Dow's average as a recording and representational technology (it has been recalibrated on several occasions, and other indices have joined in the competition to provide the best tracking device), the significance of the DJIA is that it helped consolidate the very idea of the stock market as a vast, self-contained, and self-regulating system. It was, like the ticker tape and the stock chart, a performative device that helped create the very object it claimed to so naturally represent.[20]

Economic Plumbing

Guides to the ticker tape and the stock chart were produced by a flourishing cadre of self-taught and self-designated market professionals and were aimed at clerks and other young men dreaming of getting rich through speculation.

For the most part the emerging profession of mathematically trained academic economists ignored the stock market, tending to see it as merely a sideshow to the main business of the economy, best avoided by amateurs and outsiders.[21] However, these pioneering economists grappled with similar problems of abstraction and figuration as they began to imagine the economy as a coherent whole. In addition to applying mathematical techniques to the mysteries of economic life, economists in the late nineteenth and early twentieth century began to consider the accumulated, abstracted data as part of a larger, integrated, and universal system. Where the earlier discipline of political economy had been concerned, from a moral point of view, with weighing up the competing claims to resources among social classes, the new mathematical economists were eager to discover the underlying economic relations between production and exchange, abstracted from their immediate social, class, and geographic particulars into the purer graphical language of supply and demand curves. Indeed, many of these pioneering econometricians were keen to display their data in graphical form, to make immediately apparent the underlying patterns and immutable laws that they believed themselves to be discovering.[22] For example, the British economist Alfred Marshall (whose textbook on economics became the standard work on both sides of the Atlantic) noted that "the graphical method of statistics, though inferior to the numerical in accuracy of representation, has the advantage of enabling the eye to take in at once a long series of facts."[23] What the eye was meant to take in at a single glance was a picture of a complete and coherent system of interrelated parts, with economists increasingly turning to theories that movements of the market could be explained entirely by reference to the internal structure of the economic machine itself.

As economics historian Philip Mirowski points out, neoclassical economists in the nineteenth century borrowed many of their terms and concepts from physics and engineering, not least the idea that all the individual economic impulses were in fact part of a unified force within a larger, coherent, and interconnected system (in the case of the marginalists, "utility" served as the unifying force, which therefore permitted a uniform measurement across varied economic phenomena).[24]

For some economists the physics metaphors were understood literally, with Irving Fisher, for example, setting out in his pioneering PhD dissertation of 1892 (Yale's first in economics) detailed plans for a hydraulic model of price fluctuation. He in fact built this model to use in his teaching at Yale and had another one made in 1926 when the original prototype wore out. Whatever else it purported to demonstrate, Fisher's contraption served to make visible and tangible the idea of the economy as a complex but well-ordered system, in which prices would find their equilibrium level as naturally as water under the influence of gravity.[25] As much as it brought a mathematical objectivity to the

8.

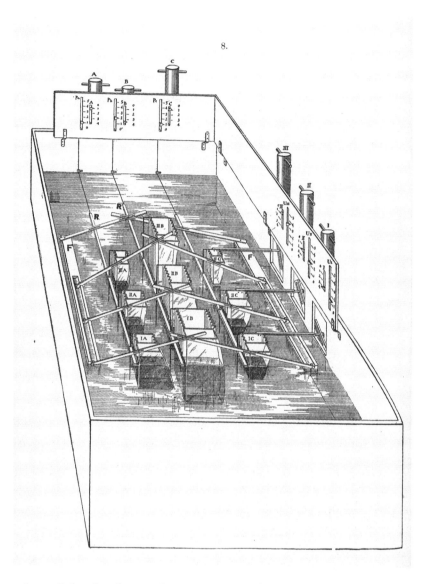

9.3 Irving Fisher, "Mathematical Investigations in the Theory of Value and Prices," *Transactions of the Connecticut Academy* 9 (July 1892): 38. Harvard College Library

representation of economics, it also portrayed the interaction of supply and demand as a quasi-autonomous machine-beast.

Like the other representational technologies examined in this essay, Fisher's all-too-solid machine allowed economic activity to be conceived as both an abstraction and a totality. This conceptual revolution involved, first, reframing the myriad data of economic life as abstracted from local particulars, and, second, portraying those diverse factors as part of a coordinated system whose patterns might not necessarily be observable at ground level.[26] As with the rhetorical transition from accounts of marketplaces to talk of the placeless market, it is important to remember that "the economy" is not a timeless and neutral category. Although it now seems obvious as the proper object of knowledge of economics, before the twentieth century the term "economy" in the writings of political economists referred simply to the idea of frugality or economizing, the proper and efficient use of resources. The use of the phrase "*the* economy"— in the sense of the whole aggregate of statistics of production, consumption, inflation, and employment that make up a bounded national entity—only emerged in interwar economic discourse as part of institutional efforts (such as the foundation of the National Bureau of Economic Research in 1920 and the Cowles Commission in 1932) designed to gather statistical information to aid state intervention and manipulation of national economic life through economic modeling.[27] Progressive Era critics originally promoted such fact-gathering institutions as the NBER with the hope that they would produce intelligible graphical representations and statistical overviews of the complex, corporate behemoths that emerged rapidly in the years around the turn of the twentieth century, in order that Congress might regulate and tax them based on objective evidence rather than on the patchy and partial information offered up by the corporations themselves. The historical irony, as Mary Poovey points out in her contribution to the present volume, is that the information on the valuation of corporations gathered for the NBER ended up helping the corporations make better accounting sense of their business and in the process improved their profitability.

Although these early twentieth-century actual and virtual models produced by professional economists were born from very different needs and institutional contexts than that of the early chartists, they share the performative capacity to make the object of their inquiry (at first the market, and then the economy) come alive. At the same time as producing an abstracting and totalizing view, these ways of imaging the market often relied on older visual tropes or homely metaphors that made the impersonal data seem more concrete and familiar. Yet the models, both mathematical and mechanical, ended up being taken for reality itself, and in so doing shaped economic practice.

Exhibit 243

The final case study is a remarkable illustration that was included as an appendix to the Pujo Committee report into the concentration of wealth and power in the nation's financial and industrial enterprises (see Figure 9.4). The diagram

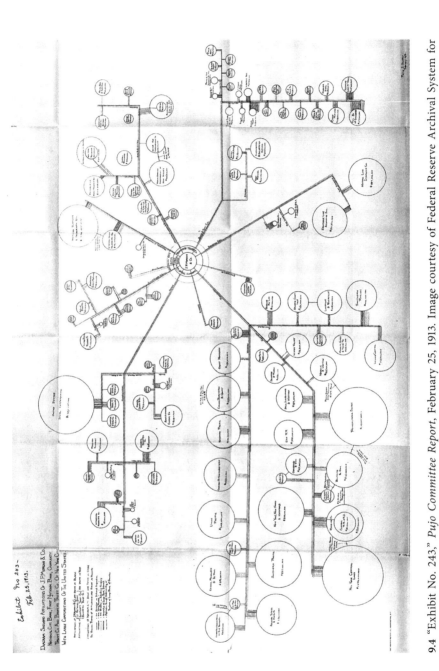

9.4 "Exhibit No. 243," *Pujo Committee Report*, February 25, 1913. Image courtesy of Federal Reserve Archival System for Economic Research, Federal Reserve Bank of St. Louis

marks a startlingly original attempt to create a panorama of high finance, but it also pushes to the limit the representational technologies of the era to combine concrete and abstract visual forms. It presents the totality of financial capitalism as both an abstract network and a quasi-conspiratorial picture of hidden intentions.

The chart was submitted as Exhibit 243 and was one of a series of diagrams that provided a schematic representation of the links between the various bankers and institutions under investigation. The diagram was derived from a huge table that plotted all the interlocking directorships of the biggest financial firms with the largest industrial and transportation companies. The table and diagrams were prepared by Philip Scudder, of the Investors' Agency, a New York firm of accountants and financial advisors. In his testimony to the committee, Scudder recounts how it took a team of twelve clerks working day and night for three weeks solid to gather the data and prepare the table and charts.[28] Exhibit 243 uses careful color coding to show the various affiliations (black for those involving J. P. Morgan & Co., green for the National City Bank, and so on), along with different lines to indicate the precise nature of the relationship (e.g., a wiggly line for a voting trustee, dashes for a director in a subsidiary company). Finally, the size of the circles is in proportion to the capital worth of each firm.

It was important to critics to find a way of rendering visible the networks of power against which they were protesting. As Louis Brandeis put it in his book that popularized the findings of the Pujo Committee, "Wealth expressed in figures gives a wholly inadequate picture of the allies' power. Their wealth is dynamic. It is wielded by geniuses in combination. It finds its proper expression in means of control. To comprehend the power of the allies we must try to *visualize the ramifications* through which the forces operate."[29] Scudder no doubt would have received his instructions from Samuel Untermyer, counsel for the committee, but there is little in the historical record about where the latter derived the specifications for Exhibit 243. Although largely forgotten now, the diagram is fascinating because it draws on a variety of different and quite contradictory representational traditions to create what is arguably one of the first attempts to provide a graphical mapping of the entire landscape of American capitalism.

We might begin by noting that the diagram has a family resemblance to the many satirical cartoons of the era that picture corporations as octopuses. With its depiction of Morgan as the central financial intelligence connected by numerous appendages to outlying parts of the national economy, Exhibit 243 resembles a structural circuit diagram of an octopus. The chart also recalls muckraking cartoons that depicted Morgan as a spider at the center of the web of "flim-flam finance," trying to lure the public to their doom.[30] With the muckraking cartoons of the era, the Pujo diagrams share a desire to see a totality

·that is more than the sum of its parts, to visualize a coordinated pattern beneath the surface detail, and, above all else, to identify the individual—or at
any rate, the individual firm—at the center of the web. Unlike the satirical cartoons, however, the Pujo diagrams unsurprisingly eschew any direct personification or anthropomorphism, relying on names, numbers, and color-coded
lines to make their argument. And yet, as illustrations, they are not entirely
mechanical and impersonal: they are painstakingly hand drawn, equally works
of art as of accountancy.

As much as the diagrams are geometric abstractions of anthropomorphic
octopuses or spiders, they also draw their visual rhetoric from the corporate
organization charts that were pioneered by the engineer Daniel McCallum for
the Pennsylvania Railroad in the 1850s.[31] In McCallum's seminal drawing, the
unprecedented organizational complexity of a large corporation was visualized
as a series of branch and trunk lines, much like the ramifying structure of the
railroad itself. What is striking, however, is that the pyramid shape that is more
familiar in twentieth-century organization charts is inverted in the railroad
chart: the managers are at the bottom, with the lowliest and remotest parts of
the New York and Erie at the top. McCallum's chart is even more intriguing
because its visual metaphor is organic rather than machinic: it resembles a
natural history drawing of a fern, or the display of a peacock's feathers (both
favored decorative motifs in Victorian America), rather than an engineering drawing. Its schematic logic also draws on the much older visual trope of
the family tree, which was beginning to be used in more systematic ways in the
mid nineteenth century.[32]

Ironically, the Pujo Committee charts, which were designed to show the
conspiratorial complicity of the corporate giants, drew on the very modes of
organizational rationality that the business historian Alfred Chandler identified as central to the rise of corporations. This irony is understandable if we
remember that Untermyer was trying to make a case for the Money Trust that
was less fevered than the Populist accusations that had led to the establishment
of the Pujo Committee, and that were in danger of getting the investigation
sunk before it could even begin. It must also be remembered that both Untermyer and Brandeis, before they turned to the antimonopoly cause, had made
their fortunes as lawyers undertaking corporate reorganizations, particularly
of railroads. It was precisely their training in the organizational efficiency of
the railroads that allowed them to visualize financial corruption as a *system*.
Exhibit 243 thus reveals insider dealing not as an occasional and incidental
corruption of proper business, but as a structural component of it, part of a
complete ecosystem.

In contrast John Moody, the American financial analyst and founder of the
bond rating agency that still bears his name, produced diagrams of corporate
interlocks in the first decade of the twentieth century that were designed not

to condemn the conspiracy of capitalism but to celebrate the emergence of the trusts as an inevitable stage in economic evolution. For Moody—as it was for Morgan—the problem of competition was to be solved through cooperation. "The modern trust," Moody asserted, "is the natural outcome or evolution of society conditions and ethical standards which are recognized and established among men today as being necessary elements in the development of civilization."[33] The diagrams are not mere illustrations but are central to Moody's overall project of trying to understand and represent industrial combinations that have grown too big to be grasped by mere mortals. He acknowledges that, because of the lack of publicly available documentation and the interconnectedness of the entity, "it is not possible to more than attempt an approximate estimate of the entire Standard Oil industrial, financial and commercial interests of the nation, as their ramifications are so varied and extensive that a clear line of demarcation could not be drawn which would absolutely distinguish the interests which are more or less dominated by them, from those which are not." However, "the chart which we publish . . . gives a fairly accurate 'bird's eye view' of the immensity of their influence and importance as the leading factors in American financial and industrial affairs" (491–92). Moody was convinced that, from this imaginary bird's-eye perspective, the two sides in fact constitute a single vast entity:

> It should not be supposed, however, that these two great groups of capitalists and financiers are in any real sense rivals or competitors for power, or that such a thing as "war" exists between them. For, as a matter of fact, they are not only friendly, but they are allied to each other by many close ties, and it would probably require only a little stretch of the imagination to describe them as a single great Rockefeller-Morgan group. (492–93)

Whereas the Pujo Committee saw the ramifications of the banking-industrial complex as something akin to a conspiracy, Moody marveled at the sublime order that emerged beneath the mundane intrigue and in-fighting. He paints a picture of a vast corporate being whose life force circulates throughout the nation, as wasteful competition between rival firms is replaced by a new cooperative and symbiotic system:

> Therefore, viewed as a whole, we find the dominating influences in the Trusts to be made up of an intricate network of large and small groups of capitalists, many allied to one another by ties of more or less importance, but all being appendages to or parts of the greater groups, which are themselves dependent on and allied with the two mammoth or Rockefeller and Morgan groups. These two mammoth groups jointly (for, as pointed out, they really may be regarded as one) constitute the heart of the business and commercial life of the

nation, the others all being the arteries which permeate in a thousand ways
our whole national life, making their influence felt in every home and hamlet,
yet all connected with and dependent on this great central source, the influence and policy of which dominates them all. (493)

Moody's written description of the Rockefeller-Morgan group is couched in
familiar terms of a central heart supplying the economic life force to the whole
body of industrial America. And although the figure is labeled a "family
tree," the picture draws more from the visual rhetoric of machine diagrams
than the organic language of biological or hereditary models. Where the Pujo
Committee perceived conspiratorial complicity and crushing size, Moody
saw "interdependence, harmony, financial strength, commercial power, [and]
ability." However, both Pujo and Moody were animated by a desire to create a
panoramic overview of industrial capitalism as a coordinated system, albeit
with very different intent. For the Pujo Committee, what began to emerge
from the diagrams was a picture of a system that in effect acted as a conspiracy,
or, at the very least, produced the kinds of effects *as if* there had been a deliberate plot.

Leaving aside the question of accuracy, the Moody and the Pujo diagrams
presented an abstracted panorama of the entire corporate economy of the
United States in a way that had not really been done before. Although they
reached wildly different conclusions, they both signal a significant departure
from earlier ways of conceiving of the power structure of large organizations—
and even the entire "economy"—as hierarchical. They both represent the
financial-industrial complex not as a pyramid in which authority flows down
from above, nor as a simple web in which control radiates outward from the
center, but as a circuit of flows in which power is dispersed throughout the
entire, interconnected system.

In *Other People's Money*, Brandeis attempted to clarify what the Pujo Committee had uncovered. "A single example," he claimed, "will illustrate the vicious
circle of control—the endless chain—through which our financial oligarchy
now operates."[34] This is not the usual hierarchical chain of command favored
by conspiracist denunciations of secret societies. Instead Brandeis describes
an interwoven pattern of control in which the ultimate source of power and
meaning is ultimately deferred: "The chain is indeed endless; for each controlled
corporation is entwined with many others."[35] Viewed in isolation, Exhibit 243
might seem to show Morgan & Co. as the controlling spider at the center of the
web, or the central octopus-like intelligence controlling the economy through
its tentacles. However, it is important to note that this was just one of several
visualizations produced by Scudder from the master table of interlocking directorships, each viewing the network of relationships through a different filter.
The individual Pujo diagrams edge toward identifying the commanding

conspirator at the heart of the system, but taken together they create a picture of power that is uncannily decentered, and that cannot be easily put together into one overarching figure. On the one hand, the individual diagrams present a level of detail that is highly personalized: they name names and document in microscopic detail the actual connections between particular capitalists. On the other hand, taken together they constitute an abstract and impersonal representation of the dense and messy entanglement of familial, social, and financial ties. The Pujo diagrams thus not only combine conspiratorial agency and impersonal system, but in effect they represent system *as* conspiracy.[36]

Representing Capitalism in the Twenty-First Century

As with the first Gilded Age, the "gilded age" of the twenty-first century has created its own crises of representation, not least with the global financial crash that began in 2007. For one thing, the mortgage-backed securities that had fueled the boom no longer corresponded to the fictional values (the AAA designation) that had been conferred on them by the ratings agencies, while the insurance contracts on the trade in credit default swaps written by firms such as AIG turned out to be merely paper promises. Likewise, it became apparent that the mathematical models of financial economics such as the Black-Scholes formula for option pricing did not so much represent economic reality as create a "reality" in its own image.[37] What also became obvious in the wake of the credit crisis was the fact that the seemingly incontrovertible truths of financial economics—not least the efficient market hypothesis (the notion that stock market prices always fully reflect all available information) and the resulting conviction that a global financial crash was beyond the realms of statistical possibility (a "black swan" event)—were ideological delusions, convenient at best and deceptive at worst.[38]

Second, the scale of the trade in the exotic products of financial engineering dwarfed comprehension: by 2007, the international financial system was trading derivatives valued at one quadrillion dollars per year, which is ten times the total worth, adjusted for inflation, of all products made by the world's manufacturing industries over the last century.[39] Third, the global financial system had also reached a level of abstraction, intangibility, and opacity that is hard to comprehend, let alone regulate. There is often literally nothing to see: the scene of frenzied traders on the floor of the stock exchange is now a quaint historical throwback, as "the market" increasingly consists of complex mathematical formulae embedded in computer code caroming around the world at close to the speed of light. The development of algorithmic trading in general and high-frequency trading in particular has raised the specter of machines trading with other machines at a speed that mere humans are incapable of following or controlling. Finally, much of the financial activity of the second Gilded Age is not only unimaginable but also invisible, deliberately hidden from regulatory oversight in the complex world of "shadow banking."

Imagining the market has become more difficult because the rising importance of finance to the economy as a whole has meant that economic reality is increasingly abstract and unrepresentable. As with the first Gilded Age, however, it is more vital than ever to understand the performative interplay between representations of the economy and representations produced by the economy. There is much to be gained from studying the formative years of financial capitalism around the turn of the twentieth century, when many of the representational technologies and conceptual frameworks that have long since become naturalized were still in formation—when, in short, they were still visible.

Notes

1. Peter Knight, *Reading the Market: Genres of Financial Capitalism in Gilded Age America* (Baltimore, Md.: Johns Hopkins University Press, 2016), 101–43. Adapted with permission of Johns Hopkins University Press.
2. Jeffrey Sklansky, "The Elusive Sovereign: New Intellectual and Social Histories of Capitalism," *Modern Intellectual History* 9, no. 1 (2012): 233–48.
3. Marieke de Goede, *Virtue, Fortune and Faith: A Genealogy of Finance* (Minneapolis: University of Minnesota Press, 2005), xiii–xxvii.
4. For an account of the rise of finance in this period, see Lawrence E. Mitchell, *The Speculation Economy: How Finance Triumphed over Industry* (San Francisco: Berrett-Koekler, 2008). In *Freaks of Fortune: The Emerging World of Capitalism and Risk in America* (Cambridge, Mass.: Harvard University Press, 2012), Jonathan Levy demonstrates how in the course of the nineteenth century many Americans became increasingly subject to the risks of the volatile economy, with the irony that they turned to financialized solutions such as life insurance to alleviate the problems caused by the market itself.
5. Cedric B. Cowing, *Populists, Plungers, and Progressives: A Social History of Stock and Commodity Speculation, 1890–1936* (Princeton, N.J.: Princeton University Press, 1965), 9. See also Levy, *Freaks of Fortune*, 231–63.
6. See Mary Poovey, *Genres of the Credit Economy: Mediating Value in Eighteenth- and Nineteenth-Century Britain* (Chicago: University of Chicago Press, 2008).
7. Although, as Julia Ott notes in *When Wall Street Met Main Street: The Quest for an Investors' Democracy* (Cambridge, Mass.: Harvard University Press, 2011), only 0.5 percent of the American population owned securities at the turn of the twentieth century (2), Wall Street already loomed large in the public imagination (not least because ordinary Americans were participating by proxy in the stock market in bucket shops which rapidly proliferated from the 1870s to the 1910s).
8. For an outline sketch of that story that includes discussion and reproductions of many of the images discussed in this essay, see Paul Crosthwaite, Peter Knight, and Nicky Marsh, eds., *Show Me the Money: The Image of Finance, 1700 to the Present* (Manchester, UK: Manchester University Press, 2014).

9. See Sarah Burns, "Party Animals: William Holbrook Beard, Thomas Nast, and the Bears of Wall Street," *American Art Journal* 30 (1999): 9–35.

10. See Robert MacDougall, "The Wire Devils: Pulp Thrillers, the Telephone, and Action at a Distance in the Wiring of a Nation," *American Quarterly* 58, no. 3 (2006): 715–41.

11. On the American public's imagination of Gould, see Richard R. John, "Robber Barons Redux: Antimonopoly Reconsidered," *Enterprise & Society* 13, no. 1 (2012): 1–38.

12. On the legal battles over access to the stock ticker, see David Hochfelder, *The Telegraph in America, 1832–1920* (Baltimore, Md.: Johns Hopkins University Press, 2012), 101–37.

13. For a more detailed account of the performative nature of this new representational technology, see Alex Preda, *Framing Finance: The Boundaries of Markets and Modern Capitalism* (Chicago: University of Chicago Press, 2009); and Urs Stäheli, *Spectacular Speculation: Thrills, the Economy, and Popular Discourse*, trans. Eric Savoth (Stanford, Calif.: Stanford University Press, 2013).

14. On the different perspectives afforded by the ticker and the chart in this period, see Preda, *Framing Finance*, 113–71.

15. *The Ticker*, February 1908, 34.

16. H. M. Williams, *The Key to Wall Street Mysteries and Methods* (New York: M. W. Hazen, 1904), 70; Lewis C. Van Riper, *The Ins and Outs of Wall Street* (New York, 1898), 72.

17. Roger Ward Babson, *Actions and Reactions: An Autobiography of Roger W. Babson* (New York: Harper, 1935). For a more detailed discussion of Babson, see Walter A. Friedman, *Fortune Tellers: The Story of America's First Economic Forecasters* (Princeton, N.J.: Princeton University Press, 2013), 12–50.

18. Preda, *Framing Finance*, 150.

19. *Wall Street Journal*, July 8, 1889, 1.

20. De Goede, *Virtue, Fortune and Faith*, 101.

21. The notable exception was Henry Crosby Emery, *Speculation on the Stock and Produce Exchanges in the United States* (New York: Macmillan, 1904).

22. On the turn to graphs in economics, see Harro Maas and Mary S. Morgan, "Timing History: The Introduction of Graphical Analysis in 19th Century British Economics," *Revue d'histoire des sciences humaines* 7 (2002): 97–127; and Judy L. Klein, *Statistical Visions in Time: A History of Time Series Analysis, 1662–1938* (Cambridge: Cambridge University Press, 1997). Klein argues that practical techniques for calculating and visualizing economic data actually preceded academic, abstract modes of analysis.

23. Alfred Marshall, "The Graphic Method of Statistics," in *Memorials of Alfred Marshall*, ed. A. C. Pigou (London: Macmillan, 1925), 175, quoted in de Goede, *Virtue, Fortune, and Faith*, 93.

24. Philip Mirowski, *More Heat than Light: Economics as Social Physics, Physics as Nature's Economics* (Cambridge: Cambridge University Press, 1989). Mirowski points out how the analogy between the conception of energy in physics and utility in economics does not hold.

25. Fisher details the development of his model in Irving Fisher, *Mathematical Investigations in the Theory of Value and Prices* (New Haven, Conn.: Yale University Press, 1925). It is important to note that the machine did not present a view of the stock market in particular or even the entire economy in general, but instead an isolated aspect of the wider economy. Fisher's device relied on the input from other economic subsystems remaining constant. In the middle decades of the twentieth century, economists began to develop more dynamic models informed by systems theory, cybernetics, and ecology with more complicated feedback loops between the various processes.

26. In "Economics Invents the Economy: Mathematics, Statistics, and Models in the Work of Irving Fisher and Wesley Mitchell," *Theory and Society* 32, no. 3 (2003): 379–411, Daniel Breslau posits a three-stage process involving abstraction, homogenization (of economic phenomena into commensurable units), and sedimentation, by which mathematically influenced economic ideas helped construct the idea of "the economy." Breslau's focus is mainly on the third stage, in which ideas became sedimented in the changing social milieu of academic economics in the early years of the twentieth century.

27. In fact, even though the econometricians of the Cowles Commission talked of the "economic system," it was only really with Keynes's *The General Theory of Employment, Interest and Money* (1936) and the institutionalization of macroeconomics that the term "the economy" began to gain any traction. In addition to Breslau, "Economics Invents the Economy," see Timothy Mitchell, "Fixing the Economy," *Cultural Studies* 12 (1998): 82–101; and Susan Buck-Morss, "Envisioning Capital: Political Economy on Display," *Critical Inquiry* 21, no. 2 (1995): 434–67.

28. *Money Trust Investigation. Investigation of Financial and Monetary Conditions in the United States under House Resolutions Nos. 429 and 504, Before a Subcommittee of the Committee on Banking and Currency*, 62nd Cong., 3rd sess. (1913) at 979–80.

29. Louis D. Brandeis, *Other People's Money: And How Bankers Use It* (New York: Stokes, 1914), 30 (emphasis added).

30. L. M. Glackens, "The Flies Got Wise," *Puck* 73, no. 1873, January 22, 1913, cover.

31. Alfred Chandler in *The Visible Hand: The Managerial Revolution in American Business* (Cambridge, Mass.: Belknap Press of Harvard University Press, 1978) credits McCallum with being the first to produce corporate organization charts (103).

32. See, for example, former railroad engineer Lewis Henry Morgan's *Systems of Consanguinity and Affinity of the Human Family* (Washington, D.C.: Smithsonian, 1870).

33. John Moody, *Truth About the Trusts* (New York: Moody, 1904).

34. Brandeis, *Other People's Money*, 51.

35. Ibid., 54–55.

36. On the paradoxical notion of representation system as conspiracy, see Timothy Melley, *Empire of Conspiracy: The Culture of Paranoia in Postwar America* (Ithaca, N.Y.: Cornell University Press, 2000).

37. The definitive account of the performative nature of the Black-Scholes model is Donald Mackenzie, *An Engine Not a Camera: How Financial Models Shape Markets* (Cambridge, Mass.: MIT Press, 2006).

38. Justin Fox, *The Myth of the Rational Market: A History of Risk, Reward, and Delusion on Wall Street* (New York: Harper Business, 2009).

39. Ian Stewart, "The Mathematical Equation That Caused the Banks to Crash," *Guardian*, February 12, 2012.

CHAPTER 10

VALUE OF LIFE

Insurance, Slavery, and Expertise

MICHAEL RALPH

The Virginia Court of Appeals judges presiding over Mr. Hill's 1836 lawsuit against Mr. Randolph were agreed on the circumstances of the case:

> Plaintiff hires a slave to defendant to work in his coal pits, and the slave being one evening at work in one of the pits with other labourers, they are all sickened by the foul air, and drawn out.

Mr. Randolph sent the enslaved worker he had rented from Mr. Hill back into the pits the following morning, "to examine with a lamp and ascertain whether the foul air has left the pit." They understood that this "is the usual course of examination in such cases" but that, this time, something had gone terribly wrong:

> The foreman reports that the foul air is gone; the laborers, ten in number, again descend, are again sickened by foul air, and the plaintiff's slave is killed by it before he can be drawn out of the pit.

The judges considering Mr. Hill's appeal affirmed that the enslaved worker he entrusted with his enterprise was the most highly regarded miner on site. "The overseer of the pits," they explained, had sent "the foreman," "a trustworthy and experienced slave," into the mines to evaluate whether working conditions were now safe. But Mr. Hill's mine was still plagued by "impure and noxious air" that not even a seasoned expert could detect:

> It was proved by the testimony of two of Mr. Randolph's overseers at his coal pits, witnesses on the part of Hill—That the slave was hired by Hill to Randolph, to work in the pits, for one year. . . . That the person sent down was the foreman, and one of the most experienced laborers at the pits, perfectly competent to make such an examination, and worthy of full confidence.

In his dissenting opinion, Judge Scott questioned the foreman's competence, dismissing the evidence presented in the case in favor of familiar racial stereotypes:

> An owner of coal mines ought not to have trusted an ignorant negro, however long he might have been accustomed to work in [the mines], to ascertain whether foul and noxious air had got into them.

Yet Judge Scott was an outlier. So, in March of 1836, the Virginia Court of Appeals upheld the ruling of the Chesterfield County Circuit Court, which had found for the plaintiff, awarding Mr. Hill $400.[1] As the expertise that made their enslaved workers so valuable undermined the legal arguments used to justify slavery, planters were reluctant to place too much faith in the courts and preferred using life insurance to guard against the potential loss of enslaved workers with premium skill sets.

Enslaved coal miners were one of several categories of bonded workers deemed highly skilled and thus highly valued.[2] As a result, these workers experienced more mobility than plantation slaves who were worked to death or beaten with impunity. To avoid the kind of loss that Mr. Hill suffered, enslaved coal miners—like other industrial workers and some favored domestic workers—were insured. Insured slaves were treated as prized assets.

The idea of speculating on someone else's life has a vexed history. The earliest known forms of life insurance entail quotidian, ad hoc strategies for betting on another person's fate.[3] These practices have historically included wagers on the life chances of marginal people, the mortality of aristocrats, or the outcome of capital punishment cases.[4] The widespread practice of generating revenue from speculation on someone else's life eventually led to the British Gambling Act of 1774. Also known as the Assurance Act, this legislation outlawed the practice of affixing a monetary value to another person's life except in cases where "the person insuring shall have an interest in the life or death of the person insured."[5]

Although the Gambling Act barred people from speculating on the life of a free citizen, it did nothing to prevent anyone from taking out an insurance policy on a slave. This practice became increasingly popular in the decades after the slave trade to the United States was outlawed in 1808. Restricting the pool of enslaved workers meant that people who owned slaves could earn more money by renting them out, over and over again, than by selling them.

The nation's emergent industries stood to profit more from renting enslaved workers than from contracting wage laborers. As they were hired out, slaves acquired skills that were highly covered in the marketplace. Planters developed unprecedented opportunities to profit from renting skilled slaves and would insure these prized possessions before loaning them out. In the decades that followed the birth of the domestic trade, slave insurance became a crucial feature of urban industry. Around the same time, northeastern urban residents began to pursue insurance policies on their own lives in large numbers.

The life insurance policies of free citizens were based on calculations about the average lifespan measured against the kinds of risk a person's life posed. Insurance firms used what are called life tables to assess the value of a policy. Slave insurance policies did not involve life tables because slaves were legally classified as property. And yet, slave insurance policies were established for the same purpose: to guard against the potential loss of revenue due to fatal accidents and other perilous circumstances.

In addition to helping people manage risk, life insurance became a way to frame, organize, and corral a person's productive potential—a key feature of growth in societies typically referred to as "capitalist." Life insurance became a handy strategy for managing the monetary value of individual members, whether free citizens concerned with providing for their next of kin or formally enslaved persons who convinced associates to purchase life insurance policies on loved ones and to hold them as collateral while they raised the money needed to purchase their freedom.

Thus, from its inception, life insurance was structured by what we might call the *forensics of capital*.[6] This idea of forensics has two dimensions. The first involves the relationship between risk and liability. The practice of insuring slaves for transport meant that if the cargo was lost or destroyed during transit, the insurer must pay the owner. But first, there was an inquiry to determine whether the loss was caused by a form of risk the insurer and cargo owner agreed upon in advance. Seeing these dynamics through the forensics of capital reminds us of the crucial role that legal and scientific inquiries play in adjudicating capital.

Forensic protocols also structure access to capital. The fact that a merchant could take out an insurance policy on a slave demonstrates that the insurer held a different legal status than the person being insured. This provokes a question central to the way capitalism works: *Under what circumstances is it possible to generate revenue from another person's life?* In the case of insurance, the more specific question is, *Under what circumstances is it possible for one person to insure the life of another?*

What I am calling the forensics of capital involves forms of legal and scientific inquiry (concerned with determining the cause of death and with establishing civil or criminal liability). It also involves strategies of bookkeeping (the means by which the profile of the person with access to capital is inscribed, as is the fate of the person whose life is capitalized). These two processes would shape access to capital from the fifteenth century to the present.[7]

That the oldest records we have for life insurance date back to the fifteenth century (1402) and center on the Iberian peninsula and the Mediterranean (a compact insuring a slave for shipment from Pisa to Barcelona)—puts life insurance at the center of European overseas exploration and the history of accounting.[8] The plantation economies of the Americas were inaugurated through fifteenth-century forms of overseas exploration that transformed into strategies of conquest and dispossession in years to follow. In the process, the forms of industry, labor organization, and accounting that merchants used to establish the plantation societies of the Americas created the material infrastructure of capitalist society.[9]

Studies of capitalism have emphasized the role of factories in building capital reserves and the role of banks in managing them. But insurance played a pivotal role in helping merchants to identify and grow capital. From the time the U.S. colonies were founded, merchants purchased marine insurance to minimize the risk of transporting commerce. Initially, they sought policies from British insurers. Eventually, they would begin to use insurers in places like Philadelphia. By 1797, Virginia merchants established the Alexandria Marine Insurance Company.[10] They were prompted by the pervasive concern that shipments could be interrupted by African adversaries[11] and by increased threats to cargo during the Napoleonic Wars. By establishing a regional center for offering insurance, the Alexandria Marine Insurance Company helped to increase local sources of capital and stimulate economic development throughout the Chesapeake region.

The practice of insurance was systematized in British coffeehouses. As sailors and merchants discussed their affairs, some investors sought the opportunity to guarantee shipments against the risks associated with seaborne transport. Merchants paid a fee to insure their cargo. If it arrived safely, the insurer kept the payment. If the cargo was lost due to an approved risk, the insurer paid an agreed-upon amount to the merchant. The practice of underwriting, or guaranteeing, cargo was based on careful scrutiny of a merchant and his affairs. In other words, insurance underwriters used careful observation, as well as gossip and correspondence with a merchant's peers and colleagues, to evaluate whether that merchant was a worthwhile risk. Insurance underwriting underscores the role of a credit profile, even at this early stage, in determining whether or not a person is granted access to capital.[12]

Most studies on life insurance in the nineteenth-century United States have emphasized why companies were reluctant to pursue slave insurance policies or how slave insurance differed from life insurance in the magnitude of capital it generated and the frequency with which it was used.[13] But more careful attention to primary sources reveals that slave insurance and life insurance evolved in tandem during the first few decades of the nineteenth century. Both forms of insurance were concentrated in urban areas. And both slave insurance and life insurance were used to secure against the potential loss of revenue from workers. Life insurance became integral to American social life during the first few decades of the nineteenth century, creating new possibilities for social mobility and new opportunities for access to capital. By the 1840s, the number of free, northeastern, urban residents who carried life insurance policies on their own lives approximated the number of enslaved workers in urban locales of the Upper South who were insured.[14] In addition to managing the problem of risk that eighteenth- and nineteenth-century capitalism posed, slave insurance and life insurance provided ways to frame, regiment, and organize the productive value of laborers in diverse sectors of U.S. society.

✳ ✳ ✳

In his memoir, Confederate General Harry Heth reminisces about adventures in a subterranean enclave that defined the family business. Against his grandfather's wishes, Heth bribed the foreman of the Black Heath coal pits to give him a tour. If Heth's memoir is marked by his amazement at the underworld labyrinth, his language is stunningly offensive, referring to the foreman who was his guide as "an old darkey."[15] The mine foreman was probably enslaved— likely insured—although slaves worked alongside free white and black miners at Virginia's antebellum coal pits.

The Chesterfield county mines are nestled in the Richmond Coal Basin. At a nearby location, coal was discovered in 1701.[16] These were the oldest coal mines in the nation, in which production was under way by the middle of the eighteenth century.[17] As the most efficient means to transport this precious resource, Virginia's Midlothian coal mines also became the site of the state's first railroad.[18]

Major Henry Heth, a British émigré to the colonies, settled in Chesterfield County, Virginia, about a decade after production began. Heth ultimately fought in the American Revolution as part of the First Virginia Regiment, shooting up through the ranks from captain to major. In the later years of his life, Major Heth honored his Second Amendment right through duty to his state militia. He also became a successful business person.[19] By 1788, the war veteran had established the Black Heath coal pits.[20]

Maybe Virginia's coal deposits are what prompted Heth to settle in this state. After leaving his native Britain, Heth had stopped in Pennsylvania, where coal was more abundant. But Virginia wound up being the first source of commercial coal production in the United States because ports close to the city of Richmond created favorable shipping routes.[21] Virginia supplied coal for homes and businesses in New York, Philadelphia, and Boston, dominating the industry until the 1840s, when Pennsylvania's extensive railroad system created unprecedented opportunities for coal merchants.[22] Among the first mines established in what would eventually become known as the Richmond Coal Basin, the Black Heath pits were renowned for the quality of their coal.[23]

The end of the transatlantic slave trade and birth of the U.S. domestic trade enticed Major Heth to make the most of his access to capital in land and slaves.[24] Heth owned twenty slaves in 1801. But he was savvy. In 1810, he placed an ad in the *Richmond Enquirer* soliciting "30 or 40 able bodied Negro Men, for whom a liberal price will be given" to "be employed in the Coal Mines."[25] By 1812, Major Heth had successfully acquired 114 slaves.[26] In addition to Harry's acquisitions, the Black Heath coal pits would employ hundreds of enslaved miners[27] rented from nearby merchants,[28] with as many as 170 workers in 1813.[29] When Henry Heth leased his Stonehenge property to a collier in 1819, he threw in more than fifty enslaved workers, including several specialists (among them a blacksmith, a striker, a cork maker, and two experts in operating machinery).[30]

Most enslaved workers were subject to harsh punishment and grueling work. Coercion was indispensable to economic production,[31] especially in the cotton kingdom. Industrial slaves like those operating in Virginia coal mines enjoyed a great deal more mobility and a different work regime. Like other chief enterprises, coal mining was understood to require tremendous skill. Consequently, mine owners fostered more favorable working conditions as a way to enhance productivity and sometimes even provided cash incentives.

Industrialists plied enslaved workers with incentives because mining was so dangerous. Chesterfield County marks the site of the first recorded explosion of a U.S. coal mine in 1810.[32] There was another in 1818.[33] Then, on March 18, 1839, a particularly gruesome explosion at the Black Heath coal mine resulted in the tragic deaths of more than forty workers.[34] At least thirty-eight of the deceased workers were slaves, although only the names of the two white mine superintendents were published in local newspapers. An 1839 article in the *Richmond Enquirer* compared these disasters to similar trends in English coal mines, where more than a hundred people had been killed between 1812 and 1815, though it concluded the report by citing scientific discoveries that were likely to reduce the rate of mortality.[35]

Despite the optimism that dominated mining ventures, coal mining continued to be an exceedingly dangerous enterprise. Some decades later, the entrepreneur Abraham S. Woolridge[36] submitted a petition to the Virginia General Assembly on behalf of his stockholders, fretting about the "deadly hazards" enslaved and free coal miners faced. These industrial workers, he noted, "must encounter dangers at every stage, from the falling or crumbling of the roofs and pillars; from the accidental fire"—a tragedy that had twice occurred at the Midlothian mines, the assembly was careful to note—"from sudden irruptions of water flooding his works; from the fearfully destructive explosions produced by inflammable gas; and from the breaking of ropes and other accidents in ascending and descending the shafts," a perennial "danger" complicated by the fact that "every laborer employed in mining is at least twice a day suspended over a depth of many hundred feet."[37] The report cited the presence of methane, "an odorless, colorless, flammable gas," that engulfed "poorly ventilated" mines as the primary cause of these calamities.[38] Even trying to investigate the source of a potential methane gas leak proved hazardous, as an 1876 article from the *Rural Messenger* stressed:

> Mr. Thomas Carol, the foreman . . . was informed that the mine was filling up with gas, and went down to the pit to see about it. He held in his hand an open lamp, such as is commonly used by the pit hands. The moment he reached the bottom of the pit, and started to go into the mouth of the shaft, the gas communicated with the lamp and a horrible explosion occurred.[39]

Thus mining was not simply hazardous to the owners of capital whose profits could literally go up in smoke but for enslaved workers who stood to die a slow, quiet death from imbibing poisonous gases. Still, these perils did little to disrupt the industry. Eager industrialists simply used insurance to protect their investments. Enslaved workers were not usually sent into the pits unless they were insured. And they were not usually insured unless they were first given medical exams.

Before insuring Thomas McTyre for $712 to work in the Black Heath coal pits in February 1857, the firm Tompkins & Company[40] had Dr. William Pollard examine him. Completing a brief questionnaire, Dr. Pollard replied to a set of standard questions:

> What are the number of respirations per minute?
>   About 78.

> What are the number of the heart's pulsations, and those of the arteries? Are they natural in regard to their force, rhythm, volume, &c.?
>   About 161.

After carefully reviewing the answers made by the applicant, and those made by the attending physician, and well weighing the result of your own examination, do you recommend the Company accept the risk?

I do.

In this way, merchants developed a calculus concerning the enslaved worker's health, the loss of his potential skill set, and the cost of insuring him.

On February 8, 1846, enslaved coal miners from Chesterfield County founded the First Baptist Church.[41] Two of the founders, Benjamin and Nathan York, were insured by Nicholas Mills with the Nautilus Insurance Company (now the New York Life Insurance Company), along with more than twenty other enslaved coal miners.[42] By the time these Chesterfield coal miners held their first service at First Baptist Church, the number of slaves insured in the Upper South approximated that of free white citizens holding insurance policies on their own lives in the metropolitan northeast.[43]

If First Baptist Church helped enslaved coal miners enhance the value of their souls, planters used insurance to generate revenue from their deaths. In January 1855, Thomas Doswell insured seven slaves to work in the coal pits of Kanawha County, in what is now West Virginia. Two older slaves named Nathan and Reuben were insured for $500 each. The rest of the slaves (a different Reuben, as well as Turner, Richard, Emanuel, and Aaron) were insured for $700 each. The average sale price for a slave at that time was $600. By 1860, Doswell held eighty-nine slaves at his plantation near Richmond, Virginia.

That same month, Richmond merchant Joseph Winston insured an eleven-year-old slave named Andrew to work in a cotton factory across the James River, in Manchester. The policy was for seven years, though Andrew died that December. Two years later, the hiring agency Tompkins & Company insured fourteen slaves, whose ages ran from twelve to fifty, to work in the Black Heath coal pits for one year. They were owned by a several different people, including Joseph Tompkins. These insurance policies amounted to $800 per slave on average during a time when the average sale price was $636.[44]

Historians have typically examined the relationship between slavery and insurance through the lens of slaves-as-cargo.[45] Considering how planters valued the expertise of enslaved workers changes the way we view the history of life insurance.

✳ ✳ ✳

Merchants who undertook the hazards of seaborne travel had used marine insurance to secure human lives since at least the fifteenth century.[46] What we now think of as the life insurance industry emerged during the seventeenth century with transformations in the science of predicting human mortality. In 1693, Edmund Halley, best known for his pioneering study of comets, created the first known mortality table, which measured life expectancy along one axis and the average year of death along the other.[47] By use of this mathematical construct, insurers assigned differential coverage based on how long someone in a given demographic was likely to live.

The London Society of Equitable Assurances on Lives and Survivorships would, in 1762, start to base life insurance premiums on age rates, or what they called "life contingencies."[48] Pricing insurance at consistent rates for people of varied age had historically discouraged younger people from contracting policies while aging and ailing persons sought them out. U.S. companies initially adapted life tables from British firms, then eventually hired actuaries to develop mathematical predictions of their own based on data unique to U.S. populations.[49]

The nature of life insurance changed even more dramatically during the nineteenth century. When abolitionist and future actuary Elizur Wright visited England in 1844, he was aghast to see men who could no longer afford to pay their insurance premiums clamor to raised platforms to sell their policies to merchants interested in turning a fast buck. Wright decided this form of auction too closely resembled slave auctions. He vowed to develop a mathematical system for tabulating the value of a human life proper to the condition of a free man in U.S. civil society.[50] In 1854, Wright shared with the New England Life Insurance Company his modified version of a British actuarial table, marking a crucial turning point in the fate of an emergent industry.[51]

By 1844, the value of the English life insurance industry already exceeded £150 million. The net worth of life insurance in the United States during the same time was merely $4.5 million. Yet in the next two decades, that figure would climb to $2.3 billion as the United States developed the world's most lucrative life insurance industry.[52]

Historians have noted that life insurance took root during the 1840s when scores of Americans abandoned rural homesteads for urban employment opportunities, leaving behind the large, agrarian households and community networks that had sustained them in times of crisis. These developments coincided with the declining significance of the church as the primary arbiter of moral judgment regarding commercial matters. In the process, many Americans found security in emergent investment strategies, like life insurance. Meanwhile, public debate about the value of a human life was shaped by the formal abolition of slavery in Britain. The status of bonded humans would, in a matter of decades, foster an attempted secession. This moment marks a watershed in American notions of mortality, both in the debate about slavery as an economic institution and moral bellwether and in the unprecedented casualties the Civil War left in its wake. These developments contributed to changing ideas about region, race, and risk.

After 1808, the most lucrative sites for slave labor shifted from Upper South regions rich in tobacco to the cotton belt that ran from South Carolina to Texas. As the demand for slave labor in the Deep South drove up prices on all enslaved workers, Maryland, Virginia, and North Carolina capitalized on their surplus of slaves. They shipped bonded human cargo by steamboat down the Mississippi River from Midwestern cities in Ohio, Indiana, and Illinois to newly settled territories like Kentucky, or down the East Coast from Chesapeake Bay port cities like Baltimore to Gulf Coast ports such as New Orleans. Between 1790 and 1860, more than 700,000 slaves were sold from the Upper South to the Lower South—more than 60 percent of the population at the time.

In urban locales like Virginia, where the demand for slave labor was high and the reserves were dwindling, workers were routinely rented out. In the process, planters took out policies on their slaves to insure against the potential loss that could result from having a slave die in someone else's possession.[53]

As planters rented bonded workers to emergent industries like railroads, steamboats, and coal mines, the value of slaves as capital was no longer determined primarily by a given slave's physical characteristics. While field hands who could gather the most cotton and women deemed fertile commanded the highest prices on auction blocks, there is no record that these kinds of slaves were ever insured. In fact, plantation slaves were often treated like livestock. Solomon Northup, the free man from Saratoga, New York, who was kidnapped in the District of Columbia and then sold into slavery and shipped to New Orleans, famously described how enslaved persons were examined like animals in the marketplace.[54]

In 1833, John O. Lay of the Baltimore Life Insurance Company (BLIC) noted that he received "frequent applications" to insure "horses and slaves."[55] In an 1847 article entitled "Statistics of Southern Slave Plantation," the celebrated scientist Josiah Nott explained the rationale:

> As long as the negro is sound, and worth more than the amount of the insured, self-interest will prompt the owner to preserve the life of the slave; but, if the slave become unsound and there is little prospect of perfect recovery, the underwriters cannot expect fair play—the insurance money is worth more than the slave, and the latter is regarded rather in the light of a superannuated horse.[56]

From this perspective, plantation slaves were like livestock: technologies for increasing the agricultural yield whose productivity could be enhanced in direct proportion to coercive violence. Enslaved women who bore children were likewise reduced to a brute calculus that overlooked the sophisticated science

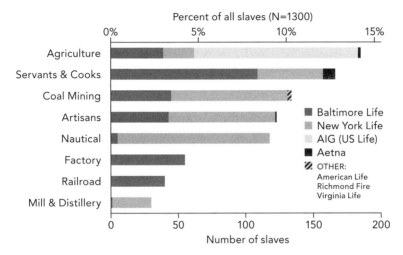

10.1 Occupations of Insured Slaves. "Servants and Cooks": general servants, house servants, cooks, nurses, and washers. "Artisans": bakers, butchers, barbers, cigar makers, book and shoemakers, blacksmiths, brick makers, masons, carpenters, cabinet makers, furniture workers, moulders, coopers, coach makers, carriage painters, wheelwrights, machine builders, manufacturers, merchants, penmen, printers, seamstresses, and tailors. "Steamboat Workers": "firemen," engineers, "stove boys," "cabin boys," cooks, and waiters. "Coal Miners": workers of mine and coal pits. "Laborers": general laborers, stevedores or draymen, and grocery servants. "Mill and Distillery": enslaved workers at mills, at distilleries, and in turpentine production facilities.

of obstetrics they had helped to pioneer. By naturalizing the skills of these laborers, planters overlooked the expertise that sustained economic growth, reserving insurance for workers with privileged skill sets.

In sharp contrast to the dehumanizing discourse of plantation slaves, insurance companies tended to view industrial slaves—and those who had extensive experience in managing plantation households—quite differently. The BLIC refused to consider insurance policies on animals but would ultimately dominate the slave life insurance industry from the time it issued its first policy on a man named Jacob in 1831 until the industry folded during the Civil War. The most highly valued slaves were domestic workers with decades of experience and intimate knowledge about how to run a household; artisans (like blacksmiths and shoemakers); workers with highly coveted expertise (like butchers and clerks); and those who excelled in especially dangerous industries (like railroad and steamboat workers, or coal miners). See Figure 10.1.[57]

Between the time that the slave trade to the United States was outlawed, in 1808, and slavery was abolished, in 1865, slave life insurance became a crucial element of industrial insurance, a key feature of slave shipping, and a central element of credit networks throughout the agrarian South. By the 1860s, approximately 31 percent of urban slaves were hired out, compared to 6 percent of rural slaves. In Virginia cities like Richmond and Lynchburg, up to two-thirds of the total enslaved population might be hired out at a given time.

Life insurance firms that sold policies on slaves included North Carolina Mutual, Greensboro Mutual, and Virginia Life of Richmond.[58] Because slaves were legally considered property, even firms specializing in fire insurance such as the Richmond Fire Association sold policies on slaves.[59]

As life insurance gained momentum in the 1830s, Northern life insurance companies moved South to pursue clientele. These firms charged Southerners higher premiums due to prejudices linking climate to disease and infirmity. Given what they deemed exorbitant rates, Southerners were reluctant to take policies on their own lives. But, from the 1830s onward, merchants peppered the BLIC with requests to take policies on enslaved workers.

Insurance firms were initially reluctant to insure slaves. As a merchant for the BLIC noted in 1836, "I have frequent applications for insurance on slaves which I have declined in obedience with former instructions." As such, one fascinating dimension of slave life insurance is the discretion agents exhibited in selling policies. Insurance firms fretted about not having reliable mortality rates or vital statistics on enslaved persons. They worried that the value of an enslaved worker might vary by age or region. Yet, whenever they discerned that an enslaved person constituted what they deemed an acceptable risk, and when they could vouch for the credibility of the merchant who sought the policy, insurance agents would initiate the transaction. As the president of BLIC John J. Donaldson suggested in correspondence with John O. Lay on February 16, 1835, "We have insured Negroes where their masters were known as persons of respectability."[60] Three months later, Donaldson likewise insisted, in correspondence with an agent of the firm, "it is important that the owner of a slave shall have a good reputation."[61]

In the effort to make sure that slave insurance policies were profitable, firms were constantly searching for ways to boost revenue. They might double the premium rate. Or, they might raise slave life insurance policies by an amount equivalent to the "climate premium" free Southerners were forced to pay for policies on their own lives. But as they began to realize how lucrative policies on enslaved workers could be, some insurance firms began encouraging their agents to sell them.

To guard against the possibility that a planter might abuse or kill a slave in order to collect insurance, BLIC's policy was to compensate owners for two-thirds of the value of a slave. In practice, this point was negligible for several reasons. First, BLIC and other firms subjected merchants to strict scrutiny when entertaining insurance policies on enslaved workers. Next, firms concerned about the problem of moral hazard could find solace in laws punishing planters for mistreatment of slaves. These statutes became increasingly frequent during the last few decades of legalized slavery—the same moment when slave life insurance took off. Finally, precisely because insured slaves possessed expertise that was highly valued in the marketplace, their skills—and thus their value—continued to increase over time. In contrast to prime field hands and woman tasked with breeding children, insured slaves typically continued to accrue value over time. Far from presenting a problem of moral hazard, insured slaves presented merchants with a bargain because the monetary value of their skill set tended to increase faster than the terms of a given life insurance contract. This phenomenon perhaps explains why some insurance firms that were initially reluctant to insure slaves and unsure about how to quantify their value would ultimately rush headlong into the industry.

Slave insurance foreshadowed postbellum genres of industrial insurance, as owners of capital sought to shield themselves against the risks associated with the loss of an individual's capacity for labor. Yet what looks like an instantaneous shift in the legal category of personhood took place against transformations several decades in the making in the way that slavery articulated with insurance.[62] These dynamics also suggest that the practice of insuring enslaved workers helped generate more enthusiasm for life insurance as a strategy for managing risk—an insight not limited to free persons.

$$* * *$$

Precocious for as long as he can recall, Noah was the playmate of the youngest child on the Davis plantation, as he explains in his autobiography, *A Narrative of the Life of Noah Davis.* As he grew older, Noah was apprenticed in the cobbler's workshop adjacent to his Virginia plantation until he caught the Holy Ghost one day. Brimming with Jesus' salvation, Noah persuaded his owner to let him tour the region raising money to buy himself out of slavery, which he managed to do after securing a position as a preacher in Baltimore. Eventually, drawing on his salary and his growing network of Christian friends, Davis managed to free his wife and seven children.

Others, like Madison Washington, sought to free their families from slavery by force. Lionized in the writings of Frederick Douglass, William Wells Brown, and Pauline Hopkins, Washington escaped from bondage and made it to Canada before returning to Virginia in the hopes of liberating his spouse. Washington promptly found himself captured, re-enslaved, and bound aboard the slave ship *Creole* for sale in New Orleans before he managed to free himself and initiate an insurrection. Washington and his comrades had hoped to commandeer the ship and navigate to the Bahamas, a feat that enslaved persons aboard the *Hermosa* had achieved one year prior.[63] Instead, Washington became embroiled in the stakes of insurance and slavery in an entirely different register when the merchants who owned him and the rest of the enslaved cargo tried to collect insurance money for the loss of their property. The courts ultimately ruled that, when enslaved persons seized their destiny, they ceased to be slaves and became free men without their consent. As the insurance company could not insure the lives of free men, it did not have to pay the owners of "cargo" that could liberate itself.[64] Given the arc of this story, and others like it, it is instructive that the Reverend Noah Davis regarded his financial acumen as his greatest asset.

When Davis first arrived in Baltimore in 1847, his initial plan was to save money from his church salary until he had enough to free his family from bondage. But a year into this plan, his wife's mistress agreed to sell her along with the couple's two youngest children to him for $800. The terms of the offer would expire in one year. This turn of events was as stressful as it was promising. "Now I had great burdens upon my mind," said the Reverend Noah Davis, "one to properly attend to my missionary duty, the other to raise eight hundred dollars":

> During this time we succeeded in getting a better place for the Sabbath school, and there was a larger attendance upon my preaching, which demanded reading and study, and also visiting, and increased my daily labors. On the other hand, the year was running away, in which I had to raise eight hundred dollars. (10)

Reverend Noah Davis spent the better part of the year collecting pledges from friends and associates and came up with nearly half of the money. But, according to the mistress, the value of his children had increased by $100. She offered to let him pay $600 in cash now, plus "a bond, with good security, for three hundred more payable in twelve months" (10) and gave him six weeks to execute the new deal. Davis sought assistance from an old friend in Fredericksburg, Virginia, a man named Mr. Wright, who agreed to provide security for the $300 bond if Davis could raise the additional $200 he needed to make the $600 cash payment. Davis returned to Baltimore to collect on the pledges he had received earlier that year and was delighted to discover that some people gave him even more money than they had promised, including a friend who made up the difference, telling him, "Go, get your wife, and you can keep on collecting, and repay the two hundred dollars when you get able" (10).

Davis promptly returned to Fredericksburg with the funds, recovered his wife and two youngest children, and brought them to Baltimore, where he continued serving his church as his wife took up domestic work. Together, they strategized about how to raise the $300 in security Mr. Wright had granted them. Davis ultimately decided to hire his daughter out as a servant for $300. As security for this contract, he took out a $700 life insurance policy on his own life, naming the man who had rented his daughter as the beneficiary (11).

Five of his children still in bondage, Davis received news that his eldest daughter would soon be "sold, and taken away South." Davis quickly raised the $850 he needed to purchase her from friends, only to learn that his eldest son was in a Richmond "[slave] trader's jail" (16). Davis promptly contacted the people who owned his son and learned that "his price was fixed at seven hundred dollars" (11). Davis did not know where to turn for the money:

> I was, of course, deeply anxious to help my boy; but I began to think that I had already drawn so heavily on the liberality of all my friends that, to appeal to them again seemed out of the question. (11)

Reverend Davis resolved to get very small donations from a lot more people: "I thought it possible that I might find three hundred persons among my friends in Baltimore, who would contribute one dollar each to save my son." As before, Davis would combine his donations with capital accrued from life insurance:

> I might then obtain some friend in Baltimore to advance four hundred dollars and let my son work it out with him: and give this friend a life insurance policy on the boy, as a security. This plan seemed practicable, and I wrote to the owners, asking for ten days to raise the money, which they granted me.

The contract secured, Reverend Davis used his connections to raise the $300 and to secure the life insurance policy. Within ten days, Davis was reunited with his son, who—by the time the Reverend penned his *Narrative*—was "doing well," busy "working out the money advanced on him" (16).

That left three of his children in bondage. When their mistress died, in 1856, Davis worried that they would "sell at auction for more money" than he could hope to raise. Indeed, Davis did not have enough money to purchase his children when his sons finally sold in an 1858 auction for $560 and $570 each, while his daughter brought in $990. But the slave trader agreed to sell Davis' daughter to two of his friends for $1,100. Davis promptly secured a $1,000 life insurance policy on the girl "as a security" for their investment and let his daughter remain in their custody while he gathered the funds to repay them.

Davis cobbled together enough money to purchase his daughter from his friends by the end of the year. Two sons remaining in bondage, he decided to pen an autobiography that he could sell for the money to free them. The autobiography ends with that wish.

We do not know if Davis was successful in freeing his remaining sons. It is hard to know how much of his story is true since the details of his life come from a narrative he wrote with his own hand and because the documentation on the overwhelming majority of slave life insurance policies have been lost to history. But in October of 1854 a woman named Lucy Shepherd took out a $300 policy with the BLIC on a "Noah Davis" of Virginia.[65] If indeed this is *the* Reverend Noah Davis, that transaction might be one of his many freedom policies.

While the story of Reverend Noah Davis is exceptional, it does not exist in isolation. Instead, it shows how life insurance became a strategy for generating capital that could later be used for manumission. This was a tactic employed by formerly enslaved people to free their family members from bondage, as did the good Reverend. But even long-time owners of enslaved persons who planned to free them later took out life insurance policies. In many of these instances, the merchant sought to preserve the family unit until the time of coerced labor had expired. Some scholars see in this practice a preoccupation with paternalism—with the idea that the careful management of slaves was essential to the task of extracting profit from bonded workers. In this fashion, the planters saw themselves as patriarchs of an extended family structure that included the people they owned and their kin. It is also possible to see this practice as completely self-serving: that slaves work better as a family—as a laboring unit. From this perspective, the life insurance policy is part of a broader concern to ameliorate working conditions for slaves whose skills were highly valued in the marketplace of the 1840s and 1850s.

These life insurance policies also mark a novel savings strategy. By treating his loved ones as collateral, Reverend Noah Davis created financial opportunities that benefited his family as well as his friends. These transactions also potentially included additional forms of exchange—would Davis' son or daughter be expected to provide uncompensated work for the friends who helped him establish the collateral needed to secure his family's freedom?

Since the industrial age, insurance—namely, life insurance—has helped people to measure the distance from familiar modes of mutual aid. But the insurance industry also illuminates the stratification that has defined finance capital in the postemancipation era.[66] The same historical moment in which slavery was abolished witnessed an uptick in sharecropping and convict leasing—institutions designed to defend forms of wealth and privilege that suddenly threatened to come undone.[67] Despite a similar emphasis on institutionalizing credit-debt relations, insurance appears benign. Even though insurance firms assign differential value to human lives, the triumph of insurance as a strategy for managing risk is frequently linked to the alleged birth of freedom. And yet, the most thoughtful scholars among us have long been wary of this conflation.[68]

In 1898, W. E. B. Du Bois of Atlanta University edited a report based on the proceedings of his "Third Conference for the Study of Negro Problems," held from May 25–26 of that year. This publication capped a three-year, three-part research investigation, an inquiry concerning "the Mortality of Negroes in Cities" in 1896; "another into the General Social and Physical Condition of 5,000 Negroes living in selected parts of certain Southern cities" in 1897; and now an examination of the "efforts Negroes" had been "making to better their social condition." It was in the context of this report that Du Bois confessed a long-standing fear that the birth of black life insurance firms would spell the official demise of the mutual aid societies formed as indigenous mechanisms of security during legalized slavery, "Negroes should be emphatically warned against unstable insurance societies conducted by irresponsible parties, and offering insurance for small weekly payments, which really amount to exorbitant rates."[69] Du Bois was right that actuaries and underwriters would saddle African Americans with higher premiums—including those who worked for black-owned life insurance firms. Of course, the demise of Reconstruction meant that African Americans would ultimately return with renewed vigor to mutual aid societies, often in the form of social clubs or fraternities and sororities, with members paying dues and pooling resources in times of crisis. Mutual aid embodies the antithesis of life insurance. Both approaches tend to members of a collective faced with trying times. But the former has historically involved kin and close friends pooling limited resources in order to support a member of their network, while the latter measures success by collecting as much money as possible through premiums and payments while dishing out as little as possible in compensation in the event of a fatality.

In 1929, Carter G. Woodson, the founder of Negro History Week, which eventually became Black History Month—who received an MA in history at the University of Chicago before becoming the second African American to get a doctorate from Harvard, after Du Bois—wrote an article entitled "Insurance Business Amongst Negroes" in which he discussed the broad range of organizations that provided aid and security for African Americans in the decades following Emancipation, from mutual aid societies modeled on fraternal lodges and burial societies to church organizations.[70] Booker T. Washington—who promoted uplift through industry and commercial aspiration in ways more acute than the academic rigor that defined Du Bois's persona, the nationalist networks for which Marcus Garvey became famous, or the strategies of labor organization that A. Phillip Randolph cultivated in his plan for a March on Washington in the 1930s, predating Martin Luther King Jr.'s march by more than thirty years—raved about the promise of black life insurance firms as a pathway to black prosperity. But Woodson was concerned that some of these groups had merely become opportunities for self-aggrandizing leaders to consolidate their power and exploit their constituencies. In exploring the plight of the many failed black life insurance firms and the few that had become successful, Woodson pointed to the challenges they faced in establishing a reliable payment schedule and viable asset base.

Pricing black lives was a fraught process. Even if mutual aid was preferable to actuarial science as a strategy for securing black life, African Americans faced a number of problems deriving from the fact that, in pragmatic terms, black life possessed such little value. As the curious case of the Reverend Noah Davis reminds us, African Americans could never extricate themselves from their monetary value in the marketplace.

Perhaps, then, Du Bois' theory of labor is even more useful than his 1898 sociological treatise for making sense of risk and liability in the postbellum age.[71] In *Black Reconstruction* Du Bois characterizes the abdication of work in which thousands of African Americans participated in the Civil War as a "general strike."[72] It follows that we should view industrial slaves as industrial workers not simply for the sophisticated forms of political engagement they developed but for the expertise they cultivated and the way they leveraged that expertise to foster enhanced appreciation for their market value. Industrial slaves were not simply deemed more highly skilled and more valuable than plantation slaves, they were routinely granted greater mobility regarding the distance between their places of residence and places of work, as well as greater say in living arrangements and romantic partnerships.[73] Insured slaves were the only assets that could enhance their value through the skills they acquired.

In that sense, the history of slave life insurance underscores the virtue of a pragmatic approach to economic and political analysis. Even while slaves were legally categorized as property, they developed expertise that enhanced their monetary value and afforded them greater mobility as well as greater control over their lives. The fact that enslaved workers could be appreciated for their expertise and still denied the rights and entitlements of other citizens is precisely what makes legalized enslavement abominable.

Notes

1. Benjamin Watkins Leigh, *Reports of Cases Argued and Determined in the Court of Appeals, and in the General Court of Virginia*, 2nd ed. (Richmond, Va.: Gary & Clemmitt, 1867), 383–89.
2. The histories of enslavement and free labor are often treated as separate and distinct, but a closer look at the antebellum era's chief industries demonstrates just how much they are intertwined. The antebellum coal industry employed enslaved workers as well as free people of color and free whites working in tandem.

3. Viviane Zelizer, *Morals and Markets: The Development of Life Insurance in the United States* (New Brunswick, N.J.: Transaction, 1983).

4. Geoffrey Wilson Clark, *Betting on Lives: The Culture of Life Insurance in England, 1695–1775* (Manchester, UK: Manchester University Press, 1999).

5. Bill Mauer, *Mutual Life, Limited: Islamic Banking, Alternative Currencies, Lateral Reason* (Princeton, N.J.: Princeton University Press, 2005), 114; L. S. Sealy and R. J. A. Hooley, *Commercial Law: Text, Cases, and Materials* 4th ed. (Oxford: Oxford University Press, 2008), 1192.

6. William Pietz coined the phrase "forensics of capital" in referring to the Fatal Accidents Act of 1846 in Britain, which reconfigured the Law of Deodand that had been on the books for more than 1,100 years. See William Pietz, "Material Considerations: On the Historical Forensics of Contract," *Theory, Culture, and Society* 19, no. 5/6 (2002): 35–50. The Law of Deodand governed circumstances in which an inanimate object injured or killed a person. The law stipulated that the "accursed" or "wicked" object must be transferred to the Crown, God's earthly representative. The birth of railroads in the 1830s prompted a change in the law. Railroads caused unprecedented injuries and fatalities. Yet merchants did not want to adjudicate these harms by transferring the value of these multimillion-dollar capitalized assets to the state. The Law of Deodand was thus replaced by the Fatal Accidents Act, which stipulated that it was not the value of the "accursed" object but the value of lost wages that would be adjudicated (the British Master and Servants Act of 1823 had established more draconic law governing labor); and that value would no longer be transferred to the government but to the injured party or to the family of the deceased. Pietz identifies this legal and economic protocol as the *forensics of capital*. I expand this concept to include the forms of profiling that structure legal standing. See Michael Ralph, *Forensics of Capital* (Chicago: University of Chicago Press, 2015).

7. This is not to say that these processes *begin* in the fifteenth century, just that they are formalized in fifteenth-century forms of capital exchange, like marine insurance. On the other hand, to the extent that capitalism is defined by the practice of treating labor/value/commodities as both concrete and abstract, fifteenth-century forms of international trade and diplomacy mark a useful point of departure for tracing the forms of finance, industry, and profiling that define social life in capitalist societies. Capital is a store of value to which a person, or firm, has exclusive access. Capitalist societies involve legal frameworks for guaranteeing unique access to capital—a phenomenon beautifully explained in Chris Desan's *Making Money: Coin, Currency, and the Coming of Capitalism* (Oxford: Oxford University Press, 2015).

   At a conceptual level, capitalist societies are defined by the tendency to treat value as both concrete and abstract—both as part of a vernacular process and part of a global system. The forms of value that labor helps to produce are treated the same way. A laborer is not merely a person performing a task but one form of a person performing a task who can be equated with all laborers everywhere performing tasks. The capitalist assumption is that all of these laborers share an economic reality. These laborers are treated as part of the same economic reality as the people who own the institutions and resources, and those who make and enforce the laws, in the societies where these laborers live and work. Capitalist societies create the possibility of generating profit from the discrepancy between the compensation a worker is given and the amount that worker is paid. But capitalism is a concept whose execution is incomplete and inconsistent. Capitalist societies systematically treat time as empty and homogenous yet there are all kinds of moments when temporality is rendered concrete and specific and meaningful. The same goes for labor and for commodities.

What we call "capitalism" or "modern capitalism" is most usefully understood as a set of historical processes and institutional protocols that gained unprecedented momentum in the fifteenth century. Modernity is a problematic concept—it is a project more than a reality and it invariably suggests that what came before it was somehow inadequate or not yet modern. But the virtue of invoking modernity here—like the promise of a careful argument about what constitutes capitalism—is that, arguably from the fifteenth century until the present, the world has witnessed global trade initiatives and forms of diplomacy that render it virtually impossible to act as outside of what is now regarded as an international community.

In its nascent stages, many of the processes that would ultimately define capitalism seemed translocal rather than truly international or global. But the point is that capitalist societies thrive on the ability to institutionalize standards for labor and exchange that are deemed universal. In practical terms, the architects of capitalist societies have treated the narrow reality of financiers, industrialists, soldiers, and rulers with leverage as a vision appropriate for the majority of the world's people. In the process, they institutionalize power through a set of cultural dictates that masquerade as scientific insights—self-serving cultural prescriptions treated as benign and self-evident.

8. Fra Luca Bartolemeo de Pacioli was an Italian mathematician and Franciscan monk who sometimes collaborated with Leonardo da Vinci on various projects. As I discuss in *Forensics of Capital*, Pacioli is the man credited with inventing double-entry bookkeeping, a method that revolutionized financial accounting between the moment it was invented sometime around 1484 and the time it was institutionalized throughout the North Atlantic as the signature strategy for keeping inventory during the century to follow. More than a mere method of keeping exchange in order, double-entry bookkeeping was a tactic for demonstrating the virtue of the merchant who prepared the books. A diligent account was equated with an earnest, noble merchant during a time when commerce was conceived as a secular version of divine grace. Here numbers spoke a divine truth rendered into numerals by God's most diligent earthly scribes. For more on the moral infrastructure of accounting, see Mary Poovey's *History of a Modern Fact: Problems of Knowledge in the Sciences of Wealth and Society* (Chicago: University of Chicago Press, 1998).

9. Eric Williams, *Capitalism and Slavery* (Chapel Hill: University of North Carolina Press, 1944); Michel-Rolph Trouillot, "North Atlantic Fictions: Global Transformations, 1492–1945," in *Global Transformations: Anthropology and the Modern World* (New York: Palgrave, 2003); Cedric Robinson, *Black Marxism: The Making of the Black Radical Tradition* (Chapel Hill: University of North Carolina Press), especially 106–20; Sven Beckert, *Empire of Cotton: A Global History* (New York: Alfred A. Knopf, 2014), especially xv–xxi and 29–98.

10. A. Glenn Crothers, "Commercial Risk and Capital Formation in Early America: Virginia Merchants and the Rise of American Marine Insurance, 1750–1815," *Business History Review* 78, no. 4 (Winter 2004): 607–33.

11. Brian Kilmeade and Don Yaeger, *Thomas Jefferson and the Tripoli Pirates: The Forgotten War that Changed American History* (New York: Sentinel, 2016).

12. I discuss this phenomenon at great length in *Forensics of Capital* (Chicago: University of Chicago Press, 2015), especially chapter 1.

13. Todd Savitt, "Slave Life Insurance in Virginia and North Carolina," *Journal of Southern History* 3, no. 4 (1977): 583–600.

14. Most of the scholarship on slave insurance is focused on slaves as cargo. For the growing body of research concerned with attempts to insure enslaved laborers, see Sharon Ann Murphy, "Securing Human Property: Slavery, Life Insurance, and Industrialization in the Upper South," *Journal of the Early Republic* 25, no. 4 (Winter 2005): 618; Sharon Ann Murphy, *Investing in Life: Insurance in Antebellum America* (Baltimore, Md.: Johns Hopkins University Press, 2010); Karen Ryder. "Permanent Property": Slave Life Insurance in the Antebellum Southern United States, 1825–1866 (PhD Diss., University of Delaware, 2012).

15. Ronald L. Lewis, "'The Darkest Abode of Man': Black Miners in the First Southern Coal Field, 1780–1865," *Virginia Magazine of History and Biography* 87, no. 2 (1979): 190–202.

16. G. P. Wilkes, *Mining History of the Richmond Coalfield of Virginia,* Virginia Division of Mineral Resources publication 85 (Charlottesville: Commonwealth of Virginia, Department of Mines, Minerals, and Energy, Division of Mineral Resources, 1988).

17. After successful extraction in 1730, the Midlothian coal mines went into production in 1748. John S. Salmon and Margaret T. Peters, *A Guidebook to Virginia's Historical Markers,* rev. and exp. ed. (Charlottesville: University of Virginia Press, 1994), 148. Samuel O. Bird, *Virginia's Coal Ages*, Virginia Division of Mineral Resources publication 149 (Charlottesville: Commonwealth of Virginia, Department of Mines, Minerals, and Energy, Division of Mineral Resources, 1997), 1.

18. Ibid., 119.

19. In 1825, Abraham S. and Archibald L. Woolridge established the mining firm A. & A. Woolridge & Co., in part by leasing land from Major Henry Heath. Woolridge and Company, *Proposals for Incorporating the Ben Lomond Coal Company* (RichWmond, Va.: T. W. White, 1837), 3.

20. The Black Heath coal pits were eventually taken over by Major Henry Heth's grandson, the Confederate general Henry Heth. See Henry Heth, *The Memoirs of Henry Heth*, ed. James L. Morrison (Westport, Conn.: Greenwood, 1974).

21. See also Ronald L. Lewis, *Coal, Iron, and Slaves: Industrial Slavery in Maryland and Virginia, 1715–1865* (Westport, Conn.: Greenwood, 1979), 4, 52.

22. Victor S. Clark, *History of Manufactures in the United States,* vol. 1, *1607–1860* (New York: Peter Smith, 1929), 331–32, 520; Samuel Harries Daddow and Benjamin Bannan, *Coal, Iron, and Oil: or, the Practical American Miner* (Philadelphia, 1866), 108; Frederick Moore Binder, *Coal Age Empire: Pennsylvania Coal and Its Utilization to 1860* (Harrisburg: Commonwealth of Pennsylvania, Pennsylvania Historical and Museum Commission, 1974), 34–35.

23. Lewis, "The Darkest Abode of Man," 191.

24. Virginia coal miners make up 10 percent of existing records on insured slaves, including the likes of Dabney Burnette, Daniel and Charles Hall, Bartlett, Isaac, Randolph, Enoch, Sam, Ben, Peter, Reuben, Stephen, Hewlett, Tom Pollard, Dick Giles, Jordan Hancock, Joe Lockett, Jim Lockett, Ned Lockett, Henry Lockett, Jordan Lockett, Henry Wright, Bob Hall, Richard Johnson, William Maston, Ampy, Edgar Porter, Jim Willis, Randolph Wright, Henry Wright, Joe Wright, Alexandria Lewis, Nelson Finley, Phillip Anderson, Patrick Cheatham, Henry Dickenson, Reuben aka Dutch, Anderson Flournoy, Henry Hanes aka Harris, Billy Harrod, John Hunt, Madison James, Anthony Jones, Sam Kiner, Ned Mills aka Miller, Jim Mills, Harry Mills, Lewis Mills, George Mills, Cyrus Mills, Ben York, Nathan York, Wilson, Godfrey, Harry aka Henry Picket, Sam Rid aka Red, Phil Moody, Henry Moody, Sam Jones, Harry Montague, Frank Porter, Henry Porter, Thomas McTyre, Horace, Gilbert Carter, Clay, Edward, George, Henry, Jefferson, Peter, Richard, Robert, Stokes, Watson, Jim Winfred, Charles, Lewis

Watkins, William Watkins. See Michael Ralph, *Treasury of Weary Souls*, www.trea suryofwearysouls.com. I began developing and constructing "The Slave Insurance Database" (now part of *Treasury*) during my tenure as a fellow at Harvard University's Charles Warren Center (CWC) for Studies in American History during the 2014–2015 academic year. "Multimedia History and Literature" was our theme, under the direction of Vince Brown and Glenda Carpio. I am grateful to them, as well as to the CWC director, Walter Johnson. I also appreciate the indefatigable work of Arthur Patton-Hock, the administrative director, and Larissa Kennedy, former coordinator to the American Studies Program and the CWC. *The Treasury of Weary Souls* is now the world's most comprehensive ledger of insured slaves, with more than 1,300 entries, culled from archives and federal records, including *California Department of Insurance Slavery Era Insurance Registry Report to the California Legislature and Registry by the Name of Slaveholder*, May 2002; Nancy Frantel, ed., *Chesterfield County, Virginia, Uncovered: The Records of Death and Slave Insurance Records for the Coal Mining Industry, 1810–1895* (Westminster: Heritage Books, 2008); *Illinois Department of Insurance Slavery Era Insurance Policies Registry Report to the Illinois Legislature*, August 2004; *Policy Books and Policy Applications*, Baltimore Life Insurance Collection (BLIC), MS 175, H. Furlong Baldwin Library, Maryland Historical Society; and Unknown No Longer: A Database of Virginia Slaves, Virginia Historical Society (VHS), accessed June 6, 2016, http://unknownnolonger.vahistorical.org/. *The Treasury of Weary Souls* also includes maps and enhancements by historian and cartographer Bill Rankin, and notes from original historical research by Sharon Ann Murphy.

25. "The Black Heath Coal Mine," *Richmond Enquirer* (VA), March 23, 1839.
26. Virginia. Auditor Public Accounts (1776–1928), Personal Property Tax Books, Chesterfield County, 1800–1843, Library of Virginia.
27. Ibid.
28. Most of the enslaved coal miners for whom we have insurance records worked in Chesterfield County. See Ralph, *Treasury*.
29. William Pennock to Harry Heth, July 10, 1813, Heth Papers, University of Virginia.
30. Agreement, Harry Heth with James and John Bavid, December 8, 1818, Heth Papers, University of Virginia.
31. This insight is most stridently developed in Walter Johnson's *River of Dark Dreams* and Ed Baptist's *The Half that Has Never Been Told*. Both texts take the cotton plantation of the nineteenth-century Mississippi River Valley, and the coercive labor regime that structured it, as their point of departure. For an especially nuanced account of the elaborate calculus concerning capital, labor, training, punishment, and geography that defined plantation work regimes, see Sven Beckert, *Empire of Cotton: A Global History* (New York: Knopf, 2015).
32. H. B. Humphrey, *Historical Summary of Coal-Mine Explosions in the United States 1810–1958*, Bureau of Mines Bulletin 586 (Washington, D.C.: Government Printing Office, 1960), 1.
33. James P. Ulery, "Explosion Hazards from Methane Emissions Related to Geologic Features in Coal Mine." National Institute for Occupational Safety and Health, Centers for Disease Control and Prevention Information Circular 9503 (Pittsburg, Pa., Department of Health and Human Services, April 2008), 1.
34. Nancy C. Frantel, *Chesterfield County Virginia Uncovered: The Records of Death and Slave Insurance Records for the Coal Mining Industry, 1810–1895* (Westminster, Md.: Heritage Books, 2008), 7; Humphrey, *Historical Summary of Coal-Mine Explosions*, 6; "The Black Heath Coal Mine," *Richmond Enquirer* (VA), March 23, 1839.
35. "The Black Heath Coal Mine." See also Frantel, *Death and Slave Insurance Records*, 8.

36. In 1825, Abraham S. and Archibald L. Woolridge established the mining firm A. & A. Woolridge & Co., in part by leasing land from Major Henry Heath. See A. S. and A. L. Woolridge and Company, *Proposals for Incorporating the Ben Lomond Coal Company* (Richmond, Va.: T. W. White, 1837), 3.

37. Virginia. General Assembly. Legislative Petitions of the General Assembly, Chesterfield County, January 1851, 2.

38. Frantel, *Death and Slave Insurance Records*, 12.

39. "Terrible Explosion—Eight Men Killed," *Rural Messenger* (Petersburg, Va.), March 27, 1876.

40. In February 1857, the firm Tompkins & Company insured fourteen miners ranging from age twelve to age fifty to work in Chesterfield County's Black Heath coal pits. These workers were insured for more than $800 on average in a year when the average slave price was $636. See Michael Ralph and William Rankin, "The Slave Insurance Market," *Foreign Policy*, January 16, 2017, accessed May 19, 2017, http://foreignpolicy.com/2017/01/16/decoder-slave-insurance-market-aetna-aig-new-york-life/.

41. Rachel L. Swarns, "Insurance Policies on Slaves: New York Life's Complicated Past," *New York Times*, December 18, 2016, https://www.nytimes.com/2016/12/18/us/insurance-policies-on-slaves-new-york-lifes-complicated-past.html?_r=0.

42. The names of the founders are Jordan Martin, Matthew Winfree, James McIntyre, Zachariah McGruder, Samuel Winfree, and Nelson Turnley. One week after the founding of First Baptist Church, the founders held another meeting at which the following names were added to their ranks: Thomas Jewett, Robert Smith, Joseph Monroe, and Matthew Ford. On the first Sunday in March of that year, they elected Benjamin York, Squire Lockett, Nathan York, and Caesar Logan to serve as deacons. They named Benjamin York to the office of treasurer, Samuel Winfree to serve as clerk, and Jordan Martin to be pastor.

    It is unclear whether Squire Lockett, Robert Smith, and the first pastor, Jordan Martin, were enslaved, but they share the last names of coal miners who were. See Ralph, *Treasury*.

43. Sharon Ann Murphy, "Securing Human Property," 618.

44. Ralph, *Treasury*.

45. Jonathan Levy, "The Ways of Providence: Capitalism, Risk and Freedom in America, 1841–1935" (PhD diss., University of Chicago, 2008).

46. Ryder, "Permanent Property," 18.

47. Nicolas Bacaër, *A Short History of Mathematical Population Dynamics* (London: Springer, 2011), 7.

48. Daniel B. Bouk, "The Science of Difference: Developing Tools for Discrimination in the American Life Insurance Industry, 1830–1930" (PhD diss., Princeton University, 2009), 26.

49. Ibid.

50. Jonathan Levy, *Freaks of Fortune: The Emerging World of Capitalism and Risk in America* (Cambridge, Mass.: Harvard University Press, 2012), 60.

51. Elizur Wright, *Politics and Mysteries of Life Insurance* (Boston: Lee and Shepard, 1873).

52. Sharon Ann Murphy, *Investing in Life: Insurance in Antebellum America* (Baltimore, Md.: Johns Hopkins University Press, 2010), 5, 300; Timothy L. Alborn, *Regulated Lives: Life Insurance and British Society, 1800–1914* (Ontario: University of Toronto Press, 2009), 4, 52.

53. Michael Ralph, "Life . . . in the midst of death": Notes on the Relationship Between Slave Insurance, Life Insurance, and Disability," *Disability Studies Quarterly* 32, no. 3 (2012), http://dsq-sds.org/article/view/3267/3100.

54. Solomon Northrup, *Twelve Years a Slave* (Auburn, N.Y.: Derby and Miller, 1853).

55. John O. Lay to John J. Donaldson, June 29, 1833, Correspondence I, BLIC.

56. Josiah C. Nott, "Life Insurance at the South," *The Commercial Review of the South and West,* vol. 3 (May 1847), 358.

57. It would have been logical to insure slave doctors—women who delivered babies and pioneered the science of obstetrics on U.S. plantations. In the nineteenth century medical expertise was based largely on practical experience rather than professional licensing, and enslaved women were often more highly prized for their knowledge of obstetrics than licensed medical doctors. Yet it is difficult to determine whether slave obstetricians were insured. Of the more than 1,300 records in the *Treasury*, the occupation "nurse" appears but three times. Tyrel Thornton of Louisville, Kentucky, employed a nurse named Lucy. John S. Primm of St. Louis, Missouri, owned a nurse named Mary Jane, who was only ten years old, and another named Polly, who was eighteen. It is possible that Polly was a wet nurse. But, as they were listed under the same occupation, it is also possible that Polly was an obstetrician and Mary Jane was her apprentice. See entries for "Mary Jane," "Polly," and "Lucy."

58. *Life Insurance: Its Principles, Operations and Benefits, as presented by the North Carolina Mutual Life Insurance Company* (Raleigh, N.C.: Seaton Gales, 1849); Greensboro Mutual Life Insurance and Trust Company policy, Joseph Aldon Linn Papers, Southern Historical Collection, Wilson Library, University of North Carolina Chapel Hill; Murphy, *Investing in Life*, 187; Savitt, "Slave Life Insurance," 587.

59. See "Unknown No Longer," Database of Virginia Slaves, Virginia Historical Society, http://unknownnolonger.vahistorical.org/. Also consider the Richmond Fire Association table of slave premiums included in correspondence from Dr. Thomas Pollard to Henry E. Thompson, January 11, 1855, Correspondence 12, BLIC.

60. John J. Donaldson to John O. Lay, February 16, 1835, Letter Book, BLIC.

61. John J. Donaldson to Duncan Robertson, May 26, 1835, Letter Book, BLIC.

62. See Figure 10.1.

63. George Hendrick and Willene Hendrick, *The Creole Mutiny: A Tale of Revolt Aboard a Slave Ship* (Chicago: Ivan R. Dee, 2003).

64. Levy, *Freaks of Fortune*, 60.

65. Ralph, *Treasury*, entry "Davis, Noah."

66. For a more explicit effort to theorize contrasting geographies of mobility, see Nicholas de Genova and Nathalie Puetz, *The Deportation Regime: Sovereignty, Space, and the Freedom of Movement* (Durham, N.C.: Duke University Press, 2010).

67. Scholars have noted how the Thirteenth Amendment provides legal justification for convict leasing by suggesting that a person cannot be enslaved unless convicted of a crime—which carries the implication that it is legally justifiable to enslave convicts. While scholars have suggested that this practice debuts in the post-Emancipation period, I trace the origin of convict leasing to the 1825 debut of Joel Scott as keeper of the Kentucky Penitentiary in an unpublished lecture entitled, "The Origin of Convict Leasing" that I delivered at the University of California, Berkeley, on February 27, 2017.

68. Michael Ralph, "*Movement* Politics," introduction to "Disability Studies and Social Movement Politics," special issue, *Disability Studies Quarterly* 32, no. 3 (2012), http://dsq-sds.org/article/view/3266/3102. The argument developed in the following paragraph borrows heavily from Ralph, "'Life in the midst of death.'"

69. W. E. B. Du Bois, "Some Efforts of American Negroes for Their Own Social Betterment," Report of an investigation under the direction of Atlanta University; together with the proceedings of the Third Conference for the Study of Negro Problems, held at Atlanta University, May 25–26, 1898.

70. Carter G. Woodson, "Insurance Business Among Negroes," *Journal of Negro History* 14, no. 2 (April 1929): 202–26.

71. Noah Davis, *A Narrative of the Life of Rev. Noah Davis, A Colored Man* (Baltimore, 1859), 37–42, 55–59.

72. W. E. B. Du Bois, *Black Reconstruction in America, 1860–1880* (1935; New York: Free Press, 1998.

73. Noah Davis' improbable trajectory is the best evidence for this assertion, but examples abound. During his famous travels Frederick Law Olmsted remarked on the unprecedented autonomy that industrial slaves enjoyed. In his incredulous words, "The the slave lumberman . . . lives measurably as a free man; hunts, fishes, eats, drinks, smokes, and sleeps, plays and works, each when and as much as he pleases. . . . No 'driving' at his work is attempted or needed. Nor force is used. . . . The overseer merely takes a daily account of the number of shingles each man adds to the general stock, and employs another set of hands, with mules, to draw them to a point from which they can be shipped, and where they are, from time to time, called for by a schooner," Frederick Law Olmsted, *The Cotton Kingdom: A Traveller's Observations on Cotton and Slavery in the American Slave States, 1853–1854* (1856; New York: Da Capo Press, 1996), 114–115. Olmsted's hyperbolic commentary can't be taken as a transparent statement of fact. Still, it illustrates the dramatic distinction between the working conditions that prevailed in many of America's chief industries with the exception of those that defined the "empire of cotton," which some publications in the "'new' history of capitalism," discuss and theorize in a way that is both compelling and illuminating. The text in this emergent tradition that possesses the most explanatory power is Sven Beckert, *Empire of Cotton* (New York: Knopf, 2015), but see also Walter Johnson, *River of Dark Dreams: Slavery and Empire in Cotton Kingdom* (Cambridge, Mass.: Harvard University Press, 2013) and Edward Baptist, *The Half That Has Never Been Told: Slavery and the Making of American Capitalism* (New York: Basic Books, 2014). In his important contribution to a largely forgotten literature on industrial slaves, Ronald L. Lewis discusses the tremendous power enslaved ironworkers sometimes wielded with regard to family arrangements and intimate partnerships. See Ronald L. Lewis, *Coal, Iron, and Slaves: Industrial Slavery in Maryland and Virginia, 1715–1865* (Westport, Conn.: Greenwood, 1979), 98–112. In addition to the ceaseless project of trying to achieve optimal profit by adjusting working conditions, planters feared that too strict a labor regime would trigger more instances of flight—or, in Du Bois's apt formulation, more labor strikes—among savvy, well-connected slaves with dense networks in the Chesapeake region.

PART IV

REFIGURING SPACE
FROM THE LOCAL TO
THE GLOBAL

CHAPTER 11

WAR BY OTHER MEANS

Mercantilism and Free Trade in the Age of the
American Revolution

ELIGA H. GOULD

The mercantilist state of early modern Europe is one of the great
bogeymen of American capitalism. Overregulated, predatory,
and inefficient, it hovers over practically every aspect of early
America's economic history, from Britain's war on piracy during the later seventeenth and early eighteenth centuries to the immediate origins and pro-
tracted aftermath of the American Revolution. In the scholarly literature no
less than in popular culture, the villains tend to be the officials charged with
enforcing British and European trade laws—naval officers, customs collectors,
admiralty judges, and colonial governors—while the heroes are usually their
opponents: pirates Ned Low and Anne Bonny, ordinary jack tars of all races
and ethnicities, and free-trading merchants and their apologists, including
people as wealthy and influential as John Hancock and Benjamin Franklin.[1] As
Adam Smith famously wrote of the "mercantile system" in *Wealth of Nations*
(1776), Europe's maritime powers all behaved as though trade with other nations was a zero-sum game. In their efforts to beggar their neighbors and en-
rich themselves, they ensured that capitalism bore little resemblance to the
peaceful, mutually beneficial force that Smith and the philosophes thought it
had the potential to be. Simply put, mercantilism was a form of war by economic means.[2]

Whatever we make of Smith's free-market remedy, this critique still reso-
nates. In this sense, at least, we are all Smithians. In Smith's day, however, there
was another way of seeing things, one that cast the regulation of international
trade as an entirely legitimate instrument of state power. For people who

thought this way, the mercantile system connoted peace and stability, and illicit trade was synonymous with war and chaos. Although it can be hard to square with the predatory ends that Britain's maritime state often served, this sort of "neomercantilism," to use a term popular with economic historians, would have been familiar to Smith's contemporaries.[3] Indeed, for neomercantilist defenders of regulated trade—and there were far more of them in both Britain and the colonies that became the United States than we usually realize—unfettered commerce was the great threat to international law and order, and it was the free-trading merchant who was engaged in what the English pamphleteer James Stephen in 1805 called "war in disguise."[4] However inefficient and intrusive Europe's maritime empires might seem, defenders of regulated trade insisted that there were equally grave dangers in the laissez faire alternative.

This way of thinking was as influential in its day as the nascent liberalism of Smith and the philosophes, and it played a significant role in shaping the political economy of British America and the early Republic. In writings on the history of capitalism, whether on a worldwide scale or in studies with a narrower focus, early America is often seen as the prototype of economic liberalism, with the American Revolution marking a crucial moment in the birth and eventual triumph of an international order based on the free flow of commerce.[5] Yet in the regulation of foreign trade, as in so many other areas of public life, Americans were willing to go only so far in breaking with the political norms of Britain and Europe.[6] Despite the founders' public commitment to free trade, most Americans accepted the need for some sort of mercantile system in 1776. More often than not, they blended the two, holding that neomercantile and free-trade principles were not the diametric opposites that Smith claimed but complementary parts of a complex and interconnected whole. In this form, mercantilism was destined to have an influence on the American Republic at least as profound as the drive to open markets, leading to the creation of what William Appleman Williams called a distinctively American economic system.[7] As with Smith's critique, that part of mercantilism's history has yet to disappear.

* * *

To understand mercantilism's influence in early America, we must begin by realizing that mercantilism was not one system but several, each with its own goals and objectives. On the most basic level, mercantilists were economic "nationalists"—in the words of William Appleman Williams—"who strove for self-sufficiency through increased domestic production and a favorable balance . . . of trade."[8] But there were various ways to achieve those ends, ranging from rigidly protective tariffs to levies designed to bolster a nation's maritime power while leaving foreign trade relatively free. Britain and the colonies that became the United States both fell somewhere on the less restrictive end of the spectrum.

This was clear from the Navigation Acts that undergirded Britain's mercantile system, the main purpose of which was to keep the regular navy supplied with ships and sailors. Toward that end, Parliament required that the colonies' most profitable "enumerated" goods, including sugar, tobacco, fish, lumber, indigo, rice, and wheat, travel in British-built merchant ships, and it stipulated that those ships had to have British crews, which could include sailors from Ireland and the colonies. Although these rules had protectionist tendencies, their chief purpose was not to secure overseas markets or tip the balance of trade in Britain's favor but to provide a cost-effective way of boosting the kingdom's maritime power.[9] In times of war, the Navigation Acts ensured a ready supply of vessels that the government could convert to military uses, either as transports for troops and military supplies or by commissioning them as privateers. No less important, the laws created a reliable pool of able-bodied seamen. "The royal navy of England," wrote Sir William Blackstone in 1765, "hath ever been it's [sic] greatest defence and ornament."[10] Though the weapon of choice was the king's ships, not the kingdom's producers, critics who saw in the mercantile system a vehicle for waging war were by no means wrong.

Insofar as Britain's regulation of overseas trade encountered opposition from Americans before the Revolution, it was the system's war-making institutions and practices that caused the most conflict. Throughout the eighteenth century, Royal Navy press gangs were a particularly disruptive and hated presence. During Boston's Knowles Riot of 1747, the most serious urban disturbance of the colonial era, protesters responded to an unusually broad impressment raid by breaking the windows of the assembly house, burning what they (mistakenly) believed to be a naval barge on the town common, and kidnapping several officers. The unrest so outraged Admiral Charles Knowles, the British commander, that he threatened to turn his guns on the town and show its inhabitants that "the Kings Government is . . . as good as a Mob."[11] Although the navy opted for less confrontational methods during the Seven Years' War, press gangs continued to have a disproportionate impact on colonial ports. In 1757, a nighttime sweep in New York took in some eight hundred men—by one estimate, more than a quarter of the city's adult male population.[12] After the return of peace in 1763, such events helped fan discontent over the parliamentary taxes and reforms that preceded the Revolution. In the Stamp Act disturbances of 1765 and again during the protests in Boston over the 1768 seizure of John Hancock's sloop *Liberty*, sailors played important and conspicuous roles.[13] "New York and Boston," wrote Benjamin Franklin, "have so often found the Inconvenience of . . . Station Ships that they are very indifferent about having them."[14] Until the eve of independence, nothing else that the British government did aroused such intense animosity.

In the decade before the Revolution, Britain's efforts to turn the trade laws into a source of revenue only inflamed these feelings. Although Parliament had regulated colonial ships and goods since the seventeenth century, there was a long history of slack enforcement, which allowed merchants to operate in many places as de facto free traders, often with the consent of British governors and local officials. In his testimony during Parliament's 1766 inquiry into the Stamp Act, Franklin noted that Pennsylvania had developed an extensive West Indian trade on this basis. Some of the commerce went "to our own islands," but a good deal was carried in foreign ships to ports belonging to the "French, Spaniards, Danes, and Dutch."[15] Although Franklin did not say how much was illegal, a lot clearly was. As Britain's tolerance for such practices diminished, starting with the navy's crackdown on merchants who traded with the enemy during the Seven Years' War and continuing with Parliament's efforts to reform the customs service after the return of peace, the judicial and bureaucratic apparatus of the maritime state became focal points for colonial opposition.[16] Although resisting naval press gangs had long been associated with plebeian activism, even wealthy merchants like Henry Laurens and John Hancock joined the fray. As Joseph Harrison, collector of customs at Boston, confided during the *Liberty* imbroglio, the "running of Goods and Smuggling," which colonial merchants long attempted to hide from view, had become public "Virtue and Patriotism" because of Parliament's revenue measures. "Hancock and Liberty [is] the cry here," wrote Harrison, "as Wilkes and Liberty is in London."[17] The result was armed resistance and, eventually, rebellion.

During the American Revolution, denouncing Britain's trade laws became a much-used weapon in the patriots' rhetorical arsenal. In *Common Sense*, Thomas Paine promised readers that freeing the former colonies from British restrictions on their exports would be one of the main benefits of independence. Significantly, the advantages that Paine envisioned had nothing to do with the trade laws' inefficiencies or the burdens that they placed on American producers and consumers. Indeed, he expected that Congress and the states would eventually adopt trade laws of their own. What Paine did object to was how, by "protecting" American maritime commerce from Britain's main imperial rivals in Europe, the Navigation Acts ensured that Britain's enemies in time of war would always be America's enemies too. If American ships and goods were allowed to sail under their own flag, Paine was sure Europe's powers would leave them alone. "The commerce by which [America] hath enriched herself," he wrote, "are the necessities of life, and will always have a market while eating is the custom of Europe." For this reason, Europe's maritime powers—including, eventually, Britain—would find that it was to their own advantage to cultivate peaceful relations with the new states, even when they were at war with each other. "It is the interest of all Europe to have America a FREE PORT," Paine assured his readers. "Our plan is commerce, and that, well attended to, will secure us . . . peace and friendship."[18] In achieving liberty for themselves, Americans would gain the right to trade freely with nations whose only interest was to trade freely with them.

In this embrace of economic liberalism, Americans were aided not only by their own experience but by growing support for free trade in Europe. During the second half of the eighteenth century, two developments in particular changed European attitudes toward mercantile regulation. One was the growing influence of writers like Smith and the French philosophes, who saw free trade as a way of encouraging the "universal society" of mankind, as Diderot wrote.[19] The other was the outrage occasioned by Britain's interference with the maritime trade of neutral powers during the mid-century wars with France and Spain. Instead of Diderot's universal society, the British government seemed to be creating a world of perpetual war and depredation. In 1780, at the height of the American Revolutionary War, the two developments converged in the formation of the so-called League of Armed Neutrality. Under the leadership of Russia's Catherine the Great, the alliance joined the Baltic states, followed eventually by the Dutch Republic, Austria, Portugal, and the Two Sicilies, in a pact to safeguard the members' trade from the warships of the main belligerents, especially Britain. Although primarily concerned with their own ships and goods, the signatories pledged, in a nod to the philosophes, to work for a "universal jurisprudence" that would protect the neutral trade of all nations, regardless of any one power's geopolitical standing or naval capacity. "We cannot give up this principle," wrote Prussia's foreign minister Count Andreas Peter Bernstorff in 1778. "War," Bernstorff explained, "does not confer the slightest right" to harm the ships of nonbelligerent powers.[20]

For free trade proponents in Europe and America, nothing showed Britain's apparent disregard for such principles more vividly than Admiral George Rodney's 1781 capture and sack of the Dutch island of St. Eustatius in the Caribbean. In an episode that triggered riots in Amsterdam, a parliamentary inquiry at Westminster, and a series of costly lawsuits in England, Romney's forces stripped everything of value that they could find on the rocky outcropping, even ransacking graves—all because the island's merchants had been trading with the United States and Britain's European enemies. St. Eustatius's 350-member Jewish community, some of whom were British subjects, suffered especially. On Rodney's orders, men were separated from their families, their clothes were ripped open "to search for concealed money," and they were banished. Convinced that Loyalist and British merchants on the island had also been trading with the enemy, Rodney had his officers confiscate their property as well. Ironically, because the logistics of selling the plunder proved so overwhelming, Rodney was unable to send warships north to assist Lord Cornwallis's beleaguered army at Yorktown and as such played an indirect role in abetting the British surrender, but that did not make the devastation any less harrowing for his victims.[21] In the accounts that inundated the press, the sack of St. Eustatius became a byword for the barbarity of using trade as an instrument of war, as well as a rallying cry for those who hoped to make commerce a vehicle for peace.

Against this backdrop, the founders' public commitment to free trade helped make the American Revolution seem like a diplomatic and commercial transformation of truly global importance—the inaugural moment, as the motto on the Union's 1782 seal suggested, of a *novus ordo seclorum*, or a new era in world history. In the Model Treaty, which John Adams drafted in 1776 to guide the Union's foreign relations with Europe, Congress insisted that prospective treaty partners, starting with France, grant Americans the right to trade on the freest possible terms in times of peace and a liberal definition of the goods that they could carry in wars where they were neutral. Had such principles been "established and honestly observed" by other nations, Adams would later write, they might have "put an end forever to all maritime war."[22] On these grounds, Congress endorsed Russia's manifesto calling for a neutral league in 1780, and the Union made the quest for free trade one of the central tenets of its postwar diplomacy.[23] Although the Washington administration declined to participate in the armed neutralities that the Baltic powers sought to revive in 1793 and 1794, the right to trade freely with other nations remained an American desideratum throughout the French Revolution and the Napoleonic Wars. Among other things, free trade was one of Washington's stated goals in his 1796 "Farewell Address," and it was equally important to Jefferson and Madison, who each made codifying the law of nations one of the main objectives of their administrations' long (and unsuccessful) effort to persuade Britain to respect the rights of American ships and sailors.[24]

In telling this part of the history of the American Revolution, historians have often focused on the new Republic's liberal underpinnings—on the founding generation's determination "to begin the world anew," in the words of Bernard Bailyn.[25] In terms of persuading the British to change their policy, the result was a failure. During the European wars that resumed in 1793, Britain proved no more willing to accommodate Americans on the question of neutral rights than it had been Europe's other maritime powers. Still, the founders' antimercantilist rhetoric had the effect of appearing to place them firmly on the side of economic liberty. In his *Report on the Commerce of the United States* (1793), written while he was secretary of state, Thomas Jefferson itemized the many ways in which the British bolstered their own power by monopolizing the trade of others, and he left no doubt that it was in the United States' interests to oppose them.[26] In 1812, such perceptions led the two nations into renewed warfare. Writing to Madame de Staël, Jefferson was clear about the war's cause. The "object of England," he wrote, is the *permanent dominion of the ocean*, and the *monopoly of the trade of the world*. To secure this, she must keep a larger fleet than her own resources will maintain. The resources of other nations, then, must be impressed to supply the deficiency of her own.... She first forbade to neutrals all trade with her enemies in time of war, which they had not in time of peace. This deprived them of their trade from port to port of the same nation. Then she forbade them to trade from the port of one nation to that of any other at war with her, although a right fully exercised in time of peace. Next, instead of taking vessels only *entering* a blockaded port, she took them all over the ocean.... And finally, that her views may no longer rest on inference, in a recent debate, her minister declared in open parliament, that the object of the present war is a *monopoly of commerce*.[27]

At the time of Jefferson's death in 1826, the system that undergirded Britain's commercial monopoly was still in place. The sage of Monticello nonetheless went to his grave believing that Americans had struck a significant blow for freedom.

✳ ✳ ✳

Even as they proclaimed the importance of commercial liberty to the newly independent United States, Americans admired the principles on which Britain's maritime empire was based, and many believed that even a nation founded on free trade would need its own mercantile system. As historians have often noted, this was partly because they recognized the need to balance idealism with realism in matters of overseas trade, doing so in the same way that they balanced the two in matters of internal governance. An unswerving adherence to principle was no more likely to ensure success in protecting American merchant ships from the Royal Navy's cruisers than it was with protecting the rights of American citizens in the new state and federal constitutions.[28] Often, though, Americans embraced mercantilist thinking on more positive grounds—doing so as a way to replicate those aspects of Britain's maritime empire that they remembered working well before the Revolution and that they believed would strengthen their new republic once the war was over.[29] In their quest to join the powers of the earth, Americans could do worse than follow Britain's example.

Paine, for one, was clear on this score. Despite venting his hostility toward Britain's trade laws and affirming his commitment to peaceful commerce, Paine predicted in *Common Sense* that Americans would find that the best means to ensure a reliable supply of ships and sailors in the event of war was by adopting policies that fostered and encouraged the building of merchant ships in times of peace. "To unite the sinews of commerce and defense," he wrote in words that could have been taken straight from a British naval treatise, "is sound policy."[30] In his 1793 report on commerce, Jefferson made a similar argument, writing that the only way to protect the Union's maritime interests was by possessing "a respectable body of citizen-seamen" and a flourishing "ship-building" industry. By endorsing what amounted to an American version of Britain's Navigation Acts, Jefferson recognized a potential contradiction with his view that the ocean ought to be "the common property of all." Because some nations—especially Britain—took a different view and sought to engross the carrying trade of others, however, Congress had no choice but "to adopt the policies of those who put us on the defensive."[31] Even as Americans pursued free trade, they assumed that their fledgling union of states would need a mercantile system of its own.

By proclaiming the compatibility of mercantilist and free trade principles, Americans were saying nothing that the British had not said many times before. Although no one doubted that the Navigation Acts' purpose was to ready the nation for a maritime war, the Royal Navy was also a bulwark against the peacetime scourge of piracy. Starting with the so-called war on pirates that followed the end of the War of the Spanish Succession in 1713, the navy checked, without entirely eliminating, the most notorious freebooters in the waters of North America and the West Indies. For the first time in British history, the Admiralty also set up permanent naval stations outside Europe, building bases in Jamaica and Antigua. Eventually, during the wars of the 1740s and 1750s, the crown also tightened its authority over colonial privateers. In the colonies that became the United States, the results helped usher in a golden age of commercial shipping, as insurance premiums on long-distance cargoes fell and merchant ships engaged in transatlantic trade were able to dispense with the weight and expense of mounting deck guns.[32] Noting the effects in 1760, Franklin wrote that the quickening pace of transatlantic commerce had brought "the banks of the *Ohio*" closer in terms of travel time "to *London*, than the remote parts of *France* and *Spain* are to their respective capitals; and much nearer than *Connaught* and *Ulster* were in the days of Queen *Elizabeth*."[33] Without this transformation, there would have been no "consumer revolution" in the colonies before the American Revolution. For that matter, it is hard to see how there could have been a political revolution either.[34]

For Franklin, who reached adulthood during the 1720s, the navy's suppression of piracy had a particular resonance. In the Boston of Franklin's youth, the executions of convicted pirates were public, highly symbolic events, which highlighted the dangers of the "privateering stroke," as Cotton Mather wrote.[35] No less important, they showed that even the most independent-minded colonies needed the protection of Britain's maritime state. In 1722, while Franklin was an apprentice in his older brother James's print shop, Massachusetts imprisoned James Franklin for appearing to suggest in the *New-England Courant* that the Bay Colony's leaders had been deliberately slow in fitting out a warship to sail against the notorious pirate Ned Low. As Philip Ashton, who was almost the same age as the younger Franklin, recalled of being taken from a fishing boat during Low's rampage, "who can express the concern and agony I was in?"[36] Over the next seventy years, one of the constants in Franklin's career was a visceral hatred for what he described in 1747 as the "unbridled Rage" of pirates and privateers and a tendency to think well of the professional military and fiscal institutions that helped keep such forces at bay.[37] In his testimony against the Stamp Act in 1766, Franklin used the navy's role in the suppression of piracy to make a distinction between Parliament's authority over seaborne trade, which he viewed as entirely legitimate, and its more limited authority on the North American mainland. "The sea is yours," Franklin said. "You maintain by your fleets, the safety of navigation in it, and keep it clear of pirates; you may have therefore a natural and equitable right to some toll or duty on merchandizes carried through that part of your dominions."[38] Although Franklin turned out to be wrong about Parliament's right to tax maritime imports for revenue, he had a keen appreciation of the benefits that he and Americans like him reaped from Britain's naval dominion.[39]

Nor was Franklin the only American who thought this way. During the mid-century colonial wars with France, some of the staunchest defenses of Britain's trade laws came from American vice-admiralty judges like Edward Long of Jamaica and New York's Lewis Morris. As Judge Morris noted in a Dutch prize case that came before his vice-admiralty court in New York in 1758, merchants who traded with Britain's enemies resorted "to all possible Arts for concealing the true Proprietors of the Cargoe" on board their ships. Often, Morris claimed, "the Covering [was] so well laid on, that a Detection of the enemys Property [could] rarely be made by the severest searching into the Ships Documents, or the Strictest Examination of the Crew."[40] In an indication of how difficult detecting such schemes could be, Captain John Gardiner of the Dutch schooner *Koninghen Esther*, who was a natural-born Englishman from Newcastle-upon-Tyne but who claimed to be a Dutch national with a wife and children on Curaçao, testified in a case from the late 1750s that before his ship was condemned in Jamaica it was stopped on the high seas by a Rhode Island privateer, "who detained her for the Space of about three Days, and searched her as thoroughly as possibly in every part." The commander eventually let the ship go, but not before his officers spent several days ransacking the vessel's cargo and papers.[41]

Not surprisingly, the efforts of judges like Morris and Long to suppress illicit trade was repeatedly a source of conflict with other colonists. Sometimes, colonial merchants evaded wartime embargos by taking out papers as naturalized subjects of foreign governments or by hiring neutral seamen to give "a foreign Name" to enemy property. "Captain Fries," wrote Rear-Admiral Charles Holmes after one of his cruisers detained the Danish trading vessel *Ravenes* off Jamaica with a cargo of French goods in 1761, "is no more than a Machine to blind the Government" to the "shameful and criminal" activities of a cabal that included merchants from Dublin and New York.[42] Colonial merchants also freighted enemy goods in British ships, using foreign entrepôt like St. Eustatius and Monte Cristi, the Spanish way station just across the border from French Saint-Domingue, to make it look as though they were carrying neutral property. "I have got from the Governor . . . a Certificate that the Cargoe I bought from [a French coasting vessel] was purchased from Spaniards," wrote Richard Mercer, one of several agents at Monte Cristi, before entrusting a shipment of French sugar to a New York privateer in 1760.[43] According to Edward Long, most of the "British" trade at Monte Cristi during the early 1760s was in fact conducted on behalf of French planters on Saint-Domingue. "[B]y this means," wrote Long, mariners in British-flagged ships "thought it no injury to their consciences to swear positively, 'That they did, dispose of, or deliver their outward cargo *to Spaniards*, and did receive the proceeds or homeward cargoe *from Spaniards* also,'" even though the cargo was invariably French.[44]

Although Long and Morris were officials of the crown, they were also Americans. In both capacities, their hostility to unbridled trade was an important counterpoint to the antimercantilism that featured so prominently in the rhetoric of the Revolution. During the 1760s and 1770s, when smuggled goods were thought to represent "about a Third of [the colonies'] actual Imports," merchants and seamen were objects of intense suspicion in colonial ports.[45] In a 1772 opinion upholding the imprisonment of a ship captain for making a false declaration, Richard Morris, who succeeded his father as New York vice-admiralty judge and whose brother Lewis signed the Declaration of Independence, wrote that shipmasters were "so much Citizens of the World that they cannot be considered as tied to this or any other province."[46] "[W]herever the Acts of Navigation are disregarded," concurred Thomas Whately in his 1765 defense of Parliament's revenue measures, Britain's colonies were "no longer *British* Colonies, but Colonies of the Countries they trade to."[47] As the governor of Massachusetts, Francis Bernard, reported in 1761, shortly after detaining a "Mississippi trader" for smuggling, the ship's master had started his voyage by sailing to Monte Cristi, where he freighted a load of Saint-Domingue sugar to Jamaica; there, "in conjunction with an English Renegade" from St. Thomas who had been "pass[ing] for a Dane," the captain fitted out the ship with naval stores for New Orleans; finally, before returning to Boston, he entered into a partnership with "a Frenchman who has been very much versed in trade with the English and is"—Bernard claimed—"familiarly known in Rhode Island." "Their purpose," warned the governor, "is to buy Shipping and freight it with provisions, naval stores and ammunition."[48] Although legally subjects of the British crown, such people were effectively in the service of whichever nation they traded with, and the trade itself was an act of war against their own country.

Despite the outcry over the British sack of St. Eustatius, this tendency to equate free trade with piracy and covert warfare played a conspicuous role in the debates that followed the island's destruction. In justifying Rodney's actions, British officials insisted that merchants who aided the enemy were "vagrants" and "renegades," who engaged in undeclared acts of war while cloaking themselves in the guise of friendship.[49] The *Annual Register* wrote that the island's "checkered and transient inhabitants" were so involved "in traffic and gain, that when Holland herself was engaged in a war," they continued to trade with the Republic's enemies "as if no rupture with the parent state had taken place."[50] Speaking of the British and Loyalist merchants whom his forces apprehended, Rodney used similar terms, noting the "respect and humanity" to which "a declared enemy" was entitled, while insisting that "a perfidious people, wearing the mask of friendship, [but] traitors to their country, . . . deserves no favour or consideration."[51] For Britain's critics, such words carried little weight, and were not nearly enough to dampen the outrage that Rodney's depredations caused in both Europe and America, but not everyone thought Rodney was in the wrong. According to Lord Germain, most of the merchants who "call[ed] themselves inhabitants" of St. Eustatius were actually English. If anyone deserved "exemplary punishment and severity," it was they.[52]

The result was an inversion—or perhaps a qualification—of Smith's famous analysis that cast mercantilism and free trade as incompatible opposites. While acknowledging that upholding Britain's maritime empire was the Navigation Acts' original purpose, Smith argued that the effect had been to sacrifice "the interest of the home-consumer . . . to that of the producer." As far as Smith was concerned, the costs far outweighed the benefits.[53] For neomercantilist defenders of Britain's trade monopoly, however, the mercantile system was better seen, not as an unfair sacrifice by British consumers to British producers, but as the price that the British government had a right to ask Britons everywhere to pay for the naval power that made it possible for British merchants to trade with extraordinary, if not complete, freedom.[54] For Smith, the smuggler was a sympathetic character who "would have been, in every respect, an excellent citizen, had not the laws of his country made that a crime which nature never meant to be so."[55] For anyone who thought the trade laws served a valid purpose, the truth could not have been more different. Merchants who refused to help pay for the protection from which they benefited were at best freeloaders, and many people viewed them as traitors to their country who, for that reason, were little better than pirates. In the words of the British pamphleteer William Allen, anyone who trafficked in "contraband Goods" strengthened the hands of "implacable" foes.[56] Only by remaining vigilant against such threats could a great maritime power like Britain hope to secure lasting peace.

In other words, from a neomercantilist standpoint, it made perfect sense for Paine and Jefferson to blend their commitment to free trade with support for an American navigation act. It was also completely understandable that Americans would worry about losing the protection of Britain's own mercantile system. Significantly, during the summer of 1776, some of the most forceful opposition to declaring independence came from people who feared that the former colonies' overseas trade would suffer irreparable harm as a result. Among the naysayers was Franklin's fellow-Pennsylvanian and delegate to the Continental Congress, John Dickinson. For Dickinson, Congress's determination to make a "brash" declaration without first obtaining commercial safeguards from another European power seemed akin to setting out to "brave the storm in a skiff made of paper." There was no way of knowing what other governments, especially France, would require as a condition for recognition and assistance. Would Europe's maritime powers "demand an exclusive trade," or would they "grant us protection against piratical states only for a share of our commerce?" Questions like these were deeply troubling to Dickinson, and they were to other Americans as well. As strangers among the "states of the world," the Union's citizens would be free to trade with whomever they pleased, but it was by no means clear that American merchants and sailors would possess anything like the commercial security that they had enjoyed as subjects of the British Empire.[57]

* * *

Because the American founders were so vocal in proclaiming their free trade principles, it can be easy to miss the extent to which Dickinson's concerns continued to resonate after the American Revolution was over. During the 1750s, Charles Jenkinson, the future baron Hawkesbury and earl of Liverpool and a man destined to play a leading role in relations with the United States after the Revolution, described Britain's maritime empire as a dominion "calculated . . . to preserve the Freedom of Navigation" for all nations.[58] Following Nelson's victory at Trafalgar in 1805, James Stephen said the same thing in *War in Disguise*, noting in particular the benefits that accrued to ships sailing under the neutral flag of the United States.[59] Although such arguments could be used to justify interfering with the trade of Britain's rivals, foreigners often quietly agreed. During the later eighteenth century, there were recurring demands that Britain protect the Mediterranean shipping of weaker powers, including Prussia, Hanover, Denmark, and the Italian states, from the depredations of Barbary corsairs, and the United States made similar demands once the Revolutionary War was over.[60] Following the Revolutionary War, American mariners often carried two sets of papers: one from the United States, the other from Britain. The first was to protect them from the Royal Navy's press gangs; the other was to claim the rights of British subjects, including British commercial rights and, presumably, the right not to be captured by North African corsairs.[61] When it came to safeguarding the freedom of the seas, Americans were as determined not to be slaves as Britons.

For citizens of the United States, the tendency to balance free trade with mercantile regulation came naturally, and it was destined to have a long history. This was particularly evident with the questions of political economy that confronted the Union during the early 1790s and that eventually helped drive a wedge between Federalists and Democratic Republicans. In the factional quarrels that marked the Washington and Adams administrations, one of the key differences between the two parties was how the United States should deal with Britain's naval hegemony. Should the new nation challenge Britain's maritime supremacy, as Jefferson and Madison both wanted to do, or should it accept the reality of British power for the time being, as Hamilton advised, and focus on creating the institutions and infrastructure that might someday make the relationship less asymmetric?[62] Although Republican calls for resistance appealed on nationalist grounds, merchants tended to accept Federalist arguments that the cost of another conflict with Britain represented the greater danger. "If England sink," declared New York's Rufus King in 1808, "her fall will prove the Grave of Our Liberties."[63] By the time King wrote, Jefferson's Republicans had won the contest at the ballot box. In some rather important ways, though, relations with Britain vindicated the Federalists. Despite the Anglo-American breach in 1812, leaders across the political spectrum realized that the Union was unlikely to prosper without some sort of accommodation with the world's leading maritime power. This included Jefferson. Writing in 1823 to President James Monroe, he confessed that while Britain was "the nation which can do us the most harm of any . . . on earth," he was sure Americans had nothing to fear "with her on our side."[64] Without always liking it, Americans would sail in the lee of British naval power for most of the nineteenth century.

Like so much else about Britain's early modern expansion, mercantilism took its rise from the urge to recreate European forms of sovereignty and control—in this case, over sea-borne trade and navigation—in a New World that lacked, or at least appeared to lack, the laws and structures of the Old World. Revisiting the connection between mercantilism and free trade accordingly has the potential to complicate our understanding of what Christopher Tomlins has called the "sovereign impulse to create 'due regulation and order'" in spaces that lay beyond the municipal jurisdiction of Europe's nation states.[65] In the age of the American Revolution, mercantilism and neomercantilism were the way that increasingly liberal powers like the British Empire and the

United States protected the economic freedom of their own people in a world that did not (yet) share their values. That Britons and Americans would see in Smith's mercantile system a means to peace, not a vehicle for war and depredation, may strike us as mistaken. Yet it ought to remind us that the gap between the liberal world of free-market capitalism whose benefits Adam Smith forcefully extolled and the mercantile one whose shortcomings he so clearly perceived was not as wide as the Scottish political economist would have had his readers believe. That is as true today as it was in 1776.

Notes

1. See, for example, Peter Linebaugh and Marcus Buford Rediker, *The Many-Headed Hydra: Sailors, Slaves, Commoners, and the Hidden History of the Revolutionary Atlantic* (Boston: Beacon, 2000); T. H. Breen, *The Marketplace of Revolution: How Consumer Politics Shaped American Independence* (New York: Oxford University Press, 2004); Paul A. Gilje, *Free Trade and Sailors' Rights in the War of 1812* (New York: Cambridge University Press, 2013).

2. Adam Smith, *An Inquiry into the Nature and Causes of the Wealth of Nations*, ed. Edwin Cannan, with a new preface by George J. Stigler (1904; Chicago: University of Chicago Press, 1976), 1:521–22. On the softening effects of laissez faire capitalism—what philosophes in France called *doux commerce*—see Albert O. Hirschman, *The Passions and the Interests: Political Arguments for Capitalism Before Its Triumph* (Princeton, N.J.: Princeton University Press, 1977). The idea of trade as a form war by other means is a deliberate play on Clausewitz's famous dictum about war being the continuation of politics by other means; see Carl von Clausewitz, *On War,* trans. and ed. Michael Howard and Peter Paret (1832; Princeton, N.J.: Princeton University Press, 1976), 605. The phrase "war by economic means" comes from Paul Langford, *A Polite and Commercial People: England 1727–1783* (Oxford: Claredon, 1989), 3.

3. See especially John E. Crowley, *The Privileges of Independence: Neomercantilism and the American Revolution* (Baltimore, Md.: Johns Hopkins University Press, 1993).

4. James Stephen, *War in Disguise; or, the Frauds of the Neutral Flags*, 3rd ed. (London, 1806).

5. For Max Weber, the quintessential Protestant capitalist was Benjamin Franklin. See Max Weber, *The Protestant Ethic and the Spirit of Capitalism*, 2nd ed., trans. Talcott Parsons (1930; London: Allen and Unwin, 1976), 48–57, 71–76, 180. On the market-friendly, individualistic basis of early American society, see Jack P. Greene, *Pursuits of Happiness: The Social Development of Early Modern British Colonies and the Formation of American Culture* (Chapel Hill: University of North Carolina Press, 1988). The classic statement of the founders' commitment to free trade is Felix Gilbert, *To the Farewell Address: Ideas of Early American Foreign Policy* (Princeton, N.J.: Princeton University Press, 1961); for a more recent iteration, see Peter S. Onuf and Nicholas Greenwood Onuf, *Federal Union, Modern World: The Law of Nations in an Age of Revolutions, 1776–1814* (Madison, Wis.: Madison House, 1993), 103–8, esp. n22.

6. See Eliga H. Gould, *Among the Powers of the Earth: The American Revolution and the Making of a New World Empire* (Cambridge, Mass.: Harvard University Press, 2012).

7. William Appleman Williams, "The Age of Mercantilism: An Interpretation of the American Political Economy, 1763 to 1828," *William and Mary Quarterly* 15, no. 4 (1958): 420; see also Crowley, *The Privileges of Independence*.

8. Williams, " The Age of Mercantilism," 422.

9. See especially Daniel Baugh, "Maritime Strength and Atlantic Commerce: The Uses of 'a Grand Maritime Empire,'" in *An Imperial State at War: Britain from 1689 to 1815*, ed. Lawrence Stone (London: Routledge, 1994), 187–88. If questions of political economy were a secondary consideration, they were the part of mercantilism that occasioned the most heated debate; see Steve Pincus, "Rethinking Mercantilism: Political Economy, the British Empire, and the Atlantic World in the Seventeenth and Eighteenth Centuries," *William and Mary Quarterly* 69, no. 1 (2012): 3–34.

10. William Blackstone, *Commentaries on the Laws of England*, 4 vols., ed. Stanley N. Katz (1765–1769; Chicago: University of Chicago Press, 1979), 1:405–6.

11. Denver Brunsman, *The Evil Necessity: British Naval Impressment in the Eighteenth-Century Atlantic World* (Charlottesville: University of Virginia Press, 2013), 233.

12. Jesse Lemisch, "Jack Tar in the Streets: Merchant Seamen in the Politics of Revolutionary America," *William and Mary Quarterly* 25, no. 3 (1968): 383, 386–87. For the somewhat different character of impressment in British ports, see Nicholas A. M. Rodger, *The Wooden World: An Anatomy of the Georgian Navy* (1986; New York: Norton, 1996), 164–88.

13. Gilje, *Free Trade and Sailors' Rights*, 87–89. See also Christopher P. Magra, *Poseidon's Curse: British Naval Impressment and Atlantic Origins of the American Revolution* (Cambridge: Cambridge University Press, 2016).

14. Quoted in Lemisch, "Jack Tar in the Streets," 385.

15. "Examination of Benjamin Franklin (February 13, 1766)," in *A Collection of Interesting, Authentic Papers Relative to the Dispute between Great Britain and America, 1764–1775*, ed. John Almon (1777; New York: Da Capo Press, 1971), 66 [hereafter cited as Almon, *Prior Documents*].

16. Gilje, *Free Trade and Sailors' Rights*, 20.

17. Joseph Harrison to the Marquis of Rockingham, June 17, 1768, in *Colonies to Nation, 1763–1789: A Documentary History of the American Revolution*, ed. Jack P. Greene (New York: Norton, 1975), 146.

18. Thomas Paine, *Common Sense* (1776), in Greene, *Colonies to Nation*, 276, 278.

19. Quoted in Anthony Pagden, *Lords of All the World: Ideologies of Empire in Spain, Britain and France c. 1500–c. 1800* (New Haven, Conn.: Yale University Press, 1995), 180–82.

20. James Scott Brown, ed., *The Armed Neutralities of 1780–1800: A Collection of Official Documents Preceded by the View of Representative Publicists* (New York: Oxford University Press, 1918), 51–52, 409.

21. The best account of the plunder of St. Eustatius is in Andrew Jackson O'Shaughnessy, *An Empire Divided: The American Revolution and the British Caribbean* (Philadelphia: University of Pennsylvania Press, 2000), 214–27.

22. Quoted in Gordon S. Wood, *Empire of Liberty: A History of the Early Republic, 1789–1815* (Oxford: Oxford University Press, 2009), 191. For the commercial provisions of the Model Treaty, see Robert J. Taylor et al., eds., *Papers of John Adams, Series III: General Correspondence and Other Papers of the Adams Statesmen*, vol. 4, *February–August 1776* (Cambridge, Mass.: Belknap Press of Harvard University Press 1977–), 262.

23. Brown, *Armed Neutralities*, 323–24.

24. Gilbert, *To the Farewell Address*; Onuf and Onuf, *Federal Union, Modern World*.

25. Bernard Bailyn, *To Begin the World Anew: The Genius and Ambiguities of the American Founders* (New York: Vintage, 2003).

26. Merrill D. Peterson, ed., *Thomas Jefferson, Writings* (New York: Library of America, 1984), 438–40.

27. Jefferson to de Staël, May 24, 1813, *Thomas Jefferson, Writings*, 1273–74.

28. On the interplay between realism and idealism in Jeffersonian foreign policy, see Robert W. Tucker and David C. Hendrickson, *Empire of Liberty: The Statecraft of Thomas Jefferson* (New York: Oxford University Press, 1990), who emphasize Jefferson's overbearing idealism; by contrast, Francis D. Cogliano, *Emperor of Liberty: Thomas Jefferson's Foreign Policy* (New Haven, Conn.: Yale University Press, 2014), casts Jefferson as a realist.

29. Williams, "Age of Mercantilism"; Curtis P. Nettels, "British Mercantilism and the Economic Development of the Thirteen Colonies," *Journal of Economic History* 12, no. 2 (1952): 105–14; Gautham Rao, *National Duties: Custom Houses and the Making of the American State* (Chicago: University of Chicago Press, 2016), 53–54. See also Steve Pincus, *The Heart of the Declaration: The Founders' Case for an Activist Government* (New Haven, Conn.: Yale University Press, 2016), who claims that the American founders' principal goal in 1776 was to create a strong, pro-growth state; for the limitations of Pincus's argument, see Eliga Gould, "It's the Economy, Stupid: An Activist History of the American Founding," *Reviews in American History* 48 (forthcoming, 2018).

30. Paine, *Common Sense*, loc 576 of 1006.

31. Peterson, *Thomas Jefferson, Writings*, 444–45.

32. Baugh, "Maritime Strength and Atlantic Commerce," 194. On the failure of the maritime powers to eradicate piracy entirely, see Guy Chet, *The Ocean Is a Wilderness: Atlantic Piracy and the Limits of State Authority, 1688–1856* (Amherst: University of Massachusetts Press, 2014).

33. Benjamin Franklin, *The Interest of Great Britain Considered, with Regard to Her Colonies, and the Acquisitions of Canada and Guadaloupe. To Which Are Added, Observations Concerning the Increase of Mankind, Peopling of Countries, &c.* (London, 1760), 41. Emphasis in original.

34. For the connection between consumer culture and the revolution, see Breen, *The Marketplace of Revolution;* Jane T. Merritt, *The Trouble with Tea: The Politics of Consumption in the Eighteenth-Century Global Economy* (Baltimore, Md.: Johns Hopkins University Press, 2016).

35. Cotton Mather, *Faithful Warnings to Prevent Fearful Judgments* (Boston, 1704), 37.

36. John Barnard, *Ashton's Memorial: An History of the Strange Adventures, and Signal Deliverances, of Mr. Philip Ashton* (Boston, 1725), 6.

37. Benjamin Franklin, *Plain Truth: Or Serious Considerations on the Present State of the City of Philadelphia, and the Province of Pennsylvania* (Philadelphia, 1747), 13.

38. "Examination of Franklin," in Almon, Prior Documents, 73.

39. Eliga H. Gould, "Empire and Nation," in *A Companion to Benjamin Franklin*, ed. David Waldstreicher (Malden, Mass.: Wiley-Blackwell, 2011), 362.

40. Captain Jacob Roome et al., v. St. Fernando and Lading (July 7 and August 25, 1758), in *Reports of Cases in the Vice Admiralty of the Province of New York and in the Court of Admiralty of the State of New York, 1715–1788*, ed. Charles M. Hough (New Haven, Conn.: Yale University Press, 1925), 131–32.

41. *Before the Lords Commissioners of Appeals in Prize Causes. Koninghen Esther, John Gardner, Master. Appendix to the Respondent's Case* ([London], [1760]), 3.

42. Holmes to Pitt, on board *Cambridge*, Port Royal, Jamaica, February 14, 1761, Colonial Office Papers [CO] 137/60, 339–340, British National Archives.

43. Long to Governor Moore, Spanish Town, Jamaica, December 31, 1760, and extract from letter of Richard Mercer to Messrs. Wm. & Jacob Walton & Co., and Messrs. Greg & Cunningham at New York, November 6, 1760, CO 137/60, 307, 309–310. See also the judgment of high treason against the Philadelphia merchant William Pickles on Antigua in January 1759, which alleges, among other things, that colonial merchants carried "stores of ammunition and provisions" to France's colonies in the West Indies, "sometimes under convoy of English privateers from N° America" (CO 152/46, 66).

44. Long to Moore, December 31, 1760, CO 152/46, 306–307. Emphasis in original.

45. Thomas Whately, *Considerations on the Trade and Finances of This Kingdom, and on the Measures of Administration, with Respect to Those Great National Objects since the Conclusion of the Peace* (London, 1766), 74–75.

46. Opinion of Judge Richard Morris in "Andrew Elliot qui tam vs. Peter Dorey" (August 28, 1772) in Hough, *Reports of Cases in the Vice Admiralty*, 240. For Britain's postwar attempts to tighten the regulation of colonial trade as a continuation of the wartime efforts to prevent colonial merchants from trading with France, see Richard Pares, *War and Trade in the West Indies, 1739–1763* (London: Cass, 1963), 467–68; Oliver M. Dickerson, *The Navigation Acts and the American Revolution* (Philadelphia: University of Pennsylvania Press, 1951), 168–70; Carl Ubbelohde, *The Vice-Admiralty Courts and the American Revolution* (Chapel Hill: University of North Carolina, 1960), 38–44.

47. Thomas Whately, *The Regulations Lately Made Concerning the Colonies, and the Taxes Imposed upon Them, Considered*, 3rd ed. (1765; London, 1775), 92. Emphasis in original.

48. Francis Bernard to William Pitt, Boston, May 5, 1761, in *Correspondence of William Pitt, When Secretary of State, with Colonial Governors and Military and Naval Commissioners in America* ed. Gertrude Selwyn Kimball (New York: Macmillan, 1906), 2:428.

49. See, for example, [James Marriott], *A Letter to the Dutch Merchants in England* (London, 1759), 6: "Every Subject of Holland, [who] acts as a real Dutchman, will . . . be treated as such, but the Dutchman who puts upon himself a borrowed Character, has little Reason to complain, if he is treated like what he appears to be, the Deserter of his own Country, and the Enemy of its Ally."

50. *Annual Register* 24 (1781): 101.

51. Copy of a letter from Admiral Rodney to the Marquis de Bouillé, in *American Journal*, May 23, 1781, 2

52. Report of House of Commons debate on St. Eustatius, May 14, 1781, in *Pennsylvania Packet*, August 23, 1781.

53. Smith, *Wealth of Nations*, 2:180.

54. Crowley, *The Privileges of Independence*, 75–93.

55. Smith, *Wealth of Nations*, 2:429.

56. William Allen, *The American Crisis: A Letter* (London, 1774), 15.

57. John Dickinson, "Arguments against the Independence of the Colonies," in Greene, *Colonies to Nation*, 293–94, 296.

58. Charles Jenkinson, *A Discourse on the Conduct of the Government of Great-Britain, in Respect to Neutral Nations, During the Present War* (London, 1758; Dublin, 1759), 54.

59. Stephen, *War in Disguise*, 188–91.
60. Emer de Vattel, *The Law of Nations, or, Principles of the Law of Nature, Applied to the Conduct and Affairs of Nations and Sovereigns*, ed. Bela Kapossy and Richard Whatmore (London, 1797 [Thomas Nugent, trans.]; Indianapolis: Liberty Fund, 2008), bk. 2, chap. 7, sec. 78, 301.
61. See, for example, Governor Sir John Orde to Thomas Townshend, Viscount Sydney, Dominica, April 26, 1787, Home Office Papers [HO] 48/1B, 131–37, British National Archives, reporting on an American ship from Casco Bay, Maine, whose American-born crew claimed to be British subjects in order to circumvent Britain's trade laws.
62. Crowley, *The Privileges of Independence*, 134–68.
63. Quoted in Bradford Perkins, *Prologue to War: England and the United States, 1805–1812* (Berkeley: University of California Press, 1961), 58.
64. Thomas Jefferson to James Monroe, Monticello, October 24, 1823, in Peterson, *Thomas Jefferson, Writings*, 1482.
65. Christopher L. Tomlins, *Freedom Bound: Law, Labor, and Civic Identity in Colonizing English America, 1580–1865* (Cambridge: Cambridge University Press, 2010), 344.

CHAPTER 12

"INNOVATIVE SOLUTIONS TO MODERN AGRICULTURE"

Capitalist Farming, Global Competition, and the Devolution of the U.S. Rice Industry

PETER A. COCLANIS

On July 1, 2011 Bayer CropScience, one of three subgroups of Bayer AG, issued a brief statement announcing that it was paying $750 million to settle a protracted legal battle with roughly 11,000 U.S. rice farmers in Arkansas, Texas, Louisiana, Mississippi, Missouri, California, and a number of other states. The settlement ended hundreds of lawsuits against the company brought by rice growers, who claimed that in August 2006 they discovered that their rice fields (and by implication the U.S. rice supply more generally) had been contaminated by trace elements of Bayer CropScience's experimental herbicide-resistant GM rice strain, Liberty Link 601 (LL601). The farmers claimed that they had lost millions of dollars after the contamination was discovered, as the EU, Japan, South Korea, and other importers either banned U.S. rice completely or accepted shipments only after it had been proven that they were not contaminated by LL601 (which had not been approved for human consumption). Rice futures fell sharply almost immediately after news of the contamination was announced, and it is estimated that the "debacle"—business magazine *Fast Company*'s description—eventually cost the industry a total of $1.2 billion.[1] After the settlement was announced, a spokesman for Bayer denied any guilt over the episode, stating:

Although Bayer CropScience believes it acted responsibly in the handling of its biotech rice, the company considers it important to resolve the litigation so that it can move forward focused on its fundamental mission of providing innovative solutions to modern agriculture.[2]

The legal brouhaha over GM-rice contamination, pitting the German pharma-chemical behemoth (over 43 billion euros in revenues in 2013) against some of the most affluent, innovative, entrepreneurial, risk-receptive farmers in the United States offers us a nice entrée into the history of the American rice in-dustry in the broader history of American capitalism.[3]

How and why? Simply put, because the American rice industry and Ameri-can capitalism had *always* been closely intertwined. Carl Degler may have oversimplified things a bit in *Out of Our Past* when he titled the opening sec-tion of chapter 1, "Capitalism Came in the First Ships," but he was clearly onto something.[4] Certainly, the history of the American rice industry can be inter-preted along capitalist lines—or at least as an expression of capitalist energy, ambition, and behaviors—almost from the start.

For example, rice—at once a basic foodstuff, industrial crop, and market staple—was one of America's first major exports and one of the first American crops to be commodified.[5] For much of the staple's history in North America, it was produced, mostly for purposes of long-distance trade, by enslaved Afri-can and African American laborers working for large, commercially minded (white) planters. To be sure, to most classical Marxists—and for Marx himself, most of the time—the fact that unfree laborers rather than laborers working for wages informed the rice industry would comprise ipso facto proof that the industry, however heavily commercialized, should not be designated capital-ist. Today, though, most commentators on capitalism, including many, if not most Marxists, approach capitalism more capaciously—and more flexibly—arguing that there are determinative variables involved other than the wage relationship, and viewing capitalism's fundamental characteristics not as indel-ible and unchanging but as constantly being shaped and reshaped as capitalism evolves.

This being the case, it is becoming more and more acceptable, even conven-tional, to view slavery and capitalism at the very least as being potentially com-plementary and reinforcing rather than antithetical or antipodal. The fact that the broad contours of the rice-production regime in the United States were not fundamentally or immediately transformed after emancipation is suggestive in this regard. For twenty years after the demise of slavery and the changes in so-cial relations arising therefrom, almost all of the rice grown in North America was still produced on lands controlled by commercially minded white plant-ers, with said landowners calling most of the shots. If rice was no longer being grown by enslaved laborers, it was nonetheless the product of African Ameri-can laborers enmeshed in very asymmetrical power relationships, whose eco-nomic freedom was perforce very narrowly circumscribed.

The question of the capitalist nature of the rice industry becomes far less controversial by the late nineteenth century as the industry evolved and, in so doing, experienced a geographic shift and a transition in key personnel. When the modern American rice industry was created as a result of a "rice revolu-tion" that began in the mid-1880s, the act of creation was again orchestrated by commercially minded (white) agriculturalists, but agriculturalists who were clearly distinguishable in origin, background, and *mentalités* from the earlier groups that had dominated the industry. The innovative, entrepreneurial, risk-receptive American rice farmers involved in the 2011 brouhaha with Bayer are the descendants—figuratively and in some cases literally—of principals in the "rice revolution" that began in the mid-1880s, an ongoing revolution that in some ways continues even today. Indeed, in some ways the history of the American rice industry—from its beginning until the present or, following our conceit here, from now back to its beginning—was part of the continuously disruptive economic process known as capitalism, wherein the leading rice planters involved have always played a most revolutionary part.

* * *

Before digging into the American rice industry, as it were, it is necessary to say a few words regarding narrativity and narration, or, to be more specific, about the rhetorical conceit pursued in this essay, following the rice industry not from its beginnings until today, but rather from present to past, tracing its de-volution, as it were. In taking this tack, the hope is that the fundamentals—the DNA, one might say—of the industry, of those that made it, and, if we are truly fortunate, of capitalism itself will be at least partially unveiled.

In light of this, a word or two regarding the guiding assumptions behind the exercise are perhaps in order. Drawing loosely from the principle of *actualism* in geology—one of the guiding principles in the discipline—the premise is that the present is the key to the past, in this case that the U.S. rice industry was shaped by long-term forces, punctuated at times by some unpredictable, often profoundly disruptive events.[6] Obviously, a social construct/process such as capitalism has a more highly contextualized history and genealogy than do Earth processes in deep time, and one can't extrapolate backward with the con-fidence that geologists sometimes do in studying the history of the Earth. But there are nonetheless certain important, even profound connections between the ideational, behavioral, and power constellations that informed the bio-prospecting—to employ Londa Schiebinger's term—that begat the American rice industry qua industry in the early modern period and the U.S. rice indus-try today (with its scientism and its own forms of bioprospecting).[7] Power asymmetries and aggressively commercialized, rent-seeking behavior were ap-parent early on and have become characteristic of the industry in the United States during all of its phases—albeit with temporally and spatially specific twists. For the record, this is not to argue that people thought and behaved in exactly the same ways in the seventeenth and eighteenth centuries as they did in the nineteenth and twentieth centuries, much less than they do today. But in the "modern" material world—a world that Hobbes at once anticipated and did so much to explain—there is certainly enough in common to render plausible and, hopefully, insightful the types of alignments proposed here.

One last matter before moving into the marrow of the piece, this one regarding precursors and precedents. For the record, the narrative strategy employed here is certainly not unknown. A similar conceit was used by Harold Pinter in structuring his well-regarded 1978 play, *Betrayal*, which traces an extramarital affair, lasting from 1968 to 1977, in reverse, and by Stephen Sondheim in his 1981 musical *Merrily We Roll Along*, which tells the story of composer Franklin Shepard backward from 1976 to 1957. While Pinter's play has been revived numerous times all over the world and been adapted into a 1983 film, the original production of Sondheim's musical, adapted from George S. Kaufman and Moss Hart's 1934 play of the same name, closed after fifty-two previews and only sixteen performances—which doesn't exactly bode well for this chapter—but it, too, has survived and sometimes thrived in revivals.[8]

So much for theatrical antecedents. One other work—a work of history—is relevant in this regard, not so much as an antecedent in a literal sense but at least as an inspiration. This work, the English version of which appeared in 1967 under the title *The Colonial Background of Modern Brazil,* was written by the brilliant Marxist historian Caio Prado Jr.[9] In this study Prado begins with the socioeconomic structure of Brazil in the early nineteenth century—on the eve of independence—then goes back to reveal to his readers how the various and sundry pathologies affecting said economy at that time came about. After situating readers in the early 1800s, however, Prado does not proceed backward in time, as we do here, but traces various social phenomena conventionally from c. 1500 to 1820 CE.

As one might imagine, it is very difficult in a narrative sense to think backward—in a devolutionary way, as it were. But when we do so, what Marx, in volume 1, chapter 32 of *Capital*, called the "integument" of capitalism is "burst asunder" and its internal structure laid out for us to see. Enough prolegomena—now back to the present.[10]

* * *

Few topics exorcize contemporary critics of capitalism, both in developed and in less developed countries (LDCs), as much as genetically modified organisms (GMOs). Indeed, from the perspective of a student of food and agriculture, GMOs seem to embody the type of "deliverables" (to use corporate-speak) associated with what Luis Suarez-Villa refers to as technocapitalism: a new form or stage of capitalism whereby or wherein research regimes controlled by corporations attempt to commodify creativity and innovation in order to produce intangibles—proprietary knowledge and intellectual property—to exploit for private gain rather than social good. Although on balance I support the development of GMOs as part of a broader breeding menu that includes gene editing and conventional methods—I don't see another realistic way to feed a wealthier world population projected to reach 9.5 to 10 billion by midcentury on less land, with less water, less fertilizer, and fewer herbicides and pesticides—I certainly understand the left critique of the technology and share some of the critics' anxieties. In particular I find worrisome the fact that GMOs up until now have been developed mainly under private auspices (Monsanto, BASF, Syngenta, Bayer CropScience, and the like) rather than under governmental auspices or under the auspices of nongovernment organizations (NGOs) or civil society organizations (CSOs) such as the Consultative Group on International Agricultural Research (CGIAR), the International Fund for Agricultural Development (IFAD), or the Food and Agriculture Organization of the United Nations (FAO). This has led among other things to what might be called "molecular divides" of one sort or another—between North and South, between big farmers and small farmers, and between agricultural research privileging soybeans, cotton, and maize over than cassava or taro, for example, and cattle and pigs over than small ruminants.[11]

In the case of rice, we find still another sort of molecular divide. On the one hand, varieties of so-called Golden Rice—genetically modified to incorporate beta carotene, and thereby to reduce vitamin A deficiency, a leading cause of blindness and malnutrition in LDCs—are being developed under the auspices of the International Rice Research Institute (an affiliate of CGIAR) in the Philippines, the national rice research institutes of Bangladesh and the Philippines, the Gates Foundation, and the Helen Keller Foundation.[12] The developers of Golden Rice, Ingo Potrykus and Peter Beyer, waived their rights to this technology in 2000, offering it to the world's farmers free of charge. Despite the exciting potential of Golden Rice, its progress has been slow, with adoption in LDCs severely impeded by hand-wringing and often tiresome opponents of GMOs, most of whom are from wealthy countries in the Organisation for Economic Co-operation and Development (OECD).[13]

LL601, on the other hand—the rice strain developed by Bayer CropScience and tested in the United States at Louisiana State University's rice research facility in Crowley, Louisiana—was bred not to enhance nutrition but for resistance to Bayer's broad-spectrum herbicide (Liberty), as was its successor seed strain, LL62.[14] Not surprisingly, Bayer CropScience—unlike Ingo Potrykus and Peter Beyer—has no intention of donating this technology, once approved, to anyone, especially not to the litigious rice grandees in Louisiana and Arkansas among other states. Ironically, once LL62 is approved for commercial use, U.S. rice planters, dollars to donuts, will be Bayer CropScience's biggest customers (provided they see greater profit possibilities from LL62 rice). For American rice farmers have been pretty avid about and receptive both to science and to productivity-enhancing innovations of one type or another for a long time, in some ways from the start.

A case in point: If German scientists Potrykus and Beyer were the coinventors of Golden Rice, U.S. scientists such as Ray Wu at Cornell also made huge contributions to the genetic modification of rice.[15] Wu was born in Beijing but took his undergraduate degree at the University of Alabama, where his father taught biochemistry. He was hardly the first "southerner" (or migrant, for that matter) to make his mark as a rice breeder. Biological innovations of one sort or another, including in breeding, have been central to American agriculture well before GMOs arrived on the scene, indeed, well before the green revolution or even hybrid corn. As Alan L. Olmstead and Paul W. Rhode demonstrate in their seminal 2008 study *Creating Abundance: Biological Innovation and American Agricultural Development*, efforts to enhance productivity in American farming via biological means began centuries earlier, laying the foundation for the giant genetic leaps since World War II.[16] And although Olmstead and Rhode do not discuss rice specifically in their book, the history of this cereal in the United States, as we shall see, is consistent with the story they tell.

To those with little familiarity with the U.S. rice industry or its history, the industry will undoubtedly seem odd, even a bit puzzling, especially at first blush. Despite the fact that the industry qua industry is over three hundred years old, the fact that we are a significant rice producer, the fact that the United States is perennially one of the world's leading exporters (usually the fourth or fifth largest), and the fact that in 2014 rice placed seventh in value among U.S. crops, relatively few people even realize that the United States produces any rice.[17] Indeed, it seems that the only time you regularly hear anything about rice is during the quinquennial debate over the farm bill, when one commentator or another mentions the cereal in the context of the "rice pudding commodities"—milk, sugar, and rice—all of which are heavily subsidized in the United States.

There are several reasons why Americans are so often rice ingenues. Rice production has always been concentrated in relatively few areas rather than broadly diffused geographically, and, while the United States grows a lot of rice, its population doesn't consume very much. There is another reason as well. By the 1890s, rice production in the United States has been based on capital-intensive, "high modernist" cultivation regimes that over time have rendered labor inputs minimal and in some cases almost negligible. Out of sight, out of mind, in a sense. Even in our foodie times—despite all the chatter about slow food, farmers' markets, organics, and locavores—the farm sector is scarcely visible to most Americans, nowhere less so than in the nation's lonely and lonesome rice zones in the Sacramento Valley of California and especially in the south central states. Indeed, for intimations of rural bleakness, isolation, estrangement, and alienation, there is little in American agriculture quite like the barren ricescape of the Grand Prairie of east central Arkansas, where today one or two hands, working now and then, can cultivate 1,000 acres or more with a little help from their friends: sophisticated university and private-sector seed breeders; advanced irrigation works and ubiquitous pumping stations; precision-farming technology characterized by computers spewing out advanced analytics, lasers, GPS-guided, self-propelled "smart" machinery—monstrous (and monstrously expensive) combines with thirty-foot headers, for example—hooked up to the National Soil Tilth Research Laboratory in Ames, Iowa, and so on.[18] If you visit the Grand Prairie it's mainly you, the machines, and the mosquitos, even as your mind drifts from Camus to Beckett, from Lydia Davis to the brothers Barthelme.

✳ ✳ ✳

How did rice—generally speaking, one of the most labor-intensive crops—come to be produced in this way? To foreground the argument, in the broadest sense because of the same constellation of forces relating to the expansion and elaboration of Atlantic capitalism that were responsible for the rise of the industry almost two hundred years earlier along the southeastern coast of North America. More specifically, because of the manner in which a network of migrant Midwestern entrepreneurs responded to said forces, perhaps not even completely wittingly, in the late nineteenth century, establishing the basic pattern of production that is still with us today.[19]

That such forces may at times have been "latent"—to use Bernard Bailyn's category—in the late nineteenth century, indeed, in the early eighteenth century and even today, does not diminish their explanatory power.[20] The fact that causative variables may be unknown or unseen by contemporaries, and the fact that people can act without being fully cognizant of, or at least articulate about the forces governing their actions does not mean that historians should relegate said variables to the dustbin of history and forego rigorous interpretation of said actions. Regarding the latter, it might be useful here to invoke Milton Friedman's famous example with regard to positive economics, to wit: A billiards player need not know the rules of geometry in any formal way in calculating his or her shots in ways that closely approximate the laws of this branch of mathematics. Given the explanatory power of Friedman's insight about economic behavior, the fact that billiards' players are imperfect and their degree of obedience to the laws of geometry partial and incomplete is, at the end of the day, small beer.[21] Arguing analogically, the same can be said with regard to the American rice industry. The trajectory of the industry is largely explainable by focusing on actions resulting from the interaction of a constellation of forces underpinning, associated with, and/or unleashed by capitalist development, and that is the case whether we trace this trajectory backward or forward.

So what was this constellation of forces? Of what classes or categories of variables was it comprised? These are tough questions to answer with a high degree of precision because the forces have been operative, informative, even determinative over several centuries. Moreover, some of these things are rather more dispositional—preferences made manifest intermittently and/or in shadowy form at the margin—than actions, behaviors, things, or states of affairs readily palpable or even visible all of the time. That said, this constellation or complex is characterized, first and foremost, by a *mentalité* or mental outlook shared by leading principals in the rice industry qua industry from the time of its inception right down to the present day. This *mentalité* can be recognized by, though not reduced to, a common adherence to certain core values, beliefs, assumptions, and norms concerning economic behavior. Among the common features of said *mentalité* were a commitment to economic rationality, not boundless but not unduly bounded either; the valorization of profit and capital accumulation; a dedication to innovation and improvement, particularly through science, broadly conceived; entrepreneurial energy (rather than lethargy, as is sometimes claimed); risk-esteem or at least tolerance rather than aversion; a willingness, indeed, eagerness to shape governmental policies to the industry's advantage; and the ability to legitimate, justify, and render moral or at least minimally acceptable a range of practices aggressively, even egregiously exploitative of labor and resources, the particular form and calibration of which varied over time and space.[22] In other words, many of the individual attributes associated over time with capitalists and capitalism. However selfish and even immoral such attributes may seem at the individual or firm level—whether to contemporaries or *sub specie aeternitatis*—at the societal level they can, depending of the circumstances, lead to a range of outcomes many if not most observers would deem favorable, including, most notably, order, economic growth, and development. Private vices, public virtues, as it were.

The particular way in which the above *mentalité* presents is neither simple not lockstep, let alone linear, but depends on interactive effects with other classes or categories of variables as well as spatial/temporal considerations. What other classes or categories? For starters, resource possibilities, under existing or plausible technology (What good were highly valued metallic ores such as coltan and rare earth elements before electronics, for example?); supply and demand considerations—prices, competition, alternative opportunities, sunk costs, and so on—regarding economically rational production possibilities; and the structures and mechanisms, formal or informal, that set the rules governing individual and group behavior, that is, the institutional framework and context within which the principals in the rice industry operated.[23] Not very elegant, much less parsimonious, to say the least, but history is more complex than many modelers believe. And this does not even include where the above recipe takes us with regard to the devolution of the American rice industry.

∗ ∗ ∗

A few more words regarding the U.S. rice industry today before detailing how the industry came about and why it looks the way it does. Again, the industry is concentrated in two general areas—the south central region and the Sacramento Valley—and almost all commercial production in the United States occurs in six states. The industry is heavily oriented toward exports—a feature characteristic of the industry since its inception in the early eighteenth century—which underscores the need always to embed the rice story in a global narrative. Despite not being one of the world's leading producers of rice—the United States accounted for only about 1.5 percent of world rice production in 2015, for example—in the postwar era the United States has consistently been one of the leading exporters. In 2015, for example, the United States was the eleventh-largest producer of rice in the world, but the fifth-largest exporter (behind India, Thailand, Vietnam, and Pakistan), accounting for about 8 percent of world exports.[24] The 2015 rankings don't diverge much from the basic pattern of the entire postwar period: The United States never ranks among the top producers but always ranks among the top exporters. Indeed, during the seventeen-year period between 1965 and 1981, the United States was the leading rice exporter in world league tables by a wide margin.[25] The United States has slipped some in a relative sense—the country was fifth in the world in both 2014 and 2015—as rice acreage is increasingly reallocated to other uses, and other large Asian producers ramp up exports, but it is still a major player in world rice markets, which, it should be noted, are much thinner (with considerably lower export/output ratios) than markets for wheat, the world's other leading cereal grain.[26]

If the U.S. rice industry has always been export-oriented, it has also long been characterized by scale and capital intensity. According to the 2012 agricultural census—the most recent available at this writing—there were 5,585 farms in the United States that grew at least some rice. According to this census, the average size of the 3,170 farms sufficiently specialized as to fit under the "rice farm" classification is much greater than the size typical of U.S. farms in general and the size of those specializing in field crops. Moreover, the vast majority of rice grown in the United States is produced on the largest rice farms.[27] And, as suggested earlier, rice, as grown in the United States, requires virtually no labor. By and large, then, rice production in the United States today means Big Agra: Wealthy, well-connected, well-subsidized agribusinesses. And it has meant that for much of yesterday too.

The modern U.S. rice industry began on the desolate prairies of southwest Louisiana in the mid-1880s, although its roots were in the corn and wheat fields of the heavily commercialized Midwest. The industry's pioneers included southerners, but its leaders comprised a loose network of white Protestant capitalists and promoters from outside the region, centered in the emerging Corn Belt and Great Plains, but stretching back to the Northeast and to Great Britain and northern Europe more generally.[28] If students today have heard anything at all about the history of the American rice industry, it is likely due to geographer Judith A. Carney, who in an influential 2001 book entitled *Black Rice* argued, at once creatively and controversially, that in the late seventeenth century and eighteenth century Africans and African Americans in South Carolina—about 900 miles farther east—were largely responsible for the beginnings of rice production in what later became the United States. She may or may not have been correct in so arguing (an interesting and intermittently intense debate continues on the subject), but of one thing we can be sure: The progenitors of the "modern" U.S. rice industry—the industry that got started in the "Old Southwest" in the mid-1880s, and our scholarly quarry here—were *white*.[29]

The network responsible for the "new" rice industry in the "old" Southwest included many important nodes (individuals and groups) with complex ties, but the nodal individual par excellence was Seaman A. Knapp, whose varied career and crowded years defy succinct encapsulation.[30] Suffice it to say that without him, his ties, and his seemingly inexhaustible stores of internally generated entrepreneurial energy, the history of the U.S. rice industry would likely have turned out quite differently.

Sometimes the temperaments and skill sets of certain individuals align closely with broader historical forces operating in, even animating, a particular place, and people such as Seaman A. Knapp and southwest Louisiana converged—harmonically or inharmoniously, depending on one's perspective—in the mid-1880s. Briefly put, at that time, southwest Louisiana was both underpopulated and underdeveloped, but, because of its propinquity to much more highly developed, commercialized areas in the eastern part of the same state—most notably, New Orleans and the cotton and sugar complexes it serviced—the area was poised for change. The area, in fact, had been so positioned for some time. The disruptions and dislocations brought about by the Civil War, however, set back "progress"—defined here as contemporary boosters did to mean railroad construction and land promotion—and things really didn't get "moving" until the postwar period.

Once they did, though, they did so in spades. In the 1880s and early 1890s both the prairies and coastal marshes of southwest Louisiana were overrun by corporate envoys—envoys representing, most notably, the Southern Pacific Railroad (which had the right of way through southwestern Louisiana and southeastern Texas), the Southwest Immigration Company, and a British concern, the North American Land and Timber Company, Ltd. They were joined by a phalanx of aggressive land agents, brokers, and speculators, who worked assiduously to lure settlers onto the area's underpopulated prairies and marshes. In a few short years, these corporate forces and expectant entrepreneurs had succeeded rather spectacularly, enticing waves of immigrants into the region and getting them so situated as to begin the farm-building process that in time would hopefully develop the area, increase the profits of these corporations, and make boosters and settlers alike rich.[31]

Among the migrants was a sizable cadre of entrepreneurially inclined small grain and corn/hog farmers from the Great Plains and Midwest. This cadre was to prove the vanguard for the so-called rice revolution that began in southwest Louisiana and spread quickly into southeast Texas and east central Arkansas, and a bit later (in somewhat different form) to the Sacramento Valley of California. But many of the early migrants who would prove so instrumental to said revolution arrived in southwest Louisiana without a clue that their fortunes—or, to be more accurate in most cases, livelihoods—would soon be inextricably tied to rice, a cultivar with which few, if any, had had any prior experience. And it is first and foremost to Knapp and a few other people—Sylvester L. Cary and Jabez B. Watkins, most notably (all three of whom were blessed or cursed with what Nelson Algren once called "hustler's blood")—that the onset of said revolution was due.[32]

Knapp is known, of course, to many agricultural historians as a plant breeder or as a farm journalist—he edited a publication in Iowa that was the progenitor of *Wallace's Farmer*—or as a leader in the movement to create a system of government-funded agricultural experiment stations (a movement that reached fruition with the passage of the Hatch Act in 1887). He was also the person most closely associated with the establishment of the modern rice industry of the United States. The abridged version of this story and his role in it goes something like this.

The almost impossibly highly networked Knapp originally got involved in land promotion in southwest Louisiana while president of the Iowa Agricultural College (now Iowa State University) in Ames. He did so at the behest of one of his colleagues at the college, Alexander Thompson, who was the brother-in-law of the aforementioned Jabez B. Watkins, one of the original organizers of the North American Land and Timber Company. This company had acquired vast amounts of undeveloped land (about 1.5 million acres) in southwest Louisiana and was looking for promoters to recruit settlers who would develop it. In 1885 Watkins recruited Thompson to join this effort, and Thompson in turn recruited Knapp shortly thereafter. Knapp agreed to travel to Louisiana on a fact-finding visit, liked what he saw, and in November 1885 moved to the region with his family, settling in the newly established town of Lake Charles in Calcasieu Parish.

Once on the job Knapp set himself to work promoting the area all over the Midwest, leveraging his relationships in farming communities, technological-educational networks, and religious circles—he was a Methodist minister who had spent two years as pastor of a rural church in Vinton, Iowa—to pique interest in an area hitherto virtually unknown to Midwesterners. Knapp and others more or less like him soon succeeded in recruiting large numbers of white Midwestern Protestant farmers down to Cajun country, but, before the region could take off, a key problem had to be solved: A viable market crop had to be found.[33]

After breaking the largely untilled prairie soils, the Midwestern migrants quickly learned that neither of the mainstays of the Midwest—corn and wheat—did well on the hardpan clay of the area. The migrants noted, however, that small quantities of rice had long been grown for home consumption by Cajun farmers in the area and that the cereal seemed to do well both on the prairies and, when properly drained, in the marshland closer to the coast. Knapp noticed this too, and, employing capital from foreign and domestic land companies and private syndicates, he soon was supporting crop experiments in the region, on which experiments rice and other crops were grown. Again, rice seemed to do well, and the entrepreneurial Midwestern farmers did not need further prompts, in short order moving to establish rice as their principal development platform.[34]

In many ways, their decision was a good one. Once the prairie was drained and irrigation works put into place—difficult tasks, to be sure, but doable since adequate credit facilities were available via the land promoters and New Orleans banking interests—production took off. But not in the manner that rice had historically been grown in the United States, or in any other part of the world for that matter. For, once in Louisiana, the white Midwestern entrepreneurial farmers, many of whom came down en masse with coreligionists from the same areas, succeeded through a process of what might be called technological transubstantiation, in turning rice into wheat.

Although rice and wheat had traditionally been grown in very different ways, they were both cereal grasses and shared some cultivation characteristics. The Midwesterners were accustomed to using a good deal of mechanized equipment on their farms, and given the prevailing factor endowment in southwest Louisiana and relative factor prices, they sensed early on that if they could adapt the mechanized technology that they previously employed in wheat production to another cereal grass, rice, they might be able to farm large acreages of cheap prairie land without employing a lot of labor, which was scarce and thus expensive. Although the adaptation process was not easy and was not done overnight—in particular it took a good deal of time to adapt the Deering binder for rice—the process went well overall and, before long, rice was being cultivated on the prairies of southwest Louisiana (and southeast

Texas, east central Arkansas, etc.) more or less like wheat, with mechanical seeders, cultivators, weeders, reapers, binders (and, later, combines)—first pulled by draft animals and later by gasoline-powered tractors—instead of with large numbers of workers seeding by hand, and using hand tools such as hoes and hooks during the cultivation and harvesting processes. Other formerly labor- intensive stages in the production sequence—field-dredging, the construction and upkeep of irrigation facilities, postharvest processing—also were mechanized in the "Old Southwest" and, later California, further reducing labor inputs, and, in so doing, facilitating the process by which rice production began to be rendered more and more capital-intensive and less and less visible on the American scene.[35]

The new production platform created in the mid-1880s changed the history of the American rice industry in many ways. Once knowledge regarding the new approach to "prairie rice" production was acquired and disseminated, and the new "package" widely adopted, production soared, and not just in southwest Louisiana and southeast Texas. During the first decade of the twentieth century, a similar, but even more modern, capital-intensive, high-tech rice complex developed in east central Arkansas—centered around Stuttgart—followed in the next decade by the broadly analogous complex in the Sacramento Valley. The complex in Arkansas was, if anything, even more Midwestern in form and style than that in southwest Louisiana. Almost all of the principals involved in the creation of the industry there were transplanted farmer-entrepreneurs—mostly from the Midwest, but some from Germany, as was the case in the Stuttgart region—who saw the possibilities for rice on the largely barren prairie lands of Arkansas and seized the main chance, adopting the farming and irrigation practices and the repurposed small-grain technology that had revolutionized the prairies of southwest Louisiana and southeast Texas (in the area around Beaumont) in preceding decades. One contemporary put the number of Midwesterners in southwest Louisiana in 1900 at 7,000—a significant number indeed, given their spearheading role—a 1933 survey of rice farmers in Arkansas found that nearly 75 percent were born out of state and that the five most common states of origin were Illinois, Iowa, Indiana, Ohio, and Missouri.[36]

Under the new cultivation regime, rice production soared in the United States, with more and more of it emanating from the new producing areas. According to the agricultural census, in 1879—that is, prior to the rice revolution in southwest Louisiana—over 75 percent of the 110 million pounds of clean rice grown in the United States came from South Carolina, Georgia, and North Carolina. The 1879 total, though up from 1869, was nonetheless more than 40 percent below the figure for U.S. rice output in 1859. By 1899—*après la révolution*—total U.S. production had grown to over 250 million pounds of clean rice, with 72 percent coming from Louisiana and Texas, and just 26 percent coming from the South Atlantic states. By 1919, the United States was producing well over a billion pounds of clean rice (1.065 billion), 79.5 percent of which came from Louisiana, Arkansas, and Texas, with another 19.6 percent originating in California. By that time, the South Atlantic states accounted for but 0.6 percent of total U.S. production.[37]

It was not just the shift in rice production that bears note, but, again, the entirely different way that rice was cultivated in the new producing areas. With land initially dirt cheap in the rice areas, the costs of capital reasonable, and labor scarce and, thus, expensive, rice farmers responded rationally and attempted to minimize the use of labor in the rice production function, while maximizing land use and substituting capital for labor whenever possible. To agricultural economists, this is all standard (Hayami-Ruttan) stuff. But, in so doing, these farmers rocked the rice world, transforming one of the most painstaking, backbreaking labor-intensive cultivations into one wherein human labor inputs were small and decreasing all the time. By the first decade of the twentieth century, one rice worker in Louisiana or Texas could work roughly eighty acres of rice—with the figure far higher in Arkansas—while nowhere else in the world at the time were rice workers able to work more than five acres.[38]

Lest we forget, though, innovation in American agriculture was hardly limited in the past to mechanical technology and to organizational changes. Throughout American history farmers could be found who pursued biological innovation, particularly through seed- or animal-breeding activities.[39] Extant evidence suggests that many rice farmers have demonstrated such interest over the centuries, including in the Old Southwest and California, which quickly became seed-breeding hotbeds, from which many important new commercial varieties and cultivars resulted—ten in Louisiana and Texas alone between 1900 and 1929.[40] Moreover, bioprospecting has long been characteristic of the American rice industry, and rice growers in the new rice zone were avidly interested in testing imported new varieties and cultivars, some of which—most notably Honduras, a long-grain variety imported (from Honduras) in 1890, and so-called Kiusha or "Jap" short-grain rices introduced in 1902—ultimately were to become extremely important in commercial terms. Interestingly, though certainly not entirely surprisingly, the Kiusha short grains were brought back to the United States by the indefatigable Seaman A. Knapp, one of the deliverables from the second of his bioprospecting trips to Asia after being named "Agricultural Explorer" for the USDA.[41]

The overall results and implications of the rice revolution were profound. The economic geography of the industry shifted dramatically, of course—from the South Atlantic Coast to the "Old Southwest" and shortly thereafter to the Sacramento Valley of California—but, more important, the industry reinvented itself in such a way as not merely to survive but to flourish for well over a century after its establishment. To be sure, the industry—by which we include not merely growers but those involved in input provision and output disposition—flourished in part because of robust institutional support from government in the form of protection, subsidies, preferments, political deals, and the like. But it cannot be denied that, working with (and through) government, those involved in the "new" industry—growers, millers, merchants, coops, trade associations, and so on—succeeded in dramatically shifting the U.S. rice industry's structure of opportunity. Their success was both surprising and shocking to established rice interests in the South Atlantic states—recall the numbers regarding the relative and absolute declines in production in South Carolina, Georgia, and North Carolina—which interests benefited not at all from said revolution but instead became one of its early victims. The traditional growing areas had been going south for a long time, as it were, for reasons that had little to do with the United States. But developments in the Old Southwest at once sealed the fate and sounded the knell for the industry that had arisen in the early eighteenth century and that for a long time had been for some the source of fabulous wealth.[42]

On the surface, the rice industry along the South Atlantic coast still seemed to many to be quite viable as late as the beginning of the Civil War. Total U.S. production in the area had grown substantially in the 1850s—from 143.6 million pounds of clean rice in 1849 to 187.2 million pounds in 1859, with South Carolina and Georgia together accounting for 92.4 percent of the total in the former year and 91.6 percent in the latter. Another South Atlantic state, North Carolina, lagged far behind, but was still the third-largest producing state in both census years, accounting for 2.5 percent of total U.S. production in 1849 and 4.1 percent in 1859.[43]

Moreover, some of the largest rice growers in the region were enormously wealthy, among the richest inhabitants in the South, with most of their wealth consisting of enslaved African Americans, human capital in literal terms. Unlike the rice-production system just discussed, which used little human labor after the production platform was established, production in the South Atlantic was very labor-intensive, based as it was on grueling hand labor in irrigated paddies with little mechanization—or even animal power—deployed in the production process. For a variety of reasons—economic and epidemiological, most notably, but, early on, perhaps for purposes of knowledge transfer as well—the vast majority of the rice work in the South Atlantic rice industry was always performed by Africans and African Americans, under conditions of slavery until the Civil War years, under a variety of conditions thereafter, some of which not far removed from slavery.[44] Before detailing how and why this production system, which seemed so strong, ultimately collapsed, a few words are in order about how it came about and evolved before it fell.

By the 1850s, the rice production complex in the South Atlantic states had been around for a long time. The first tentative efforts to grow rice in the region occurred shortly after the establishment of the colony of South Carolina in 1670, as bioprospecting Europeans (and their African and African American slaves) experimented with various and sundry cultigens hoping to find some that would help not only to sustain the inhabitants early on, but also in time to make some of them rich. Rice was but one of a number of plants tried in the first decades after settlement—it is not unlikely that African and African American slaves were involved in and may have spurred and overseen the earliest trials—but a rice industry qua industry cannot be said to have begun to emerge until the first decade or two of the eighteenth century.[45]

Cultivation may have begun dry, without irrigation or water management of any type, perhaps even on higher ground in the Lowcountry—the easternmost third of present-day South Carolina, roughly speaking, the hundred miles nearest the coast—but by the time an industry emerged, most production occurred in irrigated settings of one type or another. Until well into the second half of the eighteenth century, most of the rice produced in South Carolina—which was the epicenter of the broader South Atlantic rice industry throughout its history—was grown a good ways from the coast in scattered freshwater (inland) swamps that had been drained. Once such swamps were drained, planters constructed—or, more accurately, had their slaves construct—simple irrigation works in the vicinity, generally water impoundments. These impoundments could serve as reservoirs, holding water (often merely rainwater) for use on the rice, and could also be used as catchments when excess water had to be drained off of the same.[46]

Such water control, however rudimentary, did allow for greater regularity and routinization of production, thereby reducing planters' risk, but the enterprisers that settled the rice zone sought greater control and predictability still. As a result, during the second half of the eighteenth century—especially after the dislocations to the industry attending the American Revolution—the center of rice production in the Lowcountry of South Carolina (and Georgia, where production had started to become of some significance) shifted to drained swamps closer to the coast. Why? Because as early as the late 1730s planters had begun to learn—views differ regarding exactly how—that along certain stretches of tidal rivers in the Lowcountry they could deploy more sophisticated irrigation technology that would allow for closer calibration of the production process, better labor coordination, and greater overall efficiency. Although some rice continued to be grown in the area's inland swamps until the demise of the Lowcountry rice industry in the early twentieth century, from the late eighteenth century on most of the rice grown in the region was produced in relatively narrow bands of drained swampland along or adjacent to South Carolina's and Georgia's principal tidal rivers.[47]

In comparison to some of the technological innovations occurring more or less simultaneously in other parts of the West—innovations commonly associated with the "industrial revolution" and perhaps even with the "agricultural revolution"—the advent of tidal rice cultivation may seem modest. Indeed, seed drills, horse drills, turnip, and clover cultivation (and in America Whitney's cotton gin) all trump the coming of tidal-rice cultivation in historical importance. So, too, do innovations in textiles—flying shuttles, spinning jennys, water frames, mules, and the like—not to mention steam engines, puddling furnaces, and centralized manufactories. No one, however, can gainsay the fact that the tidal system was clever, perhaps even ingenious, and to our sensibilities rather environmentally appropriate, if it isn't anachronistic to employ such a concept.

Without getting into the intricacies of the tidal system—to do so would take us too far afield—the basic idea was to locate rice fields in drained swamps along stretches of Lowcountry rivers where the diurnal tidal action was sufficiently strong to raise and lower water levels efficiently and consistently for irrigation purposes without getting too close to the coast, where the water was too brackish and salty to use on rice fields. The sweet spot on such rivers—there were nine principal tidal rivers in South Carolina and Georgia—was generally found between about ten and twenty miles inland from the coast. Over time, such zones became the loci of rice production in the Lowcountry, with planters buying up adjacent land, draining it, and "bringing about" the arrangement of paddy fields, digging of canals, and construction of bunds, embankments, sluices, and gates so as to allow freshwater from the tidal rivers onto and off of the fields more or less as desired. The compound verb "bringing about" is a euphemism, of course, one behind which certain darker realities—the exploitation and considerable brutality associated with racial slavery—seek shelter. One must, thus, always remember that although planters may have done the buying—buying predicated, to be sure, on market awareness, risk receptiveness, the ability to mobilize capital, and, at least in some cases, considerable managerial skill—the draining, the digging, the arranging, and the constructing, and, likely, some of the technological knowledge regarding tidal cultivation emanated from slaves.[48]

That said, once the proper locations along the tidal rivers were found—the discovery costs of so doing should not be minimized—and the tidal-rice infrastructure put into place, the cultivation platform worked well for the better part of a century. Although subject to periodic breaches, breaks, and floods ("freshets"), the tidal system gave growers the ability to control water in a more exacting manner, helping better to ensure that plant-moisture requirements were met throughout the growing season. Tidal cultivation also reduced labor requirements considerably, particularly for hoeing, allowing the standard daily task expectation—rice cultivation in the Lowcountry had long been organized around the task rather than the gang system—to increase, thereby raising labor productivity.[49]

The above description, however brief, cannot help but suggest that tidal cultivation was an expensive proposition. Fertile swamp land along the proper stretches of a small number of rivers in the rice zone was limited and dear. Installing the proper infrastructure was also costly, as was amassing and retaining the labor needed to install and maintain such infrastructure and, of course, to grow and process rice. The outlays necessary to set up and then to run a tidal-rice operation in the Lowcountry were quite formidable, which, coupled with the economies of scale in rice production, meant that production of tidal rice was highly concentrated. Although there were a little over 1,600 agricultural units of three acres or more that grew rice in the Lowcountry of South Carolina and Georgia in 1859—out of 4,126 agricultural units of three acres or more in this area—most of the rice grown in the Lowcountry was grown on a small number of very sizable plantations owned by wealthy planters working large numbers of slaves.[50]

In 1859, for example, the top 10 percent of rice growers in South Carolina and Georgia were responsible for the production of 72 percent of the rice grown in these states, with the top 4 percent—each accounting for at least a million pounds of rice—alone accounting for 39 percent. In that same year, the bottom 67 percent of growers accounting for just 1 percent of production.[51] Slave ownership is characterized by similar levels of concentration. Again, using data from 1859: The modal number of slaves held by the smallest 28.5 percent of rice growers (measured by farm capitalization) was one. The largest 36 percent of producers, measured by capitalization, held at least fifty slaves, with the largest 22 percent averaging at least a hundred.[52]

Before moving on, consider Nathaniel Heyward, a planter who was hardly typical of anything or anyone, but who allows us to punctuate the points above. When Heyward—who planted rice on plantations all over the South Carolina Lowcountry—died in 1851, he held somewhere between 1,829 and 2,340 slaves, the largest total for any individual in the entire history of the American South. And there were other rice grandees in the Lowcountry c. 1850 cut out of the same (expensive) cloth. To be sure, rice production in the Lowcountry of South Carolina and Georgia was highly concentrated well before the 1850s, indeed, well before tidal cultivation carried the day. But once tidal cultivation became dominant, size, scale, and rice became bound closer and closer together in the Lowcountry.[53]

At this point, at least some readers may again be pondering the question: Why rice? What a peculiar crop for Americans to specialize in. Americans today do not eat a lot of rice, nor did they in the early twentieth century, in the antebellum era, or in the colonial period. So why did a rice-growing platform emerge along the southeastern coast of North America in the early eighteenth century. The answer, to abstract a bit, is because of the opportunities discovered and thence, aggressively seized by enterprising Europeans and European

Americans, who aimed to tap into an expanding, but incompletely integrated international market for cheap complex carbohydrates.

Unlike the situation in some other parts of the world, the hold of rice has never been broad or deep in the West in general or the Atlantic world in particular. To be sure, rice attained purchase in northwestern Italy, a few areas on the Iberian Peninsula, the eastern Mediterranean, and in some parts of West Africa well before South Carolina and Georgia were established, indeed, before the Americas were even penetrated by Europeans and Africans. And in the following centuries a few places in the Caribbean basin and South America adopted rice as *a,* if not *the* principal staple grain. But, by and large, rice in alimentary terms has generally been employed in the West either as a supplementary or complementary foodstuff, or as a substitute for more desirable small grains (or at times even pulses) if such foods were expensive or in short supply, or as a specialty food with ritualistic/ceremonial/pharmaceutical uses. Its versatility extended to other uses as well, most notably, as an animal feed and as an intermediate product in a variety of industries ranging from brewing to starch- and papermaking.[54]

Once it was discovered that rice could be grown in the South Carolina Low-country, and a viable strategy devised and operationalized to finance, assemble, and retain sufficient labor and entrepreneurial expertise to produce, process, and distribute rice of sufficient quality to market it for at least some of the uses outlined above, the possibility of establishing an economic platform based on rice became real. The criteria were met by the early eighteenth century, and, as a result, the South Atlantic rice complex began to emerge. From the start, this complex was export-based. As it would remain export-based throughout its history, it is perforce to the market for rice produced in the area that we now shall turn.

It is never easy, of course, to talk with a high degree of precision about markets in the past; both supply and demand must be ascertained and analyzed as well as the complex and variegated manner in which they interacted. Discussing the rice market in the West is particularly difficult because this cereal was never central much less indispensable there, unlike the case in Asia, for example, where it was indubitably "the primary commodity," to use A. J. H. Latham's words.[55] As a result, relevant data regarding rice are fugitive, scattered, and often incomplete, so much so that reconstructing, much less fully explaining the markets of chief interest here are formidable tasks that are best approached with interpretive modesty. With these caveats and qualifications in mind, let us consider a few broad generalizations, for which sufficient empirical evidence exists to inspire some degree of confidence.

From the late medieval period on, we know that rice had been marketed in limited ways in Europe for ceremonial and pharmaceutical purposes, as a specialty food and, now and then, even as a luxury or superior good. Even before then, the cereal was commonly grown and consumed locally in parts of Iberia,

the Valencia area in particular, and in the fifteenth century production began in in the northwestern part of the Italian peninsula, in Piedmont and
Lombardy. By the early sixteenth century, the Italian producing areas began
to trade rice beyond the growing areas, exporting the cereal in relatively
small quantities to other parts of Europe. Thence, the origins of the European
rice-export industry, which is still based in northwest Italy with attenuated
complexes in Spain, followed at farther remove by complexes in Portugal, Greece,
and France.[56]

By the end of the seventeenth century—when rice production in South Carolina was just getting going—most of the rice traded in Europe came from
northwest Italy and Valencia, with smaller amounts coming into Europe via
the Levant. Demand was not yet substantial, and few transatlantic traders
working American routes envisioned, let alone explicitly mentioned, rice as a
potential staple of note. Things changed over the course of the eighteenth
century, however, beginning relatively early on. With population growth, urbanization, and the gradual shift toward manufacturing or at least nonfarm
employment in Europe, the market there for cheap food energy in the form of
complex carbohydrates such as rice expanded substantially. In the sentence
above, close attention should be paid to the words "cheap," "food," and "energy,"
for the rice being traded was increasingly bought by (or for) commoners, the
so-called lower sorts, and various and sundry lumpen groups, when not used
for industrial purposes or as an animal feed. Not surprisingly, with these
trends accelerating in Europe in the nineteenth century—along with income
per capita—demand for rice skyrocketed. Westerners, by and large, may have
preferred wheat—they prayed for their daily bread, not their daily rice, after
all—but they would accept rice as a foodstuff for humans if the price was right
or small grains scarce, and had no problem using rice to feed their livestock or
in brewing and in making starch and paste.[57]

Thus, just as South Carolina planters—and in the early eighteenth century the
words "farmer" and "planter" were used interchangeably—working with their
local and transatlantic sources of capital, began to establish their production
units, assemble their (slave) labor forces, and establish an industry that could
produce rice efficiently, process it (fully or in part), and distribute it over long
distances, the market for the cereal grew substantially—as it continued to do
over the following three centuries.

As the complex in South Carolina (with an offshoot in Georgia) developed
and matured, it was increasingly able to do well in the European rice market,
which was centered in northern Europe, particularly in the states and princi-
palities that later comprised Germany. By the second half of the eighteenth
century, the South Carolina-Georgia complex had become the leading supplier
of rice to Europe. It retained its dominant position in most European markets
into the nineteenth century, except for Portugal, which began to source most
of its imports from its colony, Brazil, in the 1790s.

Rice proved good to those that begat and ran the South Carolina-Georgia export complex. By the time of the American Revolution, mean wealth per free capita in the Lowcountry of South Carolina—the epicenter of the rice industry—was by far the highest in British North America, with a small number of rice planters and mercantile partners (accomplices?) dominating economic, political, and social life, and at once amassing and displaying their cultural capital in myriad ways. And their brethren in the Georgia Lowcountry—sometimes brethren in a literal sense—were not far behind.[58]

This situation, however felicitous from the point of view of the principals involved, did not last all that long. Beginning in the second decade of the nineteenth century, a few potentially worrisome developments emerged that presaged the future, but such developments—"latent" phenomena, to use Bailyn's aforementioned formulation—were missed by one and all, and the rice grandees and their mercantile partners continued more or less as before, even as the growth rate of the rice economy began to slow down, especially in South Carolina. It took several more decades and an acceleration and intensification of the worrisome developments that had emerged earlier in the century before the principals involved in the South Atlantic rice complex knew what hit them.[59] And even then it didn't strike them with guillotine-like force.

What were these developments—dark ones from the perspective of the principals involved in the South Carolina-Georgia rice complex? Whence did they come and why? To foreground the ensuing discussion, the key development was the entrance into the best European markets of cheap, highly competitive rice in large quantities from South and Southeast Asia. And why? The proximate answer is because the enhanced ability of European nation-states to project power in the Indian Ocean and South China Sea, along with a series of innovations in transportation, logistics, and communications, made it possible for Western traders to procure very cheap rice in South and Southeast Asia and ship the same inexpensively to northern Europe. In essence, what these traders had done was to tap into and redirect a portion—in some cases, a very large portion—of the Asian rice trade that had been conducted for centuries. Moreover, in parts of Southeast Asia, these traders did more than tap into and redirect trade; they aggressively promoted the expansion of rice production/processing/trading facilities, in some cases dramatically. But these are still proximate considerations. The penultimate, if not ultimate cause is because the same powerful, if not irrepressible forces responsible for the rise of the South Carolina-Georgia rice-export platform in the eighteenth century—the expansion of European capitalism onto the "ghost acres" of the Americas and increased market integration—created the conditions (ironically or dialectically, depending on one's point of view) that structured and shaped, if not determined that area's later demise.[60]

Individuals/firms in South Carolina and Georgia had become viable participants in the leading European rice markets, which markets in time they came to dominate, because "Atlantic capitalism"—or, more properly, the practices and institutions associated with the same—became sufficiently developed over the course of the eighteenth century to allow the entrepreneurs who established and oversaw the rice industry in the region to acquire the resources necessary to install a competitive production platform, and to distribute the output produced/processed thereon to northern Europe via increasingly efficient transportation/communications facilities and marketing channels. The fact that South Carolina and Georgia were embedded in the British Empire until the Revolution allowed rice produced in and exported from these colonies good access to British product and capital markets, and, perhaps more important, to British commercial expertise regarding trading conditions on the Continent. Indeed, the South Atlantic rice region remained part of the British/British American trading world for decades thereafter, allowing American rice planters and merchants to leverage the valuable information networks and commercial efficiencies relating thereto.

With the benefit of hindsight, however, it is possible to point to other developments—beginning in the late eighteenth century—that were potentially troubling to the principals controlling the South Carolina-Georgia rice industry. Harvest failures in Great Britain in the 1790s opened up opportunities for Asian rice in Europe for the first time, and, as a result, significant quantities of rice from Bengal were imported into Britain. The celebrated—and keenly acute—Scottish political economist David MacPherson noticed this development, writing in 1795 that rice was the first "necessary" exported to the West from India, all previous exports being "rather of ornament and luxury than of use."[61] While this early import thrust was a bit of a one-off, as shipping costs fell through the nineteenth century cheap Asian rice looked better and better to price-conscious Europeans. And so, by the first decade of the nineteenth century, demand for Asian rice—again mainly from Bengal—had picked up considerably and rice from this area began to be imported into Europe in more regularized and substantial ways. In the 1820s and 1830s the flow of Asian rice into Europe continued to grow, with Java joining Bengal as a leading supply source.[62] For example, whereas almost no rice from Asia was imported into Great Britain before the 1790s, about 9 percent of British rice imported during that decade came from Asia. During the first decade of the nineteenth century, the proportion rose to about 31 percent, and by the 1830s to over 78 percent.[63]

This flow intensified over the next two decades, as rice from Lower Burma—mainly from Arakan and Tenasserim in the 1840s, but after the Second Anglo-Burmese War (1852) from the Irrawaddy Delta as well—began to pour into Europe, the result of growing demand for cheap foodstuffs in a time of rapid population and economic growth, urbanization, and industrialization.[64] In the 1850s, imports into Great Britain from one Burmese province—Arakan—exceeded total U.S. rice exports combined during that decade. It is at once interesting and important to note that the great increase in demand for rice in Great Britain and particularly on the Continent was tied to some of the same factors that, according to Sidney Mintz, were also driving demand for sugar, most notably, the need for calories to keep increasing stocks of urban, industrial laborers sufficiently healthy—or at least possessed of sufficient energy—to get through the work day, week, month, and year.[65]

It should be noted too that U.S. rice production grew during the 1790–1860 period. There was a big jump in the 1850s, for example, though nowhere near as great as the spike in demand for rice in Europe. Because rice from Asia always traded in Europe at far lower prices than "higher quality" U.S. rice, it is not surprising that Asia had surpassed the United States as a source of supply in the 1830s. During the 1850s, Europe's rice imports from South and Southeast Asia as a whole totally dwarfed rice imports from the United States. Indeed, total rice exports from the United States were greater in the 1790s than they were in the 1850s, and a smaller proportion of this diminished figure was going to the principal markets in Europe: In the 1790s over 72 percent of U.S. exports went to Europe whereas only 49.5 percent did in the 1850s.[66]

Instead, U.S. exports were shipped increasingly to nearby markets in the Caribbean where, because of transportation cost differentials, U.S. rice could still generally compete with Asian rice. Thus, more and more in the antebellum period, enslaved African Americans in South Carolina and Georgia produced rice to feed slaves in the late-developing Caribbean slave sugar colonies of Cuba and Puerto Rico.[67] Wheels within wheels, as it were, or speaking in formal terms, repeated and reiterative expropriation.

By the time of the Civil War—not after it, much less primarily because of it—the U.S. rice industry had lost its competitive luster. During the 1850s profits plummeted in the rice region, often turning negative. According to Dale Swan's important econometric study, returns for crop year 1859 were a shocking negative 28.3 percent.[68] And competition from cheap Asian rice was largely to blame. Lewis C. Gray found evidence that as early as the late 1830s "East Indian" rice was selling in Charleston itself at lower prices than locally grown Carolina rice, and this situation only worsened as time went by.[69] Wartime destruction and dislocations exacerbated the rice industry's problems. Emancipation and the concomitant changes in farm size/structure and labor relations in the postbellum period deepened the industry's competitive problems, which can be demonstrated most vividly by the fact that the United States lost its ability to export rice after the war and actually became a major importer of rice from Asia, despite increasing tariff barriers.[70]

But the principals in the South Carolina-Georgia rice industry gathered themselves and regrouped after the war, and attempted to carry on. They were joined in their efforts by growers in southeastern Louisiana, who grew labor-intensive swamp rice in much the same manner as in the South Atlantic states.

During the antebellum period, rice had been grown in this area—about 3.4 percent of the U.S. total in 1859—but the industry grew after the war, in part because a number of former sugar growers shifted over to rice which, while labor-intensive, was less so, all things considered, than was sugar.[71] With labor scarce and expensive in southeast Louisiana after the war, such a shift seemed to make sense (if not a lot of dollars!). Thus, as suggested earlier, rice production in the United States as a whole collapsed in the war decade of the 1860s—down to 73.6 million pounds in 1869—but recovered somewhat in the 1870s, reaching 110.1 million pounds in 1879. Demand for U.S. rice grew during the postbellum period—the population was growing rapidly and, as in Europe, was urbanizing and industrializing—which might have sparked some optimism among rice growers, especially in southeast Louisiana, the source of fully 21.5 percent of total U.S. production in 1869 and 21.1 percent a decade later.[72] There may well have been some optimism among growers in the South Atlantic states as well, but more likely it was the sunk costs that they had already invested in expensive rice infrastructure and the lack of many viable alternatives to rice in the economically limited and environmentally fragile tidal zone that kept planters plugging away at rice. In any case, although swamp rice carried on after the war, rice demand in the United States itself (and most other parts of the Americas) was increasingly met by imports from Asia. Imports from Asia continued strong even after the rice revolution began on the prairies of southwest Louisiana in the mid-1880s. This development on the prairies saved the American rice industry, but salvation, as is generally the case, took some time and was at best incomplete.

One important, but often underappreciated consideration regarding the principals involved in the first rice industry of the United States—the industry, that is to say, that began in South Carolina in the early eighteenth century—is that their behavior was generally marked by attempts at market responsiveness, by attempts to optimize within constraints, and by considerable—sometimes even formidable—entrepreneurship. That such attempts did not always succeed should not lead us to the conclusion that the principals involved were habitually inattentive or uninterested in the industry, that they lacked entrepreneurial vigor, that they were, as some imply, profligate wastrels more concerned with drinking Madeira wine and racing their horses than with making a crop of rice.[73]

Rather, when one probes deeply into the records one is impressed instead by the dedicated efforts at improvement on the part of many planters and merchants involved in the industry. Such efforts took various forms. For example, one can point to the attempts to establish huge rice-growing mega-plantations in the Lowcountry of South Carolina and Georgia in the late nineteenth century (akin in some ways to "bonanza" farms in the Dakotas) and to consistent efforts to breed better rice varieties, which efforts had led among other things to the development of Carolina's fabled "Golden" rice. There were serious attempts throughout the antebellum period to enhance labor efficiency through better organization and intensified tasking requirements. Dozens of patents relating to rice cultivation were taken out in South Carolina alone during the antebellum period and there were constant efforts to improve and enhance milling facilities, most notably, through the development of specialized steam-engines to power rice mills.[74]

The migration of production from inland swamps to tidal swamps in the second half of the eighteenth century can be viewed as a major act of entrepreneurship by the entire industry. So, too, can the spread if not the origins of the tasking system in rice, which can be interpreted as the result of a rather ingenious solution by planters to so-called principal-agent problems (relating to both hidden information and hidden actions) and to savvy efforts on their part to reduce health risks by minimizing direct supervisory responsibilities in an environmental zone highly morbid and mortal to whites.[75] Indeed, the early decision by industry principals to organize rice production overwhelmingly around the labor of enslaved Africans and African Americans, however morally repugnant to us today, was economically and epidemiologically rational, given the principals' material interests, and, well within the bounds at the time of what was considered modern in attempting to develop an agricultural colony in the semitropical periphery. The decision even earlier to experiment with rice as a potential staple was an example par excellence of bioprospecting, an example which at once succeeded and set the tone for the American rice industry as it developed over time.

In narrating the American rice story, there are in fact deep, strong, and abiding reasons to connect bioprospecting in South Carolina in the 1670s—and perhaps, by extension in West Africa even earlier—with the bioprospecting *mentalité* behind Carolina Gold, Honduras, Kiusha, Blue Rose, and Early Prolific rice, and the development today of GMOs such as Bayer's LL601 and LL62.[76] Capitalism provides these connections. The character and trajectory of the rice industry over time were related to the character and trajectory of capitalism during its various phases—from merchant capitalism to industrial capitalism to technocapitalism, as it were—and from partially to fully integrated world markets for agricultural commodities such as rice. Throughout the American rice industry's history the principal goal of those who organized and controlled the industry (which goal obviously became more explicit and self-conscious over time) was capital accumulation via the institutionalization of high levels of productivity, brought about by economically rational decision-making and the systematic employment of scientific knowledge in the economic realm. In other words, bioprospecting in West Africa and the Americas in the early modern period and the genetic modification of rice in America today, the transfer of the African heel/foot rice-sowing technique to the Americas and gene sequencing in Bayer CropScience's labs, are related, however far removed in time, via that most capacious and mutable socioeconomic complex we call capitalism.[77]

At every point in the industry's history the principals involved were motivated by and eager for "innovative solutions to modern agriculture," however much such solutions and the interpretation of "modern" changed over time. This complex structured an industry that over the course of three hundred years in North America—along the South Atlantic coast, in Louisiana and Arkansas, and in the Sacramento Valley of California—has made some individuals extraordinarily wealthy, to be sure, but at the expense of many others, and without ever succeeding in rendering any of these production centers economically developed by U.S. standards. Writing of his impoverished homeland in the mid-nineteenth century, the Portuguese Romantic philosopher/playwright Almeida Garrett formulated a question that is quite relevant in this regard:

> I ask the political economists and the moralists if they have ever calculated the number of individuals who must be condemned to misery, to excessive labour, to depravity, to villainy, to wanton ignorance, to insurmountable wretchedness, to absolute poverty, in order to produce one rich man.[78]

This question is well worth contemplating as we conclude, for the complex analyzed on the pages above continues to "roll along" in the twenty-first century, whether "merrily" or rather more as a "betrayal," depending on one's point of view.

Notes

1. "Bayer Settles with Farmers over Modified Rice Seeds," *New York Times*, July 1, 2011, http://www.nytimes.com/2011/07/02/business/02rice.html?_r=0; Ariel Schwartz, "Coming Soon: Bayer's Newest Brand of Genetically Modified Rice," *Fast Company*, December 16, 2010, http://www.fastcompany.com/1710454/coming-soon-bayers-newest-brand-genetically-modified-rice. Note that the plaintiffs included landowners and tenants involved in rice production, but not importers, exporters, millers, etc. See Robert Patrick, "Genetic Rice Lawsuit in St. Louis Settled for $750 Million," *St. Louis Post-Dispatch*, July 2, 2011, http://www.stltoday.com/news/local/metro/genetic-rice-lawsuit-in-st-louis-settled-for-million/article_38270243-c82f-5682-ba3b-8f8e24b85a92.html. As in many such cases, the settlement was not as final as it appeared to be at the time, and at the margin minor issues relating to the case continue to be litigated. See, for example, Kira Lerner, "Riceland Says Fed. Courts Can't Touch Bayer MDL Settlement," *Law 360*, October 3, 2014, http://www.law360.com/articles/584012/riceland-says-fed-courts-can-t-touch-bayer-mdl-settlement; Joe Van Acker, "Bayer Rice MDL Attys Fight to Keep Fee Class Action Alive," *Law 360*, March 10, 2015, https://www.law360.com/articles/629482/bayer-rice-mdl-attys-fight-to-keep-fee-class-action-alive.

2. "Bayer Settles with Farmers over Modified Rice Seeds."

3. On Bayer's total revenue in 2013, see *Bayer, Annual Report, 2014,* http://www.annual-report2014.bayer.com/.

4. Carl N. Degler, *Out of Our Past: The Forces That Shaped Modern America* (New York: Harper & Row, 1959), 1–8. Note that Degler approaches capitalism more or less in Weberian terms. See *Out of Our Past,* 1–8, 260–61.

5. On commodification and the commodification of the U.S. rice industry per se, see Peter A. Coclanis, "The Road to Commodity Hell: The Rise and Fall of the First American Rice Industry," in Richard Follett, Sven Beckert, Peter A. Coclanis, and Barbara Hahn, *Plantation Kingdom: The American South and Its Global Commodities* (Baltimore, Md.: Johns Hopkins University Press, 2016).

6. On "actualism" in geology, which is sometimes viewed merely as a (more nuanced) variant of the long-dominant uniformitarian approach, see, for example, Steven M. Stanley, *Earth System History,* 3d ed. (Basingstoke, UK: W. H. Freeman, 2008), 3–5.

7. Londa L. Schiebinger, *Plants and Empire: Colonial Bioprospecting in the Atlantic World* (Cambridge, Mass.: Harvard University Press, 2004). The term "bioprospecting" refers to the search or hunt for biological materials with characteristics potentially useful or at least of interest to humans. The term has been around for some time, especially in the anthropological community, the members of which generally view it with suspicion, warning that bioprospecting often bleeds into "bio-piracy" or theft of assets/knowledge/technology from indigenous peoples. See, for example, Cori Hayden, *When Nature Goes Public: The Making and Unmaking of Bioprospecting in Mexico* (Princeton, N.J.: Princeton University Press, 2003). Note that in this essay I am using the term broadly so as to incorporate searches for biological zones appropriate for the commercial application of biological materials of one kind or another, in this case, rice (*Oryza sativa*).

8. Harold Pinter, *Betrayal* (New York: Grove, 1978); Stephen Sondheim, *Merrily We Roll Along: A New Musical Comedy* [book by George Furth] (New York: Revelation Music & Rilting Music, 1981). George S. Kaufman and Moss Hart's play of the same name was published by Random House in 1934. On the (short) history of the original Broadway production, see *Merrily We Roll Along, IBDB: Internet Broadway Database,* http://www.ibdb.com/production.php?id=4144.

9. Caio Prado, *The Colonial Background of Modern Brazil,* trans. Suzette Macedo (Berkeley: University of California Press, 1967).

10. Karl Marx, *Capital,* ed. Frederick Engels, trans. Samuel Moore and Edward Aveling (New York: International Publishers, 1967), 1:763. Note that I use the term "devolution" figuratively here to suggest movement backward toward a more primitive social form—the more primitive form in this case being early capitalism. Modern scientists rightfully reject the concept of biological devolution (de-evolution).

11. See Luis Suarez-Villa, *Technocapitalism: A Critical Perspective on Technological Innovation and Corporatism* (Philadelphia: Temple University Press, 2009). Suarez-Villa elaborates further on the concept in *Globalization and Technocapitalism: The Political Economy of Corporate Power and Technological Determinism* (Farnham, UK: Ashgate, 2012). Note that the general tendencies associated with technocapitalism can be traced to earlier writers such as Harry Braverman. See Braverman, *Labor and Monopoly Capital: The Degradation of Work in the Twentieth Century* (New York: Monthly Review, 1974). On the problem of "molecular divides," see, for example, Food and Agriculture Organization of the United Nations, "FAO Warns of 'Molecular Divide' between North and South," February 18, 2003, http://www.fao.org/english/newsroom/news/2003

/13960-en.html. On the potential value of GM rice varieties, see, for example, Matty Demont and Alexander J. Stein, "Global Value of GM Rice: A Review of Expected Agronomic and Consumer Benefits," *New Biotechnology* 30, no. 5 (June 2013): 426–36, http://www.sciencedirect.com/science/article/pii/S1871678413000563.

12. On Golden Rice varieties and the institutions developing them, see, for example, International Rice Research Institute, "New Golden Rice Partners Join Forces Against Vitamin A Deficiency," April 14, 2011, http://irri.org/news/media-releases/new-golden -rice-partners-join-forces-against-vitamin-a-deficiency.

13. The landmark scientific paper on genetically modified "Golden Rice" appeared in *Science* in 2000. See Xudong Ye, Salim Al-Babili, Adreas Klöti, Jing Zhang, Paola Lucca, Peter Beyer, and Ingo Potrykus, "Engineering the Provitamin A (β-Carotene) Biosynthetic Pathway into (Carotenoid-Free) Rice Endosperm," *Science* 287, no. 5451 (January 2000): 303–5. For a historical account of the development of Golden Rice by one of the principals, see Ingo Potrykus, "The 'Golden Rice' Tale," *In Vitro Cellular & Developmental Biology—Plant* 37 (March–April 2001): 93–100. For more on IRRI's Golden Rice Project, see http://irri.org/golden-rice/the-project.

14. See, for example, United Stated Department of Agriculture, Animal and Plant Health Inspection Service, *Report on LibertyLink Rice Incidents*, Rice Report 10-2007, https://www.usda.gov/sites/default/files/documents/LLP%20Incidents%202.docx. For a broad left critique of corporate control of GMO rice varieties (in this case of Basmati by RiceTec, Inc.), see Matthew Clement, "Rice Imperialism: The Agribusiness Threat to Third World Rice Production," *Monthly Review* 55, no. 9 (February 2004): 15–22 http://monthlyreview.org/2004/02/01/rice-imperialism-the-agribusiness-threat-to -third-world-rice-production.

15. See Jeremy Pearce, "Ray Wu, 79, a Genetic Transformer of Crops, Is Dead," *New York Times*, February 25, 2008, http://www.nytimes.com/2008/02/25/nyregion/25wu.html ?_r=0; Blaine P. Friedlander Jr., "Ray Wu, Cornell's Acclaimed Pioneer of Genetic Engineering and Developer of Widely Grown, Hardy Rice, Dies at 79," *Cornell University Chronicle Online*, February 14, 2008, http://www.news.cornell.edu/stories/Feb08 /WuObit.bpf.html.

16. Alan L. Olmstead and Paul Rhode, *Creating Abundance: Biological Innovation and American Agricultural Development* (New York: Cambridge University Press, 2008).

17. U.S. Department of Agriculture, National Agricultural Statistics Service, *Crop Values, 2014 Summary* (Washington, D.C.: Government Printing Office, February 2015), 9, http://usda.mannlib.cornell.edu/usda/nass/CropValuSu//2010s/2015/CropValuSu -02-24-2015_correction.pdf. In 2015 the United States ranked as the world's fifth-largest exporter of rice, behind India, Thailand, Vietnam, and Pakistan. See U.S. Department of Agriculture, Economic Research Service, *Rice Yearbook 2016*, Table 11: "Global Rice Exporters; Calendar Year Exports, Monthly Revisions, and Annual Changes," p. 22, http://usda.mannlib.cornell.edu/usda/ers/RCS-yearbook//2010s/2016 /RCS-yearbook-09-14-2016.pdf.

18. Peter A. Coclanis, "The Rice Industry of the United States," in *Rice: Origin, Antiquity and History*, ed. S. D. Sharma (Enfield, N.H.: Science Publishers, 2010), 411–31, esp. 429–30. For a similar treatment a generation earlier, see John Fraser Hart, *The Land That Feeds Us* (New York: W. W. Norton, 1991), 301–14.

19. On the creation of the "modern," capital-intensive rice complex in the United States, See Peter A. Coclanis, "White Rice: The Midwestern Origins of the Modern Rice Industry in the United States," in *Rice: Global Networks and New Histories*, ed. Francesca Bray, Peter A. Coclanis, Edda Fields-Black, and Dagmar Schäfer (New York: Cambridge University Press, 2015), 291–317.

20. Bernard Bailyn, "The Challenge of Modern Historiography," *American Historical Review* 87, no. 1 (February 1982): 1–24, esp. 10–11.

21. Milton Friedman, *Essays in Positive Economics* (Chicago: University of Chicago Press, 1953), 21. Friedman actually used this same analogy earlier in a coauthored paper. See Milton Friedman and L. J. Savage, "The Utility Analysis of Choices Involving Risk," *Journal of Political Economy* 56, no. 4 (August 1948): 279–304, esp. 298.

22. Note that in saying that rice interests have historically been risk-receptive and (in my view) entrepreneurial is not to suggest *in extremis* that they always embrace uncertainty, are consistently willing to risk all, and are fiercely individualistic, much less antigovernment. They are, rather, risk-*receptive*, but not willing to bet the house, preferring insurable risks to extreme chance-taking—thus their willingness at times to accept, even to seek out governmental support and sustenance from other institutional sources. In their uncertain attitude toward uncertainty, they would probably not be considered truly entrepreneurial by the likes of the economist Frank Knight and those that follow his lead. For Knight's views, see Knight, *Risk, Uncertainty and Profit* (Boston: Houghton Mifflin, 1921).

23. For a robust argument on the importance of institutions in promoting or impeding growth and development, see Daron Acemoglu and James A. Robinson, *Why Nations Fail: The Origins of Power, Prosperity, and Poverty* (New York: Crown, 2012).

24. Food and Agriculture Organization of the United Nations, *Rice Market Monitor* 18, no. 2 (July 2015): 30, 32, http://www.fao.org/fileadmin/templates/est/COMM _MARKETS_MONITORING/Rice/Images/RMM/RMM_JUL15_H.pdf; see U.S. Department of Agriculture, Economic Research Service, *Rice Yearbook 2016*, Tables 10–11, pp. 21–22, http://usda.mannlib.cornell.edu/usda/current/RCS-yearbook/RCS -yearbook-09-14-2016.pdf.

25. David Dawe, "The Changing Structure of the World Rice Market, 1950–2000," *Food Policy* 27, no. 4 (August 2002): 355–70.

26. Coclanis, "The Rice Industry of the United States," 429; J. L. Maclean, D. C. Dawe, B. Hardy, and G. P. Hettel, eds., *Rice Almanac: Source Book for the Most Important Economic Activity on Earth*, 3d. ed. (Los Baños, Philippines: International Rice Research Institute, 2002), 1–9.

27. See United States Department of Agriculture, *2012 Census of Agriculture* (Washington, D.C.: Government Printing Office, 2014), vol. 1, chap. 1, table 64, http://www.ag-census.usda.gov/Publications/2012/Full_Report/Volume_1,_Chapter_1_US/st99_1 _064_064.pdf, and table 51, http://www.agcensus.usda.gov/Publications/2012/Full _Report/Volume_1,_Chapter_1_US/st99_1_051_052.pdf. The average number of acres of land on the 3,170 units classified as rice farms in the United States in 2012 was about 1,055. The average for all U.S. farms in 2012 was about 434 acres. Also see Katherine Baldwin, Erik Dohlman, Nathan Childs, and Linda Foreman, *Consolidation and Structural Change in the U.S. Rice Sector*, U.S. Department of Agriculture, Economic Research Service, RCS-11d-01, April 2011, 5–9; Coclanis, "The Rice Industry of the United States," 428.

28. See Coclanis, "White Rice." Also see Pete Daniel, *Breaking the Land: The Transformation of Cotton, Tobacco, and Rice Cultures since 1880* (Urbana: University of Illinois Press, 1985), 39–61; Henry C. Dethloff, *A History of the American Rice Industry, 1685–1985* (College Station: Texas A & M University Press, 1988), 63–109.

29. See Judith A. Carney, *Black Rice: The African Origins of Rice Cultivation in the Americas* (Cambridge, Mass.: Harvard University Press, 2001). For a systematic critique of Carney's thesis, see David Eltis, Philip D. Morgan, and David Richardson, "Agency and Diaspora in Atlantic History: Reassessing the African Contribution to Rice Cultivation in the

Americas," *American Historical Review* 112, no. 5 (December 2007): 1329–58. Also see Jessica Marie Johnson, "*AHR* Exchange: The Question of 'Black Rice,'" *American Historical Review* 115, no. 1 (February 2010): 123–71 (essays by S. Max Edelson, Gwendolyn Midlo Hall, and Walter Hawthorne, with a response by Eltis, Morgan, and Richardson).

30. Coclanis, "White Rice."

31. See Coclanis, "White Rice"; Daniel, *Breaking the Land,* 39–42; Dethloff, *A History of the American Rice Industry,* 68–76.

32. Ibid. On the early California rice industry, see, for example, Norris Arthur Bleyhl, "A History of the Production and Marketing of Rice in California" (Ph.D. diss., University of Minnesota. 1955), 83–185. The reference to "hustler's blood" is from Nelson Algren, *Chicago: City on the Make* (New York: Doubleday, 1951), 42.

33. Coclanis, "White Rice."

34. Coclanis, "White Rice"; Joseph C. Bailey, *Seaman A. Knapp: Schoolmaster of American Agriculture* (New York: Columbia University Press, 1945), 109–32.

35. Coclanis, "White Rice"; Bleyhl, "A History of the Production and Marketing of Rice," 83–185; Jenkins W. Jones, Loren L. Davis, and Arthur H. Williams, *Rice Culture in California,* U.S. Department of Agriculture, Farmers' Bulletin No. 2022 (Washington, D.C.: Government Printing Office, 1950); Jack H. Wilson, ed., *Rice in California* (Richvale, Calif.: Butte County Growers Association, 1979), 20–248.

36. Coclanis, "White Rice"; J. M. Spicer, *Beginnings of the Rice Industry in Arkansas* (Arkansas: Arkansas Rice Promotion Association and Rice Council, 1964); Daniel, *Breaking the Land*, 44–45; Dethloff, *A History of the American Rice Industry*, 87; T. C. McCormick, "Rural Social Organization in the Rice Area," *Arkansas Agricultural Experiment Station Bulletin* 296 (Fayetteville,: University of Arkansas, College of Agriculture, December 1933), 8.

37. Peter A. Coclanis, *The Shadow of a Dream: Economic Life and Death in the South Carolina Low Country, 1670–1920* (New York: Oxford University Press, 1989), 142.

38. Coclanis, "White Rice"; Seaman A. Knapp, *Rice Culture*, U.S. Department of Agriculture, Farmers' Bulletin 417 (Washington, D.C.: Government Printing Office, 1910), 20. On the situation in Arkansas, where one person could cultivate 200 acres of rice pretty much alone, see Frank L. Perrin, "Arkansas Rice," *Farm Journal* 34 (February 1910): 97. For the classic formulations of the Hayami-Ruttan approach, see Yujiro Hayami and Vernon W. Ruttan, "Factor Prices and Technical Change in Agricultural Development: The United States and Japan, 1880–1960," *Journal of Political Economy* 78, no. 5 (September–October 1970): 1115–41; Hayami and Ruttan, *Agricultural Development: An International Perspective*, rev. exp. ed. (Baltimore, Md.: Johns Hopkins University Press, 1985), 73–114. This approach, often referred to as the induced-innovation approach, views productivity gains as arising from output-augmenting and input-saving technologies involving the substitution of relatively cheap factors for relatively expensive ones. The approach has been refined and complicated since the turn of the twenty-first century, but Hayami and Ruttan's basic insight is still viewed as being important for understanding technical change in agriculture. Note that in the early 1920s an attempt was made in Sumatra to emulate the United States and establish a mechanized rice-cultivation regime. The government officials behind the initiative were impressed with what had happened in the United States—personnel visited California, Texas, and Louisiana to see the "revolution" firsthand—and tried to install a similar system on a government rice farm called Selatdjaran near Palembang in southern Sumatra. The effort came a cropper, however, ending in failure in 1924. On the attempt, see Harro Maat, "Commodities and Anti-Commodities: Rice on Sumatra 1915–1925," in *Rice: Global Networks and New Histories*, 335–54.

39. See, for example, Olmstead and Rhode, *Creating Abundance*; Jack Ralph Kloppenburg Jr., *First the Seed: The Political Economy of Plant Biotechnology, 1492–2000* (New York: Cambridge University Press, 1988); Peter A. Coclanis, "Seeds of Reform: David R. Coker, Premium Cotton, and the Campaign to Modernize the Rural South," *South Carolina Historical Magazine* 102, no. 3 (July 2001): 202–18.

40. See Hong Lu, Marc A. Redus, Jason R. Coburn, J. Neil Rutger, Susan R. McCouch, and Thomas H. Tai, "Population Structure and Breeding Patterns of 145 U.S. Rice Cultivars Based on SSR Marker Analysis," *Crop Science* 45 (January–February 2005): 66–76, esp. 68.

41. Coclanis, "White Rice."

42. On the "first" American rice industry along the South Atlantic coast, see Coclanis, "The Rice Industry of the United States," 412–22. For detailed case studies on the rice industries of South Carolina and Georgia, the epicenters of the rice industry in this region, see Coclanis, *The Shadow of a Dream*; Julia Floyd Smith, *Slavery and Rice Culture in Low Country Georgia, 1750–1860* (Knoxville: University of Tennessee Press, 1985); Mart A. Stewart, *"What Nature Suffers to Groe": Life, Labor, and Landscape on the Georgia Coastal Plain, 1680–1920* (Athens: University of Georgia Press, 1996). Note that some planters in the South Atlantic rice zone attempted to employ the new, capital-intensive methods being used in the Southwest, but such attempts failed for a variety of reasons (lack of investment capital, soils unable to bear the weight of the new machinery, sunk costs, etc.).

43. Coclanis, *The Shadow of a Dream*, 142.

44. See the works cited in note 42. Also see James H. Tuten, *Lowcountry Time and Tide: The Fall of the South Carolina Rice Kingdom* (Columbia: University of South Carolina Press, 2010).

45. Coclanis, *The Shadow of a Dream*, 58–63; Peter A. Coclanis, "Rice," in *The South Carolina Encyclopedia*, ed. Walter B. Edgar (Columbia: University of South Carolina Press, 2006), 791–94; Lewis C. Gray, *History of Agriculture in the Southern United States to 1860* (1933; Gloucester, Mass.: Peter Smith, 1958), 1:41–59, 277–84; S. Max Edelson, *Plantation Enterprise in Colonial South Carolina* (Cambridge, Mass.: Harvard University Press, 2006), 53–125.

46. See the works cited in note 42.

47. See Gray, *History of Agriculture*, 1:279–84; Coclanis, *The Shadow of a Dream*, 96–98; Joyce E. Chaplin, *An Anxious Pursuit: Agricultural Innovation and Modernity in the Lower South, 1730–1815* (Chapel Hill: Published for the Omohundro Institute of Early American History and Culture by the University of North Carolina Press, 1993), 227–76; Coclanis, "Rice," 791–94; Edelson, *Plantation Enterprise in Colonial South Carolina*, 103–13. On the development of the rice industry in the Georgia Lowcountry, see Smith, *Slavery and Rice Culture in Low Country Georgia*, 15–63; Stewart, *"What Nature Suffers to Groe,"* 98–114; Coclanis, "Rice," in *The New Georgia Encyclopedia*, ed. John C. Inscoe (Athens: University of Georgia Press, 2004), http://www.georgiaencyclopedia.org/nge/Article.jsp?id=h-899. For some of the ways in which the shift to tidal cultivation may have been financed, see Russell R. Menard, "Financing the Lowcountry Export Boom: Capital and Growth in Early South Carolina," *William and Mary Quarterly* 51, no. 4 (October 1994): 659–76.

48. See the works cited in note 42.

49. On the task system employed in rice cultivation in the South Carolina and Georgia Lowcountry, see Philip D. Morgan, "Work and Culture: The Task System and the World of Lowcountry Blacks, 1700 to 1880," *William and Mary Quarterly* 39, no. 4 (October 1982): 563–99; Peter A. Coclanis, "Thickening Description: William Washington's

Queries on Rice," *Agricultural History* 64, no. 3 (Summer 1990): 9–16; Peter A. Coclanis, "How the Low Country Was Taken to Task: Slave-Labor Organization in Coastal South Carolina and Georgia," in *Slavery Secession, and Southern History*, ed. Robert Louis Paquette and Louis Ferleger (Charlottesville: University Press of Virginia, 2000), 59–78. On the increase in tasking requirements (especially for hoeing) over time, see Morgan, "Work and Culture," 570 (table 1).

50. Coclanis, "The Rice Industry of the United States," 417–18; Dale Evans Swan, *The Structure and Profitability of the Antebellum Rice Industry 1859* (New York: Arno, 1975), 15.

51. Coclanis, "The Road to Commodity Hell"; Swan, *Structure and Profitability*, 87–89, 104–12.

52. See the works cited in note 50.

53. On Heyward, his slaveholdings, and his wealth, see Peter A. Coclanis, introduction to *Seed from Madagascar*, by Duncan Heyward (1937; Columbia: University of South Carolina Press, 1993), ix–l, esp. xxii–xxiii; Peter A. Coclanis, introduction to *Twilight on the South Carolina Rice Fields: Letters of the Heyward Family 1862–1871*, ed. Margaret Belser Hollis and Allen H. Stokes (Columbia: University of South Carolina Press, 2010), xvii–xxxi, esp. xviii. On the grandees of the Lowcountry more generally, see Chalmers G. Davidson, *The Last Foray: The South Carolina Planters of 1860: A Sociological Study* (Columbia: University of South Carolina Press, 1971), 1–17; William Kauffman Scarborough, *Masters of the Big House: Elite Slaveholders of the Mid-Nineteenth-Century South* (Baton Rouge: Louisiana State University Press, 2003), 9, 12–13, appendixes A–D, 427–84. According to Scarborough, in 1850 there were twenty-six slave owners in the United States who held five hundred or more slaves; nine were rice planters in South Carolina and Georgia. Ten years later there were fifty slave owners with fifty or more slaves. Fourteen of them were rice planters along the South Atlantic coast.

54. See Peter A. Coclanis, "Distant Thunder: The Creation of a World Market in Rice and the Transformations It Wrought," *American Historical Review* 98, no. 4 (October 1993): 1050–78, esp. 1051–55. Also see R. C. Nash, "South Carolina and the Atlantic Economy in the Late Seventeenth and Eighteenth Centuries," *Economic History Review*, New Series, 45, no. 4 (November 1992): 677–702; Kenneth Morgan, "The Organization of the Colonial American Rice Trade," *William and Mary Quarterly*, 52, no. 3 (July 1995): 433–52; Peter A. Coclanis, "Rice," *Encyclopedia of World Trade Since 1450*, ed. John J. McCusker (Detroit: Macmillan, 2006), 2:628–32. For a formal demonstration of the substitutability of rice and wheat during a later period, see A. J. H. Latham and Larry Neal, "The International Market in Rice and Wheat, 1868–1914," *Economic History Review*, New Series, 36, no. 2 (May 1983): 260–80.

55. A. J. H. Latham, *Rice: The Primary Commodity* (London: Routledge, 1998).

56. See Coclanis, "Distant Thunder," 1051–55; Aldo Ferrero and Francesco Vidotto, "History of Rice in Europe," in *Rice: Origin, Antiquity and History*, 341–72, esp. 341–48.

57. See Coclanis, "Distant Thunder"; Coclanis, "Rice," 2:628–32; Coclanis, "The Rice Industry of the United States."

58. Coclanis, *The Shadow of a Dream*, 133–35; Coclanis, "Distant Thunder."

59. Coclanis, *The Shadow of a Dream*, 111–58; Coclanis, "Distant Thunder; Coclanis, "Rice," in *The New Georgia Encyclopedia*.

60. H. J. S. Cotton, "The Rice Trade of the World," *Calcutta Review* 58 (1874): 267–302; Coclanis, "Distant Thunder"; Peter A. Coclanis, "Southeast Asia's Incorporation into the World Rice Market: A Revisionist View," *Journal of Southeast Asian Studies* 24,

no. 2 (September 1993): 251–67; Peter A. Coclanis, "ReOrienting Atlantic History: The Global Dimensions of the 'Western' Rice Trade," in *The Atlantic in Global History, 1500–2000*, eds. Jorge Cañizares-Esguerra and Erik R. Seeman (Upper Saddle River, N.J.: Pearson Prentice Hall, 2007), 111–27. "Ghost acres" is a concept used as far back as the 1960s to denote external, often underpopulated land that can be used by a given area or country for productive purposes, thereby adding to total national output/income (and, over time, to national wealth), while easing resource constraints. The concept became widely known after Kenneth Pomeranz employed it to help explain how and why parts of Europe pulled ahead of parts of Asia in the eighteenth and nineteenth centuries. See Kenneth Pomeranz, *The Great Divergence: China, Europe, and the Making of the Modern World Economy* (Princeton, N.J.: Princeton University Press, 2000), 264–97.

61. David Macpherson, *Annals of Commerce, Manufactures, Fisheries, and Navigation*, 4 vols. (London: Nichols and Son, 1805), 4:362. Note that Macpherson wrote the passage quoted in 1795, though the *Annals* was not published until a decade later.

62. See Coclanis, "Distant Thunder"; Coclanis, "Southeast Asia's Incorporation into the World Rice Market."

63. Coclanis, "Distant Thunder," 1058–59 (tables 1 and 2). Note that small amounts of Asian rice had long been shipped to West Africa by British slavers, along with much larger amounts of other Asian products, most notably cowrie shells, dyes, and textiles. See Coclanis, "ReOrienting Atlantic History."

64. See Coclanis, "Distant Thunder."

65. Sidney W. Mintz, *Sweetness and Power: The Place of Sugar in Modern History* (New York: Viking, 1985), 108–86.

66. Coclanis, *The Shadow of a Dream*, 133–42; Coclanis, "Distant Thunder," 1056–69.

67. Coclanis, *The Shadow of a Dream*, 134 (table 4-22), 134–36, 282n60.

68. See Swan, *Structure and Profitability*, preface and 75–84. Also see Coclanis, *The Shadow of a Dream*, 140–41; Coclanis, "The Road to Commodity Hell."

69. See Gray, *History of Agriculture*, 2:725–26, 1030 (table 42); Coclanis, "The Road to Commodity Hell." On the price differentials between Carolina and cheaper "East Indian" rice in Liverpool and Rotterdam in the 1820s, see, for example, the collection of "Prices Current" in the Enoch Silsby Papers, Southern Historical Collection, University of North Carolina, Chapel Hill, N.C. The "Prices Current" in the collection consistently show East Indian rice selling for considerably less than Carolina rice.

70. Cotton, "The Rice Trade of the World"; Coclanis, *The Shadow of a Dream*, 133–42; Coclanis, "Distant Thunder," 1066–70.

71. Coclanis, *The Shadow of a Dream*, 136–42; Coclanis, "White Rice."

72. Coclanis, *The Shadow of a Dream*, 136–42; Coclanis, "White Rice."

73. Tuten, *Lowcountry Time and Tide*, 27–74; Coclanis, *The Shadow of a Dream*, 48–158. Also see Coclanis, "Entrepreneurship and the Economic History of the American South: The Case of Charleston and the South Carolina Low Country," in *Marketing in the Long Run*, ed. Stanley C. Hollander and Terence Nevett (East Lansing: Department of Marketing and Transportation Administration, Michigan State University, 1985), 210–19.

74. Coclanis, *The Shadow of a Dream*, 48–158; Richard Schulze, *Carolina Gold Rice: The Ebb and Flow History of a Lowcountry Cash Crop* (Charleston: History Press, 2005); David S. Shields, "Charleston Gold: A Direct Descendant of Carolina Gold," *The Rice Paper* 5, no. 1 (February 2011), http://carolinagoldricefoundation.org/papers/ricepaper.5.1.2011 .pdf; Richard Dwight Porcher Jr., and William Robert Judd, *The Market Preparation*

of Carolina Rice: An Illustrated History of Innovations in the Lowcountry Rice Kingdom (Columbia: University of South Carolina Press, 2014); David S. Shields, *Southern Provisions: The Creation & Revival of a Cuisine* (Chicago: University of Chicago Press, 2015), 229–52; Coclanis, "'Another Faithful Index': Inventive Activity and Economic Innovation in Nineteenth-Century South Carolina," in *Scholar-Citizen: Essays in Honor of Walter Edgar,* ed. Robert H. Brinkmeyer Jr. (Columbia: University of South Carolina Press, 2016), 139–52, 241–46. Note that in research conducted for my piece on inventive activity in South Carolina I found that as of 1873 at least twenty-six patents had been awarded to South Carolinians for inventions/innovations relating to rice.

75. See Coclanis, "How the Low Country Was Taken to Task." For other interpretations of agricultural innovation in the South Atlantic rice industry in the eighteenth century, see Chaplin, *An Anxious Pursuit,* 227–76; Edelson, *Plantation Enterprise in Colonial South Carolina,* 53–125, 200–254.

76. See Coclanis, "White Rice."

77. On African rice technology and "knowledge systems" and rice cultivation in the South Atlantic rice zone and other parts of the Americas, see Carney, *Black Rice*; Carney, "Out of Africa: Colonial Rice History in the Black Atlantic," in *Colonial Botany: Science, Commerce, and Politics in the Early Modern World*, ed. Londa Schiebinger and Claudia Swan (Philadelphia: University of Pennsylvania Press, 2005), 204–20; Carney and Richard Nicholas Rosomoff, *In the Shadow of Slavery: Africa's Botanical Legacy in the Atlantic World* (Berkeley: University of California Press, 2009). Like Eltis-Morgan-Richardson (see note 29), I remain skeptical about many of the claims advanced by proponents of the "Black Rice" thesis. I do not doubt for a second, however, that the Europeans and European-Americans who created and controlled the South Carolina-Georgia rice industry *qua* industry—a big difference in terms of entrepreneurship from growing rice for subsistence—took what they could from Africa and Africans (among others) in the course of creating the production and export platform that proved so lucrative for so long.

78. Almeida Garrett, *Travels in My Homeland*, trans. John M. Parker (London: Peter Owen/UNESCO, 1987), 32. Garrett's travel account was published in serial form in the Portuguese weekly magazine *Revista Universal Lisbonense* between 1843 and 1846. It was published in two volumes late in 1846 as *Viagens na minha terra.*

CHAPTER 13

IMPORTING THE CRYSTAL PALACE

MICHAEL ZAKIM

The history of America's first world's fair begins with a tidy personal profit. Edward Riddle, who had served as a U.S. commissioner at London's 1851 Exhibition of the Works of Industry of All Nations, an event better known, both then and now, as the "Crystal Palace," returned home and convinced New York's Common Council to award him a five-year option for the purpose of organizing a similar event in Reservoir Square, situated on the northern outskirts of the city, in what is present-day Bryant Park. The site's physical dimensions were less than ideal, but all agreed that the location, lying along Manhattan's principal thoroughfares and serviced directly by railroads traveling up Fourth and Sixth Avenues, offered great advantage. The council conditioned its one-dollar-a-year lease on the erection of a modern exhibition hall of glass and iron modeled after the English archetype. The price of admission was also capped at fifty cents. Additional lobbying efforts secured the support of the state legislature, which approved a charter of incorporation authorizing an initial capitalization of $200,000, to be raised by a private stock issue. At this point, Riddle sold his rights to the lease for $10,000 to a consortium of well-heeled New Yorkers, a roster with strong political and international business connections that included August Belmont, William Cullen Bryant, and Alexander Hamilton Jr., together with representatives of the Schuyler and Livingston families. The new directors created a Crystal Palace Association which undertook the practical task of organizing an international exposition of the industrial arts, scheduled to open in the spring of 1853.[1]

This same history of America's first world's fair then ended in bankruptcy. Construction delays initially pushed the project's schedule back by two months. Even after finally opening in July, numerous displays remained in their packing cases and the exhibition space was reported to be in general disarray. Attendance figures at once fell behind the association's projections, and far behind the numbers recorded in London two years earlier. Revenue consequently fell behind expenditures as well. By December the value of Crystal Palace stock, a favorite among investors the previous winter, collapsed, precipitating a lawsuit by shareholders against the association, whose directors collectively resigned. A new committee was established with P. T. Barnum at its head, whose proven talent at producing popular spectacles might save this greatest show on earth, it was hoped. He soon lowered the price of admission, established cash-rich prizes for exhibitors, and arranged daily musical interludes for visitors to the event. But the initiatives were of little avail and Barnum was gone by the following July, at which time the "Palace" itself went into receivership.[2]

And so it was that this singularly self-conscious moment in the creation of capitalist civilization in America, an ambitious festival of material and moral surfeit, became an equally ardent display of capitalism's less redemptive infrastructure of profit and loss. The "fairer, grander, gladder Future" put on view at Reservoir Square offered a real-time exhibition of engineering incompetence, cost overruns, managerial miscues, angry confrontations over participation fees, and persistent rumors of private and public corruption.[3] Such administrative imbroglios were eclipsed, however, by a profounder set of doubts regarding the very progress and prosperity the Crystal Palace was meant to celebrate. Visitors were confronted with unsettling questions about the new industrial economy that the exhibition could not answer. Did the scientific knowledge that underwrote the new commonwealth of steam and iron belong to all of humanity, for instance, or was it the exclusive property of its owners? Was the machine the ultimate expression of industrial effort, or its very negation? Was prosperity itself a function of construction or destruction, and how was society to distribute the attendant costs and benefits? And what form should republican community assume in the insistently cosmopolitan context of free trade and the market's universalizing conceits? Because everyone recognized the Crystal Palace to be a nimbus of a future that had already, in fact, arrived, all equally strove to establish their own version of the world's fair, and the world's future.

* * *

"Let us take an inventory of the great and useful things that we have achieved," *Putnam's Monthly*, a New York journal catering to urban tastes, gushed in response to the opening of America's Exhibition of the Works of Industry of All

Nations. "Let us see how far humanity has advanced in the conquest of nature."[4] It had advanced very far indeed. Steam engines, magnetic telegraphs, hydraulic presses, adding machines, and portable pianos were just a sample of the growing catalogue of mankind's technical achievements, organized into an embracing narrative of material and ethical progress. Collectively, they heralded a new experience of command over the natural world that turned humanity into no less than "a partner in God's business," as the Rev. H. W. Bellows, the pastor at Manhattan's First Congregational Society, proclaimed in a public lecture devoted to the "Moral Significance of the Crystal Palace." Such post-Malthusian optimism promised to remove luxury from the realm of aristocratic affect and redistribute its benefits to the great body of the people, promoting the Crystal Palace into a true *Gesamtkunstwerk* of not just mechanical acumen but liberal government and the end of want. "Industry" was accordingly recast as a powerful engine of universal growth that rendered mercantilist economies resting on fixed limits and national aggrandizement as haplessly obsolete. The ensuing accumulations of wealth would be spread across the globe by a system of free trade that replaced the autarky of older, brutish struggles for survival. "Our merchants hold the peace of the world in their hands," as *Hunt's Merchant's Magazine* typically effused in conjuring this new order of things.[5]

The Crystal Palace exemplified this civilizing process, becoming a global event in its own right—the serial reproduction of exhibitions of the world's industry continued apace over the following two decades in Dublin, Paris, Istanbul, Cairo, Buenos Aires, Vienna, Berlin, Philadelphia, Chicago, and St. Louis—while at once rendering that world into an integrated model of productive energy driven by men's common aspiration for improvement. The same universalism begat calls to the workers of the world to unite as well, revealing just how much this gestalt of international cooperation founded on expanding labor and capital markets was becoming the new imaginary. It certainly captured the imagination of a broad roster of contemporary pundits that not only included Marx but Dickens, Carlyle, Whitman, Flaubert, and Dostoevsky, all of whom noted the epic quality of these spectacles of abundance and their transformative effect on cultural sensibilities, for better or worse. Later generations were no less riveted by this birth of the modern, as Georg Simmel, Max Weber, Walter Benjamin, and Siegfried Gideon also remarked on the pivotal role played by the Crystal Palace in defining the popular experience of industrial capitalism.[6]

Consensus ended there, however. The *American Whig Review*, for one, condemned the "great Peep Show" that was organized in Hyde Park in 1851 as a naked attempt to enthrall the industry of all nations to "Bullion, Bale, Bill, and Britain," and exhorted domestic manufacturing interests to avoid any association with the London event. Such vitriol was not to be dismissed as simply the latest version of a New World animus toward anything British, or a perfunctory expression of protectionist parochialisms, for it drew on a methodical critique of the low wages and growing concentrations of capital which fueled mass production but endangered the republic. At the same time, other voices, no less committed to a distinct path of American economic development, announced their support of the British undertaking, recognizing an unprecedented opportunity to test the nation's own productive prowess on the world stage and consequently form "a juster appreciation and a more perfect knowledge of what this Republic is," as Horace Greeley explained. Greeley, who boasted unimpeachable protectionist credentials, expressed every confidence that the satinets, flannels, ginghams, and drills being rolled out in increasing volume and decreasing cost from America's cotton mills were comparable in quality to any of the plainer fabrics produced in Europe, auguring new sales opportunities. No less important to the country's industrial future were the advantages to be garnered by local mechanics and engineers from the systematic exposure to foreign manufacturing know-how made possible by this first great international trade show.[7]

Greeley joined the executive committee that was established to coordinate the nation's contributions to the London World's Fair. The committee issued a formal appeal to governors, asking each to establish a separate state organization that would solicit the participation of "all the industrial classes in every department of human labor," duly undertaken in Maine, Rhode Island, New York, New Jersey, Mississippi, Illinois, Maryland, Missouri, South Carolina, Alabama, New Hampshire, Vermont, Massachusetts, Ohio, and Indiana. The *Scientific American*, a weekly journal dedicated to surveying new production technologies and whose publisher also operated a patent agency representing the property rights of the creators of those technologies, announced its support of the British initiative too, encouraging mechanic interests throughout the land to do all in their power to ensure a "good representation of American skill and genius" at the Great Exhibition. Congress refused to allocate any funds for the endeavor, but the Treasury Department provided a revenue cutter that carried the sundry specimens of American invention to New York harbor, where they were stored in the Navy Yard before being shipped across the sea. George Peabody, a Massachusetts-born banker active in transatlantic finance who became one of the industrial century's first great philanthropists, committed the $15,000 necessary for then unloading the cargo and transporting the American wares to the exhibition site, where they were arranged for display in a designated wing of the Crystal Palace adorned with an oversized replica of an American eagle.[8]

These several hundred items representing the industrial skill and genius of the former colonies constituted a meager exhibition of productive achievement, critics promptly pronounced, even failing to fill up the floor space allotted to the United States. That was a quantitative measure of what was generally adjudged to be a qualitative deficit. Surveys of the exhibition published in the English press referred to the "plain but useful products" on view in the American wing, emphasizing their "businesslike . . . and uninteresting uniformity." Others were less forgiving in conjuring up the impoverished quality of American manufactures, manifest in "tawdry," "clumsy," and even "grotesque" designs and in a consistently subpar workmanship, further testimony to the primitive condition of the industrial arts in the New World. There were exceptions, of course. These included American-made firearms, rotating chambered-breech and self-priming rifles, for instance, whose range, accuracy, rapidity of action, and safety features won accolades that might appear to contradict the reigning cant about material progress and global fraternity—a Peace Convention was convened in London the same summer in order to cement that relationship—but which were entirely consistent with the Crystal Palace's emphasis on mechanical innovation. American daguerreotypes—and daguerreotyped portraits, in particular—also elicited the praise of visitors and critics, earning Matthew Brady a coveted exhibition prize.[9]

And yet, the most noteworthy American accomplishment at the London exhibition was registered in the category of farm implements. This was no hackneyed gesture to a New World arcadia of virgin land, but recognition of the success in applying seriality, utility, and speed, among other industrial values, to that land. American-built plows became the subject of high praise for their simplicity of construction and lightness of draught, and for the fact that their shares, moldboards, and landsides were all now being produced as interchangeable parts, lowering the expense of repair and replacement while facilitating improvements. These included a steady augmentation in the number of coulters as well as greater efficiencies in their configuration, built-in gauges for measuring the depth of furrows, and cleaning mechanisms that removed refuse from the blades during the course of operations. Such technical innovations had a common aim, namely, to reduce friction in the plow's movement and so allow farmers to till more land using the same animal, or work the same amount of land with fewer animals. In either case, the marginal costs of production would be significantly reduced.[10]

The American devices were put to the test in the moderately stiff soil and light sod characteristic of suburban London. Witnesses reported that the local man assigned with carrying out the demonstration had to make a special effort in not pressing down with all his weight on the plow, unaccustomed as he was to the facility of its movement. Observers were equally struck with the regularity of the ensuing six-inch furrows that seemed to automatically issue from the plow's swift advance, and with its effectiveness in breaking up the turned soil, which further saved on time and labor since there was less need to return to the same field with harrow and cultivator prior to seeding. The plowing demonstration was followed by an even more convincing display of reaping proficiency. Cyrus McCormick's apparatus, itself the product of an auto-mated manufacturing process developed at the company's factory in far-off Chicago, attracted special attention by slicing through seventy-four yards of heavy green English wheat in seventy seconds, grasping the stalks with a spe-cial reel attachment while its patented control bar regulated the crank that drove the knives. Such mechanization achieved unrivalled rates of output, resulting in an elasticity of production that corroborated Henry Carey's char-acterization of the United States as a land where rents were transformed into profits.[11]

All the farm implements struck an admittedly plain, even odd, appearance at an exhibition devoted to the acme of production values, epitomized by "an inlaid Table or a case of Paris Bonnets," as Horace Greeley acknowledged. But the instrumental aesthetic presented by the assorted plows and reapers sig-naled a coherent production paradigm of their own, one that might diverge from standards of handicraft perfection but which also prompted a reappraisal of the imputed inferiority of the "rugged utility" of American manufactures in light of their practical success in the field. The exhibition's official *Report* ac-cordingly noted that the "expenditure of months or years of labour upon a sin-gle article," the traditional source of "its cost or its estimation as an object of virtue," proved wholly immaterial in determining the value of American wares. This was not a novel insight. Tocqueville had already noted such indifference to established rules of economy in the first volume of his *Democracy in America*, describing a distinct American tradition of the new in an allegorical encounter with an American sailor. "I ask him why his country's vessels are built to last a short time," Tocqueville recounted, "and he replies to me without hesitation that the art of navigation makes such rapid progress daily that the most beau-tiful ship would soon become useless if its existence were prolonged beyond a few years." Those notions of obsolescence and their corollary of interchange-ability—if not of "creative destruction"—offered a separate yardstick for mea-suring, and even defining, industrial enterprise, let alone establishing its value. "There is hardly anything shown by them which is not easily within the reach of the most moderate fortune," the *London Times* consequently allowed of the American industry put on display at the Crystal Palace, dedicated as it was to reducing the cost of manufacturing and the price of the resulting goods. "Every thing is entrusted to the ingenuity of individuals who look for their re-ward to public demand alone," the *London Observer* likewise acknowledged of the decisive role of the market in creating "objects of virtue."[12]

American industry was not only to be distinguished from traditional craft practices but also from the Crystal Palace's own version of the technological sublime, that which sought to promote the machine into a transcendent value in its own right by prohibiting the display of prices. The vagaries and vulgari-

ties of the marketplace would be banished from this program of polite entertainment while industry itself was to be separated out from profit and assigned
an autonomous operating principle resting on science and truth, shunting
business off to the margins, so to speak, and even out of view. But could machine logic be so cursorily divorced from the commodity form? The *Scientific
American* did not think so, and thus mobilized its columns in urging the
American commissioners on hand in London to compile a catalogue of prices
for the American goods on exhibit, in spite of official policy. That was because
price was essential to modern industrial practice. The "remarkable cheapness"
which put goods "within the reach of the most moderate fortune" constituted
the very telos of their production. This was true of all modern industry, Charles
Babbage, inventor of the "difference machine," or automated calculator, and
one of England's leading writers on technology and society, opined in arguing
that the ban on prices at the Crystal Palace effectively shunned the axioms of
speed and volume that served as the basis of mechanical production, and were
invariably calculated in terms of cost.[13]

Babbage's claims rested on an increasingly pertinent distinction between
making things and manufacturing them which he first expounded fifteen years
earlier in a treatise on the *Economy of Machinery and Manufactures*. In pointed
contrast to handicrafts, Babbage explained, the manufacturing process was not
supposed to produce articles in "perfect form." Its aim, rather, was to produce
"the greatest and most permanent profit." This turned the goods into means
rather than ends and mechanization into the means for realizing those means,
reducing the costs of manufacture and so increasing the number of persons who
could afford the finished article, which is what justified the effort and expense
invested in mechanizing production in the first place. The developing competition between industrialists striving to lower costs in order to expand their
sales is what then drove the modern spirit of invention. The subsequent earnings, moreover, were not to be compared to the profits derived from older
forms of exchange. That is why merchant circles actually supported the exhibition's ban on prices, Babbage contended in his survey of the *Exposition of 1851*, for
they sought to keep the public ignorant of the extent of their markups. Manufacturers, in contrast, together with the public able to purchase their products, subscribed to a far more transparent business metric based on the careful
calculation of inputs rather than the fortuitous machinations of arbitrage and
the hidden movement of transaction costs. Such reasoning eventually carried
the day. The prohibition on prices was reconsidered and rescinded, and jurors
were instructed to take the cost of production into consideration when awarding
prizes. By then, licenses for foreign manufacturing rights were being negotiated
for Colt pistols, Day and Newell locks, R. Hoe and Co. printing presses, and
Singer sewing machines, while British importers rushed to order McCormick's

reapers from a company that would eventually rename itself "International Harvester."[14]

* * *

There was, as such, every reason to expect that the Great Exhibition would be successfully imported to America. Early signs were certainly auspicious. The Crystal Palace Association that took over Edward Riddle's initiative mobilized its considerable influence with the nation's political class and secured a waiver from the secretary of state, Daniel Webster, suspending import duties levied on foreign goods arriving in the United States, even for display purposes. In addition to formal designation of the exposition site as a bonded warehouse, there were also plans to petition Congress should the need arise for a special extension of copyright protection to foreign exhibits, or for amendments to federal patent statutes that would allow foreign nationals to register their designs in the United States for the same thirty-dollar fee charged to citizens. This systematization of information flows marked a dramatic revision of older patterns of technology transfer that had rested on the semiofficial theft of industrial know-how from foreign countries, and particularly from Britain. Parliament had responded with legal prohibitions on the exportation of machinery for making textiles, metal, leather, paper, glass, and clocks, and with restrictions on the emigration of mechanics who knew how to build those machines. In the industrial century, in contrast, mechanization advanced under the aegis of international agreements that protected intellectual property and sought to encourage cross-border cooperation between manufacturing interests, all part of a more general political, ideological, and judicial effort to create a market economy. The Crystal Palace was part of that endeavor, resting as it did on the mobilization of municipal, state, and federal governments, as well as the collaboration of agencies at the global level—Webster himself soon issued a circular to United States consulates stationed around the world, for instance, directing them to employ their offices in promoting foreign participation in the New York exhibition. At the same time, none of those accommodations kept the association from representing its undertaking as a "purely private Enterprise." Indeed, such laissez-faire slogans had strong popular appeal, offering flattering comparisons to the stultifying reliance on state sponsorship commonly identified with Old World reaction, and providing rhetorical resonance to the "rugged utility" of American industrial enterprise inspired by the free market.[15]

And yet, America's Crystal Palace was also unabashedly modeled on its English prototype. "Every possible invention and appliance for the service of man found a place within its embracing limits," as *Tallis's History and Description* invoked the curatorial principle that guided the London undertaking, closely recapitulated two years later in *Putnam's* reference to the "inventory of the great and useful things that we have achieved" put on display in Manhattan. That collecting impulse, worthy of the most congested middle-class parlor, was born of the times, manifest, too, in the founding of the Louvre in Paris and the Smithsonian Institution in Washington; in publication of the *Oxford English Dictionary* and of Peter Force's multivolume *American Archives*; and even in the expansive taxonomy adopted for use in the decennial census of the United States in 1850, the first fully statistical digest of the nation's variable rates of mortality, mobility, property, literacy, fecundity, and, of course, industry. All these ambitious knowledge projects were dedicated to compiling an exhaustive catalogue of human experience that would reintroduce order to a society in the throes of an industrial revolution which abolished traditional hierarchies, both material and moral. The bourgeoisie might have expressed disdain for older economies that rested on dearth and a fixed fund of wealth, but they proved to be persistent system builders in their own right, anxiously indexing this brave new world of accumulating surpluses into a comprehensive ledger of art and artifice.[16]

The Crystal Palace therefore aspired to "bring within the whole field of view the surface of the globe," which meant that England's "solid wares," France's "elaborate design and exquisite finish," Belgium's "elegant fabrics," Turkey's "supremacy in those peculiarly rich and delicate textures," and Italy's "devotion to the fine arts" were respectively assigned their own floor space in representing humanity's division of its productive labor. This was the program which informed Prince Albert's panegyric to "the unity of mankind" at the inaugural ceremony of London's Crystal Palace in 1851, as well as his description of that unity as nothing "which breaks down . . . the peculiar characteristics of the different nations of the earth." The Crystal Palace constituted clear testimony of the opposite, in fact, being "the result and product of those very national varieties and antagonistic qualities." Cheap prints from Brazil were no less important to this global process of specialization—and no less worthy of a place in an exhibition promoting industrial endeavor—than were French silks, even if the former issued from a more primitive manufacturing technique, itself a function of a more primitive level of cultural development. Economic progress was not, as such, just a matter of engineering proficiency but also a recognizably liberal vision of men's shared nature based on difference, consolidating while at once ranking the contributions of each nation to a common world of plenty.[17]

A similar sense of universality bounded by hierarchy found expression in the immediate efforts of cultural authorities to marshal scientific knowledge in order to shape the "leisure" of citizens, filling those hours not contracted to anyone else—a growing portion of time due to the success of wage laborers in limiting the length of the work day—with proper examples of social order. The goal was to bestow upon an expanding public of hired hands "accessions to their stock of knowledge" that would contribute to "a liberal and enlightened condition of society," as John Griscom, a well-known New York City pedagogue, explained of the requirements for making democracy safe for everyone. The gaze of visitors to the Crystal Palace was consequently directed toward the processes of empirical reason that animated modern industry. One should look upon the great variety of exhibits, *Putnam's* advised, "not like a fairy picture in the distant clouds but close at hand; comparing, judging, scrutinizing the treasures produced by the all-bounteous earth, and the indomitable efforts of man, from pole to pole, and from east to west." Such self-conscious scrutiny was now to replace wonder as the essence of spectacle, becoming the means for what has been called the "social reproduction of seriousness," a process to which the Crystal Palace was wholly committed. The exhibition was no idle entertainment, it followed, but a user's manual that naturalized the *perpetuum mobilé* of industrial progress, casting its destruction of artisanal patriarchy as an ineluctable function of rational science. The constituent "models and representations of the real" that Timothy Mitchell identified as the means by which Europeans generated knowledge of the non-European "other" at the world's fairs thus helped capitalist society colonize itself as well. All the dedicated "comparing, judging, [and] scrutinizing" served to objectify the experience of otherness—or what some now called alienation—that was increasingly central to social life in the new economy.[18]

The most perfectly realized model of rational industry at the Crystal Palace was its own interlocking matrix of plate glass, wooden frames, iron lattice girders, and cast-iron pillars, bolted together floor by floor in standard units manufactured at workshops in New York and New Jersey and shipped to the exhibition site, where they were fitted into an edifice that wedded "remarkable cheapness" and "vast utility." The possibilities dormant in modern civilization had never been so clearly expressed, Siegfried Giedion concluded a hundred years later of this pivotal moment in the history of prefabrication, consummated in what became the largest building ever erected in America up to that time, its dome visible for miles in every direction. Horace Greeley at once grasped the dimensions of this monumental achievement when he proclaimed that "stone and timber will have to stand back for iron and glass hereafter," resulting in a new form of built environment which overturned the traditional relationship between load and support and heralded what contemporaries experienced as limitless space, if not the end of limits more generally. The acclaimed functionality of iron—most commonly associated with the railroad—reduced the number of interior columns required for buttressing the structure's massive volume, opening up lines of sight that were, in turn, illuminated by natural light pouring in through translucent naves that now became a metonym for public hygiene, and an archetype of effective retail display. Such utility also served as a conscious revolt against ornament. From now on the decorative arts would "bring out the beautiful construction of the building" rather than vice versa, *Putnam's* declared of this "miraculous . . . palace of glass" whose plain geometries were enhanced by a basic palette of reds, blues, and yellows (applied in variations of vermilion, garnet, sky-blue, and orange) that emphasized the Exhibition's organizing aesthetic of form and function.[19]

"Palace" was no misnomer, then, even if we might wonder why this representative site of industrial novelty and innovation was assigned such a premodern nomenclature. The term enjoyed considerable resonance in a constitutional monarchy, no doubt, helping the English to construct a bridge between past and present in a typical Peelite formula that integrated revolution and moderation, innovation and tradition. In that respect, "palace" was a pointed example of the European bourgeoisie's allegorical uses of the past which allowed reformers to reference older forms of social order upon embracing new ones and, in so doing, deradicalize industrial change by packaging novelty as convention. But what use did Americans have for palaces that had never been a part of their cultural or political landscape? The expression itself carried more ironic than iconic weight in a republic in which the term most usually referred to preliminary incarnations of the department store peddling an expanding inventory of dry goods, ready-mades, and home furnishings, among other cutrate merchandise flooding the country's marts. This explosion in affordable consumables signaled a diffusion of once exclusive goods among a democracy of shoppers, inverting the traditional meaning of palace while underlining American foundation myths condemning hereditary privilege and the corrupting effects of unearned advantage. The *Scientific American* could thus announce that New York's Crystal Palace "will be taken possession of by a whole army of . . . young American kings and queens" whose very commonality upended the imperious style of monarchic power.[20]

This leveling ethos was most adamantly on view in the Machine Arcade, the only gallery in the whole exhibition where "the nature of the article" rather than the "place of its origin" determined the order of display. Such criteria were the truest expression of industry's universalizing conceits, as well as its operating exigencies. Built as an annex to the basic rotunda design, the arcade abutted another of New York City's monuments to industrial civilization, the Croton Distributing Reservoir, a central component in an infrastructure project for converting Manhattan into a metropolis of European dimensions. A single row of shafting ran down the 450-foot length of the arcade floor, "straight as an arrow," delivering the requisite thrust to a Haussmanian boulevard of hydraulic pumps, automated looms, cotton gins, spinning frames, wool carders, rotary nail-plate feeders, tobacco pressers, circular saws, stave makers, cotton balers, bolts and nuts cutters, pulp strainers, clothes washers, and a Centripetal Amalgamator for separating gold from pulverized quartz. Steam was generated by five underground boilers located across Forty-second Street which fed two enormous engines built to order at workshops in Lawrence and Providence, exhibitors having specified ahead of time the amount of force their respective apparatuses needed to run. A pair of printing presses, meanwhile, were positioned at the main entrance to the arcade, attended by female operatives in an unequivocal demonstration of the demise of brawn and its replacement by machinery's "labor-crushing, time-deriding" capacities. Each press turned out a continuous run of the exhibition catalogue, one of the few objects to actually be fabricated at the Crystal Palace. Even in the absence of any other tangible output, however, the machine gallery provided an utterly convincing performance of mass production, satisfying the public's enthusiasm for the "biggest and fastest" and "largest and finest." Visitors were especially struck, if not astonished, by the vehement effect of all the automated devices acting in concert. The attendant noise and vibrations certainly resembled a working factory more than they did any kind of museum exhibit, becoming an authentic representation of the new industrial reality.[21]

∗ ∗ ∗

That cacophony sounded like a song of redemption to some, heralding a "miraculous" end to the overburdened, underfed drudgery of history's long-suffering masses of laborers. The *Scientific American*, for one, celebrated the benevolent effects of such a machine age by quoting from the prepared remarks delivered by Sir Charles Lyell at the Crystal Palace's gala dinner in 1853, where he told the assembled dignitaries of "the wonderful labor-saving inventions" he had recently encountered on a visit to Lowell, a sure sign of America's progress "in knowledge, power, and general prosperity." That progress was further exemplified for the *Scientific American* by an enormous steam engine constructed in Birmingham, Alabama, and shipped to the Crystal Palace for exhibition. Its effect was underscored by the fact that southern industry had been meagerly represented two years earlier in London, making do with a small sample of cotton plants and a single specimen of sugar. Advocates of the nation's industrial development now seized on the presence of the Birmingham engine in New York as a happy indication of the "active manufacturing spirit" taking hold in the South. Cloths and yarns produced in southern mills provided added testimony to the slave economy's ability to diversify beyond its plantation base and assume an active role in the forward march of technology. Of course, all the excitement conjured by what was little more than a modest display of industrial artifacts might prompt a different reaction, as happened when Horace Greeley summarily dismissed the colossal southern steam engine as "showy, and very useless," emblematic, if anything, of slavery's economic backwardness rather than the opposite.[22]

And yet, the place of freeborn mechanics in the Crystal Palace's vision of the industrialized future was not much more secure than that of American slaves. The "brilliant . . . revelation of . . . industry" so consciously promoted at the exhibition devoted woefully little attention to the "dignity of labor," it soon became apparent, suggesting that a less benign gloss was to be assigned slogans regarding the labor-crushing effects of machine technology. The English journal *Punch* had already taken note of the practical difficulties in organizing an exhibit of modern industry, and that because "needlewomen cannot be starved, nor tailors 'sweated,' nor miners blown up" in a museum setting. Horace Greeley was equally sardonic in deriding the bloated presence of grandees and ambassadors—"descendants of some dozen lucky Norman robbers"—who crowded around the Prince Consort at the opening festivities in London, expropriating the rightful place of Watt's and Arkwright's disciples. Much to his chagrin, however, Greeley found himself repeating the same plaint two years later in reporting on the inaugural ceremonies at Reservoir Square. True, Victoria and Albert's role had been usurped by a popularly elected representative of the people. But Franklin Pierce was likewise surrounded on the dais that day by a retinue of placeholders. Meanwhile, not "a single man eminent for the arts which the Crystal Palace was opened to celebrate" was accorded official standing. The *Scientific American* became no less exercised by the pomp and circumstance of Pierce's grandiose, if rain-soaked, procession up Broadway that morning and rendezvous with a contingent of senior military officers led by the secretaries of war and the navy. Bishop Wainwright was then invited to deliver a formal benediction before the large crowd gathered in the square, followed by a medley of homilies from Theodore Sedgwick, a New York commercial lawyer active in social reform who was president of the Crystal Palace Association. After he finished, the president of the United States himself offered brief remarks. "Inventors, artists, engineers, and mechanicians" were nowhere in sight, the *Scientific American* protested, implausibly shunted aside as "persons of no consequence," raising alarming questions about America's—and especially the exhibition's—fealty to the Republic's producerist traditions. That alarm soon escalated into a full-blown neo-Jacksonian outburst against the "petty squires, second-rate lawyers, capon-lined Aldermen, [and] hairy-faced men with epanletta on their shoulders" who denied the pride of place due men of "genius and skill," those deserving of center stage at any homage to society's productive energies.[23]

The *Scientific American* now emerged as the most consistent critic and ideological agonist of the "Wall-street clique" which had, to its mind, commandeered the industry of all nations, or at least that of America. As the self-styled "Advocate of Inventors and Mechanics in general," the journal was duty-bound to maintain a jealous eye over the operations of the association. Warning signs were already discernable the previous autumn upon announcement of the winners of the exhibition's design competition. The choice of Messrs. Carstensen and Gildemeister, the former best known as the architect of Copenhagen's new public grounds, augured a troubling preference for the cachet of foreign artists at the expense of native talent. The *Scientific American* itself had vigorously endorsed a rival proposal submitted by James Bogardus, the country's leading engineer of cast-iron construction who incorporated his method for bracing and joining building modules into his plans for the new exhibition hall. Bogardus's patented system would also allow for the structure to be dismantled and reassembled in another location, or even recycled for other purposes. Bogardus was touted as the best qualified candidate to oversee the building operations as well, a portentous claim since mismanagement of subcontracting assignments soon put the whole project behind schedule. Persistent flaws in the roof design further delayed the start of work on the foundations, which meant that the piers remained unfinished before snow and the advent of cold weather forced a suspension of construction until the spring.[24]

Such complications did not keep the value of Crystal Palace stock being traded on the city exchange from rising 40 percent over premium, however, inciting an angry wave of aspersions. The *Albany Atlas* published a report in December about "A Profitable Speculation," for instance, which effectively cast doubt over the whole project and prompted the association to defend itself by contending that no unseemly gains could possibly result from the increasing value of the stock since shares were dispersed among more than a hundred and fifty separate investors. Nor did the issue of additional shares alter that equation, since the new stock was subscribed by different parties altogether. A week later, after the appearance of another notice alluding to "one of the greatest speculations of the day," this time appearing in the *Poughkeepsie Telegraph*, Theodore Sedgwick felt compelled to issue a formal statement explaining that because a public event of such magnitude could never be organized as a "great governmental affair" in the United States, there was little choice but to rely on the "energy and activity" of private citizens in financing the undertaking. While they might consider the exhibition's success to be an opportunity for personal gain, the association itself took great umbrage at any suggestion that the Crystal Palace constituted little more than "a new money getting operation."[25]

Meanwhile, property values in Murray Hill also began to rise. Some have since claimed that this push of development up the island of Manhattan constituted the Crystal Palace's most enduring legacy. Regardless of future trends, however, it was already apparent that the real estate market, no less than the stock market, made no distinction between the "energy and activity" of private citizens, on the one hand, and the ancillary aim of turning a profit, on the other, even if the association devoted every effort to dissociating itself from such a dynamic. "I have not the smallest direct or indirect interest in that advance," Sedgwick announced in reference to the rising property values. At the same time, however, he penned a letter to Paul Lawrence in Boston, enclosing a newspaper clipping that excitedly anticipated the conversion of Reservoir Square into a local version of London's Hyde Park, which was likely to quadruple prices in the neighborhood. Rental lots fronting the exhibition site on Fortieth Street already commanded $500 a year by the end of 1852. Edward Clark, a New York City architect with close connections to the association, even sought to interest Sedgwick and the committee in extending him a mortgage for properties situated a block to the south, on the north side of Thirty-Ninth Street, which could still be had for an annual lease of $125 on a five-year contract.[26]

With the arrival of spring, new protests were to be heard, this time directed against the association's heavy-handed tactics in recruiting the exhibits themselves. Claims of limited space and of a purportedly enormous volume of applications were suspected of being no more than a subterfuge for compelling prospective exhibitors to accede to the association's stringent rules of participation, which included the delivery of all materials at one's personal expense by the first of April, even though the building still lacked a roof. Exclusive control over the specific terms of display was also to be acceded to the organizers, inviting charges of favoritism. Most irksome of all was the demand that exhibitors pay for their own admission to the very event "opened to celebrate" their industry. This struck advocates of inventors, artists, engineers, and mechanics as a cynical attempt by the association to exploit a captive market in order to bolster its bottom line, thus serving as a tax on the producing classes in favor of profiteers and speculators. The angry withdrawal by a Worcester, Massachusetts, machinist from the exhibition in response to such conditions, "so entirely different from what was represented to us by your agent when he visited our works," was recounted in detail by the *Scientific American*, provoking the association to complain about the hostility of part of the press to the whole enterprise. Discord only escalated, however, once the Crystal Palace failed to open on time. Tourists flocking to the city to attend the widely publicized event were left with nowhere to go while ships similarly languished in port for weeks on end, unable to unload their cargos. The resulting "humiliation" and "disgrace" strengthened the conviction of critics that "a private company whose object was gain, not honor to our country" was singularly ill-suited to pay homage to American industry.[27]

∗ ∗ ∗

As justified as such protests were, they also failed to recognize fundamental truths regarding the same events. The fact is, the "Wall-street clique" in charge of organizing the Crystal Palace subscribed to an increasingly prevalent view of industry that could not be divorced from the pecuniary designs of the nonproducing classes. Despite the outcry from proponents of labor theories of value and proprietary traditions pitting inventive energy against the parasitic nature of "speculation," material progress was proving to be a "new money-getting operation" whose undisguised object was "gain," that is, a value-added return on one's investment. This meant that capital had become no less critical to productive effort than any mechanic's "genius and skill." Adam Smith might still note in the first chapter of the *Wealth of Nations* that one of the "greatest improvements" made to the steam engine came when a boy assigned with co-ordinating the action of the valve and the movement of the piston tied a string between them, thus allowing the machine to open and close on its own and allowing the boy to "save his own labor." By the time Karl Marx published his aptly-entitled *Capital* almost a hundred years later, however, such tinkering had given way to a new operative logic. That was elaborated in a discussion of "Machinery and Modern Industry" which Marx opened by citing John Stuart Mill's observation about technology never relieving anyone of their toil. That was because machines, like every other aspect of the manufacturing process in a capitalist economy, were dedicated to cheapening the cost of producing commodities. If the nature of the attendant human effort was consequently transformed, that was for the sole purpose of enhancing marginal profits. The abolition of drudgery was no more than a means to that end, an end which then often resulted in the creation of entirely new forms of drudgery.[28]

This process reveals just how much republican-inflected slogans about the "dignity of labor" were turned into an oxymoron by humanity's conquest of nature with "time-deriding" machines that not only helped to accumulate capital but also constituted capital in their own right (while also requiring constant inputs of capital in order to run). Such capitalization was the source of "great suffering" for a growing number of those hired to make things, Horace Greeley acknowledged in his survey of New York's Crystal Palace, *Art and Industry*. Sewing machines were a pointed example of this turn of events. No fewer than twelve different models were on display at the exposition, attended by manufacturers' agents who distributed specimens of their automated output, which was capable of reaching the astounding rate of 1,500 stitches per minute, as I. M. Singer claimed for his own apparatus and which the *Scientific American* vociferously praised for the "excellent" quality of its operations. That very excellence made it possible for persons with little or even no experience in the art of sewing up shoes to create "a perfect article," as Greeley further remarked on the marvelous effects of mechanization. This then reduced the costs of manufacturing by half, lowering already dismal piece rates while opening up the industry to the outside control of money men who would pass the savings on to every family in the form of plain, utilitarian footwear befitting the citizens of a republic. Greeley, one of the era's foremost champions of free labor and free men, thus found himself making the best of a bad situation by abruptly shifting the narrative of industrial progress to the demand side.[29]

And so it was that the Crystal Palace became haunted by a ghostly specter, the specter of capital. While not accorded any official standing at the exhibition,

capital nevertheless emerged as its most ubiquitous display. The physical trans-
figuration of nature into use values, in other words, only seemed to be the focus
of attention. In fact, that marked no more than an intermediate step in an industrial dynamic which ultimately rendered those use values into surplus value. The
world's fair and its homage to mechanical genius therefore served as a diorama of
the great transformation from Lockean producerism to Benthamite utility, pro-
mulgating an end to the rule of thumb and its replacement by the hard-and-fast
rules of engineered precision which annexed production to the market, as
Charles Babbage explained in the *Economy of Machinery and Manufactures*,
and recast "art" for a post-artisanal world of abstraction and automation.[30] Nor
was capital's reinvention of industry restricted to the Machine Arcade. It proved
equally relevant to the charter of incorporation granted by the state legislature, to
the promises made to exhibitors about future business contracts, to transatlantic
agreements over patent rights, to the inventory of prices compiled for the wares
put on display, to fluctuations in the value of Crystal Palace stock, to retail advertisements of goods awarded exhibition prizes, to the income generated by rental
properties on Fortieth Street (after deducting the cost of the mortgage), and to
the association's own operating equity, which soon ran out.

And, indeed, the Crystal Palace's bankruptcy probably constituted the most
authentic industrial exhibit of all. It followed a December collapse in the value
of the association's stock, coming five months after the event's opening. This
was no one's fault, *Harper's* opined. Once speculators had run up the price of
shares, there was little chance of controlling their fate. The bubble would burst,
sooner or later. The *Scientific American* presented a different version of events,
predictably enough, claiming that stock prices began their precipitous decline
immediately after the Crystal Palace opened its doors, in direct response to the
general mismanagement of the event and to the association's more fundamental misconception of its very mission. This now made attendance figures into
another subject of controversy. It was officially announced, for instance, that a
million visitors had expended $330,000 to visit the exhibition by the end of the
year. Skeptics, on the other hand, basing their numbers on published records
of weekly receipts and calculations derived from a new "turnstile" technology,
determined that attendance barely reached half that figure. The lower estimate
seemed to be corroborated by steps already undertaken in early August to
boost ticket sales, which included a 50 percent reduction in the price of Satur-
day admission. Greeley's *New York Tribune* also floated a proposal to open the
exhibition on Sundays, a step that served the paper's campaign on behalf of a
ten-hour workday and the concomitant development of uplifting forms of
popular leisure. But were not such Sunday idylls most common to countries
where the Sabbath had lost its heavenly status and been transformed into an
opportunity for profaner entertainments, the *Scientific American* protested?
And was not the mechanic class habitually relegated to "the most depressed
condition" in those same Old World societies? This was no trivial dispute

between evangelical and cosmopolitan sensibilities over how to best spend one's weekend—in church or at the museum—but a confrontation over the conditions for importing the world's fair to America, importing, that is, the Republic's producerism into the industrial century.[31]

Regardless of whose numbers were judged more credible, attendance sharply plummeted once winter set in, at which point it also became clear that the springtime delay had cost the association $200,000 in lost ticket revenues, enough to cover its end-of-the-year deficit. Indeed, that debt emerged as a final symbol of the project's illusions of grandeur, an ineluctable result of the association's pomposity and accompanying disdain for virtuous industry. This was patently manifest in the $10,000 first paid out to Edward Riddle, in the $300 "puff" reportedly placed in *Putnam's* for a promotional piece on the exhibit, and, most egregious of all, in the enormous cost of the Palace itself, which ultimately exceeded half a million dollars, far above the $300,000 estimate cited in wooing investors, who were also assured that the outlay would be comfortably offset by an income certain to reach $700,000. "It is a beautiful building," the *Scientific American* conceded, but if James Bogardus's original proposal had been adopted, and Bogardus then enlisted to oversee construction, great sums would have been saved. The exhibition would also have opened on time. Instead, the association was beset with a crystal elephant that could not even be disassembled and reused for other projects.[32]

Sedgwick and the rest of the directors resigned in January. A new committee was formed, restrained by court order from paying its bills since the exhibition had exceeded the debt ceiling imposed by the state legislature. A lawsuit was also brought by a group of stockholders. P. T. Barnum, the association's new president, applied his impresario instincts to resuscitating the nearly moribund venture, further lowering the price of admission, organizing three live orchestra performances a day, offering prizes to exhibitors worth a thousand dollars "in gold," boasting the largest picture gallery ever opened "in the western hemisphere," and shipping the cross-section of a 3,241-year-old cedar tree, authenticated by Professor Benjamin Pierce of Harvard College, from California to Reservoir Square. The refitted exhibition was inaugurated in May 1854 in a ceremony shorn of the "gaud and glitter" that had marred the previous year's event, as the *Scientific American* approvingly noted. But it attracted only modest crowds, indicative of the public's indifference. Barnum himself resigned in July, after which the Crystal Palace was expected to shut its doors. The building went into receivership, hired out on occasion for Sunday School Congresses, ladies charitable bazaars, a Negro Odd Fellows function, and the Annual Fair of the American Institute for the Encouragement of Science and Invention. In 1858, upon expiration of the original five-year lease, the city took back control of the property.[33]

"They manage Worlds' Fairs better in the Old World than in the New," *Putnam's* concluded of this early American experiment in capitalist agitprop. "Like a princess born to a red republican . . . the feeling that led to its erection was a foolish imitation of foreign enterprise."[34] Visions of a world commonly transformed by the accumulation of productive wealth had provoked more acrimony than agreement in America, even among the proponents of industrial progress and machine culture. Coming at the end of what everyone acknowledged to be the most momentous half-century in the annals of material life, and at the dawn of what developed into an even more breathtaking century of economic transformation, the Crystal Palace proved singularly incompetent at establishing an embracing narrative of this unfolding revolution. The time-tested tenets of commonwealth, productive labor, inventive enterprise, and proprietary prerogative all broke down under the pressure of events, the same events that pushed "industry," an old term referring to the tangible effort required to make things, into the arms of capital, which was increasingly critical to that effort, while redefining it. The result was a peculiarly modern condition, at once conflicted and symbiotic.

"We begin to recognize the monuments of the bourgeoisie as ruins even before they have crumbled," Walter Benjamin once observed of the precarious quality of a civilization built on such dialectical foundations. Surely, the dilapidated stairways and scaffoldings described in an account of the situation of the Crystal Palace in 1857 constituted just such a monument, evincing an alternative semiotics of glass and iron that rested not on light and enlightenment but on Karl Marx's famous dictum from a few years earlier on the ephemeral nature of a commodity-driven reality in which all that is solid melts into air. The "silence and desertion" put on view at Reservoir Square was poignant testimony to this dematerializing quality of an industrial world filling up with goods, and to capitalism's consistent subversion of its own visions of a fairer, gladder future. These then found their ultimate expression on the evening of October 5, 1858, when the Crystal Palace burned to the ground within half an hour in a conflagration that attracted the largest crowd since its opening.[35]

Notes

1. New York Crystal Palace Records, 1840–1858, box 1, folder 3 (October 11, 1852), New-York Historical Society, Manuscript Collection; Charles Hirschfeld, "America on Exhibition: The New York Crystal Palace," *American Quarterly* 9, no. 2 (Summer 1957): 102. America's Crystal Palace, unlike London's Great Exhibition, has been largely ignored by historians. The outstanding exception is Hirschfeld's "America on Exhibition." Also see Ivan D. Steen. "America's First World's Fair," *New-York Historical Society Quarterly* 47 (1963).
2. Hirschfeld, "America on Exhibition," 107–8.
3. "Fairer, grander" in Horace Greeley, *Glances at Europe in a Series of Letters from Great Britain, France, Italy, Switzerland, etc. During the Summer of 1851* (New York: Dewitt and Davenport, 1851), 36.

4. *Putnam's*, August 1853, 122. A few months later, *Putnam's* published Herman Melville's two-part story, "Bartleby, the Scrivener," which presented a markedly different version of modernity.

5. Henry W. Bellows, *The Moral Significance of the Crystal Palace: A Sermon, Preached First to His Own Congregation, and Repeated in the Church of the Messiah* (New York: G. P. Putnam, 1853), 20; "Dignity of the Mercantile Profession," *Hunt's Merchant's Magazine* 35 (July 1856): 56. Werner Plum, *World Exhibitions in the Nineteenth Century: Pageants of Social and Cultural Change*, trans. Lux Furtmuller (Bonn: Friedrich-Ebert-Stiftung, 1977), 63–69; Jeffrey A. Auerbach, *A Nation on Display: The Great Exhibition of 1851* (New Haven, Conn.: Yale University Press, 1999), 162–63. See, too, Joseph Schumpeter on imperialism and capitalism in "The Sociology of Imperialism," in *Imperialism and Social Classes: Two Essays* (Cleveland: Meridian Books, 1951), 64–98.

6. John R. Davis, "The Great Exhibition and Modernization," in *Victorian Prism: Refractions of the Crystal Palace*, ed., James Buzard, Joseph W. Childers, and Eileen Gillooly (Charlottesville: University of Virginia Press, 2007), 243–47; Walter Benjamin, *The Arcades Project* (Cambridge, Mass.: Belknap Press of Harvard University Press, 1999), 182–90; Paul Greenhalgh, *Ephemeral Vistas: The "Expositions Universelles," Great Exhibitions and World's Fairs, 1851–1939* (Manchester, U.K., Manchester University Press, 1988), 3–24; Peter H. Hoffenberg, *An Empire on Display: English Indian, and Australian Exhibitions from the Crystal Palace to the Great War* (Berkeley: University of California Press, 2001), 125–28; Walt Whitman, "Great Buildings in New York," *Brooklyn Daily Times*, June 17, 1857; Francis Steegmuller, "Flaubert to Louise Colet, 1851–1854," *Grand Street*, Winter 1983; Ekaterina Tarta, "Socialist Paradise or Tower of Total Surveillance? Metamorphoses of the Crystal Palace in Chernyshevsky and Dostoevsky" (Master's thesis, University of North Carolina, Chapel Hill, 2014); Beatriz Gonzalez-Stephan, "A Gothic Glass Case in the Tropical Forest: The First Venezuelan National Exhibition of 1883," in Buzard, Childers, and Gillooly, eds., *Victorian Prism*, 221, 227; Fernando Coronil, "Toward a Critique of Globalcentrism: Speculations on Capitalism's Nature," in *Millennial Capitalism and the Culture of Neoliberalism*, ed. Jean Comaroff and John L. Comaroff (Durham, N.C.: Duke University Press, 2001), 72–73, 75; Nicholas Fisher, "'Nothing Can Be More Successful': Were the Political and Cultural Aims of the Great Exhibition Fulfilled?," in *The Great Exhibition and Its Legacy*, ed. Franz Bosbach, John R. Davis, Susan Bennett, Thomas Brockmann, and William Filmer-Sankey (Munchen: K. G. Saur, 2002), 249. More generally, see David J. Jeremy, *International Technology Transfer: Europe, Japan, and the USA, 1700–1914* (Brookfield, Vt.: Edward Elgar, 1991).

7. *American Whig Review*, February 1851; Greeley, *Glances at Europe*, 25; Merle Curti, "America at the World Fair, 1851–1893," *American Historical Review* 55 (July 1950): 833; John F. Kasson, *Civilizing the Machine: Technology and Republican Values in America, 1776–1900* (New York: Hill and Wang, 1976), 55–69, 72, 79–80, 105.

8. "Circular of the Executive Committee of the United States on the Industrial Exhibition of 1851," American Antiquarian Society, October 22, 1850; John E. Findling, "America at the Great Exhibition," in Davis, *The Great Exhibition and Its Legacy*, 197–99; Robert F. Dalzell, *American Participation in the Great Exhibition of 1851* (Amherst, Mass.: Amherst College Press, 1960), 21–22; *Scientific American*, March 1, 1851.

9. Dalzell, *American Participation*, 42; Henry Howe, *Adventures and Achievements of Americans: A Series of Narratives Illustrating Their Heroism, Self-Reliance, Genius and Enterprise of Our Countrymen* (Cincinnati: Henry Howe, 1858), 600–601. For a class statement on the relationship between capitalist progress and world peace, see Schumpeter, *Imperialism and Social Classes*, 64–98.

10. Findling, "America at the Great Exhibition," 201–2; Henry Ward Beecher, "The Right Kind of Farming," in *Eyes and Ears* (Boston: Ticknor and Fields, 1862), 126; Peter D. McClelland, *Sowing Modernity: America's First Agricultural Revolution* (Ithaca, N.Y.: Cornell University Press, 1997), 52–63; United States, *Agriculture of the United States in 1860; Compiled from the Original Returns of the Eighth Census* (Washington, D.C.: Government Printing Office, 1864), xix; see advertisement for "S. Hulbert's Patent Convex Moulboard and Iron Beam Plow" (1858), Massachusetts Historical Society; *The Reaper: Argument of William H Seward in the Circuit Court of the United States, October 24, 1854* (Albany, N.Y.: William L. Finn, 1854). See, generally, David Hounshell, *From the American System to Mass Production, 1800–1932: Development of Manufacturing Technology in the United States* (Baltimore. Md.: Johns Hopkins University Press, 1984), 153–88.

11. Howe, *Adventures and Achievements of Americans*, 602–7; Hounshell, *From the American System to Mass* Production, 156–64; Carey in Paul K. Conkin, *Prophets of Prosperity: America's First Political Economists* (Bloomington: Indiana University Press, 1980), 264–66, 269, 272.

12. Greeley, *Glances at Europe*, 289–90; Findling, "America at the Great Exhibition," 199–200; Alexis de Tocqueville, *Democracy in America*, ed. Harvey C. Mansfield and Delba Winthrop (Chicago: University of Chicago Press, 2000), 428, see also 386; Howe, *Adventures and Achievements*, 600, 613–14; Curti, "America at the World Fair," 840–41. See too Georg Simmel, "The Berlin Trade Exhibit," in *Simmel on Culture: Selected Writings*, ed. David Frisby and Mike Featherstone (London: Sage, 1997).

13. *Scientific American*, June 28, 1851; Andrew H. Miller, *Novels Behind Glass: Commodity Culture and Victorian Narrative* (Cambridge: Cambridge University Press, 1995), 63–64, 77–78, 87; Charles Babbage, *The Exposition of 1851* (London: John Murray, 1851), 21, 46.

14. Babbage, *On the Economy of Machinery and Manufactures* (London: J. Murray, 1846), 119–22; Greeley, *Glances at Europe*, 289–91; Eugene S. Ferguson, "The American-ness of American Technology," *Technology and Culture* 20 (1979), 19; Howe, *Adventures and Achievements*, 604. On the theoretical basis for such a market-driven maximization of production, see Adam Smith on the division of labor in *An Inquiry into the Nature and Causes of the Wealth of Nations*, ed. Edwin Cannan (1776; Chicago: University of Chicago Press, 1976), 17–20.

15. Horace Greeley, *Art and Industry as Represented in the Exhibition at the Crystal Palace* (New York: Redfield, 1853), vii–viii; New York Crystal Palace Records, box 1, folder 1 (September 24, 1852), box 1, folder 3 (November 29, 1852), and box 1, folder 5 (December 14, 1852); David J. Jeremy and Darwin H. Stapleton, "Transfers Between Culturally-Related Nations: The Movement of Textile and Railroad Technologies Between Britain and the United States, 1780–1840," in *International Technology Transfer: Europe, Japan, and the USA, 1700–1914*, ed. David J. Jeremy (Brookfield, Vt.: Edward Elgar, 1991), 33. Generally, see A. G. Hopkins, "The History of Globalization—and the Globalization of History?," in *Globalization in World History* (New York: Norton, 2002). More generally, Karl Polanyi, *The Great Transformation: The Political and Economic Origins of Our Time* (Boston: Beacon Press, 2001, orig. 1944), 187–209.

16. Paul Young, *Globalization and the Great Exhibition: The Victorian New World Order* (London: Palgrave, 2009), 42; *Putnam's Magazine*, August 1853, 122. Michael Zakim, "Inventing Industrial Statistics," in *Money Matters: The Law, Politics, and Economics of Currency*, special issue, *Theoretical Inquiries in Law* 11, no. 1 (2010): 283–318. Peter Force was chairman of the executive committee organizing the American display in London. Joseph Kennedy, superintendent of the 1850 federal census, was the committee's

executive secretary. Executive Committee on the Industrial Exhibition of 1851, "Circular of the Executive Committee of the United States on the Industrial Exhibition of 1851" (Washington, D.C., 1850); Thomas P. Hughes, *Human-Built World: How to Think About Technology and Culture* (Chicago: University of Chicago Press, 2004), 28–31.

17. "Introduction," in Buzard, Childers, and Gillooly, eds., *Victorian Prism*, 4; *Putnam's*, August 1853, 126; Karen Chase and Michael Levenson, "Mayhew, the Prince, and the Poor: The Great Exhibition of Power and Dispossession," in Davis, *Victorian Prism*, 127–28.

18. "Leisure—Its Uses and Abuses," *Hunt's Merchant's Magazine* 1 (November 1839): 404; John H. Griscom, *Memoir of John Griscom* (New York, 1859), 328; *Putnam's*, August, 1853, 128; the social reproduction of seriousness is borrowed and recontextualized from Allon White, "The Dismal Sacred Word: Academic Language and the Social Reproduction of Seriousness," *Journal of Literature, Teaching, and Politics* 2 (1983): 4–15; Timothy Mitchell, *Colonising Egypt* (Berkeley: University of California Press, 1991), 4–9, 12–13. Also see Bruno Latour, "Visualization and Cognition: Thinking with Eyes and Hands," in *Knowledge and Society: Studies in the Sociology of Culture Past and Present*, ed. Robert Alun Jones and Henrika Kuklick (Greenwich, Conn.: JAI, 1986), 6:1–40.

19. Greeley, *Glances at Europe*, 19; Sigfried Giedion, *Space, Time, Architecture: The Growth of a New Tradition* (Cambridge, Mass.: Harvard University Press, 1967), 246, 252–53, 259; *Putnam's*, August 1853, 121, 125; Miller, *Novels Behind Glass*, 57–60; Greenhalgh, *Ephemeral Vistas*, 142–71. This "constructive style" reached a pinnacle in the Eiffel Tower, which was erected in 1889 for yet another world's fair and marked modernity's tendency "to ennoble technological necessities through artistic ends." Walter Benjamin, "Paris, the Capital of the Nineteenth Century," in *Selected Writings*, ed. Howard Eiland and Michael W. Jennings (Cambridge, Mass.: Harvard University Press, 2002), 3:41.

20. *Scientific American*, October 23, 1852, 42; T. J. Clark, "Should Benjamin Have Read Marx?," *Boundary 2* 30 (2003): 31–49.

21. C. R. Goodrich, ed., *Science and Mechanism in the New York Exhibition, 1853–1854* (New York: G. P. Putnam, 1854), n.p. (see Sections II and III); B. Silliman Jr. and C. R. Goodrich, *World of Science, Art, and Industry Illustrated* (New York: G. P. Putnam, 1854), 70, 86; Greeley, *Art and Industry*, xxiii; *Scientific American*, July 30, 1853, 362; August 13, 378; *North American and United States Gazette*, July 19, 1852; William C. Richards, *A Day in the New York Crystal Palace, and How to Make the Most of It* (New York: G. P. Putnam, 1853), 109–18.

22. *Scientific American*, July 30, 1853, 362–63; Richard L. Stein, "National Portraits," in Davis, *Victorian Prism*, 111–12; *New Hampshire Statesman*, July 23, 1853; on the republican embrace of machinery as offering the United States a way of circumventing the industrial evils of Europe, see John F. Kasson, *Civilizing the Machine: Technology and Republican Values in America, 1776–1900* (New York: Hill and Wang, 1976), 21–33. On Southern industrialization, see *Scientific American*, June 28, 1851, 322 and September 24, 1853, 13; New York Crystal Palace Records, box 1, folder 5 (December 15, 1852); Richards, *A Day in the New York Crystal Palace*, 29; Greeley quoted in Robert C. Post, "Reflections of American Science and Technology at the New York Crystal Palace Exhibition of 1853," *Journal of American Studies* 17, no. 3 (1983): 343–44. See, too, Silliman and Goodrich, *World of Science, Art, and Industry Illustrated*, 95–97. On the broader relationship of slavery to industrial revolution, see Michael Zakim, "Slavery and Capitalism in the United States," in the *Routledge History of Nineteenth-Century America* (forthcoming).

23. Greeley, *Art and Industry*, xxiii, 18–19, 27–29, 42–46; Punch quoted in Miller, *Novels Behind Glass*, 76; Greeley, *Glances at Europe*, 22; *Scientific American*, July 23, 1853, 354. Such criticisms of the "vanity of Pomp" at the Crystal Palace's opening ceremony traveled quickly. See Henry Van Der Lyn's diary entry for July 14, 1853, written in Oxford, New York, in Henry Van Der Lyn, Papers, 1827–1857 (New-York Historical Society Manuscript Collection).

24. *Scientific American*, July 23, 1853, 354; August 6, 1853, 370; October 23, 1852, 41; Michael Borut, "The Scientific American in Nineteenth Century America" (PhD diss., New York University, 1977); Margot Gayle and Carol Gayle, *Cast-Iron Architecture in America: The Significance of James Bogardus* (New York: W. W. Norton, 1998), 70–135; Giedion, *Space, Time and Architecture*, 236–7.

25. *Cleveland Herald*, December 17, 1852; New York Crystal Palace Papers, box 1, folder 4 (December 4, December 8, December 10, 1852).

26. Chas. H. Haswell, *Reminiscences of an Octogenarian of the City of New York (1815–1860)* (New York: Harper, 1896), 488–89; Kenneth A. Scherzer, *The Unbounded Community: Neighborhood Life and Social Structure in New York City, 1830–1875* (Durham, N.C.: Duke University Press, 1992), 40–41; New York Crystal Palace Papers, box 1, folder 4 (December 4, 1852) and box 1, folder 3 (November 3, 1852).

27. *Scientific American*, March 19, 1853, 210 and April 2, 1853, 229.

28. New York Crystal Palace Papers, box 1, folder 4 (December 10 and December 4, 1852); Smith, *Wealth of Nations*, 13–14; Karl Marx, *Capital* (Moscow: Progress, 1954), 1:351. A good example of Marx's analysis of the emerging machine age, from the same chapter of *Capital*:

> A steam-plough does as much work in one hour at a cost of three-pence, as 66 men at a cost of 15 shillings. I return to this example in order to clear up an erroneous notion. The 15 shillings are by no means the expression in money of all the labour expended in one hour by the 66 men. If the ratio of surplus-labour to necessary labour were 100%, these 66 men would produce in one hour a value of 30 shillings, although their wages, 15 shillings, represent only their labour for half an hour. Suppose, then, a machine cost as much as the wages for a year of the 150 men it displaces, say £3,000; this £3,000 is by no means the expression in money of the labour added to the object produced by these 150 men before the introduction of the machine, but only of that portion of their year's labour which was expended for themselves and represented by their wages. On the other hand, the £3,000, the money-value of the machine, expresses all the labour expended on its production, no matter in what proportion this labour constitutes wages for the workman, and surplus-value for the capitalist. Therefore, though a machine cost as much as the labour-power displaced by it costs, yet the labour materialised in it is even then much less than the living labour it replaces. (*Capital*, 1:370)

29. Greeley, *Glances at Europe*, 23; Richards, *A Day in the New York Crystal Palace*, 109; *Scientific American*, September 17, 1853, 6; Ruth Brandon, *A Capitalist Romance: Singer and the Sewing Machine* (New York: Lippincott, 1977), 50; Borut, "Scientific American," 147–49; Greeley, *Art and Industry*, 242–45. See, generally, Mary Blewett, *Men, Women and Work: Class, Gender and Protest in the New England Shoe Industry, 1780–1910* (Urbana: University of Illinois Press, 1988). Lewis Mumford generalized about this development: "As production became more mechanized and the discipline of the factory became more impersonal and the work itself became less rewarding . . .

attention was centered more and more upon the product." Lewis Mumford, *Technics and Civilization* (Chicago: University of Chicago Press, 1932), 322.

30. Paul E. Johnson, *Sam Patch, the Famous Jumper* (New York: Hill and Wang, 2003), 53–61.

31. *Harper's*, April 1854, 694; *Scientific American*, July 30, 1853, 362.

32. *Scientific American*, July 23, 1853, 354; August 6, 1853, 370; August 13, 1853; *Daily South Carolinian*, July 27, 1853 and July 30, 1853; *Daily Register* (Raleigh, N.C.), November 9, 1853.

33. *Harper's*, September 1854, 553–4; *Daily National Intelligencer*, May 27, 1854 and May 13, 1854; *Scientific American*, July 22, 1854, 357 and October 7, 1854, 29; Hirschfeld, "American on Exhibition," 115.

34. *Putnam's*, March 1857, 336 and July 1857, 135.

35. Benjamin, *The Arcades Project*, 13; Hirschfeld, "America on Exhibition," 115; *Putnam's*, March 1857, 336; New York Crystal Palace Papers, box 2, folder 14 (letter, October 7, 1858). "A reward of $3000 is offered for the apprehension of whoever started the fire. The loss is estimated at half a million dollars, in addition to the value of the building, which is $635,000 and could be sold for a quarter of that sum." *Harper's*, November, 1858, 830.

CHAPTER 14

PLANTATION DISPOSSESSIONS

The Global Travel of Agricultural Racial Capitalism

KRIS MANJAPRA

Across the British West Indies and the whole British Empire, the institution of slavery was officially abolished in 1833. This is conventionally said to mark the culmination of an age of abolition, the rise of the liberal era, and the origin point of universal freedom in the nineteenth century. Abolition would reach the French Empire in 1848, the United States in 1865, the Dutch Empire in 1866, the Spanish, Portuguese, and Ottoman empires in the 1870s and 1880s, and Brazil in 1888. But during this age of abolition, new forms of forced and coerced labor arose on a global scale, and the plantation as an exploitative, racial, political-ecological complex began to expand and travel the face of earth. Just when the institution of slavery was said to die away under liberalism, the plantation complex attained new life. The turning point of 1833, with the official end of slavery in the British Empire, saw the rise of new kingdoms of sugar, coffee, cotton, and rubber across the Americas, Africa, and Asia. It saw the spread of plantation asylums ruled by the lash and worked by the chain gang. Similarly, as Sven Beckert's work discusses, the official end of slavery on the cotton plantations of the American South after 1865 led to an expansion of plantation production across the postbellum South, and an explosion of coercive cotton production across Brazil, Western Africa, Egypt, Central Asia, and India in following decades.[1] The word "abolition" supposes an end. But the plantation complex, and the modes of racial labor command endemic to it, actually flourished in abolition's aftermath.

The first doubts about the actual meaning and implications of abolition were sown on its very arrival. For example, in June 1839 on the Vreed-en-Hoop plantation in British Guyana, the following events took place. Rose, an erstwhile black slave now turned "apprentice," was deposed by an official about reports of labor abuse. She testified:

> I recollect some Coolies running away and going to Berbice long time ago; it was two or three months after they came; I heard they went to Berbice. We were free before they went away. . . . Adonis and Ramsing were sent for them. The Coolies returned before Adonis and Ramsing [came back]. . . . I saw them when they were brought to the estate, but I did not see who brought them; they were carried to the sick-house. Next day they flogged all those that ran away; they brought all from the sick-house together, and took them to the negro-yard to be flogged; I saw them flogged; Mr. Jacobs was the only white man present; the driver for them flogged them; they were flogged one after the other; they got more than three licks, but I cannot say how many, and cannot say that they got five; their backs were not cut, but in bumps. They appeared to me as severely punished as my maties were during the apprenticeship when flogged; they were flogged with a cat [cat-o'-nine-tails], the same as was formerly in use; some cried and some did not cry; there was no blood. When the blacks have been flogged I have seen blood on their backs.[2]

The testimonial speaks of the attempted escape of Indian "coolies," or indentured servants, from the plantation, after the black slaves had been supposedly freed. The audience is a fact-finding committee convened in 1838 to determine whether practices of slavery were continuing even after abolition. Note that a black and an Indian overseer were sent out to capture the absconders, and that in Rose's comparative analysis, the absconding coolies were treated just like undisciplined slaves: whipped in the same negro yards, kept in the same sick-house or plantation prison, flogged with the same whip. The only difference was in the amount of blood on their backs.

The outcome of the investigation into the punishment and torture on Vreed-en-Hoop plantation was the following: "The general manager of the estate, the manager of the Coolies, and the medical officer were all indicted and convicted of brutal assaults, before the Inferior Criminal Court of British Guiana, and either fined or imprisoned."[3] The result for the plantation owner, John Gladstone, who lived in Liverpool, is a study in contrast. He went on to become one of the most important political powerbrokers of the British Empire in the 1830s and 1840s, fashioning policies for the British West Indies and the East Indies alike as a champion of imperial monopoly and protectionism. His business interests in the East India trade, and in the trade in indentured persons from India, continued to thrive. And soon his son, William Gladstone, became British prime minister.[4]

For the four years following 1833, a halfway house institution for the ex-slaves was erected—this is the so-called "apprenticeship." During the apprenticeship period, enslaved blacks across the British Caribbean were placed in a new legal category: half property, half person. They were made into debt peons, paying off half of the price of their manumission through their work. The other half would be borne by the British state, which authorized a mind-boggling compensation package for the slave owners of the Caribbean in 1833. Damned as property, and damned as persons—the so-called apprentices were made to compensate their enslavers for the slave-owners' loss, instead of the other way around.

At the very same time, another institution was inaugurated, called the indentured laborer system. It, too, produced workers that were half property, half person. Often through kidnapping and trickery, and the use of brute force, new laborers were brought from distant lands, especially from Asia and Africa, to the plantations of the Caribbean after abolition. These workers were contract laborers, or sometimes debt peons, working under the dread of torture.

The plantation complex, an early form of prison factory, was perfected as a social and economic institution in the Caribbean. It entailed a racial system of land appropriation from indigenous peoples, and savage techniques of labor control of kidnapped and shackled labor migrants. It was based on the enclosure of lands for the intense cultivation of single crops (monocropping) that were sent into the international market. The plantation complex involved the outlay of huge amounts of credit, which served as a lever for vast infrastructure projects of agro-ecological transformation, including land enclosures, irrigation works, railways, and the dredging of ports. In short, the plantation complex was honed and streamlined in the Caribbean from the 1500s to the 1700s. It mixed together ecological extraction, racism, colonialism, financial and mercantile capitalism, militarism, and agricultural science into a destructive, cellular form that metastasized from the Caribbean across the Global South *after* abolition, creating what Shu-mei Shih has termed a global "plantation arc."[5]

Racial Capitalism and the Spread of the Plantation Complex

The history of plantations in the Caribbean is inextricably linked to the development of North American capitalism. The futures of the antebellum American South had long been tied up with the Caribbean Sea. We might even think of the American South as one precinct within a larger circum-Caribbean region of plantation colonialism. The islands in the Caribbean Sea and the land around that sea, including the plantation economies of the American South, formed an interconnected system of circulating peoples, goods, cultures, and techniques in the rise of racial slavery and the brutalizing triangular trade in kidnapped Africans. Historical connections between the Caribbean and North American capitalism extended all the way up the eastern seaboard. Plantation economies of sugar, tobacco, and, eventually, cotton fanned across colonial Virginia, the Carolinas, Barbados, and Jamaica as part of the same seventeenth-century colonial expansion. In addition, extensive webs of banking, shipping, insurance, manufacture, and trade connected the Caribbean plantation colonies to investors in the financial, milling, and transshipment hubs of Boston, Salem, Providence, New York, and Philadelphia. Finally, the rise of the "cotton kingdom" in the American South from the late eighteenth century onward depended directly on Caribbean mobilities in the wake of revolution and abolition. Louisiana, for example, became a major destination for planter-refugees fleeing the Haitian Revolution.[6] And William Faulkner's character, Thomas Sutpen, in *Absalom, Absalom,* reminds us of the ongoing circulations of slave owners between Caribbean islands and Southern states both before and after the Civil War.[7] In the mid-nineteenth century, American slavers believed their "cotton kingdom" would colonize Haiti, Cuba, Jamaica, and eventually expand into Brazil.[8] In the age of abolition, the Caribbean Sea served as a reservoir of fugitive capital, enslaved labor, coercive production techniques, racial norms, and slave owner fantasies about perpetuating the abuse of enslaved black flesh.

Racial slavery and plantation labor were key characteristics of the circum-Caribbean economy, including in the American South. And studying these racial labor relations is central to understanding the history of capitalism. We might define "capital" as value-in-motion, or the power that creates new value by putting things in accelerating motion. With roots in the late 1400s, successive phases of capitalism have constructed the colonial relations, the markets, the logistical routes, the tastes, and the cultural norms for moving and recombining productive units across globe-straddling distances in the pursuit of new value and new margins of profit. Capitalism is an ever-widening gyre for commodifying, mobilizing, recombining, redistributing, and transforming value on a global scale.

Labor power, or the biochemical and biomechanical energy concentrated in human mental and physical work, serves as an essential fuel for capitalism's perpetual motion. Capitalism could not have emerged without the ongoing short- and long-distance mobilities, reassignments, retrainings, and transformations of human beings into new kinds of workers—units of commodified labor power.[9] We understand something fundamental about how capitalism works when we consider what it does to working people—how it fetches them, commands them, moves them, and socially reconfigures them. And racist thinking is essential to capitalism's labor assignments and recombinations.

Following in the black Marxist tradition, eminent scholars have argued that the global abolitions and emancipations of racial slavery in the nineteenth century marked endings that were far from over. For example, W. E. B. Du Bois, in *Black Reconstruction in America* (1935), exposes the sources of Reconstruction's failure after 1878, which resulted in the rise of racial slavery by other means, especially through the convict lease system, debt peonage, vigilante lynchings, and the legal regime of the Jim Crow South.[10]

Meanwhile, Eric Williams, in *Capitalism & Slavery* (1944), unsettles the notion of abolition as an end to slavery in another way. Writing on slavery in the British Empire, Williams shows how "slavery helped finance the industrial revolution," and how British capitalism turned against slavery and toward abolitionism for largely opportunistic, not ideological, reasons. Only after having served its economic purpose, and not a moment sooner, was slavery abandoned by industrial and commercial interests in Britain. After abolition, British industry came to rely on the slave economies of Cuba, Brazil, and the American South for sugar and cotton. Furthermore, British capitalists opened up new plantation frontiers across Asia to obtain agricultural products to feed the hungry factories of Manchester, Birmingham, and Liverpool. Williams argues that cold economic calculus, not a philanthropic change of heart, mainly explains the coming of abolition in the British Empire. In fact, abolition marked the expansion of systems of servitude by other means, masking coercive power with liberal discourses of contract and free labor.[11]

Extending the implications of Williams' argument, a variety of scholars have shown how the racial concepts underpinning European slavery actually persisted after abolition. As opposed to the abolitions of 1833, or of 1865, marking a clean break with the past, Cedric Robinson envisioned these dates as inflexions in a continuing trajectory of "racial capitalism."[12] Capitalism is not merely a system of trade and accumulation. It is also a racialized system of dispossession and exploitation, dehumanizing some groups for the material benefit of others. As such, capitalism relies on racialized and gendered designations about the kinds of communities and peoples whose dispossession, exploitation, and obliteration is justifiable for the sake of "progress" and industrial growth. Racial categorizations organize and stabilize the capitalist mode of production, and they serve to hide and normalize capitalism's dirty work. Cedric Robinson thus argues that all capitalist enterprise is "racial capitalism," since racialization is a prime condition of possibility for capitalist exploitation and accumulation. *Racialization, like coercive force, was not vestigial to the emerging regime of liberal capitalist expansion, but integral to it.*[13]

If this is the case, then we should not be surprised that racialized labor regimes such as apprenticeship and indenture, and racialized political ecologies such as the plantation complex, continued to live on after the abolition of slavery. Abolition did not mark the end of the plantation mode of production or racial capitalism, but rather their global expansion.

The know-how, the mental models, and the methods of plantation labor control went global in the 1830s. The rise of the liberal era banked on an expanding racial extraction of labor from vast swathes of humanity, what

Table 14.1 The Global Travel of the Plantation Complex

Period	Main feature
1640s–1713	
From the First Capitalist Plantations in Barbados to the Peace of Utrecht	Sugar and tobacco mercantilism across the Caribbean
1713–1791	
From the Peace of Utrecht to the Haitian Revolution	West Indian jewels in two imperial crowns: Saint-Domingue and Jamaica
1791–1838	
From the Haitian Revolution to Emancipation in the British Empire	The first global expansion of the plantation complex
1840s–1870s	
The Liberal Era and the Bonanza of Bondage	The rise of a global colonial agrarian regime
1880s–1920s	
The Era of Corporate Agglomeration	Multinational corporations and the emergence of the Third World

W. E. B. Du Bois conjures as the "dark and vast sea of human labor in China and India, the South Seas and all Africa; in the West Indies and Central America and in the United States."[14] The 1830s were a cusp decade for this expansion, after which an emergent global racial agrarian regime emerged.

1640s–1713

The propagation of agricultural capitalism around the world occurred through discrete steps and began with the commercial cultivation of sugar. At the end of the sixteenth century, there were already 20,000 African slaves in Brazil.[15] By 1640, a new phase began, as small-hold British and French settler farms in Barbados were gradually incorporated into large-scale plantations. Brazil remained the world's largest producer and exporter of sugar until the 1680s.[16] Dutch, British, Spanish, Danish, Prussian, and Portuguese colonial powers participated in the first plantation revolution from the 1640s to the 1780s, as the circum-Caribbean region, including the North American southeastern seaboard, was transformed into commercial penal gardens for the production of sugar, cotton, indigo, and rice.[17] By the latter seventeenth century, the great potential for profits led to extensive warfare between the French and British, with major wars in 1666–1667, 1689–1697, and 1702–1713. This was a period of pillaging and widespread destruction of Caribbean plantations.

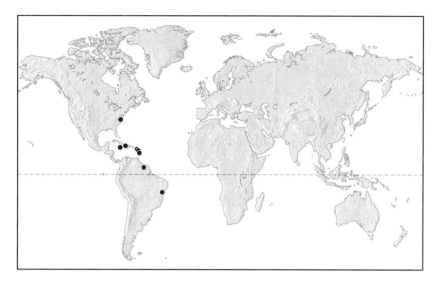

14.1 Major Sites of Capitalist Plantations, 1600s–1790s. Dots represent approximate regions of plantation production.

1713–1791

A new period opened up after the signing of the Peace of Utrecht in 1713 between the British and the French, lasting until the Haitian Revolution in 1791. The prolonged detente between British and French colonial powers in the Caribbean allowed for the stabilization of mercantilist trade. The British slave colony of Jamaica and the French slave colony of Saint-Domingue emerged as the two great centers for European sugar production and the anchors of the British and French Caribbean economies.[18] These two slave islands were the prized pearls in the imperial necklace. As Philip Curtin points out, the new version of the plantation complex that grew up in the eighteenth century "[was] more specialized, more dependent on networks of maritime trade, and on intercontinental communication."[19] C. L. R. James showed that the Saint-Domingue economy comprised two-thirds of France's overseas trade by 1789 and was the greatest single market for the European slave trade.[20] During this same period, the Spanish, who had run *ingenios,* or sugar plantations, in Cuba since the 1500s, began to implement the British and French plantation model.[21]

But Saint-Domingue and Jamaica were not considered imperial pearls just because of the level of their sugar production and their ravenous hunger for slaves from Africa, but also because of the purportedly scientific agricultural methods that characterized their enterprises. By the 1780s, Jamaica, St. Vincent, and Saint-Domingue had three of the largest botanical gardens on earth in the service of agricultural capitalism, and were exchanging and propagating lucrative specimens, such as cochineal for precious red dye and cinchona for fever medication. Even as late as the 1840s, when Jamaica and Saint-Domingue had become the iconic islands of French and British Caribbean failure, these overgrown plantation gardens were still regarded as repositories of the "West Indian method" of commercial agriculture. This "method" entailed large-scale enclosures specializing in production and export of primary commodities (such as loaves of muscovado sugar or bales of raw cotton), absentee ownership and the transfer of profits to imperial metropoles, monopolization of logistics services by metropolitan carriers, limited mechanization, chain-gang labor throughout the year, and the punishment and exhaustion of slaves, or bonded laborers.[22]

1791–1838

The subsequent decades of revolutionary instability and abolitionism, 1791–1838, witnessed the first expansion of the plantation complex to the circumferential rim of the Caribbean Sea and to the Indian Ocean. King sugar came to rule Cuba and Brazil. Levels of sugar production in both locations now exploded, surpassing the Jamaican yield after 1805.[23] Both sugar economies continued to boom under slavery well into the 1870s.[24] Following American Independence, and with the beginning of western expansion, the "cotton kingdom" arose across

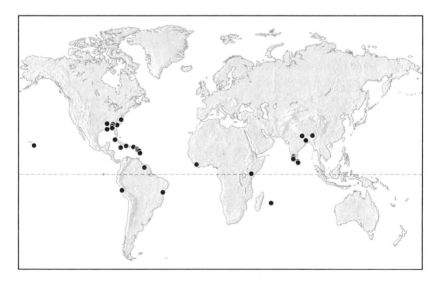

14.2 Major Sites of Capitalist Plantations, 1790s–1830s. Dots represent approximate regions of plantation production.

the American South, stretching from the old circum-Caribbean plantation centers of the Virginia, the Carolinas, and Louisiana to new frontiers across the Mississippi and the Southwest.[25]

This period, 1791–1838, was the overture to an epochal change: the emergence of a global racial agrarian regime that would soon spread across the Global South. In this period, plantation crops were coming to Asia: sugar to Mauritius, indigo to Bengal and Java, tea to Assam, coffee to Kerala. Here, for the first time, the capitalist plantation system based on monocropping and year-long production schedules tuned to global markets expanded outside the circum-Caribbean region and the American South. The islands of the Caribbean Sea, the American South, and Brazil became sources of seeds, capital, and knowledge for new plantation enterprises around the world over the course of the coming century. New Orleans cotton seeds were sent to India, Trinidad chocolate seeds to Africa, and Brazil rubber plants to Malaya.[26] In this same time, Mississippi plantation overseers were recruited by the East India Company to institute slave-like labor control on Indian plantations in Assam and around Bombay. Meanwhile, Cuban horticultural manuals were being studied by sugar entrepreneurs in the Dutch East Indies.[27]

The choreography of this expansion must be understood in terms of British imperial statecraft in the early nineteenth century, as its naval forces forcibly established a globe-straddling "imperial meridian" uncontested by any other power on earth.[28] The war with, and eventual defeat of, the Napoleonic forces allowed the British superpower to capture Java (temporarily taken from the Dutch in 1811) and Malacca, the Cape Colony (1814), Trinidad and Guyana (1814), and Ceylon and Mauritius (1815). Plantations were set up after what was alternatively called the "West Indian model" or the "American model" in all these territories by the 1820s, often under the supervision of refugee West Indian planters hungry for new land and slaves. In Mauritius, French planters who had escaped from Saint-Domingue after the revolution now brought enslaved African people to work their plantations, literally seeking to replicate the Caribbean system on new terrain. A similar history of the Saint-Domingue planter refugees played out in the well-known case of Louisiana.[29]

Imperial statecraft enabled French and British planters and their enterprises to relocate. Take the case of the reparations made to West Indian slave owners by the British government at the time of abolition. Twenty million pounds were paid to West Indian planters from the public purse beginning in 1833 to compensate them for the loss of their property in slaves.[30] This vast sum of money, obtained from British public coffers as indemnity against what the racial colonial state recognized as the loss of the planters' slave chattel, came to be reinvested in other quadrants of the empire. Reinvestments ranged from railway networks in Scotland and the United States to shipping lines in the Caribbean and banking houses in London.[31] But slave capital was not only transferred across the Americas and the Atlantic. In fact, a significant portion of slave owner compensations made what Nicholas Draper termed a "swing to the east." The actuarial pricing of black slave life was converted into money and sent to the East Indies.[32] West Indian planters got their second life in the East, and in a very material sense, the plantation complex mutated and traveled to the East with them.

For example, Leonard Wray was born in Jamaica and he owned a plantation there before departing for Bengal, India in the 1840s, where he started sugar plantations in Gorakhpur. By the late 1840s, he had moved to Malaya, establishing coffee plantations, and came to be known as "the father of Malayan coffee."[33] Robert Boyd Tytler traveled to Jamaica at age fifteen to work on plantations before journeying on to Ceylon to start his own coffee enterprises. Tytler became one of the island's biggest estate owners and a member of the legislative council. Two of his sons and his son-in-law continued as plantation entrepreneurs and political potentates. They were part of an interconnected oligarchy of Scottish families at the helm of the nineteenth-century Ceylonese colonial economy. In fact, it was estimated that by the 1880s 95 percent of the overseers on Ceylonese coffee plantations were Scottish.[34]

So far, I have traced ninety-seven instances of slave compensation capital making the "swing to the east," transferred from the Caribbean to Asia around the cusp of abolition. Sometimes, this occurred through the diaspora of planters or overseers themselves, such as in the cases of Wray and Tytler. But other times, it took place through the relocation or reinvestments of corporate entities, such as "agency houses," or British trading firms that did business in the colonies. The firm of Gladstone, Grant & Co. in British Guyana, for example, was tied to the agency house of Gillanders, Arbuthnot & Co., which became a major owner of tea plantations in Assam, an important investor in the Darjeeling Railway Co., and eventually a component of the multinational Sun Alliance Insurance Company with branches in India.[35] Other times, compensation money from the Caribbean was parlayed into other kinds of social and political capital in Asia through the institution of the East India Company. For example, at least twelve of the directors of the East India Company from the 1800s to the 1840s received compensation for the loss of Caribbean slaves. The transfer of compensation capital from the Caribbean Sea to East India could easily take the form of new kinds of investments, as "dispossessed" absentee landlords from the Caribbean moved their capital into shipping, railways, human trafficking networks of indentured labor, and other kinds of logistic and commercial infrastructure in the East.

Caribbean planters funneled a significant portion of the slave compensation paid out to them to Asia, and the forms of their reinvestments were diverse: the purchase and enclosure of lands, the development of commercial infrastructure, the consolidation of political and administrative power, the rise of small financial and credit institutions, the creation of networks to facilitate the mobility of cheap labor. All of these diversified forms of reinvestment, however, contributed to the implantation of a mutated plantation complex across the British East Indies in the decades after abolition.

Footloose plantation entrepreneurs from the Caribbean, now fattened by the Crown's massive compensation, did not only take money and influence with them to the East, they also took the West Indian method. We observe the transfer of horticultural and botanical methods—evidenced by the circulation of "master manuals" from the Caribbean across the new plantation frontiers of Asia by the mid-nineteenth century, such as Monnereau's *Complete Indigo-Maker* (first published in Saint-Domingue in the 1730s), Laborie's *Coffee Planter* (also from Saint-Domingue, and written in Jamaica, 1798), or Alvaro Reynoso guide on sugar production (*Ensayo sobre el cultivo de la caña de azúcar,* from Cuba, 1862). These texts became required reading among the planters in Asia.

The decay, and eventual death, of the planter dominion in Haiti and Jamaica led to attempted transplantation of modular forms of the plantation complex to other parts of the earth. While the transfer of liquidity was one material way in which this endeavor in transplantation took place, the reproduction and dissemination of authoritative texts about the famed West Indian method was another.

The plantations of the French and British Caribbean of the 1780s, and the American South and Spanish Caribbean by the 1830s, were considered the most mature, and most developed slave economies. They apparently held lessons that aspiring European planters in Asia were desperate to learn. But as J. E. Inikori masterfully points out, the majority of the actual innovations of West Indian or American slave horticulture and agribusiness was contributed by the conceptual and practical innovation of the slaves themselves.[36] Whether one thinks of the Rillieux vacuum pan method for sugar production or the engineering of plantation mills and machines, the expertise of enslaved peoples was the source. The conviction that West Indian planters where the ones with the methods shows a deeply skewed grasp on reality promulgated by racial capitalism.[37]

As mentioned earlier, Elias Monnereau's *The Complete Indigo-Maker* discussed indigo production in Saint-Domingue. As Prakash Kumar's study ably shows, Monnereau, who had been an indigo planter, published a work that became a staple read for aficionados of indigo cultivation in Bengal. For example, John Prinsep, the first major British planter of indigo in Bengal, was one of Monnereau's fervent readers.[38]

After sections devoted to the horticultural cultivation of indigo, Monnereau turns to questions of labor control. He instructs his readers that "every negro who leaves his master's house should be furnished with a billet . . . and his business should also be specified with the date of the day, and the time he may remain absent."[39] The negroes, Monnereau catalogues, are "great talkers, liars, cheats, lazy, lascivious and impudent, if not kept within proper bounds," and with regards to work, "they always do as little as possible."[40] And for this reason, "chastisement," counsels Monnereau, is of great importance. The negro "should be constantly watched." It is only the display of brute force that allows society to work well. Monnereau explains: "Europeans would find it very difficult to conceive how we can make use of such kinds of people; but we have recourse to a regular steadiness to keep them in order, otherwise it would be impossible to make any use of them."[41]

Pierre-Joseph Laborie, also a slave owner of Saint-Domingue, wrote another plantation manual that became required reading among planters across the Bay of Bengal. Laborie published his work in 1798 as a refugee in Jamaica after the Haitian Revolution. When he began writing his book, in 1789, Saint-Domingue was still the jewel in France's crown. In his preface, giddy with nostalgia, Laborie thanks the British governor for harboring him and offers his treatise as a gift to the Jamaican planters.

Laborie's text ranges over the full cycle of plantation operations, from obtaining a land charter from the king to clearing the "wasteland," from the horticulture of the coffee plant to the optimal organization of slave power, and the techniques for forcibly commanding labor. In Laborie's presentation, he places great emphasis on the rigors of measurement ("The outlines of the place must be measured out, and exactly drawn on paper" [36]), on calculation ("The settler must calculate carefully, and only extend his plantations in proportion to the hands he is able to supply" [34]), and on symmetry ("It costs little, and without which the best things . . . lose much of their merit" [36]). Laborie encourages the use of machines to speed up production, as well as a rudimentary division of plantation laborers: there should be field slaves, drivers, overseers, the "coffee-man," the mill hands, the hospital matron, the poultry keeper, the keeper of children, and the keeper of the provision grounds.

Slaves, Laborie councils, are best obtained directly from Guinea, where they are "docile and timid." In his grotesque menagerie of plantation life forms, Laborie categorizes the "negro" as an "animal, rational in middle degree . . . who tends to sloth." In the last section of his book, he offers detailed techniques for applying coercive force and maintains that the use of force is necessary in order to extrude the maximum amount of power from the slave's body. The slave is not a laborer for Laborie but a source of labor-power to be forcibly commandeered.

> In order to make the best of the power of the negro, and to keep him in subjection, chastisement is often necessary. . . . But, that his life may be prolonged as long as possible, the planter must not forget that chastisement ought to be neither too severe at any time, nor too often repeated.[42]

This vision of the slave as a bare container of power requiring the application of regular force infuses Laborie's way of describing the "government" of slaves. They must be "seasoned" and "made ready" for their work. They must be allowed to become "full grown for the labour," and although some are "lost in the seasoning . . . they are forged and disciplined according to the master's own ideas."

When it comes to the use of punishment and pain, Laborie presents a full syllabus of vicious techniques. He prescribes that drivers should be allowed to punish "negroes" with up to five lashes at their discretion. Faults that require more severe correction are to be punished according to the wishes of the master. Drivers should stand behind the work gang and "call the negroe back that he may rectify his faults." The most heinous misdemeanors, such as insubordination, are "never to be pardoned," and should be met with "speedy executions, and particularly on the spot, [as these have] more striking effect." Second-degree infractions, such as thefts of fruit or provisions, or faults against the general order of the plantation, should be met with the "usual penalties" of "flogging, confinement (simple or in the stocks), carrying a chain or collar." Exceptional crimes may be met with "racks, tortures, mayhems, mutilations and death." Laborie adds, assuaging his readers' concerns about the economic cost of exterminated slave property, "A state price is paid to the master, from the public revenue, for such negroes as are condemned to death or perpetual punishment" (185).

It was precisely after the abolition of slavery that the texts about how to enslave people began to circulate with unprecedented velocity and ambit. Laborie's text became a famous textbook for the establishment of plantations in Asia in the 1830s and 1840s. It was reprinted, verbatim and in full, in the *Ceylon Miscellany* of 1842. At the time, the term "negroe" served as a general concept, applicable to Tamil and Chinese indentured laborers. The text was reprinted as late as 1863, with a preface that bragged, "Laborie, though an old writer, is still *the* author on all that relates to Coffee planting. The principles laid out by him so many years ago in the West Indies, are those which will guide the managers of Ceylon properties."[43]

The challenge for planters around the earth was how to replicate the system of slave labor as it was consolidated in the West Indies and the American South, now under conditions in which slavery was formally illegal, and within new social systems. In attempting to solve this puzzle, European planters in Asia looked to the islands of Saint-Domingue, Jamaica, and Cuba, as well as Louisiana and Mississippi, as the instructive models.

Leonard Wray, of Ceylon, published his own plantation manual in 1848 and claimed it offered an advance over the West Indian method. He revived old racial fantasies and made up new ones, asserting that Indian indentured laborers were to be avoided at all costs. Indians were the "trash . . . sent from India under the general name of 'Coolies.'" Instead, Wray insists that the "intelligent, enterprising and industrious Chinese [are] the best emigrants under heaven."[44] The Chinese, Wray writes, were "like the negroes," in that they too could "withstand the effect of the West India climate." He even imagines the replacement of the African population of the Caribbean with a laboring Chinese population. The Caribbean isles of the future, for Wray, would be peopled by the "enterprising, [cheerful], and prudent" Chinese. Wray envisioned the shipment of 300,000 Chinese indentured servants to the Caribbean, doubling the island's population.[45] For Wray, who was born in Jamaica to a slave-owning family, and who had made his life as a planter in exile in Asia, Chinese indentured labor held out the hope of reconstituting the plantation complex, as well as his own abusive and profitable position within that world of force.

1840s–1870s

The decades from the 1840s to the 1870s were bonanza years for the mutating plantation complex. Between the hegemonic discourse of free trade and the rise of economic liberalism with the passing of the Sugar Duties Act and the repeal of the Corn Laws in 1846 in the British Empire, a new racial agrarian regime was established. A study of time-series data shows the rise in agricultural commodity prices during this period, attributable to a tremendous growth in demand up until about 1873.[46] Factory workers in Europe demanded tea and sugar as their morning stimulants, merchants from around the world required jute and henequen to package their goods for overseas shipment, and the middle classes purchased coffees and chocolates in their cafes and salons.[47] The boom was followed by a conjunctural fall in prices (called the "long depression," 1873–1896), which coincided with the swift multiplication of family farms in the emerging Global North and the spread of huge multinational plantation corporations across the nascent Global South.[48]

Wielding the power of military might, European imperial governments under the aegis of the British superpower sanctioned European colonists to take over the lands of colonized "natives," to cut down "wastelands" inhabited by indigenous communities, and to convert existing agricultural tenures into cash cropping. The boom years of economic liberalism were thus a peak period of primitive accumulation on a worldwide scale.

This point can be concretely traced by considering the extensive writing of land regulation acts across the Indian Ocean. The Bengal Regulation Act (1829), the Malacca Land Regulations Act (1830), the inauguration of the *Culturstelsel* system in Java (1830), the Government of India Act (1833), the Annexation of Upper Assam (1839), and the Grant of Darjeeling (1839) all legislated primitive accumulation, or the appropriation of land and labor through acts of war.[49] In Hawaii, what came to be known as the Great Māhele, or the Great Division of

Lands, took place in 1848, as 60 percent of the lands in the Hawaiian archipelago was forcibly acquired by the crown and subsequently largely claimed by American business interests.[50]

From a broader perspective, the changes to land tenure across the world, whether we think of the Prussian Reform Edict of 1807, the colonial laws of the 1820s and 1830s discussed above, the famous Act X of 1859 in British India that established peasants' rights in land, or the Emancipation of the Serfs in 1861, were all in the service of organizing agricultural production to better serve international capitalist markets. And this mass reorganization of the lands of the earth required law, militaries, scientists, and engineers—the musketeers of the plantation complex.

William Cronon describes the American mid-century project to solder the vast expanses of the "Great West" to the emerging commodity hub of Chicago.[51] Alfred Chandler points to a management revolution that began in 1840s, marked by the transition from personal to impersonal forms of commerce, and the expansion of utilities, reconnaissance, land surveying, and civil engineering services, which sustained the reorganizing of lands on an intercontinental scale.[52] Across the colonial world, new land regulations benefited European planters, as well as native landlords and big peasants who agreed to plant cash crops.

In the context of the formal abolition of slavery in the British Empire, 1834–1838, a "new system of slavery" emerged, as Hugh Tinker famously named it.[53] Not only did the system of indenture replicate the modes of labor control under slavery, but the institutions of capital, land, and labor control that were first honed on Caribbean plantations now took root in other parts of the earth.

This circulation has not been properly recognized in the historiography. Vast numbers of dispossessed Indian and Chinese peasants entered contracts for plantation labor overseas, under pressment and force.[54] But this occurred just as new plantation frontiers opened up across the Indian Ocean and as a new global racial and colonial agrarian regime was in the offing.[55] Thus, it is not only the transit of Asian bodies across geographic space that deserves our attention—conceived in terms of the study of diaspora—but also the simultaneous and interconnected expansion of the plantation complex, and agricultural racial capitalism, itself. If the study of diaspora gives us insight into the diverse subjective experiences of the plantation economy, the study of the emerging arrangement of power, land tenure, capital investment and labor control illuminates the objective structures of the plantation complex that embroiled peoples from the Americas, Africa, Asia, and Europe in each others' diasporic flows, thereby creating altogether new mobile formations.

These decades after abolition, from the 1830s onward, were also the years in which tea cultivation was forced on Assam and Ceylon, sugar and rubber on Java and Malaya, coconut and oil palm on Fiji and Papua New Guinea, sisal and coffee on Liberia and the Congo.[56] All of these plantation ventures involved the importation of bonded migrant laborers from neighboring regions, or from across the seas. Chinese indentured laborers, for example, were the first to work on the tea fields in Assam, followed thereafter by displaced tribal communities from the hill tracks of Bihar and the Gurkhas from Nepal.[57] Tamil workers, often from tribal communities or Dalit castes, were brought in large numbers to Ceylon, with 20,000 recorded deaths between 1841 and 1849 alone.[58] The indenture system coordinated distant migrations—Indian workers to Fiji and Mauritius, Chinese laborers to Peru and Queensland (Australia), and intraregional migrations of indigenous peoples and subaltern ethnic groups onto plantation enclosures. So, "tribal" or *adivasi* peoples of the Munda, Oraon, Kharia, Kol, and Bhil ethnic groups were brought from Bihar to neighboring Bengal to do the work that Bengali peasants would not do. Similarly, people from northwest Cameroon were brought down from the hills to work in the tea and coffee plantations on the coast.[59] This pattern of mixed long-distance and proximate networks of forced labor supply was repeated across Latin America, Africa, and Asia. The drift from the forests, jungles, and hills did not occur out of choice but in the context of accelerating incursions into and reclamations of "wasteland" by the colonial state.[60]

As the plantation complex traveled, it negotiated local settlement patterns and indigenous systems of rule. In South and Southeast Asia, for example, credit, coercion, and statecraft operated in very different ways than in the plantation economies of the Americas.[61] Debt bondage, as a mode of coerced labor that differed from slavery and indenture, served as the most important technique of labor control. Credit grants and the debt mechanism were used to press vast numbers of Indian peasants and landless laborers into plantation work, or into growing cash crops on small-hold farms, mediated always by caste and the strict segmentation of family lines. In Bengal, Bihar, Assam, Madras, Burma, Java, Ceylon, and Sumatra, peasants faced less the mortal fear of physical punishment and torture in the present, and more the fear of future retribution if debts were not paid back on time. Historians have pointed to the dialectic between plantation cultivation and small-hold farming, as it emerged across much of the rim of the Bay of Bengal in this period.[62] The travel of the plantation complex did not flatten the customary land tenure systems of Asia, but rather it created new relationships between land, labor, capital, and international markets for commodities. The plantation complex oriented the heavily indebted small-hold rice farmers of Burma and Bengal, the tea pluckers in Assam, the Chinese indentured servants in Fiji, and the Afro-Caribbean laborers in Guyana, to what Du Bois called "a common destiny"—the destiny of working within the agro-economy of global colonial capitalism, and of resisting, contesting, and surviving against its political, economic, social, and epistemological assignments.[63]

During the high tide of liberalism, the forms of dispossession produced on a global scale by the plantation complex engendered a chain of political rebellions and resistance movements across the colonial world. In the aftermath of perhaps the greatest revolution of modern history, the Haitian Revolution of 1791, we observe converging rebellions in colonial plantation economies in distant parts of the world, such as the Virginia Slave Rebellion in 1831, the Jamaican Revolt of 1831–32, the Malê Revolt in Brazil in 1835, the Faraizi Movement (1820–1860s), the great sepoy-led uprising in India (1857), the Blue Mutiny in Bengal (1859), the Phulaguri Uprising in Assam (1861), the General Strike by enslaved people across the American South (1865), and the Morant Bay rebellion in Jamaica (1865). These revolutionary movements shared the aim of ending racial, colonial dispossession, and suggest the strange entanglements of distant people and their fugitive, improvised forms of radicalism.

1870s–1930s

The final phase discussed here spans the period from the 1870s to the 1930s. It witnessed the consolidation of the global racial agrarian regime under the sway of great multinational corporations. The multinationalization and financialization of plantations had a major consequence: the birth of what would come to be called the Third World, between latitudes just north of the Tropic of Cancer and latitudes just south of the Tropic of Capricorn.[64]

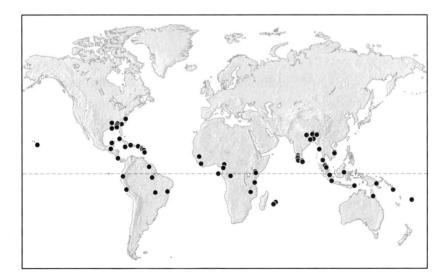

14.3 Major Sites of Capitalist Plantations, 1870s–1930s. Dots represent approximate regions of plantation production.

The plantation complex became increasingly interwoven in huge operations of monopoly capitalism with the facilitation of colonial governments. Indeed, as George Beckford shows in his classic work, *Persistent Poverty*, plantation-owning corporations became indistinguishable from colonial states by the turn of the twentieth century.[65] For example, Unilever Ltd., in many ways, *became* the state in the Solomon Islands, just as the United Fruit Company did in Honduras. The sugar giant Tate & Lyle Ltd. merged with the colonial state in Trinidad, just as Booker McConnell did in Guyana and Colonial Refining in Fiji. From the 1870s onward, we note a trend of agglomeration in plantation holdings worldwide. We might say that plantations became "Weberianized" in this period—subject to vast bureaucratization. This bureaucratization of the racial agrarian regime, which involved the emergence of new forms of governmentality, provides a proximate condition for the emergence of the Third World imagination. As Woodville Marshall observes, "A bureaucratically organized system [emerged] in which whole blocks of people [were] treated as units and [were] marched through a set of regimentation under the surveillance of the small supervisory staff."[66] Even as anticolonial activists were envisioning postcolonial nation-states in the early twentieth century, a cross-cutting Third World imagination was also on the rise—expressed in the writings of W. E. B Du Bois, or José Mariátegui, or Benoy Kumar Sarkar, or Mao Tse Tung, or Frantz Fanon, or Che Guevara. These gestures toward a political identity that cut across liberal nation-state lines represent the subjective recognition of a momentous objective transformation of geopolitics and global economy.

It is as if what the plantation complex of the mid-nineteenth century had sketched out in watercolor was now being concretized in ink through the spread of "bureaucratic rationality," and its middle managers, company executives, information gatherers, and record keepers. Here we see the historical shift taking place from the plantation complex to the Third World, which corresponded to a shift between different modes of resistance and conceptions of anticolonial struggle.

The biopolitical bureaucratized conventions of calculation and measurement did not diminish the coercive economy that operated on plantations but raised it to a higher gear. Take, for example, the role of big firms in Africa after the Berlin Conference in 1884–85. The establishment of new colonial boundaries on the African subcontinent was a joint affair of colonial states *and* multinational corporations. Plantations were rapidly established in Sub-Saharan African territories—in Togo, Namibia, in the Congo, Kenya, and Tanzania by the British, the Germans, the French, the Portuguese, and the Belgians. This led to the infamous forced labor system in the Belgian Congo and in German East Africa—where the Belgian and German governments commanded villages to grow cash crops and inflicted mortal punishments (most infamously, the cutting off of hands) when quotas were not met. In the Congo, in the advent of atrocities, Unilever had been granted the right to cultivate 74,000 hectares of land, about the size of New York City, in oil palms between 1911 and 1918. The violence of the colonial state cannot be separated from the drive for "raw material" commodity frontiers.[67] In German East Africa, the German East Africa Company not only owned the plantations but also had a controlling stake in almost every other sector of the colonial economy: local banks, retail agencies, and importantly, mining and timber firms. After multinationalization, primitive accumulation made a scalar upward shift, as big companies coordinated the extraction-to-exhaustion of wealth from many kinds of bodies—human, animal, botanical, geological. The Maji-Maji War of 1905 was as much a revolt against the totalizing logic of corporate extractivism as it was a revolt against the German colonial state.[68]

But again, multinationals became effectively indistinguishable from colonial states in the political ecologies of the plantation complex. In Guyana, 80 percent of arable land came to be owned by multinationals.[69] In Trinidad, sugar giant Tate & Lyle bought up all competing sugar plantations and became the sole sugar producer in the country by 1937. Similarly, in Assam, Malaya, Java, and Ceylon a massive corporatization of plantations was taking place.[70] Tetley Tea, Lipton's, Duncan's, and Brooke Bond emerged as the major corporations controlling thousands of acres of land across different colonies. By the time of the rubber bonanza of the 1890s, it was no longer hapless West Indian planter-refugees who established new agribusinesses, as had been the case in the 1840s. Now, corporate titans such as Goodyear, Firestone, Dunlop, and Michelin were involved in orchestrating the transfer of Brazilian rubber trees to Malaya and Vietnam and in hiring Indian *kanganies* and *maistries* (labor recruiters) to vacuum up, through violent means, the necessary number of Tamil and Bihari laborers from the countrysides.[71] The result was the expansion of the plantation complex at a mind-boggling rate: British Malaya went from having not a single *Hevea* rubber plant to producing more than 500,000 tons of rubber per year between 1900 and 1920.[72] If the construction of European territory was emerging through discourses of civil society and the welfare state, the construction of Third World territory emerged through discourses of resistance to compounding primitive accumulation and extractivism. And if postcolonial nation-states found themselves struggling to form stable civil societies once the colonizers formally left, this certainly had to do with the long legacy of extractive governmentality that had structured these political orders—and the fact that in many cases, even as the colonial governments fell, the multinationals remained. By the 1930s, 30 percent of all foreign investment in the world was made in the plantation sector, and that number grew in the 1950s.[73]

The implications were especially severe in the context of the extreme price instability for plantation commodities during the first half of the twentieth century. The severe disruptions of trade networks during World War I caused a spike in prices, followed by a precipitous crash in the early 1920s. This was soon followed by *the* Crash, as prices tumbled and remained low after the Great Depression. In the context of price instability and international turmoil, multinational firms and governments were making decisions together—the faint line between the two was ever-vanishing.[74]

The rise of multinational firms went along with a huge rise in demand for indentured labor. Hugh Tinker offers the classic comprehensive account of the indenture system, 1830–1922. His argument has a strong teleology, in which the system of indenture is "questioned," then "condemned," and finally "demolished."[75] This occludes the fact that the indenture system roared loudest in the years from 1870 to 1920. More Indians entered indenture in the decade from 1901 to 1910 than in the previous two decades combined. And more Chinese entered indenture in that decade than in the period from 1871 to 1900. In other words, the multinationalization of the plantations propelled the system of coerced labor, before its legal demise in 1922.[76] The work of Adam McKeown and Sunil Amrith shows that Asian migrations across Asia Pacific increased drastically all the way up to World War II, to places such as Malaya, Ceylon, Fiji, Hawaii, and Northern Australia.[77]

Plantation Commodities at the Heart of Empire

If European-centered markets came to depend on plantation products from the seventeenth through the twentieth centuries, plantations also possessed European societies in unsuspecting ways. Luxury goods, such as refined sugar, flavored tea, coffee, milk chocolate, and liquid soap, became necessities of daily life over the course of the nineteenth century.[78] The blood, sweat, and flesh of laboring and tortured black and brown bodies was crystallized in the form of tea, coffee, soap, and chocolate, ingested and consumed by metropolitan customers. By the late nineteenth century, Europeans used plantation commodities in ways that infiltrated all aspects of the quotidian: sugar for nutrition, cocoa for chocolate candy, fabrics and dyes for clothes, vegetable oils for soap. Without gutta-percha there could have been no telegraph wires; without rubber, no tires or bullets; without jute, no shipping sacks. Plantation inputs provided for the alimentary, clothing, and hygiene needs of the vast crowds of people pouring into European factory towns, as well as for the needs of the industrial machines. As Anne McClintock demonstrates in her study, to be a civilized and modern Victorian by the 1870s meant to consume the processed goods from plantation peripheries, and not just from local hinterlands. Civility was caught up in performances of the tasteful consumption of valuable materials rendered exchangeable across the racial and colonial line of difference. Most desirable were those refined goods purified of their "naked nature."[79]

By the late nineteenth century the extremely intimate relationship between metropolis and periphery wrought a global system of abstract exchangeability and led to the ghostly apparition of plantations in imperial centers. British corporations most involved in plantation production began establishing "model villages" in Britain, which aimed to be "total institutions" in ways that oddly evoked the logic of the plantation complex.[80] Cadbury's Bournville town (and chocolate factory), Rowntree's New Earswick settlement (also a chocolate factory), Unilever's Port Sunlight town (and soap factory), and Ripley Ville for cotton processing, all emerged as alter-forms of the plantation, organizing white laborers to refine and package plantation inputs for the market. Labor was organized in gangs (or shifts), supervised by overseers, and paid according to task-wages. Various forms of unwaging were also practiced. For example, the scrip system supplied a portion of workers' pay in the form of chits, instead of currency, which were only redeemable at the company store. The scrip system had long been honed on plantations across the Caribbean, Asia, and Latin America in the nineteenth century.[81] Seen from the opposite angle, in 1928, when Henry Ford embarked on his project to establish vast rubber plantations in "Fordlândia," on a concession from the Brazilian state of 3,900 square miles of land along the Amazon River (the equivalent of ten New York Cities), he transplanted the architecture, labor control regime, and managers from his Detroit company town to the new frontier. The project ended up a failure.[82] But by the 1930s, plantations and industrial factory enclaves were not only mirrors of each other—as they had been from the very start—but they were now increasingly owned and managed by the same multinational corporations. Even as the earth was being configured into a Global North and a Third World according to the logic of and resistance to racial colonial capitalism, the fetish of exchangeability was making specters of the Third World show up in the metropolis and specters of the Global North appear in the periphery.

The Dark and Vast Sea

By the 1890s, a world of plantations belted the Global South. Not just laboring bodies but vast ecologies had come under the sway of racial capitalism. The "sugar colonies" in the western hemisphere were matched by the "rubber colonies" in the eastern hemisphere; the iconic tea and coffee plantations of India and Ceylon counterpoised the iconic cotton plantations of the American South. The global history of plantations can be understood in terms of the material travel of the plantation complex after the collapse of the British and French slave economies in the 1830s, and as one of the afterlives of slavery.

The history of plantations sheds light on an emerging racial agrarian regime that developed over the course of the nineteenth century. The expansion of racial capitalism through the discourses of liberalism was reliant on the extension of the plantation complex across every continent on earth. The abstract, exchangeable, sovereign, and accounted financial form of money veiled the "off the books" profits and erased extractions of life-power from colonized and terrorized flesh, blood, and soil. Forced labor and dispossessed life were the conditions of possibility for the discourse of progress and industrial development in the Global North.[83] And the resistance to compounding forms of occupation and primitive accumulation, and to the governmentality of multinational firms, consolidated the discourse of the Third World in the twentieth century.

The high tide of liberalism was also a high-water mark of looting, plundering, extracting, and dispossessing within empire. In this period, primitive accumulation was at peak operation, driven by state-legislated changes to land tenure regimes, by military occupation, and by a conceptual project to think of Latin America, the Caribbean, Africa, and Asia as exchangeable terrains of resource extraction and waste reclamation. The Caribbean—that region which Jamaica Kincaid called the "Small Place"—actually served as the aperture through which a global process emerged. And this is not just because of its central position in the slave trade but also because of what happened when slavery officially ended.

Alongside the liberal universalism that developed with the wage, a fragmented, multipositional, global "public of strangers" emerged through the striations of the plantation complex.[84] This public of strangers carries the name of the Third World. For us to grasp the meaning of global history, in a way that redistributes our historical consciousness and understanding, we need to find new ways to conceive that Third World undercommons, not so as to impose false uniformity, but so as to glimpse, behind the veil of liberalism, the historical relations of those different groups who comprised the dark and vast sea.

Notes

1. Sven Beckert, *Empire of Cotton: A Global History* (New York: Knopf, 2015), 274–311.
2. House of Commons. *Hill Coolies, British Guiana. Correspondence Relative to the Condition of the Hill Coolies and Other Labourers Introduced into British Guiana* (London: 1839).
3. John Scoble, *Hill Coolies: A Brief Exposition of the Deplorable Condition of the Hill Coolies in British Guiana and Mauritius, and of the Nefarious Means by Which They Were Induced to Resort to These Colonies* (London, 1840), 12.
4. John Gladstone consulted with the 1836–37 Select Parliamentary Committee on Negro Apprenticeship, and the 1840 Parliamentary Committee on East India Produce. Other compensated slave owners from the Caribbean served on the Select Committee on Transportation (1838), the Select Committee on Sugar and Coffee Planting (1846–48), and the 1847 Committee on Commercial Relations with China. As noted earlier, John Gladstone's son, William, was already a high-ranking member of the Colonial Office in the 1830s, and went on to become the prime minister of Britain.

5. Lloyd Best and Kari Polanyi Levitt, *Essays on the Theory of Plantation Economy: A Historical and Institutional Approach to Caribbean Economic Development* (Jamaica: University of the West Indies Press, 2009); George L. Beckford, *Persistent Poverty: Underdevelopment in Plantation Economies of the Third World* (New York: Oxford University Press, 1972); Philip D. Curtin, *The Rise and Fall of the Plantation Complex: Essays in Atlantic History* (Cambridge: Cambridge University Press, 1990); Dale W. Tomich, *Through the Prism of Slavery: Labor, Capital, and World Economy* (Lanham, Md.: Rowman and Littlefield, 2004); Sidney Mintz, *Sweetness and Power: The Place of Sugar in Modern History* (New York: Viking, 1985), 19–73; Shu-mei Shih, "Comparison and Relation," in *Comparison: Theories, Approaches, Uses*, ed. Rita Felski and Susan Stanford Friedman (Baltimore, Md.: Johns Hopkins University Press, 2013), 79–98.

6. Rebecca J. Scott and Jean M. Hébrar, *Freedom Papers: An Atlantic Odyssey in the Age of Emancipation* (Cambridge, Mass.: Harvard University Press, 2012); David P. Geggus, ed., *The Impact of the Haitian Revolution in the Atlantic World* (Columbia: University of South Carolina Press, 2001).

7. Matthew Pratt Guterl, *American Mediterranean: Southern Slaveholders in the Age of Emancipation* (Cambridge, Mass.: Harvard University Press, 2008), 4.

8. Walter Johnson, *River of Dark Dreams: Slavery and Empire in the Cotton Kingdom* (Cambridge, Mass.: Belknap Press of Harvard University Press, 2013), 303–29.

9. Karl Marx, *Grundrisse: Foundations of the Critique of Political Economy* (New York: Vintage Books, 1973), 142, 274–75.

10. See W. E. B. Du Bois, *Black Reconstruction in America, 1860–1880* (New York: Free Press, 1998), 55, 670–710; as well as Eric Foner, *Reconstruction: America's Unfinished Revolution, 1863–1877* (New York: Harper and Row, 1988); Pete Daniel, *The Shadow of Slavery: Peonage in the South, 1901–1969* (Urbana: University of Illinois Press, 1972); Sarah Haley, *No Mercy Here: Gender, Punishment, and the Making of Jim Crow Modernity* (Chapel Hill: University of North Carolina Press, 2016). See also Avery Gordon's profound reflections in *Ghostly Matters: Haunting and the Sociological Imagination* (London: University of Minnesota Press, 1997).

11. Eric Williams, *Capitalism & Slavery* (Chapel Hill: University of North Carolina Press, 1944), 136, 169. See Seymour Drescher's polemic against the William thesis in *Econocide: British Slavery in the Era of Abolition* (Pittsburgh: University of Pittsburgh Press, 1977). See Hugh Tinker, *A New System of Slavery: The Export of Indian Labour Overseas, 1830–1920* (London: Hansib, 1993); Douglas A. Blackmon, *Slavery by Another Name: The Re-Enslavement of Black Americans from the Civil War to World War II* (New York: Doubleday, 2008).

12. Cedric J. Robinson, *Black Marxism: The Making of the Black Radical Tradition* (London: Zed, 1983), 1–29.

13. Tomich, *Through the Prism of Slavery*, 3–31; Kalyan Sanyal, *Rethinking Capitalist Development: Primitive Accumulation, Governmentality, and Post-Colonial Capitalism* (London: Routledge, 2007); Tinker, *A New System of Slavery*; Ann Laura Stoler, *Capitalism and Confrontation in Sumatra's Plantation Belt, 1870–1979* (New Haven, Conn.: Yale University Press, 1985).

14. Du Bois, *Black Reconstruction*, 15. This discussion of force is inspired by the writings of Sylvia Wynter, Issa Shivji, Kalyan Sanyal, Neferti Tadiar, and Douglas Hall. While, for lack of space, I do not go into a detailed discussion of their work here, I want to note some of their important conceptual contributions to the study of colonial capitalism. Sylvia Wynter's conception of "selection" and "dysselection," and the exclusive political

and racial-colonial category of "the human," continues to be a fundamental anchor in my interest in plantation histories. See Wynter, "Unsettling the Coloniality of Being/Power/Truth/Freedom: Towards the Human, after Man, Its Overrepresentation—An Argument," *New Centennial Review* 3, no. 3 (Fall 2003): 257–337. Issa G. Shivji's discussion of "disarticulated capitalism" in *Accumulation in the African Periphery: A Theoretical Framework* (Oxford: African Book Collective, 2009), 18–54, provides an indispensable genealogical study of different Marxian approaches to articulating the blind spot of Marx's own analysis when it comes to function of imperial power within capitalism.

15. P. P. Courtenay, *Plantation Agriculture* (New York: Praeger, 1966), 25.

16. Courtenay, *Plantation Agriculture*, 23.

17. Mintz, *Sweetness and Power*, 43.

18. Dale W. Tomich, *Slavery in the Circuit of Sugar* (Baltimore, Md.: Johns Hopkins, 1990), 14–32.

19. Curtin, *The Rise and Fall of the Plantation Complex*, 175.

20. C. L. R. James, *The Black Jacobins: Toussaint L'Ouverture and the San Domingo Revolution* (New York: Vintage Books, 1963 [1938]), ix.

21. Tomich, *Through the Prism of Slavery*, 75–94; Leida Fernández Prieto, "Islands of Knowledge: Science and Agriculture in the History of Latin America and the Caribbean," *Isis* 104, no. 4 (2013): 788–97; Ulbe Bosma, "Het Cultuurstelsel En Zijn Buitenlandse Ondernemers [The Dutch State Cultivation System and Its Global Entrepreneurs]," *Tijdschrift voor Sociale en Economische Geschiedenis* 2, no. 2 (2005): 3–28.; Fernando Ortiz, *Cuban Counterpoint* (New York: Knopf, 1947), 262–67.

22. Richard Drayton, *Nature's Government: Science, Imperial Britain, and the "Improvement" of the World* (New Haven, Conn.: Yale University Press, 2000); James McClellan, *Colonialism and Science: Saint-Domingue and the Old Regime* (Baltimore, Md.: Johns Hopkins University Press, 1992), 159; Richard Grove, *Green Imperialism: Colonial Expansion, Tropical Island Edens and the Origins of Environmentalism 1600–1860* (Cambridge: Cambridge University Press, 1995); Lucile Brockway, *Science and Colonial Expansion: The Role of the British Royal Botanic Gardens* (New York: Academic, 1979); Best and Levitt, *Essays on the Theory of Plantation Economy*, 20.

23. Thomas D. Rogers, *The Deepest Wounds: A Labor and Environmental History of Sugar in Northeast Brazil* (Chapel Hill: University of North Carolina Press, 2010), 38; Reinaldo Funes Monzote, *From Rainforest to Cane Field in Cuba: An Environmental History since 1492* (Chapel Hill: University of North Carolina, 2008), 128; B. W. Higman, *Plantation Jamaica 1750–1850: Capital and Control in a Colonial Economy* (Kingston, Jamaica: University of West Indies Press, 2008), 176. Cuba was the largest sugar producer in the world by the 1820s. In the 1820s and 1830s Cuban sugar production represented 13 to 20 percent of world production. Between 1850 and 1870, it was never less than 24 percent. Laird Bergad, "The Economic Viability of Sugar Production Based on Slave Labor in Cuba, 1859–1878," *Latin American Research Review* 24, no. 1 (1989): 112.

24. Stuart Schwartz, *Sugar Plantations in the Formation of Brazilian Society: Bahia, 1550–1835* (Cambridge: Cambridge University Press, 1985); Fernando Ortiz, *Cuban Counterpoint: Tobacco and Sugar*, trans. Harriet de Onís (Durham, N.C.: Duke University Press, 1995).

25. Johnson, *River of Dark Dreams*, 126; Beckert, *Empire of Cotton*, 136–74.

26. K. L. Tuteja, "American Planters and the Cotton Improvement Programme in Bombay Presidency in the Nineteenth Century," *Indian Journal of American Studies* 28, no. 1 and 2 (1998): 103–8; Tarasankar Banerjee, "American Cotton Experiments in India and the American Civil War," *Journal of Indian History* 37 (1969): 425–32.

27. Christopher M. Florio, "From Poverty to Slavery: Abolitionists, Overseers, and the Global Struggle for Labor in India," *Journal of American History* 102, no. 4 (March 2016): 1005–24. On Alvaro Reynoso's reception, see Ulbe Bosma and Jonathan Curry-Machado, "Two Islands, One Commodity: Cuba, Java, and the Global Sugar Trade (1790–1930)," *New West Indian Guide* 86, no. 3–4 (2012): 245.

28. C. A. Bayly, *Imperial Meridian: The British Empire and the World, 1780–1830* (London: Longman, 1989), 100–132.

29. Patrick Neveling, "A Periodisation of Globalisation According to the Mauritian Integration into the International Sugar Commodity Chain (1825–2005)," in *Global Histories, Imperial Commodities, Local Interactions*, ed. Jonathan Curry-Machado (London: Palgrave Macmillan, 2013), 121–42.

30. Patrick Neveling, "A Periodisation of Globalisation," 126.

31. Ibid.

32. Nicholas Draper, "Helping to Make Britain Great: The Commercial Legacies of Slave-ownership in Britain," in *Legacies of British Slave-Ownership: Colonial Slavery and the Formation of Victorian Britain*, ed. Catherine Hall et al. (Cambridge: Cambridge University Press, 2014), 93; Kumari Jayawardena and Rachel Kurian, *Class, Patriarchy and Ethnicity on Sri Lankan Plantations* (Hyderabad: Orient BlackSwan, 2015), 25.

33. Tony Webster, "An Early Global Business in a Colonial Context: The Strategies, Management, and Failure of John Palmer and Company of Calcutta, 1780–1830," *Enterprise & Society* 6, no. 1 (2005): 98–133.

34. Marjory Harper, *Adventures and Exiles: The Great Scottish Exodus* (London: Profile, 2003), 286–87n74.

35. Stephanie Jones, *Merchants of the Raj: British Managing Agency Houses in Calcutta Yesterday and Today* (Basingstoke, UK: Macmillan, 1992), 5–7.

36. Joseph E. Inikori, *Africans and the Industrial Revolution in England: A Study in International Trade and Development* (Cambridge: Cambridge University Press, 2002).

37. Johnson, *River of Dark Dreams*, 176.

38. Prakash Kumar, *Indigo Plantations and Science in Colonial India* (Cambridge: Cambridge University Press, 2012), 65.

39. Elias Monnereau, *The Complete Indigo-Maker* (London, 1769 [1736]), 48.

40. Ibid., 49, 50.

41. Ibid., 61.

42. Pierre-Joseph Laborie, *The Coffee Planter of Saint Domingo* (London: T. Cadell and W. Davies, 1798), 159.

43. Patrick Peebles, *The Plantation Tamils of Ceylon* (New York: Leicester University Press, 2001), 55.

44. Leonard Wray, *The Practical Sugar Planter: A Complete Account of the Cultivation and Manufacture of the Sugar-cane* (London: Smith, Elder & Co., 1848), 82.

45. Ibid.

46. See Jeffrey Williamson, *Trade and Poverty: When the Third World Fell Behind* (Cambridge, Mass.: MIT Press, 2011); see the Sauerbeck price index for this period provided in Jan Tore Klovland, "Zooming in on Sauerbeck: Monthly Wholesale Prices in Britain 1845–1890," *Explorations in Economic History* 30, no. 2 (April 1993): 195–228.

47. Wolfgang Schivelbusch, *Tastes of Paradise: A Social History of Spices, Stimulants, and Intoxicants* (New York: Pantheon, 1992), 194–203; Anne McClintock, *Imperial Leather: Race, Gender and Sexuality in the Colonial Contest* (London: Routledge, 1995), 207–31.

48. Harriet Friedmann, "World Market, State, and Family Farm: Social Bases of Household Production in the Era of Wage Labor," *Comparative Studies in Society and History* 20,

no. 4 (1978): 545–86; Jason W. Moore, *Capitalism in the Web of Life: Ecology and the Accumulation of Capital* (London: Verso, 2015).

49. Courtenay, *Plantation Agriculture,* 64; Vibha Arora, "Routeing the Commodities of the Empire through Sikkim (1817–1906)" in Curry-Machado, *Global Histories, Imperial Commodities*, 21.

50. Noel J. Kent, *Hawaii: Islands under the Influence* (New York: Monthly Review, 1983), 31.

51. William Cronon, *Nature's Metropolis: Chicago and the Great West* (New York: W. W. Norton, 1991), 263–309; Emily Lambert, *The Futures: The Rise of the Speculator and the Origins of the World's Biggest Markets* (New York: Basic Books, 2011).

52. Alfred Chandler, *The Visible Hand: The Managerial Revolution in American Business* (Cambridge, Mass.: Belknap Press of Harvard University Press, 1977), 79.

53. Tinker, *A New System of Slavery.*

54. Lisa Lowe, *Intimacies of Four Continents* (Durham, N.C.: Duke University Press, 2015), 101–34; Walton Look Lai, *Indentured Labor, Caribbean Sugar: Chinese and Indian Migrants to the British West Indies, 1838–1919* (Baltimore, Md.: Johns Hopkins University Press, 1993); Tinker, *A New System of Slavery.*

55. Prabhu Mohapatra, "The Hosay Massacre of 1884: Class and Community among Indian Immigrant Labourers in Trinidad," in *Work and Social Change in Asia: Essays in Honour of Jan Breman*, ed. Arvind Das and Marcel Van der Linden (Delhi: Manohar, 2003), 187–230; Madhavi Kale, *Fragments of Empire: Capital, Slavery, and Indian Indentured Labor Migration in the British Caribbean* (Philadelphia: University of Pennsylvania Press, 1998).

56. R. E. Elson, *Village Java under the Cultivation System* (Sydney: Asian Studies Association, 1994), xix; Bosma and Curry-Machado, "Two Islands, One Commodity.

57. Andrew Liu, *The Two Tea Countries: Competition, Labor, and Economic Thought in Coastal China and Eastern India, 1834–1942* (PhD diss., Columbia University, 2015), 54–58.

58. Amalendu Guha, *Planter-Raj to Swaraj: Freedom Struggle and Electoral Politics in Assam 1826–1947* (Delhi: People's Publishing House, 1977), 15; Peebles, *The Plantation Tamils of Ceylon.*

59. Piet Konings, *Gender and Class in the Tea Estates of Cameroon* (Leiden: African Studies Centre, 1995).

60. Mahesh Rangarajan, *Fencing the Forest: Conservation and Ecological Change in India's Central Provinces, 1860–1914* (New York: Oxford University Press, 1996), 95–137.

61. Sunil Kumar Sen, *Peasant Movements in India: Mid-Nineteenth and Twentieth Centuries* (Calcutta: K. P. Bagchi, 1982); Sugata Bose, *Agrarian Bengal: Economy, Social Structure and Politics, 1919–1947* (Cambridge: Cambridge University Press, 1986), 34–69.

62. Bose, *Agrarian Bengal*; Clifford Geertz, *Agricultural Involution: The Process of Ecological Change in Indonesia* (Berkeley: University of California Press, 1963).

63. W. E. B. Du Bois, *Black Reconstruction*, 15.

64. Walter Rodney, *A History of the Guyanese Working People, 1881–1905* (Baltimore, Md.: Johns Hopkins University Press, 1982). See Issa Shivji on financialization, *Accumulation in the African Periphery*, 30; see Kari Polanyi Levitt on financialization, *From the Great Transformation to the Great Financialization: On Karl Polanyi and Other Essays* (New York: Fernwood, 2013).

65. Beckford, *Persistent Poverty*, 114–53.

66. W. K. Marshall, "Social and Economic Problems in the Windward Island, 1838–65," in *Caribbean Integration: Papers on Social, Political, and Economic Integration*, ed. S. Lewis and T. G. Mathews (Río Piedras: University of Puerto Rico, 1967), 240.

67. Adam Hochschild, *King Leopold's Ghost* (Boston: Houghton Mifflin, 1998); Jules Marchal, *Lord Leverhulme's Ghosts: Colonial Exploitation in the Congo*, trans. Martin Thom (London: Verso, 2008).
68. Rene Loewenson, *Modern Plantation Agriculture: Corporate Wealth and Labor Squalor* (London: Zed Books, 1992), 5–10.
69. Clive Y. Thomas, *Plantations, Peasants, and State: A Study of the Mode of Sugar Production in Guyana* (Jamaica: Center for Afro-American Studies, 1984), 18.
70. Stoler, *Capitalism and Confrontation*, 16.
71. See Rana Behal, *One Hundred Years of Servitude: Political Economy of Tea Plantations in Colonial Assam* (New Delhi: Tulika Books, 2014), 187–251.
72. Courtenay, *Plantation Agriculture*, 115.
73. Ibid., 59.
74. Karl Polanyi, *The Great Transformation* (New York: Farrar & Rinehart, 1944), 20–30.
75. Tinker, *A New System of Slavery*.
76. David Northrup, *Indentured Labor in the Age of Imperialism, 1834–1922* (Cambridge: Cambridge University Press, 1995), 156.
77. See Adam McKeown, *Melancholy Order: Asian Migration and the Globalization of Borders* (New York: Columbia University Press, 2008), 60; Sunil S. Amrith, *Crossing the Bay of Bengal: The Furies of Nature and the Fortunes of Migrants* (Cambridge, Mass.: Harvard University Press, 2015).
78. Eric Hobsbawm, *The Age of Empire: 1875–1914* (New York: Pantheon Books, 1987), 64–65; McClintock, *Imperial Leather*.
79. See Victorian travel writer Grant Allen on the value of travel in the tropics, "Tropical Education," in *Science in Arcady* (London: 1892), 21–39.
80. Best and Levitt, *Essays on the Theory of Plantation Economy*, 41; Erving Goffman, *Asylums: Essays on the Social Situation of Mental Patients and Other Inmates* (Garden City, N.Y.: Anchor Books, 1961), 19–39.
81. Vincent C. Peloso, *Peasants on Plantations: Subaltern Strategies of Labor and Resistance in the Pisco Valley, Peru* (Durham, N.C.: Duke University Press, 1999), 44–46; Ronald Takaki, *Raising Cane: The World of Plantation Hawaii* (New York: Chelsea House, 1989).
82. Greg Grandin, *Empire's Workshop: Latin America, the United States, and the Rise of the New Imperialism* (New York: Metropolitan Books, 2006).
83. See Best and Levitt, *Essays on the Theory of Plantation Economy*, 54–56; Christopher Taylor's excellent discussion of the "incalculability" of plantation production, in "The Refusal to Work: From the Postemancipation Caribbean to Post-Fordist Empire," *Small Axe* 44 (2014): 1–17, which draws on the classic works of Douglas Hall "Incalculability as a Feature of Sugar Producing during the Eighteenth Century," *Social and Economic Studies* 10, no. 3 (September 1961): 340–52
84. Fred Moten and Stefano Harney, *The Undercommons: Fugitive Planning and Black Study* (Wivenhoe, UK: Minor Compositions, 2013), 61.

SELECTED BIBLIOGRAPHY

The following works have significantly informed the studies in this volume. The list is incomplete, but may provide a starting point for interested readers.

Adams, Sean P. *Old Dominion, Industrial Commonwealth: Coal, Politics, and Economy in Antebellum America*. Baltimore, Md.: Johns Hopkins University Press, 2004.

Akerlof, George, and Rachel Kranton. *Identity Economics: How Our Identities Shape Our Work, Wages, and Well-Being*. Princeton, N.J.: Princeton University Press, 2010.

Akerlof, George, and Robert Shiller. *Animal Spirits: How Human Psychology Drives the Economy and Why It Matters for Global Capitalism*. Princeton, N.J.: Princeton University Press, 2010.

Amadae, Sonja M. *Rationalizing Capitalist Democracy: The Cold War Origins of Rational Choice Liberalism*. Chicago: University of Chicago Press, 2003.

Amar, Akhil Reed. "Women and the Constitution." *Harvard Journal of Law and Public Policy* 18, no. 2 (1995): 465–73.

Amott, Teresa, and Julie A. Matthaei. *Race Gender and Work: A Multicultural Economic History of Women in the United States*. Boston: South End Press, 1991.

Appleby, Joyce Oldham. *Capitalism and a New Social Order: The Republican Vision of the 1790s*. New York: New York University Press, 1984.

Bailey, Ronald. "The Slave(ry) Trade and the Development of Capitalism in the United States: The Textile Industry in New England." *Social Science History* 14, no. 3 (Autumn 1990): 373–414.

Bailyn, Bernard. *The New England Merchants in the Seventeenth Century*. Cambridge, Mass.: Harvard University Press, 1955.

Balkin, Jack M. "Commerce." *Michigan Law Review* 109, no. 1 (October 2010): 1–51.

Balkin, Jack M., and Sanford Levinson. "The Dangerous Thirteenth Amendment." *Columbia Law Review* 112, no. 7 (November 2012): 1459–99.

Balleisen, Edward J. *Navigating Failure: Bankruptcy and Commercial Society in Antebellum America*. Chapel Hill: University of North Carolina Press, 2001.

Balogh, Brian. *Chain Reaction: Expert Debate and Public Participation in American Commercial Nuclear Power, 1945–1975*. Cambridge: Cambridge University Press, 1991.

Beard, Charles Austin. *An Economic Interpretation of the Constitution of the United States*. New York: Free Press, 1986.

Beckert, Jens. *Imagined Futures: Fictional Expectations and Capitalism Dynamics*. Cambridge, Mass.: Harvard University Press, 2016.

Beckert, Jens, and Patrik Aspers. *The Worth of Goods: Valuation and Pricing in the Economy*. New York: Oxford University Press, 2011.

Beckert, Sven. *Empire of Cotton: A Global History*. New York: Knopf, 2015.

——. *Monied Metropolis: New York and the Formation of the American Bourgeoisie, 1850–1896*. Cambridge: Cambridge University Press, 2001.

Beckford, George L. *Persistent Poverty: Underdevelopment in Plantation Economies of the Third World*. New York: Oxford University Press, 1972.

Beisner, Robert L., and Joan R. Challinor, eds. *Arms at Rest: Peacemaking and Peacekeeping in American History*. New York: Greenwood, 1987.

Bender, Thomas. *A Nation Among Nations: America's Place in World History*. New York: Hill and Wang, 2006.

——. *Toward an Urban Vision: Ideas and Institutions in Nineteenth-Century America*. Lexington: University Press of Kentucky, 1975.

Benedict, Michael. *The Blessings of Liberty: A Concise History of the Constitution of the United States*. Boston: Wadsworth, 2006.

——. *A Compromise of Principle: Congressional Republicans and Reconstruction, 1863–1869*. New York: W. W. Norton, 1974.

Benhabib, Seyla. *Dignity in Adversity: Human Rights in Troubled Times*. Cambridge: Polity, 2011.

Bensel, Richard Franklin. *The Political Economy of American Industrialization, 1877–1900*. Cambridge: Cambridge University Press, 2000.

——. *Yankee Leviathan: The Origins of Central State Authority in America, 1859–1877*. Cambridge: Cambridge University Press, 1990.

Berk, Gerald. *Alternative Tracks: The Constitution of American Industrial Order, 1865–1917*. Baltimore, Md.: Johns Hopkins University Press, 1994.

Berlin, Ira. *Many Thousands Gone: The First Two Centuries of Slavery in North America*. Cambridge, Mass.: Belknap Press of Harvard University Press, 1998.

Bernstein, Michael A. *A Perilous Progress: Economists and Public Purpose in Twentieth-Century America*. Princeton, N.J.: Princeton University Press, 2001.

Bértola, Luis, and José Antonio Ocampo. *The Economic Development of Latin America since Independence*. Oxford: Oxford University Press, 2012.

Blackburn, Robin. *An Unfinished Revolution: Karl Marx and Abraham Lincoln*. New York: Verso, 2011.

Blaszczyk, Regina Lee. *Imagining Consumers: Design and Innovation from Wedgwood to Corning*. Baltimore, Md.: Johns Hopkins University Press, 2002.

Blewett, Mary. *Men, Women and Work: Class, Gender and Protest in the New England Shoe Industry, 1780–1910*. Urbana: University of Illinois Press, 1988.

Blyth, Mark. *Austerity: The History of a Dangerous Idea*. New York: Oxford University Press, 2013.

Bourdieu, Pierre. *Distinction: A Social Critique of the Judgment of Taste*. London: Routledge, 1986.

Bouton, Terry. *Taming Democracy: "The People," the Founders, and the Troubled Ending of the American Revolution*. Oxford: Oxford University Press, 2007.

Boydston, Jeanne. *Home and Work: Housework, Wages, and the Ideology of Labor in the Early Republic*. Oxford: Oxford University Press, 1994.

Breen, T. H. *The Marketplace of Revolution: How Consumer Politics Shaped American Independence*. New York: Oxford University Press, 2004.

Brick, Harold. *Transcending Capitalism: Visions of a New Society in Modern American Thought*. Ithaca, N.Y.: Cornell University Press, 2006.

Brown, Roger H. *Redeeming the Republic: Federalists, Taxation, and the Origins of the Constitution*. Baltimore, Md.: Johns Hopkins University Press, 1993.

Brownlee, W. Elliot. "Economists and the Formation of the Modern Tax System in the United States: The World War I Crisis." In *The State and Economic Knowledge: The American and British Experiences*, ed. Mary O. Furner and Barry Supple, 401–35. Cambridge: Cambridge University Press, 1990.

Brunsman, Denver. *The Evil Necessity: British Naval Impressment in the Eighteenth-Century Atlantic World*. Charlottesville: University of Virginia Press, 2013.

Buck-Morss, Susan. "Envisioning Capital: Political Economy on Display." *Critical Inquiry* 21, no. 2 (1995): 434–67.

Callon, Michel, ed. *The Laws of the Markets*. Oxford: Blackwell, 1998.

——. "Some Elements of a Sociology of Translation: Domestication of the Scallops and Fishermen of St. Brieuc Bay." In *Science Studies Reader*, ed. Mario Biagioli, 67–83. New York: Routledge, 1999.

Carney Judith A. *Black Rice: The African Origins of Rice Cultivation in the Americas*. Cambridge, Mass.: Harvard University Press, 2001.

Carpenter, Daniel. *The Forging of Bureaucratic Autonomy: Reputations, Networks, and Policy Innovation in Executive Agencies, 1862–1928*. Princeton, N.J.: Princeton University Press, 2001.

Cassidy, John. *How Markets Fail: The Logic of Economic Calamities*. New York: Farrar, Straus, and Giroux, 2009.

Cattelino, Jessica. *High Stakes: Florida Seminole Gaming and Sovereignty*. Durham, N.C.: Duke University Press, 2008.

Chakrabarty, Dipesh. *Provincializing Europe: Postcolonial Thought and Historical Difference*. Princeton Studies in Culture/Power/History. Princeton, N.J.: Princeton University Press, 2000.

Chakravartty, Paula, and Ferreira da Silva, Denise. "Accumulation, Dispossession, and Debt: The Racial Logic of Global Capitalism—An Introduction." *American Quarterly* 64, no. 3 (2012): 361–85.

Chandler, Alfred D. *Strategy and Structure: Chapters in the History of the Industrial Enterprise*. Cambridge, Mass.: MIT Press, 1962.

——. *Visible Hand: The Managerial Revolution in American Business*. Cambridge, Mass.: Belknap Press of Harvard University Press, 1977.

Chernow, Ron. *Titan: The Life of John D. Rockefeller, Sr.* New York: Random House, 1998.

Clark, Christopher. *The Roots of Rural Capitalism: Western Massachusetts, 1780–1860*. Ithaca, N.Y.: Cornell University Press, 1992.

Clarke, Sally. *Trust and Power: Consumers, the Modern Corporation, and the Making of the United States Automobile Market*. Cambridge: Cambridge University Press, 2007.

Clark-Pujara, Christy. *Dark Work: The Business of Slavery in Rhode Island*. New York: New York University Press, 2016.

Clegg, John J. "Capitalism and Slavery." *Critical Historical Studies* 2, no. 2 (2015): 281–304.

Cochran, Thomas. *Frontiers of Change: Early Industrialism in America*. New York: Oxford University Press, 1981.

Coclanis, Peter A. "The Audacity of Hope: Economic History Today." *Perspectives on History* 48, no. 1 (January 2010): 21–25.

——. "Distant Thunder: The Creation of a World Market in Rice and the Transformations It Wrought." *American Historical Review* 98, no. 4 (October 1993): 1050–78.

——. "How the Low Country Was Taken to Task: Slave-Labor Organization in Coastal South Carolina and Georgia." In *Slavery Secession, and Southern History*, ed. Robert Louis Paquette and Louis Ferleger, 59–78. Charlottesville: University Press of Virginia, 2000.

——. *The Shadow of a Dream: Economic Life and Death in the South Carolina Low Country, 1670–1920*. New York: Oxford University Press, 1989.

——. "White Rice: The Midwestern Origins of the Modern Rice Industry in the United States." In *Rice: Global Networks and New Histories*, ed. Francesca Bray, Peter A. Coclanis, Edda Fields-Black, and Dagmar Schäfer, 291–317. New York: Cambridge University Press, 2015.

Coffman, D'Maris. *Questioning Credible Commitment: Perspectives on the Rise of Financial Capitalism*. Cambridge: Cambridge University Press, 2013.

Cohen, Lizbeth. *A Consumer's Republic: The Politics of Mass Consumption in Postwar America*. New York: Knopf, 2003.

——. *Making a New Deal: Industrial Workers in Chicago, 1919–1939*. New York: Cambridge University Press, 1990.

Connolly, Nathan. *A World More Concrete: Real Estate and the Remaking of Jim Crow South Florida*. Chicago: University of Chicago Press, 2014.

Cook, Eli. *The Pricing of Progress: Economic Indicators and the Capitalization of American Life*. Cambridge, Mass.: Harvard University Press, 2017.

Cooper, Carolyn C. *Shaping Invention: Thomas Blanchard's Machinery and Patent Management in Nineteenth-Century America*. New York: Columbia University Press, 1991.

Cowie, Jefferson. *Capital Moves: RCA's Seventy-Year Quest for Cheap Labor*. Ithaca, N.Y.: Cornell University Press, 1999.

Cronon, William. *Nature's Metropolis: Chicago and the Great West*. New York: W. W. Norton, 1991.

Crowley, John E. *The Privileges of Independence: Neomercantilism and the American Revolution*. Baltimore, Md.: Johns Hopkins University Press, 1993.

Currarino, Rosanne. *The Labor Question in America: Economic Democracy in the Gilded Age*. Urbana: University of Illinois Press, 2011.

Curtin, Philip D. *The Rise and Fall of the Plantation Complex: Essays in Atlantic History*. Cambridge: Cambridge University Press, 1990.

Curtis, Christopher Michael. *Jefferson's Freeholders and the Politics of Ownership in the Old Dominion*. Cambridge: Cambridge University Press, 2012.

Cutterham, Tom. "Is the History of Capitalism the History of Everything?" *The Junto* (blog). https://earlyamericanists.com/2014/09/02/is-the-history-of-capitalism-the-history-of-everything/.

Davis, Gerald F. *Managed by the Markets: How Finance Re-Shaped America*. New York: Oxford, 2011.

De Goede, Marieke. *Virtue, Fortune, and Faith: A Genealogy of Finance*. Minneapolis: University of Minnesota Press, 2005.

Desan, Christine. *Making Money: Coin, Currency, and the Coming of Capitalism*. Oxford: Oxford University Press, 2015.

——. "The Market as a Matter of Money: Denaturalizing Economic Currency in American Constitutional History." *Law & Social Inquiry* 30, no. 1 (Winter 2005): 1–60.

De Soto, Hernando. *The Mystery of Capital: Why Capitalism Triumphs in the West and Fails Everywhere Else.* New York: Basic Books, 2000.

Dew, Thomas Roderick. *Review of the Debate in the Virginia Legislature of 1831 and 1832.* Richmond, Va., 1832.

Donohue, Kathleen G. *Freedom from Want: American Liberalism and the Idea of the Consumer.* Baltimore, Md.: Johns Hopkins University Press, 2003.

Downey, Tom. *Planting a Capitalist South: Masters, Merchants, and Manufacturers in the Southern Interior, 1790-1860.* Baton Rouge: Louisiana State University Press, 2006.

Du Bois, W. E. B. *Black Reconstruction in America.* 1935. Reprint, New York: Free Press 1998.

Dunlavy, Colleen A. *Politics and Industrialization: Early Railroads in the United States and Prussia.* Princeton, N.J.: Princeton University Press, 1994.

Edling, Max M. *A Revolution in Favor of Government: Origins of the U.S. Constitution and the Making of the American State.* New York: Oxford University Press, 2003.

Edwards, Laura F. "Textiles: Popular Culture and the Law." *Buffalo Law Review* 64, no. 1 (January 2016): 193-214.

Einhorn, Robin L. *American Taxation, American Slavery.* Chicago: University of Chicago Press, 2006.

Eltis, David, Philip D. Morgan, and David Richardson. "Agency and Diaspora in Atlantic History: Reassessing the African Contribution to Rice Cultivation in the Americas." *American Historical Review* 112, no. 5 (December 2007): 1329-58.

Engerman, Stanley L., and Robert E. Gallman. *The Cambridge Economic History of the United States.* Cambridge: Cambridge University Press, 2008. http://universitypublishing online.org/cambridge/histories/subject_title_list.jsf?seriesCode=CEHU&heading=Ca mbridge+Economic+History+of+the+United+States&tSort=title+closed&aSort =author+default_list&ySort=year+default_list.

Enyeart, John P. *The Quest for "Just and Pure Law": Rocky Mountain Workers and American Social Democracy, 1870-1924.* Stanford, Calif.: Stanford University Press, 2009.

Evans, Chris. "The Plantation Hoe: The Rise and Fall of an Atlantic Commodity, 1650-1850." *William and Mary Quarterly* 69, no. 1 (January 2012): 71-100.

Ferguson, E. James. *The Power of the Purse: A History of American Public Finance, 1776-1790.* Chapel Hill: University of North Carolina Press, 1961.

Findlay, Ronald, and Kevin H. O'Rourke. *Power and Plenty: Trade, War, and the World Economy in the Second Millennium.* Princeton, N.J.: Princeton University Press, 2007.

Fink, Leon. *The Maya of Morganton: Work and Community in the Nuevo New South.* Chapel Hill: University of North Carolina Press, 2003.

Fisher, Irving. *The Nature of Capital and Income.* New York: Macmillan, 1906.

Fogel, Robert. *Without Consent or Contract: The Rise and Fall of American Slavery.* New York: W. W. Norton, 1989.

Fogel, Robert William, and Stanley Engerman. *Time on the Cross: The Economics of American Negro Slavery.* Toronto: Little, Brown, 1974.

Foley, Neil. *The White Scourge: Mexicans, Blacks, and Poor Whites in Texas Cotton Culture.* Berkeley: University of California Press, 1997.

Foner, Eric. *Reconstruction: America's Unfinished Revolution 1863-1877.* New York: Harper and Row, 1988.

Forbath, William E. *Law and the Shaping of the American Labor Movement.* Cambridge, Mass.: Harvard University Press, 1991.

Foroohar, Rana. *Makers and Takers: The Rise of Finance and the Fall of American Business.* New York: Crown, 2016.

Fox, Justin. *The Myth of the Rational Market: A History of Risk, Reward, and Delusion on Wall Street.* New York: Harper Business, 2009.

Fraser, Steve, and Gary Gerstle, eds. *Ruling America: A History of Wealth and Power in Democracy*. Cambridge, Mass.: Harvard University Press, 2005.

Fried, Barbara H. *The Progressive Assault on Laissez Faire: Robert Hale and the First Law and Economics Movement*. Cambridge, Mass.: Harvard University Press, 1998.

Frieden, Jeffry A., and David A. Lake, eds. *International Political Economy: Perspectives on Global Power and Wealth*. New York: St. Martin's, 1987.

Friedman, Tami. *Communities in Competition: Capital Migration and Plant Relocation in the U.S. Carpet Industry, 1929–1975*. New York: Columbia University Press, 2001.

Friedman, Walter A. *Business Prophets: The Rise of Economic Forecasting in American Life*. Forthcoming.

——. *Fortune Tellers: The Story of America's First Economic Forecasters* (Princeton, N.J.: Princeton University Press, 2014.

Genovese, Eugene D. *The Political Economy of Slavery: Studies in the Economy and the Society of the Slave South*. New York: Vintage Books, 1965.

Gervais, Pierre. *Les origines de la révolution industrielle aux Etats-Unis: Entre économie marchande et capitalisme industrielle, 1800–1850*. Paris: EHESS, 2004.

Gilje, Paul A. *Free Trade and Sailors' Rights in the War of 1812*. New York: Cambridge University Press, 2013.

Goldfarb, Sally. "The Civil Rights Remedy of the Violence Against Women Act: Legislative History, Policy Implications, and Litigation Strategy." *Journal of Law & Policy* 4, no. 2 (1996): 391–99.

Goldin, Claudia. *Understanding the Gender Gap: An Economic History of American Women*. New York: Oxford University Press, 1990.

Goldin, Claudia, and Larry Katz. *The Race Between Education and Technology*. Cambridge, Mass.: Belknap Press of Harvard University Press, 2008.

Goodrich, Carter. "The Virginia System of Mixed Enterprise," *Political Science Quarterly* 64, no. 3 (September 1949): 355–87.

Goodwin, Lawrence. *The Populist Movement: A Short History of the Agrarian Revolt in America*. Oxford: Oxford University Press, 1978.

Gordon, Linda. *Woman's Body, Woman's Right: A Social History of Birth Control in America*. New York: Penguin, 1977.

Gordon, Robert W. "Critical Legal Histories." *Stanford Law Review* 36 (1984): 57–125.

Graham, Willard J. "Some Observations on the Nature of Income, Generally Accepted Accounting Principles, and Financial Reporting." *Law and Contemporary Problems* 30, no. 4 (Autumn 1965): 652–73.

Gray, Lewis C. *History of Agriculture in the Southern United States to 1860*. 2 vols. Gloucester, Mass.: Peter Smith, 1958. Originally published 1933.

Gray, Thomas Ruffin. *The Confessions of Nat Turner, The Leader of the Late Insurrection in Southampton, Va, as fully and voluntarily made to Thomas Ruffin Gray, in the Prison where he was confined, and acknowledged by him to be such when read before the Court of Southampton; with the Certificate, under seal of the Court convened at Jerusalem, Nov. 5, 1831, for his Trial. Also, an Authentic Account of the whole Insurrection, with Lists of the Whites who were murdered, and of the Negroes brought before the Court of Southampton, and there sentenced, &c*. Baltimore, Md., 1831.

Gunn, L. Ray. *The Decline of Authority: Public Economic Policy and Political Development in New York, 1800–1860*. Ithaca, N.Y.: Cornell University Press, 1988.

Hahn, Steven. *The Roots of Southern Populism: Yeoman Farmers and the Transformation of the Georgia Upcountry*. Oxford: Oxford University Press, 1983.

Hall, Peter, and Soskice, David. *Varieties of Capitalism: The Institutional Foundations of Comparative Advantage*. Oxford: Oxford University Press, 2001.

Halttunen, K. *Confidence Men and Painted Women: A Study of Middle-Class Culture in America, 1830–1870*. New Haven, Conn.: Yale University Press, 1983.

Hancock, David. *Oceans of Wine: Madeira and the Emergence of American Trade and Taste*. New Haven, Conn.: Yale University Press, 2009.

Handlin, Oscar. *Commonwealth: A Study of the Role of Government in the American Economy: Massachusetts, 1774–1861*. Cambridge, Mass.: Belknap Press of Harvard University Press, 1969.

Harmon, Alexandra. *Rich Indians: Native People and the Problem of Wealth in American History*. Chapel Hill: University of North Carolina Press, 2010.

Hartmann, Susan M. *The Home Front and Beyond: American Women in the 1940s*. Boston: Twayne, 1982.

Hartz, Louis. *The Liberal Tradition in America: An Interpretation of American Political Thought Since the Revolution*. New York: Harcourt, Brace, 1955.

Harvey, David. *The Limits to Capital*. London: Verso, 2006.

Hatter, Lawrence B. A. *Citizens of Convenience: The Imperial Origins of American Nationhood on the U.S.-Canadian Border*. Charlottesville: University of Virginia Press, 2016.

Haydu, Jeffrey. *Citizen Employers: Business Communities and Labor in Cincinnati and San Francisco, 1870–1916*. Ithaca, N.Y.: Cornell University Press, 2008.

Hayek, F. A. *The Counter-Revolution of Science: Studies on the Abuse of Reason*. Glencoe, Ill.: Free Press, 1952.

Hendrickson, Mark. *American Labor and Economic Citizenship: New Capitalism from World War I to the Great Depression*. Cambridge: Cambridge University Press, 2013.

Hilferding, Rudolph. *Finance Capital: A Study in the Latest Phase of Capitalist Development*. New York: Routledge, 2006.

Hilliard, Kathleen M. *Masters, Slaves, and Exchange: Power's Purchase in the Old South*. New York: Cambridge University Press, 2014.

Hixson, William F. *Triumph of the Bankers: Money and Banking in the Eighteenth and Nineteenth Centuries*. Westport, Conn: Praeger, 1993.

Holton, Woody. *Unruly Americans and the Origins of the Constitution*. New York: Hill and Wang, 2007.

Horwitz, Morton. *The Transformation of American Law, 1780–1860*. Cambridge, Mass.: Harvard University Press, 1977.

——. *The Transformation of American Law, 1870–1960: The Crisis of Legal Orthodoxy*. New York: Oxford University Press, 1992.

Hovenkamp, Herbert. *Enterprise and American Law, 1836–1937*. Cambridge, Mass.: Harvard University Press, 1991.

Hyman, Louis. *Debtor Nation: The History of American in Red Ink*. Princeton, N.J.: Princeton University Press, 2012.

——. "Debtor Nation: How Consumer Credit Built Postwar America." PhD diss., Harvard University, 2007.

Ingham, Geoffrey. "On the Underdevelopment of the 'Sociology of Money.'" *Acta Sociologica* 41, no. 1 (1998): 3–18.

Inikori, Joseph. *Africans and the Industrial Revolution in England: A Study in International Trade and Economic Development*. Cambridge: Cambridge University Press, 2002.

Jacobs, Meg. *Pocketbook Politics: Economic Citizenship in Twentieth Century America*. Princeton, N.J.: Princeton University Press, 2005.

Jacobs, Meg, William Novak, and Julian Zelizer, eds. *The Democratic Experiment: New Directions in American Political History*. Princeton, N.J.: Princeton University Press, 2003.

Jacoby, Sanford M, ed. *Masters to Managers: Historical and Comparative Perspectives on American Employers*. New York: Columbia University Press, 1991.

——. *Modern Manors: Welfare Capitalism since the New Deal*. Princeton, N.J.: Princeton University Press, 1997.

John, Richard. *Network Nation: Inventing American Telecommunications*. Cambridge, Mass.: Belknap Press of Harvard University Press, 2010.

——. *Spreading the News: The American Postal System from Franklin to Morse*. Cambridge, Mass.: Harvard University Press, 1995.

Johnson, Paul A. *A Shopkeeper's Millennium: Society and Revivals in Rochester, New York, 1815–1837*. New York: Hill and Wang, 1978.

Johnson, Walter. *Soul by Soul: Life Inside the Antebellum Slave Market*. Cambridge, Mass.: Harvard University Press, 1999.

Johnston, Robert D. *The Radical Middle Class: Populist Democracy and the Question of Capitalism in Progressive Era Portland, Oregon*. Princeton, N.J.: Princeton University Press, 2003.

Josephson, Matthew. *The Robber Barons: The Great American Capitalists*. New York: Harcourt, Brace, 1934.

Kennedy, Duncan. "The Role of Law in Economic Thought: Essays on the Fetishism of Commodities." *American University Law Review* 34, no. 4 (1985): 939–1001.

Klarman, Michael J. *The Framers' Coup: The Making of the United States Constitution*. New York: Oxford University Press, 2016.

Knight, Frank H. Risk*, Uncertainty and Profit*. 1921. Reprint, Chicago: University of Chicago Press, 1971.

Kreitner, Roy. *Calculating Promises: The Emergence of Modern American Contract Doctrine*. Stanford, Calif.: Stanford University Press, 2007.

Krippner, Greta. *Capitalizing on Crisis: The Political Origins of the Rise of Finance*. Cambridge, Mass.: Harvard University Press, 2011.

Kulikoff, Allan. *The Agrarian Origins of American Capitalism*. Charlottesville: University Press of Virginia, 1992.

Laird, Pamela Walker. *Advertising Progress: American Business and the Rise of Consumer Marketing*. Baltimore, Md.: Johns Hopkins University Press, 1998.

——. "Looking Toward the Future: Expanding Connections for Business Historians." *Enterprise & Society* 9, no. 4 (December 2008): 575–90.

Lakwete, Angela. *Inventing the Cotton Gin: Machine and Myth in Antebellum America*. Baltimore, Md.: Johns Hopkins University Press, 2003.

Lall, Sanjaya. *Learning from the Asian Tigers: Studies in Technology and Industrial Policy*. London: Palgrave Macmillan, 1996.

Lamoreaux, Naomi. *The Great Merger Movement in American Business, 1895–1904*. Cambridge: Cambridge University Press, 1985.

Latham, A. J. H. *Rice: The Primary Commodity*. London: Routledge, 1998.

Lepler, Jessica. *The Many Panics of 1837: People, Politics, and the Creation of a Transatlantic Financial Crisis*. Cambridge: Cambridge University Press, 2013.

Lerman, Nina E. "Categories of Difference, Categories of Power: Bringing Gender and Race to the History of Technology." *Technology & Culture* 51, no. 4 (October 2010): 893–918.

Levy, Jonathan. *Freaks of Fortune: The Emerging World of Capitalism and Risk in America*. Cambridge, Mass.: Harvard University Press, 2012.

——. *The Ways of Providence: Capitalism, Risk, and Freedom*. Forthcoming from Harvard University Press.

Licht, Walter. *Industrializing America: The Nineteenth Century*. Baltimore, Md.: Johns Hopkins University Press, 1995.

Lichtenstein, Nelson. *Wal-Mart: The Face of Twenty-First-Century Capitalism*. New York: New Press, 2006.

Lipartito, Kenneth. *Constructing Corporate America: History, Politics, Culture*. Oxford: Oxford University Press, 2004.

——. *Investing for Middle America: John Elliott Tappan and the Origins of American Express Financial Advisors*. New York: Palgrave, 2001.

——. "Reassembling the Economic: New Departures in Historical Materialism." *American Historical Review* 121, no. 1 (2016): 101–39.

MacKenzie, Donald A., Fabian Muniesa, and Lucia Siu, eds. *Do Economists Make Markets? On the Performativity of Economics*. Princeton, N.J.: Princeton University Press, 2007.

Maclean, Jay L., David C. Dawe, Bill Hardy, and Gene P. Hettel, eds. *Rice Almanac: Source Book for the Most Important Economic Activities on Earth*. 3rd. ed. Los Baños, Philippines: International Rice Research Institute, 2002.

Maggor, Noam. "Politics of Property: The Boston Lower Middle Class in the Age of Capital." PhD diss., Harvard University, 2010.

Main, Jackson Turner. *The Antifederalists: Critics of the Constitution, 1781–1788*. Chapel Hill: University of North Carolina Press, 1961.

Majewski, John. *A House Dividing: Economic Development in Pennsylvania and Virginia Before the Civil War*. Cambridge: Cambridge University Press, 2000.

Mann, Bruce H. *Neighbors and Strangers: Law and Community in Early Connecticut*. Chapel Hill: University of North Carolina Press, 1987.

Marschak, Jacob. "Neumann's and Morgenstern's New Approach to Static Economics." *Journal of Political Economy* 54, no. 2 (April 1946): 97–115.

Marx, Karl. *Capital: A Critique of Political Economy*. Harmondsworth, UK: Penguin Books, 1976.

McCraw, Thomas. *Creating Modern Capitalism: How Entrepreneurs, Companies, and Countries Triumphed in Three Industrial Revolutions*. Cambridge, Mass.: Harvard University Press, 1997.

——. *Prophets of Regulation: Charles Francis Adams, Louis D. Brandeis, James M. Landis, Alfred E. Kahn*. Cambridge, Mass.: Belknap Press of Harvard University Press, 1984.

McCusker, John J., and Russell R. Menard. *The Economy of British America, 1607–1789*. Chapel Hill: University of North Carolina Press, 1985.

McLennan, Rebecca. *The Crisis of Imprisonment: Protest, Politics, and the Making of the American Penal State, 1776–1941*. Cambridge: Cambridge University Press, 2008.

Mehrotra, Ajay. *Making the Modern American Fiscal State: Law, Politics, and the Rise of Progressive Taxation*. Cambridge: Cambridge University Press, 2013.

Merrill, Michael. "Cash Is Good to Eat: Self-Sufficiency and Exchange in the Rural Economy of the United States." *Radical History Review* 13 (Winter 1977): 42–71.

——. "Putting 'Capitalism' in Its Place: A Review of Recent Literature." *William and Mary Quarterly* 52, no. 2 (April 1995): 315–26.

Merritt, Jane T. *The Trouble with Tea: The Politics of Consumption in the Eighteenth-Century Global Economy*. Baltimore, Md.: Johns Hopkins University Press, 2016.

Middleton, Simon, and Billy G. Smith. *Class Matters: Early North America and the Atlantic World*. Philadelphia: University of Pennsylvania, 2008.

Minsky, Hyman. *Can It Happen Again? Essays on Instability and Finance*. New York: Routledge, 2014.

Mintz, Sidney W. *Sweetness and Power: The Place of Sugar in Modern History*. New York: Penguin Books, 1985.

Mirowski, Philip. *More Heat Than Light: Economics as Social Physics, Physics as Nature's Economics*. Cambridge: Cambridge University Press, 1989.

Mitchell, Timothy. "Econometality: How the Future Entered Government." *Critical Inquiry* 40, no. 4 (2014): 479–507.

——. *Rule of Experts: Egypt, Techno-Politics, Modernity.* Berkeley: University of California Press, 2002.

Mitchell, Wesley C., Willford I. King, Frederick R. Macaulay, and Oswald W. Knauth. *Income in the United States: Its Amount and Distribution, 1909–1919.* Vol. 1, *Summary.* New York: Harcourt Brace, 1921.

Moreton, Bethany. *To Serve God and Wal-Mart: The Making of Christian Free Enterprise.* Cambridge, Mass.: Harvard University Press, 2009.

Moss, David. *Socializing Security: Progressive-Era Economists and the Origins of American Social Policy.* Cambridge, Mass.: Harvard University Press, 1996.

——. *When All Else Fails: Government as the Ultimate Risk Manager.* Cambridge, Mass.: Harvard University Press, 2002.

Murname, Mary Susan. "The Mellon Tax Plan: The Income Tax and the Penetration of Marginalist Economic Thought into American Life and Law in the 1920s." PhD diss., Case Western Reserve University, 2007.

Nelson, Scott Reynolds. *A Nation of Deadbeats: An Uncommon History of America's Financial Disasters.* New York: Knopf, 2012.

Nevins, Alan. *Study in Power: John D. Rockefeller, Industrialist and Philanthropist.* New York: Scribner, 1953.

Niethammer, Lutz. "Kollektive Identität." *Heimliche Quellen einer unheimlichen Konjunktur.* Reinbek: Rowolt, 2000.

Noble, David. *America by Design: Science, Technology, and the Rise of Corporate Capitalism.* New York: Knopf, 1979.

North, Douglass C. *The Economic Growth of the United States, 1790–1860.* Englewood Cliffs, N.J.: Prentice Hall, 1961.

——. *Structure and Change in Economic History.* New York: W. W. Norton, 1981.

North, Douglass C., and Barry R. Weingast. "Constitutions and Commitment: The Evolution of Institutions Governing Public Choice in Seventeenth-Century England." *Journal of Economic History* 49, no. 4 (December 1989): 803–32.

Novak, William J. *The People's Welfare: Law and Regulation in Nineteenth-Century America.* Chapel Hill: University of North Carolina Press, 1996.

Novick, Peter. *That Noble Dream: The "Objectivity Question" and the American Historical Profession.* Cambridge: Cambridge University Press, 1988.

O'Donovan, Susan. *Becoming Free in the Cotton South.* Cambridge, Mass.: Harvard University Press, 2007.

Olegario, Rowena. *A Culture of Credit: Embedding Trust and Transparency in American Business.* Cambridge, Mass.: Harvard University Press, 2006.

Olmstead, Alan L., and Paul Rhode. *Creating Abundance: Biological Innovation and American Agricultural Development.* New York: Cambridge University Press, 2008.

O'Sullivan, Mary. *Contests for Corporate Control: Corporate Governance and Economic Performance in the United States and Germany.* Oxford: Oxford University Press, 2000.

Ott, Julia. *When Wall Street Met Main Street: The Quest for an Investors' Democracy.* Cambridge, Mass.: Harvard University Press, 2011.

——. "When Wall Street Met Main Street: The Quest for an Investors' Democracy and the Emergence of the Retail Investor in the United States, 1890–1930." *Enterprise & Society* 9, no. 4 (2008): 619–30.

Peck, Gunther. *Reinventing Free Labor: Padrones and Immigrant Workers in the North American West, 1880–1930.* Cambridge: Cambridge University Press, 2000.

Peiss, Kathy L. *Hope in a Jar: The Making of America's Beauty Culture.* New York: Henry Holt, 1999.

Phelan, Craig. *Grand Master Workman: Terence Powderly and the Knights of Labor*. Westport, Conn.: Greenwood, 2000.

Phillips-Fein, Kimberly. *Invisible Hands: The Making of the Conservative Movement from the New Deal to Reagan*. New York: W. W. Norton, 2010.

Piketty, Thomas. *Capital in the Twenty-First Century*. Trans. Arthur Goldhammer. Cambridge, Mass.: Harvard University Press, 2014.

Pincus, Steve. "Rethinking Mercantilism: Political Economy, the British Empire, and the Atlantic World in the Seventeenth and Eighteenth Centuries." *William and Mary Quarterly* 69, no. 1 (2012): 3–34.

Polanyi, Karl. *The Great Transformation: The Political and Economic Origins of Our Time*. 2nd ed. Boston: Beacon, 2001.

Pomeranz, Kenneth. *The Great Divergence: China, Europe, and the Making of the Modern World Economy*. Princeton, N.J.: Princeton University Press, 2000.

Poovey, Mary. *Genres of the Credit Economy: Mediating Value in Eighteenth- and Nineteenth-Century Britain*. Chicago: University of Chicago Press, 2008.

——. *A History of the Modern Fact: Problems of Knowledge in the Sciences of Wealth and Society*. Chicago: University of Chicago, 1998.

Pope, James Gray. "The Thirteenth Amendment versus the Commerce Clause: Labor and the Shaping of American Constitutional Law, 1921–1957." *Columbia Law Review* 102, no. 1 (2002): 1–122.

Post, Robert C., and Reva B. Siegel. "Equal Protection by Law: Federal Anti-discrimination Legislation after Morrison and Kimel." *Yale Law Journal* 110, no. 3 (December 2000): 441–526.

Postel, Charles. *The Populist Vision*. Oxford: Oxford University Press, 2007.

Preda, Alex. *Framing Finance: The Boundaries of Markets and Modern Capitalism*. Chicago: University of Chicago Press, 2009.

Ralph, Michael. *Forensics of Capital*. Chicago: University of Chicago Press, 2015.

Rao, Gautham. *National Duties: Custom Houses and the Making of the American State*. Chicago: University of Chicago Press, 2016.

Rediker, Marcus. *Between the Devil and the Deep Blue Sea: Merchant Seamen, Pirates, and the Anglo-American Maritime World, 1700–1750*. Cambridge: Cambridge University Press, 1987.

Resnik, Judith. "Categorical Federalism: Jurisdiction, Gender, and the Globe." *Yale Law Journal* 111 (December 2001): 619–80.

Robinson, Cedric J. "Introduction" and "Racial Capitalism." In *Black Marxism: The Making of the Black Radical Tradition*. Durham: University of North Carolina Press, 2000.

Rockman, Seth. "Introduction: The Paper Technologies of Capitalism." *Technology & Culture* 58 (April 2017): 487–505.

——. *Landscape of Industry: An Industrial History of the Blackstone Valley*. Lebanon, N.H.: University Press of New England, 2009.

——. *Scraping By: Wage Labor, Slavery, and Survival in Early Baltimore*. Baltimore, Md.: Johns Hopkins University Press, 2009.

Rood, Daniel B. *The Reinvention of Atlantic Slavery: Technology, Labor, Race, and Capitalism in the Greater Caribbean*. New York: Oxford University Press, 2017.

Root, Erik S., ed. *Sons of the Fathers: The Virginia Slavery Debates of 1831–1832*. Lanham, Md.: Lexington Books, 2010.

Ross, Dorothy. *The Origins of American Social Science*. Cambridge: Cambridge University Press, 1992.

Rothenberg, Winifred Barr. *From Market-Places to a Market Economy: The Transformation of Rural Massachusetts, 1750–1850*. Chicago: University of Chicago Press, 1992.

Rothman, Adam. *Slave Country: American Expansion and the Origins of the Deep South*. Cambridge, Mass.: Harvard University Press, 2005.

Roy, William. *Socializing Capital: The Rise of the Large Industrial Corporation in America*. Princeton, N.J.: Princeton University Press, 1997.

Rutherglen, George. "State Action, Private Action, and the Thirteenth Amendment." *Virginia Law Review* 94, no. 6 (October 2008): 1367–1406.

Sandage, Scott. *Born Losers: A History of Failure in America*. Cambridge, Mass.: Harvard University Press, 2005.

Sandel, Michael. *What Money Can't Buy: The Moral Limits of Markets*. New York: Farrar, Straus and Giroux, 2012.

Sanders, Elizabeth. *Roots of Reform: Farmers, Workers, and the American State, 1877–1917*. Chicago: University of Chicago Press, 1999.

Scheiber, Harry. *Ohio Canal Era: A Case Study of Government and the Economy, 1820–1861*. Athens: Ohio University Press, 1987.

Schiebinger, Londa. *Plants and Empire: Colonial Bioprospecting in the Atlantic World*. Cambridge, Mass.: Harvard University Press, 2004.

Schumpeter, Joseph A. *Capitalism, Socialism, and Democracy*. 3rd ed. New York: Harper-Perennial, 1976.

Scott, Joan. "A Statistical Representation of Work: La Statistique de l'Industrie a Paris, 1847–1848." In *Gender and the Politics of History*. New York: Columbia University Press, 1988.

Scranton, Philip. *Endless Novelty: Specialty Production and American Industrialization, 1865–1925*. Princeton, N.J.: Princeton University Press, 1997.

Seligman, Edwin R. A. "Federal Taxes upon Income and Excess Profits—Discussion." In *Papers and Proceedings of the Thirtieth Annual Meeting of the American Economic Association*, supplement, *American Economic Review* 8, no. 1 (March 1918): 36–54.

Sewall, William. *Work and Revolution in France: The Language of Labor from the Old Regime to 1848*. Cambridge: Cambridge University Press, 1980.

Shammas, Carole. *A History of Household Government in America*. Charlottesville: University of Virginia Press, 2002.

Simmel, Georg. *The Philosophy of Money*. 3rd enl. ed. Ed. David Frisby. London: Routledge, 2004.

Sklansky, Jeffrey. "The Elusive Sovereign: New Intellectual and Social Histories of Capitalism." *Modern Intellectual History* 9, no. 1 (2012): 233–48.

——. *Sovereign of the Market: The Money Question in Early America (1500–1900)*. Chicago: University of Chicago Press, 2017.

Sklar, Martin. *The Corporate Reconstruction of American Capitalism, 1890–1916: The Market, the Law, and Politics*. Cambridge: Cambridge University Press, 1988.

Skocpol, Theda. *Protecting Soldiers and Mothers: The Political Origins of Social Policy in the United States*. Cambridge, Mass.: Belknap Press of Harvard University Press, 1992.

Skowronek, Stephen. *Building a New American State: The Expansion of National Administrative Capacities, 1877–1920*. Cambridge: Cambridge University Press, 1982.

Smith, Adam. *An Inquiry into the Nature and Causes of the Wealth of Nations*. 1776. 5th ed. Ed. Edwin Cannan. London: Methuen, 1904. Reprint, with preface by George J. Stigler, Chicago: University of Chicago Press, 1976.

Smith, Jason Scott. *Building New Deal Liberalism: The Political Economy of Public Works, 1933–1956*. New York: Cambridge University Press, 2006.

Sokoloff, Kenneth L. *Slavery in the Development of the Americas*. Cambridge: Cambridge University Press, 2004.

Stanley, Amy Dru. *From Bondage to Contract: Wage Labor, Marriage, and the Market in the Age of Slave Emancipation*. Cambridge: Cambridge University Press, 1998.

Stasavage, David. "Credible Commitment in Early Modern Europe: North and Weingast Revisited." *Journal of Law, Economics, and Organization* 18 (2002): 155–86.

Stein, Judith. *Pivotal Decade: How the United States Traded Factories for Finance in the Seventies*. New Haven, Conn.: Yale University Press, 2010.

——. *Running Steel, Running America: Race, Economic Policy, and the Decline of Liberalism*. Chapel Hill: University of North Carolina, 1998.

Steinfeld, Robert. *Invention of Free Labor: The Employment Relation in English and American Law and Culture, 1350–1870*. Chapel Hill: University of North Carolina Press, 1991.

Stiles, T. J. *The First Tycoon: The Epic Life of Cornelius Vanderbilt*. New York: Knopf, 2009.

Stone, Lawrence, ed. *An Imperial State at War: Britain from 1689 to 1815*. London: Routledge, 1994.

Suarez-Villa, Luis. *Technocapitalism: A Critical Perspective on Technological Innovation and Corporatism*. Philadelphia: Temple University Press, 2009.

Swan, Dale Evans. *The Structure and Profitability of the Antebellum Rice Industry 1859*. New York: Arno, 1975.

Sylla, Richard. "The American Capital Market, 1846–1914: A Study of the Effects of Public Policy on Economic Development." PhD diss., Harvard University, 1969.

——. *The Evolution of the American Economy: Growth, Welfare, and Decision Making*. New York: Basic Books, 1979.

——. *A History of Interest Rates*. New Brunswick, N.J.: Rutgers University Press, 1991.

Tadman, Michael. *Speculators and Slaves: Masters, Traders, and Slaves in the Old South*. Madison: University of Wisconsin Press, 1989.

Tilly, Charles. *Coercion, Capital, and European States, AD 990–1990*. Cambridge, Mass.: Blackwell, 1990.

——. *Trust and Rule*. New York: Cambridge University Press, 2005.

Tilly, Louise A., and Joan W. Scott. *Women, Work, and Family*. New York: Routledge, 1987.

Tinker, Hugh. *A New System of Slavery: The Export of Indian Labour Overseas, 1830–1920*. London: Hansib, 1993.

Tobin, James. "Money." In *The New Palgrave Dictionary of Economics Online*, ed. Steven N. Durlauf and Lawrence E. Blume, 1–18. Palgrave Macmillan, 2008. http://www.dictionary ofeconomics.com/article?id=pde2008_M000217.doi:10.1057/9780230226203.1126.

Tomich, Dale. *Through the Prism of Slavery: Labor, Capital, and World Economy*. Lanham, Md.: Rowman and Littlefield, 2004.

Tragle, Henry Irving. *The Southampton Slave Revolt of 1831: A Compilation of Source Material*. Amherst: University of Massachusetts Press, 1971.

Unger, Irwin. *The Greenback Era: A Social and Political History of American Finance, 1865–1879*. Princeton, N.J.: Princeton University Press, 1964.

Usselman, Steven. *Regulating Railroad Innovation: Business, Technology, and Politics in America, 1840–1920*. Cambridge: Cambridge University Press, 2002.

Van der Linden, Marcel. *Workers of the World: Essays Towards a Global Labor History*. Boston: Brill, 2008.

van der Zwan, Natascha. "Making Sense of Financialization." *Socio-Economic Review* 12, no. 1 (2014): 99–129.

Veeser, Cyrus. *A World Safe for Capitalism: Dollar Diplomacy and America's Rise to Global Power*. New York: Columbia University Press, 2002.

Wagner, Sally Roesch. *Sisters in Spirit: Haudenosaunee (Iroquois) Influence on Early American Feminists*. Summertown, Tenn.: Native Voices, 2001.

Waldstreicher, David. *Slavery's Constitution: From Revolution to Ratification*. New York: Hill and Wang, 2009.

Walpen, Bernard. *Die offenen Feinde und Ihre Gesellschaft: Eine Hegemonietheoretische Studie zur Mont Pelerin Society*. Hamburg: VSA, 2004.

Waterhouse, Ben. "A Lobby for Capital: Organized Business and the Pursuit of Pro-Market Politics, 1967–1986." PhD diss., Harvard University, 2009.

Way, Peter. *Common Labor: Workers and the Digging of North American Canals, 1780–1860*. Baltimore, Md.: Johns Hopkins University Press, 1997.

White, Richard. *"It's Your Misfortune and None of My Own": A History of the American West*. Norman: University of Oklahoma Press, 1991.

——. *Railroaded: The Transcontinentals and the Making of Modern America*. New York: W. W. Norton, 2011.

Wilentz, Sean. *Chants Democratic: New York City and the Rise of the American Working Class, 1788–1850*. New York: Oxford University Press, 1984.

Wilkins, Mira. *The Emergence of Multinational Enterprise: American Business from the Colonial Era to 1914*. Cambridge, Mass.: Harvard University Press, 1970.

Williams, Eric. *Capitalism and Slavery*. Chapel Hill: University of North Carolina Press, 1944.

Witt, John. *The Accidental Republic: Crippled Workingmen, Destitute Widows, and the Remaking of American Law*. Cambridge, Mass.: Harvard University Press, 2004.

Wolf, Eva Sheppard. *Race and Liberty in the New Nation: Emancipation in Virginia from the Revolution to Nat Turner's Rebellion*. Baton Rouge: Louisiana State University Press, 2005.

Wood, Gordon S. "Was America Born Capitalist?" *Wilson Quarterly* 23, no. 2 (1999): 36–46.

Woodson, Carter G. "Insurance Business Among Negroes," *Journal of Negro History* 14, no. 2 (April 1929): 202–26.

Wright, Gavin. *Old South, New South: Revolutions in the Southern Economy since the Civil War*. New York: Basic Books, 1986.

——. *The Political Economy of the Cotton South: Households, Markets, and Wealth in the Nineteenth Century*. New York: W. W. Norton, 1978.

——. "Quantitative Economic History in the United States." *International Encyclopedia of the Social and Behavioral Sciences*. Amsterdam: Elsevier, 2001.

Yearley, Clifton K. *The Money Machines: The Breakdown and Reform of Governmental and Party Finance in the North, 1860–1920*. Albany: State University of New York Press, 1970.

Zelizer, Julian. *Taxing America: Wilbur D. Mills, Congress, and the State, 1945–1975*. Cambridge: Cambridge University Press, 1998.

Zelizer, Vivian. *Morals and Markets: The Development of Life Insurance in the United States*. New York: Columbia University Press, 2017.

Zunz, Olivier. *Making America Corporate, 1870–1920*. Chicago: University of Chicago Press, 1990.

CONTRIBUTORS

Sven Beckert is Laird Bell Professor of History at Harvard University and Visiting
Professor of Management at Harvard Business School. He codirects, with
Christine Desan, the Harvard Initiative on the Study of Capitalism. His most
recent book is *Empire of Cotton: A Global History*, which won the Bancroft Prize,
was a finalist for the Pulitzer Prize, and was one of the *New York Times'* Ten Best
Books of 2015.

Peter A. Coclanis is Albert R. Newsome Distinguished Professor of History and
Director of the Global Research Institute at the University of North Carolina–
Chapel Hill. He works mainly on U.S., Southeast Asian, and global economic
history, and has published widely in these fields. His most recent book (coau-
thored with Sven Beckert, Richard Follett, and Barbara Hahn) is *Plantation
Kingdom: The American South and Its Global Commodities* (Johns Hopkins
University Press, 2016).

Christine Desan is the Leo Gottlieb Professor of Law at Harvard Law School and the
author of *Making Money: Coin, Currency, and the Coming of Capitalism* (Oxford
University Press, 2014), a book arguing that a radical transformation in the way
societies produce money ushered in capitalism as a public project. She is
cofounder of Harvard's Program on the Study of Capitalism, which she codirects
with Sven Beckert. Her current work considers the financial architecture
installed during the Enlightenment, and the legal components of economic
concepts like money supply and demand.

Eliga H. Gould is professor of history at the University of New Hampshire. His most
recent book is *Among the Powers of the Earth: The American Revolution and the*

Making of a New World Empire (2012; paperback, 2014), which won the SHEAR Book Prize from the Society for Historians of the Early American Republic and was a finalist for the George Washington Book Prize. He is currently writing a global history of the peace treaty that ended the American Revolutionary War.

Woody Holton is the Peter and Bonnie McCausland Professor of History at the University of South Carolina. He is the author of *Unruly Americans and the Origins of the Constitution* (which was a finalist for the National Book Award in 2007) and *Abigail Adams* (which won the Bancroft Prize in 2010).

Peter Knight is professor of American studies at the University of Manchester (UK). He is the author of *Reading the Market: Genres of Financial Capitalism in Gilded Age America* (Johns Hopkins University Press, 2016), and cocurator of the exhibition, "Show Me the Money: The Image of Finance, 1700 to the Present."

Kris Manjapra is associate professor of history and director of the Consortium of Studies in Race, Colonialism, and Diaspora at Tufts University. His research is at the intersection of social, cultural, and intellectual history in global perspective.

Julia Ott is associate professor in the history of capitalism and the codirector of the Robert L. Heilbroner Center for Capitalism Studies at the New School for Social Research and Eugene Lang College at the New School. She is the author of *When Wall Street Met Main Street: The Quest for an Investors' Democracy* (Harvard University Press, 2011) and she co-edits *Columbia Studies in the History of U.S. Capitalism* for Columbia University Press. Professor Ott's research investigates how financial institutions, practices, and theories influence American political culture and how, in turn, policies and political beliefs shape economic behavior and outcomes.

Kim Phillips-Fein is associate professor at the Gallatin School of Individualized Study and the Department of History at New York University. She is the author of *Invisible Hands: The Making of the Conservative Movement from the New Deal to Reagan* (W. W. Norton, 2009) and *Fear City: New York's Fiscal Crisis and the Rise of Austerity Politics* (Metropolitan Books, 2017). Her work has appeared in publications including the *Journal of American History*, the *Nation*, and *The New Republic*, and she has been a Distinguished Lecturer for the Organization of American Historians since 2014.

Mary Poovey is professor emeritus of English at New York University. The author of many books and articles on eighteenth- and nineteenth-century British culture, she has just co-authored (with Kevin R. Brine) *Finance in America: An Unfinished Story* (University of Chicago Press, 2017).

Michael Ralph is an associate professor in the Department of Social and Cultural Analysis at New York University, where he serves as the Director of Undergraduate Studies. Michael is the author of the University of Chicago Press book *Forensics of Capital*. He is Editor-in-Chief of *Transforming Anthropology*, the flagship journal of the Association of Black Anthropologists. Michael wrote and directed the forthcoming animated short musical "Fishing," which explores the ingenuity of people who are incarcerated. Michael is responsible for the *Treasury of Weary Souls*, the world's most comprehensive ledger of insured slaves.

Seth Rockman is associate professor of history at Brown University and the author of *Scraping By: Wage Labor, Slavery, and Survival in Early Baltimore* (Johns Hopkins University Press, 2009). He also edited *Welfare Reform in the Early Republic: A Brief History with Documents* (Bedford Books, 2003) and co-edited, with Sven Beckert, *Slavery's Capitalism: A New History of American Economic Development* (University of Pennsylvania Press, 2016).

Amy Dru Stanley is a history professor at the University of Chicago. Her work focuses on slavery and emancipation, political economy, law, and the historical experience of moral problems. She is completing a book project provisionally titled *From Slave Emancipation to the Commerce Power: An American History of Human Rights*.

Christopher Tomlins is Elizabeth Josselyn Boalt Professor of Law at the University of California, Berkeley. He writes on Anglophone legal history and on the relationships among law, legal theory, and the philosophy of history. He is currently at work on a history of the Turner Rebellion and slavery in antebellum Virginia.

Richard White is the Margaret Byrne Professor of American History at Stanford University. His last two books are *Railroaded: The Transcontinentals and the Making of Modern America* and *The Republic for Which It Stands: The United States During Reconstruction* and *The Gilded Age, 1865–1896*.

Michael Zakim is the author of *Ready-Made Democracy*, a political history of dress in the American republic, and of *Accounting for Capitalism: The World the Clerk Made*, as well as the co-editor, together with Gary Kornblith, of *Capitalism Takes Command*. He teaches history at Tel Aviv University.

INDEX